World Religions

Eastern Traditions

Fourth Edition

World Religions

Eastern Traditions

Edited by

Willard G. Oxtoby

Roy C. Amore

Amir Hussain

OXFORD

UNIVERSITY PRESS

OXFORD
UNIVERSITY PRESS

Oxford University Press is a department of the University of Oxford.
It furthers the University's objective of excellence in research, scholarship,
and education by publishing worldwide. Oxford is a registered trade mark of
Oxford University Press in the UK and in certain other countries.

Published in Canada by
Oxford University Press
8 Sampson Mews, Suite 204,
Don Mills, Ontario M3C 0H5 Canada

www.oupcanada.com

Library and Archives Canada Cataloguing in Publication

World religions : Eastern traditions / edited by Willard
G. Oxtoby, Roy C. Amore, Amir Hussain. — Fourth edition.

Includes index.
ISBN 978–0–19–900281–8 (pbk.)

1. Religions—Textbooks.   I. Amore, Roy C., 1942–, editor of
compilation   II. Oxtoby, Willard G. (Willard Gurdon), 1933–, editor
of compilation   III. Hussain, Amir editor of compilation

BL80.2.W67 2014   200   C2013-907203-9

Cover image: Cahir Davitt/AWL Images/Getty Images

Printed and bound in the United States of America

1 2 3 4 — 17 16 15 14

Brief Contents

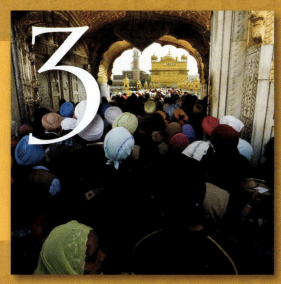

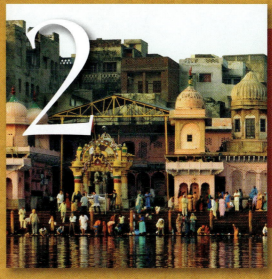

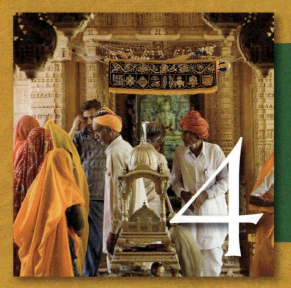

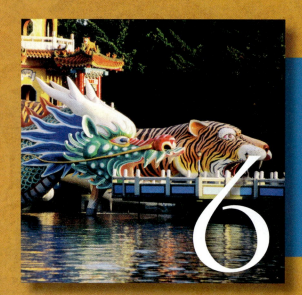

Contents

3 | Sikh Traditions   104

4 | Jaina Traditions   146

5 | Buddhist Traditions   184

6 | Chinese and Korean Traditions   262

7 | Japanese Traditions   340

8 | Current Issues   380

Contributors

Roy C. Amore is professor and an associate dean in the Faculty of Arts, Humanities and Social Sciences at the University of Windsor in Ontario. His extensive research in the areas of comparative religion and Asia has enabled him to author *Two Masters, One Message*, a book comparing the lives and teachings of Christ and Buddha, and co-author *Lustful Maidens and Ascetic Kings: Buddhist and Hindu Stories of Life*.

Amir Hussain is professor in the Department of Theological Studies at Loyola Marymount University in Los Angeles, where he teaches courses on Islam and world religions. A Canadian of Pakistani origin, he is the author of *Oil and Water: Two Faiths, One God*, an introduction to Islam for North Americans. He is also the editor of the *Journal of the American Academy of Religion* (JAAR).

Vasudha Narayanan is distinguished professor and chair, Department of Religion at the University of Florida and a past president of the American Academy of Religion. She is the author or editor of seven books and has written more than a hundred articles and chapters in books. Her current research focuses on Hindu traditions in Cambodia.

John K. Nelson is professor in the Department of Theology and Religious Studies at the University of San Francisco. Trained as a cultural anthropologist, he is the author of two books on Shinto as well as a documentary film on Yasukuni Shrine, and is the author of *Experimental Buddhism: Innovation and Activism in Contemporary Japan* (2013).

The late Willard G. Oxtoby, the original editor of this work, was professor emeritus at the University of Toronto, where he launched the graduate program in the study of religion. His books include *Experiencing India: European Descriptions and Impressions* and *The Meaning of Other Faiths*.

Pashaura Singh is professor and Dr Jasbir Singh Saini endowed chair in Sikh and Punjabi studies at the University of California, Riverside. He has authored three Oxford monographs, co-edited five conference volumes, and contributed articles to academic journals, books, and encyclopedias. His recent book, *Life and Work of Guru Arjan: History, Memory, and Biography in the Sikh Tradition* (OUP, 2006) was a bestseller in India.

Anne Vallely is associate professor in the Department of Classics and Religious Studies at the University of Ottawa, where she teaches courses on South Asian traditions (especially Jainism and Hinduism), as well as nature and religion and death and dying. Her book *Guardians of the Transcendent: An Ethnography of a Jain Ascetic Community* (2002) is an anthropological study of Jain female ascetics. Her co-edited volume *Animals and the Human Imagination* published in 2010.

Terry Tak-ling Woo teaches at York University and the University of Toronto, Scarborough. She is involved with courses that introduce the study of religion and East Asian religions. Her research interests include women in Chinese religions and Chinese religions in diaspora.

Important Features of This Edition

World Religions: Eastern Traditions, fourth edition, is a readable and reliable introduction to Eastern religions. Expert contributors thoroughly investigate Hindu, Sikh, Jaina, Buddhist, Chinese, Korean, and Japanese religious traditions. Highlights of the fourth edition include:

- **NEW "Recent Developments" sections** addressing contemporary issues and practices

- **NEW learning tools** in the form of chapter outlines, chapter summaries, discussion questions, and Sacred/Foundational Texts tables

- **NEW content on the roles and experiences of women**

Dynamic pedagogical program

Traditions at a Glance

Numbers

All numbers are based on self-assessment by the groups concerned. Because most Japanese religions are complementary rather than exclusive, the numbers of adherents reported by various sects may reflect periodic participation rather than ongoing membership.

Shinto: Estimates range from 3.5 million self-described adherents to more than 100 million if annual New Year's visits to shrines are counted as indicating "Shinto" affiliation.

Buddhism: Estimates range from 85.1 million, based on a 1999 government assessment of membership in the major denominations, to more than 100 million.

"New" religions: Estimates range from 10 to 30 million worldwide.

Christianity: Generally estimated at a little under 1 million nationwide.

Distribution

Buddhism, Shinto, and "new" religions are practised in every part of Japan, as well as in overseas communities. Japan itself counts approximately 75,000 Buddhist temples and more than 80,000 Shinto shrines, although many of the latter do not have resident priests.

Founders

Shinto is an ethnic religion with no founder. Important founders of new Buddhist schools include Saicho (Tendai), Kukai (Shingon), Eisai (Rinzai Zen), Dogen (Soto Zen), Honen (Pure Land), Shinran (True Pure Land), and Nichiren (Nichiren).

Deities

Shinto has a vast number of deities, many of which are specific to local communities. The Sun Goddess, Amaterasu, has been promoted as the supreme deity since the late 1800s because of her affiliation with the imperial household. However, one of the most widely distributed deities is Hachiman, associated with military valour.

The primary deities in Buddhism include the Medicine Buddha, the Cosmic Buddha, and Amida, the Buddha of the Pure Land, along with various bodhisattvas associated with compassion, healing, and deliverance from hell.

Authoritative Texts

Since the nineteenth century the primary texts for Shinto have been the *Kojiki: Record of Ancient Matters* and the *Nihon Shoki*. Individual Buddhist denominations and "new" religions all have their own primary texts.

Noteworthy Teachings

Shinto emphasizes harmony with nature, sincerity, and ritual purity. Each Buddhist denomination (Tendai, Shingon, Rinzai Zen, Soto Zen, Pure Land, True Pure Land, and Nichiren) and "new" religion (Tenrikyo, Omotokyo, Rissho Koseikai, etc.) likewise emphasizes key teachings that differentiate it from competing sects: secrets about the nature of reality, how universal salvation can be achieved through faith in the Buddha of the Pure Land, the perfection of the *Lotus Sutra*, the necessity of performing memorial rites for ancestral spirits, and so on.

 The great "floating" torii gate at the Itsukushima Shinto shrine (GARDEL Bertrand/hemis.fr). Each of the main posts is a giant camphor tree said to be some 500 years old.

Traditions at a Glance boxes give readers a summary of the basics at the start of each chapter.

Timelines help to place religious developments in historical context.

Timeline

c. 8000 BCE	Hunter-gatherers produce sophisticated cord-pattern pottery, arrowheads, and human figures with possible religious significance
c. 450–250 CE	Immigration from north Asia introduces new technology, cultural forms, language, religious rituals, etc.
c. 250–600	Kofun period; rulers interred in massive burial mounds (kofun), with grave goods and clay models (haniwa) of attendants that indicate complex local hierarchies in this life and the next
538	Introduction of Buddhism; Yamato clan establishes its dominance
594	"Prince" Shotoku (Shotoku taishi) promotes Confucian principles alongside Buddhism; later acknowledged as patron saint of Buddhism in Japan
600s	Early temple-building; ruler referred to as "heavenly sovereign" (tenno)
710–794	Nara period; capital city, Heijokyo, located on site of present-day Nara
712, 720	Compilation of two key texts (Kojiki, Nihon Shoki) used to legitimate imperial rule and aristocratic privileges; more than a thousand years later, these texts would be used in the campaign to revitalize "Shinto"
752	Dedication of Todaiji temple and completion of its Great Buddha image
785	Saicho, founder of Tendai sect, establishes a temple on Mount Hiei near Kyoto
794–1184	Heian period; capital city, Heiankyo, moved to what is now Kyoto
834	Kukai, founder of Shingon sect, establishes a monastery on Mount Koya
1039	Tendai monks attack monasteries of rival Buddhist sects
1052	Beginning of the "Final Decline of the Buddhist Dharma" (age of mappo) marked by fires, famines, earthquakes, wars, pestilence, etc.
1175	Honen begins propagating "Pure Land" Buddhism
1185–1333	Kamakura period, characterized by dominance of the samurai class; capital moved to Kamakura
1200	Eisai establishes Rinzai Zen school with support of the samurai
1233	Dogen establishes Soto Zen school
1253	Nichiren forms a sect centred on recitation of the Lotus Sutra
1254	Honen's disciple Shinran introduces "True Pure Land" Buddhism
1274, 1281	Attempted invasions by Mongol armies are thwarted when violent storms, called "divine winds" (kamikaze), sink many of their ships
1430–1500	Major fires, famine, epidemics, social disorder; Onin War (1467) devastates Kyoto and marks start of regional power struggles
1474–1550	True Pure Land peasant protest movement spreads throughout the country
1542	Systematization of Shinto shrines; priestly certification via Yoshida clan
1549	Christianity enters Japan with the Jesuit Francis Xavier

Informative **maps** provide useful reference points.

(Yili) for minor officials, Rites (or Institutions) of Zhou (Zhou li or Zhou guan), and the Records or Book of Rites (Liji), which explores the principles behind particular rites. The contents likely date from the mid- to late Zhou and the early Han and took their current form over time. Confucius is credited with the compilation and editing of some of these ritual texts, whose contents range from minutely detailed advice on how to live daily life to broad

philosophical discussions of the meaning of state rituals and ceremonies.

The fifth and last classic, the Spring and Autumn Annals, is a terse chronicle of events in Confucius' native state of Lu from 722 to 481 BCE. Confucius is said to have compiled it from archival materials in order to express his judgments of past events. It was therefore used as a guide to moral laws and principles in the management of human affairs.

Map 6.1 Indigenous Chinese Religions

Source: Adapted from al Faruqi and Sopher 1974: 111.

A rich and vibrant **art program** highlights practitioners' lived experience.

6

Chinese & Korean Traditions

Terry Tak-ling Woo

Sacred/Foundational Texts tables give students a convenient summary of the most important texts in each tradition, how and when they were composed, and the uses made of them.

Sacred Texts

Jaina Traditions   179

Religion (Sect)	Text(s)	Composition/ Compilation	Compilation/ Revision	Use
Jainism (Svetambara and Digambara)	Purva Agama	Ancient and timeless "universal truths" preached by all the Jinas, from the first (Rsabha) to the last (Mahavira). Communicated to disciples by Jina Mahavira and transmitted orally until the 3rd century BCE, when the verbatim recitation of teachings was no longer possible. Both Svetambara and Digambara accept that all the Purvas were eventually lost.	Reconstructed by monks mainly between the 5th and 11th centuries CE. Commentaries and narratives added by scholar-monks.	Object of study for metaphysics, cosmology, and philosophy
Jainism (Svetambara)	Anga Agama	The 12 Angas were compiled by the principal disciples of Mahavira. Svetambaras believe that the 12th Anga, called the Drstivada, contained the teachings of lost Purvas. All were transmitted orally until the 3rd century BCE (see above).	Reconstructed by monks mainly between the 5th and 11th centuries CE. Commentaries and narratives were added by scholar-monks.	Object of study for rules of mendicant conduct, stories of renouncers, karma
Jainism (Svetambara)	Angabahya (believed to contain the lost teachings of the Purva and Anga Agamas)	Compiled and orally transmitted by monks who succeeded the principal disciples of Mahavira. Contained the earliest commentaries on the Purva and Anga.	Reconstructed by monks mainly between the 5th and 11th centuries CE. Commentaries and narratives were added by scholar-monks.	Object of study for specialized topics, story literature etc.
Jainism (Digambara)	Satkhandagama (contains parts of Drstivada canon, said to mnemonically contain the lost teachings of the Purva and Anga Agamas)	Orally transmitted until 2nd century CE, when it was put in writing; the first Jaina scripture to be preserved in written form.	No substantial revisions, though commentaries are common	Object of study for entire canon: metaphysics, cosmology, karma, and philosophy
Jainism (Digambara)	Kasayaprabhrta (text based on Drstivada)	Written by Yati Vrasabha based on compilations of Gunadhara, 1st–2nd century CE	No substantial revisions, though commentaries are common	Studied for philosophy of detachment

Continued

Sites

Sites boxes draw attention to locations of special significance to each tradition.

Document

Document boxes provide a generous selection of excerpts from scripture and other important writings.

Focus

Focus boxes offer additional information on selected subjects.

End-of-chapter **discussion questions** enhance students' critical understanding of key concepts; **glossaries** explain key terms; and **further readings** and **recommended websites** provide excellent starting points for further research.

Extensive ancillary package

Instructors benefit from a suite of ancillaries designed to support their teaching goals:

- **Instructor's Manual** contains chapter overviews, lecture outlines, and tutorial discussion questions.
- **Test Generator** includes multiple-choice, true/false, short answer, and essay questions.
- **PowerPoint Slides** cover all key concepts and are easily adapted to suit your course.
- **NEW Image Bank** provides all images and captions, maps, and boxed features.

Students have access to a wealth of additional information in the **Student Study Guide**, which offers chapter summaries, multiple-choice and short-answer questions with answers, research questions, reflection questions, fieldwork guidelines, and a bonus chapter on Zoroastrianism.

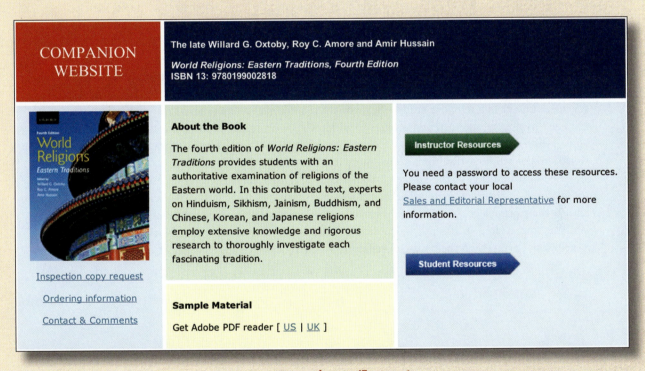

COMPANION WEBSITE

The late Willard G. Oxtoby, Roy C. Amore and Amir Hussain

World Religions: Eastern Traditions, Fourth Edition
ISBN 13: 9780199002818

Inspection copy request

Ordering information

Contact & Comments

About the Book

The fourth edition of *World Religions: Eastern Traditions* provides students with an authoritative examination of religions of the Eastern world. In this contributed text, experts on Hinduism, Sikhism, Jainism, Buddhism, and Chinese, Korean, and Japanese religions employ extensive knowledge and rigorous research to thoroughly investigate each fascinating tradition.

Sample Material

Get Adobe PDF reader [US | UK]

Instructor Resources

You need a password to access these resources. Please contact your local Sales and Editorial Representative for more information.

Student Resources

www.oupcanada.com/Eastern4e

Preface

This is the fourth edition of a successful textbook project started by the late Will Oxtoby, Professor at the University of Toronto. Will believed that only those who loved classroom teaching could write a good textbook. And he wanted authors who could write about each religion in a scholarly but appreciative way. In choosing contributors, Amir Hussain, the co-editor of the companion volume *World Religions: Western Traditions*, and I have tried to be true to Will's vision. A goal of both volumes is to include both male and female voices and to give attention to women's experience throughout each chapter.

Will wrote in his original foreword that before 1979, many people used to ask him why he was wasting his time on something as unimportant as religion, but that those questions stopped after Iran's Islamic Revolution. I have a similar story. Before I moved over to political science, I taught in a religious studies department. Sometimes political science students would ask me why anyone interested in politics would bother with religion. Since the attacks of September 2001, not a single student has raised that question. On the contrary, understanding the world's major religious traditions seems more important now than ever before.

This fourth edition of the *Eastern Traditions* volume, like its Western counterpart, updates the material, incorporates more focus and text boxes, moves the site boxes from the chapter end to their proper context, adds discussion questions, and improves the colour layout that students appreciated in the previous edition. The two new volumes share their opening and concluding chapters, on the nature of religion and current trends respectively.

✸ Acknowledgements

I wish to express my appreciation to all the teacher-scholars who have contributed to this volume. They have produced a sound and engaging text, and several of them also contributed photographs for their chapters. I enjoyed working with my co-editor Amir Hussain on the project as a whole and on the chapters that open and close this book. I also deeply appreciate the support and advice on content I have received from my wife, Michelle Morrison, and from so many of my students at the University of Windsor.

At Oxford University Press I would like to thank Katherine Skene and Stephen Kotowych for their encouragement, Meagan Carlsson for her developmental guidance, and Sally Livingston for her hands-on editorial work. I am also grateful to all the reviewers whose comments helped to shape this volume, both those whose names are listed below and those who wished to remain anonymous:

Christopher R. Austin, Dalhousie University
Adam Barkman, Redeemer University College
Larry DeVries, Langara College
Gillian McCann, Nipissing University
Justine Noel, Camosun College
Lee Rainey, Memorial University of Newfoundland

Finally, on behalf of all the authors, I wish to thank the many practitioners of Eastern religious traditions who, over the years, have answered our questions, posed for our cameras, and allowed us to observe them at worship, sometimes even inviting us to take tea with them or share their food. It is, after all, their spiritual lives that this book is all about.

Roy C. Amore
March 2013
University of Windsor

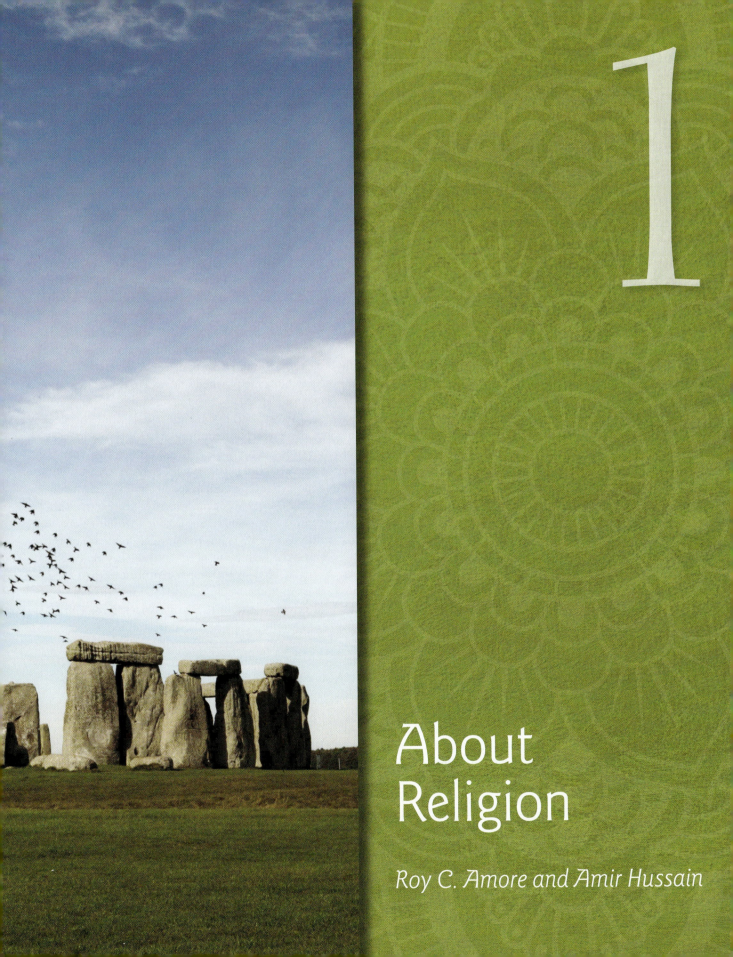

1

About Religion

Roy C. Amore and Amir Hussain

In this chapter you will learn about:

- some basic characteristics of human religion from ancient times
- a number of patterns that can be observed in more than one religious tradition
- various theories of why humans are religious
- some reasons for studying religion

⊛ Basic Human Religion: Looking Both Ways from Stonehenge

Standing on the west side of **Stonehenge**, we watch the sun rise through the circle of massive standing stones. Within the outer circle is a grouping of paired stones capped by lintels and arranged in a horseshoe pattern, opening towards the rising sun. At the centre of the horseshoe lies a flat stone that was once thought to have served as an altar for sacrifices. Today, however, it is believed that the centre stone originally stood upright, marking the spot where an observer would stand to watch the movements of the sun and stars.

The Stonehenge we know today is what remains of a structure erected between 3,500 and 4,000 years ago. But the site had already been used as a burial ground for centuries before that time: researchers believe that the remains of as many as 240 people, probably from a single ruling family or clan, were interred there between roughly 3000 and 2500 BCE.[1] The structure itself is generally believed to have been used for ceremonial purposes, and its orientation—towards the point where the sun rises at the summer solstice—has led many to think it might have been designed to serve as a kind of astronomical observatory. Another recent theory, based on excavations of a nearby Neolithic village, Durrington Walls, with a similar circular arrangement of timber posts, suggests that the two sites represented the living and the dead respectively, with Stonehenge serving as the permanent dwelling place of the ancestors. If so, there are parallels in other ancient cultures.[2]

Ignoring the crowd of tourists, we position ourselves behind the central stone to note the position of the rising sun in relation to the "heel stone" on the horizon more than 60 metres (200 feet) away. Today, on the morning of the summer solstice, the sun rises in the northeast, just to the left of the heel stone. It's easy to imagine that this day—the longest of the year and the only one on which the sun rises to the north side of the heel stone—would have been the occasion for some kind of ceremony in ancient times; that the entire community would have gathered at dawn to watch as someone with special authority—perhaps a priest, perhaps the local chief or ruler—confirmed the position of the rising sun. It's also easy to imagine the sense of order in the universe that would have come from knowing exactly when and where the sun would change course.

Tomorrow the sun will rise behind the heel stone, and it will continue its (apparent) journey towards the south for the next six months. Then in late December, at the winter solstice, the sun will appear to reverse course and begin travelling northwards again. Many centuries after people first gathered at Stonehenge, the Romans would celebrate this day as marking the annual "rebirth" of the sun—the high point of the festival they called Saturnalia. And in the fourth century CE, the Christians in Rome would choose the same time of year to celebrate the birth of their risen lord. Christmas would combine the unrestrained revelry of the Roman midwinter festival, marked by feasting, gift-giving, and general merriment, with the celebration of the coming to earth of a deity incarnate.

Looking Back from Stonehenge

There are a few concepts, shared by virtually all human cultures, which seem fundamental to what we call religion: powerful gods, sacred places, a life of some kind after death, the presence in the physical world of spirits that interact with humans in various ways. These concepts are so old and so widespread that no one can say where or when they first emerged.

Birds over Stonehenge (Tore Johannesen/Getty Images).

Three Worlds

Historically, it seems that humans around the globe have imagined the world to consist of three levels—sky, earth, and underworld. The uppermost level, the sky, has typically been considered the home of the greatest deities. Exactly how this concept developed is impossible to know, but we can guess that the awesome power of storms was one contributing factor. The apparent movement of the sun, the stars, and the planets across the sky was very likely another. Observing the varying patterns could well have led early humans to believe that the heavenly bodies were living entities animated by their own individual spirits—in effect, gods and goddesses.

The very highest level, in the heavens above the clouds and stars, was thought to be the home of the highest deity, typically referred to by a name such as Sky Father, Creator, or King of Heaven. This deity—invariably male—was the forerunner of the god of the monotheistic religions. Under the earth lived the spirits of serpents (surviving as the cobras, or **nagas**, in the religions of India) or reptilian monsters (surviving in dragon lore); perhaps because they were associated with dark and hidden places, they were usually imagined as evil. Finally, between the sky and the underworld lay the earth: the intermediate level where humans lived.

Sacred Places

Around the world, there are certain types of places where humans tend to feel they are in the presence of some unusual energy or power. Such places are regarded as set apart from the everyday world and are treated with special respect. Among those sacred places ("sacred" means "set aside") are mountains and hilltops—the places closest to the sky-dwelling deities. In the ancient Middle East, for instance, worship was often conducted at ritual centres known simply as "**high places**." People gathered at these sites to win the favour of the deities by offering them food, drink, praise, and prayer. One widely known example is the altar area on the cliff above the ancient city of Petra in Jordan (familiar to many people from the Indiana Jones films).

Great rivers and waterfalls are often regarded as sacred as well. And in Japan virtually every feature of the natural landscape—from great mountains and waterfalls to trees and stones—was traditionally believed to be animated by its own god or spirit (*kami*).

Animal Spirits

Another common and long-standing human tendency has been to attribute spirits to animals, either individually or as members of a family with a kind of collective guardian spirit. For this reason, traditional hunting societies have typically sought to ensure that the animals they kill for food are treated with the proper respect, lest other members of those species be frightened away or refuse to let themselves be caught.

In addition, body parts from the most impressive animals—bulls, bears, lions, eagles—have often been used as "power objects," to help make contact with the spirits of these animals. People in many cultures have attributed magical properties to objects such as bear claws or eagle feathers, wearing them as amulets or hanging them in the doorways of their homes as protection against evil spirits.

Death and Burial

From ancient times, humans have taken great care with the burial of their dead. The body might be positioned with the head facing east, the "first direction," where the sun rises, or placed in the fetal position, suggesting a hope for rebirth into a different realm. These burial positions in themselves would not be enough to prove a belief in an afterlife; however, most such graves have also contained, along with the remains of the dead, "grave goods" of various kinds. Some of these provisions for the afterlife likely belonged to the person in life; some appear to be specially made replicas; and some are rare, presumably costly items such as precious stones. Apparently the living were willing to sacrifice important resources to help the dead in the afterlife.

The belief that deceased ancestors can play a role in guiding the living members of their families appears to be especially widespread. Traditions such as the Japanese **Obon**, the Mexican **Day of the Dead**, and the Christian **All Saints Day** and **Hallowe'en** all reflect the belief that the souls of the dead return to earth once a year to share a ritual meal with the living.

Why Are Humans Religious?

The reasons behind human religiosity are complex and varied. All we can say with any certainty is that religion seems to grow out of human experiences: from the fear of death to the hope for a good afterlife, from the uncertainty surrounding natural events to the sense of control over nature provided by a priest capable of predicting the change of seasons and the movement of the planets. Religion emerges through the experience of good or bad powers that are sensed in dreams, in sacred spaces, and in certain humans and animals.

Religion has many emotional dimensions, including fear, awe, love, and hate. But it also has intellectual dimensions, including curiosity about what causes things to happen, a sense of order in the universe that suggests the presence of a creator, and the drive to make sense out of human experience.

The nature of religious belief and practice has changed through the centuries, so we must be careful not to take the religion of any particular time and place as the norm. What we can safely say is that religion is such an ancient aspect of human experience that it has become part of human nature. For this reason some scholars have given our species, *Homo sapiens*, a second name: *Homo religiosus*.

✸ Looking Forward from Stonehenge

Looking forward from ancient Stonehenge, we can see a number of patterns emerge in different parts of the world, some of them almost simultaneously.

Since most of the chapters in this book focus on individual religions, it may be useful to begin with a broader perspective. What follows is a brief overview of some of the major developments in the history of what the late Canadian scholar Wilfred Cantwell Smith (1916–2000) called "religion in the singular," meaning the history of human religiosity in the most general sense.

Shamanism

One very early pattern involves a ritual specialist— in essence, a kind of priest—that we know today as a **shaman**. The word "shaman" comes from a specific central Asian culture, but it has become the generic term for a person who acts as an intermediary between humans and the spirit world. Other terms include "medicine man," "soul doctor," and "witchdoctor."

Hunting Rituals

Many ancient cave drawings depict hunting scenes in which a human figure seems to be performing a dance of some kind. Based on what we know of later hunting societies, we can guess that the figure is a shaman performing a ritual either to ensure a successful hunt or to appease the spirits of the animals killed.

It's not hard to imagine why such societies would have sought ways to influence the outcome of the hunt. Indeed, it seems that the more dangerous the endeavour, the more likely humans were to surround it with rituals. As the anthropologist Bronislaw Malinowski pointed out in his book *Magic, Science and Religion*, the Trobriand Islanders he studied did not perform any special ceremonies before fishing in the lagoon, but they never failed to perform rituals before setting out to fish in the open ocean. This suggests that religious behaviour is, at least in part, a way of coping with dangerous situations.

In addition, though, as we have seen, early humans believed that the spirits of the animals they hunted had to be appeased. Thus a special ritual might be performed to mark the first goose kill of

AP photo/Jean Clottes

Animal images from the Chauvet cave in southern France, dated c. 30,000 BCE.

the season, in the hope that other geese would not be frightened away from the hunting grounds.

Such rituals reflect humans' concern over the future food supply, but they also reveal something about the nature of human belief in spirits. From very ancient times, it seems, humans have believed that the spirit—whether of an animal killed for food or of a human being—survives death and can communicate with others of its kind.

Coping with Unfriendly Spirits

The spirits associated with natural phenomena—whether animals or storms, mountains or rivers—have typically been thought to behave towards humans in the same ways that humans behave towards one another. Strategies for dealing with unfriendly spirits, therefore, are usually based on what works with humans.

Many cultures have believed wild, uninhabited areas to be guarded by resident spirits. In some cases,

these spirits have taken the form of monsters or mythical beasts; in others, of "little people" such as trolls (common in the folklore of Scandinavia, for example).

Unfriendly spirits were of particular concern to those who ventured into the forest as hunters or gatherers, but they were not confined to the wilderness. Pain and disease of all kinds—from toothache to appendicitis to mental illness—were also attributed to possession by malevolent spirits or demons. In Sri Lanka, those suffering from certain illnesses were advised to have a shaman sacrifice a chicken as an offering to the "graveyard demon," effectively bribing him to go away; in such cases a second chicken, still alive, would be given to the shaman who performed the ritual. Another approach was to frighten the demon away, either by threatening to invoke another, stronger spiritual power, such as the spirit guide of the shaman, to drive him off, or by making threatening gestures or loud noises. The firecrackers still used in some East Asian rituals are examples of the latter approach.

The Shaman

The most important resources of all, however, have been the shamans themselves. Shamans are still active in a number of cultures today. The way they operate varies, but certain patterns seem to be almost universal, which in itself suggests that the way of the shaman is very ancient. Sometimes the child of a shaman will follow in the parent's footsteps, but more often a shaman will be "called" to the role by his or her psychic abilities, as manifested in some extraordinary vision or revelation, or perhaps a near-death experience.

Candidates for the role of shaman face a long and rigorous apprenticeship that often includes a vision quest, in the course of which they are likely to confront terrifying apparitions. Typically the quester will acquire a guiding spirit, sometimes the spirit of a particular animal (perhaps a bear or an eagle, whose claws or feathers the shaman may wear to draw strength from its special powers) and sometimes a more human-like spirit (a god or goddess). That spirit then continues to serve as a guide and protector throughout the shaman's life.

To communicate with the spirit world, the shaman enters a trance state (often induced by rhythmic chanting or drumming). According to Mircea Eliade in his classic *Shamanism: Archaic Techniques of Ecstasy*, contact is then made in one of two ways. In the first, the shaman's soul leaves his body (which may appear lifeless) and travels to the realm where the spirits live; this way is described as "ecstatic" (from a Greek root meaning to "stand outside"). In the second, the shaman calls the spirit into her own body and is possessed by it; in such cases the shaman may take on the voice and personality of the spirit, or mimic its way of moving.

In either case, after regaining normal consciousness the shaman announces what he has learned about the problem at hand and what should be done about it. Typically, the problem is traced to the anger of a particular spirit; the shaman then explains the reason for that anger and what must be done to appease the spirit: in most cases the appropriate response is to perform a ritual sacrifice of some kind.

Connecting to the Cosmos

A second pattern is the one that inspired the building of structures like Stonehenge. People of the Neolithic ("new rock") era went to extraordinary lengths to create sacred areas by assembling huge stones in complex patterns. In some cases the motivation may have been political: perhaps a leader wanted to demonstrate his power over the people under his command. In others, however, the main reason undoubtedly had something to do with religion—for instance, the need for a public space where the rituals essential to the society—weddings, puberty rites, funerals—could be performed.

Discerning the Cosmic Cycles

Ritual centres such as Stonehenge may also have served purposes that we might think of as scientific or technical, but that their builders would have associated with religion. One very important function of priests was to track the seasons and determine the best time for seasonal activities such as planting. In addition to tracking the north–south movements of the sun, the people of the Neolithic era paid careful attention to the phases of the moon and the rising positions of certain constellations. The horizon was divided into segments named after the planet or constellation associated with that section. What we now call astrology developed as a way of understanding the cycle of the seasons and how humans fitted into it, collectively and individually. In ancient times no important decision would have been made without consulting an expert in the movements of the sun, moon, planets, and constellations. Even in modern times, many people, including political leaders, will consult an astrologer before making a major decision.

Hilltop Tombs

We suggested earlier that two powerful reasons behind human religion are the fear of death and the idea of an afterlife. Ancient cultures around the world appear to have favoured high places as burial sites. Where there were no hills, artificial ones were sometimes built, at least for the most important members of the society. The pyramids of Egypt and the stupas of Asia are both examples of this practice. In the pyramids, shafts extending from the burial chambers towards important stars connected the deceased with the cosmos. Similarly in Buddhist stupas, a wooden pole—later, a vertical stone structure—extended above the burial mound to connect the earth with the heavens. Scholars refer to this kind of symbolic link between earth and sky as an *axis mundi* ("world axis").

Animals and Gods

Another common feature of Neolithic religion was a tendency to associate certain animals with specific deities. One very early example comes from the ancient (c. 7000–5000 BCE) city of Catalhoyuk ("forked mound"), near Konya in modern Turkey, where a small sculpture was found of a woman flanked by two large felines. James Mellaart, the archaeologist who first excavated the site in the 1960s, believed she represented a mother goddess seated on a throne. Although this interpretation has been disputed, we know that the ancient Egyptians had a cat goddess named Bast who was revered as a symbol of both motherliness and hunting prowess. And the fierce Hindu goddess Durga is usually depicted riding either a lion or a tiger. (One Christmas card from modern India shows the Virgin Mary riding a tiger in the same fashion.)

The Bull God

A similar pattern of association links the most powerful male deities with the strength and virility of the bull. In Greek mythology, the great god Zeus took the form of a white bull when he abducted the Phoenician princess Europa. A creature known as the minotaur—half man, half bull—was said to have been kept in a labyrinth beneath the ancient palace of Knossos, on the island of Crete, where frescos show people leaping over the horns of a bull. Greek temples often displayed bull horns near

their altars. And in India a bull named Nandi is the sacred mount of the great god Shiva.

The association of the bull with the creator god can be seen even in Judaism, which strictly forbade the use of any image to represent its invisible deity. When Moses returns from the mountain and finds that his brother Aaron, the first high priest, has allowed the people to worship an image of a golden calf or bullock, he denounces this practice as idolatry. Centuries later, one of Solomon's sons is severely chastised for installing bull images in the temples he has built.

Temple Religion

A third pattern features larger temples, more elaborate sacrificial rituals, and the development of a priestly class endowed with unusual power, prestige, and wealth. This pattern, beginning at least 3,000 years ago, played an enormous role in shaping many traditions, including Judaism, Chinese religion, and Hinduism.

Indo-European Priests

"Indo-European" is a modern term referring to a language family and cultural system that eventually stretched from India all the way through Europe; it does not designate any particular ethnic group. The Indo-European (IE) cultural system has been one of the most important in human history. It may have originated in the region around the Black Sea, but that is only one of many theories that scholars have proposed. From the vocabulary of "proto-IE," as reconstructed by linguists, it is clear that the IE people hunted, practised metallurgy, rode horses, drove chariots, and waged war, among other things. Farming, however, appears not to have been part of their culture: the fact that the IE vocabulary related to agriculture differs from one place to another suggests that in farming the Indo-Europeans simply adopted existing local practices.

Everywhere the IE warriors conquered, they set up a social system with four basic divisions, the top three of which consisted of priests, warriors, and

Document

The Sacrifice

When they divided the Man [*Purusha*, the primal Person sacrificed by the gods to create the world], into how many parts did they disperse him? What became of his mouth, what of his arms, what were his two thighs and his two feet called? His mouth was the brahmin, his arms were made into the nobles, his two thighs were the populace, and from his feet the servants were born (Doniger O'Flaherty 1975: 26).

Three times a year all your males shall appear before the Lord your God at the place which he will choose: at the feast of unleavened bread, at the feast of weeks, and at the feast of booths. They shall not appear before the Lord empty-handed: All shall give as they are able, according to the blessing of the Lord your God that he has given you (from Moses' instructions to the people of Israel; Deuteronomy 16: 16–17).

middle-class commoners. In India these groups are known respectively as the brahmins, kshatriyas, and vaishyas. In ancient times each of these groups had a special clothing colour; thus today in India *varna* ("colour") is still the standard term for "class." The priests performed rituals, kept the calendar, taught the young, and advised the kings; within the warrior class, the top clans were the rulers, while the middle-class "commoners" earned their living as merchants or farmers. Finally, all people of local origin, no matter how wealthy or accomplished, were relegated to the servant (shudra) class.

The four-level social system was given mythic status in the *Rig Veda*, according to which the world came into being through the sacrifice of a "cosmic person" (*Purusha*). Out of his mouth came the brahmin priests, whose job was to chant the sacred hymns and syllables. The warriors came from his arms, the middle class from his thighs, and the servants from his feet. Even today, this ancient hymn continues to buttress the social class structure of India.

Over a period of about a thousand years, beginning around 2500 BCE, the Indo-Europeans took control of the territories that are now Afghanistan, northwest India, Pakistan, Turkey, Greece, Rome, central Europe, and, for a while, even Egypt. Their religious culture was similar to most of its counterparts four to five thousand years ago, with many deities, including a "sky father" (a name that survives in Greek Zeus Pater, Latin Jupiter, and Sanskrit Dyaus Pitar) and a storm god (Indra in India, Thor in Scandinavia); they sang hymns to female deities, such as the goddess of dawn; and they had a hereditary priesthood to offer sacrifices to the gods.

Although the IE people did not necessarily invent the system of hereditary priesthood, they certainly contributed to its spread. In addition to Hindu brahmins, examples include the ancient Roman priests and Celtic Druids. These priests enjoyed great power and prestige, and sometimes were resented by non-priests. (One ancient Indian text includes a parody in which dogs, acting like priests, dance around a fire chanting "*Om* let us eat, *om* let us drink."[3])

Priests and Temples Elsewhere

We actually know when the first Jewish temple was built. After David had been chosen as king of both the northern kingdom of Israel and the southern kingdom of Judah, he captured the Jebusite city now known as Jerusalem. He transformed the city into a proper capital, complete with a grand palace for himself and an organized priesthood. His son Solomon took the next step, building the first temple in the mid-tenth century BCE. The priests attached to the temple soon made it the only site where sacrificial rituals could be performed.

The Jewish priesthood was hereditary. All those who served in the temple as assistants to the priests were required to be Levites (from the tribe of Levi), and priests themselves had to be not only Levites but direct descendants of Aaron, the brother of Moses who was the original high priest.

Priests became a powerful social class in many other parts of the world as well, including Africa, Asia, and the Americas. In some cultures they were a hereditary class, and in others they were recruited. Typically, the role of priest was reserved for males, females being considered impure because of the menstrual cycle; the Vestal Virgins of ancient Rome, who tended the sacred fires and performed rituals, were among the very few exceptions to the general rule.

Prophetic Religion

By 700 BCE or even earlier, several new religious traditions had begun to form under the leadership of a great prophet or sage. The word "prophet" derives from Greek and has two related meanings, one referring to a person who speaks on behalf of a deity and one referring to a person who foresees or predicts the future. The terms are often conflated because prophets delivering messages from the deity often warned of disasters to come if God's will was not obeyed. The site of the temple at Delphi, Greece, where a virgin priestess under

Document

Ritual Sacrifice in the Hebrew Bible

Long before the establishment of the temple in Jerusalem, where priests would perform ritual sacrifices, God commanded the Hebrew patriarch Abram (later renamed Abraham) to sacrifice several animals to mark the covenant that was about to be made between them.

Then [God] said to [Abram], "I am the Lord who brought you from Ur of the Chaldeans, to give you this land to possess." But he said, "O Lord God, how am I to know that I shall possess it?" He said to him, "Bring me a heifer three years old, a female goat three years old, a ram three years old, a turtledove, and a young pigeon." He brought him all these and cut them in two, laying each half over against the other; but he did not cut the birds in two. And when birds of prey came down on the carcasses, Abram drove them away.

As the sun was going down, a deep sleep fell upon Abram, and a deep and terrifying darkness descended upon him. Then the Lord said to Abram, "Know this for certain, that your offspring shall be aliens in a land that is not theirs, and shall be slaves there, and they shall be oppressed for four hundred years; but I will bring judgment on the nation that they serve, and afterward they shall come out with great possessions. As for yourself, you shall go to your ancestors in peace; you shall be buried in a good old age. . . ."

When the sun had gone down and it was dark, a smoking fire pot and a flaming torch passed between these pieces [the halved carcasses]. On that day the Lord made a covenant with Abram, saying, "To your descendants I give this land, from the river of Egypt to the great river, the river Euphrates, the land of the Kenites, the Kenizzites, the Kadmonites, the Hittites, the Perizzites, the Rephaim, the Amorites, the Canaanites, the Girgashites, and the Jebusites" (Genesis 15: 7–21).

the inspiration of Apollo delivered prophecies, had been considered sacred for centuries, maybe millennia, before the glory days of classical Greece. It must have seemed a natural spot for making contact with the divine and receiving sacred knowledge: high up a mountainside, close to the gods, with a natural cave that resembled the entrance to a womb (*delphys* in Greek, representing the mysterious female energy) and a standing stone or *omphalos* (navel of the earth), representing the male energy and the connection between heaven and earth.

This sacred site dates back at least 3,000 years, to a time before the rise of classical Greece, when the oracle was believed to be inspired not by Apollo but by the earth goddess Gaia. Eventually males took control of the sacred site, but even in classical times the virgin priestesses would prepare themselves to receive Apollo's message by bathing in an artesian spring and breathing intoxicating fumes from a fissure in the earth—both water and fumes issuing from Gaia, the earth.

Those wishing to consult the oracle had to climb the mountain, make known their request, pay a fee, and sacrifice a black goat before their question would be put to the oracle. The priestess would take her place over the fissure and, in an ecstatic trance, deliver Apollo's message, which was typically unintelligible and had to be translated into ordinary language by a male priest. Interpreting the real-world significance of a prophecy was not so simple, however. In one famous case, a Greek leader who asked what would happen if he went to war with another state was told that a great country would fall; accordingly, he went to war—but the country that fell was his own. Similarly in the Oedipus myth, the oracle's prophecy that the infant would grow up to kill his father and marry his mother was fulfilled in spite of the measures taken to avoid that fate.

Abrahamic Prophetic Traditions

In 586 BCE the people of Israel were forcibly removed from their homeland and exiled to Babylon. The centuries that followed the "Babylonian captivity" were the defining period for the concept of prophecy as it developed in the three monotheistic traditions that trace their origins to the prophet Abraham. Often, the Jewish prophets' messages were directed towards the people of Israel as a whole, warning of the disasters that loomed if they did not follow God's demands. Christianity saw Jesus and certain events surrounding his life as the fulfillment of Hebrew prophecies. And Islam in turn recognized the Hebrew prophets, beginning with Abraham and including Jesus, as the forerunners of the Prophet Muhammad, the last and greatest of all, the messenger (*rasul*) who received God's final revelations. Muslims understand Muhammad to have been the "seal of the prophets": no other prophet will follow him, since he has delivered the message of God in its entirety. As with earlier prophetic traditions, the Day of Judgment (or Day of Doom) and the concepts of heaven and hell are central to Islam.

Zarathustra, Prophet of the Wise Lord

Zarathustra (or Zoroaster) was a prophet figure who lived more than 2,500 years ago, probably in the region of eastern Iran or Afghanistan. Although we know little about his life, he left behind a collection of poems devoted to a "wise lord" called Ahura Mazda. The religion that developed around his teachings, which came to be known as Zoroastrianism, played an important part in the development of monotheism. The concepts of heaven and hell also owe a lot to the Zoroastrians, who believed that evildoers were condemned to hell at their death, but that eventually a great day of judgment would come when the souls of all the dead would be made to pass through a fiery wall. Those who had been virtuous in life would pass through the fire without pain, while the rest would be cleansed of their remaining sin and permitted to enter paradise (a term believed to derive from a Persian word meaning garden). The threat of hell and the promise of heaven were powerful tools for any prophet seeking to persuade people to behave as they believed the deity demanded.

Sites

Tell Megiddo, Israel

Tell Megiddo is an archeological mound in Israel, southeast of the modern city of Haifa. The ancient city of Megiddo was strategically located near a pass used by the trade route connecting Egypt and Assyria. The site of a battle with Egypt in the sixteenth century BCE, Har ("Mount") Megiddo is mentioned numerous times in the Hebrew Bible, and is referred to by the Greek version of its name, Armageddon, in the Book of Revelation 16: 16—a passage that some Christians interpret to mean that a final battle will be fought there at the end of time.

© Richard T. Nowitz/Corbis

The remains of Har Megiddo, the site known to Christians as Armageddon. The circular rock structure is thought to have been an altar.

The Energy God

Yet another important pattern emerged around 2,500 years ago. In it the divine is understood not as a human-like entity but as the energy of the cosmos. The Energy God does not issue commandments, answer prayers, or in any way interact with humans as a human. It does not create in the usual fashion of gods; it does not direct the course of history, or dictate the fate of individuals. In fact, some have suggested that this god may have more in common with the principles of modern physics than with

Document

Divine Energy

The Dao that can be told of
Is not the Absolute Dao;
The Names that can be given
Are not Absolute Names.
The Nameless is the origin of Heaven and Earth;
The Named is the Mother of All Things
(from Laozi in the *Daodejing*; Lin Yutang 1948: 41).

This finest essence, the whole universe has it as its Self: That is the Real: That is the Self: That *you* are, Svetaketu! (from the *Chandogya Upanishad* 6.9; Zaehner 1966: 110).

the traditional gods of most religions. This divinity simply exists—or rather, "underlies" everything that exists. Among the traditions that developed around the Energy God concept were Chinese Daoism, the Upanishadic wisdom of India, and the pre-Socratic philosophy of the early Greek world.

Finding the Dao Within

The sage who became known as Laozi ("Master Lao") lived in northern China around 600 BCE. According to legend, he worked for the government as an archivist. At night students would visit his home to hear his words of wisdom about life, especially how to live in harmony with one's inner nature. But Lao had what we might call a mid-life crisis. Dissatisfied with his job and the social and political life of his time, he is said to have left home and set out to the west, riding on a water buffalo (an event that became a favourite subject for artists). Apparently he had not even said goodbye to his students, but one of them happened to be working as a guard at the border. Shocked to learn that his master was leaving China, he begged Lao to record his teachings before leaving.

So Lao paused at the border long enough to write down the fundamentals of his thought in a series of beautiful, if cryptic, verses that were eventually collected in a small volume called **Daodejing** (or *Tao De Ching*), meaning the book (*jing*) about the

Dao and its power (*de*). It became and remains one of the world's most influential books.

What did Laozi write that has spoken to so many through the millennia? He begins with what became one of the most famous opening lines in history: "The Dao that can be described is not the eternal Dao. The name that can be named is not the eternal name." In general usage the word "Dao" means "the way," but here it refers to the mysterious energy that underlies all things. Laozi is warning readers that words cannot adequately describe the Dao. Ogden Nash, a twentieth-century poet noted for combining insight and humour, captured the same idea this way: "Whatever the mind comes at, God is not that."

In traditional cultures, people talk about the characteristics of various deities—their loving nature, or anger, or jealousy, or desire for a particular kind of behaviour. But the absolute, the eternal Dao, has no such attributes. Thus Laozi uses poetic imagery to give us some insights into its nature. Unlike Athena, Zeus, Yahweh, or Indra, the Dao does not have a "personality," and there is no reason for humans to fear, love, or appease it.

Rather, Laozi says, the Dao is like water: it will take on the shape of whatever container we pour it into. Falling from the sky, it may seem content to lie in the hollow made by the hoof of an ox in the muddy road. Raining on the rocky mountaintop, it tumbles all the way down. Water seems malleable, passive and without a will of its own. Yet a mountain will be worn down by the water over time. The water in the hoofprint will evaporate and return to the sky, to fall again when the time is right.

"That Is You": Sitting near the Sages of Old India

A worldview similar to that of Daoism took shape in northern India around the same time. It is reflected in the **Upanishads** (a Sanskrit term meaning literally "sitting-up-near" the master), a series of philosophical texts composed beginning around 600 BCE.

What the Daoist sages called the Dao the Upanishadic masters called *sat* (usually translated as "being," "truth," or "the real"). One Upanishad tells the story of a young man named Svetaketu who has just completed his studies with the brahmin priests. Back at home, his father, who is a king and therefore a member of the warrior class, asks Svetaketu what his priestly teachers taught him about the original source of all things. When Svetaketu admits that he was not taught about that subject, his father undertakes to instruct him in the secret wisdom.

The first lesson has to do with the need for sleep and food; then the real teaching begins. The father has Svetaketu bring a bowl of water and taste it. Then he has him put a lump of sea salt into the water. The next morning Svetaketu sees that the lump of salt is no longer visible; he tastes the water and finds it salty. We can imagine his impatience at being instructed in something he already knows. But his father has a bigger point in mind. He tells Svetaketu that just as the salt is invisible yet present in the water, so also there is a hidden essence present throughout the world. That hidden essence, the force that energizes everything, is the highest reality, the father says, and that reality is you (*tat tvam asi*; "that you are"). The Upanishadic master is initiating his son into a new religious worldview that understands "god" as an energy hidden within and sustaining everything. And that great energy, that ultimate reality, "*tat tvam asi*"—that is you.

The First Principle: Greek Philosophy before Socrates

Around 2,500 years ago the Greek-speaking philosophers of Ionia (now southwestern Turkey) began to ask the same questions as Svetaketu's father: What is the first principle, the first cause, the source from which all else comes? Starting from the science of the day, which held there to be four primal elements—earth, air, fire, and water—they wanted to determine which of the four came first. Although their methods were those of philosophy rather than scientific experimentation, their attempt to understand the causal principle underlying all things—without bringing in a god as the final cause—marked a major advance towards the development of the scientific worldview.

Later Theistic Mysticism

European religious thought eventually reflected mysticism as well. German Christian mystics such as Jacob Böhme (1575–1624) would use terms such as *Ungrund* ("ungrounded") or *Urgrund* ("original ground") to refer to the divine as primal cause. Christian, Jewish, and Muslim mystics all believed in a god beyond the reaches of human understanding.

Purity and Monasticism

At almost the same time that the "Energy God" worldview was establishing itself in China, India, and Greek culture, another spiritual movement of great importance was developing in India. The earliest historical records come from the region of what is now northern India around 2,500 years ago, but the tradition itself claims to have much older roots. Its followers typically sought spiritual enlightenment through asceticism—intense bodily discipline. Their ethic was one of non-violence towards all creatures, and their goal was perfect purity of mind.

Ganges Spirituality

English has no specific term for the new type of religion that came into bloom in the region of the Ganges river around 500 BCE. By that time the Indo-European cultural system, including the religion of the brahmin priests, was firmly established in what is now northern India. We can never know for certain what earlier traditions that religion displaced, since the written sources we rely on were the products of the brahmins themselves. However, linguistic and archaeological data lend support to the theory that two of the world's great living religions—Jainism and Buddhism—were rooted in the pre-brahminic traditions of the Ganges region.

Along the banks of the river were many camps where spiritual masters of various persuasions operated what were in effect open-air seminaries. Though some of the teachers were brahmins, others were committed to the idea that it was wrong to harm any living creature. Their followers rejected the killing of animals for food, and some even objected to farming, because hoeing and plowing would harm organisms living in the soil. While the brahmin masters continued to perform their animal sacrifices, the masters committed to the principle of non-harm (*ahimsa*) denounced that tradition. Some of the latter—among them the Jaina master Mahavira—went so far as to require their disciples to cover their mouths and noses and strain their drinking water, in order to avoid causing harm to microscopic insects.

Leaving the world of day-to-day life to follow the path of spiritual enlightenment through rigorous ascetic discipline, the students who gathered around these masters took vows of poverty and celibacy, and considered themselves to have "departed the world." The Buddhist and Jaina monastic traditions trace their roots to these ascetics, and it is possible that Indian monasticism played a role in the development of Western monasticism as well.

One more difference between the Indo-European and "Gangetic" cultural systems is worth mentioning here. In the IE system, priests were recruited only from the brahmin social class. In the Ganges tradition, by contrast, the notion of a hereditary priesthood is rejected entirely: anyone, however humble, can choose to lead the life of a holy person. As the Buddha would teach his followers, the status of the "true brahmin" is not a birthright, but must be earned through meritorious conduct.

Mystery Religion

"Mystery religion" refers to a type of Greek and Roman tradition in which the core teachings and rituals were kept secret from outsiders and were revealed only to those who were prepared to undergo initiation in the hope of securing blessings during this life and a heavenly paradise in the afterlife. Such religions became so popular during the Roman period that they presented a threat to the power and influence of the official Roman priesthood (not to be confused with the Roman Catholic priesthood).

The Eleusinian mystery tradition may be the oldest. Named for an ancient Greek town called Eleusis, it grew out of the myth of the young Persephone or Kore ("girl") who is abducted by the god of the dead (Hades) and taken down into the underworld. With the disappearance of this young girl—a potent symbol of growth and fertility—everything on earth begins to die. This imperils not only humans but the gods themselves, who depend on humans to feed them through sacrifices. The girl's mother, Demeter, is therefore allowed to descend into the underworld and bring her back. Scholars understand the Persephone myth to be based on the seasonal cycles of stagnation during the winter and renewal in the spring. Members of her cult believed that by identifying themselves with the dying and rising goddess through the celebration of seasonal rituals, they too would triumph over death.

Initiates into the mysteries associated with the god Dionysus were also following a very ancient tradition. Through rituals that included the drinking of wine, ecstatic dancing, and, perhaps, the eating of mind-altering plants, participants were able to enter into ecstatic states of consciousness in which they believed that their god would ensure

Document

Avatar Gods

For the protection of the good,
For the destruction of evildoers,
For the setting up of righteousness,
I come into being, age after age.
(Krishna to Arjuna in the *Bhagavad Gita*; Zaehner 1966: 267).

Have this mind among yourselves, which you have in Christ Jesus, who, though he was in the form of God, did not count equality with God a thing to be grasped, but emptied himself, taking the form of a servant, being born in the likeness of men. And being found in human form he humbled himself. . . . (St Paul to the Christians of Philippi: Philippians 2: 6–7).

a pleasant afterlife. Another popular mystery cult, dedicated to the goddess Isis, had Egyptian origins.

Many scholars have suggested that mystery cults such as these may have influenced the development of Christianity. The early Christians were initiated into the new cult by undergoing baptism. They then joined an inner circle of people whose faith centred on the death and resurrection of Jesus and who hoped that by following Christ they would secure blessings during this life and a place in heaven after death. Although Christianity developed out of Judaism, its theological structure does seem to have been influenced, however indirectly, by mystery religion.

Avatar: God on Earth

The Avatar

Long before anyone thought of an "avatar" as either a blue-skinned movie humanoid or the on-screen image representing a player in a computer game, *avatar(a)* was a Sanskrit theological term for the "coming down" to earth of a god. By the first century of the Common Era, the idea of a god born in human form was taking root in many parts of the world. In the earlier stages of religion there were many stories of gods and goddesses who came down to earth, but there are two major differences in the avatar stories.

First, whereas the ancient gods came down to earth as gods, the avatar is a god in a truly human form—as a later Christian creed put it, "fully God and fully man." For example, in the ancient Indian story of Princess Dhamayanti, her father holds a party to which he invites all the marriageable princes from various kingdoms. Four gods also attend the party, however, all disguised as the handsome prince Nala, whom the princess already plans to choose. At first she is disturbed to see five look-alikes, but finally finds that she can distinguish the four divine imposters because they do not sweat and are floating slightly above the ground. She marries the human prince, and they live happily ever after.

Unlike the gods at Dhamayanti's party, the avatar gods walk on the ground, sweat, get hungry, sleep, and are in every way human. They are incarnated in a human womb, are born, grow up, teach, save the world from evil, and eventually die. As a Christian layman once explained, "You have to understand that we Christians worship a god in diapers." His choice of words was unusual, but his theology was solid, and it leads us to the second major innovation that came with the concept of the avatar god.

This second innovation is the idea that the avatar god is a saviour figure in at least two ways. Not only does he save the world from some evil power, such as Satan or a demonic king: he also saves from hell those who put their faith in him and secures them a place in heaven. In avatar religions, the ritual of sacrifice is replaced by the ritual of placing faith in the saviour god.

The biography of the saviour gods follows a well-known pattern. Typically, the avatar god has a special, non-sexual conception. His mother is chosen to bear him because she is exceptionally pure, and an angel or prophet announces to her that the child she is carrying has a special destiny. The saviour's birth, usually in a rustic setting, is surrounded by miracles, which often include a fortuitous star or constellation pattern in the night sky. Wise persons foresee the child's greatness. An evil king tries to kill the baby, but kills another baby, or other babies, instead. The child has special powers, and as an adult is able to work miracles. He typically marries and has a child before embarking on his religious mission. His death represents a triumph over evil and the cosmos responds with earthquakes and other natural signs. Upon dying, he returns to the heavens to preside over a paradise in which his followers hope to join him after they die.

The avatar concept took root in Asia and the Middle East at least two thousand years ago. Among Hindus its impact was reflected in the worship of Krishna; among Buddhists in the veneration of Amitabha Buddha (the figure who would become Amida in Japan); and among Jews in the rise of Christianity.

The name Krishna means "dark one," and he is usually pictured as dark blue or black. Here the youthful Krishna and his older brother Balarama are pictured stealing ghee (Indian-style butter) from storage pots, thus earning his nickname "The Butter Thief." He is both an avatar of God and a naughty human boy.

Krishna, Avatar of Vishnu

In some Hindu stories Vishnu is the ultimate deity, the god who lies at the origin of everything there is, including the creator god Brahman. Vishnu lies on his cosmic serpent, sometimes identified with the Milky Way, and out of his navel grows a lotus plant. From the lotus Brahman is born as the first of all creations; then the universe and all its material and spiritual energies follow. This is not exactly a mythic version of the big bang theory, but it comes close. Life evolves, over an unimaginable number of years, out of the divine energy at the centre of the universe. After the universe has run its allotted course, the process reverses from evolution to involution. Over an equally long period of time, eventually all things return into Vishnu, as if crossing the event horizon into a black hole. There all energy lies dormant as Vishnu sleeps, before the whole process begins again.

Another story about Vishnu sees him as the protector of the world. When earth gets into trouble, he comes down to save us. The first five *avatars* of Vishnu take the form of animals that protect the world from natural disasters in its formative millennia. The next four avatars are humans, the most important of whom is Krishna. His exploits are narrated in several different Hindu sources. The most famous is the *Bhagavad Gita*—the "Song of the Lord." A small section of the epic *Mahabharata*, the *Gita* tells of a great war between two houses of the royal family. Krishna is a relative of both houses and is recruited by both armies, but chooses to fight for neither. Instead, he agrees to drive the chariot of Arjuna, one of the five princes who lead one army.

At the beginning of the *Gita*, just before the battle, Arjuna asks Krishna to drive the chariot into the neutral zone between the two great armies, so that he can get a better look at the enemy. But when he sees his adversaries more closely, he loses his will to fight, telling Krishna that he recognizes among them his cousins, his old teachers, and others he remembers from childhood.

Krishna counsels him to take up his bow and fight, for that is his duty as a warrior. Arjuna has misgivings, however, and they begin a long conversation about morality or duty (*dharma*) and the eternal soul that cannot die even though the body may be killed in battle. Krishna teaches with such great authority that soon Arjuna asks how he knows so much. Krishna replies that he is a god of gods, that he is the energy behind all the categories of spirits and gods. When Arjuna asks for proof, Krishna grants him the eye of a god, with which he sees the splendours and mysteries of the universe as a god would.

In the end, Arjuna accepts the divinity of his chariot-driving cousin, acts on his advice, fights alongside his brothers, and wins the war. More important, however, is what Arjuna learns from Krishna about the many ways to lead a good religious life. These include the *yoga* (way) of good works (*karma yoga*), the way of deep spiritual wisdom (*jnana yoga*), and the way of faithful devotion to Krishna (*bhakti yoga*). Of these, the path of faithful devotion is the most highly recommended because it is the easiest and the most certain. The real saving power comes not from the wisdom or discipline of the individual, but from the saving power of the god. Krishna promises that those who practise devotion to him will go to his heaven when they die.

Another source offers stories about other parts of Krishna's life. We learn from it that Krishna was born under the rule of an evil king who was secretly part of a demonic plot to take over the world. One day King Kamsa is driving the wedding chariot of a female relative when an old man—a prophet figure—yells out to the king and tells him he is assisting in the marriage of a woman whose eighth child will grow up to kill him. The king is about to call off the wedding, but the bride pleads with him to reconsider, even promising that when she has children, Kamsa can do with them as he wishes. Kamsa agrees, the marriage takes place, and he proceeds to kill her children as they are born. On the night of the fateful eighth birth, the father is told in a dream to take the baby to safety with relatives across the river. This he does, replacing his child with a baby girl born the same evening.

When the king's guards hear the baby crying, they awaken the king, who smashes the infant's head on the ground. As the baby's soul rises towards heaven, it tells Kamsa that the baby who will grow up to kill him is still alive. That child is Krishna, and when he grows up he fulfills his destiny, saving the world from the evil represented by Kamsa and his demons.

Amitabha, the Buddha of Saving Grace

The avatar concept gave Buddhism the story of Amitabha Buddha, in which a prince intent on achieving buddhahood makes 48 vows, a number of which focus on helping others towards the same goal. Among them is a promise to establish a paradise free of all suffering, disease, and ill will, in which those who put their trust in Amitabha Buddha will be reborn after their death. His followers hope that if they sincerely profess their faith in his saving power, they will be rewarded with rebirth in that "Pure Land."

Jesus the Christ: God Come Down

The Christian doctrine of the trinity affirms that the one God exists in three persons: those of the father, the son, and the holy spirit. In formulating this doctrine, the Christians departed radically from the theology proclaimed by Abraham and Moses. There is no room in Jewish thought for an avatar god, but that was the direction in which Christian thought developed. The prologue to the Gospel of John identifies Jesus with the divine Logos—the word of God that was present before creation. The New Testament says that Jesus "emptied himself of divinity" and came down for the salvation of the world. He is conceived in the womb of a virgin by the spirit of God. An angel announces the pregnancy and its significance to his mother. The birth is associated with a special star. Shepherds overhear the angels rejoicing and come to revere the infant, according to Luke's gospel. In Matthew's gospel, magi (wise men) from the East follow a special star and bring gifts to the child.

For Christians, Jesus became the ultimate god who died on the cross on behalf of his followers and rose on the third day. By participating in the sacred rituals—the sacraments of baptism and the eucharist (in which consecrated bread and wine are consumed in commemoration of the Last Supper)—and placing their trust in Jesus as Lord, Christians hoped to secure a place in heaven after their death.

So Christianity starts with the Hebrew scriptures and the monotheism of Moses and incorporates into them the avatar pattern, along with elements of the mystery traditions, to form a new religion. Many Jews resisted these changes, but some accepted them in the belief that God had in fact offered the world a new dispensation.

Scriptural Religion

The beginning of scriptural religion is hard to date. The earliest scriptures we have are the Zoroastrian Avesta of Persia, the Hindu Vedas, and the Torah of Judaism, all of which took shape approximately 3,000 years ago. Religions based primarily on scripture came much later, however, when different groups began to insist that their particular scriptures were the literal words of God, and to make adherence to those scriptures the focus of their religious life.

Scripturalism manifested itself in Rabbinic Judaism in the centuries that followed the destruction of the Jerusalem temple in 70 CE. It emerged in full force with the rise of Islam, destined to become one of the two most influential religions of all time, in the seventh century. It also played a large role in Protestant Christianity, starting in the sixteenth century, in which the authority of scripture replaced that of tradition and the papacy.

Living by Torah

During the Jews' exile in Babylon the priests were not able to perform the traditional temple rituals, and so the Jews turned to the rabbis—scholars of the Torah with special expertise in Jewish law and

Document

The Word of God

We have sent it down as an Arabic Qur'an, in order that you may learn wisdom (from the Qur'an, 12: 2).

In the beginning was the Word, and the Word was with God, and the Word was God. The same was in the beginning with God. All things were made by him, and without him was not any thing made that was made (John 1: 1–3, KJV).

And the Word was made flesh and dwelt among us (John 1: 14, KJV).

ritual. In this way scripture began to play a more important role in Jewish life, a role that became even more important after the destruction of the second temple in 70 CE. Since that time, Jewish religious life has centred on interpretation of the scripture.

The Word of God

The gospels were not written until two or three generations after the death of Jesus, and the Christian canon did not take final shape until well into the third century CE. But once the books of the canon were fixed, the Church came to emphasize scripture as a divinely inspired source of faith and practice. The Bible became as central to Christianity as the Torah was to Judaism. Christians commonly refer to the scripture as the word of God, and some believe that the Bible was literally dictated by God to its human authors.

God's Final Prophet

The scriptural approach to religion reached its greatest height in Islam. The *surahs* that make up the Qur'an are believed to be the sacred words of God as revealed to the Prophet Muhammad by an angel, recorded by scribes, and compiled as a collection after his death. In its essence, therefore, the Qur'an is considered to be an oral text, meant to be recited—always in the original Arabic—rather than read. Nevertheless, the written Qur'an is treated with great respect. No other book is to be placed on top of the Qur'an, and before opening the book, the reader is expected to be in the same state of ritual purity required to perform the daily prayers.

The Lotus Sutra

The teachings of the Buddha were transmitted orally for centuries before they were first written down, some 2,000 years ago. Although Buddhists revered these texts, their practice did not centre on them. Later, the Mahayana and Vajrayana schools added many more texts to their respective canons, but Buddhists in general did not attribute any special properties to the scriptures themselves. That changed in the 1200s, when a Japanese monk named Nichiren instructed his followers to place their faith in the power of his favourite scripture, the *Lotus Sutra*, and chant their homage to it, just as followers of the Pure Land school chanted homage to Amitabha/Amida Buddha.

Creation through the Word of God

A number of scriptural traditions have maintained that their scriptures were in existence before the world was created. The medieval book of Jewish mysticism known as the *Zohar*, for example, teaches that the Torah played a role in the creation. The prologue to the Gospel of John in the New Testament talks about creation through the Word (*logos*

School children in Ibadan, Nigeria, learning to read the Arabic of the Qur'an.

in Greek). And Islam understands the Qur'an to have existed in the mind of God before the world itself was brought into existence.

This idea has very old roots. In ancient Israel, Egypt, India, and elsewhere, it was assumed that the deities would not have performed the physical work of creation themselves, like ordinary humans: rather, like kings, they would have commanded that the work be done: "Let there be light." Thus the divine word took on a special role in later theologies. In traditional Hindu thought, the goddess of speech, Vac, played this role. How could the scriptures—the actual words of the Torah, Bible, or Qur'an—be present in the mind of God at the time of creation, thousands of years before the historical events they describe? The answer for believers is that God knows the future. Outsiders might argue that this calls into question the concept of free will: If the deity knows everything in advance, how can humans be free to choose? What use is it to try to persuade people to do the right thing if the deity

has already determined what each of them will do? Such questions have led to lively theological debates in many religious traditions.

Some branches of scriptural religions place such total authority in their scripture that outsiders have branded them **fundamentalists**. As we will see in Chapter 8, the term "fundamentalism" was first used in the early twentieth century to refer to a variety of American Protestantism characterized by a fervent belief in the absolute, literal truth of the Bible. Similar movements exist within most religious traditions.

✸ What Is Religion?

Many scholars trace the derivation of the word "religion" to the Latin verb *religare*, "to bind." Yet others argue that the root is *relegere*, "to go over again." From the beginning, then, there is no universal definition of religion. We can describe religion as being concerned with the divine, but even that raises questions. Is there one god that is worshipped, or many gods? What about atheism, or no gods? Most of us would probably not think of atheism as a religion, but what about Theravada Buddhism, which is clearly a religion but has nothing to do with an Abrahamic-style god? The same problem arises with religious texts. Is there one text or a set of texts that is particularly authoritative for a particular tradition? Is that set a closed "canon," or can new materials be added to it? What are the distinctions between established religions and newer ones (sometimes referred to pejoratively as "cults")? We may accept, for example, the validity of a man (Moses) receiving revelations from God on Mount Sinai 3,200 years ago, or another man (Muhammad) receiving similar revelations in Mecca 1,400 years ago, but reject the idea of a third man (Joseph Smith) receiving revelations in upstate New York 200 years ago. There is some truth in the saying "today's cult, tomorrow's religion." Although this text focuses mainly on established traditions, it will discuss several newer religious movements in Chapter 7.

Another way of looking at religion is in terms of its functions. For example, a simple functional definition might be that religion is a way of creating community. For some people, "church" has less to do with piety or Sunday worship than with a community that offers a sense of belonging and activities to participate in. Karl Marx defined religion in terms of economics; Sigmund Freud, in terms of interior psychological states. Other scholars have approached the question from the perspective of sociology or anthropology, looking at religion as a social phenomenon or a cultural product. The academic study of religion is usually a secular, non-confessional enterprise, undertaken without a particular faith commitment. One of the key scholars in this area is Jonathan Z. Smith at the University of Chicago. His work on the history of religions has had a profound impact on scholarly understanding of key terms such as "myth" and "ritual," and the way comparisons are made both within a single religious tradition and across different traditions.

⊛ Why Study Religion?

The first and most obvious reason to study religion is that it exists. Not all humans would lay claim to religious beliefs, but humans in general have been religious from time immemorial.

A closely related reason is that religion has played such an important role in human affairs. People organize their communities around religious identities, go to war over religious beliefs, make great art in the service of religion, seek to change social norms, or to prevent change, out of religious conviction. In short, religion so pervades the human world that it demands our attention regardless of whether it plays a direct role in our own lives.

It is also common to study religion for more personal reasons. You may want to know more about the tradition you, or someone close to you, grew up in. You may want to study other religions in order to understand other people's beliefs, or to look at your own beliefs from a different perspective. You may also want to arm yourself with knowledge in order to bring others around to your way of thinking, or to defend your beliefs against the arguments of those who might try to convert you to theirs.

Insider versus Outsider

Most people learn about their own religion from their parents, their teachers at religious schools, or other members of the same religious community. Naturally, we tend to accept the teachings of our own religion as true and assume that the teachings of other religions are false, or at least less true. As "insiders" we may find it disturbing when "outsiders" challenge our beliefs or suggest that the history of "our religion" may not be exactly as we have been taught. In his 1962 book *The Meaning and End of Religion*, Wilfred Cantwell Smith famously wrote: "Normally persons talk about other people's religions as they are, and about their own as it ought to be."

One of the advantages of a book such as this is that it helps us appreciate our own traditions from both insider and outsider points of view. When approaching an unfamiliar religious tradition, outsiders need to be sensitive to the ways in which it serves the needs of its followers. For their part, insiders need to understand how their own tradition looks from the outside.

The insider–outsider matter is more complex than we might imagine, for there are many kinds of insiders. Is your Muslim friend a Sunni or a Shi'i? If a Shi'i, does she belong to the Twelver branch or one of the Sevener branches? Which variety of Buddhism does your classmate practise—Theravada, Mahayana, or Vajrayana? If Mahayana, which school? Is your Christian neighbour Protestant, Catholic, or Orthodox? A Protestant may well be an "outsider" to other Protestant groups, let alone to Catholic Christianity. A Zen Buddhist could have trouble seeing any connection between his practice and an elaborate Vajrayana ritual. Because each religion has many subdivisions, in these volumes we will speak of traditions in the plural. We hope our readers will keep in mind the diversity behind the monolithic labels.

Some Practical Matters

The East–West division of our two volumes is quite conventional, but it's problematic for several reasons. For one thing, the so-called "Western" religions arose in what we now term the Middle East: they are Western only in the sense that they were widely adopted in the West. A related problem is that there is no clear dividing line between East and West. As the late Will Oxtoby pointed out in an earlier edition of this text,

> Well into the twentieth century, the East was everything to the east of Europe. The Orient

began where the Orient Express ran: Istanbul. For some purposes, it even included North Africa and began at Morocco. A century ago, Islam was thought to be an Eastern religion, and Westerners who studied it were called orientalists.

For those of us living in the twenty-first century, the biggest problem with the East–West division is that all the religions discussed in these volumes may be found anywhere in the world. In any event, our Eastern volume focuses on traditions that developed in the East and are still centred there, while its Western counterpart focuses mainly on traditions that developed in the Middle East and now predominate in the Middle East, Europe, Africa, and the Americas.

For dates we use BCE ("Before the Common Era") rather than BC ("Before Christ"), and CE ("Common Era") rather than AD ("Anno Domini," Latin for "in the year of our lord"). For dates that are obviously in the Common Era, the "CE" will be implied.

Finally, it is difficult to decide whether a book like this should use diacritical marks on foreign words. Scholars of religion writing for other scholars typically use diacritics for precision in transliterating foreign terms into English. Since this is an introductory text, we have chosen not to use diacritics because students often find them more confusing than helpful. Anyone who wishes to do more research on a religious tradition will soon encounter them, however.

Whether or not you are religious yourself, we invite you to delve into the study of several religious traditions that have played central roles both in the lives of individual humans and in the civilizations they have built around the world.

Discussion Questions

1. What are some concepts that are fundamental to what we call religion?

2. What are some of the major developments or patterns in the history of human religiosity?

3. What is an avatar? Give an example from both an Eastern and a Western tradition to illustrate your answer.

Glossary

All Saints Day A Christian festival honouring all the departed saints; held in the West on 1 November.

Daodejing The Daoist "Classic of the Way and Power," compiled roughly 2,500 years ago and traditionally attributed to Laozi.

Day of the Dead A Mexican festival honouring the dead.

fundamentalists/fundamentalism Persons who ascribe total authority to their scriptures or doctrines, rejecting any conflicting secular or religious alternatives.

Hallowe'en Now a popular secular holiday, held on 31 October; originally celebrated as the "Eve" of All Saints Day.

high places Sacred areas located on hill- or mountain tops; such places existed throughout the ancient Near East.

naga A mythical cobra living in the underworld, often associated with water and fertility in Indian religions.

Obon A Japanese festival honouring ancestors.

shaman A type of priest, widespread among hunter-gatherer societies, who communicates with the spirit world on behalf of the people.

Stonehenge One of several ancient rock structures thought to have been constructed for ritual purposes.

Upanishads Hindu religious texts thought to have been composed around 600 BCE.

References

Ballter, Michael. 2005. *The Goddess and the Bull: Catalhoyuk: An Archaeological Journey to the Dawn of Civilization*. New York: Free Press.

Doniger O'Flaherty, Wendy. 1975. *Hindu Myths: A Source Book*. Translated from the Sanskrit. Harmondsworth: Penguin Classics.

Eliade, Mircea. [1951] 1964. *Shamanism: Archaic Techniques of Ecstasy*. Translated by Willard R. Trask. Princeton: Princeton University Press.

Lin, Yutang. 1948. *The Wisdom of Laotse*. New York: The Modern Library.

Malinowski, Bronislaw. 1948. *Magic, Science and Religion*. Boston: Beacon Press.

Zaehner, R.C., ed. 1966. *Hindu Scriptures*. London: Everyman's Library.

Notes

1. Marc Kaufman, "Researchers Say Stonehenge Was a Family Burial Ground," *Washington Post*, 30 May 2008: A1.

2. Mike Parker Pearson, *Stonehenge: Exploring the Greatest Stone Age Mystery* (London: Simon and Shuster, 2012).

3. *Chandogya Upanishad* I, xii, in Zaehner 1966: 84.

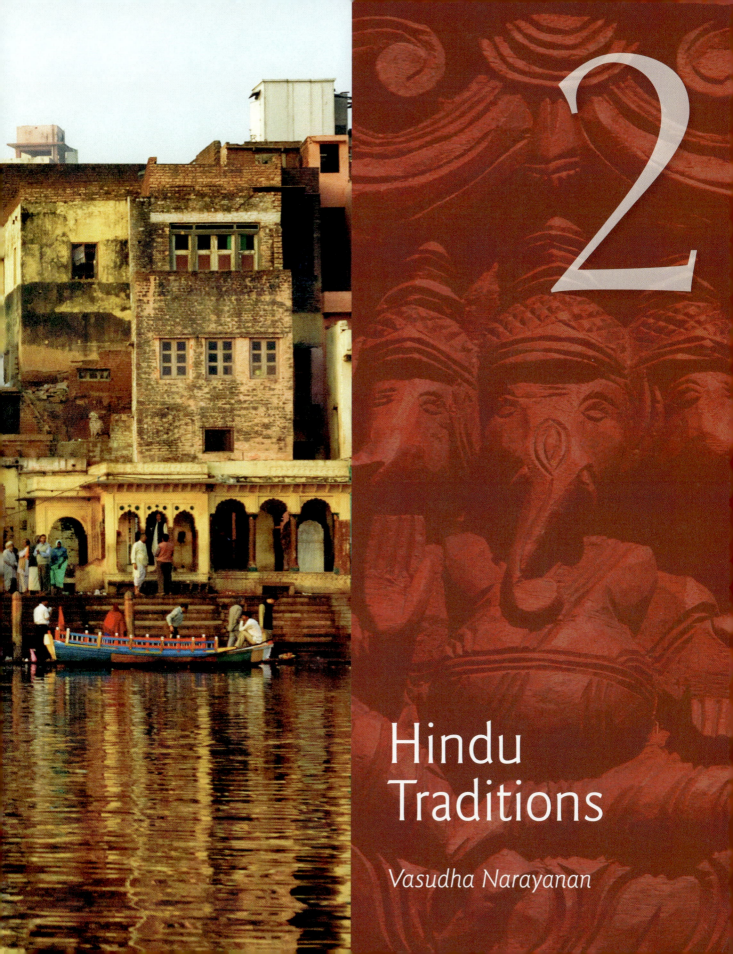

2

Hindu Traditions

Vasudha Narayanan

Traditions at a Glance

Numbers

Approximately 950 million to 1 billion around the world.

Distribution

Primarily India; large numbers in other regions of South Asia, as well as the United States, Canada, Australia, Western Europe, and many parts of Southeast Asia.

Principal Historical Periods

c. 2500–600 BCE	Indus Valley civilization; composition of the Vedas
c. 500 BCE–1000 CE	Composition of epics and *Puranas*
600–1600	Devotional poetry in local languages, building of major temples in South and Southeast Asia
13th–18th centuries	Northern India under Muslim rule
mid-1700s–1947	British colonial period

Founders and Leaders

Important figures include Shankara, Ramanuja, Madhva, Vallabha, Ramananda, Chaitanya, Swami Narayanan, Ramakrishna, and Vivekananda. Among the hundreds of teachers who have attracted followings in the last century alone are Aurobindo, Ramana Maharishi, Maharishi Mahesh Yogi, Sathya Sai Baba, Anandamayi Ma, and Ma Amritananda Mayi.

Deities

Hindu philosophy recognizes a supreme being (the ineffable Brahman) who is not limited by gender and number and who may take countless forms; classical rhetoric typically refers to 330 million. Some sectarian traditions identify the supreme deity as Vishnu, some as Shiva, and some as a form of the Goddess. The supreme being may be understood as male, female, androgynous, or beyond gender.

Authoritative Texts

The Vedas are technically considered the most authoritative texts, though the epics (the *Ramayana* and the *Mahabharata*, including the *Bhagavad Gita*), the *Puranas*, and several works in regional languages have also been very important.

Noteworthy Teachings

In general, most Hindus recognize a supreme being, variously conceived—personal for some, impersonal for others. Most think of the human soul as immortal and believe that when it reaches liberation it will be freed from the shackles of karma and rebirth. Specific teachings vary depending on sectarian tradition, region, and community.

In this chapter you will learn about:

- The history of the Hindu traditions in South Asia
- The diversity of Hindu traditions and the common threads they share
- Significant texts, in Sanskrit and in vernacular languages
- Major philosophical traditions and religious teachers
- The importance of devotion (*bhakti*)
- The significance of temples in South and Southeast Asia and North America
- The place of the performing arts in the Hindu traditions.

The earliest compositions in any Hindu tradition are the **Vedas**: four collections of hymns and texts that are said to have been "revealed" to **rishis** (visionaries or seers) through both sight and sound; thus

 The Vishram Ghat, Mathura (© 2008 Himanshu Khagta/Getty Images).

the sacred words are called **shruti** ("that which is heard"). This dual emphasis on seeing and hearing the sacred is characteristic of all Hindu traditions.

When Hindus go on a pilgrimage or visit a temple, they seek an experience known as a *darshana*: to see and be seen by a particular deity or **guru**. But Hindus also believe in the importance of uttering prayers aloud. Reciting Sanskrit and vernacular texts in the temple and at home, telling stories of the gods, chanting prayers or singing devotional songs or meditating on a holy **mantra**—these are just some of the ways in which Hindus actively live their tradition through its sacred words. In short, Hindus experience the divine through both sight and sound. Although sacred texts have been important, for most Hindus the primary source of knowledge about their traditions has been performance: rituals, recitations, music, dance, and theatre.

It is hard to identify common denominators in Hinduism. While some texts and some deities are widely accepted, there is no single text, deity, or teacher that all Hindus would consider supremely authoritative. There is a corpus of holy works, but many non-literate Hindus may not even have heard of them. Similarly, there are many local deities with local names who may or may not be identified with pan-Indian gods. The Hindu tradition is in fact many traditions encompassing hundreds of communities and sectarian movements, each of which has its own hallowed canon, its own sacred place, and its own concept of the supreme deity.

"Hinduism"

The word "Hinduism" itself has often been contested. It is used here as a very fluid shorthand for the diverse philosophies, arts, branches of knowledge, and practices associated with people and communities who have some connection (geographic, biological, intellectual, or spiritual) with the Indian subcontinent. Knowledge of the Vedas is not necessarily required in order to qualify as Hindu. In fact, there are probably millions of people in India who have never heard of them. Yet all of those people would be considered Hindu as long

they do not belong to a faith tradition that explicitly denies the exalted status of the Vedas. In other words, "Hindu" is a kind of default category.

The word "Hinduism," like "India" itself, is derived from "Sind": the name of the region—now in Pakistan—of the river Sindhu (Indus). The term was given currency by the British colonizers of India in the eighteenth and nineteenth centuries. To them, "Hinduism" essentially meant the religion of those Indians—the majority of the population—who were not Muslims, although a few smaller groups, including Jainas, Parsis, Christians, Jews, and sometimes Sikhs, were also recognized. As a term for a religious identity, "Hinduism" did not catch on until the nineteenth century. Thus anyone who tries to look for the term in books printed earlier is unlikely to find it.

There are approximately a billion Hindus in the world today. Yet when they are asked about their religious identity, they are more likely to refer to their particular caste or community than to Hinduism. An alternative term designating a comprehensive tradition is *sanatana dharma* ("eternal faith"), but it is common in only a few parts of India and only certain classes of society. The term is seldom used to refer to local manifestations of the faith.

Under Indian law, the term "Hindu" applies not only to members of a Hindu "denomination" such as Vira Shaiva or Brahmo Samaj, but also to "any other person domiciled in the territories to which [the Hindu Family Act] extends who is *not a Muslim, Christian, Parsi, or Jew* by religion" (italics added). In effect, India's legal system uses "Hindu" to refer to anyone who does not profess one of the specified religions, all of which originated outside India. Thus while we can make some generalizations and trace some important lines of historical continuity, we must keep in mind their limitations.

The very concept of religion in the Western, post-Enlightenment sense is only loosely applicable to the Hindu tradition. Some Hindus think that the Sanskrit word **dharma** comes close to "religion," but they recognize that this is true in only a limited way. "Dharma" for Hindus means righteousness, justice, faith, duty, religious and social obligation,

Timeline

c. 3300–1900 BCE	Evidence of Indus Valley civilization (early to mature phases)
c. 1750?–1500	Earliest Vedic compositions
c. 600	Production of *Upanishads*
c. 500	Production of Hindu epics begins
326	Greek armies in India under Alexander
c. 272	Accession of King Ashoka
c. 200	First contacts with Southeast Asia
c. 200 BCE–200 CE	Composition of *Bhagavad Gita*
c. 200 CE	Compilation of *Laws of Manu* and *Natya Sastra* completed
c. 500	Beginnings of tantric tradition
c. 700–900	Alvars and Nayanmars, Tamil *bhakti* poets
c. 700–800	Shankara's Advaita Vedanta
c. 1008–1023	Mahmud of Ghazni raids kingdoms in India several times, strips temples of their wealth; Somnath Temple in Gujarat destroyed
1017	Traditional birth date of Ramanuja, Vaishnava philosopher (d. 1137)
1100–1150	Angkor Wat built in Cambodia
1398	Traditional birth date of Kabir, North Indian *bhakti* poet (d. 1518)
c. 1400	Major endowments at Tirumala–Tirupati temple
1486	Birth of Chaitanya, Bengali Vaishnava *bhakti* leader (d. 1583)
c. 1543	Birth of Tulsidas, North Indian *bhakti* poet (d. 1623)
1757	British rule established in Calcutta
1828	Ram Mohan Roy founds Brahmo Samaj
1836	Birth of Ramakrishna Paramahamsa (d. 1886)
1875	Dayananda Sarasvati founds Arya Samaj
1893	Vivekananda attends World's Parliament of Religions in Chicago
1905–6	Vedanta Temple built in San Francisco
1926	Birth of Sathya Sai Baba
1947	Partition of India and Pakistan on religious lines resulting in almost a million deaths
1959	Maharishi Mahesh Yogi brings Transcendental Meditation to America and Europe
1965	A.C. Bhaktivedenta Swami Prabhupada, founder of ISKCON, sails to America
1977	Hindu temples consecrated in New York and Pittsburgh

but it does not cover all that is sacred in specific contexts for Hindus. Hindus may consider many things—from astronomy and astrology to music and dance, from phonetics to plants—essential to the practice of their religion. Therefore the following discussion will include a number of features not usually covered by the term "religion" in the Western world.

⊛ Origins

The origins of Hinduism have been much debated. The view in the early twentieth century was that it had grown from a fusion of the indigenous religions of the Indus Valley with the faith of the Aryans, an Indo-European people usually thought to have migrated there sometime between 1750 and 1500 BCE. More recently, however, other theories have been proposed. Some scholars maintain that the Indo-Europeans migrated into India from other parts of Asia; others insist there is demonstrable evidence that the Indian subcontinent itself was their original homeland.

The Harappa Culture

In 1926 excavations revealed the remains of several large towns on the banks of the Indus River in what is now Pakistan. Two of these towns, known today as Mohenjo Daro ("Mound of the Dead") and Harappa, were more than 480 kilometres (300 miles) apart. Yet archaeological evidence suggested a certain uniformity in the culture across the entire northwestern part of the subcontinent. Similar objects found in towns hundreds of kilometres apart suggest continuous travel and communication between them, and although the culture is still widely identified with the Indus Valley, some scholars prefer to call it the Harappa culture because it extends well beyond the Indus basin itself.

It is generally believed that the towns were in existence by about 2750 BCE, though some historians push the date back several centuries. Inscriptions on carved seals show that this culture had a written language, though no one has yet been able to decipher the script with any assurance. What we do know is that the people of the Harappa civilization were impressive builders who lived in what appear to have been planned cities. In the citadel mound at Mohenjo Daro there is a huge swimming-pool-like structure (archaeologists call it "the Great Bath"), surrounded by porticos and flights of stairs. The care with which the complex was built has led scholars to believe that it was designed for religious rituals of some sort. Some of the houses also appear to have included a room with a fire altar, suggesting a domestic fire ritual. Stone sculptures and terracotta statuettes of what looks like a mother goddess may have been used as icons in worship.

The figure identified as a mother goddess wears a short skirt, abundant jewellery, and a fan-shaped headdress with two little cups on either side. Smoke stains in these cups suggest that they were used for offerings of fire or incense. Some Western scholars believe that goddess worship is indicative of a society in which women enjoyed high status, but we have no hard evidence to support this thesis in the case of the Harappan civilization. And though goddesses have certainly been worshipped in the later Hindu tradition, women were not necessarily held in high esteem in all strata of society.

In addition, excavations around the Indus River have yielded approximately two thousand flat seals and many amulets. A few of the seals represent a man seated on a low throne in what looks like a **yoga** posture. The man's headdress and the animals around him suggest that this figure may be a prototype of the deity who came to be known as Shiva. On some seals a horned person is emerging from a *pipal* tree in front of which stand seven figures with long braids. Pointing out that the notion of seven beings is important in later Hindu mythology, some commentators have identified those figures as seven holy men (*rishis*); others, as seven goddesses.

Scholars are not yet sure how the people who lived in these cities disposed of their dead. Since the manner of disposal frequently reveals religious convictions, this is an important gap in our knowledge. No large burial sites have been found, though it is possible that some land used for this purpose was later flooded and now lies under water. Of the few graves that have been discovered, most are oriented on a north–south axis. In a small number of them objects were buried with the bodies, perhaps to serve the dead in an afterlife. It is possible that both cremation and burial were practised.

What might have brought the Indus Valley civilization to an end? Some scholars think it was the arrival of the Indo-Europeans around 1750 BCE. Others suggest that flooding, drying of the river, or epidemics might have driven the population farther east. Whatever the answer, from the fragmentary evidence found in the Indus Valley we can tentatively say that some features of the Hindu religion as practised today go back before 1750 BCE to Mohenjo Daro and Harappa.

We know even less of the early history in other parts of the subcontinent than we do of the Indus Valley civilization. Nevertheless, scholars have noticed an intriguing correspondence between sites that were inhabited between four and five thousand years ago and sites that are of religious significance today. It seems likely that at least some elements of Hinduism as we know it have been part of the religious culture of the subcontinent for as long as five millennia.

The Indo-Europeans

The language of the Vedas, the earliest Hindu compositions, is Sanskrit, a member of the language family known as Indo-European (or "Indo-Aryan"). Western scholars in the nineteenth century noted the similarities between some Indian and European languages. For example, the Sanskrit word **jnana** is a cognate of the English word "knowledge"; "lack of knowledge" is *ajnana* in Sanskrit and "ignorance" in English. There are hundreds of similar cognates, including the words for "father" and "mother." The Indo-European languages also have many grammatical structures in common. Based on linguistic evidence, nineteenth-century scholars posited a theory of migration according to which people from Central Asia began migrating to widely distant regions at some time between 2000 BCE and

1500 BCE. Some moved west and north into what is now Europe, from Ireland to Scandinavia. Others headed south or east and settled in the region of Iran, where they called themselves Aryans—a name that eventually acquired a class connotation, coming to mean "noble ones."

Many scholars believe that the Indo-Europeans originated in Central Asia and that the migration began around 2000 BCE. Others think the migrants originated in the general region of modern Turkey and began spreading out as much as 4,000 years earlier. The latter suggest that it was a peaceful migration undertaken by a growing agricultural population in need of additional land.

Yet another school of thought holds that the original home of the Indo-Europeans was actually the Indian subcontinent. Proponents of this theory base their arguments on astronomical data and evidence concerning a great river that was said to have flowed from the mountains to the sea in the region of the Harappan civilization. They identify this river as the legendary Sarasvati, which according to the ancient Hindu text known as the *Rig Veda* had five Aryan tribes living on its banks, yet has been shown by geologists to have run dry by the time that the Aryans were supposed to have entered India (i.e., around 1750 BCE). If the Aryans were actually there before the Sarasvati dried up, the theory goes, their dates must be pushed back to the time of the Harappan civilization or even earlier.

None of the evidence is conclusive, and some theories have been motivated by political, racial, religious, and nationalist agendas. Evidence from many areas of study has been drawn into the debate: Vedic philology, comparative philology, linguistic paleontology, linguistics, archeology, astronomy, geography, and geology, as well as religious traditions.

What we do know is that the Indo-Europeans composed many poems and, eventually, manuals on rituals and philosophy. They committed these traditions to memory using various mnemonic devices to ensure correct pronunciation, rhythm, and intonation, and passed them from generation to generation by word of mouth.

Map 2.1 Hinduism

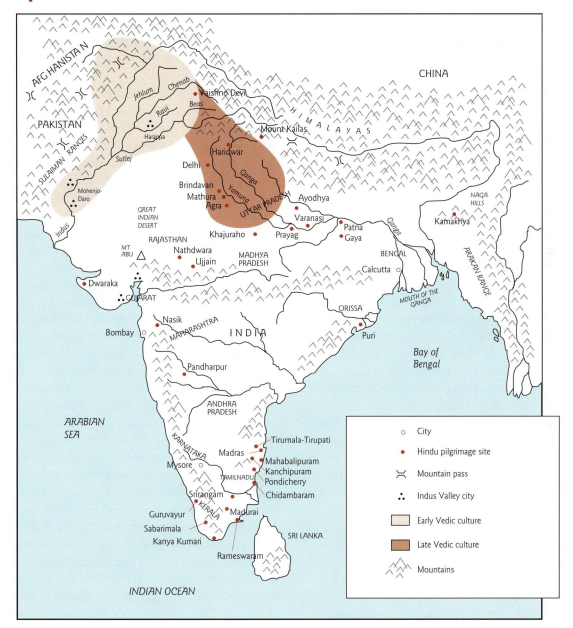

Source: Adapted from Nielsen et al. 1993: 85.

The Vedas

The earliest surviving Indo-European compositions are the **Vedas** (from the Sanskrit for "knowledge"); these are the works collectively known as *shruti* ("that which was heard"). The Vedic *rishis* "saw" the mantras and transmitted them to their disciples, starting an oral tradition that has continued to the present.

Traditionally regarded as revealed scripture, the Vedas are now generally thought to have been composed between roughly 1500 BCE (some scholars put the earliest date closer to 1750 BCE) and 600 BCE. There are four Vedic collections: *Rig, Sama, Yajur,* and *Atharva*. Each of these collections in turn consists of four sections: hymns (*Samhitas*; the earliest parts), directions for the performance of sacred rituals (**Brahmanas**), "compositions for the forest" (*Aranyakas*), and philosophical works called the **Upanishads** ("sitting near [the teacher]").

The earliest section of the *Rig Veda* contains 1,028 hymns. The hymns of the *Sama Veda* and *Yajur Veda* are largely borrowed from the *Rig*, and the *Sama Veda* was meant to be sung. The *Upanishads* are the most recent sections of each collection, composed around 600 BCE. The famous *Chandogya Upanishad* belongs to the *Sama Veda*, and the *Brihadaranyaka* and *Taittiriya Upanishads* to the *Yajur Veda*.

The *Atharva Veda* differs from the other three Vedas in that it includes material used for purposes other than sacrificial rituals, such as incantations and remedies to ward off illness and evil spirits. One verse (7.38), for example, refers to the use of herbs to make a lover return, and another (7.50) requests luck in gambling.

In the Hindu tradition, the term "Vedas" denotes the whole corpus, starting with the hymns, continuing through the ritual treatises, and concluding with the texts of a more philosophical character. Many Orientalists and Western Indologists, however, have used "Veda" only for the hymns, the *samhita* portion of each collection. This narrower use of the term is generally not accepted by Hindus.

The Status of the Vedas

Almost all educated Hindus would describe the Vedas as their most sacred texts; yet most would be hard pressed to identify their contents. Despite their importance to philosophers and theologians, the Vedas are not books that people keep in their homes. Rather, they are ritual texts that are understood to represent eternal sound, eternal words passed on through the generations without change. A few hymns from them are recited regularly at

home as well as in temple liturgies, and the philosophical sections have often been translated and commented upon, but the rest of the Vedas are known only to a handful of ritual specialists and to Sanskrit scholars familiar with the early Vedic form of the language.

The Vedas are particularly significant to the **brahmins**, the class that has historically considered itself the "highest" in Hindu society. For many centuries, acceptance as an orthodox member of the society we call Hindu depended on acceptance of the Vedas as authoritative. As custodians of the Vedas, the brahmins reserved for themselves the authority to study and teach these holy words. Though members of two other classes were technically "allowed" to study the Vedas, in time this privilege was lost and, in some cases, abandoned.

Historically, the Vedas were treated as "revealed" scripture, though the source of the revelation was not necessarily a deity. In medieval times brahmin commentators considered the Vedas to represent "eternal truth," coeval with God. All schools of medieval thought agreed that the Vedas have a transcendental aspect and an authoritative nature. Where they differed was on the significance of their status as divine (*apauruseya*, literally "superhuman": not composed by man).

Followers of the Nyaya ("logic") school of philosophy believed that God was the author of the Vedas and that, since God is perfect, the Vedas were infallible. Many other Hindu schools took different views. Two that continue to be influential, the Mimamsa and Vedanta schools, say that the Vedas are eternal and of non-human origin. The Vedic seers (*rishis*) "saw" the mantras and transmitted them; they did not invent or compose them. The words have a fixed order that must be maintained by a tradition of recitation. The Vedic seers transmitted the words to their disciples, establishing an oral tradition that has come down to the present. Not being composed by human beings, the Vedas are considered faultless, the perfect and supreme source of knowledge. From them we can learn about the Supreme Being, and their authority grants credibility to particular doctrines. The Vedic collections have served as manuals of ritual for all the many strands of the Hindu tradition. Some sections have been recited and acted on without major changes for more than 2,000 years. Interpretations have not been static, however. In every generation, specialists in Vedic hermeneutics have worked to make the texts' messages relevant to the particular time and place.

Several works have been more popular among Hindus generally, but the theoretical, ritual, and epistemological significance of the Vedas has been unquestioned. Thus the highest honour that could be given to any Hindu religious text was to describe it as a "Veda."

Among the works that have been accorded this title are the **Mahabharata**, one of two great Hindu epics; Bharata's *Natya Sastra*, an important treatise on dance and performance composed around the beginning of the Common Era; and a number of Tamil-language compositions from South India, especially the *Tiruvaymoli* ("sacred utterance") of Nammalvar (ninth century) and the *Periya Puranam* (twelfth century), a collection of the life stories of saints who were devotees of Shiva.

These texts made no attempt either to imitate the Vedas or to comment on them. They are called "Vedas" only because Hindus thought they reflected the wisdom embodied in the four original Vedas, making their eternal truth relevant to a new place and time.

The Vedic Hymns

The figures that were to become the principal Hindu deities—goddesses like Lakshmi and gods like Narayana (Vishnu)—are rarely mentioned in the *samhitas*; only the later Vedic hymns address them directly. Rather, the earliest hymns of the Vedas speak of many deities who in time would be superseded, and many of the stories they allude to would not be familiar to most Hindus today.

Indra, for instance, is a warrior god who battles other cosmic powers. Agni is the god of fire who was believed to serve as a messenger, carrying to the deities the offerings that humans placed in the sacrificial fire. Soma is the name of a god identified with the moon, but also of a plant-based elixir, used for ritual purposes.

Sarasvati, as we have seen, was the name given to a great river. But Sarasvati was also a goddess described in the *Rig Veda* as beautiful and fortunate, the inspirer of noble thoughts, giving rise to truthful words. By the time the ritualistic sections called the *Brahmanas* were composed, Sarasvati had taken over the attributes formerly associated with the goddess Vac ("speech"). Now Sarasvati is speech incarnate, the power of the word, and the mother of the Vedas.

In addition, some texts refer to Sarasvati as Gayatri ("singer") and Savitri ("sun"), and in this guise she is associated with learning. To this day, young boys recite the *Gayatri* mantra, dedicated to the sun, as part of the ceremony that marks their initiation into the life of a student.

The early hymns typically offer praise to the gods; thus the river Indus is praised for giving cattle, children, horses, and food. But many of them also include petitions—not for salvation or eternal bliss (in fact, the idea of an afterlife is rarely mentioned), but rather for a good and happy life on this earth. Thus Agni is asked to protect those who praise him, and Indra is asked to crush the worshipper's enemies. A *rishi* named Sobhari simply requests "all good things," but a woman poet named Ghosa specifically asks to be cured of her white-tinted skin, so that she may marry and live happily with her husband. One of the dominant features of Vedic religious life was the ritual sacrifice (*yajna*), typically performed using fire. From simple domestic affairs to elaborate community events, these sacrifices were conducted by ritual specialists and priests who supervised the construction of altars, the sacrifice of animals, and the recitation of the hymns. Many rituals also involved the making, offering, and drinking of the *soma* elixir.

A delicate connection was understood to exist between the rituals and the maintenance of cosmic and earthly order, or *rta*. *Rta* is truth and justice, the rightness of things that makes harmony and peace possible on earth and in the heavens.

Document

The Creation Hymn, *Rig Veda* 10.129

There was neither non-existence nor existence then; there was neither the realm of space nor the sky which is beyond. What stirred? Where? In whose protection? Was there water, bottomlessly deep?

There was neither death nor immortality then. There was no distinguishing sign of night nor of day. That one breathed, windless, by its own impulse. Other than that there was nothing beyond.

Darkness was hidden by darkness in the beginning; with no distinguishing sign, all this was water. The life force that was covered with emptiness, that one arose through the power of heat.

Desire came upon that one in the beginning; that was the first seed of mind. Poets seeking in their heart with wisdom found the bond of existence in non-existence.

Their cord was extended across. Was there below? Was there above? There were seed-placers; there were powers. There was impulse beneath; there was giving-forth above.

Who really knows? Who will here proclaim it? Whence was it produced? Whence is this creation? The gods came afterwards, with the creation of this universe. Who then knows whence it has arisen?

Whence this creation has arisen—perhaps it formed itself, or perhaps it did not—the one who looks down on it, in the highest heaven, only he knows—or perhaps he does not know (Doniger O'Flaherty 1981: 25–6).

Although it is an impersonal cosmic principle, it was upheld by Vedic gods like Varuna.

A number of hymns composed around 1000 BCE speculate on the origins of the universe. One, entitled "The Creation Hymn," expresses wonder at the creation of the universe from nothing and ends with the suggestion that perhaps no one knows how it all came to be.

Another account, however, describes how the universe itself was created through the cosmic sacrifice of the primeval man (*Purusha*). This account, entitled the "Hymn to the Supreme Person" (*Purusha Sukta*), is important even today in both domestic and temple rituals, and has figured continuously in the tradition for some 3,000 years. Straining to capture infinity in words, the composer uses the notion of "a thousand" to evoke what cannot be measured or perhaps even imagined:

(1) The cosmic person has a thousand heads
      a thousand eyes and feet

It covers the earth on all sides
and extends ten finger-lengths beyond

(2) The cosmic person is everything
      all that has been and will be. . . .

Various elements of the universe are said to have arisen from this sacrifice:

(13) From his mind came the moon
      from his eye, the sun
      Indra and Agni from his mouth
      the wind came from his breath.

(14) From his navel came space
      from his head, the sky
      from his feet, earth;
      from his ears, the four directions
      thus the worlds were created.

In this context an idea is introduced that will change forever the religious and social countenance of the Hindu tradition:

(12) From his mouth came the priestly class
      from his arms, the rulers.
      The producers came from his legs;
      from his feet came the servant class.

Thus the origins of the four classes (*varnas*) of Hindu society are traced to the initial cosmic sacrifice. Although this verse is the first explicit reference to what came to be called the caste system, it is likely that the stratification of society had already taken place long before the *Rig Veda* was composed.

The Upanishads

By the time of the *Aranyakas* and *Upanishads*, in the seventh and sixth centuries BCE, the early Vedic emphasis on placating the gods through ritual sacrifice had given way to critical philosophical inquiry. This period, a little before and perhaps during the lives of Gautama Buddha and the Jaina teacher Mahavira, was a time of intellectual ferment, of questioning—and rejecting—authoritarian structures.

Yet the *Upanishads* do not totally reject the early hymns and sacrificial rituals. Instead, they rethink and reformulate them. Thus some rituals are interpreted allegorically, and the symbolic structures of the sacrifices are analyzed in some detail.

Most of the *Upanishads* take the form of conversations—between a teacher and a student, between a husband and wife, or between fellow philosophers. In the beginning of one study session a teacher exclaims: "May we work with vigour; may our study illumine us both. May there be no discord between us. *Om.* Let there be peace, peace, peace" (*Taittiriya Upanishad* 11.1.1). After years of Vedic instruction, a departing student receives moving advice from his guru (teacher):

Speak the truth. Practice virtue. Do not neglect to study every day. Do not neglect truth, virtue, studying or teaching. . . . Be one to whom your mother is a god, your father is a god, your teacher is a god, a guest is like a god. . . . Give with faith . . . give liberally, give with modesty . . . give with sympathy. . . . This is the command. This is the teaching. This is the secret of the Veda. . . . (*Taittiriya Upanishad* 1.11.1–6).

Karma and Samsara

It is in the *Upanishads* that we find the earliest discussions of several concepts central to the later Hindu tradition, among them the concept of **karma**. The literal meaning of "karma" is "action," especially ritual action, but in these books the word eventually comes to refer to a system of rewards and punishments attached to various actions. This system of cause and effect may require several lifetimes to work out. Thus the concept of karma implies a continuing cycle of death and rebirth or reincarnation called **samsara**. To achieve liberation (**moksha**) from this cycle, according to the *Upanishads*, requires a transforming experiential wisdom. Those who attain that wisdom become immortal (*a-mrta*, "without death").

A frequent theme of the *Upanishads* is the quest for a unifying truth. This "higher" knowledge is clearly distinguished from the "lower" knowledge that can be conceptualized and expressed in words. Its nature cannot be explained or taught: it can only be evoked, as in this question posed by the seeker in the *Mundaka Upanishad*: "What is it that, being known, all else becomes known?" (1.1.3). The *Brihadaranyaka Upanishad* of the *Yajur Veda* reflects the quest for enlightenment in these lines:

Lead me from the unreal to reality
Lead me from darkness to light
Lead me from death to immortality
Om, let there be peace, peace, peace.

Significantly, in later centuries the "higher wisdom" is not connected with any Vedic or book learning or conceptual knowledge. It is only through the experience of enlightenment that one is freed from the birth-and-death cycle.

© Vasudha Narayanan

Stone shrine (c. 1500 CE), modelled after a wooden processional chariot, in the Vitthala (Vishnu) temple complex in Hampi, northern Karnataka. The two elephants pulling the chariot date from a later time.

Atman and Brahman

At the heart of this wisdom is experiential knowledge of the relationship between the human soul (**Atman**) and the Supreme Being (**Brahman**). Brahman pervades and at the same time transcends not only human thought but the universe itself. Ultimately, Brahman cannot be described any more than infinity can be contained.

To know Brahman is to enter a new state of consciousness. The *Taittiriya Upanishad* associates Brahman with existence or truth (*satya*), knowledge (*jnana*), infinity (*ananta*), consciousness (*chit*), and bliss (*ananda*); elsewhere Brahman is described as the hidden, inner controller of the human soul.

Many passages of the *Upanishads* discuss the relationship between Atman and Brahman, but invariably they suggest rather than specify the connection between the two. In one famous conversation in the *Chandogya Upanishad*, a father asks his son to dissolve salt in water and says that Brahman and Atman are united in a similar manner. The father ends his teaching with a famous dictum—*tat tvam asi* ("you are that")—in which "that" refers to Brahman and "you" to Atman. More than a thousand years later, philosophers still differed in their interpretations of this passage. For Shankara in the eighth century, "you are that" indicated that Brahman and Atman were identical. On the other hand, for Ramanuja in the eleventh century it meant that the two were inseparably united but not identical.

We learn more of the relationship between Brahman and Atman elsewhere in the *Upanishads*. In some passages, the sage Yajnavalkya refers to Brahman as the hidden, inner controller of the human soul (Atman); in others, as the frame and the substance of the universe. In the latter analogy the reference is to a weaving loom: the universe is said to be woven over Brahman.

The *Upanishads* represent the beginnings of Hindu philosophical thought; in the opinion of some, they also represent the best. The quest for a unifying knowledge or higher wisdom is a recurring theme in various systems of Hindu philosophical reasoning, and continues to preoccupy thinkers today.

Women in the Vedas

Ghosa, Apala, and Lopamudra are all poets named in the early part of the Vedas. The *Upanishads* also identify a number of women who participated in the quest for ultimate truth and sought salvific knowledge in both domestic and public forums. In the *Brihadaranyaka Upanishad*, for instance, Maitreyi, the wife of the sage Yajnavalkya, questions

him in depth about the nature of reality, and a woman philosopher named Gargi Vachaknavi challenges a scholar with the same name in a public debate. When he does not answer to her satisfaction, Gargi presses the question, and eventually she pronounces a judgment about him to her fellow philosophers, saying that he is indeed wise. Apparently Gargi and Maitreyi were honoured and respected for their wisdom, as were dozens of other women whose names appear in the *Upanishads* and elsewhere in the *Vedas*.

These women were among the teachers through whom the sacred knowledge was probably transmitted. While the fathers of the teachers listed in the *Upanishads* are frequently named, in some cases the teachers are identified as the sons of particular women. In the *Brihadaranyaka Upanishad* (VI.5.1) roughly 45 teachers are listed with their mothers' names instead of their fathers'. So, while it is clear that a male spiritual lineage is generally accepted (after all, it is the male teachers who are being named), it is possible that some teachers received spiritual instruction from their mothers.

Document

How Many Gods Are There?

Vidagdha Shakalyah asked: "Yajnavalkya, how many gods are there?"

He answered . . . in line with the formulaic [mantra], ". . . three hundred and three, and three and three thousand."

"Yes, but Yajnavalkya, how many gods are there, really?"

"Thirty-three."

"Yes, but really, how many gods are there, Yajnavalkya?"

"Six."

"Yes, but really, how many gods are there, Yajnavalkya?"

"Three." . . .

"Yes, but really, how many gods are there, Yajnavalkya?"

"One and a half."

"Yes, but really, how many gods are there, Yajnavalkya?"

"One."

"Yes, but who are those three hundred and three and three thousand and three?"

"They are but the powers of the gods; there are only thirty-three gods" (*Brihadaranyaka Upanishad* 3.9.1–2; trans. Vasudha Narayanan).

Document

Gargi Vachaknavi Questions Yajnavalkya

Then Vachaknavi said, "Venerable Brahmanas, I shall ask him two questions. If he answers me these, none of you can defeat him in arguments about Brahman." "Ask, Gargi" [said he].

She said, "As a warrior son of the Kasis or the Videhas might rise up against you, having strung his unstrung bow and having taken in his hand two pointed foe-piercing arrows, even so, O Yajnavalkya, do I face you with two questions. Answer me these." "Ask, Gargi."

She said, "That, O Yajnavalkya, of which they say, it is above the heaven, it is beneath the earth, that which is between these two, the heaven and the earth, that which the people call the past, the present and the future, across what is that woven, like warp and woof?"

He said, "That which is above the heaven, that which is beneath the earth, that which is between these two, heaven and earth, that which the people call the past, the present, and the future, across space is that woven, like warp and woof."

She said, "Adoration to you, Yajnavalkya, who have answered this question for me. Prepare yourself for the other." "Ask, Gargi."

She said, "That, O Yajnavalkya, of which they say, it is above the heaven, it is beneath the earth, that which is between these two, the heaven and the earth, that which the people call the past, the present, and the future, across what is that woven like warp and woof?"

He said, "That which is above the sky, that which is beneath the earth, that which is between these two, sky and earth, that which the people call the past, the present, and the future, across space is that woven like warp and woof."

"Across what is space woven like warp and woof?"

He said, "That, O Gargi, the knowers of Brahman call the Imperishable. It is neither gross nor fine, neither short nor long, neither glowing red (like fire) nor adhesive (like water). (It is) neither shadow nor darkness, neither air nor space, unattached, without taste, without smell, without eyes, without ears, without voice, without mind, without radiance, without breath, without a mouth, without measure, having no within and no without. It eats nothing and no one eats it."

"Verily, at the command of that Imperishable, O Gargi, the sun and the moon stand in their respective positions. At the command of that Imperishable, O Gargi, heaven and earth stand in their respective positions. At the command of the Imperishable, O Gargi, what are called moments, hours, days and nights, half-months, months, seasons, years stand in their respective positions. At the command of that Imperishable, O Gargi, some rivers flow to the east from the white (snowy) mountains, others to the west in whatever direction each flows. By the command of that Imperishable, O Gargi, men praise those who give, the gods (are desirous of) the sacrificer and the fathers are desirous of the darvi offering."

"Whosoever, O Gargi, in this world, without knowing this Imperishable performs sacrifices, worships, performs austerities for a thousand years, his work will have an end; whosoever, O Gargi, without knowing this Imperishable departs from this world, is pitiable. But, O Gargi, he who knowing the Imperishable departs from this world is a Brahmana (a knower of Brahman)."

"Verily, that Imperishable, O Gargi, is unseen but is the seer, is unheard but is the hearer, unthought but is the thinker, unknown but is the knower. There is no other seer but this, there is no other hearer but this, there is no other thinker but this, there is no other knower but this. By this Imperishable, O Gargi, is space woven like warp and woof."

She said, "Venerable Brahmana, you may think it a great thing if you get off from him though bowing to him. Not one of you will defeat him in arguments about Brahman." Thereupon [Gargi] Vachaknavi kept silent (*Brihadaranyaka Upanishad* 3.8; Radhakrishnan 1953: 230–4).

✺ Classical Hinduism

The literature that was composed after the Vedas, starting around 500 BCE, was recognized to be of human origin and was loosely called **smrti** ("that which is remembered"). Though theoretically of lesser authority than the "revealed" *shruti*, this material was nonetheless considered inspired, and it has played a far more important role in the lives of Hindus for the last 2,500 years. There are three types of *smrti*: epics (*itihasas*), ancient stories (**Puranas**), and codes of law and ethics (*dharmashastras*). (The term *smrti* can also refer to the codes alone.)

For many Hindus the phrase "sacred books" refers specifically to two epics, the **Ramayana** ("Story of Rama") and the *Mahabharata* ("Great [Epic of] India" or "Great [Sons of] Bharata"). The best-known works in the Hindu tradition, these stories are told to children and invariably constitute their first and most lasting encounter with Hindu scripture.

The Ramayana

The *Ramayana* has been memorized, recited, sung, danced, enjoyed, and experienced emotionally, intellectually, and spiritually for 2,500 years. A source of inspiration for Hindus all over the world, it is performed as a drama, often in dance, in places of Hindu (and Buddhist) cultural influence throughout Southeast Asia, and its characters are well known in Cambodia, Thailand, and Indonesia.

The hero of the *Ramayana* is the young prince Rama, whose father, Dasaratha, has decided to abdicate in favour of his son. On the eve of the coronation, however, a heartbroken Dasaratha is forced to exile Rama because of an earlier promise made to one of his wives. Rama accepts cheerfully and leaves for the forest, accompanied by his beautiful wife, Sita, and his half-brother Lakshmana, who both refuse to be separated from him. Bharata, the brother who has now been named king, returns from a trip to discover that Rama has gone into exile and his father has died of grief. He finds Rama and begs him to return, but Rama refuses because he feels he must respect his father's decision to banish him. He asks Bharata to rule as his regent.

While in the forest, Sita is captured by Ravana, the demon king of Lanka. Rama, full of sorrow at being separated from his wife, sets out to search for her with the aid of his brother and a group of monkeys led by Hanuman, a monkey with divine ancestry. It is Hanuman who finds Sita and reports her whereabouts to Rama, who, with the monkeys' help, goes to war with Ravana. After a long battle, Rama kills Ravana and is reunited with Sita. They eventually return to the capital and are crowned. Rama is considered such a just king that *Ram rajya* ("kingdom or rule of Rama") is the Hindu political ideal.

Rama is also the ideal son and husband, and Sita as well has been idealized both for her own qualities and for her relationship with her husband. In a sequel to the *Ramayana*, however, Rama's subjects become suspicious about Sita's virtue following her captivity in Ravana's grove. Because there is no way of proving her innocence, and possibly because he does not want to create a legal precedent for excusing a wife who has slept outside her husband's home, Rama banishes his own wife, who by now is pregnant.

The exiled Sita gives birth to twins. Some years later, the twins prepare to meet Rama in battle, and it is then that Sita tells them he is their father. There is a brief reunion. Rama asks Sita to prove her innocence in public by undergoing some ordeal, but Sita refuses and asks Mother Earth to take her back. She is then swallowed by the ground.

Many Hindus have considered Sita the ideal wife because she follows her husband to the forest. Others see her as a model of strength and virtue in her own right. She complies with her husband as he does with her; their love is one worthy of emulation. Yet she is also a woman who stands her ground when asked by her husband to prove her virtue. On one occasion, in Lanka, she acquiesces, but the second time she gently but firmly refuses and so rules out any possibility of a reunion. The tale has sometimes been retold from Sita's viewpoint under the title *Sitayana*, and even conservative commentators agree with the time-honoured saying *"sitayas chari-tam mahat"* ("the deeds of Sita are indeed great").

Rama is a paragon of human virtue, and in later centuries he came to be seen as an incarnation of Vishnu. Temples dedicated to Rama and Sita are found in many parts of the world.

The *Mahabharata* and the *Bhagavad Gita*

With approximately 100,000 verses, the *Mahabharata* is said to be the longest poem in the world. It is not found in many homes, but many people own copies of an extract from it called the **Bhagavad Gita**.

The *Mahabharata* is the story of the great struggle among the descendants of a king named Bharata. The main part of the story concerns a war between two families, the Pandavas and the Kauravas. Though they are cousins, the Kauravas try to cheat the Pandavas out of their share of the kingdom and will not accept peace. A battle ensues in which all the major kingdoms are forced to take sides. Krishna, by this time considered to be an incarnation of the god Vishnu, is on the side of the Pandavas, but refuses to take up arms. Instead, he agrees to serve as charioteer for the warrior Arjuna, who in later centuries would be understood to symbolize the human soul in quest of liberation.

Just as the war is about to begin, Arjuna, who has hitherto been portrayed as a hero, emerging victorious from several battles, becomes distressed at the thought of fighting his relatives. Putting down his bow, he asks Krishna whether it is correct to fight a war in which many lives will be lost, especially when the opposing forces are one's own kin. Krishna replies that it is correct to fight for what is right; peaceful means must be tried, but if they fail one must fight for righteousness ("dharma"). The conversation between Arjuna and Krishna, which unfolds across 18 chapters, constitutes the *Bhagavad Gita*.

One of the holiest books in the Hindu tradition, the *Gita* teaches loving devotion to Krishna and the importance of selfless action as Krishna instructs Arjuna on the nature of God and the human soul, and how to reach liberation. It was probably written sometime between 200 BCE and 200 CE, and for centuries people learned it by heart. In verses that are still recited at Hindu funerals, Krishna describes the soul as existing beyond the reach of the mind and the senses, unaffected by physical nature. Just as human beings exchange old clothes for new ones, so the human soul discards one body and puts on another through the ages, until it acquires the knowledge that will free it forever from the cycle of birth and death.

Thus Arjuna is told not to grieve at what is about to take place; however, he is also warned that if he does not fight for righteousness, he will be guilty of moral cowardice and will have to face the consequences of quitting at a time when it was his duty (dharma) to wage a just war and protect the people.

Krishna also makes several statements about himself in the *Gita* that mark an important shift in Hindu theology. The *Upanishads* presented the Supreme Being, Brahman, as beyond human conceptualization, but in the *Gita* Krishna speaks of himself as both a personal god, one so filled with love for human beings that he will incarnate himself when necessary in order to protect them, and the ultimate deity, the origin, dissolution, and maintenance of the universe. When Arjuna is unsure about Krishna's claim to be God incarnate, Krishna reveals his cosmic form. Arjuna quakes at this vision and is filled with love and awe. Trembling, he seeks forgiveness of Krishna and implores him to resume his normal form.

The Three Ways to Liberation

In the course of the *Gita*, Krishna describes three ways to liberation from the cycle of birth and death: (1) the way of action, (2) the way of knowledge, and (3) the way of devotion. (Some Hindus would argue that they are three aspects of the same way.) Each way (*marga*) is also a discipline (*yoga*).

The way of action (*karma yoga*) is the path of unselfish duty performed neither in fear of punishment nor in hope of reward. Acting with the expectation of future reward leads to bondage and unhappiness. If our hopes are disappointed, we may

Document

From the *Bhagavad Gita*

On the immortality of the soul:
Our bodies are known to end, but the embodied self is enduring, indestructible, and immeasurable; therefore, Arjuna, fight the battle!

He who thinks this self a killer and he who thinks it killed, both fail to understand it does not kill, nor is it killed.

It is not born, it does not die; having been, it will never not be; unborn, enduring, constant, and primordial, it is not killed when the body is killed. . . .

As a man discards worn-out clothes to put on new and different ones, so the embodied self discards its worn-out bodies to take on other new ones.

Weapons do not cut it, fire does not burn it, waters do not wet it, wind does not wither it. It cannot be cut or burned; it cannot be wet or withered; it is enduring, all-pervasive, fixed, immovable, and timeless. . . .

On the way of action:
Be intent on action, not on the fruits of action; avoid attraction to the fruits and attachment to inaction!

Perform actions, firm in discipline, relinquishing attachment; be impartial to failure and success—this equanimity is called discipline. . . .

When he shows no preference in fortune or misfortune and neither exults nor hates, his insight is sure. . . .

On the mystery and purpose of incarnation:
Whenever sacred duty decays and chaos prevails, then, I create myself, Arjuna.

To protect men of virtue and destroy men who do evil to set the standard of sacred duty, I appear in age after age. . . .

On the nature of God and the way of devotion:
Always glorifying me, striving, firm in their vows, paying me homage with devotion, they worship me, always disciplined. . . .

I am the universal father, mother, granter of all, grandfather, object of knowledge, purifier, holy syllable OM, threefold sacred love.

I am the way, sustainer, lord, witness, shelter, refuge, friend, source, dissolution, stability, treasure, and unchanging seed.

I am heat that withholds and sends down the rains; I am immortality and death; both being and nonbeing am I. . . .

The leaf or flower or fruit or water that he offers with devotion, I take from the man of self-restraint in response to his devotion.

Whatever you do—what you take, what you offer, what you give, what penances you perform—do as an offering to me, Arjuna!

You will be freed from the bonds of action, from the fruit of fortune and misfortune; armed with the discipline of renunciation, yourself liberated, you will join me. . . .

Keep me in your mind and devotion, sacrifice to me, bow to me, discipline your self toward me, and you will reach me!

(Miller 1986: 32–87)

respond with anger or grief, and even if we do receive the expected reward, we will not be satisfied for long. Soon that goal will be replaced with another, leading to further action—and further accumulation of karma, which only leads to further rebirth.

Other books of the time pointed out that even the "good" karma acquired by performing good deeds is ultimately bad, because to enjoy the good karma we must be reborn. A thirteenth-century Hindu philosopher, Pillai Lokacharya, described good karma as "golden handcuffs." Therefore Krishna urges Arjuna to act without attachment to the consequences. Evil will not touch the person who acts according to his dharma, just as water does not cling to a lotus leaf. All actions are to be offered to Krishna. By discarding the fruits of our action, we attain abiding peace.

Krishna also explains the way of knowledge (*jnana yoga*): through scriptural knowledge, we may achieve a transforming wisdom that also destroys our past karma. True knowledge is an insight into the real nature of the universe, divine power, and the human soul. Later philosophers say that when we hear scripture, ask questions, clarify doubts, and eventually meditate on this knowledge, we achieve liberation.

The third way—the one emphasized most throughout the *Gita*—is the way of devotion (*bhakti yoga*). If there is a general amnesty offered to those who sin, it is through devotion. Ultimately, Krishna promises Arjuna that he will forgive all our sins if we surrender and devote ourselves to him (*Gita* 18: 66).

The Deities of Classical Hinduism

The period of the Gupta empire (c. 320–540) was one of great cultural and scholarly activity. In mathematics the concept of zero was introduced along with the decimal system. Around 499 Aryabhatta established both the value of pi (3.14) and the length of the solar year (365.3586 days); he also proposed that the earth is spherical and rotates on its axis. As commercial activity increased, so did contact with Greek and Roman trade missions from the Mediterranean, and coastal towns flourished, particularly in southern India.

The Gupta period also saw a surge in religious and literary activity. Temple building was encouraged, pilgrimages were undertaken, and playwrights used religious themes in their dramas. Hindus, Jainas, and Buddhists all composed poems and plays that reveal a great deal about the religious trends of the time. Temple architecture, literature, astronomy, and astrology received royal patronage.

Hinduism had by no means been dormant during the previous seven centuries; the *Bhagavad Gita* is only one example of the Hindu traditions from that era. Nevertheless, those traditions had been overshadowed to some degree by the spread of Buddhist teachings and institutions. Now, under the Guptas, Buddhist influences receded and Hinduism became the dominant faith in India. Eventually, some Hindu texts would even assimilate Siddhartha Gautama, the Buddha, as an incarnation of Vishnu.

It would be impossible to identify the precise time when the transition occurred, but from the Gupta era onward three deities become increasingly prominent: Vishnu, Shiva, and Shiva's consort, variously known as Parvati, Durga, Devi, or simply "the Goddess." Devotees who give primacy to Vishnu are termed Vaishnavas; those who focus on Shiva are termed Shaivas; and followers of the Goddess are called Shaktas, in reference to her role as the *shakti* ("power") of her divine consort.

Starting around 300 BCE and continuing until a little after 1000 CE, numerous texts known as *Puranas* (from the Sanskrit for "old") were composed

Sites

Kamakhya, Assam

One of the most important Shakti *peethas* (sites where the power of the Goddess is said to be palpably felt). The temple is dedicated to the goddess Kamakhya, a form of Shakti/Parvati/Durga.

that retold the "old tales" or ancient lore of the Hindu tradition, shifting the emphasis away from the major Vedic gods and goddesses in favour of other deities. In the Hindu tradition nothing is ever really discarded. Older deities or concepts may be ignored for centuries, but eventually they are discovered afresh. As we have seen, a prototype for Shiva may have existed as long ago as the ancient Harappa culture, and Vishnu was mentioned as a minor figure in the early Vedic hymns. It was as these gods moved to the forefront, in the first millennium of the Common Era, that the Hindu tradition as we know it today crystallized.

Vishnu

Vishnu ("the all-pervasive one") is portrayed as coming to Earth in various forms, animal and human, to rid the world of evil and establish dharma or righteousness. In the first of these incarnations (**avataras**) he appears as a fish who saves Manu, the primeval man. This story was originally part of the Vedic literature, but is expanded in the *Puranas*.

While bathing in a lake, Manu finds a small fish in his hand. The fish speaks to him and asks him to take it home and put it in a jar. The next day it has expanded to fill the jar. Now Manu is asked to put

© Vasudha Narayanan

The Hindola Torana at Gyaraspur, Madhya Pradesh, dates from the tenth or eleventh century and was probably a gateway to a temple. The ten incarnations of Vishnu are carved on the pillars. Gyaraspur is near the famous Buddhist Sanchi stupa, and Vidisha, the site of a fifth-century Gupta-era temple complex.

the fish into a lake, which it outgrows, then into a river, and finally into the ocean. The fish, who is really Vishnu, then tells Manu that a great flood is coming, and that he must build a boat and put his family in it, along with the seven sages or *rishis*, and "the seeds of all the animals." Manu does as he is told, and when the flood sweeps the earth, those on the ship survive. This story is strongly reminiscent of flood myths in other religious traditions.

Eventually, Vishnu will have ten incarnations in the present cycle of creation. Nine are said to have taken place already, and the tenth is expected at the end of this age. Vishnu's incarnations appear in some of the earliest carvings both in India and in Southeast Asia. Some of the earliest carvings of

the Gupta period, dated c. 400 CE, depict Vishnu's second and third incarnations, as a tortoise and as a boar who saves the earth goddess Bhu. These magnificent carvings are in the Udayagiri caves, in the modern state of Madhya Pradesh. The story of the tortoise incarnation is relatively unimportant in India, but it became very popular in Cambodia. In this powerful narrative, the celestial beings (*devas*) and demons (*asuras*) churn an ocean of milk to make the nectar of immortality, using a (good) snake, Vasuki, as the churning rope. In 2004, when a memorial was built in Siem Reap, Cambodia, for those killed in previous wars, the entire park was circled by *devas* and *asuras* holding a rope, in the act of churning for *amrita*, the nectar of immortality.

© Vasudha Narayanan

Vishnu in his boar incarnation, saving the earth goddess Bhu from the demon Hiranyaksha; Udayagiri caves, Madhya Pradesh, India, c. 400 CE.

Vishnu's seventh incarnation was Rama, the hero of the epic, and according to some narratives the ninth was the Buddha, who may have diverted attention away from Hindu teachings but is admired for his emphasis on non-violence.

In other texts Vishnu's ninth incarnation is Krishna, whom we have already met in the *Bhagavad Gita*. The *Puranas* tell other stories from the life of Krishna: the delightful infant, the mischievous toddler who steals the butter he loves, the youth who steals the hearts of the cowherd girls and dances away the moonlit nights in their company. Some of the later *Puranas* celebrate the love of Krishna and his beloved Radha.

In many other incarnations Vishnu is accompanied by his consort Sri (Lakshmi), the goddess of good fortune, who bestows grace in this world and the next, blessing her worshippers not only with wealth but eventually with liberation. All stores display pictures of her, and so do most homes.

Shiva

Like Vishnu, Shiva emerged as a great god in the post-Upanishadic era. Unlike Vishnu, however, he does not reveal himself sequentially, in a series of incarnations. Instead, Shiva expresses the manifold aspects of his power by appearing simultaneously in paradoxical roles: as creator and destroyer, exuberant dancer and austere yogi. The wedding portrait of Shiva and his divine consort, Parvati, is an important part of his tradition, and his creative energy is often represented in the symbolic form of a **linga** (a conical or cylindrical stone column). Popular throughout India, stories of Shiva and his local manifestations—for instance, as Sundaresvara in the city of Madurai—are beloved by Hindus.

The Goddess

The great Goddess also appears in multiple forms, although the lines between them are not always clearly defined (Western scholars tend to emphasize the distinctions, while Hindus tend to blur them). Though many goddesses appear in the Vedas, none of them were all-powerful. Likewise, the epics and the early *Puranas* honour many consort goddesses, but no supreme female deity. It is only in the later *Puranas* that we begin to see explicit references to worship of a goddess not just as an appendage to a male deity but as the ultimate power, the creator of the universe, and the redeemer of human beings. She was sometimes considered to be the *shakti* or power of Shiva, but frequently her independence from the male deity was emphasized.

The most familiar manifestation of the Goddess is Parvati, the wife of Shiva. Durga is her warrior aspect, represented iconographically with a smiling countenance and a handful of weapons. As Kali, the Goddess is fierce and wild, a dark, dishevelled figure who wears a garland of skulls; yet even in this manifestation, her devotees call her "mother." In addition there are countless local goddesses with distinctive names and histories.

Festivals like the autumn celebration of **Navaratri** ("nine nights") are dedicated to the Goddess, and millions of Hindus offer her fervent devotions every day. The continuing importance of the Goddess is a distinctive characteristic of the Hindu tradition.

Sarasvati

In the *Puranas* the Vedic goddess Sarasvati becomes the goddess of learning. Although she is the consort of a creator god named **Brahma** (a minor deity, not to be confused with Brahman), their relationship is not celebrated iconographically, as the unions of Vishnu and Lakshmi or Shiva and Parvati are.

Rather, Sarasvati seems to enjoy a certain autonomy: portraits usually depict her alone, without any male god. She is a beautiful young woman with a white sari and a golden crown over flowing hair, radiant with wisdom, sitting gracefully on a rock beside a river. She has four hands; two of them hold a stringed musical instrument called a *vina*, another holds a string of beads, and the last holds a manuscript. The *vina* symbolizes music and the manuscript learning, while the beads signify the counting and recitation of holy names, which leads

© Vasudha Narayanan

A modern icon of the goddess Durga, who has eight arms and rides a tiger. Enshrined in the Hindu Society of Calgary (Canada) Temple, she is carved of marble in the "north Indian" style.

to transformative knowledge or wisdom. All these themes would eventually coalesce to form the composite picture of Sarasvati as the patron goddess of arts and education, music and letters.

Other Deities

Three other gods are also very popular. Ganesha, the elephant-headed son of Shiva and Parvati, is probably the most beloved of all the Hindu gods. He is the remover of obstacles and hindrances, and no new project or venture begins without a propitiatory offering for him, or at least a prayer. Murugan, another son of Shiva, is popular among Tamil-speaking people in India, Sri Lanka,

Malaysia, and Canada. And the monkey god Hanuman (also known as Maruti), a model devotee of Rama and Sita, is everyone's protector.

In South India Vishnu, Shiva, and Devi are frequently known by local names, and temples devoted to them are seldom referred to as Vishnu or Shiva temples. Thus Vishnu is known in the Tirupati hills and Srirangam as Venkateshwara ("lord of the Venkata hill") or Ranganatha ("lord of the stage" or *ranga*). Each manifestation has not only a unique personality, but a mythical history that links it with a particular place. These myths are recorded in books called *Sthala Puranas* ("*Puranas* about the place"). Local manifestation is extremely important in Hinduism. Every village has its own deity, and it can take considerable effort to connect those deities with pan-Indian gods and goddesses.

Sri or Lakshmi is called the mother of all creation, who bestows wisdom and salvation and is grace incarnate. Many teachers have composed hymns celebrating her compassion and wisdom. Vedanta Desika (1268–1369) describes her thus:

> She fulfills all [our] desires. She is noble, she gives prosperity, she is filled with good thoughts; she gives righteousness, pleasure, attainment and liberation. She gives the highest state (parinirvana) . . . she helps one cross the ocean of life and death. . . .

The Hindu "Trinity"

The notion of the *trimurti* ("three forms") seems to have been part of the Hindu tradition since at least the fourth century.

In the symbolism of *trimurti*, the gods Brahma, Vishnu, and Shiva either coalesce into one form with three faces, or are represented as equal. This has sometimes been interpreted as implying a polytheistic belief in three gods: Brahma the creator, Vishnu the preserver, and Shiva the destroyer. This interpretation contains a grain of truth, for the *trimurti* concept does effectively bring together the three great functions of a supreme god and distribute them among three distinct deities. But it is more misleading than informative in two ways.

First, it suggests that Hindus give equal importance to all three gods. In practice, however, most sectarian Hindu worshippers focus their devotions on only one supreme deity, whether Shiva, Vishnu, the Goddess in one of her multiple forms, or a local deity who may be unknown in other parts of India. Such devotees consider the other deities important but secondary to their own faith and practice. Furthermore, Brahma is not worshipped as a supreme deity. Though portrayed in mythology as the creator god, he himself is only the agent of the supreme deity who created him; that deity, at whose pleasure Brahma creates the universe, may be Vishnu, Shiva, or the Goddess, depending on the worshipper's sect.

Second, the "polytheistic" interpretation of *trimurti* suggests that creation, preservation, and destruction are functions that can be performed separately. But in fact followers of Vishnu or Shiva commonly understand creation, preservation, and destruction to be three parts of an integrated process for which their own particular supreme god is responsible. In this context, destruction is not unplanned, nor is it final: it is simply one phase in the ongoing evolution and devolution of the universe. All of creation temporarily enters or becomes one with Vishnu or Shiva until a new cycle of creation begins again. The cycle of creation will continue as long as there are souls caught up in the wheel of life and death. It is in this sense that devotees of Shiva, Vishnu, or the Goddess see their own chosen deity as the creator, the maintainer, and the destroyer of the universe.

Ages of Time

The *Puranas* refer to those cosmic cycles of creation and destruction as the days and nights of Brahma. Each day of Brahma contains approximately 4,320 million earthly years, and the nights of Brahma are equally long. A year of Brahma is made up of 360 such days, and Brahma lives for 100 years. Each cycle therefore amounts to 311,040,000 million earthly years, at the end of which the entire cosmos is drawn into the body of Vishnu or Shiva (depending on which *Purana* one is reading), where it remains until another Brahma is evolved.

Each day of Brahma contains 14 secondary cycles of creation and destruction called *manavantara*s, each of which lasts 306,720,000 years. During the long intervals between *manavantara*s, the world is recreated and a new Manu or primeval man appears and once again begins the human race.

Each *manavantara* in turn contains 71 great eons (*maha yugas*), each of which is divided into four eons (*yugas*). A single one of these eons is the basic cycle. The golden age (*krta yuga*) lasts 1,728,000 earthly years. During this time dharma or righteousness is envisioned as a bull standing firmly on all four legs. The Treta age is shorter, 1,296,000 earthly years; dharma is then on three legs. The Dvapara age lasts half as long as the golden age; thus for 864,000 earthly years dharma hops on two legs. Finally, during the *kali yuga*, the worst of all possible ages, dharma is reduced to one leg. This age lasts for 432,000 earthly years, during which the world becomes progressively worse. It is in this degenerate *kali yuga*—which, according to traditional Hindu reckoning, began around 3102 BCE—that we live today.

There is a steady decline in morality, righteousness, life span, and human satisfaction through the *yugas*. At the end of the *kali yuga*—obviously still a long time off—there will be no righteousness, no virtue, no trace of justice. When the world ends, seven scorching suns will dry up the oceans, there will be wondrously shaped clouds, torrential rains will fall, and eventually the cosmos will be absorbed into Vishnu. The *Puranas* deal with astronomical units of time; the age of the earth, let alone the human being, is infinitesimally small in relation to the eons of time the universe goes through. Although, according to many Hindu systems of thought, it is entirely possible for human beings to end their own cycle of birth and death through transforming wisdom and/or devotion, the cycles of creation and destruction of the universe are independent of the human being's attaining *moksha* or liberation.

Temples represent the spatial and temporal cosmos. Thus their architecture sometimes reflects the Puranic cycles of time. At the great Vishnu temple of Angkor Wat in Cambodia, for instance, the causeways and passages were designed so that their measurements (when calculated in the units used in the building of the temple) represent the numbers of years in various cycles of time.

Caste and the *Laws of Manu*

"Caste" is used as a shorthand term to refer to the thousands of social and occupational divisions that have developed from the simple fourfold structure laid out in the "Hymn to the Supreme Person": priests, rulers, merchants, and servants. There are said to be more than one thousand *jatis* ("birth groups") in India, and people routinely identify themselves by their *jati*. Ritual practices, dietary rules, and sometimes dialects differ between castes. Although the modern word "caste" signifies both the four broad *varnas* and the minutely divided *jatis*, Western scholars sometimes translate *varna* as "class" and *jati* as "caste."

By the first centuries of the Common Era, many treatises had been written regarding the nature of righteousness, moral duty, and law. Called the *dharmashastras*, these are the foundations of later Hindu laws. The most famous is the *Manava Dharmashastra* (*Laws of Manu*). These "laws" were probably codified around the first century, for they reflect the social norms of that time: the caste system is firmly in place, and women have slipped to an inferior position from the relatively high status they

Document

Becoming a Brahmin

Nahusha asked Yudhishthira:
"Who can be said to be a brahmin, O King?"
Yudhishthira replied:
"O lord of Serpents! The one who is truthful, is generous, is patient, is virtuous, has empathy, is tranquil, and has compassion—such a person is a brahmin" (*Mahabharata Vana Parva*, 177.15, trans. Vasudha Narayanan).

enjoyed in the period of the Vedas. When reading this text we have to understand that in many parts of India the rules it laid down were not followed strictly. We also have to take its pronouncements on women with a grain of salt.

The upper classes were generally called "twice born," in reference to the initiatory rite by which the males of these social groups were spiritually reborn as sons of their religious teachers. This rite, the **upanayana**, marked a boy's initiation into studenthood—the first of four stages in life. The *dharmashastras* set out the roles and duties of the four principal castes that make up Hindu society: brahmins (priests), **kshatriyas** (rulers, warriors), **vaishyas** (merchants), and **shudras** (servants). The brahmins were (and are still) the priestly class, the only group in Hindu society supposedly authorized to teach the Vedas. Although not all members of the brahmin community were priests, all enjoyed the power and prestige associated with spiritual learning.

The dharma of the kshatriya class, which was permitted only to study the Vedas, not to teach them, was to protect the people and the country. In the Hindu tradition, past and present, lines of descent are all-important. Thus many kings sought to confirm their legitimacy by tracing their ancestry to the primeval progenitors of humanity—either the sun or the moon—and even usurpers of thrones invoked divine antecedents. Later Hindu rituals explicitly emphasized kshatriya families' divine connections. The *Laws of Manu* describe in detail the duties of a king. He must strive to conquer his senses, for only those who have conquered their own senses can lead or control others. He must shun not only the vices of pleasure—hunting, gambling, drinking, women—but also the vices that arise from wrath, such as violence, envy, and slander.

The dharma of the vaishya (mercantile) class made them responsible for most commercial transactions, as well as agricultural work, including the raising of cattle. The power of wealth and economic decisions lay with the vaishyas, who were likewise permitted only to study the Vedas.

The last class mentioned formally in the *dharmashastras* is the shudras. The *dharmashastras* say that it is the duty of shudras to serve the other classes; they would not be permitted to accumulate wealth even if they had the opportunity to do so. As the *Laws of Manu* put it, "The seniority of brahmins comes from sacred knowledge, that of kshatriyas from valour, vaishyas from wealth, and shudras, only from old age."

In practice, however, the caste system is far more complex and flexible than the *dharmashastras* suggest. For example, the Vellalas of South India wielded considerable economic and political power, even though the brahmins considered them a shudra caste. They were wealthy landowners, and the *dharmashastra* prohibitions do not seem to have had any effect on their fortunes.

The *Laws of Manu*, as well as the *Bhagavad Gita*, tell us that it is better to do one's own dharma imperfectly than to do another person's well. However, the *dharmashastras* acknowledge that in times of adversity one may do other tasks, and they list these in order of preference for each class. Although they emphasize the importance of marrying within one's own class, they also recognize that mixed marriages do take place, and so they go on to list the kind of sub-castes that emerge from various permutations. A marriage is generally acceptable if the male partner is of a higher caste, but if the woman is higher, their offspring are considered to be of a lower caste than either parent.

Also part of India's social fabric are various "outcastes": groups officially excluded from the caste system either because they originated in mixed marriages in the distant past or, more often, because they are associated with occupations deemed polluting, such as dealing with corpses or working with animal hides (the English word "pariah" comes from the Tamil for "drummer"—an outcaste occupation because drums were made of animal hides stretched taut over a frame). Until the nineteenth century, caste was only one factor among the many considered in the judicial process and in society itself. Legal cases were decided with reference to the immediate circumstances, and local customs were no less important than written texts—sometimes more so. It was India's British colonial rulers who, assuming that the caste laws were binding, attributed a new authority to them.

The caste system is such a strong social force in India that even non-Hindu communities such as the Christians, Jainas, and Sikhs have been influenced by it. Nadar Christians from the south, for instance, will marry only people of the same caste, and similar restrictions are observed all over India. In Southeast Asia, on the other hand, the caste system bears little resemblance to the Indian model. Inscriptions after the eighth century show that Manu was known, as were the *varna* and *jati* systems, and brahmins were honoured and several held high positions. However, the rest of society seems to have been organized in different ways, and, in some cases, the king actually awarded specific caste status to various groups. The caste system still functions to a limited extent in some diasporas but has been significantly diluted among Hindu groups in North America.

The Stages and Goals of Life

The dharma texts of the classical period recognized four stages of life (**ashramas**) for males from the three higher classes in society. First, a young boy was initiated into studenthood, during which he was to remain celibate and concentrate on learning. Education was to be provided for all those who desired it, and families were to support students. Although the early epics suggest that girls could also become students, it is likely that this right had been withdrawn by the first century, when the *Laws of Manu* were codified.

In the next stage the young man was to repay his debts to society and his forefathers, and his spiritual debt to the gods, by marrying and earning a living to support his family and other students. It was the householder's dharma to be employed and lead a conjugal life with his partner in dharma. Few men went beyond these two stages, and it is likely that most people never had the opportunity to study at all.

Nevertheless, the *Laws of Manu* describes two more stages. When a man's children have grown and become householders themselves, he and his wife may retire to the forest and live a simple life. Finally, in the last stage, an elderly man would renounce the material world altogether and take up the ascetic life of the **samnyasin**. His old personality was now dead; he owned nothing, relied on food given as alms, and spent the rest of his days seeking enlightenment and cultivating detachment from life. This kind of formal renunciation became rare with the increasing popularity of the *Bhagavad Gita*, which stresses controlled engagement with the world.

The literature of the period just before the beginning of the Common Era also recognized a number of aims that human beings strive for. These are neither good nor bad in themselves, but may become immoral if they are pursued at an inappropriate time of life or with inappropriate intensity. The aims are dharma, the discharging of one's duties; **artha**, prosperity and power; **kama**, sensual pleasure of many types, including sexual pleasure and the appreciation of beauty; and finally, *moksha*, or liberation from the cycle of birth and death. The last was sometimes seen as belonging to a different category, but texts like the *Gita* made it clear that we may strive for liberation even in daily work as long as we act without attachment.

Attitudes towards Women

The Hindu scriptures were written by men, and many of their statements about women's position in society may seem contradictory, alternately honouring, respecting, and even venerating women, but also scorning them. The *Laws of Manu* make it only too clear that women's status in Hindu society in the early Common Era was inferior. For example: "Though destitute of virtue, or seeking pleasure elsewhere, or devoid of good qualities, a husband must be constantly worshipped as a god by a faithful wife" (*Manu* 5.154). Male commentators through the centuries have quoted such statements approvingly.

The text goes on to say that a wife is the goddess of fortune and auspiciousness (*Manu* 9.26) and that only if women are honoured will the gods be pleased and the religious rituals prove beneficial (*Manu* 3.56). On balance, however, the negative statements outweigh the positive ones. Perhaps the most famous of his pronouncements on women is the following:

By a girl, by a young woman or even by an aged one, nothing must be done independently, even in her own house. In childhood a female must be subject to her father, in youth to her husband, when her lord is dead, to her sons; a woman must never be independent (*Manu* 5.147–8).

Statements like that, and the weight given to them by later commentators, did much to shape Western notions of Hindu women. As influential as *Manu* has been in some communities and at certain times, however, the views it presents cannot be considered prescriptive or normative. Women in the Vedic age composed hymns and took part in philosophical debates. In fact, *Manu*'s dictates were not necessarily followed. As we will see, medieval women were more than dutiful wives: they composed poetry, endowed temples, gave religious advice and wrote scholarly works, including commentary on scripture. Far from being ostracized or condemned, those women were respected, honoured, and in some cases even venerated. Despite *Manu* and its proponents, many women of the upper socio-economic groups enjoyed both religious and financial independence and made substantial contributions to literature and the fine arts.

Some of the contradictions in Hindu thinking about women can be traced to the concept of auspiciousness. "Auspiciousness" refers primarily to prosperity in this life—prosperity being associated above all with wealth and progeny. Thus cattle, elephants, kings, and married women with the potential to bear children are all said to be auspicious, as are birth and marriage rituals, because they are associated with the promotion of three human goals recognized by classical scriptures: dharma (duty), *artha* (prosperity), and *kama* (sensual pleasure). There is also a second level of auspiciousness, however, that is related to the fourth and ultimate human goal: *moksha* (liberation). The two levels of auspiciousness have been implicit in Hindu religious literature and rituals. In many contexts, women have auspiciousness in different degrees, which determine the levels of their acceptance in society.

In the classical literature of the *dharmashastra*s and in practice, it is auspicious to be married because it is only in marriage that one can fulfill one's dharmic obligations. The ideal is the *sumangali*, the married woman who is a full partner in dharma, *artha*, and *kama*, through whom children are born, and wealth and religious merit are accumulated. Only a married woman may be called *Srimati* (the one with *sri* or auspiciousness). Traditionally, a Hindu wife's dharma included not only total obedience and loyalty to her husband in life but fidelity to his memory after his death. While some of these notions are still adhered to in Hindu life, there is a wide array of role models for women, and a woman's position in society depends on a variety of factors, including religious culture.

⊛ Schools and Communities of Theology

Vedanta

Six schools of "philosophy" are recognized within the Hindu tradition—Samkhya, Nyaya, Vaisheshika, Mimamsa, Yoga, and Vedanta—and elements of all six can be seen in modern Hinduism. Although popularly called "philosophy," these traditions are closer to theological enterprises as they accept and build on many Hindu texts. Yoga has attracted a wide popular following in recent years, but as a philosophical school Vedanta is by far the most important. Vedanta ("end of the Vedas") has engaged Hindu thinkers for more than a thousand years. Although the term "Vedanta" traditionally denoted the *Upanishads*, in popular usage it more often refers to systems of thought based on a coherent interpretation of the *Upanishads* together with the *Bhagavad Gita* and the *Brahma Sutras* (a collection of roughly 500 aphorisms summarizing the teachings of those texts).

An important early interpreter of Vedanta was Shankara (fl. c. 800). For him, reality is non-dual (**advaita**): the only reality is Brahman, and this reality is indescribable, without attributes. Brahman and Atman (the human soul) are identical; Shankara interprets the Upanishadic phrase "you are that" in a literal way and upholds the unity of what most people perceive as two distinct entities. Under the influence of *maya* we delude ourselves into believing that we are different from Brahman, but when the illusion is dispelled, the soul is liberated by the realization of its true nature. Liberation, therefore, is the removal of ignorance and the dispelling of illusion through the power of transforming knowledge. That goal can be reached in this life; human beings can achieve liberation while still embodied. But final release will come only after the death of the body. Those liberated in this life act without binding desire and help others to achieve liberation.

Shankara also posits three levels of reality. He recognizes that human beings believe life is real, but points out that when we are asleep we also believe that what happens in our dreams is real. Only when we wake up do we discover that what we dreamt was not real. So too in this cycle of life and death, we believe that everything we experience is real. And it is—until we are liberated and wake up to the truth about our identity. One might argue that there is a difference: that the dream seems true only to the individual dreamer, whereas the phenomenal world appears real to millions who seem to share the same reality. But the school of Shankara would say that our limited reality is the result of ignorance and illusion. With the transformative knowledge spoken of in the *Upanishads*, we recognize that we are in reality Brahman and are liberated from the cycle of life and death. But that cycle goes on for the other souls still caught in the snares of *maya*.

Shankara's philosophy was criticized by later philosophers like Ramanuja and Madhva. One of their principal objections is connected with the status of *maya*: if *maya* is real, then there are *two* realities: Brahman and *maya*. If *maya* were unreal, Shankara's critics argue, surely it could not be the cause of the cosmic delusion attributed to it. Shankara tries to circumvent this objection by saying that *maya* is indescribable, neither real nor unreal, and his followers would say that in the ultimate state of liberation, which is totally ineffable, such criticisms are not valid in any case.

Ramanuja (traditionally 1017–1137) was the most significant interpreter of theistic Vedanta for the Sri Vaishnava community—the devotees of Vishnu and his consorts Sri (Lakshmi) and Bhu (the earth goddess)—in South India. In his commentaries on the *Brahma Sutras* and the *Gita*, as well as his independent treatises, Ramanuja proclaims the supremacy of Vishnu–Narayana and emphasizes that devotion to Vishnu will lead to ultimate liberation. He challenges Shankara's interpretation of scripture, especially regarding *maya*, and his belief that the supreme reality (Brahman) is without attributes. For Ramanuja, Vishnu (whose name literally means "all-pervasive") is immanent throughout the universe, pervading all souls and material substances, but also transcending them. Thus from one viewpoint there is a single reality, Brahman; but from another viewpoint Brahman is qualified by souls and matter. Since the human soul is the body and the servant of the Supreme Being, liberation is portrayed not as the realization that the two are the same, but rather as the intuitive, joyful, and total realization of the soul's relationship with the lord.

The Sri Vaishnava community differs from other Hindu traditions in that it reveres as sacred not only Sanskrit texts like the Vedas, the *Bhagavad Gita*, the epics, and the *Puranas* but also the Tamil compositions of the **Alvars**: twelve South Indian poet-saints who lived between the eighth and tenth centuries CE. Specifically, the Sri Vaishnavas hold the *Tiruvaymoli* of Nammalvar to be the *Tamil* (or *Dravida*) *Veda* and refer to their scriptural heritage as *ubhaya vedanta* or dual Vedic theology.

The temple tower at Tirukoshtiyur, Tamilnadu. One of the 108 places sung about by the Alvars, this temple was made famous by Ramanuja in the eleventh century CE. Given a secret mantra that would grant salvation, he is said to have climbed the tower and shouted the powerful mantra to all the devotees in the area, so they too could receive the grace of Vishnu.

The community also considers the 108 temples that the Alvars glorified in their poems to be heaven on earth. Worship in these Vishnu temples includes selections from both Sanskrit and Tamil scripture. In the Sanskrit devotional hymns of the Sri Vaishnava community, following the Puranic literature, Vishnu is portrayed as reigning over heaven. The liberated human soul, after cleansing itself in the waters of the river Viraja, which encircles heaven, approaches Vishnu and his consort Sri, renders loving service, and is never separated from them. The Sri Vaishnava tradition reveres Ramanuja as a saviour of the community, and his image is found in many temples.

The philosopher Madhva (c. 1199–1278) is unique in the Hindu tradition in classifying some souls as eternally bound. For him there are different grades of enjoyment and bliss even in liberation. He is also one of the explicitly dualistic Vedanta philosophers, holding that the human soul and Brahman are ultimately separate and not identical in any way.

Yoga

"Yoga" has had many meanings in the history of the Hindu tradition. In general, though, it is the physical and mental discipline through which practitioners "yoke" their spirit to the divine. The origins

Sites

Badrinath, Uttaranchal

An important pilgrimage site, high in the Himalayas, with a temple of Vishnu in the form of the sages Nara and Narayana (twin manifestations of the god who are sometimes considered to be his incarnations); one of 108 sacred places for the Sri Vaishnava community.

of yoga are obscure, though (as we saw) some scholars have pointed out that seals from the Harappan culture portray a man sitting in what looks like a yogic position.

For many Hindus the classic yoga text is a collection of short, aphoristic fragments called the *Yoga Sutras*, finalized sometime in the early centuries of the Common Era and attributed to Patanjali. We do not know who Patanjali was, but he is said to have lived in the second century BCE. It's likely that yoga had been an important feature of religious life in India for centuries before the text was written.

Patanjali's yoga is a system of moral, mental, and physical discipline and meditation with a particular object, either physical or mental, as the "single point" of focus. It is described as having eight "limbs" or disciplines. The first of these, *yama*, consists of restraints: avoidance of violence, falsehood, stealing, sexual activity, and avarice. (Interestingly, the same prohibitions are part of the "right conduct" taught by the Jaina tradition.) The second, *niyama*, consists of positive practices such as cleanliness (internal and external purity), equanimity, asceticism (what Patanjali calls "heat," a kind of energetic concentration), the theoretical study of yoga, and the effort to make God the focus of one's activities. In addition Patanjali recommends a number of bodily postures and breathing techniques.

A crucial aspect of yoga practice is learning to detach the mind from the domination of external sensory stimuli. Perfection in concentration (*dharana*) and meditation (*dhyana*) lead to *samadhi*: absorption into and union with the divine. There are various stages of *samadhi*, but the ultimate stage is complete emancipation from the cycle of life and death. This state is variously described as a coming together, uniting, and transcending of polarities; empty and full, neither life nor death, and yet both. In short, this final liberation cannot be adequately described in human language.

Although Patanjali's yoga is widely considered the classical form, there are numerous variations. "Yoga" is often used in a general way to designate any form of meditation or practice with ascetic tendencies, and in the broadest terms it may refer to any path that leads to final emancipation. Thus in the *Bhagavad Gita* the way of action is called *karma yoga* and the way of devotion is *bhakti yoga*. In some interpretations of these forms, the eight "limbs" of classical yoga are not present; *bhakti yoga* simply comes to mean *bhakti marga*, the way of devotion. In this context yoga becomes a way of self-abnegation, in which the worshipper seeks union with the Supreme Being through passionate devotion. Some philosophers, including Ramanuja, have said that *bhakti yoga* includes elements of Patanjali's yoga, but many Hindus use the term "yoga" much more loosely. Although its theoretical aspects have had considerable importance in particular times and traditions, Patanjali's yoga has not enjoyed mass popularity over the centuries, and few religious teachers have regarded it as a separate path to liberation. Recent decades have seen increasing interest in the physical aspects of yoga, especially in the West, but that interest does not always extend to the psychological and theoretical foundations of the practice.

Tantra

The tantric component of the Hindu tradition is hard to define, partly because advocates and detractors portray it in very different lights. Essentially **tantra** consists of a body of ritual practices and the texts interpreting them, which appear to be independent of the Vedic tradition.

"Tantra" may be derived from a root word meaning "to stretch" or "expand." It began to gain importance in the Hindu and Buddhist traditions in about the fifth century. Some scholars believe it originated in the indigenous culture of the subcontinent and re-emerged in later centuries. Others see it as a later development external to the Vedic tradition (though not in opposition to it). One may also see divisions in tantra along sectarian lines: the Shaiva, Shakta, and Vaishnava communities all have their own texts called *tantras*.

Tantra is perhaps more difficult to define than most other Hindu systems of thought and ritual, partly because of the esoteric nature of tantric texts and practices, partly because of regional and sectarian variations, and partly because of its interpenetration with other systems of philosophy and practice. In general, tantric systems have four components: *jnana* (knowledge of the deities and divine powers), *yoga* (forms of praxis including, but not limited to, the use of mantras); *kriya* (praxis and rituals), and *carya* (conduct and behaviour). The Shaiva, Shakta, and Vaishnava communities incorporated elements of tantra in their own practice. For example, when an image of a deity is installed in a temple, a large geometric drawing (*yantra*; sometimes called a *mandala*) representing gods or goddesses and the cosmos is drawn on the floor and used as an object of meditation and ritual. Worship of the deities in temples is explicitly based on tantra texts and practices. The use of *mantras*—words or short, formulaic phrases that are said to have transformational potency—is also important in the practice of tantra.

Tantrism developed its own form of yoga, known as *kundalini*, centred on the *shakti* or power of the Goddess, which is said to lie coiled like a serpent at the base of the spine. When awakened, this power rises through six chakras or "wheels" within the body to reach the final chakra under the skull known as the thousand-petalled lotus.

The ultimate aim of this form of yoga is to awaken the power of the *kundalini* and allow it to unite with the divine being who is in the thousand-petalled lotus. When this union is achieved, the practitioner is granted visions and psychic powers that eventually lead to emancipation (*moksha*).

There are many variants of tantrism, but the main division is between the "left-handed" and "right-handed" schools. As the left hand was considered inauspicious, the term "left-handed" was applied to movements that did not meet with the approval of the larger or more established schools. "Left-handed" practices centred on the ritual performance of activities forbidden in everyday life, such as drinking liquor, eating fish and meat, and having sexual intercourse with a partner other than one's spouse. These activities were disapproved of in many other Hindu circles, so that to a large extent left-handed tantrism remained esoteric. The "right-handed" school was more conservative.

Hinduism in Southeast Asia

Hindu culture today is associated almost exclusively with the Indian peninsula, but its influence can still be seen across Southeast Asia. Archeological evidence suggests that extensive trade links were established by the second century CE, and both Hindu and Buddhist texts in India refer to Southeast Asia as the land of gold (*suvarna bhumi*) and gems. Chinese texts from about the third century CE refer to kings of Funan (a kingdom in ancient Cambodia) with Indian names. Sanskrit inscriptions are seen in the Khmer empire beginning about the late fifth century CE. Until the fourteenth century, Hindu narratives and temple-building traditions were popular across much of Southeast Asia, especially in Cambodia.

Cultural connections between India and Southeast Asia were also widespread. Many Sanskrit inscriptions and thousands of icons and sculptures portraying Hindu deities indicate that Hindu influences were pervasive in Cambodia, Thailand, Laos, Vietnam, Java, Indonesia, and Bali. One of the largest Hindu temples in the world is Angkor Wat, built by King Suryavarman II in the twelfth century CE and dedicated to Vishnu. Kings and queens of Cambodia had names reminiscent of Indian–Hindu royalty—names such as Jayavarman, Indravarman, Mahendravarman, and Indira-lakshmi.

Even so, Hindu traditions in Southeast Asia, as in every part of India, have distinctive local characteristics. The Khmer people of Cambodia, for instance, emphasized some stories that were not so important in India, and temples in Cambodia, Laos, and Indonesia are often strikingly similar to their counterparts on the subcontinent in their basic design, yet strikingly different in effect.

Shiva, Vishnu, and Lakshmi were all popular in Southeast Asia, but so was a god—an amalgam of Vishnu and Shiva—named Hari-Hara, particularly in Cambodia. Portrayed in relief in the Badami caves (c. sixth century CE, Northern Karnataka) but otherwise little known in India, Hari-Hara appears in many Cambodian inscriptions after the seventh century; we also see him represented in many icons. In addition, icons of Brahma, Vishnu, Ganesha, Murugan, Nandi (a bull sacred to Shiva), Garuda (the "eagle mount" of Vishnu), the nine planets worshipped by Hindus, and other deities have been found all over Southeast Asia.

One of the most widely worshipped deities across Southeast Asia was Shiva, particularly as represented by the creative symbol of the *linga*. In Cambodia, Shiva is usually depicted with two wives, Uma and Ganga. In the *Puranas*, the river Ganga is said to reside in Shiva's hair, but other narratives refer to the river itself as a deity, a

© Vasudha Narayanan

Vishnu reclining on a snake called Ananta, surrounded by emblems of Shiva (Shiva lingas) carved on the rocks in the Kbal Spean river, about 30 km from Siem Reap, Cambodia. The Kbal Spean is considered sacred and compared to the Ganga in India.

consort of Shiva. In this way, local rivers in Cambodia came to be considered holy. Their sacred nature was proclaimed in carvings made on rocks on their banks, which emphasized their identification with the Ganga.

Carvings of Vishnu in various incarnations can also be found in temples across South and Southeast Asia. Starting with the endowments of Queen Kulaprabhavati in the late fifth century, we find many endowments to Vishnu temples in Cambodia. Knowledge of Indian Vaishnava texts, including the two epics, was widespread, at least among the elite, and even though Shaivism and other forms of Hinduism were largely displaced by Buddhism by the fifteenth century, the *Ramayana* continues to thrive through the performing arts. The Prambanan temple near Yogyakarta, Indonesia, is just one of many in the region whose walls are carved with scenes from the *Ramayana* and the *Puranas*.

The Prambanan temple also has shrines for Brahma and Vishnu, although the main shrine is dedicated to Shiva. In fact, most of the temples in Southeast Asia were home to more than one deity: Shiva, Vishnu, and Devi—the Goddess—were frequently worshipped in the same building. Sectarian affiliation and devotion to either Shiva or Vishnu seems to have been flexible within families as well.

Many inscriptions, especially in Cambodia, trace matrilineal as well as patrilineal descent. We can also note the importance given to biological ancestry, the pride taken in brahmin ancestors who were learned in the Vedas. However, despite the great respect shown to the brahmins in Cambodian (as well as Thai) culture, the caste system as we know it in India did not exist in that region. Studies show that new castes were created by the king, who seems to have had the power to bestow caste identities on his subjects. It may be that the caste system in Cambodia was largely ceremonial, or of relevance only to brahmins and royalty.

The famous inscription called the Sdok Kok Thom (c. 1052), one of the most important sources of information about Cambodian culture, traces many generations of kings and priests, often through matrilineal descent. Many women seem to have held royal offices, and they certainly executed many pious and charitable works. We also hear of three queens—Indira-lakshmi, Kambuja-raja-lakshmi, and Jayaraja-devi—who seem to have wielded considerable power. Apparently claims were made to the throne by royal women as well as men.

Although Hinduism is not widely practised in Southeast Asia today except in the island of Bali and among descendants of Indian immigrants, cultural traditions associated with it still linger. Dances with Indian themes, particularly stories connected with the *Ramayana* and Tamil works such as the *Manimekalai* (c. second to fifth centuries CE) are part of almost every cultural event, and names of Indian origin are still common among people in Indonesia, Thailand, and Cambodia.

South Indian Devotion (*Bhakti*)

The standard portrait of Vedic and classical Hinduism is based on the culture of the northern part of the Indian subcontinent. But South India—that is, the region south of the Vindhya mountains—had

Sites

Guruvayur, Kerala

This temple dedicated to the youthful Krishna draws millions of pilgrims every year. It is one of the largest temples in India. The deity enshrined in Guruvayur is the subject of a famous Sanskrit poem by Melpathur Narayana Bhattathiri (1559–1645) called the *Naraayaneeyam*.

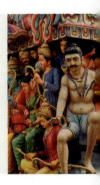

a flourishing cultural life of its own by 400 BCE and possibly earlier. It was here that an entirely new type of Hindu devotion (**bhakti**) emerged and spread throughout India.

A sophisticated body of literature in the Tamil language existed 2,000 years ago. Its earliest components are a number of poems on secular themes that are thought to have been composed at the time of three great Tamil academies. Known as the *Sangam* (Academy) poems, they fall into two groups: one dealing with the outer (*puram*) world of warfare, the valour of kings, and honour, the other with the inner (*akam*) world of love and romance, of secret meetings, anguished separation, and the overwhelming joy of union.

The Tamil language has a long history of sophisticated poetry, drama, and grammatical analysis. The earliest extant Tamil composition shows some undeniable similarities to Sanskrit literature, and the early poems of love and war include many words borrowed from Sanskrit. Yet Tamil literature on the whole is neither derived from nor imitative of Sanskrit material.

The oldest collections of Tamil poems, known as the *Ettutokai* (Eight Anthologies) and the *Pattupattu* (Ten Songs) were probably composed between the first and the third centuries. Lost for more than a thousand years, they were rediscovered in the nineteenth century. Five basic situations or moods are associated with five distinct landscape settings (*tinai*). In the *akam* poems, for example, the seashore represents separation between lovers, and a jasmine flower symbolizes a woman patiently waiting for her beloved. The underlying meaning of each poem would have been instantly clear to the audiences that heard it recited.

Religious literature apparently began to flourish after the fifth century. Several poems are addressed

Document

From the Songs of Andal

Andal ("she who rules") was an eighth-century Alvar who is worshipped in many South Indian temples dedicated to Vishnu. Her passionate poetry is not only recited and sung by the Vaishnava community today, but is broadcast over every radio station in Tamilnadu and Karnataka in the month of December. Tradition says that she refused to marry and longed for union with Vishnu—a wish that her biographers claim was fulfilled. Thus in her life as well as her work Andal represents a radical alternative to Manu's view of women and their role. Icons of Andal can be found in major South Indian Hindu temples across North America as well as in many other parts of the world.

A thousand elephants circle,
as Narana, Lord of virtues,
walks in front of me.

Golden jars brim with water;
Festive flags and pennants fly through this town,
eager to welcome him—
I saw this in a dream, my friend!
Drums beat happy sounds; conches were blown.
Under the canopy strung heavy with pearls,
Madhusudha, my love, filled with virtue,
came and clasped the palm of my hand
I saw this in a dream, my friend!
Those with eloquent mouths recited the good Vedas,
With mantras they placed
the green leaves and the grass in a circle.
The lord, strong as a raging elephant,
softly held my hand as we circled the fire.
I saw this in a dream, my friend!
(*Nachchiyar Tirumoli* 1.1 and 1.6–7; trans. Vasudha Narayanan)

to Vishnu, Shiva, and Murugan (the son of Shiva and Parvati).

The *bhakti* movement represented a major shift in Hindu culture. It arose sometime around the seventh century, when poet-devotees of Vishnu and Shiva began travelling from temple to temple singing the praises of their chosen deity not in formal Sanskrit but in Tamil—the mother tongue of the people, the language of intimacy and powerful emotion. By the twelfth century, 75 of these devotees had been recognized as saints: 63 devotees of Shiva known as the Nayanmars ("masters") and 12 devotees of Vishnu known as the Alvars ("those 'immersed deep' in the love of Vishnu").

Composed between the seventh and ninth centuries, the vernacular songs of the Alvars were introduced into the temple liturgy as early as the tenth century, challenging orthodox claims that Sanskrit was the exclusive vehicle for revelation and theological communication. Moreover, brahmin theologians honoured their authors as ideal devotees. This response was extraordinarily significant, for some of the Alvars came from lower-caste (perhaps even outcaste) backgrounds and one of them—Andal—was a woman. Selections from their works, collected in the eleventh century as the *Nalayira Divya Prabandham*, or *Sacred Collect of Four Thousand Verses*, are recited daily in temples and in homes by the Sri Vaishnava community, which considers them the Tamil equivalents of the Sanskrit Vedas.

The poems of the Alvars follow the literary conventions of earlier Tamil poetry, incorporating the symbols of the *akam* and *puram* poems. Vishnu is seen as a lover and a king, accessible and remote, gracious and grand. In their songs of devotion, the Alvars seek from Vishnu both the embrace of the beloved and the protection of the king.

Many incidents from the *Ramayana*, *Mahabharata*, and *Puranas* make their way into the Alvars' songs, along with some stories not found in any of these sources. Above all, the poets focus on the supremacy of Vishnu–Narayana, emphasizing that his incarnations as Rama or Krishna and his presence in the temple point to both his ability and his desire to save all beings. In the eighth century, Kulacekara Alvar expressed his longing to see Rama in the temple at Tillai (the modern city of Chidambaram):

In the beautiful city of Ayodhya, encircled
by towers,
a flame that lit up all the worlds
appeared in the Solar race
and gave life to all the heavens.
This warrior, with dazzling eyes,
Rama, dark as a cloud,
the First One, My Lord,
is in Chitrakuta, city of Tillai.
When is the day
when my eyes can behold him
and rejoice? (*Perumal Tirumoli* 10.1)

Sometimes the Alvars identify themselves with characters from the epics or the *Puranas*, expressing their longing for Vishnu by speaking in the voice of one who is separated from Rama or Krishna. A royal devotee of Rama, Kulacekara Alvar, imagines the grief felt by Dasaratha, the father of Rama, after banishing his son to the forest:

Without hearing him call me "Father" with
pride and with love,
Without clasping his chest adorned with
gems to mine,
Without embracing him, without smoothing
his forehead,
Without seeing his graceful gait, majestic
like the elephant,
Without seeing his face [glowing] like the
lotus,
I, wretched one,
having lost my son, my lord,
Still live (*Perumal Tirumoli* 9.6).

Many of the Tamil saints, both Vaishnava and Shaiva, travelled all over South India and parts of the north, visiting temples in which their chosen deity was enshrined. In this way pilgrimage became an important feature of the Hindu tradition, and as the character of Vishnu or Shiva varied from one

Document

From the *Tiruvaymoli*

Although philosophical texts say that the soul is beyond gender, devotional poets have often used the language of human love to express their feelings for the divine. In the following extracts from the Tiruvaymoli—*the ninth-century masterpiece that is considered to be a "fifth Veda"—the poet Nammalvar speaks in the voice of a young girl who longs for Vishnu as she would for a human lover (the indented lines refer to various incarnations of Vishnu).*

Where do I go from here?
I can't stand the soft bells, the gentle breeze,
the dark water-lily, darkness that conquers day,
dulcet notes, jasmines, the refreshing air.
The Lord, my beguiling one,
    who creates, bores through,
    swallows and spews this earth,
    who measures here and beyond,
does not come.
Why should I live? (*Tiruvaymoli* 9.9.2; trans. Vasudha Narayanan)

In another section Nammalvar speaks in the voice of a cowherd girl longing for Krishna (addressed here as "Kanna"):

My fragrant shoulders, slender as bamboo shoots,
have become weak, alas!
Blind to my pining,
not heeding of my loneliness,
The cuckoo birds coo, alas!
Peacocks mate and dance, alas!
When you go to graze the cattle,
a day seems like a thousand ages, alas!
Your lotus eyes pierce me;
Kanna, you're unfair, you're unfair.

You're unfair, Kanna, you're unfair!
When you make love and embrace my full breasts,
a tidal wave of pleasure, unchecked by our union,
rises to the firmament, and soars beyond,
making my wits drown in the flood.
And then it all recedes like a dream.
My passion permeates my inner life
and throbs in every cell of my body.
My soul cannot bear the burden
when I am separated from you.
Every time you go to graze the cows,
    I die.
I shall die if you go to graze the cows,
for my soul is ablaze with the fire of my breath,
I have no companion.
I shall not live to see your dark body dance.
When you leave me, the day never ends;
my twin eyes, shaped like *kayal* fish,
swim in tears that never end.
Born as cowherd girls in a herder clan,
a humble state,
Our loneliness is death.
You were gone the whole day,
grazing cows, Kanna!
Your soothing words burn my soul.
Evening tramples like a rogue elephant
and the fragrance of jasmine buds,
loosening my bonds, blows upon me.
Embrace my beautiful breasts
with the fragrance of the wild jasmine
upon your radiant chest.
Give me the nectar of your mouth,
and adorn my lowly head
with your jeweled lotus hands.
    (*Tiruvaymoli* 10.3.1, 2, 3, and 5; trans. by Vasudha Narayanan)

region to another, individual places were glorified along with the lord himself. Eventually, 108 sites came to be known as sacred places in which Vishnu abides, and the number was even higher for the Shaiva tradition. The Vira Shaiva movement gained popularity in what is now the state of Karnataka, in the twelfth century. The *vachana*s, or sayings, of their poet-saints—who also included a woman, Akka Mahadevi—made explicit their contempt for the caste system. Rejecting temple worship, the Vira Shaivas preferred to express their devotion to Shiva symbolically, by carrying a small *linga*.

North Indian Bhakti

North Indian *bhakti* resembled its southern counterpart both in its use of vernacular languages (rather than Sanskrit) and in the fact that it was open to people of every caste, from high to low. It differed, however, in the focus of devotion. Whereas South Indian *bhakti* was generally addressed to a particular deity—either Vishnu or Shiva—the object of devotion in the north was often Rama or Krishna

(*avataras* of Vishnu), or sometimes the divine being without a form.

An early exponent of Krishna devotion was the twelfth-century poet Jayadeva, who is thought to have lived in the eastern city of Puri on the Bay of Bengal. His Sanskrit work *Gita Govinda* ("Song of the Cowherd") extols the love of Radha and Krishna; it also contains a reference to the Buddha as an incarnation of Krishna–Vishnu, filled with compassion. His songs are a regular feature of music and dance concerts in many parts of India.

The sometimes synergistic relationship that developed between Hindus and Muslims in northern India (see Focus box, below) was reflected in the delightful, sometimes poignant works composed in the vernacular by poet-singers of the Sant ("holy person" or "truth") tradition. Emphasizing the *nirguna* ("without attributes") Brahman of the *Upanishads*, the Sants held the divinity to be without form. Hence their worship had nothing to do with physical images, and—unlike the Tamil poet-saints, who travelled from temple to temple precisely in order to express their devotion

Focus

Hindu–Muslim Relations

Islam arrived in India around the middle of the eighth century CE. In southern India the first Muslims were seafaring Arab traders who visited the region's many ports on their way to and from Southeast Asia. Over time, a minority Muslim population became established that was well integrated into the larger society.

Early encounters in northern India took a more hostile form. The invasions led by Muhammad of Ghazni (971–1030) and Muhammad of Ghor (1150–1206) in particular are seen as seminal events, paving

the way for the installation of Ghor's general Qutbuddin Aibak as the first Muslim ruler in northern India, and the establishment of a dynasty and, eventually, an empire. The plundering and destruction of sacred Hindu monuments such as the Somnath temple in Gujarat in 1025 have long been a part of the Hindu collective memory. On the other hand, the synergy made possible by the confluence of cultural influences from the Middle East and India gave rise to extraordinary innovations in all the arts, from painting and architecture to music, dance, and poetry.

to local manifestations of their chosen deity—they expressed their devotion either in poetry or in silent meditation. At the same time they rejected distinctions between religious communities.

Among the most important Sant poets was Kabir, whose life is shrouded in legend. Said to have been both Hindu and Muslim, he is reputed to have lived more than a hundred years (1398–1518?). In his insistence that God is beyond the particularities of any religious community, Kabir had much in common with a Punjabi religious leader named Nanak (1469–1539) and a Sufi Muslim teacher named Dadu (1544–1603). In time, the disciples of Kabir and Dadu were reabsorbed into the general populations of Hindus and Muslims, but Nanak's ultimately formed a separate community—the Sikhs. Kabir was one of several Sant poets whose works became part of the Sikh scripture.

Two other important poets in North India were Surdas and Tulsidas. Surdas (c. 1483–1563), who settled just south of Delhi near Agra, was a blind singer and poet whose compositions, in a dialect of Hindi, celebrate the youthful Krishna and Radha's devotion to him as a model of *bhakti*. Tulsidas (1543?–1623) is perhaps best known for his *Lake of the Deeds of Rama*, a retelling in Hindi of the ever-popular *Ramayana* in verses that have their own beauty and have inspired hundreds of traditional storytellers and millions of Rama devotees. Large sections of this work are learned by heart: sidewalk vendors, shopkeepers, housewives, and learned people can all quote from it even today and his work formed the basis for the *Ramayan*, a block-buster TV serial in Hindi screened in the 1980s.

Finally, a Bengali contemporary of Surdas was Chaitanya (1486–1583), who took the religious name Krishna-Chaitanya, "he whose consciousness is Krishna." Chaitanya's theology and practices have been tremendously influential not just in India but in many parts of the world. Like many other theologians who have emphasized the importance of *bhakti*, he maintained that in the *kali yuga*, our present degenerate age, humans lack the capacity to fulfill all the requirements of religious action and duty; therefore the only way to liberation is through trusting devotion to a loving and gracious deity.

For Chaitanya, however, the ultimate goal was not liberation from attachment in the traditional sense but rather the active enjoyment of his intense love of Krishna—a passionate spiritual love

Document

From Kabir

Go naked if you want,
Put on animal skins.
What does it matter till you see the inward Ram?
If the union yogis seek
Came from roaming about in the buff,
Every deer in the forest would be saved. . . .
Pundit, how can you be so dumb?
You're going to drown, along with all your kin
Unless you start speaking of Ram.
Vedas, *Puranas*—why read them?
It's like loading an ass with sandalwood!
Unless you catch on and learn how Ram's name goes,

How will you reach the end of the road?
You slaughter living beings and call it religion:
Hey brother, what would irreligion be?
"Great Saint"—that's how you love to greet each other:
Who then would you call a murderer?
Your mind is blind. You've no knowledge of yourselves.
Tell me, brother, how can you teach anyone else?
Wisdom is a thing you sell for worldly gain,
So there goes your human birth—in vain (Hawley and Juergensmeyer 1988: 50–1).

Document

From Mirabai

Mirabai (1450?–1547) was a Rajput princess in Gujarat. Left a widow when she was still a young woman, she became a devotee of Krishna and wrote passionate poetry about her love for him.

Sister, I had a dream that I wed
the Lord of those who live in need:
Five hundred sixty thousand people came
and the Lord of Braj was the groom.
In dream they set up a wedding arch;
in dream he grasped my hand;
in dream he led me around the wedding fire
and I became unshakably his bride.
Mira's been granted her mountain-lifting Lord:
from living past lives, a prize (Caturvedi, no. 27;
Hawley and Juergensmeyer 1988: 137).

equivalent to the passion that the cowherd girls felt for him. Chaitanya is said to have led people through the streets, singing about his lord and urging others to join him in chanting Krishna's names. Eventually, many of his followers came to believe that both Krishna and Radha were present in Chaitanya himself.

Chaitanya's movement had waned somewhat by the late nineteenth century, but it was revived through the efforts of a government official named Kedarnath Datta (1838–1914) who took the name Bhaktivinode Thakur, and his son Bhaktisiddanta Sarasvati (1874–1937). A pupil of Sarasvati's, Abhaycaran De (1896–1977), who took the name A.C. Bhaktivedanta, then carried this lineage abroad, launching the International Society for Krishna Consciousness (ISKCON)—better known as the Hare Krishna movement—in New York in 1966. Both the Hare Krishnas' theology, locating divine grace in Krishna, and their practice, centred on devotional chanting, can be traced directly to Chaitanya.

What has been the legacy of the *bhakti* movement? With its spread, the message of the Sanskrit scriptures was reinforced by powerful devotional works in vernacular languages, many of which have come to function as scripture themselves. These poems and songs offer the faithful far more guidance, inspiration, consolation, hope, and wisdom than the Vedas do. This is not to say that the vernacular literature is at variance with the Vedas. Rather, the poet-saints made what they perceived to be the messages of the Vedas accessible to everyone, inspiring devotion and preparing devotees to receive the shower of divine grace.

The period of Mughal rule, from the early sixteenth century to the early eighteenth, was characterized by a growing sense of "Hindu-ness" among some strata of the North Indian population. Eventually, the British used "Hindu" as an umbrella term for all the religious traditions perceived to be indigenous to the subcontinent. There was also considerable antagonism against Aurangzeb, the last Mughal emperor, whose policies caused severe hardship to large segments of the population, as well as against other Muslim rulers in the Deccan area, in central India. It was in this political climate that several leaders emerged to fight for Hindus' religious and political freedom. Notable among them was Shivaji (c. 1630–80) from what is now the state of Maharashtra. A hero of national proportions, he is credited with developing the concept of *Hindavi Swarajya* or independent self-rule for Hindus. Shivaji is revered as a courageous fighter who stood up for the rights of the Hindus against the authority of some Muslim rulers and is a symbol of religious and national honour.

It was during the rule of the Mughals that many European states began sending emissaries to India.

While there had been contact between Hindus and a small population of Christians in south India since the first millennium CE, missionary as well as trade efforts were gradually stepped up after the seventeenth century.

Colonialism and Beyond

It was the Portuguese explorer Vasco da Gama (1469–1524) who fulfilled Columbus's ambition of finding a sea route to India from Europe. When he landed in Calicut, on the western coast of India in 1498, he opened the way to the Indian subcontinent for a long line of traders, missionaries, and eventually rulers. Before long, the Dutch, English, and French were also travelling to India, where they soon established settlements. Early European scholarship in Indian languages, especially Sanskrit, led to the historical reconstruction of the movements of the Indo-European people from Central Asia. Studies in comparative philology pioneered the theory of a common Indo-European ancestry. This was the first glimpse that Hindus received of their pre-Vedic historical antecedents.

In time the foreign powers became involved in local politics, and possession of territory became one of their goals. As the Mughal empire disintegrated in the early eighteenth century, many chieftains attempted to acquire parcels of land and to enlist English or French help in their efforts. Eventually large parts of the Indian subcontinent were loosely united under British control. In the past, most Hindu and Muslim rulers had accepted a large degree of local autonomy, but the British felt a moral and political obligation to govern and impose sweeping changes without regard to local tradition or practice. At the same time, foreign missionaries were severely critical not only of what they saw as Hindu "idolatry," but of the caste system and practices such as **sati** (the self-immolation of widows on their husbands' funeral pyres). The foreigners were not the only ones to call for change, however: some Hindu intellectuals were equally convinced of the need for reform. Among them was Ram Mohan Roy.

The Brahmo Samaj

Ram Mohan Roy (1772–1833) was born into an orthodox brahmin family in western Bengal. He is said to have studied the Qur'an as well as the Vedas, and may also have explored Buddhism. Eventually joining the East India Company, he became familiar with the Christian scriptures and formed close ties with members of the Unitarian movement. He rejected the Christian belief in Jesus as the son of God, but admired him as a compassionate human being, and in 1820 he published a book called *The Precepts of Jesus: The Guide to Peace and Happiness*, in which he emphasized the compatibility of Jesus' moral teachings with the Hindu tradition.

Roy believed that if Hindus could read their own scriptures they would recognize that practices such as *sati* were not part of classical Hinduism and had no place in Hindu society. Therefore he translated extracts from Sanskrit texts into Bengali and English and distributed his works for free. In 1828 he established a society to hold regular discussions on the nature of Brahman as it is presented in the *Upanishads*. This organization, which came to be called the Brahmo Samaj ("congregation of Brahman"), emphasized monotheism, rationalism, humanism, and social reform. Although Roy rejected most of the stories from the epics and the *Puranas* as myths that stood in the way of reason and social reform, he drew on the Vedas, particularly the *Upanishads*, to defend Hinduism against the attacks of Christian missionaries. At the same time, together with the Unitarians, he accused the missionaries, who taught the doctrine of the Trinity (God as three persons, father, son, and holy spirit), of straying from monotheism. A pioneer in the area of women's rights, including the right to education, he fought to abolish *sati* and child marriage. He also founded a number of periodicals and educational institutions.

The Brahmo Samaj has never become a "mainstream" movement. Nevertheless, it revitalized Hinduism at a critical time in its history by calling attention both to inhumane practices and to the need for education and reform, and in so doing played a major part in the modernization of Indian society.

The Arya Samaj

The Arya Samaj was established in 1875 by Dayananda Sarasvati (1824–83). Born into a brahmin family in Gujarat, he left home at the age of 21 to take up the life of an ascetic. After 15 years as a wandering yogi, he studied Sanskrit under a charismatic guru named Virajananda, who taught that the only true Hindu scriptures were the early Vedas and rejected as false all later additions to Hindu tradition, including the worship of images. On leaving his teacher, Dayananda promised that he would work to reform Hinduism in accordance with the true teachings of the Vedas.

Dayananda believed that the Vedas were literally revealed by God, and that the vision of Hinduism they presented could be revived by stripping away later human accretions such as votive rituals and social customs such as *sati*, and teaching young people about their true Vedic heritage. To that end, he founded many educational institutions.

Dayananda also believed that the Vedic teachings were not at variance with science or reason. He rejected the notion of a personal saviour god; in fact, he rejected any anthropomorphic vision of the divine. He believed that the human soul is in some way coeval with the deity. A radical feature of Dayananda's teaching is the idea that total elimination of karma is virtually impossible, and that the goal of eternal liberation is therefore unattainable. In his view, the ideal was not renunciation but rather a full, active life of service to other human beings: working to uplift humanity in itself would promote the welfare of both the body and the soul.

The Ramakrishna Movement

Ramakrishna Paramahamsa (1836–86; born Gadadhar Chatterjee) was a Bengali raised in the Vaishnava *bhakti* tradition, cultivating ecstatic trance experiences. In his early twenties he was employed as a priest by a wealthy widow who was building a temple to the goddess Kali, and by his account he experienced the Divine Mother as an ocean of love. From the age of 25 he took instruction in tantra as well as Vedanta. He concluded that all religions lead in the same direction and that all are equally true.

Following his death, his disciples in Calcutta formed the Ramakrishna Mission to spread his eclectic ideas. Among them was Swami Vivekananda (Narendranath Datta, 1862–1902), a former member of the Brahmo Samaj who believed that Western science could help India make material progress, while Indian spirituality could help the West along the path to enlightenment. As a Hindu participant in the 1893 World's Parliament of Religions in Chicago, and subsequently as a lecturer in America and Europe, he presented an interpretation of Shankara's non-dualist (*advaita*) Vedanta in which Brahman is the only reality. As a consequence of the attention he attracted, it was this philosophy that the West generally came to consider the definitive form of Hinduism.

Under Vivekananda's leadership, the movement established a monastic order and a philanthropic mission, both dedicated to humanitarian service. In keeping with Ramakrishna's ecumenical vision, it encouraged non-sectarian worship. It also ignored caste distinctions, opening hundreds of educational and medical institutions for the welfare of all. The Ramakrishna movement's introduction of a Hindu presence into this field of activity was particularly significant because until then most of India's new medical and educational institutions had been run by Christian missionaries.

The monastic wing of the movement maintains that renunciation promotes spiritual growth. Unlike other monastic orders, however, it insists that its members should not be isolated ascetics, but should live in and for the world, giving humanitarian service to others.

The Struggle for India's Independence

Hindus and Muslims came together to fight for independence from British colonial rule. The earliest eruption was India's First War of Independence, which is better known in Europe as the "sepoy mutiny" of 1857. Although that "rebellion" was put down by the British, the struggle would continue for another 90 years. Of the many leaders, Hindu and Muslim, who contributed to the achievement of independence in 1947, undoubtedly the best known is the one to whom Rabindranath Tagore, India's famed poet and Nobel laureate, gave the title "Mahatma" ("great soul"): Mohandas Karamchand Gandhi (1869–1948).

Born in coastal Gujarat and trained as a barrister in England, Gandhi practised law in South Africa from 1893 to 1915. It was there, in response to the racial discrimination faced by the Indian minority, that he began experimenting with civil disobedience and passive resistance as vehicles for protest. After his return to India, where he became the leader of the Indian National Congress in 1921, he combined the techniques he had developed in South Africa with practices drawn from India's Hindu and Jaina religious traditions and applied them to the campaign for India's freedom.

In particular, Gandhi emphasized the principle of non-violence (*ahimsa*) and developed a strategy of non-violent resistance called *satyagraha* ("truth-force"). Also borrowed from religious observances was his practice of fasting, which he used both as a means of "self-purification" and as a psychological weapon. Gandhi's fasts drew attention to social injustices and the atrocities perpetrated by the British authorities. Faced with brutality, he refused to retaliate, saying that "An eye for an eye makes the world blind." Another major influence was the *Bhagavad Gita*, which he first became acquainted with as a student in England and understood as an allegory of the conflict between good and evil within human beings. It remained his guide throughout his life.

In addition to his political work, Gandhi promoted social reform, especially with respect to the notion of "untouchability." He gave the generic name "Harijan" ("children of God") to outcaste communities such as the Dalits. Although outcastes today reject the name as patronizing, it drew attention to discriminatory practices within Hindu society.

Less successful were Gandhi's efforts to promote peace between Muslims and Hindus in the context of the achievement of independence. Some scholars hold that the British, to stave off further problems, resorted to a "divide and rule" policy, fostering and amplifying underlying tensions between Hindus and Muslims. The complex issues involving leadership and electoral representation, among other factors, eventually led the Muslims to demand their own independent state, to be formed out of the Muslim-dominated areas of the subcontinent. The name of the new country, Pakistan, means "land of the pure," but is also an acronym representing the regions where it was claimed that Muslims were dominant: Punjab, Afghania (an old name for the North Western Frontier province), Kashmir, Sindh, and Baluchistan.

In the process of partition, some 12 million people were displaced, and approximately 1 million were killed in bloody riots and massacres. For Gandhi, the violence that accompanied independence represented a major failure. Within a few months, on 30 January 1948, he was assassinated by a Hindu incensed by what he perceived to be Gandhi's championing of the Muslim cause. Since then, Gandhi's influence has been felt in many parts of the world, but perhaps most notably in the US civil rights movement under the leadership of Martin Luther King, Jr.

Independence and the Secular State

India became independent from British rule on 15 August 1947. Although India is a secular state, its legal system is unique in that personal and/or family law differs depending on the religious tradition that the individual belongs to. In 1771 Warren Hastings, the first Governor-General, proclaimed that "in all suits regarding inheritance, marriage, caste and other religious usages or institutions, the laws of the Koran with respect to the Mohamedans and those of the Shaster [*dharmashastra*] with respect to the Gentoos [an archaic word referring to the inhabitants of India] shall invariably be adhered to." *Dharmashastra* prescriptions were flexible, and Hindus did not consider them "laws" in the Western sense; nevertheless, they became the framework for "Hindu" law under the British. In an effort to respect and accommodate the different religions, the British and later the Indian government upheld the traditional legal structures of Islam, Christianity, and Zoroastrianism (a Persian tradition whose adherents, known as "Parsees," had sought refuge in India many centuries earlier). Thus how people marry, divorce, adopt children, inherit property, etc., all depends on their religious affiliation. Legislation was passed in the 1950s to codify the Hindu laws regarding marriage, succession, and so on, but the fact that the new laws did not reflect the rich diversity of the Hindu traditions eventually led to further tensions between Hindus and Muslims because the laws in the other traditions were not codified. There had been some hope of moving towards a uniform civil code with the same laws for all citizens, but at present the different legal regimes remain in effect.

Contemporary Religious Leaders

For more than 2,000 years Hindus have venerated holy men and women. The *Taittiriya Upanishad* exhorts a departing student to think of his **acharya** (religious instructor) as a god, and there have been countless other gurus, ascetics, mediums, storytellers, and **sadhus** ("holy men") who have commanded anything from obedience to veneration. It would not be an exaggeration to say that for many Hindus, the primary religious experience is mediated by someone they believe to be in some way divine.

This is no less true of modern times than of the ancient past. Followers of Sri Sathya Sai Baba (Sathya Narayan Raju, 1926–2011), a charismatic teacher from Andhra Pradesh in the south, believe him to be an *avatara*. The heads of the monasteries established by the philosopher Shankara in the eighth century continue to exercise considerable influence among educated urban people, as do a number of intellectual Vedantic commentators.

In their interpretation of the ancient scriptures and their mediation of traditional values, we see the dynamic and adaptable nature of the Hindu tradition.

All *acharyas* are gurus, but not all gurus are *acharyas*. Most *acharyas* belong to a specific lineage and teach a particular sectarian tradition. Gurus, by contrast, are not necessarily connected to any particular tradition, and they tend to emphasize more "universal" and humanist messages, stressing the divinity in all human beings and encouraging their followers to transcend caste and community distinctions. Another difference is that whereas *acharyas* are almost invariably male, many women have been gurus. An example is Ma Amritananda Mayi ("Ammachi"; b. 1953), the leader of a movement that sponsors an international network of charitable, humanitarian, educational, and medical institutions. Known as the "hugging guru," she is one of the most popular religious leaders in the world today.

Many charismatic teachers are called *swami* ("master") by their followers. Others take their titles from the ancient Vedic "seers" known as *rishis*. An example is the founder of the Transcendental Meditation movement, popularly known in the West as TM. Maharishi ("great seer") Mahesh Yogi (1911?–2008) was one of the most influential teachers in the Western world.

❋ Practices, Rituals, and Arts

Many Hindus are fond of the dictum that "Hinduism is not a religion, it is a way of life." While most know very little about the texts, beliefs, and philosophies of their tradition, they are generally familiar with the practices they have observed since birth. Performances of various kinds—from music and dance, both folk and classical, to drama and ritual enactments of devotional poetry—are just as important as rituals, since it is through them that most Hindus learn the stories of the epics and *Puranas*.

Temple Worship

It is not clear when exactly temples began to figure in Hindu worship. Even though it appears that the Harappa culture may have set some buildings apart for worship, and certain figures seem to have had iconic status, the Vedic literature contains no indication of temple worship. While South India has a number of temples that have survived from about the fifth century CE, in the north many older temples were destroyed either by Muslim rulers or by various invaders. However, carvings depicting incarnations of Vishnu as well as icons of Shiva, found in the Udayagiri caves near Bhopal, in the modern state of Madhya Pradesh, suggest that worship at public shrines was established by the early fifth century. (Equally magnificent carvings from the sixth century can be seen at the Badami caves in Karnataka.) Some temples to Shiva and Vishnu in Southeast Asia may also have been built as early as the fifth century.

Deities in Hindu temples are treated like kings and queens. (The Tamil word for temple is *koil*, "house of the king.") The **murtis**—variously translated as "idols," "icons," "forms," or "objects to be worshipped"—are given ritual baths, adorned, carried in procession, and honoured with all the marks of hospitality offered to royal guests, including canopies to shelter them, and music and dance to entertain them. In the Srirangam temple in South India, there are special festivities for 250 days a year.

This treatment reflects the fact that in most cases, once consecrated, the *murti* becomes the deity him- or herself. Devotees believe that the presence of a deity in the temple does not detract from his or her presence in heaven, immanence in the world, or presence in a human soul. The deity is always complete and whole, no matter how many forms he or she may be manifest in at any given time. Generally, in Hinduism, there is no tradition of congregational prayer in the style of Christian or Muslim worship. Rather, the priest prays on behalf of the devotees, presents offerings of fruit, flowers, or coconut to the deity, and then gives back some of the blessed objects to the devotees. The food thus presented is considered ennobled because it is now **prasada** (literally "clarity," but meaning "divine favour"), a gift from the deity. Traditionally, Hindu priests have been primarily ritual specialists rather than counsellors, although those in North America may be taking on a more pastoral role today.

Because there are so many philosophical and sectarian traditions within Hinduism, understandings of the *murti* vary widely. As we noted above, many Hindus believe that the image enshrined in the temple is not a symbol of God but God himself, fully present in image form in order to make himself accessible. For them, the *murti* is a direct analogue to an incarnation (*avatara*) of Vishnu as Rama or Krishna in times past. Others, however, believe that the image in a temple is only a symbol of a higher reality, and some—including members of the Brahmo Samaj and Vira Shaiva movements—have rejected images altogether. Adherents of Shankara's non-dual Vedanta, for their part, believe that the supreme reality, Brahman, is identical to the human soul, Atman, and that it is transforming

Sites

Srirangam, Tamilnadu

An island temple-town in the Kaveri river, where Vishnu, here called Ranganatha ("Lord of the stage"), reclines on the serpent Ananta ("infinity"); one of the most important pilgrimage sites for the followers of Vishnu, celebrated in the poems of the Alvars.

The strings of flowers sold outside temples may be worn by devotees themselves or presented to the deities inside.

© Vasudha Narayanan

wisdom, not *bhakti*, that leads to liberation. Thus we might assume that Vedantins would have no reason to worship in a temple; yet in practice they flock to shrines to express their devotion.

Temple festivals celebrate events portrayed in the local myths as well as more generic observances. At Madurai in Tamilnadu, for instance, the Meenakshi–Sundaresvara temple complex honours Meenakshi, a manifestation of Parvati who is also portrayed as a princess of the local Pandyan dynasty. After a military career in which she is said to have conquered many chiefs, she marries Sundaresvara, who is understood to be Shiva himself. The wedding of the god and goddess is celebrated with much pomp and joy every year at a festival attended by pilgrims in the hundreds of thousands.

Vishnu temples in South India also have large shrines for the goddess Sri (Lakshmi). Similarly, temples dedicated to a manifestation of Shiva or Parvati usually include a shrine for that deity's consort. The processional image of Vishnu in the inner shrine always shows him with his consorts Sri (Lakshmi) and Bhu, the earth goddess. In Sri's own shrine, however, she is represented alone and is only occasionally accompanied by an image of Vishnu. In other words, while Vishnu is worshipped only in conjunction with Sri, Sri may evidently be worshipped alone, and several festivals are celebrated for her exclusively.

Temples to Murugan, a son of Shiva and Parvati, are popular among Tamil-speaking people in India, Sri Lanka, and Canada but are not found in north

Sites

Madurai, Tamilnadu

A large city, important for more than 2,000 years and home to dozens of temples including a famous complex dedicated to the goddess Meenakshi (a form of Parvati) and the god Sundaresvara (Shiva).

India. Hanuman, who figures in the story of Rama and Sita, is venerated both at temples and at home shrines. Many south Indian temples also contain representations of the "nine planets," which may cause harm if they are not propitiated. Especially dreaded is Shani or Saturn, who is said to wreak havoc unless he is appeased by the correct prayers or rites.

Temples to the creator god Brahma or his consort Sarasvati, the goddess of learning, are rare. The reason is usually associated with a Shaiva story in which Brahma is said to have told a lie, for which he is cursed and told that he will not be worshipped in any temple; the curse seems to include Sarasvati. Nevertheless, there are a few temples dedicated to them. Karambanur or Uttamar koil, near Srirangam in Tamilnadu, for instance, is an early syncretic temple with separate shrines to Shiva, Parvati, Vishnu, Lakshmi, Brahma, and Sarasvati. Devotion to Sarasvati is most evident in domestic worship, however. Children recite prayers to her daily, and students carry little pictures of her to school.

Although most of the temples in northern India today date from after the end of the Mughal period, architectural guides from as early as the fifth century suggest that at least some elements of temple design and construction have remained constant.

A temple has a correlation to the universe itself and to the body of divine beings, and is therefore planned with care. In the Sri Vaishnava community, the temple is said to be heaven on earth. Although most temples do not meet these standards, an ideal temple is supposed to have seven enclosures and be located near a body of water—whether the sea, a river, a pond, a spring, or an artificial pool (called a "tank" in India)—which automatically becomes holy. Devotees making a formal pilgrimage from a faraway place will sometimes bathe in the water before entering the temple. In South India, the temple enclosures have gateways over which stand large towers (*gopuras*). The towers are an essential part of the religious landscape, and in popular religion even a vision of the temple tower is said to be enough to destroy one's sins.

Devotees frequently walk around the temple inside one of the enclosures; this "circumambulation" of the deity is an essential part of the temple visit. They may sponsor an *archana* ("formal worship") in which the priest praises the deity by reciting his or her names. Devotees also bow down before the deity. Afterwards, they may go to the temple kitchen for *prasada*. In some temples devotees must buy the *prasada*, but in others it is provided at no charge from endowments made by patrons in the past. Patrons frequently earmark their donations for particular charitable deeds or functions in the temple, and their donations are inscribed on stones of the temple walls.

Women, especially those from royal families, were liberal benefactors of temples and other institutions. In the year 966, in Tirumala-Tirupati, a woman called Samavai donated money for the temple to celebrate some festivals and consecrate a silver processional image of Vishnu (known here as Venkateshwara). A record of her endowments, inscribed in stone, says that within a short time Samavai donated two parcels of land and ordered that the revenues derived from them be used for

Sites

Tirumala-Tirupati (also known as Tiruvenkatam), Andhra Pradesh

Probably one of the most important pilgrimage sites in India. The temple, located on seven hills, is dedicated to Venkateshwara (Vishnu) and is said to be one of the richest religious institutions in the world.

major festivals. She also gave a large number of jewels to the temple for adorning the image of the deity. Until the discovery of a large treasure trove in the Padmanabhaswamy temple in Kerala in 2012, the Tiruvenkatam temple had the largest endowments and revenues in India.

Studies by epigraphers and art historians show that Samavai was not an isolated example. We know, for instance, that queens of the South Indian Chola dynasty (c. 846–1279) were enthusiastic patrons of Shiva temples and religious causes around the tenth century. At that time, a South

© Vasudha Narayanan

Angkor Wat in northern Cambodia was built by King Suryavarman II in honour of Vishnu. Its unusual three-level structure may indicate a connection with South India, which also has a handful of three-storeyed Vishnu temples.

Indian queen called Sembiyan Mahadevi gave major endowments to many Shiva temples.

The inscriptions recording endowments represent a tangible honour for the many patrons over the centuries who have generously donated funds. In addition, the large amounts of money received point to the temples' power as economic institutions. Inscriptions are an important source of information about a temple and the social life of the times. The fact that women like Samavai were able to make such donations suggests a certain independence both of lifestyle and of income.

Hindu temples made of perishable materials may have been built in Vietnam as early as the fourth or fifth century, and some of the largest temples to Shiva and Vishnu are found in the region of the Khmer empire, which stretched from modern Cambodia to parts of Thailand and Laos. Although there are striking similarities to temples and iconographic styles in different parts of India, including the states along the eastern coast, the Southeast Asian buildings have their own architectural idiom. Shiva temples are shaped like mountains; the large mountain-temples at Bakheng and Bakong in the Siem Reap area of Cambodia, for instance, look more like the Buddhist temple of Borubodor in Indonesia than their counterparts in India. The large Vishnu temple of Angkor Wat in Cambodia, like many temples in India (and Central America as well), is situated and built according to astronomical calculations: the sun rises directly behind the central tower at the time of the spring and autumn equinoxes. The Udayagiri cave complex may also reflect astronomical knowledge, since it is situated close to the latitude where the Tropic of Cancer—the northernmost point where the sun appears to stand directly overhead at noon on the summer solstice—would have been around 400 CE.

Sculptural and Pictorial Symbolism

The Naga

One of the earliest symbols in the Hindu tradition may be the *naga* (serpent). In many towns and villages there are sacred trees surrounded with small stone images of intertwined snakes, which are venerated with spots of red powder (the same kumkum powder that is used to adorn women's foreheads). Women come to these open-air shrines to worship at particular times of the year, or when they want to make a wish regarding a matter such as childbirth. *Nagas* are also important in the iconography of Shiva and Vishnu.

In Cambodia balustrades in the form of large *nagas* are an integral part of both Hindu and Buddhist temple landscapes. Cambodian narratives trace the descent of the kingdom from a *naga* princess and a Hindu prince from India.

The Dance of Shiva

Iconographically, Shiva is often portrayed as a cosmic dancer known as Nataraja, the king of the dance. In this form Shiva is the archetype of both the dancer and the ascetic, symbolizing mastery over universal energy on the one hand and absolute inner tranquillity on the other.

In the classic Nataraja representation, Shiva has four hands. One of the right hands holds an hourglass-shaped drum, symbolizing sound—both speech and the divine truth heard through revelation. The other right hand is making a gesture that grants fearlessness to the devotee. One of the left hands holds a flame, symbolizing the destruction of the world at the end of time. The feet grant salvation and are worshipped to obtain union with Shiva. The left foot, representing the refuge of the devotee, is raised, signifying liberation. The other left hand points to this foot.

Dancing through the creation and destruction of the cosmos, Shiva–Nataraja is the master of both *tandava*, the fierce, violent dance that gives rise to energy, and *lasya*, the gentle, lyric dance representing tenderness and grace. The entire universe shakes when he dances; Krishna sings for him, the snake around his neck sways, and drops of the Ganga River, which he holds in his hair, fall to the earth.

The Linga

In temples, Shiva is usually represented by a *linga*: an upright shaft, typically made of stone, placed

© Vasudha Narayanan

The dancing Shiva.

in a receptacle called a *yoni*, which symbolizes the womb. Although *linga* is generally translated into English as "phallus," and in Sanskrit *linga* means "distinguishing symbol," Hindus do not normally think of it as a physical object. Rather, it serves as a reference point to the spiritual potential in all of creation, and specifically to the energies of Shiva. The union of the *yoni* and *linga* is a reminder that male and female forces are united in generating the universe. Although Shiva is stereotyped as the "destroyer" in some literature, it is his creative role that is represented in the temple.

Erotic Sculpture

People from other cultures have often been shocked by Hindu temple sculptures celebrating *kama*, sensual love. Probably the most famous examples are found at Khajuraho (c. 1000 CE) in Madhya Pradesh, southeast of Delhi, and Konarak (c. 1250), in the eastern coastal state of Orissa. Although many other temples also contain erotic sculptures, they are often kept in inconspicuous niches or corners.

Some art historians have speculated that the sculptures may have been intended to serve an educational purpose for young men who as students were isolated from society, in order to prepare them for adult life in a world where sensual enjoyment of all kinds was considered a legitimate goal and spouses were expected to be partners in *kama* as well as dharma. Other scholars have suggested that such scenes illustrate passages from various myths and literary works such as the *Puranas*.

Focus

The Significance of Food

The Hindu tradition is preoccupied with food: not just what kind of food is eaten, where and when it is consumed, and how it is prepared, but who prepares it, who has the right to be offered it first, and who may be given the leftovers. Certain dates and lunar phases require either fasting or feasting. Furthermore, there are technical distinctions among fasts: some demand abstention from all food, others only from grain or rice. According to some texts, one can win liberation from the cycle of life and death simply by observing the right kinds of fast.

Contrary to a common Western stereotype, most Hindus are not vegetarians. Nor does vegetarianism for Hindus mean abstaining from dairy products. Generally speaking, vegetarianism is a matter of community and caste. The strictest Hindu vegetarians are generally the Vaishnavas, who are found all over India. In addition, most brahmins are vegetarian—except in Bengal, Orissa, and Kashmir. In the West, members of the International Society for Krishna Consciousness (the Hare Krishna

movement) not only abstain from meat, fish, and fowl, but also avoid certain vegetables that are thought to have negative properties, such as onions and garlic.

These dietary prohibitions and habits are based on the idea that food reflects the general qualities of nature: purity, energy, and inertia. The properties of food include both those that are intrinsic to it and those that are circumstantial. Pure foods such as dairy products and many vegetables are thought to foster spiritual inclinations. By contrast, meat, poultry, and onions are believed to give rise to passion and action, while stale food and liquor are seen as encouraging sloth. Thus a strict vegetarian diet is prescribed for people who are expected to cultivate spiritual tranquillity and avoid passion.

In addition, the nature of a given food is thought to be influenced by the inherent qualities of the person who cooks it. For this reason it was common even in the mid-twentieth century for strictly

Forehead Marks

Perhaps the most common visual sign of Hindu culture is the forehead mark or **tilaka** ("small, like a *tila* or sesame seed"), especially the red dot (*bindi*) traditionally worn by married women. Yet in many parts of India, male ascetics and temple priests also wear various forehead marks in the context of religious rituals. Like many elements in the Hindu traditions, a forehead mark may be interpreted in various ways, depending on the gender and marital status of the person wearing it, the occasion for which it is worn, the sectarian community from which the wearer comes, and, occasionally, his or her caste.

At the simplest level, the forehead mark is decorative. In this spirit, unmarried and Christian as well as married Hindu women today wear *bindis*, and the traditional dot of kumkum powder has been largely replaced by stickers in a wide variety of shapes and colours. Thus many people today do not think of forehead marks as having anything to do with religion. Yet their value is more than cosmetic. Married women see the *bindi* as a symbol of the role that they play in society. Other marks indicate the wearer's sectarian affiliation. When worn correctly in ritual situations, the shape and colour indicate not only which god or goddess the person worships, but also the socio-religious community to which he or she belongs.

observant Hindus to eat only food prepared by people of their own caste.

Food is also auspicious and inauspicious. Weddings, funerals, ancestral rites, and birthdays require the use of auspicious lentils, spices, and vegetables. What one feeds the forefathers is different from what one feeds the gods and human beings; rituals associated with death involve different kinds of food from life-promoting rituals. Turmeric powder, for example, is auspicious, while sesame seed is inauspicious. Similarly, food prepared for ritual use in temple and death ceremonies is restricted to traditional ingredients; innovations such as potatoes and red peppers (both hot and sweet), introduced to India by Europeans in the last few centuries, are to be avoided.

A central element in temple rituals is the offering of food to the deity, after which the "leftovers" are served to devotees as *prasada*. Inscriptions on the walls of medieval temples show that most endowments were intended for food offerings, and in the case of the temple at Tirumala-Tirupati they include detailed instructions for the preparation of offerings. The latter is one of a number of pilgrimage centres that eventually became famous for particular kinds of *prasada*. The cooking and distribution of *prasada* is now a multi-million-dollar industry at such temples.

Beyond the practicalities of use or avoidance, food appears in Hindu thought as an important symbol of spiritual experience. The idea of a mystical union between food and the person who eats it is suggested in the *Taittiriya Upanishad* (part of the *Yajur Veda*):

Oh, wonderful! Oh, wonderful!
Oh, Wonderful!
I am food! I am food! I am food!
I am a food-eater! I am a food-eater! I am a food-eater! (*Taittiriya Upanishad* III.10.5)

Theologians through the centuries have debated the significance of this passage, but most have interpreted it as referring to the experience of the Vedic sacrificer, who identifies himself with Brahman both as food and as eater. This verse is recited as part of the weekly temple liturgy in Vishnu temples all over the world.

Food also plays an important role both in Ayurvedic medicine and in various regional traditions that rely on different foods to rectify imbalances of "cold" and "heat" accumulated in the body.

The materials used to create the mark depend on the wearer's sectarian affiliation and the purpose for which the mark is worn. Marks denoting affiliation to a particular deity may be made with white clay, sandalwood paste, smoke-collyrium, flower petals, or ash. In general, followers of Vishnu, Krishna, and Lakshmi wear vertical marks; worshippers of Shiva and Parvati wear horizontal or slightly curved crescent marks made of ash or other substances with a red dot in the middle; and a combination of dots and crescents usually indicates a preference for the Goddess (Devi) in one of her many manifestations. Other variations are instantly identifiable to those familiar with India's many philosophical traditions.

Domestic Worship

One of the most significant ways in which Hindus express their devotion to a deity or a spiritual teacher is through rituals performed in the home; such worship is usually called **puja**. Many Hindu households set aside some space—if only a cabinet shelf—for a shrine to hold pictures or small images of the revered figure, whether god or guru.

The rituals performed in the home are simplified versions of temple rituals, led by family members rather than priests. In the home as in the temple, the deity is treated with all the hospitality accorded to an honoured guest. Daily puja typically consists of simple acts in which all family members can take part, such as lighting oil lamps and incense sticks, reciting prayers, or offering food to the deity. More elaborate rituals, however—such as the puja offered to Satyanarayana (a particular manifestation of Vishnu) on full-moon days—may involve a priest or other specialist.

Significantly, a number of domestic rituals are specific to the women of the household. In many parts of India, women gather on certain days of the year to celebrate the goddess by fasting and feasting, and then perform what are called "auspiciousness" rituals for the happiness of the entire family. Other women's rituals are found only in certain geographic regions. In the south, for example, women will often gather before a major family celebration (such as a wedding) to ask for the blessing of a particular group of female ancestors: those who have had the good fortune to die before their husbands and therefore have preserved their status as *sumangalis* or "auspicious women." Such women are believed to have immense power to influence the success of any ritual. In northern India, during some domestic festivals such as Navaratri (see below) young virgin girls are venerated by other women who believe that they are temporary manifestations of the Goddess.

In the home as in the temple, worshippers participate in the stories associated with the various deities. At the same time, in speaking a prayer or singing a hymn, they take part in the passion of the composer. Thus in Sri Vaishnava worship, devotees who recite a verse of Andal's are to some extent participating in Andal's own devotion, and through this identification they link themselves with the devotional community extending through time.

Ayurvedic Medicine

Medicine made great progress in the Hindu world in the first millennium. One of the most important systems was called **Ayurveda**: the *veda* (knowledge) of enhancing life. The physician or *vaidya* ("one who is learned") promotes both longevity and quality of life. The prototype is a deity called Dhanavantari,

sometimes identified as an incarnation of Vishnu. The South Indian parallel to Ayurveda is the Tamil system called Siddha.

Ayurveda is considered to be an ancillary to the Vedas. While healing and medicine may not be central to religion in some cultures, they have remained part of the larger religious culture in the Hindu traditions. An early compendium on the subject, written by a physician named Charaka (c. third century BCE) frames it in a larger humanistic discourse and says that every human being should have three desires: the will to live, the drive for prosperity, and an aspiration to reach the world beyond. As with many other subjects, including astrology and the performing arts, treatises on healing and medicine are often framed as conversations between two sages or between a god and a sage. Sometimes the text in question is understood to have been revealed by a gracious deity.

At some time during the last three centuries BCE, both the surgeon Sushruta and the physician Charaka presented theories that they claimed had been transmitted to them by the gods. These teachings reflected an understanding of illness as a lack of balance among three elements: air, phlegm, and bile. This analytic approach recalls Greek and Chinese medical theories of roughly the same period. The *Sushruta Samhita* begins by declaring that the physician's aim is "to cure the diseases of the sick, to protect the healthy, to prolong life," while the *Charaka Samhita* includes a detailed statement of the ethics required of a physician. In these respects, the ancient roots of Ayurvedic medicine seem strikingly modern.

Today in India, Ayurveda serves as a bridge between modern international medicine and traditional Indian religio-philosophical theories. Ayurvedic clinical practice relies on specific remedies and therapies, just as modern medicine does, while Ayurvedic theory, as expounded in books and on websites draws on elements of tantra and yoga. It shares those disciplines' outlook on life and the world, but puts greater emphasis on health than on spiritual attainment.

The Annual Festival Cycle

In the Hindu tradition there is a festival of some kind almost every month of the year. The most popular are the birthdays of Rama, Krishna, and Ganesha; the precise dates for these celebrations vary from year to year with the lunar calendar, but they always fall within the same periods.

Some festivals are specific to certain regions. **Holi**, for instance, is a North Indian festival celebrated in March or April with bonfires to enact the destruction of evil, and exuberant throwing of coloured powder to symbolize the vibrant colours of spring. It commemorates the fourth incarnation of Vishnu, when he took the form of a man-lion in order to save the life of his devotee Prahlada. Vishnu's fifth incarnation, as a dwarf-brahmin, is celebrated in the state of Kerala in a late-summer festival called Onam. Other festivals, like Navaratri and **Deepavali** (known colloquially as Diwali in some areas) are more or less pan-Hindu. A detailed discussion of Navaratri will give us an idea of the complexity of the variations in observance across the many Hindu communities.

© Jonathan Irish/National Geographic Society/Corbis

Celebrating Holi in Jaipur.

Navaratri

The festival of Navaratri ("nine nights") begins on the new moon that appears between 15 September and 14 October and is celebrated all over India, but in different ways and for different reasons.

In Tamilnadu, for instance, Navaratri is largely a festival for women. Exquisite dolls representing the goddesses Sarasvati, Lakshmi, and Durga are arranged in elaborate tableaux depicting scenes from the epics and *Puranas*. Every evening, women and children dressed in bright silks visit one another, admire the dolls, play musical instruments, and sing songs from the classical repertoire in praise of one or another of the goddesses. It is a joyous time of music and beauty, and a glorious celebration

Sites

Haridwar, Uttaranchal

One of seven holy sites identified in the *Puranas*. Located on the banks of the river Ganga, it is one of the cities where a great festival called Kumbha Mela is held.

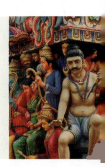

Sites

Puri, Orissa

Site of a temple dedicated to Jagannath (a form of Vishnu), his brother Balabhadra, and their sister, Subhadra. Also the site of a famous festival (Ratha Yatra) in which Lord Jagannath (the origin of the English word "juggernaut") is taken through the streets on a huge chariot.

of womanhood. On the last two days—a special countrywide holiday—large pictures of Lakshmi and Sarasvati, draped with garlands of fresh flowers, are placed in front of the display of dolls and worshipped.

In the state of West Bengal, the same nine or ten days are dedicated to a festival called Durga Puja, commemorating the goddess Durga's killing of the buffalo-demon Mahisa. Local communities make extravagant statues of Durga for her spirit to inhabit; then, after nine nights, they immerse the statues in water to symbolize her return to the formless state.

In the state of Gujarat, Navaratri is celebrated with two special dances. In the circular dance called *garbha*, a sacred lamp is kept in the centre of the circle as a manifestation of the goddess. The second dance, called *dandiya*, is performed with sticks and recalls the dance that Krishna is said to have performed with the cowherd girls.

In many parts of northern India, women will invite seven pre-pubescent girls to a home during Navaratri for veneration as representatives of the goddess Durga.

According to some traditions, it was during the same nine nights and ten days that Rama battled Ravana. In Ramnagar, a city near Varanasi (Banaras) on the river Ganga, people act out the story of the *Ramayana* in a play called *Ramlila* and on the tenth day celebrate Rama's victory. Little boys play the parts of Rama and his brothers in what is considered to be India's largest outdoor theatre, spanning several hectares.

Some Hindus believe that it was on the ninth day of Navaratri that Arjuna found the weapons he had hidden a year before and paid respect to them before entering battle. Because of this story, the last two days, dedicated to Lakshmi and Sarasvati, are called *Ayudha Puja* ("veneration of weapons and machines"): cars and buses are draped with garlands, while computers and typewriters are blessed with sacred powders and one acknowledges their importance in one's life. The ninth day of the festival honours Sarasvati, the patron of learning and

Sites

Vaishno Devi, Jammu and Kashmir

Located at an elevation of more than 1,580 metres, this temple is dedicated to the Goddess Vaishno Devi, who is sometimes perceived as a form of Durga and sometimes as an amalgamation of all the major goddesses.

music. All the musical instruments in the house, any writing device, and selected textbooks are kept in front of her image, to be blessed by her for the rest of the year.

In many parts of India, the last day of the festival is dedicated to Lakshmi. This is a time for fresh starts: to begin new ventures and new account books, to learn new prayers and music, to acquire new knowledge, and to honour traditional teachers. On the last days of the Navaratri festival, the fortune of learning, the wealth of wisdom, and the joy of music are said to be given by the grace of the goddesses. While most Indians do celebrate Navaratri, then, it is in different ways and for different reasons.

Deepavali

Deepa means "lamp" and *vali* means "necklace" or "row." Thus Deepavali (or Diwali) means "necklace of lights." It is celebrated at the time of the new moon between 15 October and 14 November. Hindu families all over the world decorate their houses with lights, set off firecrackers, and wear new clothes. In some parts of India, Deepavali marks the beginning of a new year, but that is only one of several reasons for the festival. As in the case of Navaratri, the significance of Deepavali varies from region to region.

In South India, for instance, Deepavali celebrates the dawn when Krishna is said to have killed Narakasura, a demon from the nether world, thus ensuring the victory of light over darkness. In North India, Deepavali marks the return of Rama to Ayodhya and his coronation. And in Gujarat it is the beginning of the new year, when new account books are opened and new clothes are worn. Presents are exchanged in some communities, and it is generally a time of feasting. In Tamilnadu, it is said that the river Ganga itself is present in all the waters on Deepavali day. People get up at three or four in the morning for a special purifying bath, and members of some communities greet one another by asking "Have you had a bath in the river Ganga?" Whatever the local customs associated

with the festival may be, the celebrations are always family-centred.

Life-Cycle Rites

Every culture has its rites of passage: rituals that mark the transitions from one stage of life to another. In some of the *dharmashastra* texts the discussion of the life-cycle sacraments begins with the birth of a child. In others the first sacrament is marriage, for it is in this context, properly speaking, that each new life will begin.

Two factors are important to note in discussing life-cycle rites. First, not all are pan-Hindu, and even those that are do not necessarily have the same importance in all communities. Some of the life-cycle rites discussed here are practised only by the "upper" castes and those in higher economic classes. Second, many important rites, especially those involving girls or women, are not discussed in the classical texts—possibly because those texts were written by men. Women were considered merely as partners to males, who were the main focus of the books. It may also be that some of these rites developed after the texts were written. We will discuss the normative *dharmashastra* sacraments first, and then look at a few rites of passage that have more localized regional importance.

The English word "auspiciousness" has become the standard translation for what in Sanskrit may be called *mangala*, *shubha*, or *sri*. Certain kinds of people, animals, rituals, smells, sounds, and foods are considered auspicious: that is, they are thought to have the power to bring about good fortune and a good quality of existence. Marriage is called "the auspicious (*kalyana*) ceremony" in Tamil, and in some North Indian usage the word *shubha* ("auspicious") precedes the word *vivaha* ("marriage"). Auspicious times are chosen for the performance of all sacraments; these times depend on the horoscope of the person concerned, which is cast at birth.

The right hand is associated with auspicious activities, such as gift-giving, eating, and wedding rituals. The left hand is associated with the inauspicious and the impure: insults, bodily hygiene, funerary rituals, and rituals honouring ancestors.

Birth Rituals

The cycle of sacraments (*samskaras*; literally, "perfecting") begins before birth. The time at which a child is conceived, the rituals administered to a pregnant woman, and her behaviour during pregnancy are all thought to condition the personality of the child. The *Upanishads* describe specific rituals to be followed if one wanted a learned daughter or a heroic son; in later times, however, daughters were rarely desired. Although the conception sacrament has been largely discarded, it survives in some communities as one of the rituals observed on the wedding night. Some *dharmashastras* suggest that it is a husband's duty to approach his wife for intercourse at particular times of the month, and a few even go so far as to say that a man who does not do so is guilty of abortion. Abortion has generally been considered sinful, but the texts apparently have little influence on modern Hindu life: abortion is legal in India today and is rarely a subject of debate in Hindu religious discourse.

Many communities in India also follow two other prenatal rites called *pumsavana* ("seeking a male offspring") and *simanta* ("hair parting"). Although they used to be performed in the fifth month of pregnancy, today they are performed much later and are said to ensure the safe birth of a son.

At the moment of birth, care must be taken to note the exact time, to ensure an accurate horoscope. The first ceremony performed after the birth, called *jatakarma* ("birth ritual"), was supposed to precede the cutting of the umbilical cord, but it is now done a few days or even weeks later. The *jatakarma* rites include *medhjanana* ("birth of intelligence"), in which the father prays for the intellectual well-being of the child, and *ayushya*, in which he prays for longevity for himself and for the child: "May we see a hundred autumns, may we hear a hundred autumns." The ceremony ends with a request for the infant's physical strength and well-being.

Initiation Rituals

The ritual that initiates a young brahmin boy into the study of the Vedas is called *upanayana* or *brahma upadesha*. *Upanayana* can mean either "acquiring the extra eye of knowledge" or "coming close to a teacher" to get knowledge; *brahma upadesha* refers to receipt of the sacred teaching (*upadesha*) concerning the Supreme Being (Brahman).

The *upanayana* ritual was traditionally performed when the boy was eight or nine, to initiate him into the first stage of life, which was studenthood. Students were supposed to concentrate on acquiring knowledge, not wealth. Therefore they did not work for a living; rather, it was the society's duty to support and feed them. In the past, students would often live in their teacher's house. It has been suggested that girls may have undergone a similar initiation in the early Vedic era, but if that was the case, the practice had been discontinued by the time the *Upanishads* were composed (c. 600 BCE).

The *upanayana* ceremony takes two days to complete. On the first day, the boy is bathed in water into which the essence of all the sacred and life-giving waters has been invoked through the recitation of sacred verses from the *Vedas*. This ritual is called *udaga shanti* ("peace brought on the waters"), and in a larger sense it seeks peace on all the waters and lands of the earth. The verses end with repeated requests for *shanti* (peace): peace for the individual, the soul, the body, the divine beings, the family, the community, and the entire earth. On the second day the boy is given a sacred "thread" or cord to wear over his left shoulder. The meaning of this cord is unclear. Some think it represents an upper garment that the student would wear when he was fit to perform a sacrifice. Others think it symbolizes a spiritual umbilical cord representing the boy's connection to his teacher—the spiritual parent through whom he will be reborn. The boy is now taught how to eat properly, thanking the earth for his food and asking divine beings to bless it. Then comes the central part of the ritual: the actual *brahma upadesha*, or imparting of the sacred teaching. As the boy sits with his father and the priest sits under a silk cloth (thought by some scholars to symbolize the spiritual womb) a sacred mantra is given to him that he will be expected to chant 108 times in succession, three times each day. Known as the *Gayatri* or sun mantra, it is very short—"I meditate on the brilliance of the sun; may it illumine my mind"—but it is considered the most important of all mantras. The boy is then taken outside and shown the sun, the source of light, knowledge, and immortality. He must twine his fingers in a particular way to ward off the harmful rays while looking directly at the heart of the sun.

Today, of course, the initiate no longer goes to live with his teacher, and most boys do not undertake any Vedic studies. The initiation ceremony was traditionally part of the life cycle for male members of all three of the higher castes, but it is now rarely performed outside the brahmin community. Efforts are underway to introduce similar initiation ceremonies for young girls.

Weddings

According to the *dharmashastras*—the texts of theoretical reflection on law and ethics—a man is born with debts to the sages, the gods, and the ancestors. A wife helps him repay these debts. The debt to the gods is discharged through the correct performance of domestic and social rituals with—and only with—his wife; the debt to the ancestors, by having children. A wife is a man's partner in fulfilling dharma, and without her a man cannot fully perform his religious obligations.

Hindu scriptures suggest that there is no higher ideal for a woman than to be a faithful wife. In the myth of Savitri, for example, the princess Savitri chooses to marry Satyavan even though it has been predicted that he has just one more year to live. She repeats a prayer taught to her by a divine minstrel for the longevity of her husband. A year later, Yama, the god of death, comes to claim Satyavan, but Savitri follows them to the end of the earth. Touched by her devotion, Yama grants her three wishes—anything she desires, except the life of her husband.

As her third wish, Savitri asks for a hundred sons, and since at that time no Hindu wife could properly have sons out of wedlock, Yama is forced to relinquish his grip on Satyavan's life. In this way Savitri became the symbol of the faithful wife. In South India her triumph over death is celebrated in a domestic ritual in which married women request happiness with their husbands, and unmarried girls request a happy married life.

Wedding ceremonies in India vary widely from region to region. In some communities in Kerala, the rite may take less than a half hour; in other areas it may last five days.

Before a wedding can be arranged, the parents of the prospective bride must find a suitable bridegroom; for this they often rely on the help of friends and extended family. Ideally, he will come from the same geographic region, speak the same language, and belong to the same community and sub-community, though he must belong to a different *gotra* or clan. He should be compatible with the bride in education, looks, age, and outlook, and the two families should be of similar socio-economic status.

When a potential husband is found, the family sometimes compares the horoscopes of the bride and the groom. The purpose of this reading is not only to assess compatibility and character but also to balance the ups and downs in the partners' future lives. To select a mate, parents sometimes obtain several horoscopes and have them analyzed in order to eliminate unsuitable candidates from the start. In the past the search for prospective partners was conducted largely through informal networks, but today much of this work is done through the Internet and social media. The Sunday newspapers devote three or four pages to matrimonial advertisements listing all the qualifications required of a prospective mate, from caste and community background to language and dietary preferences. Today computers are often used to cast children's horoscopes as soon as they are born. When the horoscopes are compatible, the young people and their families meet to decide whether they like each other—a decision that sometimes takes little more than a brief look at one another. At this point both parties have the right either to opt out or to request more time to get acquainted.

Obviously, arranged marriages are less common today than they were when young women were largely sheltered from the world outside the home. Now that men and women increasingly study and work together, a couple may meet and decide to get married with or without the families' approval. Such marriages often cross boundaries of caste and community—even language and geography.

The marriage ceremony itself must include several basic features if it is to be considered legal. These include the *kanya dana* (the gift of the virgin by her father), *pani grahana* (the clasping of hands), *sapta padi* (taking seven steps together around fire, which is the eternal witness), and *mangalya dharana* (the giving of "auspiciousness" to the bride). In addition, the bride and bridegroom usually give one another garlands.

Some weddings include lavish exchanges of presents with friends and extended family members, processions on horseback or in antique cars, feasting, entertainment, and fireworks. The festive atmosphere often recalls a fairground, with vibrant splashes of colour and plenty of noise. Everyone has a good time, and relatively little attention is paid to the bride and groom.

The ceremony itself lasts several hours and for the bride may involve several changes of elaborate clothing and jewels. Often the couple sits on a platform near a fire, to which offerings are made. At particular moments in the ritual the bride's parents have an active role to play, as do the groom's sister and the bride's brother and maternal uncle, but the hundreds of guests are free to come and go as they please. During the *kanya dana* or "giving away of the girl," the father of the bride quotes from the *Ramayana*, reciting the words spoken by Janaka, the father of Sita, as he gives her in marriage to Rama: "This is Sita, my daughter; she will be your partner in dharma."

In many communities, though not all, the groom's family then presents the bride with the "gift of auspiciousness": a gold necklace, a string of black beads, or a simple yellow thread carrying the insignia of the particular god that the family worships (a conch and discus symbolizing Vishnu, for instance, or a *linga* symbolizing Shiva).

In South India the groom fastens this string or necklace around the bride's neck as her symbol of marriage (corresponding to a wedding ring in the West). She will wear it for the duration of her marriage. There is no equivalent symbol for the groom, although men who have put on the sacred thread will wear a double set of threads after they marry. In many communities in Northern and Eastern India, the bridegroom anoints the bride with a red powder, *sindoor*, near the parting of her hair on her forehead.

In the central rite of the wedding, when the bride and the bridegroom take seven steps around the fire together, the groom says:

> Take the first step; Vishnu will follow you. You will not want for food for the rest of your life. Take the second step; Vishnu will guard your health. Take the third step; Vishnu will follow you and see that you may observe all religious rituals. Take the fourth step; Vishnu, following you, will grant you happiness. Take the fifth step; Vishnu will follow and grant you cattle and kine. Take the sixth step; let Vishnu follow you and let us enjoy the pleasures of the season. Take the seventh step; Vishnu will follow you. We shall worship together.

Then, clasping the bride's hand (*pani grahana*), the groom says:

> You have taken seven steps with me; be my friend. We who have taken seven steps together have become companions. I have attained your friendship; I shall not forsake that friendship. Do not discard our relationship.
>
> Let us live together; let us think together. We have come to a right and fitting stage of our lives; let us be happy and prosperous, thinking good thoughts.

Let there be no difference in our hopes and efforts; let us attain our desires. And so we join ourselves (our lives). Let us be of one mind, let us act together and enjoy through all our senses, without any difference.

You are the song (Sama), I am the lyric (Rig), I am Sama, you are Rig. I am the sky, you are the earth. I am the seed; you shall bear my seed. I am thought; you are speech. I am the song, you are the lyric. Be conformable to me; O lady of sweet unsullied words, O gem of a woman, come with me; let us have children and attain prosperity together.

Many of these verses come from sections of the Vedas that explain how to perform rituals. The officiating priest recites the mantras, which the bride and groom repeat after him. It is worth noting that these passages from the Vedas refer to the wife not as her husband's possession or servant, but rather as his partner in dharma and his companion and friend in love. In most communities, the central rituals must be conducted near a sacred fire. The importance of fire (*agni*) can be traced as far back as the coming of the Indo-European people to India around 1500 BCE. Fire was considered the master of the house, the eternal witness to all the rituals marking the milestones in a human life. Oblations are made to the fire as part of the prenatal rites, when the child is one year old, when a man reaches 60, and yet again if he reaches 80. Finally, when life is over, the body is committed to fire. Without a fire as witness, therefore, the wedding will not be valid. In another ritual, the groom bends down and places the bride's foot on a firm, heavy stone. The fact that he touches her feet is significant in itself, for this is an unequivocal gesture of respect in Hindu culture. He then places rings on her toes, saying, "Stand on this stone, be firm and steady as this stone. Stand conquering those who oppose you; be victorious over your enemies." Like the passages from the Vedas cited above, this rousing speech suggests a view of a wife's role that has nothing to do with servitude.

Later in the evening the new husband and wife are taken outside for a ritual called *Arundhati*

darshana ("the sighting of Arundhati"). In Indian astrology, the seven brightest stars of the Great Bear constellation (the Big Dipper) represent the seven sages, one of whom (Vasistha) is accompanied by a companion star identified as his wife, Arundhati—a symbol of fidelity throughout India. Just as the stars Vasistha and Arundhati remain close through the years, so the newlyweds are urged to stay together forever.

Funeral Rites

We have noted elsewhere that nothing in the Hindu tradition is ever really discarded. Funeral rites reflect different combinations of elements from the Vedas and the *Bhagavad Gita* with elements specific to individual regions and communities (Shaiva, Vaishnava, etc.). Except for infants and ascetics (who may be buried), cremation by fire is the final sacrament in most communities. No fire is to be lit or tended in the house where the death occurred until the cremation fire has been lit, and the family of the deceased is considered to live in a state of pollution for a period of time that varies from 12 days to almost a year after the death. Each religious community has its own list of scriptures to recite from. Although the funeral rituals for most Hindu communities would include portions of the Vedas and the *Bhagavad Gita*, many would also include recitations from texts sacred only to that specific community.

The funeral rituals are usually performed by the eldest son of the deceased. For the first few days the spirit of the deceased is a *preta* (ghost). To quench the thirst resulting from the body's fiery cremation, the spirit is offered water, as well as balls of rice for sustenance. Some of these rituals go back to the earliest Vedic times, when the dead were thought to live on the far side of the moon and thus to need food for their journey.

After a designated period of time, the length of which varies depending on caste, the injunctions relating to pollution are lifted in an "adoption of auspiciousness" ceremony. On every new-moon day, the departed soul is offered food in the form of

Sites

Varanasi, Uttar Pradesh

Also known as Kasi or Banaras; one of the holiest cities in India, located on the banks of the river Ganga. After cremation, many Hindus' ashes are brought here to be ritually submerged in the waters.

libations with sesame seeds and water. After a year, the anniversary of the death is marked with further ceremonies, and the family is then freed from all constraints.

Women's Rituals

Most women's rituals are domestic, undertaken for the welfare of the family and earthly happiness, but a few are intended solely for personal salvation or liberation. Many practices, such as worship at home shrines or temples, pilgrimages, and the singing of devotional songs, are similar to those undertaken by men, but some are unique to married women whose husbands are alive. Underlying many of the rites is the notion that women are powerful and that the rites they perform have potency. Though many women's rituals share certain features, the differences among the many communities, castes, and regions are so great that generalizations should be avoided.

Early History

We have already noted that upper-caste girls may have been permitted to study the Vedas in the ancient past. The epics tell of women lighting and tending the sacrificial fire used to make ritual offerings to the gods. They also refer to women ascetics, who would presumably have undergone renunciatory rites similar to those required of men. These privileges appear to have disappeared by the beginning of the Common Era, however.

Calendrical Rituals

Many traditional women's rituals are no longer practised today, but a number of votive rituals (*vrata*) are still observed on particular days during specific lunar months. These rituals involve the welfare of others—whether the husband and children, the extended family, or the community. Although Sanskrit manuals say that performing these rites will enable a woman to attain final liberation from the cycle of birth and death, most participants ask only for more worldly rewards, such as marriage, or a long life for their husbands.

After prayers to the family deity, the women may eat a meal together and distribute emblems of auspiciousness such as betel leaves, bananas, coconuts, turmeric, and kumkum powder. The rituals may take anywhere between a few minutes and five days to complete, with periods of fasting alternating with communal eating.

In South India many women's rituals are performed during the month of Adi (approximately 15 July–14 August). Married women were traditionally enjoined to stay celibate during this month. There are a variety of rituals connected with various castes. Women of some castes carry special pots of water and other ritual items to the temples of local goddesses and perform rites in their honour for the benefit of the entire family. Others cook rice and milk dishes in the temples of the local goddesses and distribute the food. In the temple of Draupadi Amman, women and men alike enter a trance state and walk over hot coals in a ceremony called "walking on flowers."

Reuters/Ajay Verma

Karva Chauth is a North Indian festival celebrating married women's devotion to their husbands. Participants observe a 24-hour fast, during which they pray for their husbands' well-being.

In North India many women's rites focus on the welfare of male relatives. In late summer, for example, girls tie a protective cord around the wrists of their brothers. And in October–November, women undertake two fasts (*karva chauth* and *hoi ashtami*) for the well-being of their husbands, as well as one for the health of their sons. These daytime fasts are broken only after the stars come out in the evening.

Women's Life-Cycle Rituals

In the upper castes the standard life-cycle rituals associated with childhood, marriage, and death are much the same for both sexes. There are many other sacraments associated with women, however, that have not received scriptural ratification. Some of these rites are local in nature, specific to certain regions and communities.

In the past, for instance, many communities would celebrate a young girl's first menstrual period, since this "blossoming" meant that she was ready for marriage. Today urban communities tend to consider this tradition old-fashioned, but it is still practised in rural areas. The girl is showered with gifts of money or clothing by her family, and the ritual celebration often resembles a mini-wedding.

Special rituals may also attend pregnancy, especially the first. In a popular South Indian ritual called "bracelets and amulets," the pregnant woman is dressed in a heavy silk sari, and women of all ages slip bangles and bracelets onto her arm. In earlier days a bangle-seller was invited and the woman's parents gave all the guests glass bracelets that were supposed to safeguard them from evil spirits.

In another rite the expectant mother's hair is adorned with flowers, to enhance the natural radiance that is often said to accompany pregnancy. In the Hindu tradition married women often wear flowers in their hair, but normally only a bride's hair is completely woven with flowers. Rituals such as these acknowledge the importance of a woman's body and celebrate its life-bearing potential.

Women and Pollution

With a few exceptions (among them the Vira Shaiva), most Hindu communities have traditionally regarded menstruation as physically polluting. Menstruating women were excluded from everyday life, and even though strict segregation is no longer widespread, vestiges of the old attitudes remain. Frequently, menstruating women were prohibited from cooking and most communities still do not permit menstruating women to attend a place of worship or participate in any religious ritual; even Vira Shaiva households may prohibit menstruating women from cooking. Virtually all Hindu women take a purifying ritual bath on the fourth day.

The same concept of pollution extends to childbirth. Even though the birth of a child is a happy and auspicious occasion, it is thought to render the entire family ritually impure. For several days after the birth, the family cannot go to a temple or celebrate an auspicious event.

The Performing Arts

The Hindu tradition, like many others, has been very favourably disposed towards both the visual and the performing arts. *Gandharva veda*, the knowledge related to music and dance, was considered to be an "upa" or ancillary branch of the Vedas.

A treatise on theatre and dance called the *Natya Sastra* is attributed to a legendary sage named Bharata, but was said to have originated with the creator god Brahma, who took the reading text from the Rig Veda, the music from the Sama Veda, gestures from the Yajur Veda, and *rasa*—literally, "essence" or "juice"; the aesthetic element—from the Atharava Veda and combined them to create the fifth Veda. In oral tradition, the very name "Bharata"

is said to incorporate the main elements of music and dance: *Bha-* stands for "*bhava*," a state of mind, an attitude; *-ra-* for "raga" (melody or pattern of notes); and *-ta* for "tala" or rhythm. Together, music and dance were also known as the *Gandharva Veda*.

Acting, music, and dance have even been considered ways to liberation. Classical dance requires total control of the body—the same control that is central to the physical discipline of yoga. Theoretically speaking, all dance is divine, but many dances are explicitly devotional in tone. This is particularly true of Bharata Natyam, the classical dance form of South India. While the dancer expresses the human soul's longing for union with the Lord in erotic terms, the audience may also participate in the divine joy of movement, whether that of the dancer, of Krishna with his cowherd friends, or of Shiva Nataraja, the King of the Dance, and through this participation attain the frame of mind that leads to liberation.

Sanskrit texts on dance such as the *Natya Sastra* usually make a distinction between classical and folk dance. These categories have not been immutable; sometimes the boundaries have been fluid, and both forms have derived inspiration from each other. A striking example of public singing and dancing (though originally performed in the home) is the *garbha* dance of Gujarat, in which women and young girls celebrate the Mother Goddess by dancing around a *garbha*: a clay pot holding a lamp. This is frequently classified as "folk" dancing, but as in any other tradition, one cannot draw hard lines between classical and popular dance forms: these were in dialectical relationship with each other. *Garbha* or *garbhi* means "womb," the source of all creative energy; it is the Mother Goddess who is present in the lamp inside the clay pot. It seems that when the focus is on *moksha* (liberation), rather than *dharma* (issues of righteousness), women have more freedom to take part in public activities. The androcentric controls imposed on the public activities of women are simply bypassed in contexts where the focus is on the potential for liberation that is inherent in all human beings; thus even though society may disapprove of a woman

Dancing the *garbha* during Navaratri celebrations in Mumbai.

who has rejected marriage, the women poets who rejected marriage in favour of union with their deity are venerated.

To study dance forms such as Bharata Natyam, Manipuri, Kathak, Kathakali, or Kuchipudi—classical forms from different regions of India—is to do more than simply learn a fine art. Through them dancers (and audiences) learn not only the stories of the Hindu gods but their physical appearance, their insignia, their demeanour. Whether in India or outside, in Fiji, Trinidad, or South Africa, the classical dances introduce new generations to the affective ethos of the Hindu traditions. To watch them is to know the body languages of Hindu heroes and heroines, and to learn to perform them is to plug into patterns of Indian corporeal knowledge. At the same time the dances offer insight into the allegorical structures of Hindu devotional songs, in which the love between the deity and the human being is often portrayed as that between a man and a woman. To know Indian dance forms is also a way of participating in power structures, whether spiritual or social. One Hindu text says that dance invites the blessings of the righteous, counsels the fool, cheers the depressed, enhances happiness for women, and gives prosperity in this world and in the next; above all, it pleases Vishnu.

The ostensible reason for the "revelation" of the treatise on dance was to make the Vedas accessible to *all* human beings. However, it is interesting to note that at least after the fifteenth century (and possibly earlier), the only women who sang and danced in public seem to have been courtesans. This was apparently not the case in earlier times; even as late as the twelfth century, sculptures of women dancers, perhaps royalty, adorned the niches of the Belur temple in Karnataka. The apparent prohibition against women from "decent families" dancing in public may have come from a gradual coalescence of the conservative attitudes explicit in many Hindu *dharmic* texts and Islamic mores, as well as the puritanical perspectives of Christian missionaries from Europe.

As for sound, it has been part of Hindu worship since the time of the Vedas. The holy word "Om," which is chanted at the beginning and end of all Hindu and Jaina prayers and recitations of scripture, and is central to Buddhist practice as well, is perceived to be filled with power. It is understood to have three sounds, *a–u–m*, with the diphthong *au* producing an *o* sound. The sound of *om*, which begins deep in the body and ends at the lips, is considered auspicious. Its history in the Hindu tradition is ancient; the *Mandukya Upanishad* discusses its meaning and power. Hindu philosophers and sectarian communities all agree that *om* is the most sacred sound.

Yet that sound does not have a particular meaning. Almost every Hindu community has speculated about the meaning of *om*, and the meanings vary widely. Some say it represents the supreme reality or Brahman. Many Hindu philosophers have believed that *om* was present at the beginning of the manifest universe and that it contains the essence of true knowledge. Some say that its three sounds represent the three worlds: earth, atmosphere, and heaven. Others say that they represent the essence of the three Vedas: Rig, Yajur, and Sama. Some trace its origins to the Sanskrit verbal root *av-*, meaning "that which protects."

According to followers of the non-dualist philosopher Shankara, the three sounds *a*, *u*, and *m* have the following experiential meanings:

- *A* stands for the world that we see when we are awake, the person who is experiencing it, and the waking experience.
- *U* stands for the dream world, the dreamer, and the dream experience.
- *M* represents the sleep world, the sleeper, and the sleep experience.

These three states we experience on this earth, while a fourth, unspoken syllable represents the state of liberation.

Some Vaishnava devotees, on the other hand, say that *a* represents Vishnu, *u* denotes the human being, and *m* denotes the relationship between the two. Other Vaishnavas say that the sounds represent Vishnu, Sri, and the devotee. Thus Hindus agree that *om* is the most sacred sound but disagree regarding its meaning. In a sense, then, the sound of *om* is a whole greater than the sum of its parts, exceeding in significance the many meanings attributed to it.

Music, too, from the times of the Sama Veda, has been perceived as sacred in both origin and function. Knowledge of the nature of sound and its proper expression was therefore considered to be religious knowledge. The Vedas specify the different pitches and tones in which the verses were to be recited. The exalted status of the Sama Veda was in part a reflection of the melodious sounds produced when it is sung according to the instructions.

Classical music was largely religious in nature. Treatises on music refer to a divine line of teachers, frequently beginning with the deities Shiva and Parvati, and honour Sarasvati as the patron goddess

of the fine arts. Some later Puranas, such as the Brhaddharma, say that Vishnu and Sri are manifested as Nada Brahman or the Supreme Being in the form of sound.

Properly controlled and articulated, sound itself could lead to mystical experience. Thus the sound of a hymn was considered no less important than the words. *Nadopasana*, meditation through sound, became a popular religious practice. The Alvars composed their poems to be sung and danced. Many devotional poet-composers addressed their songs to the deities.

✸ Recent Developments

Global Hinduism, Interaction, and Adaptation

Ideas, texts, sectarian movements, rituals, and arts connected with the religion that we now call "Hinduism" have been travelling, along with Hindu material culture, to other parts of the world for more than two millennia. Hinduism is a global religion in at least three ways. First, there are sizeable numbers of Hindus in almost every part of the world who trace their roots to the Indian subcontinent; second, local people in various countries have accepted Hindu teachers, doctrines, beliefs, or practices, from the Khmer aristocracy in the ninth century to the "Hare Krishnas" in the twentieth; and third, Hindu ideas and practices have been decontextualized from their original socio-cultural milieu, separated from the name "Hindu," and become part of cultures outside India. An example of the last point can be seen in the United States. Since the time of the New England Transcendentalists in the early nineteenth century, generations of Americans have engaged with ideas, philosophies, and practices rooted in Hindu traditions without identifying them as such: instead, ideas such as reincarnation and practices such as meditation or yoga have been labelled as "spiritual" or "universal."

In general, one could say that Hinduism comes in both brand name and generic forms. It is rare to find a generic Hindu in India; everyone belongs to a particular caste, community, and sectarian group, all of which are further sub-divided along linguistic and geographic lines. However, Hindu texts and practices have been mined for "universal" messages that have been popularized as applicable to all human beings. Thus Hindu teachers beginning with leaders such as Vivekananda and Yogananda, who travelled to North America in the late nineteenth and early twentieth centuries, have stressed the "timeless" and "universal" quality of Hindu concepts and practices.

The Hindu Diaspora

There have been at least three major waves of Hindu migration outside the Indian subcontinent. The first was a gradual process that took place over several centuries in the first millennium and probably involved mainly small groups of influential elites who carried Hindu ideas and practices to Southeast Asia. The second major migration was the movement of workers (free or indentured) seeking employment in the nineteenth century. The third large wave began in the second half of the twentieth century and has been more varied in its composition. The watershed year in the US was 1965, when immigration laws were relaxed to allow skilled, educated professionals such as engineers, physicians, and, towards the end of the century, software professionals to enter the country. Since 1965 diasporic communities in Europe and the Americas have also received political refugees and members of second diasporas (descendants of earlier immigrants from India who are now immigrating themselves).

Temples in the Diaspora

Perhaps the most noticeable feature of global Hindu communities is the tremendous amount of time, money, and energy they devote to the building of temples. From the time of the Mi Son temple in Champa (Vietnam), which was rebuilt in the early seventh century after a fire had destroyed the earlier shrine, temples have been the centres of Hindu communities. Since the 1970s in particular, Hindu immigrants to North America have been transforming their new homes into sacred places.

Places of worship were established as early as 1906 in the San Francisco area, but the first really ambitious attempt to reproduce the traditional architecture and atmosphere of a Vaishnava sacred place came in 1976 with the construction of the Sri Venkateshwara temple in Penn Hills, a suburb of Pittsburgh, Pennsylvania. The Penn Hills temple enshrines a manifestation of Vishnu as Venkateshwara, lord of the hill in the South Indian state of Andhra Pradesh known as Venkata ("that which can burn sins"). (Other Venkateshwara temples or shrines have been established in many parts of the United States and Canada.) The Penn Hills temple was built with the help, backing, and blessing of one of the oldest, richest, and most popular temples in India, the Venkateshwara temple at Tiruvenkatam.

Despite devotees' desire to maintain sacred traditions, some compromises and innovations have been necessary. As far as possible, for example, the ritual calendar has been adapted to fit the American secular calendar, since many festival organizers live far from the temple and long weekends are often the only time they can travel. Nevertheless, the land on which the temple is located is considered no less sacred than the land in India where Tiruvenkatam stands. The devotees celebrate the significance of having Venkateshwara dwelling on American soil with his consort Sri (known locally as Padmavati, "the lady of the lotus"). In a popular song that was recorded and sold to temple visitors in the 1980s, the following verse is sung in Sanskrit:

> Victory to Govinda [Krishna], who lives in America,
> Victory to Govinda, who is united with Radha who lives on Penn Hills,
> Victory to the Teacher, Victory to Krishna.

The idea that the Penn Hills temple is located on sacred land is not merely abstract. Devotees see the entire Pittsburgh area as geographically similar to the sacred land of India. Drawing on Puranic lore, the Penn Hills devotees think of their temple's physical location—at the confluence of three rivers, one of them subterranean—as recalling the sacred place in India where the rivers Ganga and Yamuna meet the underground Sarasvati. As they described it in 1986:

> Pittsburgh, endowed with hills and a multitude of trees as well as the confluence of the three rivers, namely, the Allegheny, the Monongehela, and the subterranean river (brought up via the 60 foot high fountain at downtown) to form the Ohio river is indeed a perfect choice for building the first and most authentic temple to house Lord Venkateshwara. The evergrowing crowds that have been coming to the city with the *thriveni Sangama* [confluence of three rivers] to worship at the Temple with the three *vimanas* [towers] reassure our belief that the venerable Gods chose this place and the emerald green hillock to reside in.

The concept of sacred land is not unique to the Penn Hills devotees. Hindus have built temples and gardens in other parts of the world to replicate or mimic the sacred geography in India. In every one of these institutions, there is continuity and innovation.

The particular place from which Hindu immigrants come has an influence on the kinds of temples they build. In Canada, Australia, and parts of Europe such as France and Switzerland, the numbers of Tamil-speaking immigrants, among them political refugees from Sri Lanka, are reflected in an emphasis on Tamil deities. Temples and shrines dedicated to Murugan, the son of Shiva and Parvati, and an important deity among Tamil-speaking people, are popular in many parts of Canada; both Toronto (Richmond Hill) and Montreal, for instance, have Murugan temples, but also have shrines to other deities within the main temple to accommodate their devotees. The icon of Murugan in the Richmond Hill temple near Toronto is said to be the tallest in the world. This is also the temple that proudly claims to have been the first in North America to consecrate images of the Vaishnava philosopher Ramanuja and the twelve Alvars, the Tamil poets who lived between the eighth and tenth centuries CE. Maintaining the community's ethno-linguistic identity is also culturally and politically significant in other temples in the world; the devotees of Sri Venkateswara Temple, Helensburgh (near Sydney, Australia), for instance, showed their strong Tamil identity by consecrating images of the 63 Nayanmars: the poets devoted to Shiva who were contemporary with the Alvars.

Temples in the diaspora often take decades to build because of the incremental nature of fundraising. Typically, by the time one section is completed, the needs in other areas have grown to the point that further additions are required. The Murugan temple near Toronto, for example, was chartered in 1973 but the land had to be bought and was not consecrated until 1983, and it was only after the influx of immigrants in the 1980s, including the surge in the Sri Lankan Tamil/Hindu population, that the temple began to take shape. Religious services were first held in the main complex after the icon of Murugan was installed there in 1988. In 1992 two towers were constructed above the shrines of Murugan and Venkateshwara in this temple, and today this is said to be the largest temple complex in North America. People from other parts of India as well as members of the second diaspora, such as immigrants from Guyana, Trinidad, and South Africa, have also built temples in the Toronto area, making this one of the religiously most diverse areas for Hindu worship in the world.

Miracles and Temple Building

Occasionally, there are miracles connected with temples in North America. An origin myth involves a dream or vision, or the "discovery" of the form of the deity in natural formations such as mountains

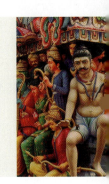

Sites

Mount Kailas, Tibet

An important peak in the Himalayan range, said to be the abode of Lord Shiva; sacred to Jainas and Buddhists as well as Hindus. Pilgrims circle Lake Manasarovar (also in Tibet) to have a *darshana* of Mount Kailas and then return home.

or caves. Generally these origin myths are associated with Shaiva temples, especially if there is a strong connection with American devotees. Thus the Light of Truth Universal Shrine temple at Yogaville, Virginia, was established in response to a vision experienced by Swami Satchidananda (b. 1919) of the Divine Life Mission. Overlooking the temple is a mountain called Kailas, after the traditional abode of Shiva.

The Kadavul temple on Kauai, Hawaii, was built in 1970 by Swami Shivaya Subramuniyaswami (1927–2001), who was born in the United States and initiated in Sri Lanka. In 1975 he had three visions of Shiva walking in the meadows near the Wailua River. Twelve years later, a rare Shiva *linga*, a six-sided quartz crystal, was discovered and taken to Kauai from Arkansas. A new Iraivan ("God") temple is now being built of stone carved in Bangalore and shipped to Hawaii.

Community Life

When overseas Hindu communities build a temple, they gain a local place of worship with formally consecrated icons, where sacraments can be conducted and offerings of devotion made.

In both the daily and seasonal routines of prayers and services, Hindu temples in North America try to remain faithful to Indian traditions. The morning wake-up prayers, the offering of food to the deity, the daily round of worship (*archana*), and the recitation of prayers at specific points of the day are all followed correctly; here, however, community participation tends to be limited to weekends, since many devotees must travel significant distances. Although seasonal festivals such as Navaratri and Deepavali are celebrated at the traditional times, for the most part, as we have noted, temples try to plan big events around the North American holiday calendar. Thus in the United States most of the major festivals are scheduled to take advantage of the long weekends between Memorial Day (May) and Labor Day (September). The sacred-time orientation of the temple is made to coincide, as far as the ritual almanac will allow, with the secular schedule of the new homeland. Following the secular holiday calendar helps to ensure full participation from devotees.

In addition to serving as places of worship, temples in the diaspora serve as community centres, with regular newsletters and website updates to provide "outreach." They have also taken on the responsibility of educating the younger generation in their ancestral traditions through weekly language and religion classes, frequent religious discourses, study circles, classical music and dance lessons, and summer camps. In addition, many new Hindu temples in North America offer SAT and other preparation courses as a way of encouraging families to come to the temple and of investing in the success of the younger generation. Since many of the founding trustees of Hindu temples in Australia, Canada, and the United States have been physicians, temples frequently organize events such as blood drives and health screenings. In the home country, temples do not serve any of these functions.

While there are many differences in architecture and modes of worship, the temples of the Hindu diaspora tend to share at least two elements in common. First, most of them focus primarily on devotional practices as opposed to meditational or yogic exercises. Second, many of them—whether in Fiji, Mauritius, or the United States—sponsor classes or programs in classical Indian dance forms such as Bharata Natyam. Learning classical dances and performing them in public during festivals is one of the most important avenues for young girls to participate in the larger Hindu community.

An important feature of the diaspora is a blurring of lines between domestic, community, and temple rituals. In the diaspora, rituals that in India are conducted in the home, such as the prenatal rites outlined above, are conducted in the temple; family festivals like Deepavali are celebrated in

Focus

Yoga in North America

Since it was introduced to the West, in the late nineteenth century, yoga has become one of the most popular activities among middle-class Americans, especially women. Today somewhere between 16 to 18 million people in the United States say that they either practise or plan to practise yoga. The fact that Americans spend as much as $27 billion a year on yoga-related products suggests that commodification has played an important part in the popularization process.

Is yoga Hindu? Some people answer in the affirmative because its roots are in traditions that eventually came to be called Hindu, but others consider it to be independent of any religious framework: if yoga deepens practitioners' spirituality, it is only in a generic way. Certainly, most people would say that practising yoga outside the religio-spiritual context does not make one Hindu.

In India the word "yoga" has been used to refer to a wide range of physical, mental, and emotional disciplines involving devotion (*bhakti*), knowledge (*jnana*), and action (*karma*) leading to emancipation from the cycle of life and death. As we saw earlier, it is one of the six orthodox schools of "philosophy" in India.

To appreciate how different "American yoga" is from "Indian yoga," recall the normative forms that are said to go back to Patanjali. As we saw, Patanjali's yoga centred on moral discipline and meditation; although he recommended the kinds of bodily postures and breathing techniques that are at the core of American yoga, for Patanjali these were just two aspects of a much more complex discipline.

Perfection in concentration (*dharana*) and meditation (*dhyana*) lead to *samadhi*, the final state of absorption into and union with the supreme being or higher consciousness. Anyone who reaches this stage is well on the way to emancipation from the cycle of life and death. Obviously, the scope of the yoga taught in North American church basements and fitness centres is much more limited. The kinds of yoga that have been made popular since the 1970s by B.K.S Iyengar and Pattabhi Jois, two prominent disciples of Sri Krishnamacharya, focus mainly on physical well-being and stress reduction rather than "spirituality." The same is true of popular gurus such as Maharishi Mahesh Yogi, Sri Sri Ravi Shankar (not to be confused with the late sitar master), and Deepak Chopra: they do not connect their teachings with any specific "religion," and they say that the techniques they advocate are not incompatible with anyone's religious beliefs.

the diaspora with community gatherings held in a school gym or church auditorium if there is no temple nearby.

Finally, among the features of life on the subcontinent that diaspora communities lack is the tradition of making pilgrimages to certain Muslim and Christian shrines. In India, many Hindus will visit *dargahs* (literally, "doorways"; here the term refers to the shrines of Muslim holy men) to make offerings to the saints who have answered their petitions. The *dargahs* of the Sufi saints Khwaja Moinuddin Chishti (1141–1236) in Ajmer, Rajasthan; Hazrat Nizamuddin (1238–1325) in Delhi; and Shahul Hamid (1490–1579) in Nagore, Tamilnadu, are shared ritual spaces at which Hindus and Muslims alike offer prayers. Hindus in South India also make pilgrimages to Catholic sites such as the basilica at Vailankanni, Tamilnadu, and the Infant Jesus Shrine in Bengaluru (Bangalore), Karnataka. Since most Hindus have an eclectic view of religion and believe that divinity manifests itself in many ways, they have been enthusiastic pilgrims to shared ritual spaces, even if they generally do not attend regular church services or prayers at a mosque. To a large extent, of course, the loss of that tradition can be attributed to the absence of *dargahs* or shrines in the new world, but it is also possible that Hindus in the diaspora are more concerned than those on the subcontinent with demarcating their religio-cultural identity.

Hinduism and the Environment

The history of environmental activism in India is sometimes traced as far back as the late fifteenth century, when a guru named Jambho—inspired by the pastoral life of Krishna the cowherd—taught his followers to minimize harm to the natural world. The community he established took the name Bishnoi, after the 29 ("bish-noi") most important of his teachings, which included everything from vegetarianism to water conservation and the protection of trees. Based in Rajasthan, the Bishnoi have continued to follow those teachings for more than 500 years.

Environmental responsibility is by no means confined to the Bishnoi, however. Today, growing numbers of Hindu leaders and institutions are drawing on the classic texts to encourage eco-activism. Visitors to the Venkateshwara temple in Tirumala-Tirupati, for instance, are greeted by billboards proclaiming *vriksho rakshati: rakshatah* ("Trees, when protected, protect us"), and the temple authorities draw attention to a line from the *Matsya Purana* in which the goddess Parvati declares that "One tree is equal to ten sons." In a culture where sons are so highly prized, the force of this statement is striking.

The Tirumala-Tirupati temple has also established a large nursery on the surrounding hills. In addition to plants of many varieties, it grows tree saplings that are given as *prasada* to pilgrims, who are encouraged to plant them at home. In addition to this consciousness-raising venture, the temple invites pilgrims to offer donations for the purchase and planting of trees and plants. Donors are honoured with a special *darshana* (viewing of the deity) in the inner shrine, and their names are displayed on the trees they pay for.

Religious teachers and institutions retrieve and re-envision the meaning of the Vedas by emphasizing the sections that speak of peace and harmony. The *Song of Peace* (*shanti path*), for example, composed more than three millennia ago, has become a source of inspiration for environmental activists:

> May there be peace in the skies, peace in the atmosphere, peace on earth, peace in the waters. May the healing plants and trees bring peace; may there be peace [on and from] the world, the deity. May there be peace in the world, peace on peace. May that peace come to me! (Yajur Veda 36.17).

Modern Reproductive Technology

Of all the technological innovations developed in recent years, those associated with reproduction tend to be among the most controversial. Yet Hindus appear on the whole to be quite accepting of intervention in this area. In the case of assisted reproduction, this acceptance is probably not surprising: the traditional teachings on dharma have always emphasized that reproduction is a primary duty. Thus many Hindus today accept artificial insemination, although for most couples the husband is the only acceptable donor.

In fact, many stories about supernatural or "unnatural" means of conception and childbirth can be found in the classic literature. In the *Mahabharata*, a queen named Gandhari grows one hundred sons in brass jars. In other texts, an embryo is transplanted from one woman to another, Krishna's brother Balarama is transplanted into another womb, and deities are invoked to "fertilize" women whose husbands cannot procreate.

The ethical considerations become more complex where issues such as contraception and gender selection are concerned. For thousands of years, male children were more welcome than females, largely because of the traditional duty to the ancestors: in a patriarchal, patrilineal society, sons would continue the family line and could be counted on to look after their parents in old age, whereas daughters would be of benefit only to their husbands' families. Indeed, the cost of providing a dowry for a daughter represented a significant financial burden for many families.

Although illegally, sonograms and amniocentesis are sometimes used for the express purpose of ascertaining the sex of the fetus early in pregnancy, so that female fetuses can be aborted. As a result, the numbers of female births have dropped in recent years.

The *dharmashastra* texts maintain that the unborn fetus has life; according to popular belief and stories from the *Puranas*, it is even capable of hearing and learning from the conversations that take place around it. Nevertheless, abortions are legal in India and are accepted without any strong dissent from religious leaders or prolonged editorial, legislative, or judicial debate.

Thus it appears that the dharma texts do not have the compelling authority for Hindus (and probably never did) that their counterparts in some other religious traditions do for their adherents.

⚛ Summary

As the communities in the diaspora face the challenges of raising a new generation in the faith, Hindus in many parts of the world are actively working to define Hinduism. Examples include statements such as "Hinduism is not a religion, it is a way of life," or "Hinduism is a tolerant religion." The difficulty of proving or disproving such claims only underscores the complexities of a religious tradition that has evolved through more than 3,000 years of recorded history—5,000 if the Harappa culture is included.

The dynamism of the many Hindu traditions is unmistakable. Vedanta is continually being interpreted. People continue to experience possession by deities, to situate their homes in auspicious directions, and to choose religiously correct times for happy events. Temples continue to be built, consecrated, and preserved. The sacred words of the Vedas and the *smrti* literature are still broadcast widely. Manuscripts are being restored, edited, and published, and new technologies are making the literature more widely accessible; the tradition confining the sacred word to particular castes is gone forever. The airwaves are flooded with religious programs, horoscopes are cast and matched by computer, surgeries are scheduled for auspicious times. In short, Hinduism continues to adapt to changing times and different lands.

Sacred Texts

Religion (Sect)	Text(s)	Composition/ Compilation	Compilation/ Revision	Use
Hinduism	Vedas (Sanskrit)	Composed between c. 1500 and 600 BCE		Considered the most authoritative of all texts. Parts of the Vedas were used in both domestic and temple rituals.
	Upanishads: the last section of the Vedas, focusing on philosophy (Sanskrit)	c. 6th century BCE	Most Vedanta philosophers used these texts in commentaries or wrote commentaries on them. The commentarial tradition continues today.	Philosophical
	Ramayana (Sanskrit)	c. 5th century BCE– 1st century CE Very approximate dates	Periodically rendered in local languages. Tulsidas' *Ramcharitmanas* in Hindi is very important.	Doctrinal, ritual, performative, inspirational, devotional, narrative, educational
	Mahabharata (Sanskrit)	c. 5th century BCE– 2nd century CE		Doctrinal, ritual, narrative, performative, inspirational, devotional, educational
	Bhagavad Gita (part of the *Mahabharata*; Sanskrit)	c. 2nd century BCE– 2nd century CE	Extensive tradition of commentary	Doctrinal, ritual, performative, devotional, inspirational, narrative, educational
	Puranas (Sanskrit)	1st millennium CE	Often recreated in local languages	Doctrinal, ritual, devotional, narrative, inspirational, educational
Vaishnava, (specifically Gaudiya and ISKCON)	*Bhagavata Purana* (Sanskrit)	c. 1st millennium CE		Doctrinal, ritual, devotional, narrative, inspirational, educational
	Dharmasutras followed by the *Dharmashastras* Many texts, of which the *Manava Dharmashastra* ("Laws of Manu") is the most important (Sanskrit).	Dharmasutras composed in the 1st millennium BCE; dharmashastras in the 1st millennium CE	Extensive tradition of commentary. Medathithi (c. 9th–11th centuries CE?) commented on *Manu*.	Ritual, moral, and legal prescriptions on all aspects of life: personal, domestic, and public; discussions of right behaviour
	Yoga Sutras of Patanjali	c. 200 BCE–300 CE	Commentarial tradition	Classical philosophical text for yoga

Continued

Sacred Texts (Continued)

Religion (Sect)	Text(s)	Composition/ Compilation	Compilation/ Revision	Use
Vaishnava (Tamil)	*Nalayira Divya Prabandham* Sacred Collect of 4,000 verses by the Alvars (Tamil)	c. 8–10th centuries CE; said to have been "revealed" in 11th century	Extensive commentarial tradition	Doctrinal, ritual, performative, devotional, inspirational, narrative, educational use
Shaiva (Tamil)	Tirumurai	c. 8th–12th centuries		Devotional and philosophical use
Vaishnava	Poems of Surdas (Hindi/Braj Bhasha)	16th century		Doctrinal, ritual, performative, devotional, inspirational, narrative, educational use
Vaishnava (Marathi)	*Dnyaneshwari* or *Jnaneswari*	Composed by *Dnyaneshwar*, c. 13th century		Doctrinal, devotional, and educational use

Discussion Questions

1. What is the origin of the word "Hindu"? What elements of the Harappa culture suggest connections with Hindu traditions?

2. Why are the *Ramayana* and *Mahabharata* central to Hinduism?

3. What role do sacred texts play in Hinduism?

4. Identify some of the deities, major and minor, that Hindus worship. How is it that Hindus describe themselves as monotheistic?

5. Who or what is Brahman? What is the relationship between Brahman and deities such as Vishnu, Shiva, and the Goddess?

6. What is *bhakti*? What role does it play in Hinduism?

7. What are the three ways to liberation discussed in the *Bhagavad Gita*?

8. Describe some of the distinctive features of Hinduism as it developed in Southeast Asia.

9. What is the role of the performing arts in Hinduism?

10. What are the primary ways in which women historically contributed to various Hindu traditions?

Glossary

acharya The leading teacher of a sect or the head of a monastery.

advaita Shankara's school of philosophy, which holds that there is only one ultimate reality, the indescribable Brahman, with which the Atman or self is identical.

Alvars Twelve devotional poets whose works are central to the South Indian *bhakti* tradition.

artha Prosperity; one of the three classical aims in life.

ashramas Four stages in the life of an upper-class male: student, householder, forest-dweller, and ascetic.

Atman The individual self, held by Upanishadic and Vedantic thought to be identical with Brahman, the world-soul.

avatara A "descent" or incarnation of a deity in earthly form.

Ayurveda A system of traditional medicine, understood as a teaching transmitted from the sages.

Bhagavad Gita A section of the *Mahabharata* epic recounting a conversation between Krishna and the warrior Arjuna, in which Krishna explains the nature of God and the human soul.

bhakti Loving devotion to a deity seen as a gracious being who enters the world for the benefit of humans.

Brahma The creator god; not to be confused with Brahman.

Brahman The world-soul, sometimes understood in impersonal terms; not to be confused with Brahma.

Brahmanas Texts regarding ritual.

brahmin A member of the priestly class.

darshana Seeing and being seen by the deity (in the temple) or by a holy teacher; the experience of beholding with faith.

Deepavali (Diwali) Festival of light in October–November, when lamps are lit.

devanagari The alphabet used to write Sanskrit and northern Indian vernacular languages such as Hindi and Bengali.

dharma Religious and social duty, including both righteousness and faith.

guru A spiritual teacher.

Holi Spring festival celebrated by throwing brightly coloured water or powder.

jnana Knowledge; along with action and devotion, one of the three avenues to liberation explained in the *Bhagavad Gita*.

kama Sensual (not merely sexual) pleasure; one of the three classical aims of life.

karma Action, good and bad, as it is believed to determine the quality of rebirth in future lives.

kshatriya A member of the warrior class in ancient Hindu society.

linga A conical or cylindrical stone column, symbolizing the creative energies of the god Shiva.

Mahabharata A very long epic poem, one section of which is the *Bhagavad Gita*.

mantra An expression of one or more syllables, chanted repeatedly as a focus of concentration in devotion.

moksha Liberation from the cycle of birth and death; one of the three classical aims in life.

murti A form or personification in which divinity is manifested.

Navaratri "Nine nights"; an autumn festival honouring the Goddess.

om A syllable chanted in meditation, interpreted as representing ultimate reality, or the universe, or the relationship of the devotee to the deity.

prasada A gift from the deity, especially food that has been presented to the god's temple image, blessed, and returned to the devotee.

puja Ritual household worship of the deity, commonly involving oil lamps, incense, prayers, and food offerings.

Puranas "Old tales," stories about deities that became important after the Vedic period.

Ramayana An epic recounting the life of Lord Rama, an incarnation of the god Vishnu.

rishi A seer; the composers of the ancient Vedic hymns are considered *rishis*.

sadhu A holy man.

samnyasin A religious ascetic; one who has reached the last of the four stages of life for a Hindu male; see *ashramas*.

samsara The continuing cycle of re-births.

sati The self-sacrifice of a widow who throws herself onto her deceased husband's funeral pyre.

shruti "What is heard"; the sacred literature of the Vedic and Upanishadic periods, recited orally by the brahmin priests for many centuries before it was written down.

shudra A member of the lowest of the four major classes, usually translated as "servant," though some groups within the *shudra* class could be quite prosperous.

smrti "What is remembered," a body of ancient Hindu literature, including the epics, *Puranas*, and law codes, formed after the *shruti* and passed down in written form.

tantra An esoteric school outside the Vedic and brahminical tradition, which emerged around the fifth century and centred on a number of controversial ritual practices, some of them sexual.

tilaka A dot or mark on the forehead made with coloured powder.

upanayana The initiation of a young brahmin boy into ritual responsibility, in which he is given a cord to wear over his left shoulder and a mantra to recite and is sent to beg for food for the day.

Upanishads Philosophical texts in the form of reported conversations on the theory of the Vedic ritual and the nature of knowledge, composed around the sixth century BCE.

vaishya A member of the third or mercantile class in the ancient fourfold class structure.

Vedas The four collections of hymns and ritual texts that constitute the oldest and most highly respected Hindu sacred literature.

yoga A practice and discipline that may involve a philosophical system and mental concentration as well as physical postures and exercises.

Further Reading

Baird, Robert D. 1993. *Religions and Law in Independent India*. New Delhi: Manohar. Takes up some problems of the status of various groups.

———, ed. 1995. *Religion in Modern India*. 3rd ed. New Delhi: Manohar. Good individual chapters on nineteenth- and twentieth-century sectarian movements.

Basham, Arthur Llewellyn. 1954. *The Wonder That Was India*. London: Sidgwick & Jackson. Arguably still the definitive introduction to the pre-Muslim culture of the subcontinent.

Brill's Encyclopedia of Hinduism, 4 vols. 2009–12. Knut Jacobsen (chief editor), Helene Basu, Angelika Malinar, and Vasudha Narayanan, (associate editors). Leiden: Brill. An excellent and comprehensive resource on the Hindu traditions.

Bryant, Edwin. 2003. The *Quest for the Origins of Vedic Culture: The Indo-Aryan Migration Debate*. New York: Oxford University Press. A balanced and thorough discussion of a controversial topic.

———, ed. *Krishna: A Sourcebook*. 2007. New York: Oxford University Press. A good introduction to one of the most important deities in the Hindu tradition from a variety of sectarian and regional perspectives.

Bryant, Edwin, and Maria Eckstrand. 2004. *The Hare Krishna Movement: The Postcharismatic Fate of a Religious Transplant*. New York: Columbia University Press. An eclectic collection of essays on the International Society for Krishna Consciousness.

Chapple, Christopher, and Mary Evelyn Tucker, eds. 2000. *Hinduism and Ecology: The Intersection of Earth, Sky, and Water*. Cambridge, MA: Center for the Study of World Religions, Harvard Divinity School. Part of an important series in which various traditions address current environmental issues.

Coward, Harold. 2005. *Human Rights and the World's Major Religions.* Vol. 4. *The Hindu Tradition.* Westchester Books. A good introduction to an important topic.

Craven, Roy C. 1976. *A Concise History of Indian Art.* New York: Praeger. Remains one of the best introductions to Indian art.

Dalmia, Vasudha, and Heinrich von Steitencron. 1995. eds. *Representing Hinduism: The Construction of Religious Traditions and National Identity.* New Delhi: Sage. A good set of essays discussing whether Hinduism is one or many traditions.

de Bary, William Theodore, ed. *1958 Sources of Indian Tradition.* New York: Columbia University Press. The classic sourcebook: well selected, well introduced.

Dimock, Edward C., Jr, and Denise Levertov, trans. 1967. *In Praise of Krishna: Songs from the Bengali.* Garden City, NY: Doubleday. Lyrical expressions of devotion from eastern India.

Doniger O'Flaherty, Wendy, ed. and trans. 1988. *Textual Sources for the Study of Hinduism.* Manchester: Manchester University Press. A good sourcebook in a rather compressed format, covering the main phases of the Hindu tradition.

Eck, Diana L. 1981. *Darsan: Seeing the Divine Image in India.* Chambersburg, PA: Anima Books. On the significance of coming into the presence of the deity; brief but authoritative.

Embree, Ainslie T., ed. *Sources of Indian Tradition.* 2nd ed. 2 vols. New York: Columbia University Press. 1988. Expands on the de Bary first edition but drops a few items in the process.

Erndl, Kathleen M. 1993. *Victory to the Mother: The Hindu Goddess of Northwest India in Myth, Ritual, and Symbol.* New York: Oxford University Press. Well focused on one region.

Findly, Ellison B. 1985. "Gargi at the King's Court: Women and Philosophic Innovation in Ancient India." In Yvonne Y. Haddad and Ellison B. Findly, eds. *Women, Religion and Social Change,* 37–58. Albany: State University of New York Press. Shows that intellectual activity was not entirely limited to males.

Flood, Gavin. ed. *The Blackwell Companion to Hinduism.* London: Blackwell, 2003. Good essays on a variety of topics in the Hindu tradition.

González-Reimann, Luis. 2009. "Cosmic Cycles, Cosmology and Cosmography." In *Brill's Encyclopedia of Hinduism* vol. 1, 411–28.

Hawley, John S. and Mark Juergensmeyer. 1988. *Songs of the Saints of India.* New York: Oxford University Press. Excellent translations of the works of four medieval saints of North India.

Hawley, John S., and Donna M. Wulff. 1982. *The Divine Consort: Radha and the Goddesses of India.* Berkeley: Berkeley Religious Studies Series. Another useful work on feminine aspects of the Hindu tradition.

———. 1996. *Devi: Goddesses of India.* Berkeley: University of California Press. Expands on the theme of the previous work.

Huntington, Susan L. 1985. *The Art of Ancient India: Buddhist, Hindu, Jain.* New York: Weatherhill. A good introduction to ancient Indian monuments.

Leslie, Julia, ed. 1991. *Roles and Rituals for Hindu Women.* London: Pinter; Rutherford, NJ: Fairleigh Dickinson University Press. A coherent set of essays on the subject.

Lopez, Donald S., Jr., ed. 1995. *Religions of India in Practice.* Princeton: Princeton University Press. A sourcebook containing a fine range of material; strong on ritual.

Manu, Patrick Olivelle, and Suman Olivelle. 2005. *Manu's Code of Law: A Critical Edition and Translation of the Manava-Dharmasastra.* Oxford: Oxford University Press.

Marglin, Frédérique, and John B. Carman, eds. 1985. *Purity and Auspiciousness in Indian Society.* Leiden: E.J. Brill. A useful collection, in an anthropological series.

Miller, Barbara Stoler, trans. 1977. *Love Song of the Dark Lord: Jayadeva's Gitagovinda.* New York: Columbia University Press. An important *bhakti* text.

———, trans. 1986. *The Bhagavad Gita: Krishna's Counsel in Time of War.* New York: Columbia University Press. A good translation, accessible to undergraduates.

Mittal, Sushil, and Gene Thursby, eds. 2004. *The Hindu World.* Routledge. Fairly comprehensive coverage, using Sanskrit terms, concepts, and categories.

Narayan, R.K. 1972. *Ramayana: A Shortened Modern Prose Version of the Indian Epic.* New York: Viking. A useful point of access to this classic.

Narayanan, Vasudha. 1994. *The Vernacular Veda: Revelation, Recitation, and Ritual Practice.* Columbia: University of South Carolina Press. The ritual use of the *Tiruvaymoli* among India's scheduled castes as well as brahmins.

———. 1996. "'One Tree Is Equal to Ten Sons': Hindu Responses to the Problems of Ecology, Population, and Consumption." *Journal of the American Academy of Religion* 65: 291–332. Discusses some classic resources for addressing concerns of today.

Nelson, Lance E. ed. 1998. *Purifying the Earthly Body of God: Religion and Ecology in Hindu India.* Albany: State University of New York Press. One of the earliest and best collections of essays on an important topic.

Olivelle, Patrick, trans. 1996. *Upanisads.* New York: Oxford University Press.

———, trans. 1997. *The Pancatantra: The Book of India's Folk Wisdom.* New York: Oxford University Press.

———, trans. 1999. *Dharmasutras: The Law Codes of Atastamba, Gautama, Baudhyayana, and Vasistha.* New York: Oxford University Press. This and the two foregoing items are lucid translations of influential texts.

Orr, Leslie C. 2000. *Donors, Devotees, and Daughters of God: Temple Women in Medieval Tamilnadu.* New York: Oxford University Press. A useful corrective to prescriptive male writings in Sanskrit on Hindu women.

Patton, Laurie L., ed. 2002. *Jewels of Authority: Women and Text in the Hindu Tradition.* New York: Oxford University Press. A wide-ranging collection of essays on Hindu and Buddhist women's relationship to sacred text and mantras.

Pechilis, Karen, ed. 2004. *The Graceful Guru: Hindu Female Gurus in India and the United States.* New York: Oxford University Press. A good set of essays on women gurus, with an excellent introduction by the editor.

Radhakrishnan, Sarvepalli, and Charles A. Moore, eds. 1957. *A Source Book in Indian Philosophy.* Princeton: Princeton University Press. A very good anthology of philosophical texts.

Rajagopalachari, Chakravarti. 1953. *Mahabharata.* Bombay: Bharatiya Vidya Bhavan. A sampling from this vast epic.

Ramanujan, A.K. 1979. *Speaking of Siva.* Harmondsworth: Penguin. Lyrical and moving translations of Kannada poems written by three men and one woman saint from 12th–13th century south India.

———, trans. 1981. *Hymns for the Drowning: Poems for Vishnu by Nammawvar.* Princeton: Princeton University Press. An excellent source for Tamil *bhakti*.

Rangacharya, Adya, trans. 1986. *The Natyasastra: English Translation with Critical Notes.* Bangalore: IBH Prakashana. A text frequently considered India's fifth Veda, important for the role of the performing arts in modern Hindu tradition.

Richman, Paula, ed. 1991. *Many Ramayanas: The Diversity of a Narrative Tradition in South Asia.* Berkeley: University of California Press. Reflects the importance of the *Ramayana* in vernacular South Asian traditions.

———, ed. 2000. *Questioning Ramayanas: A South Asian Tradition.* Delhi: Oxford University Press.

Soneji, Davesh. ed., 2012. *Bharatanatyam: A Reader.* New York: Oxford University Press. A scholarly and multi-disciplinary set of essays on the most popular classical form of dance in India.

Sweetman, Will. 2003. *Mapping Hinduism: "Hinduism" and the Study of Indian Religions, 1600–1776.* Halle: Franckesche Stiftungen.

Tharu, Susie, and K. Lalita. 1991. *Women Writing in India: 600 BC to the Present.* New York: Feminist Press. A must-read for all those interested in hearing women's voices from the past. Includes literature not necessarily perceived to be religious or Hindu.

von Stietencron, Heinrich. 1989. "Hinduism: On the Proper Use of a Deceptive Term." In Günther D. Sontheimer and Hermann Kulke, eds. *Hinduism Reconsidered*, 11–27. New Delhi: Manohar. One of the best discussions of the nomenclature of "Hinduism."

Waghorne, Joanne P., Norman Cutler, and Vasudha Narayanan, eds. 1985. *Gods of Flesh, Gods of Stone: The Embodiment of Divinity in India.* New York: Columbia University Press. Explores a range of forms in which Hindus see deity manifested.

Williams, Raymond Brady, ed. 1992. *A Sacred Thread: Modern Transmission of Hindu Traditions in India and Abroad.* Chambersburg, PA: Anima. A good description of the diaspora in the 1970s and 1980s.

Wujastyk, Dominik, intro. and trans. 1998. *The Roots of Ayurveda: Selections from Sanskrit Medical Writings.* Delhi: Penguin. Useful for the relationship between traditional Indian medicine and religion.

Zimmer, Heinrich. 1946. *Myths and Symbols in Indian Art and Civilization.* New York: Pantheon. A classic study, still often cited.

Recommended Websites

www.sacred-texts.com/hin/index.htm

Free online translations (mostly late-nineteenth to early-twentieth century) of the Vedas, epics, *Puranas*, *Yoga Sutras*, *smrti* literature, etc.

www.sscnet.ucla.edu/southasia/

Very good links for South Asian culture, religions, and history.

www.harappa.com/har/haro.html

Many links to various aspects of the Indus Civilization.

www.wabashcenter.wabash.edu/resources/result_ browse.aspx?topic=569&pid=361

A meta-site with links to many useful resources, including course syllabi.

www.columbia.edu/itc/mealac/pritchett/00 generallinks/index.html

A good site with links to many resources on South Asia.

http://virtualvillage.wesleyan.edu/

An on-the-ground look at a "virtual village" in North India.

www.veda.harekrsna.cz/encyclopedia/index.htm

Links to articles on various topics in Hinduism from an ISKCON perspective.

www.sathyasai.org/

The official site of Sri Sathya Sai Baba, maintained by his devotees.

http://prapatti.com/

Texts and MP3 audios of several Tamil and Sanskrit Vaishnava prayers.

www.hindupedia.com/en/Main_Page

An online encyclopedia offering "a traditional perspective" on the Hindu religion and way of life.

www.hinduismtoday.com/

A popular magazine based in Hawaii, rooted in the classical Shaiva tradition, but offering articles of interest to Hindus all over the world.

References

Carman, John B., and Vasudha Narayanan, trans. 1989. *The Tamil Veda: Pillan's Interpreta-tion of the Tiruvaymoli*. Chicago: University of Chicago Press.

Doniger, Wendy, and Brian K. Smith, trans. 1981. *The Laws of Manu*. London: Penguin.

Doniger O'Flaherty, Wendy, ed. and trans. 1981. *The Rig Veda: An Anthology, One Hundred and Eight Hymns*. Harmondsworth: Penguin.

Hawley, John S., and Mark Juergensmeyer, trans. 1988. *Songs of the Saints of India*. New York: Oxford University Press.

India. Ministry of Education and Social Welfare. 1984. *Toward Equality: Report of the Status of Women in India*. New Delhi: Ministry of Education and Social Welfare.

Jackson, William J., trans. 1991. *Tyagaraja: Life and Lyrics*. Delhi: Oxford University Press.

Lipski, Alexander. 1977. *Life and Teachings of Sri Anandamayi Ma*. Delhi: Motilal Banarsidass.

Miller, Barbara Stoler, trans. 1986. *The Bhagavad-Gita: Krishna's Counsel in Time of War*. New York: Columbia University Press.

Radhakrishnan, Sarvepalli, trans. 1953. *The Principal Upanisads*. London: Allen and Unwin.

Sengupta, D. n.d. *"The Historic Healing Stone—L.O.T.U.S."* Kauai: Lord of the Universe Society.

Tagore, Rabindranath, trans. 1915. *One Hundred Poems of Kabir*. London: Macmillan.

Venkateshwara Temple. 1986. *"Kavachas for the Deities."* Pittsburgh: Venkateshwara Temple.

3

Sikh
Traditions

Pashaura Singh

Traditions at a Glance

Numbers

25 million around the world.

Distribution

Primarily northern India, especially Punjab, Haryana, and Delhi, with minorities in other provinces of India and many other countries, including Canada, the United States (especially California), and Britain.

Founders and Leaders

Founded by Guru Nanak c. 1500 CE, and developed over the following two centuries by a succession of nine other inspired teachers, the last of whom, Guru Gobind Singh, died in 1708.

Deity

The Supreme Being is considered to be One and without form. Guru Nanak refers to the deity as Akal Purakh ("Timeless Person"), Kartar ("Creator"), and Nirankar ("Formless"), among many other names.

Authoritative Texts

The Adi Granth (also known as Guru Granth Sahib) is a compilation of divinely inspired hymns by six Gurus, fifteen poet-saints, and fifteen Sikh bards; the Dasam Granth, a collection of hymns made in the time of the tenth Guru, is also revered as a secondary scripture.

Noteworthy Teachings

There is One Supreme Reality, never incarnated. In addition to reverence for the Gurus and the sacred scriptures, Sikhs emphasize egalitarianism, tolerance, service to others, and righteous life in this world as the way to ultimate liberation from the cycle of rebirth.

In this chapter you will learn about:

- The origins of Sikhism, the Sikh Panth, and the Ten Gurus
- Sikh–Mughal conflict and the creation of the Khalsa
- Sikh teachings and sacred scriptures
- Sikh reform movements and variations in modern Sikhism
- Sikh social norms, culture, and institutions of doctrinal authority
- The Sikh Diaspora and recent developments.

"Sikh" is a Punjabi word meaning "disciple." People who identify themselves as Sikhs are disciples of **Akal Purakh** ("Timeless Being," God), the ten Sikh **Gurus**, and the sacred scripture called the **Adi Granth** ("Original Book"). The youngest of India's indigenous religions, Sikhism emerged in the Punjab approximately five centuries ago and quickly distinguished itself from the region's other religious traditions in its doctrines, practices, and orientation—away from ascetic renunciation (withdrawal from worldly life) and towards active engagement with the world.

Today the global Sikh population numbers approximately 25 million, of whom more than 20 million live in India, mainly in the state of Punjab. Sikhs make up only about 2 per cent of the country's 1 billion people, but their contributions to its political and economic life are significant. The rest of the world's Sikhs are part of a global diaspora that includes substantial communities in Southeast Asia, Australia, New Zealand, East Africa, Britain, and North America, established through successive waves of emigration.

Overview

The religious environment of the fifteenth-century Punjab was suffused with the thought of the North

Entering the Darbar Sahib (Golden Temple) in Amritsar (Ashok Sinha/Getty Images).

Timeline

1469	Birth of Guru Nanak, the founder of the Sikh tradition
1499	Guru Nanak's mystical experience
1519	Establishment of the first Sikh community at Kartarpur
1539	Guru Nanak is succeeded by Guru Angad
1577	Guru Ram Das establishes the town of Ramdaspur (Amritsar)
1604	The Adi Granth is compiled under Guru Arjan's supervision
1606	Guru Arjan's martyrdom on the orders of Emperor Jahangir
1675	Guru Tegh Bahadur's martyrdom on the orders of Emperor Aurangzeb
1699	Guru Gobind Singh organizes the Khalsa
1708	The succession of human Gurus ends with the death of Guru Gobind Singh; from now on the Guru is the scripture, known as Guru Granth Sahib
1765	Sikhs capture Lahore
1799	Punjab united under Maharaja Ranjit Singh
1849	Annexation of the Punjab by the British
1865	Publication of the first printed edition of the Guru Granth Sahib
1873	Singh Sabha movement is established
1892	Singh Sabha establishes Khalsa College in Amritsar
1920	Shiromani Gurdwara Prabandhak Committee (SGPC) is established
1925	Sikh Gurdwara Act gives the SGPC legal authority over all gurdwaras
1947	Punjab is partitioned between India and Pakistan
1973	The Sikh political party, the Akali Dal, passes the Anandpur Sahib Resolution, demanding greater autonomy for all Indian states; relations with the central government become increasingly strained
1984	Indian army attacks the Darbar Sahib and other gurdwaras in the Punjab
1999	Sikhs celebrate the tri-centenary of the Khalsa
2004	Manmohan Singh is elected the first Sikh prime minister of India
2008	Tri-centenary celebration of the installation as Guru of the Guru Granth Sahib
2010	Tri-centenary celebration of Sikh rule established by Banda Singh Bahadur in 1710
2012	Indian Parliament passes the Anand Marriage (Amendment) Act, 2012 to register Sikh marriages

Indian **Sants**. The founder of the Sikh tradition, Guru Nanak (1469–1539), shared both the mystic and the iconoclastic tendencies of "poet-saints" such as Kabir, Ravidas, and Namdev. Nevertheless, Nanak declared his independence from the prevailing thought forms of his day and sought to kindle the fire of independence in his disciples.

The foundation of the tradition he created was his own belief in the possibility of achieving spiritual liberation in a single lifetime through meditation on the divine Name (**nam**), the constant presence of Akal Purakh in the heart, and the living of an ethical life in the world. The interaction of this ideology with two environmental factors—the rural base of Punjabi society, which is suffused with the cultural traditions of agriculturalist Jats ("peasants"), and the historical circumstances of the period during which Nanak's successors elaborated on the foundations he laid—determined the historical development of Sikhism.

The name "Punjab" (literally, "five waters") refers to the five rivers (Jehlum, Chenab, Ravi, Beas, and Sutlej) that define the region, all of which are tributaries of the Indus. The central Punjab has a rich layer of fertile soil resulting from heavy rainfall and changes in the courses of rivers. Historically, this region was a geographical crossroads where the cultures of the Middle East, Central Asia, and India interacted in various ways, and through which a series of Muslim invaders—Afghans, Arabs, Iranians, Turks—made forays into the subcontinent.

Sufi Islam had already become established in the Punjab by the eleventh century, and with the establishment of the Delhi Sultanate, in the thirteenth century, three Sufi orders from Iraq and Persia moved into northern India. By the fifteenth century the Buddhists had disappeared from the Punjab, although a few Jaina ascetics had survived. There were also three distinct Hindu communities devoted to Shiva, Vishnu, and Devi (the Goddess), along with a cluster of tantra-influenced yogic sects known collectively as the Nath tradition. It is only in the context of this diverse religious universe that the development of the Sikh tradition can be understood, for it required the Sikhs to define themselves in an ongoing process of interaction and lively debate.

Guru Nanak

Guru Nanak was born in 1469 to an upper-caste professional khatri ("merchant") family in the village of Talwandi (Nankana Sahib), not far from what is now Lahore, Pakistan. At the time of his birth, much of northern India, including the Punjab, had been under Muslim control for more than two centuries. In his lifetime Guru Nanak witnessed the dominance of the Lodhi Sultanate and its final defeat in 1526 by the Mughal Emperor Babur (1483–1530). By the time Babur came to power, Guru Nanak had already established a community of his followers in the village of Kartarpur ("The Creator's Abode"). For the next two centuries the Sikh tradition evolved in the historical context of the Mughal regime.

Focus

The Nath Tradition

The various Nath sects all claimed descent from a semi-legendary yogi named Gorakhnath and all promulgated hatha yoga—a formidably difficult system of physical postures and breath control—as the means of spiritual liberation. Nath doctrine affirmed that the rigorous practice of hatha yoga induced a psycho-physical process whereby the spirit could ascend to mystical bliss (**sahaj**). Stressing the irrelevance of caste to spiritual liberation, the folly of sacred languages and scriptures, and the futility of temple worship and pilgrimage, while emphasizing interior devotion, the Nath yogis had a strong influence on the Sant tradition of North India. During the period of Guru Nanak, the Nath yogis were an important force in the religious milieu of the Punjab, and the use of Nath terminology in Guru Nanak's hymns suggests that he engaged in a number of debates with them.

Guru Nanak's Mystical Experience

Much of the material concerning Guru Nanak's life comes from hagiographical *janam-sakhis* ("birth narratives") that were first written down roughly seven decades after his death but began circulating orally during his lifetime. His life may be divided into three distinct phases: an early contemplative period; a mystic enlightenment followed by years of pilgrimage and debate; and a conclusion in which

Map 3.1   The Punjab

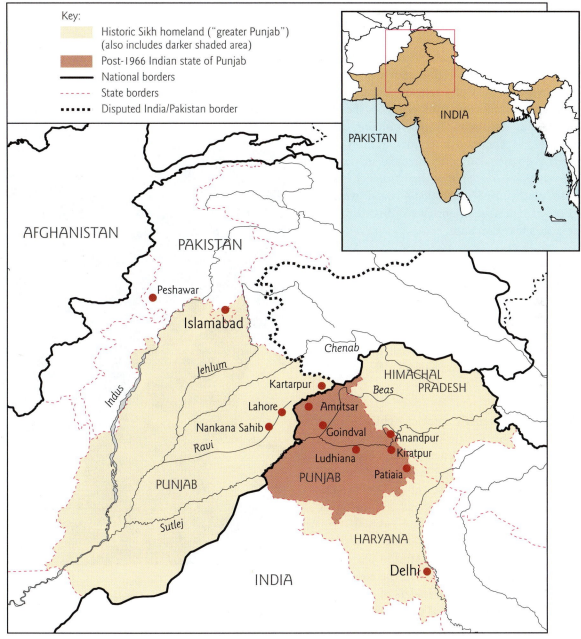

Key:

- ▢ Historic Sikh homeland ("greater Punjab") (also includes darker shaded area)
- ▢ Post-1966 Indian state of Punjab
- ▬ National borders
- ┄ State borders
- ▪▪▪ Disputed India/Pakistan border

Source: Adapted from Nesbitt 2005: 9.

he and his growing community of disciples established the first Sikh community.

Employed as a steward by a local Muslim nobleman, the young Nanak worked diligently at his job. But his mind was preoccupied with spiritual matters, and he spent long hours at the beginning and end of each day absorbed in meditation and devotional singing. Early one morning, while he was bathing in the Vein River, he disappeared without a trace. Family members gave him up for dead, but three days later he stepped out of the water and proclaimed: "There is no Hindu, there is no Muslim."

The significance of this statement becomes clear in the context of a religious culture divided between the conflicting truth claims of the Islamic and Hindu traditions. Nanak pointed the way towards the common humanity underlying the external divisions. After his three-day immersion in the waters—a metaphor of dissolution, transformation, and spiritual perfection—Nanak was ready to proclaim a new vision. One of his own hymns describes his experience:

> I was a minstrel out of work; the Lord assigned me the task of singing the Divine Word day and night. He summoned me to his Court and bestowed on me the robe of honour for singing his praises. On me he bestowed the Divine Nectar (**amrit**) in a cup, the nectar of his true and holy Name (M1, *Var Majh* 27, Adi Granth/AG 150).[1]

This hymn is intensely autobiographical, explicitly pointing out Guru Nanak's own understanding of his divine mission and marking the beginning of his ministry to preach the message of the divine Name. He was then 30 years of age, had been married for more than a decade, and was the father of two young sons, Sri Chand and Lakhmi Das. Yet he left his family behind to set out on a series of journeys to both Hindu and Muslim places of pilgrimage in India and abroad. In the course of his travels he encountered the leaders of different religious persuasions and tested the veracity of his own ideas through dialogue with them.

Foundation of the Sikh Panth

At the end of his spiritual travels, Guru Nanak purchased a parcel of land on the right bank of the Ravi River in central Punjab, where he founded the village of Kartarpur in 1519. There he lived for the rest of his life as the "spiritual guide" of a new religious community. His charismatic personality and teaching won him many disciples, who received the message of liberation through religious hymns of unique genius and notable beauty. They began to use these hymns in devotional singing (**kirtan**) as part of congregational worship. The first Sikh families who gathered around Guru Nanak at Kartarpur formed the nucleus of the Nanak-**Panth** (Path of

© Andrea Magugliani/Alamy

Dhadhis are traditional singers and musicians who specialize in martial ballads. This *dhadhi* is playing a *sarangi* outside the Darbar Sahib in Amritsar.

Nanak), the community who followed his path to liberation. In his role as what the sociologist Max Weber called an "ethical prophet," Nanak called for a decisive break with existing formulations and laid the groundwork for a new, rational model of human behaviour based on divine authority.

The authenticity and power of Guru Nanak's spiritual message derived from his direct access—through personal experience—to Divine Reality itself, which gave him a perspective from which he was able to interpret and assess the various elements of existing traditions. He conceived of his work as divinely commissioned, and he demanded the obedience of his followers as an ethical duty.

The 974 hymns of Guru Nanak that are preserved in the Adi Granth offer the most authoritative account of his teachings. Thoroughly familiar with the texts, beliefs, and practices of the existing traditions, Guru Nanak made a very clear distinction between their teachings and practices and his own. He frequently refers to contemporary Hindus, Vaishnavas, Jainas, Nath yogis, Sufis, and Muslim scholars (the ulama or "theologians"). In his *Siddh Gosti* ("Discourse with the Siddhas," AG 939–46), for instance, he critiques Nath beliefs and contrasts his own path of spirituality with theirs. In another composition he offers a critique of a ritual dance of Vaishnavas (AG 465). Defining his own path against the Hindu and Muslim conventions of the day, including rituals and pilgrimages, temples and mosques, brahmins and mullahs, Vedas and Qur'an, at the same time he recognized "true Hindus" and "true Muslims"—as opposed to false believers who continued to follow the conventional forms—and invited them to follow his own path of inner spirituality based on ethical values.

Guru Nanak rightly understood that his listeners would comprehend his message more clearly if

Document

Guru Nanak's Message to Different Audiences

Guru Nanak addressed his Muslim audience as follows:
Make mercy your mosque and devotion your prayer mat,
    Righteousness your Qur'an;
Meekness your circumcising, goodness your fasting;
    For thus the true Muslim expresses his faith.
Make good works your Ka'bah, take truth your Pir
    Compassion your creed and your prayer.
Let service to God be the beads which you tell
    And God will exalt you to glory.
    (M1, *Var Majh*, AG 140–1)

To the "twice-born" Hindus, he said:
Make compassion the cotton, contentment the thread,
    Continence the knot, and truth the twist.
This is the sacred thread of the soul,
    If you possess it, O Brahmin, then place it on me.

It does not break or become soiled with filth.
    This can neither be burnt, nor lost.
Blessed are the mortals, O Nanak,
    Who wear such a thread round their neck.
    (M1, *Var Asa*, AG 471)

Guru Nanak encountered the Nath yogis on their own terms:
Make contentment your earrings, modesty your begging-bowl and wallet,
    And meditation on the Lord your ashes.
Let the fear of death be your patched garment;
    Be chaste like a virgin; make faith in God, your staff.
Your great Yogic sect (*ai panthi*) should be universal brotherhood,
    And self-control the conquest of the world.
    (M1, *Japu* 28, AG 6)

it was expressed in the language of their own religious heritage. Thus he reached out to his Muslim audience by using Islamic concepts and used Nath terminology with the yogis. In each case, however, the message reflected Guru Nanak's own understanding of the divine truth.

Guru Nanak, as founder, was the central authority for the Kartarpur community. He prescribed the daily routine, in which communal devotions—Nanak's Japji ("Honoured Recitation") was recited in the early hours of the morning, and So Dar ("That Door") and Arti ("Adoration") were sung in the evening—were balanced with agricultural work for sustenance. He defined the ideal person as a **Gurmukh** ("one oriented towards the Guru") who practised the threefold discipline of *nam dan ishnan*, "the divine Name, charity and purity" (AG 942). Corresponding to the cognitive, the communal, and the personal aspects of the evolving Sikh identity, these three features—*nam* (relation to the Divine), *dan* (relation to the society), and *ishnan* (relation to self)—established

a balance between the development of the individual and the society. For Guru Nanak, the true spiritual life required that "one should live on what one has earned through hard work and share with others the fruit of one's exertion" (AG 1245). Service, self-respect, truthful living, humility, sweetness of the spoken word, and taking no more than one's rightful share were among the virtues most highly prized in the pursuit of liberation.

Guru Nanak's spiritual message found expression at Kartarpur through three key institutions: the **sangat** ("holy fellowship") in which all felt that they belonged to one large spiritual fraternity; the *dharamsala*, the original form of the Sikh place of worship; and the **langar**, the communal meal that is served to everyone attending the **gurdwara** (the Sikh place of worship) and is prepared as a community service by members of the *sangat*. As established by Guru Nanak, the *langar* tradition requires people of all castes and conditions to sit side-by-side in status-free rows—female next to male,

Document

Guru Nanak on Women

Guru Nanak spoke out clearly against the inferior position assigned to women in Punjabi society, as the following verse from his celebrated Asa Ki Var *("Ballad in the Asa mode") shows:*

From women born, shaped in the womb,
To woman betrothed and wed;
We are bound to women by ties of affection,
On women man's future depends.
If one woman dies he seeks another;
With a woman he orders his life.
Why then should one speak evil of women,
They who give birth to kings?
Women also are born from women;
None takes birth except from a woman.

Only the True One [Akal Purakh/God], Nanak [Guru Nanak often addresses himself],
needs no help from a woman.
Blessed are they, both men and women,
Who endlessly praise their Lord.
Blessed are they in the True One's court,
There shall their faces shine.
(M1, **Var Asa**, AG 473; McLeod 1997: 241–2)

Nanak's egalitarian ideas about women set him far apart from the medieval poet-saints of North India, particularly Kabir, who described woman as "a black cobra," "the pit of hell," and "the refuse of the world" (Kabir Granthavali: 30.2, 30.16, and 30.20).

Langar at a gurdwara in Siliguri, India.

© Rupak De Chowdhuri/Reuters/Corbis

socially high next to socially low, ritually pure next to ritually impure—and share the same food. This was the first practical expression of Guru Nanak's spiritual mission to reform society. The institution of the *langar* promoted egalitarianism, community service, unity, and belonging while striking down a major aspect of the caste system. In so doing it marked a major step in the process of defining a distinctive Sikh identity.

The Lineage of Gurus

Finally, Guru Nanak created the institution of the Guru, who became the central authority in community life. Before his death in 1539, he designated his disciple Lehna as his successor by renaming him Angad, meaning my "own limb." Thus a lineage was established that would continue from the appointment of Guru Angad (1504–52) to the death

Sites

Patna, Bihar

Guru Gobind Singh was born in Patna, the capital city of Bihar state. This is the site of the Takhat Sri Patna Sahib, one of the most important of the five seats of authority in the Sikh world.

of Guru Gobind Singh (1666–1708), the tenth and the last human Guru of the Sikhs.

The Ten Gurus

Guru Nanak's decision regarding the succession was the most significant step in the development of the early Sikh Panth, for he not only promoted Angad to the status of "Guru" within his own lifetime, but bowed before his own successor, becoming a disciple himself. In this act of humility, Guru Nanak clearly asserted both the primacy of the message over the messenger and the objective independence of the power behind divine revelation. In this way he gave the office of Guru charismatic authority and established that the Guru is "one," whatever form the occupant of the office may take.

Guru Angad consolidated the nascent Sikh Panth in the face of a challenge mounted by Guru Nanak's eldest son, Sri Chand, the founder of the ascetic Udasi sect. The 62 *shaloks* ("couplets" or "stanzas") composed by Guru Angad throw light on the historical situation of the Panth during his period and mark the doctrinal boundaries of the Sikh faith in strict conformity with Guru Nanak's message. He established a new Sikh centre at Khadur, where his wife Khivi ran the community kitchen (also called the *langar*) and added a dessert of rice boiled in milk to the standard vegetarian meal. This addition was a sign of the Sikhs' ability to attract contributions substantial enough to offer generous meals to one and all.

Guru Angad refined the **Gurmukhi** ("from the Guru's mouth") script in which the Guru's hymns were recorded. The original Gurmukhi script was a systematization of the business shorthand that Guru Nanak used to write the Punjabi language as a young man. Apparently the early Gurus had no objection to the idea of an overlap between everyday life and the life of the spirit. Thus the use of the Gurmukhi script signals the early Sikhs' emphatic rejection of the hegemonic authority attributed to Sanskrit, Arabic, and Persian in the scholarly circles of the period. At the same time, the use of Gurmukhi reinforced the distinct identity of the Sikhs.

In fact, language has been the single most important factor in the preservation of the Sikh cultural heritage. For Punjabis, the idea that spiritual truth could be inscribed in their own native language created a sense of empowerment that had been conspicuously absent.

The third Guru, Amar Das (1479–1574), introduced a variety of institutional innovations that helped to reinforce the cohesion and unity of the ever-growing Sikh Panth. In addition to founding the town of Goindval (southeast of Amritsar on the river Beas), he established two annual festivals (Divali and Baisakhi) that provided regular opportunities for the growing community to get together and meet the Guru; introduced a system of 22 **manjis** ("cots" or seats of authority) as bases for missionaries seeking to attract new converts, and oversaw the preparation of the Goindval **pothis** ("volumes"): the initial collection of the compositions of the first three Gurus and some of the medieval poet-saints.

These early steps towards the establishment of a more comprehensive administrative system speak of the rapidity with which Guru Nanak's message was gaining ground, and also of the practical wisdom of those charged with sustaining the movement. The second- and third-generation disciples had to find ways to convey that message without the benefit of direct emotional experience. In every religious tradition, translation into a standard written form and objectification in rituals and ceremonies become imperative as time removes new converts further and further from the lives of the founder and the original disciples.

As the geographical base of the Panth expanded, missionaries needed copies of the **bani** ("divine Word") that they could carry with them, and growing numbers of Sikhs needed a common frame of reference for communal worship. Thus Guru Amar Das had scribes make copies of the hymns for distribution.

As important as these innovations were, the reforms that Guru Amar Das instituted regarding women were perhaps even more significant. He abolished not only the wearing of the veil but the practice of **sati**, and permitted widows to remarry.

Sites

Amritsar, Punjab

The holiest of all places for Sikhs, Amritsar is the site of the Darbar Sahib (the Golden Temple) and was named for the "pool of nectar" that surrounds the shrine. Facing the Darbar Sahib and connected to it by a causeway is the Akal Takhat ("Throne of the Timeless Being"), the most important of the five seats of authority within the Sikh world.

He also appointed women as missionaries (roughly half of the original 22 *manjis* were held by women) and gave all Sikh women equal rights with men to conduct prayers and other ceremonies in the congregational setting.

The fourth Guru, Ram Das (1534–81), established a town called Ramdaspur in 1577 and ordered the construction of a large bathing pool there. (After the pool was completed, the town was renamed Amritsar, "nectar of immortality.") The new building projects required considerable financial and logistical mobilization for which the appointment of "deputies" (*masands*) became necessary to deal with increasingly complex administrative demands. The fact that the Panth was equal to such an endeavour is an indication of the support that Guru Nanak's message had attracted in just a few decades.

In addition, Guru Ram Das contributed 679 new hymns to the collection that made up the Sikh scripture, and expanded the number of melodies (*ragas*) specified for their singing from 19 to 30. Together, the musicality and the emotional appeal of his hymns had a tremendous impact on his audience. The liturgical requirement not only to recite but to sing the sacred Word became part of the very definition of Sikhism, and contributed significantly to Sikhs' self-image as a distinct and cohesive community. Indeed, the process of distinguishing between "us" and "them" was effectively completed during the period of Guru Ram Das, who proclaimed the "loyal Sikhs of the Gurus (*gursikhs*)" to be spiritually greater than the "Bhagats, Sants, and Sadhs" (AG 649).

The fifth Guru, Arjan (1563–1606), inherited a vibrant religious community. His 25 years as Guru were marked by several far-reaching institutional developments. First, he built the Darbar Sahib ("Divine Court," also known as Harimandir Sahib and, later, as the "Golden Temple") in the sacred pool of Amritsar, a shining monument that remains the central symbol of the Sikh faith to this day. Its foundation was laid in January 1589 and the construction was completed in a decade. Second, he took it on himself to organize the scriptural corpus he had inherited into the Adi Granth, the definitive statement of Sikhism's unique spiritual stance. Third, by the end of the sixteenth century the Sikh Panth had developed a strong sense of independent identity: as Guru Arjan asserted, "We are neither Hindu nor Musalman" (AG 1136).

By the mid-seventeenth century, the author of a Persian study of different religious systems (*Dabistan-i-Mazahib*) was able to comment that "there were not many cities in the inhabited countries where some Sikhs were not to be found." Indeed, the growth of Sikhism was so significant that it attracted the unfavourable attention of the Mughal authorities. The fact that, ethnically, the majority of Sikhs were Jats—agriculturalists with distinctly martial cultural traditions—played a significant role in this development.

Rise of Sikh–Mughal Conflict

To a large extent, the peaceful growth of the Sikh Panth through the sixteenth century can be

© Raghu Rai/Magnum Photos

Bathing in the Pool of Nectar.

attributed to the liberal policy of Emperor Akbar (r. 1556–1605). Within eight months of Akbar's death, however, Guru Arjan himself was dead, executed at Lahore by order of the new emperor, Jahangir (r. 1605–28). This "first martyrdom" was a turning point in Sikh history, pushing the community in the direction of self-consciousness, separatism, and militancy. In short, Guru Arjan's martyrdom became the decisive factor in the crystallization of the Sikh Panth.

The sixth Guru, Hargobind (1595–1644), signalled this new direction when, at his investiture, he donned two swords, one symbolizing spiritual (**piri**) and the other temporal (**miri**) authority. One symbol of this new temporal authority was Hargobind's construction, in 1609, of the Akal Takhat ("Throne of the Timeless Being") facing the Darbar Sahib, to resolve internal disputes within the community. Under his direct leadership the Sikh

Panth took up arms to defend itself against Mughal hostility. The new emphasis on worldly affairs did not mean that the Sikhs had abandoned their spiritual base. Rather, as a Sikh theologian of the period, Bhai Gurdas, explained, in adopting a martial orientation the Guru was simply "hedging the orchard of the Sikh faith with the hardy and thorny *kikar* tree." After four skirmishes with Mughal troops, Guru Hargobind withdrew from Amritsar to the Shivalik hills—beyond the jurisdiction of the Mughal state—and Kiratpur became the new centre of the mainline Sikh tradition.

Relations with the Mughal authorities eased under the seventh and eighth Gurus, Har Rai (1630–61) and Harkrishan (1655–64), although the Gurus held court to adjudicate on temporal issues within the Panth and kept a regular force of Sikh horsemen. But the increasing strength of the Sikh movement during the period of the ninth Guru,

Tegh Bahadur (1621–75), once again attracted Mughal attention in the 1670s. Guru Tegh Bahadur encouraged his followers to be fearless in their pursuit of a just society: "He who holds none in fear, nor is afraid of anyone, is acknowledged as a man of true wisdom" (AG 1427). In so doing, he posed a direct challenge to Emperor Aurangzeb (r. 1658–1707), who had imposed Islamic laws and taxes, and ordered the replacement of Hindu temples with mosques. Guru Tegh Bahadur was summoned to Delhi, and when he refused to embrace Islam he was publicly executed on 11 November 1675. If the martyrdom of Guru Arjan had helped to bring the Sikh Panth together, this second martyrdom helped to make human rights and freedom of conscience central to its identity.

The Khalsa

Tradition holds that the Sikhs who were present at Guru Tegh Bahadur's execution concealed their identity for fear of meeting a similar fate. For this reason the tenth Guru, Gobind Singh, resolved to impose on his followers an outward form that would make them instantly recognizable. He restructured the Panth and created the **Khalsa** ("pure"), an order of loyal Sikhs bound by a common identity and discipline (**rahit**). On **Baisakhi** Day 1699 at Anandpur, Guru Gobind Singh called for volunteers and initiated as the nucleus of the new order the "Cherished Five" (**Panj Piare**) who were the first to respond. To this day, the Khalsa initiation ceremony follows the pattern established in 1699: initiates drink sweet "nectar" (*amrit*) that has been stirred with a two-edged sword and sanctified by the recitation of five liturgical prayers.

The Khalsa

Three aspects of the institution created by Guru Gobind Singh on Baisakhi Day 1699 are particularly significant. First, it was understood that, in undergoing the *amrit* ceremony, the Khalsa initiates were "reborn" in the house of the Guru. From that day forward, Guru Gobind Singh would be their spiritual father and his wife, Sahib Kaur, their spiritual mother. As part of their new identity, male members of the Khalsa were given the new surname *Singh* ("lion") and female initiates were given the surname *Kaur* ("princess"). Their birthplace became Kesgarh Sahib (the gurdwara that commemorates the founding of the Khalsa) and their home Anandpur Sahib (the town where Kesgarh Sahib is situated). The new collective identity conferred on the Khalsa initiates gave them a powerful sense of belonging.

Second, the Guru himself received the nectar of the double-edged sword from the hands of the Cherished Five, becoming part of the Khalsa Panth, subject to its collective will. In so doing, he symbolically transferred his spiritual authority to the Cherished Five, paving the way for the termination of the office he occupied as a human Guru. At the same time he abolished the institution of *masands* ("deputies"), which was becoming increasingly disruptive; several of them had refused to forward the offerings they had collected to the Guru, and were trying to cultivate their own factions within

Sites

Anandpur, Punjab

The birthplace of the Khalsa; the Takhat Sri Kesgarh Sahib stands on the spot where Guru Gobind Singh is said to have created the "Cherished Five" (*Panj Piare*) in 1699. This is one of the five important seats of authority within the Sikh Panth.

the Sikh Panth. In addition, Guru Gobind Singh removed the threat posed by the competing seats of authority when he declared that the Khalsa should have no dealings with the followers of Guru Arjan's elder brother Prithi Chand (the Minas), Dhir Mal (Guru Har Rai's elder brother, who established his seat at Kartarpur, Jalandhar) and Ram Rai (Guru Harkrishan's elder brother, who established his seat at Dehra Dun). The severing of relations with these five dissident groups (*panj mel*) led to greater awareness of boundaries and a heightened consciousness of identity.

Finally, it was at the inauguration of the Khalsa that Guru Gobind Singh delivered the nucleus of what would become the order's *Rahit* ("Code of Conduct"). To ensure that Khalsa members would never seek to conceal their identity as Sikhs, he made five physical symbols mandatory:

1. *Kes*, unshorn hair, symbolizing spirituality and saintliness;
2. *Kangha*, a wooden comb, signifying order and discipline in life;
3. *Kirpan*, a miniature sword, symbolizing divine grace, dignity, and courage;
4. *Kara*, a steel "wrist-ring," signifying responsibility and allegiance to the Guru; and
5. *Kachh*, a pair of short breeches, symbolizing moral restraint.

Known (from their Punjabi names) as the **Five Ks** (*panj kakke*), these outward symbols of the divine Word imply a direct correlation between *bani* ("divine utterance") and **bana** ("Khalsa dress").

Every morning, in putting on the various items of dress (including the turban, in the case of male Sikhs) while reciting prayers, Khalsa Sikhs dress themselves in the word of God; their minds are purified and inspired, and their bodies are girded to do battle with the day's temptations.

In addition to cutting the hair, three other sins are specifically prohibited: using tobacco (this injunction was later expanded to include all intoxicants); committing adultery; and eating meat that has not come from an animal killed with a single blow.

The launch of the Khalsa was the culmination of the formative period in the development of Sikhism. But it was only one in a series of major reforms instituted by Guru Gobind Singh. After adding a collection of the works of his father, Guru Tegh Bahadur, to the Adi Granth, he closed the Sikh canon. And before he passed away in 1708, he brought to an end the succession of human Gurus. Thereafter, the authority of the Guru would be invested not in an individual but in the scripture (Guru-Granth) and the corporate community (Guru-Panth). Together, Guru-Granth and Guru-Panth would continue the process of consolidating the Sikh tradition through the eighteenth century.

⊛ Crystallization

The term "crystallization" comes from Wilfred Cantwell Smith, who identified a number of standard stages in the development of a religious tradition. The process begins with the vision of a mystic whose preaching attracts followers and continues with the organization of a community, the positing

Sites

Talwandi Sabo, Punjab

Guru Gobind Singh stayed at Talwandi Sabo, Punjab for several months c. 1705 where he prepared the final Damdama version of the Adi Granth. This is also the site of the Takhat Sri Damdama Sahib, one of the five most important seats of authority in Sikhism.

of an intellectual ideal of that community, and the development of its institutions. Smith maintains that in the case of Sikhism the last two stages were reached under the fifth Guru, Arjan, and the tenth, Gobind Singh. In his view, the concept "Sikhism" must be understood as the "total complex of Sikh religious practices and rites, scriptures and doctrines, history and institutions" as they developed over a period of two centuries. Of course crystallization is an ongoing process, one that continues as the community is obliged to respond to changing conditions.

Document

From the Sacred Writings of the Sikhs

Guru Nanak exalts the divine Name:

If in this life I should live to eternity, nourished by nothing save air;

If I should dwell in the darkest of dungeons, sense never resting in sleep;

Yet must your glory transcend all my striving; no words can encompass the Name.

> (*Refrain*) He who is truly the Spirit Eternal, immanent, blissful serene;
>
> Only by grace can we learn of our Master, only by grace can we tell.

If I were slain and my body dismembered, pressed in a hand-mill and ground;

If I were burnt in a fire all-consuming, mingled with ashes and dust;

Yet must your glory transcend all my striving, no words can encompass the Name.

If as a bird I could soar to the heavens, a hundred such realms in my reach;

If I could change so that none might perceive me and live without food, without drink;

Yet must your glory transcend all my striving; no words can encompass the Name.

If I could read with the eye of intelligence paper of infinite weight;

If I could with the winds everlasting, pens dipped in oceans of ink;

Yet must your glory transcend all my striving; no words can encompass the Name.

(M1, *Siri Ragu* 2, AG 14–15; McLeod 1984: 41)

The third Guru, Amar Das, addresses the Brahmins' pride in the traditional learning that they had monopolized:

He who is truly a dutiful Brahmin will cast off his burden of human desire,

Each day performing his God-given duty, each day repeating God's Name.

To such as submit God imparts divine learning, and those who obey him live virtuous lives.

He who is truly a dutiful Brahmin wins honour when summoned to God.

(M3, *Malar* 10, AG 1261; McLeod 1984: 47)

The tenth Guru, Gobind Singh, praises the sword. This passage, often repeated at Sikh functions, has now come to serve as the national anthem of the Khalsa:

Reverently I salute the Sword with affection and devotion.

Grant, I pray, your divine assistance that this book may be brought to completion.

Thee I invoke, All-conquering Sword, Destroyer of evil, Ornament of the brave.

Powerful your arm and radiant your glory, your splendour as dazzling as the brightness of the sun.

Joy of the devout and Scourge of the wicked, Vanquisher of sin, I seek your protection.

Hail to the world's Creator and Sustainer, my invincible Protector of the Sword!

(*Bachitar Natak*, Dasam Granth, 39; McLeod 1984: 58)

The Sacred Scriptures

The Adi Granth is the primary scripture of the Sikhs. It includes the hymns of the first five Gurus and the ninth, plus material by four bards (Satta, Balvand, Sundar, and Mardana), 11 Bhatts ("court poets" who composed and recited panegyrics in praise of the Gurus), and 15 Bhagats ("devotees" of the Sant, Sufi, and Bhakti traditions, including the medieval poets Kabir, Namdev, Ravidas, and Shaikh Farid)—a total of 36 contributors ranging historically from the twelfth century to the seventeenth. The standard version of this collection contains a total of 1,430 pages, and every copy is identical in terms of the material printed on each page.

The text of the Adi Granth is divided into three major sections. The introductory section includes three liturgical prayers. The middle section, which contains the bulk of the material, is divided into 31 major *ragas*, or musical patterns. The final section includes an epilogue consisting of miscellaneous works.

The second sacred collection, the **Dasam Granth**, dates from the 1690s and is attributed to the tenth Guru, Gobind Singh. During the eighteenth century subsequent collections added Guru Gobind Singh's *Zafarnama* ("Letter of Victory"; see p. 125) and fixed the sequence of composition. However, its final form was not approved until the nineteenth century. It contains four major types of compositions: devotional texts, autobiographical works, miscellaneous writings, and a collection of mythical narratives and popular anecdotes.

The third category of sacred literature consists of works by Bhai ("Brother") Gurdas (c. 1558–1637) and Bhai Nand Lal Goya (1633–1715). Along with the sacred compositions of the Gurus, their works are approved in the official manual of the *Sikh Rahit Maryada* ("Code of Conduct") for singing in the gurdwara.

The last category of Sikh literature is made up of three distinct genres. The *janam-sakhis* ("birth narratives") are hagiographical accounts of Guru Nanak's life dating from the seventeenth century but based on earlier oral traditions. The *rahit-namas* ("manuals of code of conduct") provide rare insight into the evolution of the Khalsa code in the course of the eighteenth and nineteenth centuries. And the *gur-bilas* ("splendour of the Guru") literature of the eighteenth and nineteenth centuries praises the mighty deeds of the two great warrior Gurus, Hargobind and Gobind Singh, in particular.

Finally, it is important to emphasize that the Adi Granth is set apart from other Sikh texts not only by the richness and semantic density of its content, but because it is inextricably embedded in daily life. For Sikhs, the scripture is not merely to be read, or even to be understood, but to be appropriated and interiorized, to be practised and lived.

Sikh Doctrine

The primary source of Sikh doctrine is the Adi Granth. Its first words are Guru Nanak's invocation of One God (*1-Oankar*) in the **Mul Mantar** ("Seed Formula"). Sikh tradition maintains that one cannot understand the meanings of any parts of the Sikh scripture without testing them on the touchstone of the Mul Mantar. At the same time, one cannot understand the Mul Mantar without insightful understanding of the Adi Granth as a whole. This succinct expression of the nature of the Ultimate Reality is the fundamental statement of Sikh belief:

> There is One ("1") Supreme Being, the Eternal Reality, the Creator, without fear and devoid of enmity, immortal, never incarnated, self-existent, known by grace through the Guru. The Eternal One, from the beginning, through all time, present now, the Everlasting Reality (AG 1).

By beginning with "One" (the original Punjabi text uses the numeral rather than the word), Guru Nanak emphasizes the singularity of the divine; as he put it in a later hymn, the Supreme Being has "no relatives, no mother, no father, no wife, no son, no rival who may become a potential contender" (AG 597). At the same time he draws attention to the unity of Akal Purakh, the Eternal One, the source as well as the goal of all that exists. The Mul Mantar illuminates the way Sikh doctrine understands a Divine Reality that is at once transcendent and immanent, a personal God of grace for his humblest devotee. The vital expression of the One is through the many, through the infinite plurality of creation. This understanding of the One distinguishes the Sikh interpretation of "monotheism" from its interpretation in the Abrahamic traditions.

The Sikh Gurus were fiercely opposed to any anthropomorphic conception of the divine—that is, any notion of God that imagines him in the form (Greek *morphe*, shape) of a human being (*anthropos*, man). Nevertheless, Akal Purakh is the creator and sustainer of the universe who watches over it as lovingly as any parent. Like a father, he runs the world with justice, destroys evil, and supports good, and like a mother she is the source of love and grace, and responds to the devotion of her humblest followers. Simultaneously "Father, Mother, Friend, and Brother" (AG 268), God is without gender.

In general, then, Sikh tradition worships a transcendent (*nirguna*, "without attributes"), non-incarnate, universal God. Yet this God is also described as immanent (*saguna*, "with attributes"), and is partly embodied in the divine Name (*nam*) as well as the collective Words (*bani*) and persons of the Gurus. Only through personal experience can he be truly known.

Creation

According to Guru Nanak's cosmology hymn, the universe was brought into being by the divine order, will, or command (**hukam**). This *hukam* is an all-embracing principle, the sum total of all divinely instituted laws; and it is a revelation of the nature of God:

> For endless eons, there was only darkness.
> Nothing except the divine order existed.
> No day or night, no moon or sun.
> The Creator alone was absorbed in a primal state of contemplation . . .

When the Creator so willed, creation came into being . . .
The Un-manifest One revealed itself in the Creation (AG 1035–6).

Elsewhere Guru Nanak describes how "From the True One came air and from air came water; from water he created the three worlds [sky, earth, and netherworld] and infused in every heart his own light" (AG 19). As the creation of Akal Purakh, the physical universe is real but subject to constant change. In Sikh cosmology, the world is divinely inspired, the place that provides human beings with the opportunity to perform their duty and achieve union with Akal Purakh. Since "all of us carry the fruits of our deeds," the actions we take during our earthly existence are important (AG 4).

The Value of Human Life

A human being is a microcosm (*pind*) of the macrocosm (*brahmand*) in the Sikh worldview. For Guru Nanak, human life is worth a "diamond," but its value drops to a "farthing" if we do not realize our true spiritual nature (AG 156). In his *Suhi* hymn, he proclaims:

> One is blessed with the rarest opportunity of the human birth through the grace of the Guru. One's mind and body become dyed deep red (with the love of the divine Name) if one is able to win the approval of the True Guru (AG 751).

For Guru Arjan, human life is the most delightful experience possible (AG 966), and the human being is the epitome of Creation: "All other creation is subject to you, O man/woman! You reign supreme on this earth" (AG 374). Like Guru Nanak, he emphasizes the opportunity that human life provides to remember the divine Name and ultimately to join with Akal Purakh: "Precious this life you receive as a human, with it the chance to find the Lord" (AG 15). But those who seek the divine beloved while participating in the delights of the world are rare.

Karam, Sansar, and Divine Grace

The notions of **karam** (karma, "actions," the principle of moral cause and effect) and **sansar** (samsara, "reincarnation") are fundamental to all religious traditions originating in India. In other Indian religions, karma is popularly understood as an inexorable, impersonal law. In Sikh doctrine, however, karam is not inexorable, not absolute. Rather, it is subject to the "divine order" (hukam), a higher, all-embracing principle that is the sum total of all the divinely instituted laws in the cosmos. For Sikhs, karam is not an impersonal law, but a principle that can be overridden in the name of justice by Akal Purakh's omnipotent grace. In fact, divine grace always takes precedence over the law of karam in the Sikh teachings, and can even break the chain of adverse karam.

Divine Revelation

Guru Nanak used three key terms to describe the nature of divine revelation in its totality: nam ("divine Name"), **shabad** ("divine Word"), and guru ("divine Preceptor"). Nam refers to the divine presence that is manifest everywhere around and within us, though most people fail to perceive it because of the self-centred desire for personal gratification. This self-centredness (**haumai**, meaning "I, I" or "me, mine") separates us from Akal Purakh, and thus we continue to suffer within the cycle of rebirth (sansar). Akal Purakh, however, takes pity on human suffering. Thus he reveals himself through the Guru by uttering the shabad ("divine Word") that will communicate a sufficient understanding of the nam ("divine Name") to those who are able to "hear" it. The shabad is the utterance that, once heard, awakens the hearer to the reality of the divine Name, immanent in all that lies around and within.

Remembering the Divine Name

Traditionally, haumai is the source of five evil impulses: lust, anger, covetousness, attachment to worldly things, and pride. Under its influence humans become "self-willed" (manmukh), so attached to worldly pleasures that they forget the divine Name and waste their entire lives in evil and suffering. To achieve spiritual liberation within one's lifetime it is necessary to transcend the influence of haumai by adopting the strictly interior discipline of **nam-simaran** or "remembering the divine Name."

There are three levels to this discipline, ranging from the repetition of a sacred word, usually Vahiguru ("Praise to the Eternal Guru"), through the devotional singing of hymns with the congregation, to sophisticated meditation on the nature of Akal Purakh. The first and the third levels are undertaken in private, while the second involves public, communal activity. The main purpose of nam-simaran is to bring practitioners into harmony with the divine order (hukam). Ever-growing wonder in spiritual life ultimately leads to a condition of blissful "equanimity" (sahaj), when the spirit ascends to the "realm of Truth": the fifth and last stage, in which the soul finds mystical union with Akal Purakh.

The primacy of divine grace over personal effort is fundamental to Guru Nanak's theology. Yet there is neither fatalism nor passive acceptance in this view of life. Rather, personal effort in the form of good actions is seen as an integral part of spiritual discipline: "With your own hands carve out your own destiny" (AG 474). By teaching his followers to see their own "free" will as part of Akal Purakh's will, Guru Nanak encouraged them to create their own destinies. The necessity of balance between meditative worship and righteous life in the world is summed up in the following triple commandment: earn your living through honest labour, adore the divine Name, and share the fruits of your labour with others.

Four Notions of Guruship

In Indic traditions the guru is a human teacher who communicates divine knowledge and guides disciples along the path to liberation. In Sikhism, however, the term "guru" has evolved over time to encompass four types of spiritual authority: the eternal Guru, the personal Guru, Guru-Granth, and Guru-Panth.

God as Guru

Guru Nanak uses the term "Guru" in three basic senses: to refer to Akal Purakh himself, to the voice of Akal Purakh, and to the Word, the Truth of Akal Purakh. To experience the eternal Guru is to experience divine guidance. Guru Nanak himself acknowledges Akal Purakh as his Guru: "He who is the infinite, supreme God is the Guru whom Nanak has met" (AG 599). In Sikh usage, therefore, the Guru is the voice of Akal Purakh, mystically uttered within the human heart, mind, and soul (**man**).

Akal Purakh is often characterized as *Nirankar*, "the One without Form." Guru Arjan states explicitly that "The True Guru is *Niranjan* [the One who is wholly apart from all that is darkness and untruth—hence the "One who is himself Truth," God]. Do not believe that he is in the form of a human being" (AG 895).

Sikhs evoke the absolute knowledge and power of the divine Name by chanting "*Vahiguru! Vahiguru!*" ("Hail the Guru"). The sound vibrations of this phrase are believed to be supremely powerful.

In addition, the Sikh scripture often uses Hindu and Muslim names for God. Hindu (particularly Vaishnava) names such as Ram, Hari, Govind, Mukand, Madhav, Murari, Sarangpani, Parmeshvar, and Jagdish, and Muslim names such as Allah, Khuda, Rahim, Karim, and Sahib, express different aspects of Akal Purakh, as Guru Nanak recognized (AG 1168). And Guru Arjan provided a comprehensive list of the names from various contemporary religious traditions associated with different attributes of God (AG 1083). These names acquire meaning and significance in the Sikh context, however, only when they are viewed through the lens of the Mul Mantar. Most important, the "truth of the Name" (*satinamu*) is a reality that lies beyond any name.

The Teacher as Guru

The personal Guru functions as the channel through which the voice of Akal Purakh becomes audible. Nanak became the embodiment of the eternal Guru only when he received the divine Word and conveyed it to his disciples. The same spirit manifested itself in his successors. In fact, Guru Nanak bypassed the claims of his own son, Sri Chand, who was disqualified by his ascetic ideals, in favour of a more worthy disciple. Guru Angad followed the example of his Master when he chose his elderly disciple Amar Das over his own sons. The third Guru, however, designated as his successor his son-in-law, Ram Das. The latter's youngest son, Arjan, was the direct ancestor of all the later Gurus. Nevertheless, in each case the succession went to the most suitable candidate, not automatically from father to eldest son.

In Sikh doctrine, a theory of spiritual succession known as "the unity of the office of the Guru" meant that there was no difference between the founder and the successors: all represented one and the same light, just as a single flame ignites a series of torches. The same principle can be seen in the Adi Granth, where all the Gurus sign their compositions "Nanak" and each is identified by the code word *Mahala* ("King") with an appropriate number. Thus the compositions labelled "Mahala 1" (M 1) are by Guru Nanak, while those labelled M 2, 3, 4, 5, and 9 are by Guru Angad, Guru Amar Das, Guru Ram Das, Guru Arjan, and Guru Tegh Bahadur, respectively (the sixth, seventh, and eighth Gurus did not contribute any hymns to the corpus).

The Scripture as Guru

Sikhs normally refer to the Adi Granth as the Guru Granth Sahib ("Honourable Scripture Guru"). In so doing, they acknowledge their faith in the scripture as the successor to Guru Gobind Singh, with the same status, authority, and functions, in terms both of personal piety and of collective identity, as any of the ten personal Gurus. The Adi Granth has become the perennial source of divine guidance for Sikhs, and it is treated with the most profound respect.

The Adi Granth is more authoritative than the secondary Sikh scripture, the Dasam Granth, which contains the works attributed to the tenth (*dasam*) Guru, Gobind Singh. It is also the authoritative basis of the most important Sikh doctrines, rituals, and social and ethical positions. Simply to see the Guru Granth Sahib, or to hear a sentence read aloud from it, makes Sikhs feel they are in the presence of something sacred.

The Community as Guru

The phrase "Guru-Panth" is employed in two senses: one, "the Panth of the Guru," refers to the Sikh community; the other, "the Panth as the Guru," refers to the Guru-Panth doctrine, which developed from the earlier idea that the Guru is mystically present in the congregation. At the inauguration of the Khalsa in 1699, Guru Gobind Singh symbolically transferred his authority to the "Cherished Five" when he received initiation from their hands. Sainapati, the near-contemporary author of *Gur*

Sobha (1711 CE), recorded that Guru Gobind Singh designated the Khalsa as the collective embodiment of his divine mandate:

> Upon the Khalsa which I have created I shall bestow the succession. The Khalsa is my physical form and I am one with the Khalsa. To all eternity I am manifest in the Khalsa. Those whose hearts are purged of falsehood will be known as the true Khalsa; and the Khalsa, freed from error and illusion, will be my true Guru.

As the elite group within the Panth, the Khalsa has always claimed to speak authoritatively on behalf of the whole, although at times non-Khalsa Sikhs have interpreted the doctrine of Guru-Panth as conferring authority on the broader community. In

© Sanjeev Gupta/epa/Corbis

The *Panj Piare* (Cherished Five) take part in a procession to celebrate the 347th birth anniversary of Guru Gobind Singh, in Bhopal, India, 16 January 2013.

practice, consensus is achieved by following democratic traditions.

Sikh Ethics

The Adi Granth opens with a composition of Guru Nanak's known as the *Japji*, in which a fundamental question is raised: "How is Truth to be attained, how the veil of falsehood torn aside?" The Guru answers his own question: "Nanak, thus it is written: Submit to the divine Order (*hukam*), walk in its way" (AG 1). In other words, Truth is obtained not by intellectual effort or cunning, but by personal commitment alone. To know Truth one must live it. The seeker of the divine Truth must live an ethical life. In this context Guru Nanak explicitly says: "Truth is the highest virtue, but higher still is truthful living" (AG 62). Indeed, truthful conduct is at the heart of Guru Nanak's message. Cultivating virtues such as wisdom, contentment, justice, humility, truthfulness, temperance, love, forgiveness, charity, purity, and fear (in the sense of "reverence") of Akal Purakh not only enriches personal life but also promotes socially responsible living, hard work, and sharing. In contrast to the Hindu tradition, in which holy men live by begging alms, Sikhism rejects both begging and withdrawal from social participation.

Service

The key to a righteous life is to render service (*seva*) to others. Such service must be voluntary and undertaken without any desire for self-glorification. Nor should the one who gives aid sit in judgment on those who receive it. The Sikh Prayer (*Ardas*) emphasizes the importance of "seeing but not judging," urging the faithful to reflect on the merit of those "who magnanimously pardoned the faults of others." The ideals are social equality and human brotherhood. Therefore any kind of discrimination based on caste or gender is expressly rejected. The Gurus also emphasized the importance of optimism in the face of adversity, and preferred moderate living and disciplined worldliness to asceticism and self-mortification.

Justice

Guru Nanak held justice to be the primary duty of the ruler and the administrator. Thus he severely condemned the contemporary Muslim jurists (*qazi*) who were believed to take bribes and have no concern for truth. "To deprive others of their rights must be avoided as scrupulously as Muslims avoid the pork and the Hindus consider beef as a taboo" (AG 141). In short, Guru Nanak regarded the violation of human rights as a serious moral offence.

The Sikh view of justice is based on two principles: first, respect for the rights of others; second, the non-exploitation of others. To treat everyone's right as sacred is a necessary constituent of justice. Those who are truly just will not exploit others even if they have the means and opportunity to do so.

Guru Gobind Singh taught that, in the pursuit of justice, peaceful negotiation must be tried. Only when all such efforts have failed does it become legitimate to draw the sword in defence of righteousness. A famous verse from the *Zafarnama* ("Letter of Victory")—a long poem addressed to Emperor Aurangzeb after the latter, instead of negotiating, had sent his forces against the Sikhs—makes this point explicitly: "When all other methods have been explored and all other means have been tried, then may the sword be drawn from the scabbard, then may the sword be used" (verse 22). The use of force is allowed in Sikh doctrine, but only in defence of justice and then only as a last resort. Moreover, in the face of tyranny no sacrifice is too great: "It does not matter if my four sons have been killed; the Khalsa is still there at my back" (verse 78). For the Sikhs of the Khalsa, the quest for justice is the primary ethical duty.

Oneness of Humankind and Religion

Sikhism is dedicated to the defence of human rights and resistance against injustice. It strives to eliminate poverty and to offer voluntary help to the less privileged. It is committed to the ideal of universal brotherhood, with an altruistic concern for humanity as a whole. In a celebrated passage from the *Akal*

Ustat ("Praise of the Immortal One"), Guru Gobind Singh declares that "humankind is one, and all people belong to a single humanity" (verse 85). Here it is important to underline the Guru's role as a conciliator who tried to persuade the Mughals to walk the ways of peace. Even though he had to spend the greater part of his life fighting battles forced on him by Hindu hill rajas and Mughal authorities, a longing for peace and fellowship may be seen in a passage from the *Akal Ustat*:

> The temple and the mosque are the same, so are the Hindu worship (*puja*) and Muslim prayer (*namaz*). All people are one; it is through error that they appear different. . . . Allah and Abhekh are the same, the Purana and the Qur'an are the same. They are all alike, all the creation of the One (verse 86).

The above verses emphasize the belief that the differences dividing people are in reality meaningless. In fact, all people are fundamentally the same because they are all the creations of the same Supreme Being. To this day, Sikhs conclude their morning and evening prayers with the words "In thy will, O Lord, may peace and prosperity come to one and all."

☸ Practice

Prayer

Devout Sikhs rise during the "ambrosial hours" (*amritvela*, the last watch of the night, between 3 and 6 a.m.) and begin their daily routine with approximately an hour of devotions, beginning with meditation on the divine Name and continuing with recitation of five liturgical prayers, including Guru Nanak's *Japji* ("Honoured Recitation") and Guru Gobind Singh's *Jap Sahib* ("Master Recitation"). Evening prayers are selected from a collection of hymns entitled *Sodar Rahiras* ("Supplication at That Door"), and the *Kirtan Sohila* ("Song of Praise") is recited before retiring for the night. These prayers are learnt by heart in childhood and recited from memory every day. Thus they are always available to provide guidance. In fact, knowing the *gurbani* ("Guru's Utterances") by heart is often compared with having a supply of cash on hand and ready for use whenever it may be needed.

Focus

Daily Routine of Liturgical Prayers

The individual recitation of morning prayers takes about an hour. One can recite them at home from memory or even listen to them on a CD while driving to work. Similarly, one can recite evening prayer at home alone or with other family members. There are no strict formalities to be followed in the daily routine.

The Early Morning Order (3–6 a.m.)
1. *Japji* ("Honoured Recitation")
2. *Jap Sahib* ("Master Recitation")
3. The Ten *Savayyas* ("Ten Panegyrics")
4. *Benati Chaupai* ("Verses of Petition")
5. *Anand Sahib* ("Song of Bliss")

The Evening Prayer
   Sodar Rahiras ("Supplication at That Door")
The Bedtime Prayer
   Kirtan Sohila ("Song of Praise")

Congregational Worship

In every gurdwara a large copy of the Guru Granth Sahib is reverently wrapped in expensive cloth and installed ceremoniously every morning on a cushioned, canopied stand called the *palki* ("palanquin"). There is a broad aisle leading from the main entrance to the Guru Granth Sahib at the opposite end of the hall. All who enter the gurdwara are expected to cover their heads, remove their shoes, and bow before the sacred volume by touching the floor with their foreheads. Worshippers sit on the floor, and it is the Punjabi custom for men to sit on the right side of the hall and women on the left, but this is not mandatory.

Sikhism has no ordained priesthood. Instead, every gurdwara has a **granthi** ("reader") who, in addition to reading from the Guru Granth Sahib, takes care of the book and serves as custodian of the gurdwara. The office is open to men and women alike, though in practice most *granthis* are men.

Worship consists mainly of *kirtan*: the congregational singing of devotional hymns, led and accompanied by musicians (*ragis*) playing harmoniums and the small drums called *tabla*. Through *kirtan* the devotees attune themselves to the divine Word and vibrate in harmony with it. Many today believe that this traditional practice helps them cope with the additional obstacles that a modern technological society puts in the way of their spiritual life.

At some time during the service, either the *granthi* or a traditional Sikh scholar (*giani*) may deliver a homily (*katha*) based on a particular hymn or scriptural passage appropriate to the occasion. Then all present will join in reciting the *Ardas* ("Petition," the Sikh Prayer), which invokes divine grace and recalls the rich heritage of the community.

AP Photo/Appeal-Democrat, David Bitton

The *granthi* reads from the Guru Granth Sahib in Yuba City, California.

The Sikh understanding of the Adi Granth as living Guru is most evident in the practice known as "taking the Guru's Word" (*vak laina*) or "seeking a divine command" (*hukam laina*). As a mark of respect, a ceremonial fan (***chauri***) is waved over the Guru Granth Sahib. Then the book is opened at random and the first hymn on the left-hand page is read aloud in its entirety (beginning on the previous page if necessary). In this way the congregation hears the Guru's **Vak** ("Saying") for that particular moment or occasion. Taken in the morning, the Vak is the divine lesson that will serve as the inspiration for personal meditation throughout the day; taken in the evening, it brings the day to a close with a new perspective on its particular joys and sorrows. The whole *sangat* (congregation) receives the Vak at the conclusion of different ceremonies.

The reading of the Vak is followed by the distribution of **karah prashad**—a sweet, rich paste of flour, sugar, and butter that has been "sanctified" first by the recitation of prayers during its preparation and then by resting next to the scripture during the service. Symbolically, it represents the bestowal of divine blessings on all who receive *karah prashad*. At the end of congregational worship everyone shares in the *langar* prepared and served by volunteers as part of the community service expected of all Sikhs. All present, Sikhs and non-Sikhs alike, sit together to share a traditional vegetarian meal—usually flat bread, bean stew, and curry. This custom is a powerful reminder of the egalitarian spirit that is so central to Sikhism.

The Annual Festival Cycle

The most important festival day in the Sikh calendar is Baisakhi (Vaisakhi) Day, which usually falls on 13 April. Celebrated throughout India as New Year's Day, it has been considered the birthday of the Sikh community ever since Guru Gobind Singh inaugurated the Khalsa on Baisakhi Day in 1699. Sikhs also celebrate the autumn festival of

© Munish Sharma/Reuters/Corbis

The Darbar Sahib is illuminated during the Divali celebration.

lights, Divali, as the day when Guru Hargobind was released from imprisonment under the Mughal emperor Jahangir. The Darbar Sahib (Golden Temple) in Amritsar is illuminated for the occasion. These two seasonal festivals were introduced by the third Guru, Amar Das, and Guru Gobind Singh added a third: Hola Mahalla, the day after the Hindu festival of Holi (March/April), is celebrated with military exercises and various athletic and literary contests.

The anniversaries of the births and deaths of the Gurus are marked by the "unbroken reading" (*akhand path*) of the entire Sikh scripture by a team of readers over a period of roughly 48 hours. Such occasions are called *Gurpurbs* ("holidays associated with the Gurus"). The birthdays of Guru Nanak (usually in November) and Guru Gobind Singh (December–January) and the martyrdom days of Guru Arjan (May–June) and Guru Tegh Bahadur (November–December) in particular are celebrated around the world.

Life-Cycle Rituals

At the centre of every important life-cycle ritual is the Guru Granth Sahib.

Naming a Child

When a child is to be named, family members take the baby to the gurdwara and present the *karah prashad* that will be distributed after the actual ceremony to the Guru Granth Sahib. After various prayers of thanks and a recitation of *Ardas*, the Guru Granth Sahib is opened at random and the first letter of the first composition on the left-hand page is noted; then a name beginning with the same letter is chosen. In this way the child takes his or her identity from the Guru's Word and begins life as a Sikh. Then a boy is given the second name *Singh* ("Lion") and a girl the second name *Kaur* ("Princess"). *Amrit* is applied to the eyes and head; the infant is given a sip of the sweetened water to drink; and the first five stanzas of Guru Nanak's *Japji* are recited.

Marriage

"They are not said to be husband and wife, who merely sit together. Rather, they alone are called husband and wife who have one soul in two bodies" (AG 788). This proclamation of the third Guru, Amar Das, has become the basis of the Sikh view of marriage, which emphasizes the necessity of spiritual compatibility between the spouses. In a traditional society where the family is more important than the individual, the fact that Sikh marriages have traditionally been arranged is not inconsistent with that principle.

To be legal, a Sikh wedding must take place in the presence of the Guru Granth Sahib. The bride and groom circumambulate the sacred scripture four times, once for each of their four vows:

1. to lead an action-oriented life based on righteousness and never to shun obligations of family and society;
2. to maintain bonds of reverence and dignity between one another;
3. to keep enthusiasm for life alive in the face of adverse circumstances and to remain detached from worldly attachments; and
4. to cultivate a balanced approach in life, avoiding all extremes.

The circular movement around the scripture symbolizes the primordial cycle of life in which there is no beginning and no end, while the four marital vows reflect the ideals that the Sikh tradition considers the keys to a blissful life.

Khalsa Initiation

The Khalsa initiation ceremony (*amrit sanskar*) must also take place in the presence of the Guru Granth Sahib. There is no fixed age for initiation: all that is required is that the candidate be willing and able to accept the Khalsa discipline. Five Khalsa Sikhs, representing the original Cherished Five (*Panj Piare*), conduct the ceremony. Each recites from memory one of the five liturgical prayers while stirring

Document

From Sikh Hymns and Prayers

Despite his militancy, Guru Gobind Singh shared with Guru Nanak a sense that religious boundaries are irrelevant to God:

There is no difference between a temple and a mosque, nor between the prayers of a Hindu and a Muslim. Though differences seem to mark and distinguish, all men/women are in reality the same. Gods and demons, celestial beings, men called Muslims and others called Hindus—such differences are trivial, inconsequential, the outward results of locality and dress. With eyes the same, the ears and body, all possessing a common form—all are in fact a single creation, the elements of nature in a uniform blend.

Allah is the same as the God of the Hindus, Puran and Qur'an are the same. All are the same, none is separate; a single form, a single creation (*Akal Ustat, Dasam Granth,* 19–20; McLeod 1984: 57).

Bhai Gurdas likewise declares the irrelevance of external religious observances:

If bathing at *tiraths* ["pilgrimage centres"] procures liberation, frogs, for sure, must be saved;

And likewise the banyan, with dangling tresses, if growing hair long sets one free.

If the need can be served by roaming unclad the deer of the forest must surely be pious;

So too the ass which rolls in the dust if limbs smeared with ashes can purchase salvation.

Saved are the cattle, mute in the fields, if silence produces deliverance.

Only the Guru can bring us salvation; only the Guru can set a man free (*Varan Bhai Gurdas,* 36:14; McLeod 1984: 67).

The Sikh Prayer called the Ardas, standardized by the 1930s, contains a roll call of the ten Gurus. Sri Hari Krishan, included in it, is the child who became the eighth Guru, and should not be confused with the Hindu Hare Krishna movement:

Having first remembered God, turn your thoughts to Guru Nanak; Angad Guru, Amar Das, each with Ram Das grant us aid.

Arjan and Hargobind, think of them and Har Rai.

Dwell on Sri Hari Krishan, he whose sight dispels all pain.

Think of Guru Tegh Bahadur; thus shall every treasure come.

May they grant their gracious guidance, help and strength in every place.

May the tenth Master, the revered Guru Gobind Singh, also grant us "help and strength in every place.

The light which shone from each of the ten Masters shines now from the sacred pages of the Guru Granth Sahib.

Turn your thoughts to its message and call on God, saying, *Vahiguru!* (*Chandi di Var, Dasam Granth,* 119; McLeod 1984: 104).

Martyrdom is a frequent theme in Sikh history, motivating Sikhs to persevere in struggles today:

These loyal members of the Khalsa who gave their heads for their faith; who were hacked limb from limb, scalped, broken on the wheel, or sawn asunder, who sacrificed their lives for the protection of hallowed gurdwaras never forsaking their faith; and who were steadfast in their loyalty to the uncut hair of the true Sikh: reflect on their merits, O Khalsa, and call on God, saying, *Vahiguru!* (*Ardas*; McLeod 1984: 104).

the sweetened water (*amrit*) with a double-edged sword.

The novices then drink the *amrit* five times so that their bodies are purified of five vices (lust, anger, greed, attachment, and pride), and five times the *amrit* is sprinkled on their eyes to transform their outlook towards life. Finally, the *amrit* is poured on their heads five times, sanctifying their hair so that they will preserve its natural form and listen to the voice of conscience. At each stage of the ceremony, the initiates repeat the words *Vahiguru Ji Ka Khalsa! Vahiguru Ji Ki Fateh!* ("Khalsa belongs to the Wonderful Lord! Victory belongs to the Wonderful Lord!"). Thus a person becomes a Khalsa Sikh through the transforming power of the sacred word and the sacred nectar (*amrit*). At the conclusion of the ceremony, a Vak is read aloud and *karah prashad* is distributed.

Death

For a dedicated Sikh (*Gurmukh*), death is a joy to be welcomed when it comes, for it means the perfecting of his or her union with Akal Purakh and a final release from the cycle of rebirth. For a self-willed person (*Manmukh*), by contrast, death means the culmination of his or her separation from the Divine and perpetuation of the process of reincarnation.

Hymns from the Guru Granth Sahib are sung both in the period preceding the cremation and in the post-cremation rites. In India, the body of the deceased is bathed, dressed in new clothes, and placed on a pyre for cremation. The ashes are then disposed of in a nearby stream or river. In the diaspora, however, the rituals associated with death have had to undergo significant changes. Family and friends gather around the body at a funeral home with the necessary facilities for cremation. The body is placed in a casket where people may scatter flower petals as a tribute. Following devotional singing and eulogy, *Ardas* is offered by the *granthi*. Then the casket is pushed on a trolley to the cremation furnace, usually accompanied by family and friends. While the casket is burning, the congregation recites the late-evening prayer, *Kirtan Sohila*.

In addition, a reading of the entire scripture takes place either at home or in a gurdwara—a process that may take up to 10 days to complete. At the conclusion of the reading a "completion" ceremony is held when the final prayers are offered in the memory of the deceased.

✸ Differentiation

The Encounter with Modernity

The Khalsa spent most of its first century fighting the armies of Mughals and Afghan invaders. Immediately after the death of Guru Gobind Singh in 1708, Khalsa Sikhs rose in rebellion under the leadership of Banda Singh Bahadur, contributing to a widespread civil war that ended in 1710 with the defeat of the Mughals and the establishment of Sikh rule in Punjab. Although the Mughals returned to power in 1716, Khalsa Sikhs were able to establish multiple Sikh kingdoms in the mid- to late eighteenth century. Finally, in 1799, Ranjit Singh (1780–1839) succeeded in unifying the Punjab, taking control of Lahore, and declaring himself Maharaja. For the next four decades the Sikh community enjoyed more settled political conditions, and with territorial expansion as far as Peshawar in the west, people of different cultural and religious backgrounds were attracted into the fold of Sikhism. The appearance of the Darbar Sahib today owes a great deal to the generous patronage of the Maharaja, who also employed scribes to make beautiful copies of the Sikh scripture that were sent as gifts to the Sikh *Takhats* ("Thrones," the traditional seats of authority at Amritsar, Anandpur, Talwandi Sabo, Patna, and Nander) and other major historical gurdwaras.

Although Maharaja Ranjit Singh himself was a Khalsa Sikh, his rule was marked by religious diversity within the Sikh Panth. Khalsa members, in their drive to carve out an empire for themselves, realized that for their project to succeed they required allies both inside and outside the Sikh Panth. Therefore they forged an internal alliance with the **Sehaj-dharis** ("gradualists"): Sikhs who lived as members of the Nanak-Panth but did not accept the Khalsa code of conduct. The Khalsa conceded the religious culture of the *Sehaj-dharis* to be legitimate even though, in keeping with the inclusive approach of the Maharaja, the latter revered Hindu scriptures as well as the Guru Granth Sahib and the Dasam Granth, and in some cases even worshipped Hindu images.

Sikh Reform Movements

After the death of Maharaja Ranjit Singh in 1839, his successors could not withstand the pressure exerted by the advancing British forces. After two Anglo–Sikh wars, in 1846 and 1849, the Sikh kingdom was annexed to the British empire. With the loss of the Punjab's independence, the Sikhs were no longer the masters of their own kingdom. It was in this context that three reform movements emerged in the second half of the nineteenth century, each attempting to restore the sense of a distinct spiritual identity to a people whose religious tradition was just one among a vast array of traditions now encompassed within colonial India.

The Nirankaris

Baba Dayal Das (1783–1853) was the founder of a renewal movement devoted to purging Sikhism of Hindu influences (especially image worship) and recalling Sikhs to the worship of the "formless and invisible God" (*Nirankar*). Dayal Das's followers revered his *Hukam-nama* ("Book of Ordinances") alongside the Guru Granth Sahib and recognized a line of personal Gurus descending from him. Although they did not equate this line with the succession of ten Gurus ending with Guru Gobind Singh, and did not reject the orthodox doctrine according to which the Guru is eternally present in the sacred scripture, they believed that Baba Dayal was dispatched by God to recall the Panth to obedience and renew the Sikh tradition.

The Nirankari movement survives today, although its numbers do not exceed a few thousand and they have remained on the periphery of the Panth. They claim that it was Baba Dayal Das who instituted the distinctively Sikh marriage ceremony, in which the Sikh scripture replaced the fire at the centre of the older Hindu rite.

The Namdharis

The Namdharis took their name from their emphasis on the divine Name. Their leader, Baba Ram Singh (1816–84), was the first reformer to stress the importance of the Khalsa under colonial rule. He reinstituted the order of Sant ("Devout") Khalsa in 1862, creating his own initiation ritual and an austere rule of conduct stressing a vegetarian diet and all-white dress, as well as the chanting of the divine *nam*.

As the number of his followers grew, Baba Ram Singh took on an increasingly active role in the public sphere, promoting boycotts of various kinds as a form of non-violent resistance to the British occupation of the Punjab. After the British gave permission to resume the slaughter of cows (banned under Maharaja Ranjit Singh)—a number of Muslim butchers in Amritsar and Ludhiana were killed by Namdhari extremists. In the background of the mutiny of 1857, the British crushed the Namdhari movement, sending Baba Ram Singh into exile and executing more than 60 Namdharis without trial in a particularly horrifying way—tying them over the mouths of canons and blasting their bodies to pieces. The Namdharis came to be seen as political martyrs and forerunners of the Gandhian movement for the independence of India.

After Ram Singh's death, the Namdharis developed a doctrine of religious authority similar to the Shi'i Muslim doctrine of the hidden Imam, maintaining that Guru Gobind Singh did not die in 1708 but went into hiding; that Baba Ram Singh succeeded him as the twelfth Guru; and that although Ram Singh in turn went into hiding as well, he will return some day.

The Singh Sabha Movement

Among the most important contributions to the modernization of the Sikh tradition were the educational initiatives of the **Singh Sabha** ("Society of the Singhs"). Established in 1873 by four prominent Sikh reformers, the Singh Sabha sought to reaffirm Sikh identity in the face of two threats: the casual reversion to Hindu practices during the period of Punjabi independence under Maharaja Ranjit Singh and the active proselytizing efforts not only of the Hindu Arya Samaj, but of Christian missionaries.

By the end of the nineteenth century the Tat ("Pure" or "True") Khalsa, the dominant wing of the Singh Sabha, had eradicated the last traces of religious diversity within the Sikh Panth and established clear norms of belief and practice. In effect, they made the Khalsa tradition the standard of orthodoxy for all Sikhs.

In the twentieth century the Tat Khalsa reformers also contributed to two important legal changes. First, in 1909, they obtained legal recognition of the distinctive Sikh wedding ritual in the Anand Marriage Act (1909). Then in the 1920s they helped to re-establish direct Khalsa control of the major historical gurdwaras, many of which had fallen into the hands of corrupt **mahants** ("custodians") supported by the British. Inspired by the Tat Khalsa ideal, the Akali movement of the 1920s eventually secured British assent to the Sikh Gurdwara Act (1925), under which control of all gurdwaras passed to the Shiromani Gurdwara Prabandhak Committee (SGPC; "Chief Management Committee of Sikh Shrines"). The Akalis were the forerunners of the modern political party known as the Akali Dal ("army of the immortal").

SGPC Rahit Manual

Control of the gurdwaras gave the SGPC enormous political and economic influence. By 1950 it had established itself as the central authority on all questions of religious discipline, and in that year it published a manual entitled *Sikh Rahit Maryada*, which has been regarded ever since as the authoritative guide to orthodox Sikh doctrine and behaviour.

Based on the teachings of the Guru Granth Sahib, supplemented with teachings from revered Sikh leaders, the *Sikh Rahit Maryada* enjoins Sikhs

to cultivate a pure and pious inner spirituality (*bani*), to adopt the Five Ks as external signs of virtuous conduct (*bana*), and to abstain from the four cardinal sins (hair-cutting, adultery, intoxicants, and consumption of meat from animals that have not been killed with a single blow).

The manual encourages the worship of God and meditation on his name, undergoing Khalsa initiation, and attending divine services. It also calls on Sikhs to earn a living honestly and truthfully, to share selflessly with the needy and less fortunate in order to further the well-being of all, to nurture virtues such as compassion, honesty, generosity, patience, perseverance, and humility, and to avoid superstitions, idols, and images.

Not punitive in intent or effect, the *Sikh Rahit Maryada* encourages devotees to attune their daily lives to the will of God. It calls for tolerance of those who stray as well as the *Sehaj-dharis* who, though they follow the teachings of Guru Granth Sahib, have not yet accepted the full discipline of the Khalsa; instead of condemning these gradualists, it assumes that in time they will progress to the point where they will join the Khalsa. The only code of conduct sanctioned by the Akal Takhat—the highest seat of religious and temporal authority among Sikhs—the *Sikh Rahit Maryada* is distributed free of charge by the SGPC, and is now available in Hindi and English as well as Punjabi, in acknowledgement of the needs of Sikhs living outside their historical homeland.

Variations in Modern Sikhism

Although the *Sikh Rahit Maryada* tends to represent Sikhism as a single coherent orthodoxy, at the popular level the Sikh Panth today encompasses a number of variations. For instance, the Khalsa itself includes a distinctive order called the Nihangs, who are rigorous in the observance of the *Khalsa Rahit* and, having renounced all fear of death, are ready to die for their faith at any time. Their garments are always blue, with some saffron and white, and on their heads they wear a high turban surmounted by a piece of cloth called a *pharhara* ("standard" or "flag"). In North America some Sikhs occasionally wear Nihang dress on special occasions such as Baisakhi Day.

Another group within the Khalsa calls itself the Akhand Kirtani Jatha ("continuous singing of the Sikh scriptures") and follows its own special discipline, which includes an entirely vegetarian diet and requires that female members wear a small turban.

In fact, the Sikh Panth has never been monolithic or homogeneous, and in recent years the Internet has allowed many groups to claim that they represent the "true" Panth. Of the 25 million Sikhs in the world today, only about 20 per cent are orthodox **Amrit-dharis** ("initiated"). But many other Sikhs follow most of the Khalsa code even though they have not been initiated. (Those who "retain their hair" are known as **Kes-dharis**.)

Less conspicuous are the many Sikhs (especially in North America and the United Kingdom) who do cut their hair but do not consider themselves to be "lesser Sikhs" in any way. Many of these people use the Khalsa names "Singh" and "Kaur" without inhibition. In fact, they are the majority in the diaspora, and they play active roles both in the community's ritual life and in the management of the gurdwaras.

These semi-observant Sikhs are often confused with the *Sehaj-dharis* who have never accepted the Khalsa discipline. Although the *Sehaj-dharis* practise *nam-simaran* and follow the teachings of the Adi Granth, they do not observe the *Khalsa Rahit*. The number of *Sehaj-dharis* has declined in the last few decades, but they certainly have not disappeared completely.

Finally, there are Khalsa Sikhs—especially in the diaspora—who have committed one or more of the four sins after initiation. These lapsed *Amrit-dharis* are known as "Patit Sikhs" ("Apostates"). It should be emphasized that none of these categories are necessarily permanent. Individuals go through different stages in life and their status within the Panth changes accordingly. In short, there is no single way of being a Sikh.

☸ Cultural Expressions

Social Norms

Guru Nanak believed that the key to liberation lay not in ascetic renunciation but in the life of the householder. His successors shared that belief, upholding the ideal of family life in their own lives as well as in their teachings. The third Guru, Amar Das, proclaimed, "Family life is superior to ascetic life in sectarian garb because it is from householders that ascetics meet their needs by begging" (AG 586). To understand family relationships, one must address issues of caste and gender from the Sikh perspective. Doctrinally, rejection of caste-based discrimination was a fundamental feature of Sikhism from the beginning. Moreover, the *Sikh Rahit Maryada* explicitly states that "No account should be taken of caste" in the selection of a marriage partner. This is the ideal; in practice, however, most Sikhs still marry within their own caste group, though inter-caste marriages are becoming more common among urban professionals, in India and elsewhere.

In Punjabi society, marriage creates a connection not just between two individuals but, more important, between two groups of kin. It is in this context that the concept of honour (*izzat*) continues to play a significant role in family relationships.

The Role of Women

The Sikh Gurus approached issues of gender within the parameters of a traditional patriarchal society. Thus despite their egalitarian principles and efforts to foster respect for womanhood, their ideas about women were inseparable from their ideas about family: in their view, the ideal woman was defined by her conduct in the context of family life, as a good daughter, a good sister, a good wife and mother. They condemned men as well as women who did not observe the cultural norms of modesty and honour in their lives. There was no tolerance for any kind of premarital or extramarital sexual activity, and rape was regarded as a particularly serious violation, for the dishonour it brought to the family meant the loss of social standing in the community. Furthermore, the rules governing the Khalsa are clearly egalitarian in principle. Those who seek initiation cannot be accepted without their spouses; hence the proportions of male and female initiates are roughly equal. And Khalsa women wear all of the Five Ks.

A number of women are remembered for their contributions to the Panth, some but not all of them the sisters, wives, and daughters of the Gurus. Guru Nanak's older sister Nanaki, for instance, was unfailing in her love for her brother and supported his travels while his wife Sulakhani raised their two children through his long absences from home. Mata Khivi, the wife of the second Guru, is praised in the Guru Granth Sahib for her contributions to the development of the *langar* tradition. In 1705, when the forces of Guru Gobind Singh had abandoned him in battle, a brave woman named Mai Bhago persuaded them to return and fight. And after the Guru's death in 1708, his wife Sundri played a major role in guiding the destiny of the Khalsa. She appointed Bhai Mani Singh to compile the Dasam Granth, and a number of the edicts (*hukam-namas*) she issued to various Sikh congregations survive, reflecting her deep concern for the welfare of the Panth.

In modern times, Bibi Jagir Kaur became the first woman to be elected president of the SGPC twice, in 1999 and 2004—a sign of real progress towards equality. Other exceptional women include the mystic Bibi Nihal Kaur; Bibi Balwant Kaur, who established both a gurdwara and a women's group in honour of Bebe Nanaki in Birmingham (UK); and Bibi Jasbir Kaur Khalsa, who devoted her life to the promotion of Sikh music and established a Chair for its study at the Punjabi University in Patiala, India. Female musicians often perform in the gurdwaras. Women have also played important roles in the operations of the Akhand Kirtani Jatha and the Healthy, Happy, Holy Organization (3HO; now known as Sikh Dharma).

In general, however, males still dominate most Sikh institutions, and many Sikh women continue to live in a society based on patriarchal cultural assumptions. In this respect they differ little from their counterparts in any of India's major religious communities. Even so, Sikh women have been asserting themselves with growing success in recent years.

Music

Sikhism is the only world religion in which song has been the primary medium for the founder's message. Sacred music has been at the heart of the Sikh devotional experience from the beginning. In specifying the *ragas* (melodies) to which the hymns were to be sung, Guru Nanak and his successors sought to promote harmony and balance in the minds of listeners and performers. Thus any *raga* likely to arouse passion was either excluded altogether or adapted to produce a gentler effect.

Sites

Nanded, Maharashtra

Guru Gobind Singh died in Nanded, which is also the site of the Takhat Sri Hazur Sahib, one of the five important seats of authority within Sikhism. It was at Hazur Sahib that, before his death in 1708, the tenth Guru installed the Adi Granth as the "Eternal Guru" of the Sikhs.

Art

The earliest examples of Sikh graphic art are illuminated scriptures dating from the late sixteenth and early seventeenth centuries. Sikh scribes followed the Qur'anic tradition of decorating the margins and the opening pages of the text with abstract designs and floral motifs. The earliest extant paintings of Guru Nanak appear in a *janam-sakhi* (birth-narrative) from the mid-1600s.

Both fine and applied arts flourished under the patronage of Maharaja Ranjit Singh. In addition to painting, sculpture, armour, brassware, jewellery, and textiles, a distinctive architecture developed at his court in the first half of the nineteenth century. Murals and frescoes depicting major events from Sikh history can still be seen at historic gurdwaras including the Darbar Sahib in Amritsar.

Two great Sikh artists emerged in the twentieth century. Sobha Singh (1901–86) was skilled in the Western classical technique of oil painting, but he drew his themes from the romantic lore of the Punjab, the Indian epics, and the Sikh tradition; he is particularly well known for his portraits of the Gurus. Kirpal Singh (1923–90) specialized in realistic depictions of episodes from Sikh history, including appalling scenes of battle and martyrdom. Some of his works are displayed in the Central Sikh Museum in the Darbar Sahib complex.

A number of Sikh women have also made names for themselves as artists. Amrita Shergill (1911–41), for instance, has been described as the Frida Kahlo of India. Raised largely in Europe, she studied art in Paris but returned to India in 1934 and explored village life in a series of paintings that have been declared National Art Treasures. Arpana Caur (b. 1954) is a bold modern painter who addresses current issues and events directly. The Singh Twins (b. 1966), born in England, apply styles and techniques of the classic Indian miniature tradition to contemporary themes. Their painting *Nineteen Eighty-Four*, inspired by the storming of the Darbar Sahib, is a powerful reflection not only on the event itself but on the responses it evoked in the Sikh diaspora.[2]

Literature

A rich literary tradition began with the introduction of the Gurmukhi script used to record the hymns of the Gurus. The influence of the Adi Granth is clear in the works of early poets such as Bhai Gurdas.

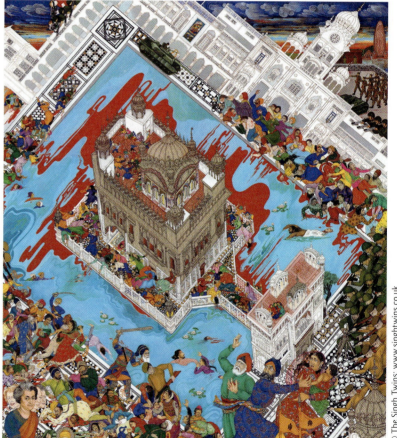

Nineteen Eighty-Four, by The Singh Twins, 1998.

The first Punjabi prose form was the *janam-sakhi*, which remained the dominant literary genre before the emergence of the twentieth-century novel. It is easy to see the impact of Sikh devotional literature on the writings of celebrated early modern authors such as Kahn Singh Nabha (1861–1938), the poet Bhai Vir Singh (1872–1957), and Mohan Singh Vaid (1881–1936), who wrote stories, novels, and plays as well as many works of non-fiction. All these writers emphasized optimism, resolute determination, faith, and love towards fellow human beings. Max Arthur Macauliffe (1837–1913) was an administrator in the British colonial government who became interested in Sikhism in the 1860s and devoted his life to the translation of the Sikh scriptures. Writers played a leadership role in the Singh Sabha reform movement of the late nineteenth and early twentieth centuries.

Although much contemporary Punjabi literature reflects Western influences, Sikh devotional literature is still a source of inspiration for the passionate lyricism of the new generation of writers such as Harinder Singh Mehboob, the author of the much-acclaimed *Saheje Rachio Khalsa* ("The Gradual Creation of the Khalsa"; 1988).

❂ Interaction and Adaptation

Twentieth-Century India

Doctrinal Authority

By 1950, as we have seen, the Shiromani Gurdwara Prabandhak Committee (SGPC) had become the principal voice of authority in both religious and political affairs for the worldwide Sikh community. Although it has often been challenged by Sikhs living outside the Punjab, the SGPC is a democratic institution that claims to speak on behalf of the majority of Sikhs, and hence to represent the authority of the Guru-Panth.

Still, the ultimate authority is the Akal Takhat in Amritsar. The most important of the five *Takhats*, the Akal Takhat may issue edicts (*hukam-namas*) that provide guidance or clarification on any aspect of Sikh doctrine or practice. It may punish any

Sikh charged with violating religious discipline or engaging in activity "prejudicial" to Sikh interests and unity; it may also recognize individuals who have made sacrifices or performed outstanding services for the sake of the Sikh cause.

The Partition of India

In 1947 the British withdrew from India and the subcontinent was partitioned to create two independent republics of India and Pakistan. Partition was especially hard for the Sikhs because it split the Punjab into two. Most of the 2.5 million Sikhs living on the Pakistani side fled as refugees; though many settled in the new Indian state of Punjab, some moved on to major cities elsewhere in India.

Since 1976 the Constitution of India has defined the republic as a secular state, and Article 25 guarantees the right to freedom of religion. However, a sub-clause of the same Article states that "persons professing the Sikh, Jaina, or Buddhist religion" will be considered to fall within the general category of Hinduism. When the original Constitution was drafted, the Sikh members of the Constituent Assembly refused to sign the document because it did not recognize the Sikhs as a group with an independent identity. Since that time, Sikh and Hindu politicians alike have deliberately stirred up popular resentment on both sides for political purposes.

In 2002 the National Commission to Review the Constitution recommended that the wording of Article 25 be amended to refer specifically to the three religious groups—Sikhs, Jainas, and Buddhists—that are currently covered under the default term "Hindu." To date, however, this amendment has not been enacted.

"Operation Blue Star"

In 1973 the main political party of the Sikhs, Akali Dal, passed the Anandpur Sahib Resolution, demanding greater autonomy for all the states of India. As a result, relations with the Indian government became increasingly strained over the following years. In an apparent attempt to sow dissension in the Akali ranks, the Congress government encouraged the rise of a charismatic young militant named Jarnail Singh Bhindranvale (1947–84). But this strategy backfired in the spring of 1984, when a group of armed radicals led by Bhindranvale decided to provoke a confrontation with the government by occupying the Akal Takhat building inside the Darbar Sahib complex. The government responded by sending in the army. The assault that followed—code-named "Operation Blue Star"—resulted in the deaths of many Sikhs, including Bhindranvale, as well as the destruction of the Akal Takhat and severe damage to the Darbar Sahib itself.

A few months later, on 31 October 1984, Prime Minister Indira Gandhi was assassinated by her own Sikh bodyguards. For several days unchecked Hindu mobs in Delhi and elsewhere killed thousands of Sikhs. As a consequence of these events, 1984 became a turning point in the history of the Sikhs, precipitating an identity crisis within the Panth and dividing Sikhs around the world into two camps, liberal and fundamentalist.

The Sikh Diaspora

Over the last century more than 1 million Sikhs have left India for foreign lands. Wherever they have settled—in Singapore, Malaysia, Thailand, Hong Kong, Australia, New Zealand, East Africa, and the United Kingdom, as well as Canada and the United States—they have carried their sacred scripture with them and established their own places of worship. Today there are more than 500 gurdwaras in North America and the United Kingdom alone.

New cultural environments have required some adaptation. In diaspora gurdwaras, for instance, congregational services are usually held on Sunday, not because it is the holy day—in India there is no specific day for worship—but because it is the only day when most Sikhs are free to attend services.

Western societies have also presented Sikh spirituality with serious challenges. Turban-wearing Sikhs have frequently faced discrimination from prospective employers, and Khalsa Sikhs have had to negotiate with various institutions for permission to wear the *kirpan* as a religious symbol. At the same time, a gradual loss of fluency in the Punjabi language means that younger Sikhs are at growing risk of theological illiteracy. Diaspora Sikhs, fully aware that assimilation is making steady progress among the second and third generations, have responded with concerted efforts to revive interest in Sikh traditions and identity.

To meet the challenges of life in Western societies, many gurdwaras now hold "Sunday school" classes for children, and many Sikh families now worship at home—in both Punjabi and English—as well as at the gurdwara. Another innovative response has been to organize Sikh Youth Camps offering continuous exposure to Sikh spirituality, values, and traditions.

Punjabi Sikhs and White Sikhs

Around 1970 a number of yoga students in Toronto and Los Angeles were inspired by their teacher, a

In 2006 Gurbaj Singh Multani won his right to wear a kirpan to school against a Montreal school board in the Supreme Court of Canada.

CP Photo/Fred Chartrand

Sikh named Harbhajan Singh Puri (Yogi Bhajan), to convert to the Sikh faith and join his Healthy, Happy, Holy Organization ("3HO"). Eventually renamed Sikh Dharma, the organization has since established chapters or *ashrams* in various North American cities.

All members of this organization—male and female—wear the same costume of white turbans, tunics, and tight trousers, and for this reason they have come to be known as "White Sikhs." They live and raise families in communal houses, spending long hours in meditation and chanting as well as yoga practice.

Punjabi Sikhs in general praise the strict Khalsa-style discipline of the White Sikhs. In other respects, however, the White Sikh culture is seen as quite alien. In the Punjab, for instance—as in India as a whole—white clothing is normally a sign of mourning; only the Namdharis dress entirely in white. And the only Sikh women who wear turbans are members of the Akhand Kirtani Jatha. Finally, the concept of *izzat* ("prestige" or "honour"), which plays such an important part in Punjabi culture and society, is irrelevant to the White Sikhs. Even in North America, therefore, Punjabi Sikhs have tended to distance themselves from the White Sikhs.

☸ Recent Developments

Religious Pluralism

The beginning of the third millennium has brought the issue of religious pluralism into sharper focus. The coexistence, in a single society, of multiple religious worldviews, some of which may be incompatible with one another, has always been a fact of life. But awareness of that fact has increased sharply in recent times with increasing urbanization, mass education, international migration, and advances in communications. Especially in democratic states that do not attempt to impose a single worldview, people of different faiths must learn how to live together harmoniously.

Acceptance of religious pluralism is a condition of religious understanding. Dialogue and interaction with people of other faiths provide opportunities for spiritual reflection and growth. It is in this context that Sikhism emphasizes the importance of keeping an open mind and being willing to learn from other traditions, while preserving the integrity of one's own tradition. The Sikh Gurus strongly opposed any claim, by any tradition, to possession of the sole religious truth. A spirit of accommodation has always been an integral part of the Sikh attitude toward other traditions.

Sikhs are enthusiastic participants in interfaith dialogue. The fact that the Adi Granth includes works by 15 non-Sikh poet-saints suggests a four-part theory of religious pluralism. First, participants in interfaith dialogue must recognize that the religious commitments of others are no less absolute than their own. Thus the quest for a universal religion must be abandoned, along with any attempt to place one religious tradition above others. Second, doctrinal differences must be respected. Third, interfaith dialogue requires an open mind that allows for recognition of the points on which different traditions agree, but also disagreement on crucial points of doctrine. Finally, one must be willing to let the "other" become in some sense oneself. In this way the experience of dialogue can enrich one's own spiritual life.

Sikh Militancy in Politics

Another issue confronting Sikhs around the world is the tendency to associate their tradition with violence. The use of warrior imagery to evoke the valour of the Sikhs has been standard since colonial times. Relatively little attention has been directed to the other, perhaps more demanding, dimensions of Sikhism. What is expected of the Sikh warriors is not violence but militancy in the sense that they are prepared to take an active and passionate stand on behalf of their faith.

In Canada the association between Sikhs and violence was underlined by the 1985 bombing of Air India Flight 182, in which 329 people—most of them Canadian citizens—were killed. This happened in the highly volatile context of the Indian army's assault on the Darbar Sahib in 1984. Nearly two decades passed before the two Vancouver men suspected of masterminding the attack were brought to trial, and in the end they were acquitted. It took more than 20 years and several government inquiries for the Canadian public in general to recognize that the bombing was a Canadian tragedy, the result of a Canadian plot and the failure of Canadian security officials—a conclusion that was made luminously clear by former Supreme Court Justice John Major in his 2010 report on the investigation into the attack.

In India separatist violence was contained within a decade and the main Sikh political party (Akali Dal) reasserted its right to work within the democratic system for greater justice and transparency. In the long run, peaceful public demonstrations and engagement in the political process have proved more effective than violent struggle. In response to a long-standing demand of the Sikhs, the Indian Parliament recently passed the Anand Marriage (Amendment) Act, 2012, lifting the requirement that Sikh marriages be registered under the Hindu Marriage Act.

Sexuality and Bioethical Issues

The Adi Granth and the Sikh Rahit Maryada are silent on homosexual activity. The official Sikh response to same-sex marriage has been negative, and the Akal Takhat has issued a decree forbidding the performance of any such marriage in the gurdwara. Since the life of the householder is the Sikh ideal, any form of family or sexual relationship that is not procreative and within the bounds of a marriage is opposed. Thus the official position strongly upholds heterosexuality, sanctioning union (*sanjog*) between a man and a woman only.

For centuries in Punjab, as elsewhere throughout the subcontinent, sons have tended to be preferred to daughters. The Gurus explicitly prohibited female infanticide, and the *rahit-namas* include specific injunctions against it. Yet in recent years the proportion of females to males in the Punjabi population has declined, and it seems clear that this decline can be attributed to the abortion of female fetuses. This is contrary to the Sikh principle of gender equality. Thus Sikhism does not condone abortion for the purpose of sex selection; however,

it does permit medical abortion when the mother's life is in danger, or in cases of incest or rape.

In the diaspora setting Sikhs are beginning to debate issues such as organ donation, genetic engineering, surrogacy, and the use of embryos in medical research. Sikhs often refer to the martyrdom of Guru Tegh Bahadur, who sacrificed himself to defend the rights of the Hindus, as an example that should encourage families to donate the organs of their deceased loved ones to save the lives of others. However, many Sikhs believe that life begins at conception, and that to alter the genetic makeup of a human being would amount to interfering with the natural order. On the other hand, some argue that scientific knowledge is God-given and should be used to benefit humanity.

Environmental Issues

Guru Nanak himself spoke of the natural world with great tenderness: "Air is the Guru, water the Father and earth the mighty Mother of all. Day and night are the caring guardians, fondly nurturing all creation" (AG 8). Today environmental issues are coming into prominence both in the Punjab and in the diaspora. The celebration of Guru Har Rai's birthday in March has been fixed as "Sikh Environment Day." And in recent years the environmentalist Balbir Singh Seechewal has made it his mission to spread ecological awareness. He singlehandedly organized the restoration of the river associated with Guru Nanak's mystical experience, and he encourages Sikh congregations across the Punjab to plant trees in every available space.

Internet Technology

The twenty-first century promises to be both challenging and rewarding for Sikhs. It is astounding to see how fast Sikh websites are multiplying. The ability to locate a reference from the Guru Granth Sahib in seconds, or listen to *kirtan* and the daily Vak from the Darbar Sahib, is inspiring for Sikhs around the world. Online courses offer instruction in everything from the Gurmukhi script to playing the harmonium and other instruments associated with Sikh worship. The diversity of Sikh life is now visible in a global context, and webmasters have become the new authorities speaking on behalf of Sikhism, eroding the power of institutional structures. Websites such as Gurmat Learning Zone (GLZ), Sikh-Diaspora, Sikhchic, and SikhNet are among many forums that now host discussions of contemporary Sikh issues. Of course, Sikhism is not the only tradition in which institutional authority is eroding; in an increasingly secular, globalized world, all religions are facing similar challenges.

Sikh Visibility

On 15 September 2001, an American Sikh became the first victim of the racial backlash that followed the 9/11 terrorist attacks. Balbir Singh Sodhi was shot dead in Phoenix, Arizona, by a self-described "patriot" who mistook him for a Muslim. More recently, on 5 August 2012, a gunman burst into the gurdwara in Oak Creek, Wisconsin, and opened fire, killing five men and one woman, ambushing one police officer, and injuring three others before dying of a self-inflicted shot to the head. The dominant narrative that has emerged in both media coverage and public discourse since then has been one of mistaken religious identity. It presumes that the killer, identified as a white supremacist named Wade Michael Page, shot the Sikhs because he ignorantly believed they were Muslim. Even today it is painfully clear that too many people in the West simply do not know who Sikhs are.

Organizations such as the Canadian Sikh Coalition are working to raise awareness of Sikhs in Canada and elsewhere. American Sikhs are leading the way with major civil rights organizations such as the Sikh Coalition, SALDEF (Sikh American Legal Defense and Education Fund), and Sikhs For Justice (SFJ), which are providing legal aid and have dynamic information systems and extensive data bases.

© AP Photo/Appeal-Democrat. Nate Chute

A prayer vigil in memory of the six people who died when a gunman opened fire in a Sikh temple in Oak Creek, Wisconsin, in 2012.

The situation is somewhat better in academic circles. The first North American conference on Sikh studies was held in 1976 at the University of California, Berkeley. Participants at that conference generally felt that Sikhism was indeed "the forgotten tradition" among scholarly circles in North America. This is no longer the case. In the last two decades the scholarly literature on Sikhism has grown steadily, and the mistaken notion that Sikhism represents a synthesis of Hindu and Muslim ideals has been almost entirely abandoned. Today there are eight endowed chairs in Sikh studies in North America, and Sikhism is increasingly recognized in undergraduate academic programs.

❀ Summary

Over the last five centuries the Sikh tradition has evolved in response to four motivating factors. First and foremost were the religious and cultural innovations proposed by Guru Nanak and his nine successors. The second was the martial character of Punjabi society's rural base, which appears to have brought the Sikh Panth into conflict with Mughal authorities and helped to shape the future direction of the Sikh movement. The third element was the conflict created within the Sikh community by dissident groups such as the Minas, which at first hampered the crystallization of the Sikh tradition but in the longer term, paradoxically, enhanced it. The fourth and last factor was the ongoing tension of the period in which the Sikh Panth evolved, when Punjab was governed by Mughal rulers and under constant threat of invasion from Afghanistan.

The Sikh community has been involved in a process of "renewal and redefinition" throughout its history, and that process has only intensified in recent years. Today, the question "Who is a Sikh?" is the subject of often acrimonious debate in online discussions among the various Sikh networks. Each generation of Sikhs has had to respond to this question in the light of new historical circumstances while addressing the larger issues of orthodoxy and orthopraxy. Not surprisingly, diaspora Sikhs approach these issues from different perspectives, depending on the cultural and political contexts they come from. In many cases they rediscover their identity through their interaction with other religious and ethnic communities. New challenges demand new responses, especially in a postmodern world where notions of self, gender, and authority are subject to constant questioning. Thus the process of Sikh identity-formation is a dynamic and ongoing phenomenon.

Sacred Texts

Religion	Texts	Composition/ Compilation	Compilation/ Revision	Use
Sikhism	The Adi Granth/ Guru Granth Sahib; the primary scripture	The first collection of Guru Nanak's hymns was compiled in the 1530s. This *pothi* ("sacred volume") was expanded by the succeeding Gurus. A four-volume collection produced in 1570, under Guru Amar Das, came to be known as the Goindval Pothis.	The fifth Guru, Arjan, produced a prototype of the Adi Granth in 1604. The tenth Guru, Gobind Singh, added the works of his father and closed the canon in the 1680s. Before he passed away in 1708, he installed the Adi Granth as Guru Granth Sahib.	In worship, the hymns of the Guru Granth Sahib are sung in melodic measures (*ragas*), while prayers are recited. The sacred text also plays a pivotal role in all Sikh ceremonies, including life-cycle rituals, and is the central authority regarding both personal piety and the corporate identity of the Sikh community.
	The Dasam Granth; the secondary scripture	The first collection of works attributed to the tenth Guru, Gobind Singh, dates to the 1690s.	18th–19th centuries: subsequent collections added the *Zafarnama* of Guru Gobind Singh and fixed the sequence of compositions.	Portions of the Dasam Granth are used as liturgical texts in the daily routine of the Sikhs and the Khalsa initiation ceremony.

Discussion Questions

1. Do you think that Guru Nanak intended to establish a new religion, independent of Hindu and Muslim traditions? What is the evidence in his works?

2. How did Sikhism evolve in response to changing historical circumstances during the time of the ten Gurus?

3. How did the martyrdoms of Guru Arjan and Guru Tegh Bahadur contribute to the emergence of militancy as a core tradition within the Panth?

4. How did modern Sikhism come into being? What role did the Singh Sabha reform movement play in defining Sikh doctrine and practice?

5. What is the role of the Guru Granth Sahib in Sikh life?

6. Why is the practice of *kirtan* (devotional singing) central to Sikh congregational worship?

7. What role has the institution of the gurdwara played in the Sikh diaspora?

Glossary

Adi Granth Literally, "original book"; first compiled by Guru Arjan in 1604 and invested with supreme authority as the Guru Granth Sahib after the death of Guru Gobind Singh.

Akal Purakh "The One Beyond Time," God.

Amrit "Divine Nectar"; the Khalsa initiation nectar.

Amrit-dhari "Nectar-bearer"; an initiated member of the Khalsa.

Amrit sanskar The formal ceremony initiating Sikhs into the Khalsa.

Baisakhi An Indian new year's holiday in mid-April, when Sikhs celebrate the birthday of the Khalsa.

Bana The Khalsa dress.

bani "Divine Utterance"; the works of the **Gurus** and the **Bhagats** recorded in the Adi Granth.

Bhagat "Devotee"; one of the poets of traditions other than Sikhism whose work is included in the Adi Granth (e.g., Kabir, Ravidas, Namdev).

chauri A ceremonial whisk (made of yak hair or man-made fibre attached to a wooden handle) that is waved over Guru Granth Sahib as a mark of respect.

Dasam Granth "The Book of the Tenth Guru"; secondary Sikh scripture attributed to Guru Gobind Singh.

Five Ks The Panj Kakke, or five marks of Khalsa identity: *kes* (uncut hair), *kangha* (wooden comb), *kirpan* (sword), *kara* (wrist-ring), and *kachh* (short breeches).

granthi "Reader"; the reader and custodian of the Guru Granth Sahib who performs traditional rituals in the gurdwara.

gur-bilas "Splendour of the Guru"; Sikh literature of eighteenth and nineteenth centuries praising the martial traits of two warrior Gurus, Hargobind and Gobind Singh.

Gurdwara Literally, "Guru's door"; the Sikh place of worship.

Gurmukh One who faces the Guru, a follower of the Divine and of the Guru.

Gurmukhi Literally, "from the Guru's mouth"; the vernacular script in which the compositions of the Gurus were first written down. It has since become the script of Punjabi language.

gursikhs Literally, "Disciples of the Guru."

guru "Teacher"; either a spiritual person or the divine inner voice.

haumai "I-ness, my-ness"; self-centred pride.

hukam "Divine order, will, or command"; an all-embracing principle, the sum total of all divinely instituted laws; a revelation of the nature of God.

janam-sakhis "Birth testimonies"; traditional accounts of the life of Guru Nanak.

karah prashad A sweet pudding or paste of flour, sugar, and butter that is prepared in an iron (*karah*) bowl with prayers, placed in the presence of the Sikh scripture during worship, and then distributed in the congregation.

karam "Actions" or karma; the destiny or fate of an individual, generated in accordance with deeds performed in one's present and past existences.

Kes-dhari Literally, "hair-bearer"; a Sikh who affirms his identity by wearing unshorn hair.

Khalsa Literally, "pure" or "crown estate"; hence an order of Sikhs bound by common identity and discipline.

kirtan The singing of hymns from the scriptures in worship.

langar The term for both the community kitchen and the meal that is prepared there and served to all present in the congregation.

man The complex of heart, mind, and spirit.

manji Literally, "cot"; administrative subdivision of the early Sikh Panth.

miri-piri The doctrine that the Guru possesses both temporal (*miri*) and spiritual (*piri*) authority.

Mul Mantar Literally, "Basic Formula"; the opening creedal statement of the Adi Granth, declaring the eternity and transcendence of God, the creator.

nam "The divine Name."

nam-simaran "Remembrance of the divine Name," especially the devotional practice of meditating on the divine Name.

Panj Kakke See **Five Ks**.

Panj Piare The "Cherished Five"; the first five Sikhs to be initiated as members of the Khalsa in 1699; five Sikhs in good standing chosen to represent a *sangat*.

Panth Literally, "path"; hence the Sikh community.

pothi Volume or book.

raga A series of five or six notes on which a melody is based.

Rahit The code of conduct for the Khalsa.

sahaj The condition of ultimate bliss resulting from the practice of *nam-simaran*.

Sangat Congregation; group of devotees in Sikhism.

sansar "Cycle of birth and death"; Transmigration in Sikh terminology.

Sants Ascetic poets who believed divinity to exist beyond all forms or description.

sati The immolation of a widow on her husband's funeral pyre.

Sehaj-dhari Literally, a "gradualist"; a Sikh who follows the teachings of the Gurus but has not accepted the Khalsa discipline.

shabad Literally, "divine Word," a hymn of the Adi Granth.

Singh Sabha Literally, "Society of Singhs"; a revival movement established in 1873 that redefined the norms of Sikh doctrine and practice.

Vak "Saying"; a passage from the Guru Granth Sahib that is chosen at random and read aloud to the congregation as the lesson of the day.

Further Reading

Dusenbery, Verne A. 2008. *Sikhs at Large: Religion, Culture, and Politics*. New Delhi: Oxford University Press. A collection of essays bringing together different perspectives on the cultural and political dimensions of the Sikh diaspora and of Sikhism as a global religion.

Fenech, Louis E. 2008. *The Darbar of the Sikh Gurus: The Court of God in the World of Men*. New Delhi: Oxford University Press. Traces the evolving nature of the court of the Sikh Gurus in the broader historical context of Indo-Persian courtly tradition.

Grewal, J.S. 1991. *The New Cambridge History of India: The Sikhs of the Punjab*. Cambridge: Cambridge University Press. A classic chronological study of Sikh history from the beginnings to the present day.

Jakobsh, Doris R. 2012. *Sikhism*. Honolulu: University of Hawai'i Press. A comprehensive overview of Sikhism in its Indian context and as an increasingly global tradition.

Mandair, Arvind-pal S. 2010. *Religion and the Spectre of the West: Sikhism, India, Postcolonialism, and the Politics of Translation*. New York: Columbia University. A recent study of the Sikh tradition from a postcolonial perspective.

McLeod, W.H. 1984. *Textual Sources for the Study of Sikhism*. Manchester: Manchester University Press. An anthology of selections covering all aspects of Sikh belief, worship, and practice.

——. 1999. *Sikhs and Sikhism*. New Delhi: Oxford University Press. An omnibus edition of four classic studies on the history and evolution of Sikhs and Sikhism by one of the world's leading scholars in the field.

——. 2002. *The Sikhs of the Khalsa*. New Delhi: Oxford University Press. A study of how the *Rahit* or "Code of Conduct" came into being, how it developed in response to historical circumstances, and why it still retains an unchallenged hold over all who consider themselves Khalsa Sikhs.

Nesbitt, Eleanor. 2005. *Sikhism: A Very Short Introduction*. Oxford: Oxford University Press. An ethnographic introduction to Sikhism, its teachings, practices, rituals, and festivals.

Oberoi, Harjot. 1994. *Construction of Religious Boundaries*. New Delhi: Oxford University Press. A major reinterpretation of Sikh religion and society during the colonial period.

Singh, Harbans, ed. 1992–8. *The Encyclopaedia of Sikhism*, 4 vols. Patiala: Punjabi University. A four-volume reference work covering Sikh life and letters, history and philosophy, customs and rituals, social and religious movements, art and architecture, and locales and shrines.

Singh, Nikky-Guninder Kaur. 2011. *Sikhism: An Introduction*. London and New York: I.B. Tauris. An introduction to Sikh religion and culture, highlighting various issues related to doctrine, worship, ethics, art, architecture, and diaspora.

Singh, Pashaura. 2006. *Life and Work of Guru Arjan: History, Memory and Biography in the Sikh Tradition.* **New Delhi: Oxford University Press.** A reconstruction of the life and work of the fifth Guru, based on history, collective memory, tradition, and mythic representation.

Recommended Websites

www.columbia.edu/itc/mealac/pritchett/ oogenerallinks/ index.html

A good site with links to many resources on South Asia.

www.sikhs.org

The Sikhism Home Page, Brampton, ON.

www.sikhnet.com

SikhNet, Espanola, New Mexico.

www.sgpc.net

Shiromani Gurdwara Parbandhak Committee, Amritsar.

www.sikhchic.com

Online magazine: journey through the Sikh universe.

www.sikhcoalition.org

Sikh advocacy group in the United States of America

www.saldef.org

Sikh American Legal Defense and Education Fund

www.sikhsforjustice.org

Sikhs for Justice (SFJ) is a human rights organization

References

McLeod, W.H. 1984. *Textual Sources for the Study of Sikhism.* Manchester: Manchester University Press.

———. 1989. *Who Is a Sikh? Problem of Sikh Identity.* Oxford: Clarendon Press.

———. 1997. *Sikhism.* London: Penguin Books.

Singh, Pashaura. 2006. *Life and Work of Guru Arjan: History, Memory and Biography in the Sikh Tradition.* New Delhi: Oxford University Press.

Notes

This chapter is dedicated to the memory of my teacher, Professor Willard G. Oxtoby.

1. This reference means that the passage quoted comes from the 27th stanza of the ballad (*Var*) in the musical measure *Majh*, by Guru Nanak (M1), on page 150 of the Adi Granth (AG).

2. For a discussion of this work by the artists themselves, see www.sikhchic.com/article-detail.php?cat=21&id=747. *Nineteen Eighty-Four and the Via Dolorosa Project* (2009) is a semi-autobiographical documentary film in which the artists draw parallels with the Christian faith.

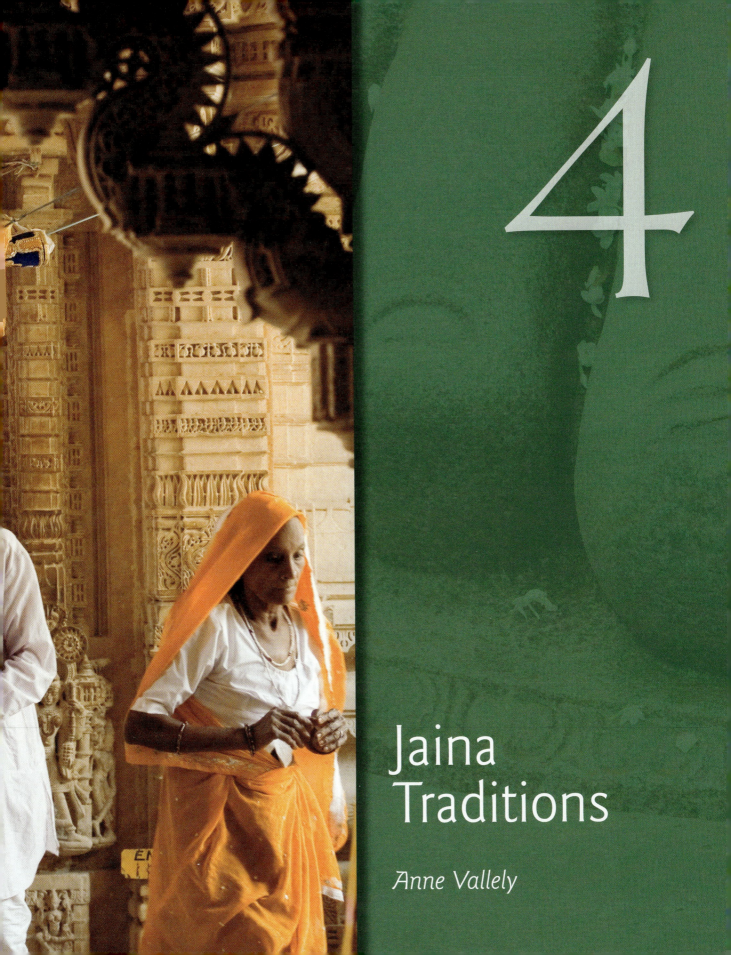

4

Jaina
Traditions

Anne Vallely

Traditions at a Glance

Numbers

Estimates range from 5 to 8 million worldwide.

Distribution

Primarily India; smaller numbers in East Africa, England, and North America.

Principal Historical Periods

599–527 BCE	Traditional dates of Mahavira
c. 310 BCE	Beginning of the split within the Jaina community
2nd century BCE	Possible composition of *Kalpa Sutra*
6th century CE	Crystallization of Svetambara sect
17th century	Emergence of the Svetambara Sthanakvasi subsect
18th century	Emergence of the Svetambara Terapanthi subsect

Founders and Leaders

The 24 Jinas or Tirthankaras: a series of "ford-builders" who achieved perfect enlightenment and serve as guides for other human beings. The most important Tirthankaras are the two most recent, Parsavanath and Mahavira.

Deities

None in philosophy; a few minor deities in popular practice; some Jainas also worship Hindu deities such as Sri Lakshmi. Although the Tirthankaras are not gods, their images are revered by many Jainas.

Authoritative Texts

All Jainas agree that the earliest texts were lost long ago. The Svetambara sect reveres a collection called the *Agama*, consisting of various later treatises known as the *Angas*, as well as the *Kalpa Sutra*, which contains the life stories of the Tirthankaras. The Digambara sect believes that the original *Angas* were lost as well and focus instead on a set of texts called *Prakaranas* (treatises).

Noteworthy Teachings

The soul is caught in karmic bondage as a result of violence, both intended and unintended, done to other beings. Non-violence is the most important principle, in thought, word, and deed. Freed from karma, the soul attains crystal purity.

In this chapter you will learn about:

- the socio-cultural context in which Jaina traditions emerged in northwestern India between the ninth and sixth centuries BCE
- the geographic spread of the early Jaina community and the concomitant rise of distinctive branches of belief and practice, including an overview of their historical development until the modern period
- the singularity of the soul in Jainism's intricate cosmology, its need to free itself from the material world, and the centrality of non-violence for its liberation
- the rigorous demands of the idealized renouncer path, as well as the mainstream householder path and its relationship with the ideals of Jainism
- the central teachings, prayers, practices, and festivals that constitute the lifeblood of Jainism for the millions of its adherents.

A frail monk sits cross-legged on a bed, leaning against the wall for support as his followers enter the room. Everyone knows this is the last time they will gather for *darshana*—to pay homage to their guru and receive his blessing—for he has taken the vow of **sallekhana** and the process is nearing its

---

Jaina pilgrims at a temple in the Jaisalmer Fort, Rajasthan (© Craig Lovell/Eagle Visions Photography/Alamy).

end. *Sallekhana* is the ritual death achieved at the end of a long fast. No Jaina is required to undertake such a fast; in fact, Jainas are expressly forbidden to cause harm to any living being, whether in thought, speech, or action. But the Jaina path is one of **renunciation**—of departure from life during life—and *sallekhana* is merely its logical end. Voluntary death is the most radical statement possible of detachment from the body and the world. A dispassionate death is a triumph for the eternal soul on its journey towards perfection.

⊛ Overview

Jainism confronts us with a simple yet extraordinary message: the path to happiness, truth, and

Sites

Gwalior Fort, Madhya Pradesh

The Gwalior Fort in the central Indian state of Madhya Pradesh contains architectural treasures from several historic northern Indian kingdoms. Colossal rock-cut sculptures of the Tirthankaras (dating from the ninth to the fifteenth century) gaze down on Gwalior city below. According to legend, the city was named for a Jaina saint named Gwalipa after he cured a Rajput chieftain of leprosy.

© Atlantide Phototravel/Corbis

Timeline

c. 850 BCE	Parsavanath, the 23rd Tirthankara
599–527	Traditional dates of Mahavira
4th century	Possible beginning of split within Jaina community with southward migration of one group
2nd century CE	Umasvati, Digambara author of the *Tatthvartha Sutra*
5th century	First Jaina temples
9th century	Jinasena, Svetambara philosopher
10th century	Colossal statue of Bahubali erected in Shravanabelagola, Karnataka
11th century	Dilwara temple complex in Rajasthan
12th century	Hemachandra, Svetambara philosopher
15th century	Lonkashaha initiates reform in the Svetambara tradition
16th century	Banarsidass initiates reform in the Digambara tradition
17th century	Formation of Svetambara Sthanakvasi subsect
18th century	Formation of Svetambara Terapanthi subsect
20th century	Revitalization of the Bhattaraka tradition within the Digambara sect

self-realization is the path of restraint. Happiness is the product not of doing but of not-doing; not of embracing the world but of disengaging from it.

It is this emphasis on restraint that gives Jainism its distinctive ascetic character. To study the Jaina tradition, however, is to realize that it cannot be contained within such narrow bounds. For one thing, the Jaina community is equally well known for its business acumen, worldly success, and strong social identity—in other words, for its effective, dynamic engagement with the world.

Outsiders often perceive a paradoxical disjunction between the Jaina community's this-worldly achievements and its other-worldly ethos. But this seeming paradox reflects the spirit of the tradition: the path of renunciation is a path of transformative power. The power of renunciation lies not in opposing worldly power, but rather in transcending and subsuming it. Some of the most interesting dimensions of Jainism can be traced to this interplay between the worldly and the other-worldly, both in scripture and in lived practice. Ultimately, following the Jaina path means withdrawing from the world—not just from its sorrows but also from its ephemeral joys, from family and community, from desires and pride, even from one's own body. Conquering our attachment to the world is the most difficult of all battles, but for Jainas it is the only battle worth engaging. Such is the message of the **Jinas** ("victors" or "conquerors"), the 24 ascetic–prophets—the most recent of whom was **Mahavira** (c. 599–527 BCE)— who taught the path to eternal happiness.

Jainism is a tradition that expresses itself ritually through the veneration and emulation of the Jinas (also known as "**Tirthankaras**"—builders of bridges across the ocean of birth and death, or *samsara*). The Jina is the highest expression of the Jaina ideal, and the focus of the Jaina devotional apparatus. A commanding figure who could just as easily have been a worldly *chakravartin*—the ideal benevolent ruler—endowed with all the powers and possessions the world has to offer, the Jina "conquers" the world by turning his back on it. Indeed, the Jina is venerated in both his potentialities: as the regal *chakravartin*, magnificently bejewelled and crowned, and as the unadorned **Arhat** (perfected being), deep in meditation, entirely detached from worldly concerns. World renouncer and world conqueror, though antithetical in their orientations, both trace their beginnings to the auspicious karma accrued through a life of non-violence. Restraint, self-discipline, and commitment not to harm are the starting points for the Jina and the *chakravartin* alike.

To grasp the vigorous, even forceful character of Jainism, we need to keep in mind that the Jaina path of renunciation is one not of retreat from the harshness of the world, but of triumph over it. The world surrenders its bounty spontaneously to those who conquer it through detachment—though of course the true renouncer is indifferent to such rewards.

For Jainas the highest possible value is non-violence. So central is this value that Jainas commonly express the essence of their tradition in three words: "*ahimsa paramo dharma*" ("non-violence is the supreme path"). This is not to say that Jainas seek to eradicate the violence of the world. In a universe where every life exists only at the expense of others, such a commitment would be futile; furthermore, any engagement with the world only causes us to sink deeper into its depths, generating ever more karma to fasten to our souls. Rather, the Jaina commitment to non-violence is a commitment to radical non-interference.

Jainas equate non-violence with renunciation because it is only through the total cessation of activity—of mind, speech, and body—that one can truly avoid harming others and, consequently, oneself.

We are surrounded by countless life forms, many of which are invisible to the eye. All possess an eternal soul (*jiva*), and none desires to be harmed. Yet their omnipresence means that we cannot perform any action without causing them harm. And in causing them harm, we harm ourselves, for every act of violence we perpetrate increases the negative karma attached to our souls, impeding our ability to know our true selves. Lack of intention to commit harm is an important mitigating factor. But even unintended acts of harm still result in some degree of karmic bondage—though that karma is

less heavy, dark, and damaging than the kind created when the harm is intentional.

Jainism tells us that attachment to the world, our bodies, and the cultivation of our personalities comes at the expense of knowing our true Self. The Self has nothing to do with this world—not with its sounds, its colours, or its rhythms, nor with our own talents, aptitudes, or experiences, nor even with the relationships we forge with others. The worldly, social selves constructed with such care from the time of our birth are no more than elaborate sand castles, washed away with each wave of the ocean of *samsara*.

The Self is fundamentally other. Its deep, silent tranquillity is indifferent to the cacophony of the world. And precisely because the soul does not lobby for the attention of our consciousness, its presence is easy to ignore amidst the endless distractions created by the demands of the body. Nevertheless, the soul is luminous, radiating peace, and on very rare occasions our conscious minds may catch a glimpse of its magnificence. Jainas call this momentary awakening **samyak darshan** ("right faith" or "correct intuition" into the workings of the world), and it is the starting point of Jainism.

In the absence of *samyak darshan* Jainism makes little sense. The restraint and self-discipline it calls for are challenges to be undertaken only by those with an awareness of both the uniqueness of human birth—the only incarnation from which liberation can be attained—and the perils of worldly attachment.

According to Jainas, there is only one path to emancipation: the path of self-discipline and non-harm. Yet this singular path leads to a remarkable range of Jaina communities, and the lived traditions of Jainism vary widely in both interpretation and practice. In fact, diversity is one of the distinguishing characteristics of Jainism.

The most fundamental distinction is the one between the two Jaina sects: **Digambara** (naked or "sky-clad") and **Svetambara** (white-clad). This sectarian split occurred some 200 years after the death of Mahavira, and was the product of enduring differences in views regarding ascetic practice, women's spiritual capacity, and the nature of the Jina, among other things.

Other issues that divide Jainas include the worship of images or idols and the use of "living beings" such as flowers, water, and fire in worship. Despite the diversity of their interpretations, however, all Jainas share the commitment to renunciation and non-violence that is the heart of the tradition. The message of restraint is unambiguously conveyed by the "sky-clad" ascetics who literally embody the principle of renunciation, but it is also present in the beliefs and practices of lay Jainas, including those who live in a context of plenty. Out of the clamorous diversity of Jaina expression emerges the unbroken and unvarying message that non-violence is the only path to liberation.

◉ The Shramana Revolution

Jainism appeared on the historical scene sometime between the ninth and sixth centuries BCE as part of the same *shramana* ("world-renouncing") movement that gave rise to Buddhism. The imprecise dating reflects the meagre data that historians have at their disposal. The later date is the more commonly accepted because the historicity of Mahavira (born Vardhamana Jnatrpura) has been widely established. The earlier date is associated with the life of the twenty-third Tirthankara, Parsavanath, for which the evidence is limited to the occasional scriptural reference (for instance, Mahavira's parents were said to be devotees of the lineage of Parsavanath).

The followers of Mahavira, like other *shramana* groups (most notably the followers of the Buddha), rejected the brahminical orthodoxy of the day. As their name implies, the "world renouncers" considered the brahmins' preoccupation with cosmic and social order to be fundamentally flawed. All the elements that went into maintaining that order—the hierarchical caste system, the elaborate liturgy, the rituals, and above all the cult of sacrifice—were anathema to the renouncers.

United in their condemnation of the status quo, the *shramanas* also held similar views regarding the need for salvation from a meaningless cosmos. All

regarded the cosmic order not as the creation of a transcendent, cosmic god—the existence of which they denied—but rather as a purposeless place of suffering that must be transcended. Finally, each *shramana* group claimed a unique insight into the workings of the cosmos, as well as the means to escape its confines and attain **moksha** (liberation/ nirvana). Despite their similarities, therefore, the various *shramana* groups developed as distinct traditions and even rivals.

Mahavira is said to have been born to a ruling family in the region of Nepal–northeastern India. Our knowledge of his life is derived from very limited scriptural sources (Jaina texts and parts of the Buddhist Pali canon). Almost all that can be said with any authority is that he was a historical personage whose teachings on restraint attracted a considerable number of disciples and lay followers.

Nevertheless, the Jaina tradition has many tales of the teacher they call Mahavira, or "Great Hero," beginning with the miraculous transfer of his embryo from the womb of a brahmin woman named Devananda to that of Queen Trisala (which unequivocally established the supremacy of the kshatriya caste over the brahmins). Indeed, Jainas are familiar not only with Mahavira's life story, but with the stories of his previous lives. Accounts of his life are retold and re-enacted throughout the year, but especially during the festival known to Svetambara Jainas as Paryushana and to Digambara Jainas as Daslakshana.

Discussion of origins in any religion is often fraught with ambiguities, as historicity and mythology are interwoven in such complex ways that they become hard to separate. The ambiguities are multiplied in the case of Jainism, because the Jainas have both a strong sense of historical continuity and an equally strong sense of being embedded in a system of eternally recurring time, cycles of generation and degeneration so vast that mytho-historical particularities, though "real" (never illusory), are ultimately meaningless.

Jainas believe that the cycles of generation (*utsarpini*) and degeneration (*avasarpini*) produce predictable patterns in social, moral, and physical life. Thus within each cycle of generation and

Map 4.1 Origin and dispersion of Jainism

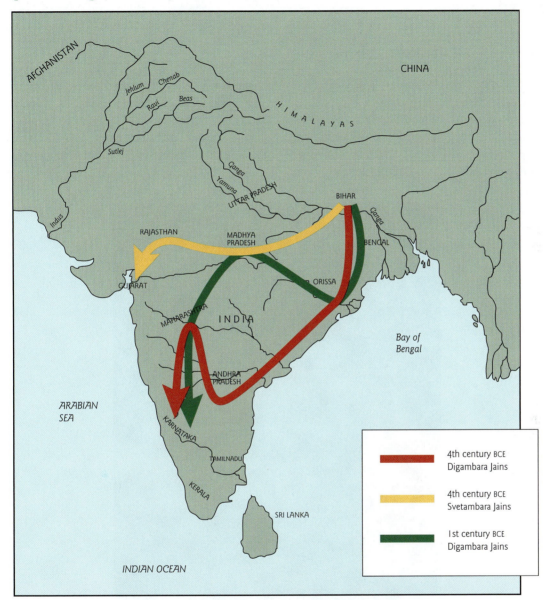

	4th century BCE Digambara Jains
	4th century BCE Svetambara Jains
	1st century BCE Digambara Jains

Today most Svetambara Jainas live in central and western India (Gujarat, Rajasthan, Madhya Pradesh, Uttar Pradesh) and most Digambara Jainas in the south, but communities of both sects can be found throughout the country, as well as abroad.

degeneration alike there are periods that favour the emergence of Jinas who teach the path of liberation. For Jainas, therefore, Mahavira—far from being the founder of Jainism—is merely the final Jina of the current degenerate time period. In the next cycle, which will be one of generation, another 24 Jinas will appear, preaching the same wisdom. And during the cycle of decline that will inevitably follow, yet another 24 will appear, and so on, in an unending cycle of decay and growth.

Sites

Shravanabelagola, Karnataka

Home of the colossal 18-metre (57-foot) statue of the renouncer Bahubali (also known as Gomateshwara), a prince who, in the midst of a battle, gained sudden insight into the senselessness of violence (*samyak darshan*) and renounced all attachment to worldly existence, including his kingdom.

Digambaras believe he was the first person in our time cycle to attain *moksha*. Every 12 years, thousands of pilgrims make their way to Shravanabelagola for the Mahamasthaka Abhisheka (Great Head Anointing Ceremony) of Bahubali.

© Frederic Soltan/Sygma/Corbis

Perched on scaffolding constructed especially for the festival, Jainas bathe the head of the Bahubali statue with substances that range from milk and sugarcane juice to saffron, sandalwood, vermilion, and flowers. Technically, these are not "offerings" since Bahubali, in a state of *moksha*, can neither receive anything from, nor give anything to, devotees. Instead, the ritual is understood as an act of pure devotion.

Focus

The Life of Mahavira in the Kalpa Sutra

Mahavira's Birth

[When] the Venerable Ascetic Mahavira was born, . . . [there] rained down on the palace of King Siddhartha one great shower of silver, gold, diamonds, clothes, ornaments, leaves, flowers, . . . sandal powder, and riches.

. . . [His parents] prepared plenty of food, drink, spices, and sweetmeats, invited their friends, relations, kinsmen. . . . His three names have thus been recorded: by his parents he was called Vardhamana; because he is devoid of love and hate, he is called sramana (i.e., Ascetic); because he stands fast in the midst of dangers and fears, patiently bears hardships and calamities, adheres to the chosen rules of penance, is wise, indifferent to pleasure and pain, rich in control . . . the name Venerable Ascetic Mahavira has been given him by the gods (Jacobi 1884: 251–6).

Enlightenment

When the Venerable Ascetic Mahavira had become a Jina and Arhat, he was a Kevalin [liberated one], omniscient and comprehending all objects; he knew and saw all conditions of the world, of gods, men, and demons: whence they came, whither they go, whether they are born as men or animals or become gods or hell beings, the ideas, the thoughts of their minds, the food, doings, desires, the open and secret deeds of all the living beings in the whole world; he, the Arhat for whom there is no secret, knew and saw all conditions of living beings in the world, what they thought, spoke, or did at any moment (Jacobi 1884: 263–4).

Mahavira's Physical Death

In the fourth month of that rainy season . . . in the town of Papa . . . the Venerable Ascetic Mahavira died, went off, quitted the world, cut asunder the ties of birth, old age, and death; became a Siddha [a liberated being], a Buddha, a Mukta, a maker of the end (to all misery), finally liberated, freed from all pains . . . [that night, the kings who had gathered there said]: "since the light of intelligence is gone, let us make an illumination of material matter" (Jacobi 1884: 264–6).

In this context linear time carries very little weight. Jainas can be said to be both diachronically and synchronically oriented, moving nimbly between the two perspectives. Most crucially, however, Jainas assert that Jainism—like the cosmos itself—has no point of origin. Just as the cosmos has existed from "beginningless time," so too has the struggle for liberation from it—as well as the truth about how to attain salvation. "Jainism" is simply the name we give to this path. By declaring the cosmos to be eternal, Jainism directs our attention away from the fruitless question of origins to the more pressing existential issue of our bondage in *samsara* (the cycle of birth and death).

Jainism is overwhelmingly concerned with conveying its message of liberation through restraint.

This task is urgent because, even though the message is eternal, it is accessible only to specific incarnations (human beings), residing in specific regions of the cosmos (the *karmabhumi*, or realms of action) and, as noted above, during specific time periods. Under any other conditions the message would not reach us. Thus we who have the good fortune to hear it must not squander our chance to learn from it how to escape.

⚛ The Early *Sangha*

Mahavira established Jainism as a four-fold community (*caturvidhyasangha*) made up of monks, nuns, laymen, and laywomen. His open acceptance of women in his sangha is noteworthy, particularly

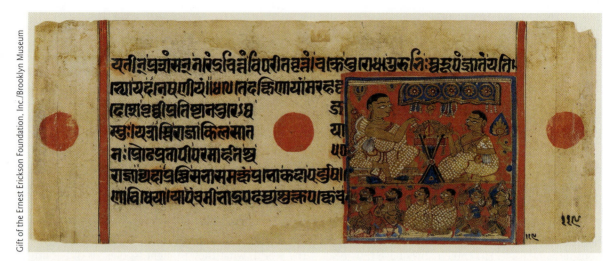

A page from a fifteenth-century copy of the *Kalpa Sutra*, the devotional text narrating the lives of the Jinas. Here Mahavira is shown preaching to renouncers and householders.

since the *shramana* groups generally regarded women as "objects of desire," to be avoided lest they distract male ascetics from their path. (The Buddha's initial reluctance to permit women to join his order is well known.)

For its first 30 years the sangha was held together by the charismatic example of the living Jina. It is said that Mahavira's sangha grew to include 36,000 nuns and 14,000 monks, as well as 318,000 laywomen and 159,000 laymen (Jaini 1979: 37). The preponderance of nuns over monks—highly unusual for a religious order in India—has remained a distinguishing feature of Jainism throughout its history.

At the age of 72 Mahavira "left his body" and attained *moksha*. For Jainas, *moksha* is a state of complete detachment from the world, a state from which communication with those still in the cycle of *samsara* is impossible. Thus Mahavira's followers were deprived of the sort of post-mortem cult typical of some other religious traditions, in which followers have sought to maintain contact with their central figures through prayer. Instead, the Jainas faced the enormous challenge of sustaining their tradition without any hope of spiritual guidance from the Jina.

Mahavira's disciples assumed leadership of the community, but the process of institutionalization soon gave rise to dissension. Within two centuries of Mahavira's death, the once cohesive Jaina community had begun to split into two discrete traditions. The precise causes of the split remain unknown, but many sources suggest that the turning point came in the fourth century BCE, when one group moved south (possibly in response to a severe famine in the north). Thereafter the two groups developed in isolation. Differences inevitably arose, and in time each group came to see the other as deviating from the vision of Mahavira, and therefore as inauthentic.

That the northern group had abandoned Mahavira's principle of nudity and begun wearing a white robe was a particular abomination to the southerners, for whom nudity was among the most elemental expressions of non-attachment and non-violence. The northerners argued that a simple garment had no bearing on spiritual progress. Nevertheless, the matter of clothing was such a central and visible difference that it became the basis for the two groups' self-identification. Eventually, in the early centuries of the Common Era, the northerners came to be known as the Svetambara (white-clad) and the southerners as the Digambara (sky-clad, or naked). The lay followers of both groups (including the fully clothed lay followers of the naked monks) likewise took on these appellations as markers of their religious identity.

This was not the only point of division, however. Another important disagreement involved women's eligibility for initiation into the order. The Digambaras' insistence on nudity meant that women were, *a priori*, disqualified from taking the vows of renunciation. The Svetambaras, by contrast, imposed no such condition and therefore did permit women to join them.

Both groups regard women's bodies as inferior to men's in that they are weaker by nature. Therefore the ascetic path is more difficult for them. For the Svetambaras, however, the female body is not an insurmountable obstacle; they permit women full initiation, and even maintain that the nineteenth Jina (Mallinath) was female. Digambaras vehemently disagree, arguing that asceticism requires a powerful, "adamantine" body, which women lack (Jaini 1979: 39). They believe that rebirth in a male body is a prerequisite for full renunciation, but in the interim they permit women to become *aryikas* (noble women) and lead a life of semi-renunciation.

Finally, the nature of the Jina's omniscience when embodied (that is, while in life) came to be a point of contention between the two groups. According to the Digambaras, one who is omniscient must already have transcended bodily appetites and functions. Thus the Jina has no need of normal bodily activities such as sleep or the consumption and elimination of food, and does not preach but rather communicates by a divine, supernatural sound. The Svetambaras, by contrast, believe that all embodied beings are subject to bodily demands; therefore the omniscient Jina eats, sleeps, and communicates in the regular way through the spoken word.

Sacred Literature

Scholars of religion today acknowledge that the boundaries separating one religion from another have never been as watertight as the scriptures of those religions suggest they are. The creation of a sacred literature or canon might seem to require the existence of a well-defined community. But in practice the development of such a community may depend (at least in part) on the creation of such a canon. While a socially recognized community of some kind must have existed in order for a canon to develop, it would always have been, and continues to be, more porous than scriptures suggest.

The sacred literature of the Jainas is said to have been transmitted by the Jina Mahavira to his followers, but it is not believed to have originated with him. In our time cycle, the eternal teachings were first propounded by the Jina **Rsabha**, and then promulgated anew by each succeeding prophet. Mahavira's teachings were committed to memory by his closest disciples, the *ganadharas*, who then transmitted them orally to other disciples, who in turn passed them along down the generations. Thus the

Sites

Sammet Shikarji, Jharkand

Known as the "King of the Tirths" (*tirthraj*), Sammet Shikar (or Sammed Shikar) is said to be the place where 20 of the 24 Jinas achieved omniscience. Part of a remote mountain range in the western state of Jharkhand, in the deep forest of Madhuban, the hilltop is adorned with temples and shrines dedicated to the 20 Jinas and countless renouncers who attained *moksha* here. To reach it, pilgrims must make an arduous trek of more than 30 kilometres (18 miles).

Jaina canon (*Agama*) for many years existed as a purely oral tradition.

The entire *Agama* consists of three main branches: the *Purva* ("the ancient"), concerned with Jaina metaphysics, cosmology, and philosophy; the *Anga* ("the limbs"), which includes discussion of mendicant conduct, doctrine, karma, and religious narratives; and the *Angabahya* ("ancillary limbs"), a subsidiary collection of commentaries on the above topics, along with dialogues on topics such as astrology and the cycles of time.

The canon was faithfully preserved and transmitted orally from generation to generation within the ascetic orders for more than 200 years. In the early fourth century BCE, however, northern India was struck by a devastating famine that is said to have continued for 12 years. The Jaina canon was nearly lost altogether as both the ascetics and the householders, whom they depended on for sustenance, struggled to survive.

From this point on, what actually happened to the *Agama* becomes sketchy and contentious. The *Purvas*—the most ancient section, believed to date back to the time of Parsavanath, in the ninth century BCE—disappeared, although it is thought that much of the content was contained in the final section of the *Anga*, called the *Drstivada*. Unfortunately, according to the Svetambaras, the *Drstivada* was also lost to memory, but its essence was preserved through mnemonic allusions in a text contained within the *Angabahya*.

The Digambaras, however, claim that they managed to retain much of the *Drstivada*, and they eventually put it in writing around the second century CE. This work, called the *Satkhandagama*, was the first Jaina scripture to be preserved in written form, and it is one of very few canonical works that the Digambaras recognize as authoritative. They reject the scriptures retained by the Svetambaras as inauthentic deviations from the original canon.

In addition to the *Agamas*, vast collections of post-canonical writing were produced by the learned *acharyas* (mendicant scholars) of both the Svetambara and Digambara sects, including

Document

From the Bhaktamara Stotra

The Bhaktamara Stotra *is one of the most beloved Jaina texts. It is addressed to Adinatha—another name for Rsabha, the first Tirthankara.*

In the fullness of faith
I bow
to the feet of the Jina,
shining as they reflect the gems in the crowns of the gods
who bow down in devotion,
illuminating the darkness
of oppressive sin,
a refuge in the beginning of time
for all souls
lost in the ocean of birth (1)

. . .
Praising you
instantly destroys
the sinful karma that binds
embodied souls
to endless rebirth
just as the sun's rays
instantly shatter
the all-embracing
bee-black
endless dark night (7)
. . .

(*Bhaktamara Stotra, Manatunga*, 1, 7, 20–1, 26, 44; Cort 2005: 95–8).

Jinasena, Hemachandra, Kundakunda, Haribhadra, and Umasvati. Known collectively as *Anuyogas* ("branches of scripture"), their writings achieved canonical status within their respective traditions and are today among the most celebrated works of ancient and medieval Indian philosophy.

The seemingly intractable dispute over the Svetambara and Digambara canons aside, the gulf between the two groups is not as wide as it may appear. Many fundamental ideas—on the nature of the soul, karma, non-violence, the cosmos—are common to both groups, as are many practices. It would be patently wrong to suggest that differences do not exist within Jainism on these fundamentals, but there is enough consensus across sectarian lines to permit us to consider them "tenets" of the tradition.

The **Tatthvartha Sutra** of Umasvati (second century CE) merits special note here. It is an extraordinarily comprehensive treatment of the fundamentals of the tradition, and remains a cherished manuscript among both Svetambara and Digambara communities. Finally, the recent text *Saman Suttam* (1974)[1] is the first cross-sectarian effort to produce a concise summary of Jaina thought. Following are the fundamentals of Jaina cosmology on which the two sects agree.

Cosmology

Jainas believe that the entire cosmos (*loka*) is made up of six eternal substances, called *dravya*, and that knowledge of these *dravya* is an important step towards self-perfection. These substances are classified in two broad categories—*jiva* (soul) and **ajiva** (non-soul). *Jiva* is an eternal substance with consciousness. *Ajiva* is a substance without consciousness and consists of five types: *pudgala* (pure matter), *kala* (time), *dharma* (principle of motion), *adharma* (principle of rest), and *akash* (space). The latter four—all variants of *pudgala*—are "supportive" forms, without which existence would not be possible.

Pudgala is a concrete substance with the attributes of touch, taste, smell, and colour. Although it has no special function, in its most subtle form it is the basis of all matter and energy. All activities of the mind and body, including thought and speech, are considered to be *pudgala*. All worldly knowledge is acquired by means of *pudgala*—including the knowledge of how to free ourselves from it! Indeed, it is only through perception, which is also a form of *pudgala*, that we can know the cosmos and its contents.

Thus *pudgala* is not antithetical to *jiva*. It is neutral in this regard, although its natural tendency is to become attached both to other forms of matter and to *jiva*. This is an important point, because the renouncers typically speak of matter in highly negative terms (for example, referring to the world as vomit, or the body as a trap). Those terms are chosen largely for rhetorical impact, however, for *pudgala* is *jiva*'s friend as well as its foe. The effective omnipresence of *pudgala* makes this unavoidable. The worldly soul that seeks release from it is nevertheless utterly dependent on it.

The most fundamental existential problem, shared by all beings in the cosmos, is the fact that *jiva* and *ajiva* are thoroughly enmeshed. This is what prevents the soul from achieving a state of bliss, for bliss can be experienced only in a state of purity and separation from all that is not-soul. Jainas do not posit an original state of separation from which there was a "fall." Instead they assert that this state of entanglement is eternal, "without beginning," and that we are constantly exacerbating it, since every activity of the mind as well as the body causes vibrations that create ever more particles of sticky, binding karma. These karmic particles come in two types—auspicious ("good karma," called **punya**) and inauspicious ("bad karma," called **paap**)—but ultimately all forms of karma must be purged. The forces behind those karma-creating activities, and hence the root causes of our bondage, are the passions.

This is the quandary from which the Jaina path of self-restraint offers a coherent way out. By limiting—eventually, eliminating—the inflow of karma and cleansing the soul of all the karmic particles that have become encrusted on it through eternity, we can eliminate the cause of the soul's suffering. The process of purging is called *nirjara*, and it is the purpose behind most Jaina practices. Normally, karma dissolves when (after giving its pain or pleasure) it comes to fruition. But karma can be made to "ripen" and vanish prematurely through the practice of certain austerities, and this is the aim of ascetic discipline.

◉ Major Developments

As a tiny, heterodox minority within the vast Indian mosaic, Jainas have always been vulnerable to assimilation. How they have managed to differentiate themselves, expand, and thrive when other world-renouncing traditions have not remains a curiosity. Paradoxically, the success of "other-worldly" Jainism likely owes much to its "this-worldly" know-how. The skills required to forge alliances with ruling elites and make inroads into established economic structures were key to its survival in the medieval period (fifth through seventeenth centuries). The Jaina tradition developed those skills early on, in the first two centuries of its existence, when it enjoyed the patronage of the kshatriya rulers.

In the final centuries before the beginning of the Common Era, the fate of all the *shramana* groups, including the Buddhists as well as the Jainas, depended on their ability to secure royal patronage. The socio-political "alliance" between the kshatriyas and the various *shramanas* was rooted in a shared ideological opposition to brahminic orthodoxy. The fact that Mahavira came from a kshatriya clan was a sign of the kshatriyas' ascent. The alliance was mutually beneficial: the *shramanas*

prospered with the economic support of the kshatriyas, while the latter gained in a myriad of ways through the extension of their popular support.

In the fourth century BCE, however, Emperor Ashoka converted to Buddhism and the balance of power shifted. The Jainas slowly retreated from their original centres of power in eastern India (Magadha), towards the more peripheral (at that time) northwestern regions of Rajasthan, Gujarat, and Punjab, as well as into the southern areas of what are now Maharashtra and Karnataka. Nevertheless, the wealth and—more important—the political skills that Jainas had acquired from serving (in legal positions, as advisers, etc.) at the various kshatriya courts gave them a worldly acumen that would serve them well long after their royal support had disappeared.

By the third century BCE, the once unified Jaina *caturvidhyasangha* had begun to separate into the two groups that, centuries later, would become the Svetambaras and Digambaras. The split was reinforced by the geographical repositioning of the Svetambaras in the northwest and the Digambaras in the south. Yet Jainas of both sects managed to prosper and gain positions of importance in their new environments. Although their influence with local elites was always limited, their skills, especially in trade, enabled them to establish secure communities.

Jaina philosophy flourished over the following centuries. Among the *acharyas* who produced important treatises were the Digambaras Umasvati

Sites

Rajasthan, India

Rajasthan is a large state in northwestern India bordering Pakistan. Though it is renowned as the ancient land of the Rajputs, Jainism has also had a presence there for more than 2,000 years and has given Rajasthan the world famous Dilwara temple complex near Mount Abu. Built between the eleventh

and thirteenth centuries CE, the temples are stunningly beautiful marble architectural monuments and a major Jain pilgrimage centre. In western Rajasthan is the important Jain pilgrimage site of Ranakpur, home to the exquisite fifteenth-century marble temple dedicated to the first Tirthankara, Adinath.

(the second-century author of the *Tatthvartha Sutra*), his contemporary Kundakunda, and Haribhadra in the seventh century, and the Svetambaras Jinasena in the ninth century and Hemachandra in the twelfth. Together, the philosophical works of the *acharyas* constitute an enormous and celebrated body of sacred literature.

The social organization of the Jaina community retained its "fourfold" character throughout the medieval period, preserving the interdependence of householders and renouncers. Instead of establishing large monasteries, as the Buddhists did, the Jaina ascetics continued to rely directly on householders for sustenance. Rules of ascetic practice placed severe restrictions on personal possessions and comforts. Householders were keenly aware of these rules, and because of their direct involvement in the lives of renouncers, they acted as unofficial enforcers of proper conduct. These factors likely account for the fact that no large Jaina monasteries were ever established. It has been suggested that the Jainas resisted the wave of Hindu devotionalism, and the arrival of Islam, in the twelfth century far more successfully than the Buddhists did, precisely because of their social organization. The Buddhist monasteries also relied on the support of their lay followers, but never to the extent that the Jaina ascetics relied on Jaina householders, who provided **mendicants** with sustenance as often as three times a day. The latter played a central role in the perpetuation of Jaina tradition, and for that reason they may have been less vulnerable than their Buddhist counterparts to the rise of the Hindu *bhakti* movement. Furthermore, whereas the concentration of the Buddhist monks and scriptures in large, wealthy monasteries made them easy targets for marauding armies, the Jainas were dispersed throughout the society and had no property to plunder. Thus the decentralized nature of Jaina groups may have inadvertently contributed to their survival.

Reform

Idol (*murti*) veneration became an established feature of Jainism very early in its history (third century BCE), but the first Jaina temples did not appear

until the early medieval period (c. fifth century CE)—an era of widespread temple construction. With time and growing affluence, the temples became the anchors of Jaina religious life, sites not only of devotion but of interaction between householders and the mendicants who gathered there.

Temple building and maintenance continue to be central religious activities for most Jainas. Today, however, the care and management of temples is almost exclusively the responsibility of the laity. The general absence of settled, temple-based communities of mendicants today can be traced to a number of powerful reform movements that arose between the fifteenth and seventeenth centuries and effectively reinvigorated the tradition of ascetic discipline among both Svetambara and Digambara Jainas.

The reformers saw a direct correlation between the proliferation of temples and what they considered to be a growing laxity on the part of many Jaina ascetics, who gradually abandoned their itinerant way of life for the relative comfort of a settled life in and around the temples.

The first in the Svetambara tradition to question the wealth and power of the *caityavasis* (temple-dwelling renouncers) was a fifteenth-century lay reformer named Lonkashaha. He also challenged their deviation from the principle of *samyama* (restraint), and criticized idol worship and temple building as contrary not only to the ethos of renunciation but also to the vow of non-violence, given that the construction of idols and temples involved unnecessary violence to living beings. Lonkashaha's uncompromising critique effectively put an end to the institution of the *caityavasis* and eventually gave rise to two sects that remain highly influential among Svetambara Jainas: Sthanakvasis (who oppose temple-based Jainism and reside in halls known as *sthanaks* on their peripatetic travels), and Terapanthis (reformers who oppose the use of *sthanaks* as well as temples).

Major changes took place in the Digambara tradition as well, initiated by the lay poet Banarsidass in the sixteenth century. Like Lonkashaha, Banarsidass criticized what he considered to be the excessive ritualism and unnecessary violence (the use of flowers, for instance) associated with temple worship. At the same time he denounced a group of quasi-ascetic clerics called the *bhattarakas*. Analogous to the Svetambara *caityavasis* but with greater political clout, the *bhattarakas* served both as guardians of the temples and as intermediaries between the naked ascetics and the ruling elites—a role that, in addition to gaining them power and wealth, made them vulnerable to corruption.

The Digambaras responded to these critiques with sweeping reforms that led to the decline (though not the disappearance) of the *bhattarakas*. The revitalization sparked by the reformers' critiques put both the Svetambara and Digambara orders in positions of significant strength as they entered the modern period.

⚛ Practice

The importance that Jainism attaches to practice is one of the tradition's defining features. Correct practice (*samyak caritra*) constitutes one of the "Three Jewels" of Jainism, along with correct intuition (*samyak darshan*) and correct knowledge (*samyak jnana*). Although all three are equally fundamental, correct practice tends to overshadow the others because it is so conspicuous. Jainas are everywhere known by their practices—from their strict avoidance of certain very common foods to the Digambara ascetics' insistence on nudity. Before we look at specific practices, however, it is important to grasp the special significance that the concept of practice has in Jainism, and how it is grounded in Jaina metaphysics.

The Jaina emphasis on practice reflects an understanding of the world and human suffering as *real*—not illusory—and in need of active human intervention. This understanding stands in sharp contrast to that of Vedanta-Hinduism and Buddhism, which essentially see the world and human suffering as products of thought and perception, and therefore focus on changing consciousness as the way to freedom. While Jainas recognize that lack of consciousness plays a key role in the problems of earthly existence, they also believe that those problems are constituted from physical realities that must be dealt with physically through practices such as penance and fasting.

We have already described the Jaina view of the eternal soul (*jiva*) and matter (*ajiva*) as enmeshed in a labyrinthine web that will never be untangled without concrete action. Because our entrapment is real in a physical sense—not just an illusory state that can be dispelled through clearer thinking—our enlightenment hinges as much on our practice as it does on our worldview. Good intentions, for Jainas, can never be enough; action must always be the foremost consideration. It is for this reason that renouncers follow an ascetic discipline designed to heighten their awareness of how they move their bodies in and through space—how they walk, sit, lie down, speak, hold items, collect alms, sleep, go to the toilet, etc. It is no exaggeration to say that the focus on practice is a defining feature of the Jaina path.

The elaborate edifice of Jaina practice aims to purify the soul of the *pudgala* that clings to it. By shedding obstructive karma, the soul becomes free to manifest its true nature, radiant and powerful. Practices are of two types: defensive and offensive. In the process known as *samvara*, defensive strategies, such as inculcating detachment and mindfulness, are used to impede the accumulation of new karma, while *nirjara* (purging) uses practices such as fasting, meditation, and various forms of physical discipline to "burn off" old karma.

The hallmarks of Jaina practice—ascetic discipline, dietary restrictions, fasting, **samayika** (state of equanimity), **pratikramana** (repentance of sins), *sallekhana* (fast to death), even Jina puja (worship of the Jinas)—are undertaken, by both renouncers and householders, with the aim of purification through the dual processes of *samvara* and *nirjara*. The main difference between the paths of the renouncer and the householder lies in the degree of purification they permit; the renouncer's life is structured by a series of vows (**mahavratas**) that make it nearly impossible for new karma to develop.

Because renouncers are largely shielded from the risk of accumulating new karma, they can devote their time to whittling away the karmic load they carry. Householders, immersed as they are in worldly activities—working, raising families, preparing food—are awash in karmic influences. Nevertheless, they can limit the influx of negative karma (*paap*) through lay practices (**anuvratas**) such as fasting or limiting possessions, travel, cosmetics, and so on; many women in particular undertake these moderate exercises in restraint. What marks such activities as characteristically Jaina is that they all involve disengagement from the world. Even devotional activities (Jina puja, for example) that outwardly resemble Hindu forms of worship are interpreted by Jainas as practices that foster worldly detachment.

Ideally, the lives of Jainas, whether renouncers or householders, are governed by a series of vows (*mahavratas* and *anuvratas* respectively) that limit worldly engagement, discipline the body, and help the soul develop the tools it will need for its eventual liberation. Thus Jainism is unequivocally a *shramana* or renouncer tradition, even though the vast majority of Jainas at any given time have always been householders enthusiastically, and successfully, involved in worldly pursuits.

Jainism is a *shramana* tradition because its defining framework is thoroughly ascetic in character. It creates and moulds religious identity by asking the faithful to accept increasingly restrictive boundaries. The main difference between the *mahavratas* of the mendicants and the *anuvratas* of the householders is the degree to which the vows restrict worldly engagement.

Ascetic Practice

The *mahavratas* are five "great vows" accepted by everyone who takes up the life of a Jaina ascetic (*muni* or *sadhvi*): *ahimsa* (non-harm), *satya* (truthfulness), *asteya* (non-stealing), *brahmacharya* (celibacy), and *aparigraha* (non-possession/non-attachment). It is said that Mahavira established celibacy as a separate vow, independent of the fourth vow of non-attachment under which it had been incorporated during the time of Parsavanath.

Although the discourse of renunciation refers often to the poetic image of the solitary wanderer, initiation into the renouncer path is very much a collective endeavour. Aspiring ascetics must first seek and receive permission from their families (or spouses), as well as from the leader of a mendicant order.

In addition, the ascetic orders impose certain restrictions themselves. Neither sect accepts individuals who are physically, emotionally, or mentally fragile. The renouncer path was not designed as a refuge for those on the margins of conventional society; it is an arduous path suitable only for the courageous, committed, and stalwart. It is for this reason that the Digambara sect continues to claim that women's physical and emotional natures make them unsuitable for the ascetic life. The female body's "femaleness"—determined as it is by karma—is seen as too great an impediment, making the already challenging life of mendicancy impossible. In other words, the renouncer path is to be undertaken only by those who have both the spiritual desire and the physical fortitude for a life of denial.

By drawing the self back from worldly concerns, the vows create the conditions in which its true vitality and force can be unveiled. The first vow (*ahimsa*) is the weightiest of the five; Jainas commonly say that it effectively encompasses all the others. In effect, *ahimsa* forbids all involvement with the world and ensures that no action is undertaken spontaneously, without restraint. Because the vow of *ahimsa* is total and unconditional in its application, renouncers must be concerned to cause no harm—through speech, action, or thought—even to "one-sensed" beings (invisible air-bodied beings, water, fire, earth) as well as plants, insects, animals, and fellow human beings. Avoiding harm to human beings and animals is easy compared to avoiding harm to water and air and other minute forms of life (all of which are equally endowed with an eternal soul); this is a monumental challenge and is the main reason behind the Jaina insistence on correct practice.

Munis and *sadhvis* are not permitted to prepare their own food, since even harvesting plants

A Jaina woman in New Delhi gives food to a nun. Such women are very conscious of the strict dietary rules that govern the renouncers' lives, and take care to ensure that all offerings have been rendered *ajiv* (without life).

or boiling water inevitably causes harm to living beings. Thus the ascetics depend entirely on the generosity of householders, and even so they must be vigilant to maintain their vow of *ahimsa*. They are permitted only a small portion of the householder's "leftovers"; they cannot accept food that has been prepared expressly for them, as this would implicate them in whatever violence that preparation entailed; and the food and water they receive in their alms bowls must already have been cooked, boiled, or peeled (in the case of fruits) to ensure that it is *ajiv* (without life).

It is critical to understand the rationale underpinning these practices. The path of renunciation is open to all, irrespective of caste, gender, or social position. But it is extremely demanding, and Jainas know that very few will ever be able to undertake

it. The overwhelming majority who remain householders therefore accept, implicitly or explicitly, that a certain amount of violence will be a regular part of their lives. For these people, support for the renouncers is both a duty and an honour—with the additional benefit of earning them merit or good karma (*punya*). More important, it sustains a system in which the ideal of living without doing harm remains a genuine possibility for anyone with the requisite strength of character.

The *mahavrata* of *ahimsa* prohibits outright many aspects of the renouncers' former householder lives, and no aspect of embodied existence escapes the framework of restraint: eating, talking, sleeping, walking, defecating, urinating, thinking, even dreaming—all must be disciplined in non-harm. Renouncers must not walk on grass, for to

Document

From the Acaranga Sutra on Good Conduct

He who injures these (earth bodies) does not comprehend and renounce the sinful acts; he who does not injure these, comprehends and renounces the sinful acts. Knowing them, a wise man should not act sinfully towards the earth, nor cause others to act so, nor allow others to act so. He who knows these causes of sin relating to earth, is called a reward-knowing sage. Thus I say (Jacobi 1884: 10–11).

. . . the sage who walks the beaten track (to liberation), regards the world in a different way. "Knowing thus (the nature of) acts in all regards, he does not kill," he controls himself, he is not overbearing.

Comprehending that pleasure (and pain) are individual, advising kindness, he will not engage in any work in the whole world: keeping before him the one (great aim, liberation), and not turning aside, "living humbly, unattached to any creature." The rich in (control) who with a mind endowed with all penetration (recognizes) that a bad deed should not be done, will not go after it. What you acknowledge as righteousness, that you acknowledge as sagedom . . . ; what you acknowledge as sagedom, that you acknowledge as righteousness. It is inconsistent with weak, sinning, sensual, ill-conducted house-inhabiting men. "A sage, acquiring sagedom, should subdue his body." "The heroes who look at everything with indifference, use mean and rough (food, &c.)." Such a man is said to have crossed the flood (of life), to be a sage, to have passed over (the samsara) to be liberated, to have ceased (from acts). Thus I say (Jacobi 1884: 46–7).

do so would cause it harm; they must look carefully wherever they step to be sure they do not harm anything on the ground; they are forbidden from using electricity and flush toilets (which cause harm to fire-bodied and water-bodied beings respectively); and their minds are subject to continuous self-censure as they try to eliminate anger, jealousy, greed, and desire. Negative or aggressive thoughts are believed to accrue bad karma (paap) in much the same way that stepping on an insect would. The restrictions on speech, body, and thought contained within the principle vow of ahimsa are potentially limitless.

The subsidiary vows of non-attachment, truthfulness, non-stealing, and celibacy reinforce and enlarge the vow of ahimsa. The vows of truthfulness and non-stealing forbid false speech and the use of anything that has not been freely given. Brahmacharya is more than a vow of celibacy: it is a vow to renounce all desire. Even dreams of a "carnal"

Focus

The Mahavratas

1. Non-violence (*ahimsa*)
2. Truth (*satya*)
3. Non-stealing (*asteya*)
4. Chastity (*brahmacharya*)
5. Non-possession/non-attachment (*aparigraha*)

nature have the power to attract karma, and therefore require penance. The vow of *aparigraha* entails the renunciation not only of all possessions (home, clothing, money, etc.) but of all attachments, whether to places, people, things—or even dogmatic ideas.

In addition to the *mahavratas*, which specify actions to be avoided, there are six "obligatory actions" that renouncers are required to perform, some of which will be discussed in detail below. In brief, they are equanimity (*samayika*), praise to the Jinas (Jina puja), homage to one's teachers (*vandana*), repentance (*pratikramana*), body-abandonment (*kayotsarga*), and, finally, the more general pledge to renounce all transgressions (*pratyakhyana*).

Taken together, the *mahavratas* and obligatory actions can appear overwhelming. But it is important to bear in mind that the constraints they impose are not seen as barriers to freedom. Rather, they are understood as catalysts to self-realization, the means to the sublime state of unconditional freedom, permanent bliss, and omniscience. Furthermore, each step along the way to self-realization is believed to bring benefits for the community as well as the individual. For Jainas, the renouncers embody a spiritual power that can work miracles—though of course they are not supposed to use their powers for "worldly" purposes.

The path to the very highest levels of self-realization has 14 stages (**gunasthanas**). Householders rarely rise above the fifth step, and must fully renounce worldly life if they wish to go beyond it. Nevertheless, the householder path offers considerable opportunities for spiritual progress as well.

Householder Practice

The *anuvratas* are the "small (or lesser) vows" that govern lay life and are normally taken without any formal ceremony. Modelled on the mendicant's *mahavratas*, they reflect the same aspiration to limit worldly engagement. They are identical in name and number to the *mahavratas*, but are interpreted and applied more leniently.

For instance, the *ahimsa anuvrata* is partial, not total. It prohibits the consumption of certain foods,

as well as eating after dark (when injury to insects is more likely). But it does not concern itself with one-sensed beings, accepting that harm to them is unavoidable for householders. The subsidiary vows work in a similar manner: truthfulness and non-stealing are emphasized in much the same way as in the *mahavratas*, but celibacy is redefined to mean chastity in marriage.

Similarly, the *anuvrata* of *aparigraha* does not require householders to live without possessions. Instead, it demands that they scrutinize their psychological attachment to their possessions.

The *anuvratas* are seen as establishing a compromise between worldly existence and spiritual progress. They do not interfere with the householder's ability to lead a "normal" existence. Quite the contrary: Jainas have long been among the wealthiest, most literate, and most accomplished communities in India. And from the Jaina perspective, there is a direct connection between their socio-economic success and their religious vows.

Reflection–Meditation

Whereas the *mahavratas* and *anuvratas* seek to discipline embodied activities, the practice of *samayika* seeks to halt them altogether. *Samayika* is a daily period of 48 minutes reserved for meditation or reflection, during which the practitioner seeks to leave the concerns of body behind and "dwell in the soul." Through the practice of *samayika*, the Jaina seeks a state of equanimity by striving to remain indifferent to attachments and aversions, sufferings and pleasures. In the absence of such ultimately meaningless distractions, the Self can experience and enjoy itself. Jainas believe that the practice of *samayika* offers a foretaste of the joyous state that final release will bring.

Fasting and Dietary Practices

Closely connected in intent with *samayika* is fasting, a practice so widespread among Jainas that it can be considered emblematic of the tradition. The word Jainas use for "fast" is **upvas** (literally, "to be near the soul"); this term underscores their belief that in order to get close to the soul we must get away from the worldly demands of the body and ego. Like the daily practice of *samayika*, fasting facilitates withdrawal from worldly activities so as to focus on the soul. At the same time fasting is considered a highly effective means of eliminating karma.

Jainas are renowned for their fasts, which are legendarily long, frequent, and arduous. Laywomen, in particular, are celebrated for their heroic fasting, which is believed to benefit their families as well as themselves. The entire household gains social prestige from the pious acts that the women perform, and the auspicious karma created by fasting can bring karmic rewards for the family.

Jaina dietary restrictions are the culinary expression of a philosophy of non-attachment that is most forcefully expressed in the practice of *sallekhana*, the ritual fast that brings life to an end.

The Fast to Death

Jainas boast that whereas other traditions celebrate birth, they celebrate death. This statement is a powerful reminder that they trace their origins to the *shramana* tradition in which the highest goal was to escape embodied existence. A death that is "celebrated" is one that has been accepted voluntarily and with equanimity, indicating total detachment from the body and the world. We recall that the root of "Jainism" is the Sanskrit word *Jina*—the "one who has conquered" his ego, greed, and attachment to the world, even his body.

For Jainas the ideal death is voluntary, achieved through the ritual fast called *sallekhana*. Although *sallekhana* is not the universal practice, it is not uncommon even among householders. It is seen as a fitting and highly auspicious conclusion to a life dedicated to self-discipline and detachment. To be able to "discard the body" without pain or fear, and greet death with calmness and equanimity, is to reap the ultimate reward of a life lived in accordance with Jaina principles.

In addition, *sallekhana* is believed to be highly advantageous for the soul as it journeys forward.

A dispassionate death results in a powerful expulsion of *paap* (bad karma) while attracting the *punya* (good karma) required to ensure a good rebirth either in a heavenly realm or in a spiritually advanced human state. Jainas believe that at the moment of physical death, the karma-saturated soul will be instantaneously propelled into a new incarnation, determined by its karma. (A soul free of all karma, instead of being reborn, would ascend to the realm of liberation, **siddha loka**; but that is not possible in the current time cycle.)

If the Jaina ideal is detachment, a progressive withdrawal from life during life, then *sallekhana* becomes its logical conclusion. The title of an essay on the subject by James Laidlaw captures this idea beautifully: "A Life Worth Leaving" (2005). For

Digambara mendicant in prayer, fingering *mala* beads.

© Frédéric Soltan/Sygma/Corbis

Jainas, *sallekhana* is the natural culmination of a life dedicated to the discipline of detachment from the world; it is the ultimate embodiment of Jaina values, paradoxically achieved through a kind of disembodiment. Whether or not they choose *sallekhana*, Jainas endeavour to accept the inevitability of death with self-control and serene detachment.

Jaina Astrology

Jaina astrology has received relatively little scholarly attention, but it is a subject of great interest in the community itself. The complex and unique ways in which Jainas use astrological charts is beyond the scope of this chapter. Nevertheless, it is worth noting that the practice points to an aspect of Jainism that is easily overlooked, namely its recognition of the role that external forces play in the process of self-realization. We have seen that Jainas eschew any notion of a creator god, and—with no hope of divine assistance—emphasize self-reliance along the path to liberation. Under these circumstances it is essential to make use of all possible means. Astrology, as it turns out, is one means, especially useful for the insight it offers into the manipulation of karma for both spiritual and worldly benefit.

The Jaina interest in astrology is noteworthy for at least two reasons. First, it sheds light on the Jaina understanding of karma/*pudgala* as something with positive as well as negative aspects. Second, to the extent that astrology is a proactive art that seeks to pre-empt misfortune and take advantage of opportunity, it reminds us that Jaina renunciation is not a matter of flight from the world but rather of a resolute fight to overcome it.

Jina Worship

The objects of Jaina worship are the 24 perfected beings known as the Jinas. Temples are constructed to house icons of them, pilgrimages are made to places associated with them, and they are worshipped daily in prayer. Although four of the Jinas are especially revered (Mahavira, Parsavanath, Neminath, Rsabha), all receive regular devotions.

The main Jaina festivals celebrate events in the lives of the Jinas, as do the exquisite Jaina miniature paintings, while Jaina sculpture is devoted almost exclusively to portraits of the Jinas in meditation. Even among the Sthanakvasis and Terapanthis, who reject image worship, the Jinas are ubiquitous in narrative and prayer. Clearly, then, to be a Jaina is to be a worshipper of the Jinas.

And yet the Jinas are profoundly absent. Having perfected themselves, they are indifferent to their worshippers, whose transient worldly concerns are literally "beneath them." The existence of a lively, emotional cult of devotion within a tradition centred on dispassionate renunciation of all attachments may seem paradoxical, but Jainas insist that the real purpose of devotion is self-transformation through surrender to the ideal that the Jina embodies.

The central prayer in Jainism, called the **Namokar Mantra**, suggests how the devotional cult operates. The first part begins by proclaiming homage to the Jinas ("Namo Arihantanum"), then to all liberated beings ("Namo Siddhanum"), to *acharyas*, ("Namo Ayariyanam"), to religious leaders ("Namo Uwajayahanum"), and finally to all renouncers everywhere ("Namo loe savva sahunam"). The second part consists of the statement "This five-fold mantra destroys all sins and is the most powerful of all auspicious mantras." The words of the Namokar Mantra simply indicate praise, not supplication. The beings most revered (Jinas and *Siddhas*) are incapable of response, as they are in a state of liberation and therefore outside the world of give and take. Jains insist that they recite the mantra as a way of inculcating in themselves the ideals of detachment and non-violence that the praiseworthy represent. Nevertheless, they do not treat the recitation of the mantra as a purely symbolic gesture; instead they readily acknowledge its power to effect transformation. It is widely held that its sincere recitation can be extremely effective both as an apotropaic or protective mantra, as well as one that leads to the inflow of good merit. It is commonly recited before the start of an undertaking, whether a pilgrimage, a sermon, a ritual, school exam, or business endeavour. The Namokar Mantra is the supreme mantra

Sites

Palitana, Gujarat

Palitana in the western state of Gujarat, is famous for the magnificent complex of nearly 900 marble temples on Shatrunjaya hill. Constructed over hundreds of years, beginning in the late tenth century, the complex remains a major pilgrimage centre.

© Francis Leroy/Hemis/Corbis

A lay Jaina worshipping at Palitana adopts the attire of an ascetic for the duration of the *puja*.

Table 4.1 The Ṇamōkāra Mantra

Ṇamō arihantāṇaṁ	I bow to the arihants (Jinas).
Ṇamō siddhāṇaṁ	I bow to the siddhas (liberated souls).
Ṇamō āyariyāṇaṁ	I bow to the acharyas (mendicant leaders).
Ṇamō uvajjhāyāṇaṁ	I bow to the mendicant teachers.
Ṇamō lōē savva sāhūṇaṁ	I bow to all mendicants everywhere.
Ēsōpanñcaṇamōkkārō, savvapāvappaṇāsaṇō Maṅgalā ṇaṁ ca savvēsiṁ, paḍamama havaī maṅgalaṁ	This five-fold mantra destroys all sins and obstacles and of all auspicious mantras, is the first and foremost one.

within Jainism, equally revered among Svetambara and Digambara Jainas. Like so many prayers the world over, it is also often put to music and collectively chanted. But it can also be recited privately and silently, at any time of the day.

Terapanthis and Sthanakvasis are uncomfortable with the quasi-miraculous language of the latter section of the mantra (beginning with "This five-fold mantra . . .") and therefore omit it. But most Jainas consider it an integral part of the prayer.

Document

The Sakra Stava (Hymn of Indra)

"Sakra" is an alternative name for the god Indra. This hymn, in which the god praises the Jinas, is recited by observant Jainas.

[Indra, the god of the celestial one, spoke thus]:
"My obeisance to my Lords, the Arhats, the prime ones, the Tirthankaras, the enlightened ones, the best of men, the lions among men, the exalted elephants among men, lotus among men.
Transcending the world they rule the world, think of the well-being of the world.
Illuminating all, they dispel fear, bestow vision, show the path, give shelter, life, enlightenment.
Obeisance to the bestowers of *dharma*, the teachers of *dharma*, the leaders of *dharma*, the charioteers of *dharma*, the monarchs of the four regions of *dharma*,
To them, who have uncovered the veil and have found unerring knowledge and vision, the islands in the ocean, the shelter, the goal, the support.

Obeisance to the Jinas—the victors—who have reached the goal and who help others reach it.
The enlightened ones, the free ones, who bestow freedom, the Jinas victorious over fear, who have known all and can reveal all, who have reached that supreme state which is unimpeded, eternal, cosmic and beatific, which is beyond disease and destruction, where the cycle of birth ceases; the goal, the fulfillment,
My obeisance to the *Sramana Bhagvan Mahavira*
The initiator, the ultimate Tirthankara, who has come to fulfill the promise of earlier Tirthankaras.
I bow to him who is there—in Devananda's womb from here—my place in heaven.
May he take cognizance of me."
With these words, Indra paid his homage to *Sramana Bhagvan Mahavira* and, facing east, resumed his seat on the throne (*Kalpa Sutra* 2; Lath 1984: 29–33).

Puja assists the devotee in two ways, helping him or her along the path of self-realization and at the same time bringing "worldly" benefits. The beneficent power of good karma (*punya*), earned through devotional practice, makes a reciprocal relationship with a god unnecessary (see Cort 2001). It's important to add here that even though the Jaina devotional cult operates within its own non-theistic framework, Jainas also venerate gods and goddesses who are believed to reside in heavenly realms. These divinities (e.g., Padmavati, the female guardian deity of Parsavanath, or the Hindu god Ganesha) *are* capable of interceding on behalf of their followers. Jainas worship and pray to them for assistance in worldly matters, but not for assistance along the path of liberation.

❀ Expressive Dimensions

The Jaina community is rich in cultural expression, with celebrated temples, festivals, art, and literature, as well as active philanthropy. How can a tradition dedicated to renunciation have such a robust culture? Before we look at the most significant examples of Jaina cultural expression, it's worth considering how it is that Jainas have such a solid presence in the world, despite their ethos of withdrawal from mundane temporal concerns.

Although Jainas maintain that the path to freedom is one of restraint and withdrawal, this is not a forcefully normative message: from the Jaina perspective it simply reflects a sober assessment of the way the world works. To be a "good" Jaina does not require adoption of a mendicant's life, though this is unequivocally the ideal. The tradition accommodates varying degrees of renunciation, and overtly recognizes human shortcomings in this regard.

Each living being is a bundle of karmic proclivities that compel us to engage with the external world. Only human beings are capable of taming these proclivities; yet very few of us even recognize their presence, let alone seek to eradicate them. Jainas use the epithet "Maharaja" ("Great King" or "Great Ruler") for those who try (the renouncers).

The best that most of us can aim for is to control our inclinations by living our lives in a framework of *samyak darshan* ("correct faith"). To lead the life of a disciplined householder is perfectly respectable, as long as it is done in the context of *samyak darshan*.

What ignites the spark of spiritual awareness depends on the individual. For some it may be a powerful artistic experience; for others it may be a philosophical tract, or participation in a public festival. Therefore all cultural expressions that inculcate *samyak darshan* are valued. Building a temple, creating a work of art, taking part in a festival—all help to bring a community together in celebration of shared Jaina values. The tenth-century Digambara *acharya* Nemicandra praised "the great monks and *acharya*s who have established the celebration of festivals . . . due to which even the downtrodden and condemned people become religious" (cited in Jain 2008).

Music, art, temple architecture, festivals, and rituals are all vehicles for celebration of the tradition. Their ultimate purpose, writes Shugan C. Jain, is to "take followers away from worldly pleasures and bring them back to the path of spiritual purification" (2008).

Festivals

The Jaina ritual calendar revolves around three major festivals, with many minor ones in between. The three are Divali, which coincides with the start of the New Year in November–December; **Mahavira Jayanti** in spring; and, most important, Paryushana/Daslakshana, in August–September.

Although it is common to think of Divali as a Hindu or even pan-Indian festival of light, many Jainas believe it began as a Jaina commemoration of the *moksha* of Mahavira. For Jainas, the "light" that Divali celebrates is the light of omniscience. While Hindus celebrate the defeat of the evil King Ravana and the establishment of social and cosmic order with the return of Lord Rama, Jainas commemorate their Lord's transcendence of society and the cosmos altogether.

A devotee offers flowers at the Adinath Temple in Ranakpur, Rajasthan.

Even so, Jaina celebrations of Divali do not differ markedly from those of their Hindu neighbours. For example, because Divali coincides with the new year, the Hindu goddess of wealth, Sri Lakshmi, is enthusiastically worshipped by all. And because the festival marks the start of a new financial year, members of the business community (of which Jainas constitute an important segment) are especially fervent in showing their appreciation of the goddess. Of course, the ascetics are never too far away to remind the Jainas that the greatest wealth is *moksha* itself.

Mahavira Jayanti is a joyous festival held in the month of *caitra* (March–April). Celebrating the birth of Lord Mahavira, it is an occasion for great pageantry, with shops, streets, and temples all sumptuously decorated. Jainas enthusiastically undertake pilgrimages, listen to sermons, sing devotional hymns, and take part in pujas as well as ritual re-enactments of the wondrous events associated with Mahavira's birth. Ritual actors in heavenly costume play the roles of the adoring gods and goddesses, who descend from the heavens to pay the baby homage and carry him to the mythical Mount Meru, where he is ceremoniously given his first bath and his name.

The most important of all Jaina festivals, however, is Paryushana/Daslakshana (the Svetambara and Digambara names for the festival, respectively). This festival is celebrated at the end of the summer rainy season—a four-month period of such lush fecundity that renouncers are forbidden to travel during it, lest they cause unnecessary violence to the innumerable sentient beings that the rains bring to life.

The literal meaning of Paryushana is "abiding together"—a reference to the sustained interaction that takes place between householders and renouncers during the summer. Obliged to stay in one place, the renouncers must seek alms from the same local householders for several months, and the latter take advantage of this daily contact to seek the renouncers' advice on spiritual and worldly issues of all kinds. Paryushana comes at a time of transition in the annual calendar, marking the end of the rains and the resumption of the renouncers' peripatetic rounds. It is the climax of a period of heightened religiosity. The end of the eight-day festival, called Samvatsari Pratikraman, is a day of introspection, confession of sins, and fasting. The penultimate day is celebrated as the Day of Forgiveness (Kshamavani), when Jainas seek to wipe the slate clean with one another and with the world itself by asking and offering forgiveness for all, and by reciting the prayer *Micchami Dukkadam*:

> We forgive all living beings
> We seek pardon from all living beings
> We are friendly towards all living beings,
> And we seek enmity with none.

Almost all Jaina cultural expressions (art, ritual, iconography) are tied in one way or another to the Five Auspicious Events (*Panch Kalyanaka*) in the lives of the Jinas: conception, birth, renunciation, omniscience, and *moksha*. These five paradigmatic events are universally celebrated and powerfully inform the Jaina religious imagination. They are vividly represented in sculptures and miniature paintings, re-enacted in theatre and ritual, and devotedly described in narrative—most famously in the ancient *Kalpa Sutra* text. They are also closely associated with pilgrimages, since every *tirtha* (site of devotion) is linked with one or more of them.

The centrality of the Jinas in the cultural expressions of Jainism—in its rituals and iconography, and as an ethical archetype—is overwhelming. Ultimately, however, Jainism insists that the Jinas are irrelevant: self-realization is not dependent on them, and since the Jinas have by definition passed out of this world into a state of liberation, any connection they might have had with life in this world is radically absent. Clearly, the Jina is not central to Jaina metaphysics in the way that God is central in theistic traditions. Nevertheless, the Jina is the bedrock on which the Jaina imagination has developed and around which Jaina devotional life revolves.

Jainas Among Others

Because Jainas have never made up more than a small proportion of the communities they live in, a capacity for effective interaction with non-Jainas has been essential. Jainas themselves credit their adaptive success to their commitment to *ahimsa*: non-violence in thought, speech, and deed makes for easy friendship. Another factor encouraging broad-mindedness and compromise is the doctrine of *anekantavada*: literally meaning "not one-sided," it teaches that all human truth claims are partial and context-bound, and that intolerance is the product of confusing partiality with truth.

Of course Jainism is not a relativist epistemology. It unequivocally affirms the existence of Truth, as well as its ultimate attainability, but argues that among those who have not reached enlightenment,

no one can claim more than partial understanding. This perspective may very well foster—as Jainas claim it does—a general attitude of tolerance towards difference.

We have seen how Jainism's ethical principles—the restrictions it places on dietary practices, livelihoods, and so on—serve as "fences" to keep the violence of worldly life at bay. Socially, however, Jainism has never erected fences to ensure religious purity. To insist on exclusion would likely have doomed a community so small and vulnerable. Instead, Jainas seek the closest possible integration with their neighbours, adopting local languages and customs while safeguarding their fundamental practices and beliefs.

According to Padmanabh Jaini, a prominent scholar of Jainism and Buddhism, the Jaina *acharyas* were prescient when they recommended "cautious integration" with neighbouring peoples and practices. Well aware of the risk of assimilation into Hindu culture, they also recognized the necessity of forging close social and economic ties with non-Jainas.

Perhaps because of its individualist ontology, emphasizing the solitary nature of the soul, Jainism is not inclined to question the "authenticity" of its followers. So, for instance, Jainas rarely debate who is and who is not a "true" Jaina. This is not necessarily the case with the question of "true" Jaina practices, however. The absorption of Hindu influences into Jainism (e.g., theistic elements, ritual practices) has gone on for a long time, and for most Jainas it has not been a cause for anxiety. This situation may be changing somewhat today. In the current climate of religious revival, as the symbolic boundaries between traditions are hardening, these issues appear to be taking on increasing significance.

Women

Renunciation—Jainism's most (perhaps only) truly venerated path—has been available to Jaina women and men alike. And since the time of Mahavira, the majority of those who have responded to its call have been women. This is highly unusual in the

Nuns descend the steps of the major Jaina temple complex and pilgrimage site of Mount Shatrunjaya, Palitana, Gujarat.

South Asian context, where asceticism has been, and remains, forcefully associated with maleness.

Women played a central role in Jaina asceticism from the beginning, embodying its most venerable ideals. In so doing, they repudiated the "feminine" obligations of wife- and motherhood. Nuns' writings became part of the philosophical tradition, and their roles were recognized in the narrative literature. Furthermore, most rules of ascetic discipline were applied to nuns in much the same way as they were to monks.

Nevertheless, women at no time came near a position of equality with men. Although women scholar-ascetics are known, they are few in number. Furthermore, religious narratives often contain ambivalent messages, extolling women for their piety and chastity, but condemning them as capricious and sexually predatory. While women were permitted to renounce marriage and motherhood

for spiritual advancement, those belonging to the Digambara tradition are still not allowed to take the full vows of ascetic initiation. Furthermore, Digambaras hold that *moksha* is not achievable from within a female body. Svetambaras part company with the Digambara sect here, permitting women full entry into mendicancy and not considering the female body to be an obstacle to liberation. Yet even in the Svetambara sect, nuns are not equal in status to monks, and senior nuns are expected to demonstrate their ritually subordinate status through gestures of deference to junior monks.

Nonetheless, the numerical strength of nuns—a phenomenon that has endured from the time of Mahavira—may to some extent have offset the ideological bias in favour of monks. In the contemporary period, it means that nuns are a regular presence in Jain communities, serving as role models and teachers, and they are able to operate with considerable autonomy. For instance, within the Terapanthi Svetambara order, the *pramukha* (female leader) has near-absolute control over the order of nuns. Although she remains formally subject to the ultimate authority of the *acharya* (male leader), she effectively governs nearly 600 nuns.

Despite the numbers, vigour, and symbolic importance of Jaina nuns, they constitute a tiny portion of the overall Jaina population. The vast majority of Jaina women (and men) choose a far more "worldly" life that includes family, career, and community. Monks and nuns may be the religious heroes of Jainism, but they are utterly dependent on lay women and men for their existence. In defining itself as a four-fold community, Jainism explicitly acknowledges this dependence, and hence the religious importance of the laity. Renouncers could not set themselves apart from the violence of worldly existence if it were not for the householders who shield them from it. Lay Jainas willingly act as buffers between renouncers and the world, enabling the heroic endeavours of the ascetics to bear fruit and in the process creating good karma for themselves. Importantly, it is mainly women who daily provide the necessities of life to mendicants of both sexes. This role is so significant that the entire Jaina infrastructure can be said to rest upon it.

It is only through the efforts of laywomen that the institution of mendicancy exists: they are the ones who grow or purchase the fruits and vegetables, who perform whatever preparation is necessary to make them acceptable as food (i.e., without life), and who follow the detailed rules that govern the offering. The sustenance they provide is the foundation that makes everything else possible: the tradition, the knowledge, the teachings, the experience, the living role models, and the ascetic ideal itself.

✸ Recent Developments

Jainism—like many of the world's religious traditions—has been undergoing a profound revitalization over the last century. This renewal is expressing itself in many ways: a growth in Jaina educational institutions, the wide dissemination of Jaina publications (including sacred texts), the emergence of nationwide Jaina organizations, a rise in the numbers of mendicants, a revival of naked mendicancy in the Digambara sect, the birth of a strong and vocal diaspora Jainism, and the development of a more muscular political identity. All these changes have had the effect of creating a Jainism that is both more visible and more self-conscious, and whose followers are increasingly concerned to define what is (and what isn't) "correct" Jaina belief and practice.

Twentieth-Century Reform Movements

The roots of these changes can be traced to India's turbulent colonial period (1857–1947), which saw the rise of reform movements seeking to modernize the Jaina tradition and give it a greater national presence alongside its Hindu, Muslim, and Christian counterparts. Reformers worked to move Jainism away from the narrow socio-cultural and spiritual concerns of particular communities of adherents. From the perspective of the reformers, the Jainism of their day was deeply conservative and defensive, under the control of insular mendicants whose obsession with purity limited access to the tradition's scriptures and condemned Jaina teachings to public obscurity. The reformers launched a two-pronged attack: they sought to have Jainism recognized as an essential part of India's national cultural heritage, integrated into its secular educational institutions; and they fought to combat the prejudice against those institutions within their own communities, which feared that secular education would endanger Jaina spiritual goals (Flügel, 2005). Their successes were swift and momentous: within a century Jainas would be among the most educated communities in India (their literacy levels second only to those of the tiny Parsi community); their cultural achievements would be recognized as part of India's national heritage (symbolized by the issuance of India's first "Jainism stamp" in 1935); and their scriptures would be widely accessible.

Jaina Identity

The decades since Indian independence (1947) have witnessed simultaneous efforts to define more clearly the boundaries of Jaina identity and to gain recognition of Jainism as a world religion with universal appeal. Although these endeavours might seem contradictory—one constrictive and introverted, the other expansive and extroverted—both are fundamental characteristics of Jainism today. Indeed, far from being peculiar to Jainism, the tension between those two poles is characteristic of identity politics in all world religions today.

Relationship with Hinduism

The effort to define Jaina identity took a more political turn in the second half of the twentieth century, focusing on the community's status as an explicit minority, distinct from and vulnerable to the overwhelmingly dominant Hindu majority. This was a new development, and must be seen as part of the trend towards pluralistic identity politics that can be seen in all of the world's religious and cultural traditions today. It is certain that the communities devoted to the teachings of the Jinas over the last 2,600 years have not understood and defined themselves in the same way. Being "a follower of the Jina" may or may not have been a significant marker of identity, and it was almost certainly not predicated on exclusion of non-Jaina ideas and practices. To the contrary, as was mentioned earlier, the Jaina community traditionally followed a strategy of "cautious integration" in its relations with cultural others. In recent decades, this strategy has become anachronistic for a sizeable number of Jainas. In an environment where Hindu, Muslim, and Sikh nationalisms find frequent and flamboyant public expression, Jainism's low-key strategy has been criticized as ineffective, insufficient to safeguard a robust identity. Reform-minded Jainas have gained momentum in their efforts to have

Jainism recognized as an independent and historically discrete minority tradition in India. In particular, contemporary reformers demand recognition of fundamental differences between the two traditions: Jainas do not consider the Vedas to be sacred, for instance, nor do they believe in any creator God, and they reject the treatment of Jainism as a sect of Hinduism under Indian law.

On the other hand, the demand for minority status is by no means universally supported by Jainas themselves, and some Jaina organizations have spoken out against it. Stressing the overwhelming social fact of cultural integration (including marriage) between Jainas and Hindus, and the harmonious relations that have existed between the two groups throughout history, they see no reason to upset the status quo. Those who oppose recognition of the Jaina community as an official minority within India do not deny that differences of a theological or religious nature exist between Jainas and Hindus; however, they consider the social, cultural and ideological commonalities to supersede the differences.

Jainism Around the World

Far less divisive for the Jaina community have been contemporary efforts to establish Jainism as a world religion. The coexistence of expansive with constrictive tendencies is not unique to Jainism; it is characteristic of all contemporary traditions, being an expression of modernity itself. To be "modern" is to be simultaneously universal and distinctive; to be globally relevant and utterly singular. Interestingly, one factor that has bolstered both tendencies in Jainism has been the rise of the Jaina diaspora. There are now sizeable Jaina communities in England, the United States, and Canada that are forging their own understanding of what constitutes Jainism. The kind of Jainism that is taking root outside India—removed from the immediate influence of the mendicant tradition—is contributing to significant new developments.

Outside India, for example, the renunciatory ethos becomes harder to sustain, and seemingly

Sites

Jain Centre, Leicester, England

The Jain Centre in Leicester is the first such centre to be established outside India. In 1979, the community bought an old church and transformed it into a temple, importing intricately carved pillars as well as both Svetambara and Digambara Jina *murtis* (statues of the Tirthankaras) from India. The temple serves Jains of all sectarian affiliations.

less important for Jaina religious identity. Although Jainas everywhere retain their philosophical commitment to the *ahimsa* principle, in diaspora communities it is often expressed in the "worldly" terms of animal rights, ecological health, and societal improvement; aspirations to self-purification and world transcendence seem to be less common. A similar shift is occurring with respect to dietary practices, which are no longer inextricably tied to the ideology of renunciation; the connection with

© Gideon Mendel/Corbis

Very few Jain renouncers ever leave India, as most are not permitted to travel by any means other than foot. An exception is the Veerayatan order (established in 1973), which has relaxed many of the traditional rules in order to focus on social work. Here a Veerayatan sadhvi offers religious discourse to lay Jainas in the UK.

Sites

Jain Center of Greater Boston

The Jain Center of Greater Boston describes itself as "primarily a religious social non-profit organization." Established in 1973, it was the first such centre in North America. Eight years later the community inaugurated a temple that now serves more than 300 families.

the *ahimsa* principle remains close, however. What we seem to be witnessing is a redefinition of *ahimsa* and a de-coupling of the previously inseparable relationship between *ahimsa* and renunciation.

Diaspora Jainas are far less inclined to describe Jainism as an ascetic, renunciatory ideology than as one that is progressive, environmentally responsible, egalitarian, non-sectarian, and scientifically avant-garde. In the same way, the cosmological dimensions of Jainism have been eclipsed by its ethical dimensions. This shift marks Jainism's universalizing aspirations; its message of *ahimsa* as globally relevant establishes its credentials as a world religion.

Finally, Jainism's sectarian differences are less salient in the diaspora than in India, partly because the community's small numbers make them largely irrelevant. To identify oneself as "Jaina" is already to identify with a sub-category within the general category of "Indian," so for many (especially those of the second generation) additional identifiers carry little significance. The markers distinguishing the two Jaina sects may remain meaningful within families, but they carry little currency on the cultural or societal level. As a consequence, Jaina identity is increasingly emphasized, and this development in turn may play a role in the arena of identity politics in India.

⊛ Summary

This chapter has explored the historical roots of the Jaina path in ancient India, its flourishing over the past three millennia, and its emergence as a global tradition in the twentieth century. Its beginnings as a world-renouncing tradition have informed its social, cultural, and artistic development, so much so that even its tremendous worldly successes (in business and the professions) and its celebratory festivals are not without their renunciatory dimensions. Jainism communicates a message of restraint, detachment, and non-violence in all its expressions.

The Jaina community has undergone dramatic changes since the appearance of Mahavira on the historical scene more than 2,500 years ago, but the centrality of *ahimsa* as the tradition's defining principle has remained constant. Though variously understood, it remains the unquestioned foundation that underpins the many and varied expressions of Jainism that now exist, both in India and outside it. The resilience of Jaina teachings must be credited, at least in part, to their effectiveness; that they are now gaining the attention of many well beyond the borders of the Jaina community is testimony to their enduring relevance.

Sacred Texts

Religion (Sect)	Text(s)	Composition/ Compilation	Compilation/ Revision	Use
Jainism (Svetambara and Digambara)	Purva Agama	Ancient and timeless "universal truths" preached by all the Jinas, from the first (Rsabha) to the last (Mahavira). Communicated to disciples by Jina Mahavira and transmitted orally until the 3rd century BCE, when the verbatim recitation of teachings was no longer possible. Both Svetambara and Digambara accept that all the Purvas were eventually lost.	Reconstructed by monks mainly between the 5th and 11th centuries CE. Commentaries and narratives added by scholar-monks.	Object of study for metaphysics, cosmology, and philosophy
Jainism (Svetambara)	Anga Agama	The 12 Angas were compiled by the principal disciples of Mahavira. Svetambaras believe that the 12th Anga, called the Drstivada, contained the teachings of lost Purvas. All were transmitted orally until the 3rd century BCE (see above).	Reconstructed by monks mainly between the 5th and 11th centuries CE Commentaries and narratives were added by scholar-monks.	Object of study for rules of mendicant conduct, stories of renouncers, karma
Jainism (Svetambara)	Angabahya (believed to contain the lost teachings of the Purva and Anga Agamas)	Compiled and orally transmitted by monks who succeeded the principal disciples of Mahavira. Contained the earliest commentaries on the Purva and Anga.	Reconstructed by monks mainly between the 5th and 11th centuries CE. Commentaries and narratives were added by scholar-monks.	Object of study for specialized topics, story literature etc.
Jainism (Digambara)	Satkhandagama (contains parts of Drstivada canon, said to mnemonically contain the lost teachings of the Purva and Anga Agamas)	Orally transmitted until 2nd century CE, when it was put in writing; the first Jaina scripture to be preserved in written form.	No substantial revisions, though commentaries are common	Object of study for entire canon: metaphysics, cosmology, karma, and philosophy
Jainism (Digambara)	Kasayaprabhrta (text based on Drstivada)	Written by Yati Vrasabha based on compilations of Gunadhara, 1st–2nd century CE	No substantial revisions, though commentaries are common	Studied for philosophy of detachment

Continued

Sacred Texts (Continued)

Religion (Sect)	Text(s)	Composition/ Compilation	Compilation/ Revision	Use
Jainism (Digambara)	Nataktrayi (Samaysara, Pravanasara and Pancastikaya)	Written by Kundakunda between 1st century BCE and 2nd century CE	No substantial revisions, though commentaries are common	Object of study for mysticism, doctrine/ philosophy, and ontology; the most sacred Digambara author and texts
Jainism (Svetambara and Digambara)	Anuyogas ("Expositions")	From 1st century BCE to 6th century CE		Object of study for philosophy, etc.
Jainism (Svetambara and Digambara)	Tatthvartha Sutra	Written by Umasvati in 2nd century CE	Many commentaries were written by Svetambaras between the 2nd and 8th centuries CE, but the process of commenting continues.	Object of study for doctrine, cosmology, ethics, philosophy, etc.
Jainism (Svetambara and Digambara)	Bhaktamara Stotra	Written by Acharya Mantunga in 3rd century CE		Used in devotion
Jainism (Svetambara)	Kalpa Sutra (lives of the Jinas, especially Parshvanath and Mahavira, and doctrine)	3rd century CE		Used in devotion and ritually during Paryushana
Jainism (Digambara)	Adi Purana/Mahapurana	Written by Acharya Jinasena between 6th and 8th centuries CE		Object of study for life stories of Tirthankaras and all Digambara rituals

Discussion Questions

1. Lay (householder) Jainas are integral to the tradition, which has always recognized the centrality of their role. Explain.

2. What are some of the major differences between Svetambara and Digambara Jainism?

3. What are the main reasons believed to be responsible for the split that gave rise to the Svetambara and Digambara sects?

4. How are women understood in Jainism? What are some of the main differences between Svetambaras and Digambaras with regard to women?

5. Although Jainism envisions final liberation (*moksha*) as a purely spiritual state, it does not see the spiritual and the material in oppositional terms. Explain.

6. Non-violence (*ahimsa*) informs every aspect of Jainism, from cosmology to dietary practices and devotional rituals. Elaborate.

7. How do Jainas understand their acts of devotion to beings (the Jinas) they believe to be removed from all worldly matters and unresponsive to their concerns?

8. What is the significance of "right faith" (*samyak darshan*) in Jainism?

9. How do Jainas understand the final state of liberation (*moksha*)?

10. What are some of the main ways in which expressions of Jainism in the diaspora differ from expressions in India today?

Glossary

ajiva Non-soul, non-consciousness; also referred to as "matter" or "karma."

anuvratas Five vows modelled on the great vows of the renouncers but modified to make them practicable in lay life: non-violence, truthfulness, non-stealing, non-attachment, and chastity.

Arhat A perfected, omniscient being (male or female) who teaches the Jaina dharma while embodied in the world and who upon death will attain *moksha*. All the Jinas were called *Arhats* during their final incarnation on earth.

caturvidhyasangha Literally, "fourfold community"; the community consisting of monks, nuns, laymen, and laywomen.

chakravartin Universal monarch; one who governs the world ethically.

Digambaras Early Jaina sect with its own sacred scriptures; identified by male mendicants' practice of nudity.

gunasthanas Stages or steps of spiritual progress, numbering 14 in all.

Jina Literally, "conqueror"; an epithet for the 24 ascetic–prophets who conquered the world of desire and suffering, and taught the path to eternal happiness; alternatively called Tirthankara.

jiva Eternal soul/consciousness; all living beings are endowed with *jiva*.

Mahavira Literally, "Great Hero"; epithet of the twenty-fourth and final Jina of our time cycle, born Vardhamana Jnatrpura in the sixth century BCE.

Mahavira Jayanti A joyous spring festival celebrating the birth of Mahavira.

mahavratas The five "great vows" adopted by renouncers: absolute non-violence, truthfulness, non-stealing, non-attachment, and celibacy.

mendicants Jaina men and women who renounce all worldly attachments to seek self-realization (and eventually, *moksha*) by pursuing the difficult path of detachment and non-violence. Male mendicants (monks) are called *sadhus* or *munis*, and female mendicants (nuns) are called *sadhvis*.

moksha The ultimate goal of the Jaina path: release from the cycle of birth and death; nirvana.

Namokar Mantra The central prayer in Jainism.

paap Karmic particles of an inauspicious nature ("bad karma").

pratikramana Ritual practice of repentance.

punya Karmic particles of an auspicious nature ("good karma").

renunciation The Jaina ideal: the giving up of all worldly attachments (family, friends, wealth, pride etc.) in order to pursue the path of detachment and non-violence. Though a powerful ideal for all Jains, it is practised fully only by **mendicants**; also referred to as *shramanism*.

Rsabha The first Tirthankara of our current time cycle; also called Adinath.

sallekhana A ritual fast to death undertaken voluntarily, usually in old age or illness.

samayika A desired state of equanimity; ritual practice of meditation.

samsara The endless cycle of rebirth from which Jains seek release.

samyak darshan Right vision, faith, or intuition into the basic truth of the cosmos; spiritual growth depends on the attainment of *samyak darshan*.

shramana A renouncer; one who has given up worldly attachments to pursue spiritual release.

siddha loka Final abode of the liberated *jiva*.

Svetambara One of the two early sectarian nodes within Jainism; mendicants wear simple white robes.

Tatthvartha Sutra An important philosophical text accepted by all Jaina sects, composed by Umasvati in the second century CE.

Tirthankara Literally, "ford-maker"; epithet for the 24 Jinas who, through their teachings, created a ford across the ocean of *samsara*.

upvas Literally, "to be near the soul"; a term used to denote ritual fasting.

Further Reading

Babb, Lawrence A. 1996. *Absent Lord: Ascetics and Kings in a Jain Ritual Culture.* Berkeley: University of California Press. A wonderful exploration of the place of worship in Jaina ritual culture.

Banks, Marcus. 1992. *Organizing Jainism in India and England.* Oxford: Clarendon. An ethnographic study of the historical, sociological, and cultural ties between the Jaina communities of Leicester, England, and Saurashtra, India.

Carrithers, Michael, and Caroline Humphrey, eds. 1991. *The Assembly of Listeners: Jains in Society.* Cambridge: Cambridge University Press. An outstanding edited volume exploring sociological dimensions of the Jaina community by leading scholars in the field.

Cort, John E. 2001. *Jains in the World: Religious Values and Ideology in India.* New York and Delhi: Oxford University Press. A detailed and insightful ethnographic study of the religious lives of contemporary lay Jainas.

Dundas, Paul. 2002. *The Jains.* 2nd edn. London: Routledge. A comprehensive overview of Jainism and an excellent introduction to the subject.

Jaini, Padmanabh S. 1979. *The Jaina Path of Purification.* Berkeley: University of California Press. The standard general study of Jainism.

Laidlaw, James. 1995. *Riches and Renunciation: Religion, Economy, and Society among the Jains.* Oxford: Oxford University Press. Explores the place of renunciation in the life of North India's thriving Jaina business community.

Recommended Websites

www.jaindharmonline.com
A portal dedicated to Jainism and Jaina dharma; it contains information and links to news articles.

www.jainstudies.org
The International Summer School for Jain Studies.

www.jainworld.com
Jainism Global Resource Center, USA.

http://pluralism.org/wrgb/traditions/jainism
Resources from Harvard University's Pluralism Project.

References

Cort, John E. 2001. *Jains in the World: Religious Values and Ideology in India*. New York and Delhi: Oxford University Press.

———. 2005. "Devotional Culture in Jainism: Manatunga and His Bhaktamara Stotra." In James Blumenthal, ed., *Incompatible Visions: South Asian Religions in History and Culture*. Madison, WI: Center for South Asia, University of Wisconsin-Madison.

Gelra, M.R. 2007. *Science in Jainism*. Ladnun, Rajasthan: Jain Vishva Bharati Institute.

Jacobi, Hermann, trans. 1884. "Jaina Sutras, Part I." In F. Max Müller, ed., *Sacred Books of the East*, 22. Oxford: Clarendon Press.

Jain, S.C. 2008. "Jain Festivals." Unpublished manuscript prepared for the International Summer School of Jain Studies.

Jaini, Padmanabh S. 1979. *The Jaina Path of Purification*. Berkeley: University of California Press.

———. 1990. "Ahimsa." Inaugural Roop Lal Jain Lecture, Centre for South Asian Studies, University of Toronto.

Laidlaw, James. 2005. "A Life Worth Leaving: Fasting to Death as Telos of a Jain Religious Life." *Economy and Society* 34, 2: 178–99.

Lath, M., trans. 1984. *Kalpa Sutra*. V. Sagar, ed. Jaipur: Prakrit Bharati.

Note

1. This text was compiled by Jinendra Varni and published by Sarva Seva Sangh Prakashan, India. It was translated into English in 1993 by T.K. Tukol and K.K. Dixit.

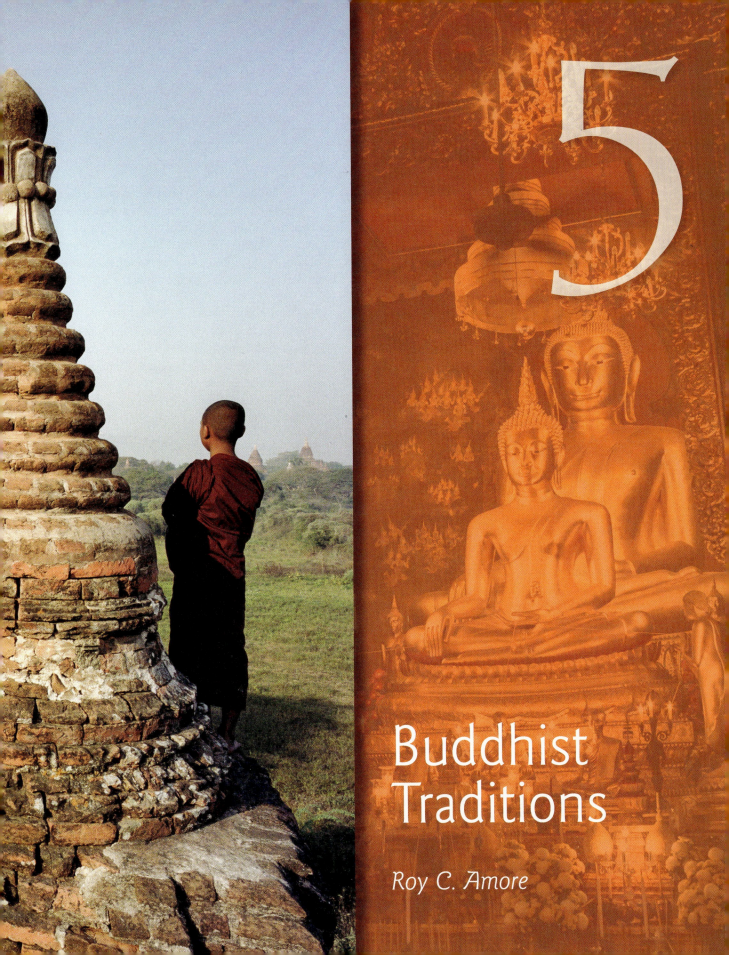

5

Buddhist
Traditions

Roy C. Amore

Traditions at a Glance

Numbers

Most estimates range between 200 and 300 million.

Distribution

South, Southeast, and East Asia, plus minorities on all continents.

Founder

Shakyamuni Buddha, who taught in northern India 2,500 years ago and is believed to be the most recent in a long line of major buddhas.

Principal Historical Periods

5th to 1st century BCE	Early Indian Buddhism; the roots of the Theravada tradition, which eventually spread to Sri Lanka and Southeast Asia
1st century CE	Mahayana emerges and later spreads to Southeast, Central, and East Asia
5th century CE	Vajrayana emerges and begins spreading to the Himalayan region

Deities

The Buddha is not worshipped as a god; rather, he is venerated as a fully enlightened human being. Regional variants of Buddhism have often incorporated local gods and spirits. Mahayana developed a theory of three bodies of the Buddha, linking the historic buddhas to a cosmic force.

Authoritative Texts

Theravada has the *Tripitaka* ("Three Baskets"): *Vinaya* (monastic rules), *Sutras* (discourses), and *Abhidharma* (systematic treatises). Mahayana has a great number of texts in various languages, including Chinese, Japanese, and Tibetan. Vajrayana has the *Kanjur* (tantric texts) and *Tanjur* (commentaries).

Noteworthy Teachings

The Three Characteristics of Existence are suffering, impermanence, and no-self. The Four Noble Truths are suffering, origin of suffering, cessation of suffering, and the Eightfold Path. Other notable teachings include karma, rebirth, and nirvana. In addition, the Mahayana and Vajrayana schools stress the emptiness (non-absoluteness) of all things. All schools emphasize non-violence and compassion for all living beings.

In this chapter you will learn about:

- The origins of Buddhism in ancient India as part of an ascetic spirituality
- The life and teachings of Shakyamuni Buddha
- The spread of the conservative Theravada Vehicle (major division) into Southeast Asia and beyond
- The rise of the Mahayana Vehicle and its spread into East Asia and beyond
- The rise of the Vajrayana Vehicle and its current status in the Tibet Autonomous Region of China
- The nature and impact of Buddhism in the West
- Some of the issues facing Buddhism today.

At the heart of Buddhism are three elements known as the "Three Jewels" or the "Triple Gem": the Buddha, the **Dharma** (teachings), and the **Sangha** (congregation). Buddhists express their faith in these elements by saying they "take refuge" in them. Recitation of the "Three Refuges" mantra remains a regular part of many Buddhist ceremonies.

⊛ Overview

With his last words to his disciples—"Everything that arises also passes away, so strive for what has not arisen"—the Buddha passed into **nirvana** some 2,500 years ago. After a deep enlightenment experience at the age of 35, he had spent the remaining 45 years of his life teaching that all worldly phenomena are transient, caught up in a cycle of arising and passing away. He set the wheel of dharma (teaching) in motion, established a community (sangha) of disciples, and charged his followers to carry the dharma to all regions of the world. The missionary effort succeeded. Today there are Buddhists in nearly every country, and Buddhism is the dominant religion in many parts of East, South, and Southeast Asia.

Buddhism has three main traditions or "vehicles," all of which originated in India. The earliest is **Theravada** (also known as **Hinayana**), which spread to Sri Lanka and Southeast Asia; the second is **Mahayana**, which became the principal school in East Asia; and the third is **Vajrayana**, which developed out of Mahayana and became closely associated with the Himalayan region. All three traditions also have followers in most parts of the world.

⊛ The First Gem: The Buddha

Religious Life in Ancient India

By 500 BCE, the tradition that we have called "Ganges Spirituality" was flourishing in northern India. Located in "The Middle Country," halfway between the Bay of Bengal to the east and the Arabian Sea to the west, the region had easy access to a trading route that stretched across the Indian subcontinent. Trade enriched the merchant (vaishya) class and gave

rise to a new money-based economy, while agriculture flourished on large estates that were owned by the two highest classes (brahmins and kshatriyas) and were worked by commoners and slaves.

Hidden beneath the peace and prosperity, however, were social and ideological tensions that went beyond the usual tensions between the upper and lower classes. The new money economy had created a large urban merchant class with wealth and financial power but without either the land or the social status of the traditional landowning classes. The brahmins and kshatriyas who considered themselves to represent the mouth and arms of the "Cosmic Person" (Purusha) looked down on the new urban rich.

Perhaps the most important cultural tension, however, was between the religion of the brahmins and the other traditional religious beliefs and practices of the region. While the brahmins considered animal sacrifice central to their sacred tradition, the ascetic masters—among them the Jaina master Mahavira—took the ethic of *ahimsa* (non-violence) so seriously that they denounced animal sacrifice.

Another major difference between the brahmin and ascetic traditions had to do with the role of deities. In the former, the deities required regular praise and ritual offerings, and in return they would respond to devotees' requests for assistance. Some of the major deities were recognized by the ascetic traditions as well—especially the creator god Brahma and the storm god Indra. For the most part, though, deities played quite a small role in the non-brahminic traditions. Minor gods might provide practical help from time to time, but there was no question of asking the gods for assistance along the spiritual path. The liberation that the ascetics sought could be achieved only through their own efforts. As an East Asian Zen Buddhist master put it much later, "If there is anything to take hold of, you must take hold of it for yourself." The spiritual masters led the way, but the disciples had to walk the path themselves, without any supernatural assistance. A verse of the *Dhammapada*, a collection that is a favourite of Buddhists everywhere, puts it this

Timeline

c. 531 (or 589 or 413) BCE	Shakyamuni's enlightenment
c. 496 (or 544 or 368)	Shakyamuni's *parinirvana* or passing
c. 395	First Buddhist council
c. 273	Accession of King Ashoka
c. 225	Mahendra takes Theravada Buddhism to Sri Lanka
c. 67 CE	Buddhism takes root in China
c. 100	Emergence of Indian Mahayana
c. 200	Nagarjuna, Madhyamaka philosopher
c. 350	Asanga and Vasubandhu, Yogacara philosophers
372	Buddhism introduced to Korea from China
c. 500	Emergence of tantra in India
604	"Prince" Shotoku, Japanese regent and patron of Buddhism, issues Seventeen-Article Constitution
c. 750	Padmasambhava takes Vajrayana Buddhism to Tibet
806	Shingon (tantric) Buddhism introduced to Japan
845	Persecution of Buddhism in China
1173	Birth of Shinran, Japanese Pure Land thinker (d. 1262)
1222	Birth of Nichiren, founder of the Japanese sect devoted to the *Lotus Sutra* (d. 1282)
1603	Tokugawa regime takes power in Japan; Buddhism is put under strict state control
c. 1617	Dalai Lamas become rulers of Tibet
c. 1900	Beginnings of Buddhist missionary activity in the West
1956	B.R. Ambedkar (1891–1956) converts to Buddhism, leading to the conversion of 380,000 other Dalits and re-establishing Buddhism in India
1959	China takes over Tibet; the Dalai Lama and many other Tibetans flee to India
1963	Thich Quang Duc immolates himself in protest against the persecution of Buddhists in South Vietnam
2001	Taliban forces destroy colossal Buddhist statues along ancient trade route in Afghanistan
2008	Tibetan protests against Han Chinese domination erupt into violence in the lead-up to the Beijing Summer Olympics. The Dalai Lama denounces the violence while sympathizing with the Tibetans' concerns.
2011	The Dalai Lama renounces his role as the temporal ruler of Tibet.

way: "You must strive for yourselves. The Tathagatas [buddhas] are only your guides. Meditative persons who follow their path will overcome the bonds of Mara [death]" (*Dhammapada* no. 276).

It was in this environment that Buddhism originated. Some aspects of Buddhist thought were major innovations: the concept of the impermanence of the human self or soul, for instance, and the idea of social egalitarianism. But others—including the notions of **karma** and successive reincarnations, the ideal of ascetic withdrawal from the world, and the belief that numerous gods, demons, and spirits play active roles in human life—were common to all the traditions of the Ganges region.

The Bodhisattva Vow and Previous Lives

Buddhism, like Hinduism and Jainism, understands the cosmos in terms of an endless succession of universes arising and passing away. Our current universe, having evolved millions of earthly years before the present, was already in the declining phase of its life cycle when the Buddha of the present age, Siddhartha Gautama—also known as **Shakyamuni**, the "sage of the Shakya clan"—was born. In every era, when the inevitable decline in morality and truth—that is, dharma—becomes severe, a highly developed being is born to become the buddha for that era. (In the same way, Hindu tradition maintains that the lord Krishna comes to save the earth when dharma has declined.)

Although many Buddhists believe in gods and spirits, no almighty god is needed to mastermind the arrival of a new buddha: such a highly developed being is aware of the state of the world and knows when the time has come. Buddhists tell the story of Shakyamuni as the Buddha for our era with the understanding that there have been buddhas in previous eras and there will be buddhas in subsequent ones. Each era is considered to have only one fully enlightened, teaching buddha, but there are numerous other beings in every age who are thought to have achieved some degree of enlightenment. Among them are *pratyeka buddhas* (hermits who live in isolation from the world and do not teach), **Arhats** ("worthy ones," or "saints"), and **bodhisattvas** (those who have dedicated themselves to achieving buddhahood). All the Buddhist traditions agree that Shakyamuni lived to the age of 80, but the traditions hold to different dates. Theravada tradition sets the birth at 624 BCE (the "older date"), while Mahayana Buddhists hold to a later date. As for Buddhologists, some correlate Buddhist and Greek evidence to fix the date at 566 or 563 BCE, while others rely on Chinese and Tibetan texts to argue for 448 BCE. Recent excavations at the Buddha's birthplace (Lumbini, Nepal) may support the older date range.

It is significant that Shakyamuni achieves enlightenment through his own efforts; however, he has nearly perfected his "mind of enlightenment" through hundreds of previous lives. Unlike the Hindu *avatara* or the Christian god incarnate, the Buddha, Shakyamuni, is not a god on earth but simply a human being who has perfected the spiritual potential of all living creatures.

What is special about the Buddha is the spiritual and intellectual power of his insight. That manifestation of power, the ability to free people from entrapment in suffering, is what Buddhists have in mind when they say that they "take refuge" in the Buddha.

Before we relate the narrative of Shakyamuni, we must clarify a matter of terminology. Usage distinguishes between a buddha as an already enlightened being and a bodhisattva as one who has vowed to seek enlightenment but has not yet attained it. Thus for the period of his younger years in quest of enlightenment, Shakyamuni is termed a bodhisattva, but in his mature teaching following his enlightenment he is referred to as the Buddha. This chapter will refer to Shakyamuni as "the Buddha" (with a capital "B"), but to any other enlightened being, in the generic sense, as "a buddha" (lower-case).

The story of the Buddha, as Buddhists tell it, has its beginning in earlier ages. During the lifetime of one previous buddha, a young man comes upon a crowd of people filling mud holes in the road in anticipation of the arrival of the buddha of that era. But the buddha comes before one mud hole is filled, and so the young man puts himself into the hole to serve as a stepping-stone. Instead of stepping on him, however, the buddha announces that the young man will become a buddha himself in the distant future.

The young man takes the startling prophecy to heart and vows to work towards full enlightenment. The act of solemnly promising to work towards buddhahood is called taking a "bodhisattva" vow. The term *bodhi* in the first part of the compound means "enlightenment," and *sattva* means "being," as in the phrase "human being." After the young man in our story dies, his karma complex—the matrix of all his past actions—gives rise to a new being. In short, he is reborn, as are all living beings. Over many lives he makes progress towards purifying his inner nature. Stories of more than 500 of his lives are preserved in a collection called *Jataka* ("birth stories").

The best known and most beloved of the *Jataka* tales is the final one, which tells the story of the bodhisattva's last incarnation before he becomes the Buddha. Here the bodhisattva is reborn as a prince named Vessantara, who as a young boy takes a vow to perfect the virtue of generosity: whenever he is asked for something, he will give it. The consequences of this promise are not terribly serious as long as he is a child, but eventually his father, following an old royal custom of India, retires and passes the throne to him.

No one complains much when Vessantara gives food and clothing from the public treasury to the poor, for his generosity is credited with bringing rains and prosperity to the kingdom. But when he gives the kingdom's lucky white elephant to citizens of a rival kingdom, the people demand that his father resume the throne and banish Vessantara. Yet even in exile he continues to give away everything he is asked for, up to and including his wife and children. Finally his father intervenes, Vessantara is reunited with his family, and we learn that the gods have been guiding events in order to give him the opportunity to test his resolve. Vessantara's strict adherence to his vow serves as a model for Buddhist self-discipline.

The Buddha's Birth and Childhood

After Vessantara dies, he is not reborn immediately. Rather, the new being generated by his karma complex waits in one of the heavens until the time comes when the dharma of the previous buddha has been lost and a new "wheel-turner" is needed to set the wheel of dharma (the *dharmachakra*) in motion once again. Finally, when the world needs him, he chooses to be born into the ruling family of a small kingdom in what is now southern Nepal.

The story of the Buddha's birth and childhood varies to some extent among the Buddhist traditions. What follows is a very brief version, based on the early Pali-language account preserved in the Theravada tradition. (Later versions tend to be longer and to include many more miracles.) According

Sites

Lumbini Park, Nepal

Located in southern Nepal, Lumbini Park preserves the sacred area where the Buddha was born, with old stupas, the pond where Mahamaya bathed, a Bodhi tree, and a park surrounded by monasteries for visiting monks. This is the first of the four major pilgrimage sites of India/Nepal.

to this early account, the queen of the Shakya people, Mahamaya, is keeping a vow of sexual abstinence in observance of a festival. One afternoon she takes a nap and dreams she is carried by the four "world protectors" to a pleasant grove of trees. (The world protectors are minor gods who look after the earth, one for each cardinal direction. Although Buddhists do not believe that enlightenment requires any kind of divine intervention, they do imagine minor gods to play an active role in the unfolding of events.)

In the grove, a spiritual being in the form of a sacred white elephant (albino elephants were associated with good fortune) descends from the heavens and miraculously enters through her side, where it becomes the embryo of the Buddha-to-be. After a pregnancy marked by supernatural signs (including the ability to see the child in her womb), Mahamaya sets out for her home city, intending to give birth there. But along the way she stops to rest at a roadside park known as Lumbini, and the baby is born through her right side as she holds on to a tree branch for support. In later Buddhist accounts,

the tree miraculously lowers its branch to assist her, flowers appear out of season, and streams of hot and cold water rain down from the sky to wash the baby. In the Theravada tradition, the birth takes place on the full-moon day of the month called **Vaishakha** ("rains"), which usually falls in April or May of the Western calendar (East Asian Buddhists follow a different tradition). That night a bright light illuminates the world to mark the holy event. In the ancient world, the birth of an extraordinary person was often associated with unusual astral events, such as a bright light or an auspicious alignment of the planets.

The infant bodhisattva is presented to his father, King Shuddhodana, who holds a naming festival. The name chosen for him, Siddhartha, can be translated as "he who achieves success." But Buddhists rarely use it, preferring the titles related to his spiritual role, such as Shakyamuni or (Lord) Buddha.

During the naming ceremony, various brahmin sages offer predictions based on their reading of his physical features. Later Buddhist texts report that

Focus

Shakyamuni and Jesus of Nazareth: Life-Story Parallels

Although Shakyamuni and Jesus of Nazareth lived in very different times and places, there are several parallels in their life stories. Whether coincidental, the reflection of common narrative themes, or the result of historical influence, the parallels include the following:

- both infants are conceived without normal intercourse (Mahamaya is a married woman under a temporary vow of celibacy; Mary is a virgin)
- both infants are born in an unusual setting (Shakyamuni in a grove of trees in a park, Jesus in a stable)

- the birth is announced by angels (to a meditating sage in the case of Shakyamuni, to shepherds in the case of Jesus)
- birth under a special star or constellation
- adoration by sages or wise men, who foresee spiritual greatness (Asita with Buddha, Simeon with Jesus)
- departure from home
- temptation by the Lord of Death (Mara, Satan)
- recruitment of disciples who are sent out as missionaries
- miracle-working

they find 32 major bodily signs and more than 80 minor ones. The most significant features can be seen in the Buddha statues that became popular approximately five centuries after his death. His unusually long ear lobes are a sign of great spiritual wisdom; his golden complexion shows his inner tranquillity, and the wheel patterns on the soles of his feet point to his role as "wheel-turner." On the basis of these signs, the brahmins predict an extraordinary destiny for the young prince. If he stays "in the world," he will become a great emperor, ruling far more than the little Shakya kingdom. But if he "departs the world," he will achieve the highest possible goal for a monk, becoming a fully enlightened buddha.

His father, the king, wants Siddhartha to become a great emperor, so he orders that no evidence of sickness, old age, or death be allowed near the boy, lest knowledge of life's inevitable suffering lead him to renounce the world and become a monk. Evidently the early Buddhists who told this story shared the view of those modern scholars who see religion as a response to the adversities of life and suggest that, in the absence of adversity, humans would have little reason to pursue the spiritual path. As the Buddha explained to his followers, his early life was that of a pampered prince:

> I was delicate, most delicate, supremely delicate. Lily pools were made for me at my father's house solely for my benefit. Blue lilies flowered in one, white lilies in another, red lilies in a third. I had three palaces; one for the Winter, one for the Summer and one for the Rains (*Anguttara Nikaya* iii.38; Nanamoli 1972: 8).

There are only a few stories of the bodhisattva's childhood. In one of them he amazes his first teacher when he shows that he already knows the various alphabets. In another he wins a martial arts tournament even though he has shown little interest in war. In the most significant of these stories, the boy is sitting in the shade of a rose-apple tree watching his father perform a spring groundbreaking ritual when he enters a meditational trance, during which the shadow of the tree miraculously stands still even though the sun moves. The memory of this wakeful meditation state will play a role in his eventual achievement of enlightenment.

The Four Sights and the Great Departure

Despite all King Shuddhodana's precautions, Siddhartha learns the bitter truth of life's sorrows around the time of his thirtieth birthday. By then he is happily married (the earliest sources do not refer to his wife by name, but later texts call her Yasodhara) and the father of a son named Rahula. Going for a chariot ride through the royal park, the prince happens to see four sights that will alter the course of his life. The first three—a sick man, a suffering old man, and a dead man—awaken him to life's problems. When he asks what is wrong with these men, his chariot driver answers honestly, revealing to him for the first time the harsh realities of life. The Buddha would later explain to his disciples what he learned from seeing the reality of sickness:

> When an untaught ordinary man, who is subject to sickness, not safe from sickness, sees another who is sick, he is shocked, humiliated and disgusted; for he forgets that he himself is no exception. But I too am subject to sickness, not safe from sickness, and so it cannot befit me to be shocked, humiliated and disgusted on seeing another who is sick. When I considered this, the vanity of health entirely left me (*Anguttara Nikaya* iii. 38; Nanamoli 1972: 8).

The fourth and final sight is an ascetic whose aura of tranquil detachment from the world suggests that there is a way to overcome the suffering of life after all. To this day, Buddhist monks often say that what first attracted them to join the sangha (the monastic order) was seeing, as children, the calmness and serenity of the older monks and nuns

Document

From the *Dhammapada*

Many of the Buddhist sutras include one or more verses that sum up the teaching. These memory verses were eventually collected as a separate work called the Dhammapada, *"fundamentals of Dharma." The verses from Chapter One concern the pure mind.*

1. The mind is the source of all mental actions [dharmas],
   mind is the chief of the mental actions, and they are made by the mind.
   If, by an impure mind, one speaks or acts, then suffering follows the mind as a cartwheel follows the footprint of the ox.
2. The mind is the source of all mental states, mind is their leader, and they are made by the mind.
   If, by a pure mind, one speaks or acts, then happiness follows the mind like a shadow.
3. "I was abused." "I was beaten." "I was hurt." "I was robbed."
   Those who dwell excessively on such thoughts never get out of their hating state of mind.
4. "I was abused." "I was beaten." "I was hurt." "I was robbed."
   Those who leave such thoughts behind get out of their hating state of mind.
5. In this world hatreds are never ended by more hating.
   Hatreds are only ended by loving kindness.
   This is an eternal truth [dharma].
6. Some people do not know that we must restrain ourselves.
   But others know this and settle their quarrels.
7. One who dwells on personal gratifications, overindulges the senses, overeats, is indolent and lazy, that person is overthrown by Mara [Death] like an old, weak tree in a windstorm.
8. One who dwells in meditation on the bodily impurities, keeps the senses under control, eats moderately, has faith and disciplined energy, that person stands against Mara like a rocky mountain.
9. Whoever puts on the ochre robe but lacks purity, self-control, and truthfulness, that person is not worthy of the robe.
10. Whoever puts on the ochre robe and is pure, self-controlled, and truthful, that person is truly worthy of the robe.
11. Mistaking the unessential for the important, and mistaking the essential for the unimportant, some persons, dwelling in wrong-mindedness, never realize that which is really essential.
12. Knowing the essential to be important, and knowing the unessential to be unimportant, other persons, dwelling in rightmindedness, reach that which is really essential.

as they passed through the streets on their daily alms-seeking rounds.

On returning home, the bodhisattva ponders the four sights. That night, with the help of the four world protectors, he flees the palace, taking along his horse and servant. Many Buddhist temples have murals depicting this event, known as the Great Departure.

Having departed the worldly life, the bodhisattva dismisses his servant and horse, exchanges his princely clothes for those of a poor hunter, obtains an alms bowl, and begins a new life as one of the wandering students seeking spiritual truth along the banks of the Ganges. Determined to learn all eight levels of classical yoga, he soon masters the six levels known to his first guru. He then finds another guru who is able to teach him the seventh level, but even the deep tranquillity he experiences there is not enough to satisfy the bodhisattva.

Therefore, with five other students, he embarks on an independent program of rigorous ascetic discipline. After six years he is subsisting on nothing more than one palmful of water and one of food per day. He becomes so emaciated that he loses consciousness, but the four world protectors preserve him.

Enlightenment

Now convinced that even the most extreme asceticism cannot bring about the enlightenment he seeks, the bodhisattva leaves the cave where he has been living and goes to a pleasant town now called Bodh Gaya ("bodh" being short for "enlightenment"). There he resumes eating and drinking, but he still needs a method. Then he remembers the wakeful meditational trance he experienced spontaneously as a child:

> I thought of a time when my Sakyan father was working and I was sitting in the cool shade of a rose-apple tree: quite secluded from sensual desires, secluded from unprofitable things I had entered upon and abided in the first meditation, which is accompanied by thinking and exploring with happiness and pleasure born of seclusion. I thought: Might that be the way to enlightenment? Then, following up that memory there came the recognition that this was the way to enlightenment (*Majjhima Nikaya*; Nanamoli 1972: 21).

Choosing a pleasant spot beside a cool river, under a *pipal* tree (a large fig tree considered sacred in India at least as far back as the Harappa civilization, known thereafter to Buddhists as the Bodhi tree), he sits to meditate and vows that he will not get up until he has achieved nirvana.

According to some versions of the story, it is at this point, just before dusk on the evening of the full-moon day in the month of Vaishakha, that Mara, the lord of death, arrives. Mara plays a role in Buddhism similar in some ways to that of Satan in Christianity. His main function is to come for people at death and oversee their rebirth in an appropriate place. But he wants to exercise power over events in this world as well. Determined to thwart the bodhisattva's attempt to achieve enlightenment, Mara summons his daughters—whose names suggest greed, boredom, and desire—to tempt him. When that fails, Mara offers him any worldly wish, if only he will return home and live a life of good karma (merit) as a householder. The bodhisattva refuses.

Now Mara becomes violent. He sends in his sons—whose names suggest fear and anger—to assault the bodhisattva. But the bodhisattva's spiritual power is so great that it surrounds and protects him from attack like a force field.

Having failed in his efforts to tempt and threaten the bodhisattva, Mara challenges him to a debate. Mara himself claims to be the one worthy to sit on the Bodhi Seat—the place of enlightenment—on this auspicious night, and he accuses the bodhisattva of being unworthy. With his sons and daughters cheering him on, Mara thinks he has the upper hand. But the bodhisattva has the truth on his side. He responds that he has the merit of the generosity, courage, and wisdom perfected through countless previous lives, and calls upon the Earth herself to stand witness on his behalf. The resulting earthquake drives Mara away. Buddhists today understand this story as symbolizing the surfacing of the last remnants of the mind's deep impurities, which the bodhisattva must overcome before he can attain liberation.

With Mara defeated, the bodhisattva begins to meditate in his own way—the reverse of the way taught by the yoga masters. A yogi seeks to move ever deeper into unconsciousness, drawing in the conscious mind as a turtle draws in its head and limbs, in effect shutting out the world. The bodhisattva, by contrast, meditates to become more conscious, more aware, more mindful.

In ancient India soldiers divided the night into three watches. The same concept can be seen in

Buddhism. During the first watch, the bodhisattva remembers his own past lives; the ability to do this is considered one of the psychic powers that come with spiritual advancement, but it should not be a goal in itself. During the second watch, he acquires deeper insight into the working of karma, understanding how the past lives of various people have been reflected in later incarnations. During the third watch of the night, he turns his awareness to the question of how to put an end to suffering and in due course arrives at what will become known as the Four Noble Truths.

Sites

Bodh Gaya, India

Bodh Gaya in northeastern India preserves the place where the Buddha was enlightened. In addition to a huge Bodhi tree (said to be descended from the tree under which the Buddha sat) there is a temple, and the park is surrounded by temples and monasteries representing different schools of Buddhism. Many Tibetans come here in the winter for a festival that is usually attended by the Dalai Lama. Bodh Gaya is the second of the four great pilgrimage sites of India/Nepal.

Young monks in the Tibetan tradition pay their respects to the Buddha by circumambulating the Bodh Gaya Bodhi tree.

Finally, just before dawn, the bodhisattva enters the state of complete awareness, of total insight into the nature of reality. After hundreds of lives, he has fulfilled his bodhisattva vow. He is no longer a being (*sattva*) striving for enlightenment (*bodhi*); he is now a buddha, a "fully enlightened one": "I had direct knowledge. Birth is exhausted, the Holy Life has been lived out, what was to be done is done, there is no more of this to come" (*Majjhima Nikaya*; Nanamoli 1972: 25).

Having completed his journey to full enlightenment, he has earned the title Tathagata ("thus-gone one"). It is by this title that the Buddha will most often refer to himself. For example: "Whatever a Tathagata utters, speaks, and proclaims between the day of his enlightenment and the day he dies, all that is factual, not otherwise, and that is why he is called 'Tathagata'" (*Anguttara Nikaya* ii.22; Dhammika 1989: 50).

Another term for the state of enlightenment or *bodhi* that the Buddha has reached is "nirvana" ("*nibbana*" in Pali). This state has two aspects, negative and positive. In its negative aspect nirvana has the sense of "putting out the fires" of greed, hatred, and delusion. In its positive aspect nirvana is the experience of transcendent happiness. A poem by Patacara—one of the first ordained Buddhist women—expresses the way the positive and negative meanings of nirvana come together in the perfect happiness that arrives when evil desires have been extinguished. In the first verse she expresses her longing for nirvana and her frustration at not attaining it despite all her efforts; in the second verse she recalls how the breakthrough finally came as she was turning down the wick on her oil lamp:

> With ploughshares ploughing up the fields, with seed
> Sown in the breast of earth, men win their crops,
> Enjoy their gains and nourish wife and child.
> Why cannot I, whose life is pure, who seek
> To do the Master's will, no sluggard am,
> Nor puffed up, win Nibbana's bliss?
> One day, bathing my feet, I sit and watch

> The water as it trickles down the slope.
> Thereby I set my heart in steadfastness,
> As one doth train a horse of noble breed.
> Then going to my cell, I take my lamp,
> And seated on my couch I watch the flame.
> Grasping the pin, I pull the wick right down
> Into the oil . . .
> Lo! the Nibbana of the little lamp!
> Emancipation dawns! My heart is free!
> (*Songs of Sisters*, Rhys Davids 1964: 73)

Reflecting on his experience, the new Buddha wonders whether the way to enlightenment can be taught. He decides that it can, and so begins a teaching career motivated by compassion for all living beings.

Setting the Wheel in Motion

The new Buddha's first impulse is to seek out and teach his two former yoga teachers, but one of the by-products of his enlightenment is heightened psychic powers, and by telepathy he realizes that both have died. Thus he decides to begin by teaching the five *shramanas* (ascetic students) who were his companions during his years of ascetic discipline. Perceiving (again using his psychic powers) that they can be found at a deer park known as Sarnath near Varanasi (Banaras), he sets out and on the way encounters two merchants, sometimes said to be Burmese, who show their respect by offering him food.

In a sense, this act marks the beginning of institutional Buddhism, which depends on the material support (food, medicine, robes, financial donations) given by laypeople in return for the spiritual gifts offered by ordained Buddhists (dharma teaching, chanting, guidance). This pattern of reciprocal giving has remained central to all forms of Buddhism to the present day.

On arriving at the deer park, the Buddha is at first shunned by his five friends because he has abandoned the rigorous discipline they so value, but when they see his aura they recognize that he has attained nirvana and ask to know how he did it. He responds with his first **sutra**, often referred

Sites

Sarnath, India

Sarnath, the third of the four great pilgrimage sites of India/Nepal, is the deer park near Varanasi in northern India where the newly enlightened Buddha found his former companions, preached his first sermon, and ordained them as his disciples. Sights include a new temple, several old stupas and temples, and a museum.

to as the "Wheel Turning" sermon or discourse because it marks the moment when the wheel of true dharma is once again set in motion.

Another name for this first discourse is the "Instruction on the Middle Path," for in it the Buddha encourages his former companions to follow a path of moderation between indulgence and asceticism. As long as he lived the life of a pampered prince he did not advance spiritually. Yet the years of ascetic discipline left him too weak to

Roy C. Amore

Shakyamuni and his five fellow ascetics in the deer park at Sarnath, the site of his first sermon; from a series of illustrations of the life of Buddha on a temple wall.

make any real progress. Only after he began to eat, drink, and sleep in moderation was he able to reach enlightenment. In time, this principle of moderation would be developed into a general ethic of the Middle Way. Some interpreters consider this principle so central to the tradition that they refer to Buddhism itself as "the Middle Way."

Having counselled the five to abandon their ascetic practices, the Buddha begins to explain the insight into suffering that he gained while meditating under the Bodhi tree. After a few days of instruction in the Four Noble Truths and the Eightfold Path for overcoming suffering, the Buddha ordains the five as his first disciples and sends them forth to teach the dharma to others.

Entering Parinirvana

For the next 45 years the Buddha travels throughout the Middle Region, ordaining disciples and teaching thousands of lay followers, including various local kings. He also ordains several members of his own family, one of whom—his cousin Devadatta—eventually leads a group of dissident disciples in revolt, and makes more than one attempt on his life.

His body is becoming weak as he nears 80, but he continues to travel. Finally, one day he and his disciples are dining with the leader of a local tribal group when an odd-smelling dish is brought to the table. He asks his host to serve it only to him, not to his disciples. On eating the dish, he falls ill. When it becomes apparent that he is dying,

the Compassionate One tells his disciples not to blame the host, who meant well. They ask whom they should follow if he dies, and he tells them to follow the dharma. Thus in Buddhism no individual has absolute authority, although there are senior authorities in particular traditions (the Dalai **Lama** in the Gelugpa sect of Vajrayana, for example).

On his deathbed—in a grove of trees at Kushinagar—the Buddha meditates up through the eight yoga stages, back down through them, and finally back up through the first four. Then, at the moment of death, he experiences *parinirvana*: the final end of the cycle of rebirth, the total cessation of suffering, the perfection of happiness. Until that moment he has been in the state known as nirvana "with remainder"—the highest level of nirvana possible for one still living.

Buddhism does not elaborate on the nature of *parinirvana*—"nirvana without remainder": such a state is by definition beyond human understanding. What is important, and fundamental to Buddhism, is the reality of that state and the potential of all living beings to attain it.

☸ The Second Gem: The Dharma

> Avoid doing all evil deeds,
> cultivate doing good deeds,
> and purify the mind—
> this is the teaching of all buddhas
> (*Dhammapada* 183).

Sites

Kushinagar, India

It was in a grove of trees near this town in northeastern India that the Buddha is said to have entered *parinirvana*. At the time Kushinagar was a small town in a forested area inhabited by a people known as the Mallas. King Ashoka (see p. 206) and

at least one Chinese Buddhist made pilgrimages to the site in ancient times, before it fell into a state of ruin. Today it is being restored as the fourth great pilgrimage site of India/Nepal.

Document

A Woman's Compassionate Wisdom

Compassion is a major value in Buddhism. In this story, a woman's compassion for her sick husband not only comforts him but brings him back to health.

Once, while the Lord [Buddha] was staying among the Bhaggis on the Crocodile Hill . . . , the good man Nakulapita lay sick, ailing and grievously ill. And his wife Nakulamata said to him: "I beg you, good man, do not die worried, for the Lord has said that the fate of the worried is not good. Maybe you think: 'Alas, when I am gone, my wife will be unable to support the children or keep the household together.' But do not think like that, for I am skilled in spinning cotton and carding wool, and I will manage to support the children and keep the household together after you are gone.

"Or maybe you think: 'My wife will take another husband after I am gone.' But do not think that, for you and I know that for sixteen years we have lived as householders in the holy life [that is, as celibates, practising strict sexual abstinence].

"Or maybe you think: 'My wife, after I am gone, will have no desire to see the Lord or to see the monks.' But do not think like that, for my desire to see them shall be even greater.

"Or maybe you think: 'After I am gone, my wife will not have a calm mind.' But do not think like that, for as long as the Lord has female disciples dressed in white, living at home, who gain that state, I shall be one. And if any doubt it, let them ask the Lord.

"Or maybe you think: 'My wife will not win a firm foundation, a firm foot-hold in this Dhamma and discipline. She will not win comfort, dissolve doubt, be free from uncertainty, become confident, self-reliant, and live by the Teacher's words.' But do not think like that, either. For as long as the Lord has female disciples dressed in white . . . I shall be one."

Now, while Nakulapita was being counselled thus by his wife, even as he lay there his sickness subsided and he recovered. And not long after, he got up, and leaning on a stick, Nakulapita went to visit the Lord and told him what had happened. And the Lord said: "It has been a gain; you have greatly gained from having Nakulamata as your counsellor and teacher, full of compassion for you, and desiring your welfare" (adapted from Dhammika 1989: 111–13).

The crystallization of the Buddhist tradition began with the transformation of the Buddha's discourses into a set of doctrinal teachings, the dharma, and the movement towards an institutionalized monastic system. To "take refuge in the dharma" is to have confidence in the eternal truth of the Buddha's teachings. "Dharma" (in Pali, *dhamma*) is a central concept in Buddhist thought, and the range of its meanings and associations extends well beyond the meaning of "dharma" in the Hindu context.

In classical Indian culture generally, the Sanskrit word "dharma" carries the sense of social and moral obligation. The *Bhagavad Gita*, for instance, assumes that each individual's dharma is the duty appropriate to the caste and the life situation into which he or she born. (Thus the law codes governing Hindu society came to be called the *dharmashastras*.)

It is no surprise, then, that the "dharma" referred to in Buddhist texts is sometimes translated as "law." Buddhist usage, however, reflects the root meaning of "dharma": "that which holds." In fact, the Sanskrit "dharma" is related to the Latin word *firma*; thus in English we could understand "dharma" to mean "teachings that are firm"—that is, eternal truths. For Buddhists those eternal truths include the laws of nature, the reality of spiritual forces such as karma,

Document

From the Itivuttaka

The Itivuttaka *("So I heard") is a collection of the Buddha's teachings said to have been made by Khujjuttara, a lay woman of the servant class who was held up by the Buddha himself as an exemplary lay disciple. She would listen to the Buddha's talks and then pass along what she had learned to other women; hence the phrase "So I heard" ("Itivuttaka"), which begins each section of the collection and became its title.*

Even if one should seize the hem of my robe and walk step by step behind me, if he is covetous in his desires, fierce in his longings, malevolent of heart, with corrupt mind, careless and unrestrained, noisy and distracted and with sense uncontrolled, he is far from me. And why? He does not see the Dhamma, and not seeing the Dhamma, he does not see me. Even if one lives a hundred miles away, if he is not covetous in his desires, not fierce in his longings, with a kind heart and pure mind, mindful, composed, calmed, one-pointed and with senses restrained, then indeed, he is near to me and I am near to him. And why? He sees the Dhamma, and seeing the Dhamma, sees me (Dhammika 1989: 49–50).

and the rules of moral conduct or duty. Believing the Buddha's understanding of those realities to be definitive, generations of thinkers studied and systematized his insights, creating a program of instruction that anyone seeking enlightenment could follow.

The Four Noble Truths and Eightfold Path

At the core of the Buddha's first sermon in the deer park were the Four Noble Truths about suffering and the Eightfold Path to overcoming it. The Truths are:

1. The Noble Truth of Suffering: No living being can escape suffering (**dukkha**). Birth, sickness, senility, and death are all occasions of suffering, whether physical or psychological.
2. The Noble Truth of Origin: Suffering arises from craving (*trishna*), from excessive desire.
3. The Noble Truth of Cessation: Suffering will cease when desire ceases.
4. The Noble Truth of the Eightfold Path: It is possible to put an end to desire, and hence to suffering, by following eight principles of self-improvement.

The eight principles that make up the Eightfold Path are not sequential, like the steps on a ladder. All are equally important, and each depends on all the rest. Thus none of them can be properly observed in isolation. They must work in concord, like the petals of a flower unfolding together. They are:

1. right understanding (specifically of the Four Noble Truths),
2. right thought (free of sensuous desire, illwill, and cruelty),
3. right speech,
4. right conduct,
5. right livelihood,
6. right effort,
7. right mindfulness, and
8. right meditation.

The Three Characteristics of Existence

Existence has three characteristics, according to the Buddhist dharma: suffering, impermanence, and no-self. "Suffering," as a characteristic of existence, refers to all the varieties of pain and deprivation, physical and psychological, that humans are subject to. "Impermanence" is the passing nature of all things. Remember the last words of the Buddha: "Everything that arises also passes away." With the exceptions of empty space and nirvana, nothing in life is static: everything is in process. Some philosophies, both in India and in the West, treat change as a problem to be overcome and attribute permanence to what they value most highly; by contrast, Buddhist thought regards change as a fact.

Finally, the concept of no-self draws attention to the psychological implications of that existential impermanence. The Sanskrit term **anatman** means "without Atman": but what is Atman? The Hindu understanding at the time of Shakyamuni is reflected in the *Upanishads*, where Atman represents the eternal self or soul in humans and is related to Brahman, the underlying energy of the universe. For many Hindus, the innermost self is the most stable and abidingly real feature of the individual, because it participates in the reality of the universe.

The Buddha proposed that no such eternal, unchanging self exists. And in denying the existence of a self, he made the concept of ownership radically unsustainable for his followers: if there is no "I," there can be no "mine." The *anatman* concept does not mean that there is "no person" or "no personality" in the ordinary English sense of those terms. In fact, Buddhist teachings about the self address the components of personality, the *skandhas*, in some detail, suggesting that personality is the product of shifting, arbitrary circumstance. In that respect, Buddhist notions of personality have more in common with modern psychological theory than they do with either Hindu or Western religious notions of an eternal soul. What Buddhist personality theory implies is that wise people, recognizing the impermanence of all things—including themselves—will not become emotionally attached either to material goods or to fixed images of themselves.

The Three Instructions

There is a story about a young Buddhist monk named Buddhaghosa, who goes to the main monastery in ancient Sri Lanka, requesting permission to use its library for his research and writing on the dharma. To test him, the abbot assigns him the task of commenting on a verse to the effect that once one has become established in morality (*sila*) one should go on to perfect one's concentration (**samadhi**) and wisdom (**prajna**). In response, Buddhaghosa writes what was to become a very famous commentary called *The Path of Purity* in which he expands on the meaning of the three instructions.

Morality, *sila*, is the essential foundation. Perfecting concentration means developing a mental state in which one is focused, tranquil, and alert. This *samadhi* state of mind is helpful in every aspect of life, but it is especially important if one is to move to the third level, the state of higher wisdom, without which one cannot attain nirvana. One of the central insights gained at that third level is the nature of causality.

The principle of causality is a thread that runs throughout the Buddha's dharma. To appreciate its function, think of a pool table. To observe this world of changing circumstances is like observing a pool table where the balls are colliding with one another and the cushions, repeatedly causing one another to change directions: each time you blink, you see a new configuration of pool balls, caused by the previous configuration. With this image in mind, we can now turn to one of the more difficult expressions of Buddhist higher wisdom.

The Stages of Dependent Origination

The standard term for this understanding of causality—in which everything that arises does so in response to other factors, and will in turn cause changes in other things—is *pratitya-samutpada*, usually translated as "dependent origination" or "conditioned coproduction." Because early Buddhist teachers delivered the dharma teachings orally, they tended to use visual images and numbered lists to help fix them in listeners' minds. Thus Buddhist dharma uses the image of a "wheel of becoming" (Bhava Chakra) with 12 spokes (not to be confused with the eight-spoked Dharma Chakra, the wheel that symbolizes the Eightfold Path) to express the view of life as a cycle of interdependent stages or dimensions.

The 12 links of the chain of dependent origination may be further divided into three stages, reflecting the movement from a past life through the present one and on to the future:

Past	1.	Ignorance, leading to
	2.	karma formations, leading to
Present	3.	a new individual "consciousness," leading to
	4.	a new body-mind complex, leading to
	5.	the bases of sensing, leading to
	6.	sense impressions, leading to
	7.	conscious feelings, leading to
	8.	craving, leading to
	9.	clinging to (grasping for) things, leading to
	10.	"becoming" (the drive to be reborn), leading to
Future	11.	rebirth, leading to
	12.	old age and death

The process does not stop with the twelfth link, of course, since old age and death lead to yet another birth, and so the wheel of rebirth turns on and on. Buddhists have analyzed this wheel from many viewpoints and with many similes, but the heart of the matter is always the same: all living beings are in process and will be reborn over and over again until they realize nirvana.

The *Tripitaka*: Three Baskets of Sacred Texts

Shakyamuni did not write down any of his teachings, nor did he assign anyone the task of recording his words. This was entirely in keeping with the Hindu tradition, in which writing was associated with commerce. The sacred teachings of the Hindus were the exclusive preserve of the priests, who committed them to memory and transmitted them by sound alone. In fact, the Hindu ritual

formulas were understood to have an acoustic effectiveness that would be lost if they were not spoken and heard. Thus for its first 400 years or so, the Buddhist sangha was content to recite the teachings from memory.

To manage the work of passing along the teachings, various **bhikshus** (monks) were assigned the task of memorizing selected portions. At the early conferences of all sangha members, one of the most important tasks was to recite the teachings in their entirety.

At the first council, held not long after Shakyamuni's death, *Bhikshu* Ananda, who had been his travelling companion, is said to have recited the discourses (*sutras*) on dharma ascribed to Shakyamuni. *Bhikshu* Upali is credited with reciting the section on monastic rules (**vinaya**). The systematic treatises (*abhidharma*) composed after Shakyamuni's *parinirvana* were recited at a later meeting. The oral teachings were finally put into writing by the Theravada monks of Sri Lanka in the first century CE, after a famine had reduced the monks' numbers so drastically as to threaten the survival of the oral tradition. The fact that Theravada Buddhists refer to their scriptures as the **Tripitaka** ("three baskets") suggests that the manuscript copies of the three types of texts—written on palm leaves strung together and bundled like Venetian blinds—may have been stored in three baskets. The collection survives in the Pali language (a vernacular derived in part from Sanskrit) and is therefore referred to as the Pali canon.

The *Sutra Pitaka*, or "discourse basket," contains the talks on dharma attributed to Shakyamuni or his early disciples. The discourse is often presented as a response to a question from a disciple. The beginning of the *sutra* gives the setting in a stylized manner. The following opening of the "Discourse on the Lesser Analysis of Deeds" is typical:

Thus have I heard: At one time the Lord was staying near Savatthi in the Jeta Grove in Anathapindika's monastery. Then the brahmin youth Subha, Todeyya's son, approached the Lord; having approached, he exchanged greetings with the Lord; having conversed in

Figure 5.1 The Wheel of Becoming (Bhava Chakra) represents the 12 stages of dependent origination. At the centre are three animals representing the three evil root tendencies of human consciousness: greed represented by a rooster with endless desire for more hens; hate represented by a snake spitting venom; and delusion represented by a boar (perhaps because boars were thought to have poor eyesight or bad judgment). The surrounding 12 pictures illustrate the spokes of the wheel of becoming (see list on page 202). The wheel is held in the teeth of the demon of death, whose head, hands, and feet are visible behind the wheel.

a friendly and courteous way, he sat down at a respectful distance. As he was sitting down at a respectful distance the brahmin youth Subha, Todeyya's son, spoke thus to the Lord: "Now, good Gotama, what is the cause, what the reason that lowness and excellence are to be seen among human beings while they are in human form?" (Horner 1967, 3: 248–9)

Subha has asked the timeless question of why bad things happen to apparently good people. Shakyamuni, referred to here by the title *bhaga-van* ("Lord"), then explains to Subha how the karma accumulated through actions in past lives causes some people to suffer short, unhappy lives and others to enjoy long, blessed lives.

There are five sections (*nikayas*) of the *Sutra Pitaka*, the first "basket." In the ancient world, texts were usually organized not chronologically or alphabetically but by length, from longest to shortest. (The same principle was followed by the early Muslims in organizing the sequence of the *surahs* that make up the Qur'an.) There are a few exceptions, however. The *sutras* in the "Kindred Sayings" section are organized around topics, while the "Gradual Sayings" are arranged in numerical lists (four truths, four kinds of humans, and so on).

The other early basket, the *Vinaya* ("discipline") *Pitaka*, contains both the rules of monastic discipline and stories about how Shakyamuni came to institute each rule.

Finally, the *Abhidharma* (Further Discourses) *Pitaka* contains seven books by unnamed early Buddhists who systematically analyzed every conceivable aspect of reality in the light of various Buddhist principles. For example, the first book of *abhidharma* classifies all mental phenomena according to their karmic consequences, good, bad, or neutral. Other books deal with the various physical elements of nature.

The development of *abhidharma* is associated with Sariputra, one of the brightest of the Buddha's disciples. He lived in a city called Nalanda, where a large university—perhaps the world's first—was flourishing by the first century. The *abhidharma* books formed the basis of the physical and psychological sciences taught at Nalanda and other Buddhist universities of India. The goal, however, was not so much the advancement of the physical sciences as it was the spiritual advancement of the students. Throughout the *abhidharma* works runs the basic Buddhist teaching that no physical or mental reality is eternal, and that all are subject to constant change.

◉ The Third Gem: The Sangha

The third part of the Triple Gem has two components: the monastic community of ordained men (*bhikshus*) and women (*bhikshunis*), and the broader community, the universal sangha of all people who follow the Buddha's path.

Bhikshus and Bhikshunis

Shakyamuni began accepting disciples from the time of his first sermon in the deer park at Varanasi. Within a short time, an ordination ritual took shape in which the new disciples recited the Triple Refuge and took vows of chastity, poverty, obedience, and so on (similar vows would play an important role in Christian monasticism), and put on the distinctive robes of a monk. In early Indian Buddhism, monks' robes were usually dyed with saffron—made from the dried stigmas of certain crocuses—which produces a bright orange-yellow. Most Theravada monks still wear saffron robes, but in East Asia other colours were eventually adopted, such as red and brown. There is no special meaning to the colour, although all members of a particular branch of Buddhism wear the same one.

Ordained and Lay Women

Unlike many other religious traditions, Buddhism never defined women as the "property" of men. Nevertheless, the early texts in particular indicate a profound ambiguity about the status of women in Buddhism. Shakyamuni himself is said to have

cautioned the *bhikshus* against allowing themselves to be distracted by women:

> "How are we to conduct ourselves, Lord, with regard to womankind?"
> "Don't see them, Ananda."
> "But if we should see them, what are we to do?"
> "Abstain from speech, Ananda."
> "But if they should speak to us, Lord, what are we to do?"
> "Keep wide awake, Ananda" (Rhys Davids 1881: 91)

Shakyamuni is also said to have resisted the formation of an order for women, the *bhikshuni* sangha, and to have predicted that such an order would be detrimental to the survival of his teachings. On the other hand, he did agree to its establishment, and encouraged close relatives, including his stepmother, to join it, maintaining that women were no less capable than men of becoming Arhats (saints), and that the way to nirvana was the same regardless of gender:

> And be it woman, be it man for whom
> Such chariot doth wait, by that same car
> Into Nirvana's presence shall they come
> (Horner 1930: 104).

Other early Buddhist texts are similarly ambiguous about women. On the positive side, they describe approvingly the support provided to the early sangha by some wealthy women. And one book of the Pali canon, the Therigatha, contains poems by early *bhikshunis*. On the negative side, there was a distinct difference in status between *bhikshus* and *bhikshunis*, who were not allowed to teach their male counterparts.

Ordination

Eventually, as Buddhism became more institutionalized, a preliminary level of ordination was introduced during which novices were required to master the basics of dharma before becoming *bhikshus* or *bhikshunis*. Each novice (*shramanera*) was assigned both a rigorous, demanding teacher and a supportive spiritual guide.

The full ordination ritual can be performed only in certain designated areas, which some ordination traditions still mark off with "boundary stones," as in ancient India. The ordination ceremony takes several hours to complete. Friends and relatives of the candidates for ordination attend and pay their respects to the new sangha members, who give presents to their teachers and counsellors in gratitude for their assistance. Because seniority plays a large role in monastic life, careful attention is paid to the exact time and date of the ordination.

The Lay Sangha

Lay Buddhists are considered members of the sangha in its wider sense, which includes all those following the path laid down by the Buddha. The sangha of all disciples includes eight categories of "noble persons," according to the progress they have made towards nirvana. There are four levels: "those who have entered the stream (to nirvana)," those who have advanced enough to return (be reborn) just once more, those who are so advanced that they will never return, and those who have advanced to the state of realizing the Arhat (worthy) path. At each of the four levels, Buddhists distinguish the person who has just reached the new level from one who has matured at that level, making a total of eight classifications of noble persons.

All Buddhist traditions maintain that laypeople are capable of advancing towards nirvana. However, some traditions expect lay members of the sangha to seek ordination at some stage, so that they can devote themselves full-time to the spiritual quest.

Controversies, Councils, and Sects

The defection of some *bhikshus* under the leadership of Devadatta shows that sectarian problems could

A Theravada *bhikshu* with a palm-leaf umbrella.

Roy C. Amore

arise even during the Buddha's lifetime. Other divisions followed.

In the fourth century BCE, for instance, trouble arose when a *bhikshu* visiting the city of Vaishali found that his colleagues there were accepting donations of gold and silver from the laypeople. He criticized them publicly, and they demanded that he apologize in front of their lay supporters. As a consequence, a meeting of all the *bhikshus* in the area had to be convened.

Because there was no central individual, court, or committee that held authority in Buddhism, the monks had to settle disputes collectively on the basis of their interpretations of the Buddha's discourses—a challenging task in an era when the scriptures had not yet been written down.

The meeting, called the Vaishali Council, decided that monastic discipline did indeed forbid the acceptance of gold and silver. Most of the Vaishali *bhikshus* agreed to abide by the ruling, but a schism soon developed when one dissident monk raised five points of controversy concerning the status of Arhats, the "worthy ones" or saints. Was an Arhat subject to the same limitations as an ordinary *bhikshu*? Was an Arhat susceptible to sexual misconduct? Was it possible for an Arhat to be ignorant of some doctrine or to have doubts about doctrine? Could one become an Arhat merely by instruction, without spiritual practice?

Behind those questions lay an issue that was to fuel even more serious divisions later on. That issue was the level of spiritual attainment possible for Buddhists in this life. The majority of the monks took a relatively liberal position, holding out the prospect of enlightenment for ordinary people, but many of the *sthavira* ("elders" or senior monks) disagreed, arguing that attaining the Arhat level was beyond the reach of all but a few. In this way a division arose between the majority group, who formed the Mahasanghika or "Great Sangha" sect, and the Sthavira group, who formed the Sthaviravada or Theravada sect. This debate gave the *bhikshus* a foretaste of the split that would lead to the development of the Mahayana and Theravada schools as distinctly different forms of Buddhism.

By the time of King Ashoka, in the third century BCE, there were 18 sects, each with its own oral version of the Buddhist teachings, although from the few later-written texts that have survived, we can imagine that the versions did not differ very much. They all shared a similar ordination tradition and all followed more or less the same *vinaya* rules.

It is unlikely that the laity paid much attention to the divisions, which were minor compared to the differences between the various denominations in Protestant Christianity. The monks of the various sects sometimes lived together in one monastery, especially at the major training centres, which evolved into Buddhist universities. The same was true of the *bhikshunis*, who always resided in their own monasteries, separate from the men.

King Ashoka's Conversion

The spread of Buddhism within India was quite remarkable. Unlike many reformers, Shakyamuni had succeeded in gaining converts across a broad social spectrum, ranging from the lowest classes of labourers through the rich merchant class to the powerful rulers of newly formed kingdoms. But the conversion of the kings in Shakyamuni's lifetime did not necessarily mean that their successors were Buddhists as well. There was a long-standing Indian tradition that the king had a duty to defend and support all the legitimate religious traditions of his kingdom. It seems that Buddhism became one among several legitimate dharma systems.

Approximately 150 years after the passing of Shakyamuni, Greek-speaking rulers came to power in northwestern India as a result of Alexander's conquest in 326 BCE. An Indian king of the Mauryan dynasty later drove the Greek rulers out of central India, and his son expanded the newly formed kingdom. When the latter's son, Ashoka (r. c. 273–232 BCE), inherited the throne, he embarked on a series of wars to expand his territory to the south and west. Eventually he ruled an empire that included most of modern India.

Buddhist accounts claim that it was Ashoka's reflection on the horrible carnage of his bloody war with the kingdom of Kalinga on the eastern coast that led him to convert to Buddhism and begin promoting the ethic of non-violence. It is possible that his family had been supporters of other non-brahminical traditions such as Jainism, however, and so his conversion to Buddhism likely did not represent a major shift.

Under the patronage of Ashoka, Buddhism enjoyed its golden age in India. Buddhist accounts say that Ashoka turned from military conquest to dharma conquest. To spread the dharma of non-violence, he ordered that large stones or pillars be erected at the principal crossroads throughout his empire, with messages carved on them for the moral instruction of his subjects. Some of these stones and pillars have been recovered by archaeologists, and the messages are still readable.

In the message carved on the rock erected in the coastal Kalinga area of eastern India, he expresses remorse for the death and suffering he caused to so many people:

> When the king, Beloved of the Gods and of Gracious Mien, had been consecrated eight years Kalinga was conquered, 150,000 people were deported, 100,000 were killed, and many times that number died. But after the conquest of Kalinga, the Beloved of the Gods began to follow Righteousness (dharma), to love Righteousness, and to give instruction in Righteousness. Now the Beloved of the Gods regrets the conquest of Kalinga, for when an independent country is conquered people are killed, they die, or are deported, and that the Beloved of the Gods finds painful and grievous. . . . The Beloved of the Gods will forgive as far as he can, and he even conciliates the forest tribes of his dominions; but he warns them that there is power even in the remorse of the Beloved of the Gods, and he tells them to reform, lest they be killed (*Thirteenth Rock Edict*; de Bary 1958: 146).

He then lays out his ideals for governing his new subjects, saying that he desires security, self-control, impartiality, and cheerfulness for all living creatures in his empire. Ashoka spells out his "conquest by dharma" and claims that it is spreading not only within the Indian continent but westward among the various Alexandrian kingdoms, whose kings he names. Ashoka states that real satisfaction in ruling over people comes only from inducing them to follow dharma:

> Thus he achieves a universal conquest, and conquest always gives a feeling of pleasure; yet it is but a slight pleasure, for the Beloved of the Gods only looks on that which concerns the next life as of great importance. I have had this inscription of Righteousness engraved that all my sons and grandsons may not seek to gain new victories, . . . that

they may consider the only [valid] victory the victory of Righteousness, which is of value both in this world and the next (*Thirteenth Rock Edict*; de Bary 1958: 147).

Although he reminds his Kalinga subjects and the tribal people of the surrounding forest areas that he will not hesitate to deal firmly with rebels and criminals, he promises that his punishments will be just and moderate. Ashoka's promotion of dharma became a model for later Buddhist rulers. Like "Dharma-Ashoka," as Buddhists later called him, they were willing to sentence criminals (and rebels) to punishment or even death, but they remained committed to non-violence in other matters. Ashoka himself went so far as to encourage his subjects to become vegetarian and give up occupations such as hunting.

Buddhism and the State

The King as Wheel-Turner

Indian tradition had long used the term *chakravartin* or "wheel-turner" to refer to kings as world rulers. On one level, the image suggests a ruler whose chariot wheels encounter no opposition. On another level, it evokes the wisdom of the ruler who in meditation perceives a wheel turning in the heavens and understands it to represent the orderly process of the universe. Thus the true world ruler has both the spiritual wisdom to perceive the cosmic order and the political power to impose a similar order in the world.

When the early Buddhists began to refer to Shakyamuni as a *chakravartin*, they were in one sense according him the honour due to one of his princely birth—an honour that Shakyamuni himself may or may not have sought. In another sense, however, they were redefining the concept of political power, shifting the emphasis away from unchallenged military strength and towards the notion of wisdom in the guidance of society.

From the time of Shakyamuni, Buddhism understood rulers to have special duties with regard

Document

King Milinda Questions Nagasena

The military campaigns of Alexander the Great in the late fourth century BCE *left a number of Greek-derived regimes in eastern Iran and northwestern India. These may have been the "Yavanas" (presumably "Ionians") to whom the Buddhist King Ashoka reported sending missions. The following extract recounts a meeting, real or imagined, between a foreign king and a Buddhist sage.*

Now Milinda the king went up to where the venerable Nagasena was, and addressed him with the greetings and compliments of friendship and courtesy, and took his seat respectfully apart.

And Milinda began by asking, "How is your Reverence known, and what, Sir, is your name?"

"I am known as Nagasena, O king. But although parents, O king, give such a name as Nagasena . . . [it] is only a generally understood term, a designation in common use. For there is no permanent individuality (no soul) involved in the matter."

"If, most reverend Nagasena, there is no permanent individuality (no soul) involved in the matter, who is it, pray, who gives to you members of the Order your robes and food and lodging and necessaries for the sick? Who is it who enjoys such things when given? Who is it who lives a life of righteousness? . . . You tell me that your brethren in the Order are in the habit of addressing you as Nagasena. Now what is that Nagasena? Do you mean to say that the hair is Nagasena?"

"I don't say that, great king."

"Or is it the nails, the teeth, the skin, the flesh, the nerves, the bones . . . or any of these that is Nagasena?"

And to each of these he answered no.

"Is it the outward form then (*rupa*) that is Nagasena, or the sensations, or the ideas, or the confections, or the consciousness, that is Nagasena?"

And to each of these he answered no.

"Then is it all these *skandhas* [physical and mental "heaps" or processes] combined that are Nagasena?"

"No! great king."

"But is there anything outside the five *skandhas* that is Nagasena?"

And he still answered no.

"Then thus, ask as I may, I can discover no Nagasena. Nagasena is a mere empty sound. . . ."

[*Now Nagasena asks the king how he travelled to their meeting. When the king says he came in a chariot, the sage asks him to explain what a chariot is.*] "Is it the pole that is the chariot?"

"I did not say that."

"Is it the wheels, or the framework . . . ?"

"Certainly not."

"Then is it all these parts that are the chariot?"

"No, Sir."

"Then . . . I can discover no chariot. Chariot is a mere empty sound."

"It is on account of its having all these things— the pole, and the axle . . .—that it comes under the generally understood term, the designation in common use, of 'chariot.'"

"Very good! Your Majesty has rightly grasped the meaning of 'chariot.' And just even so it is on account of all those things you questioned me about . . . that I come under the generally understood term . . . 'Nagasena.' For it was said, Sire, by our Sister Vajira in the presence of the Blessed One: 'Just as it is by the condition precedent of the coexistence of its various parts that the word "chariot" is used, just so is it true that when the *skandhas* are there we talk of a "being".'"

"Most wonderful, Nagasena, and most strange. Well done, well done, Nagasena" (abridged from Rhys Davids 1890: 40–55).

to the dharma. Kings were expected not only to provide for the physical welfare of their subjects (for example, by distributing food in times of need) but to promote dharma by setting a good example and sponsoring lectures, translations, and the distribution of literature. The king who promoted dharma would be a true successor to the Buddha, the definitive wheel-turner.

As Buddhism spread throughout Asia, so did its social and moral ideals regarding kingship. A Zen Buddhist story tells of a Chinese king named Wu who has dedicated himself to doing all the good works expected of a Buddhist king, probably with the goal of winning a long and pleasant rebirth in heaven. When Wu learns that Bodhidharma, a monk newly arrived from India, has taken up residence in his kingdom, he summons the monk to court and proudly shows him everything he has accomplished. Wu has established rice kitchens for feeding the poor; filled a new wing of the palace with scribes who are busy translating and copying the sacred texts to be read aloud and explained to the people at Buddhist festivals; and set up an altar for daily worship.

After the tour, the emperor asks Bodhidharma, "How much merit do you think I have made from all this?" "None whatsoever!" is the famous response. Bodhidharma proceeds to explain that true merit comes only from activities that increase one's wisdom and purify the mind. It seems that the emperor has been doing all the right things for the wrong reason. With regard to Buddhism and the state, what this story tells us is that although the rulers were encouraged to support the sangha and actively promote dharma in their realms, the ultimate goal was the ruler's own spiritual advancement. This helps to explain why Buddhist kings sometimes abdicated at a fairly early age in order to take ordination as *bhikshus*.

Non-violence as a Public Ethic

One characteristic of Buddhist political rule, at least ideally, was promotion of non-violence. Unnecessarily harsh punishment was forbidden, and kings were expected to release prisoners during Buddhist festivals. (Even today, some Buddhist festivals include the release of caged birds or other animals into the wild.) Justice was to be administered fairly, regardless of the social status of the accused, and quickly. A particularly pious king of ancient Sri Lanka is remembered for instructing his staff to wake him even in the middle of the night if a citizen came seeking justice. A rope attached to a bell was installed outside the palace walls so that anyone could pull it to awaken the king and present their case to him.

At the same time, the Buddhist king was expected to maintain an army and a police force, to defend the public against criminals and foreign enemies. There is no such thing in Buddhist scripture as a "just war" of aggression, but many Buddhists have believed that a defensive war is not against dharma, and that the state may use force as necessary to maintain law and order.

With very few exceptions, Buddhism spread by missionary conversion rather than by force. The adoption of Buddhism in new regions was helped by the dedicated, spiritual lifestyle of the monks and nuns and the fact that Buddhist missionaries allowed new converts to continue venerating their traditional gods and goddesses as well as the spirits of their ancestors. There were territorial wars between Buddhist kingdoms in Southeast Asia, however, and Sri Lanka has a long history of conflict between the Buddhist Sinhalese and Hindu Tamils.

☸ Early Buddhism

By Ashoka's time, in the third century BCE, Buddhism had split into 18 distinct sects. Over the following centuries most of these disappeared. The main survivor, Theravada, is one of the three major divisions of Buddhism that exist today. The second major school, which emerged around the first century CE, called itself Mahayana, "Great Vehicle," in contrast to what it considered the Hinayana, "Lesser Vehicle," of Theravada and its contemporaries. The third division, Vajrayana, emerged some 500 years

Map 5.1 The Spread of Buddhism

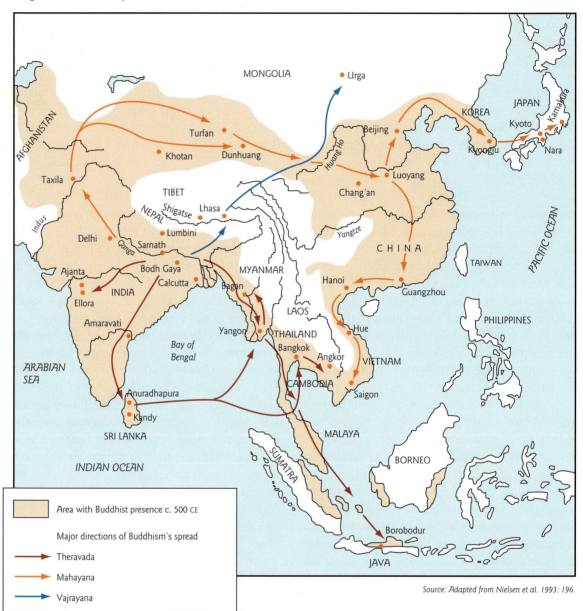

Area with Buddhist presence c. 500 CE

Major directions of Buddhism's spread

→ Theravada
→ Mahayana
→ Vajrayana

Source: Adapted from Nielsen et al. 1993: 196.

later and considered itself the third vehicle or the third turning of the wheel of dharma.

Theravada Buddhism

We know very little about the early history of the "Way of the Elders" (Sthaviravada in Sanskrit and Theravada in Pali). However, it appears to have been widespread in India by the time of Ashoka, and the Pali dialect associated with it was said to come from the ancient north Indian kingdom of Magadha, one of the four where Shakyamuni himself taught.

We do know that the Theravada tradition was conservative, as its name suggests. Rejecting all

Focus

Buddhist Vehicles and Schools

1. Theravada (sometimes called Hinayana, the "Little Vehicle"), now dominant in Sri Lanka and Southeast Asia: a survivor of the 18 sects that existed in the third century BCE
2. Mahayana (the "Great Vehicle"), now dominant in East Asia and Vietnam:
   - Madhyamaka in India, Sanlun in China
   - Yogacara in India, Faxiang in China
   - Tiantai in China, Tendai in Japan
   - Huayan in China, Kegon in Japan
   - Zhenyan in China, Shingon in Japan
   - Pure Land, Jingtu in China, Jodo in Japan
   - Chan in China, Seon in Korea, Zen in Japan
   - Linji in China, Rinzai in Japan
   - Caodong in China, Soto in Japan
   - Nichiren in Japan
3. Vajrayana (the "Diamond Vehicle"), now dominant in Tibet and the Himalayas:
   - Gelugpa ("Yellow Hats")
   - Kargyu ("Red Hats")
   - Karma-pa ("Black Hats")
   - Nyingma ("Ancient" school)

scriptures composed after the formation of the *Tripitaka*, it considers itself the preserver of Buddhism in its original form.

Theravada in Sri Lanka

A monk named Mahinda (Mahendra in Sanskrit), who was Ashoka's son, is said to have taken Theravada Buddhism to Sri Lanka in the third century BCE. The story of his conversion of the Sri Lankan people is told in the island's *Great Chronicle* (*Mahavamsa*). Mahinda and his assistant monks use psychic powers to travel through the air, and arrive on a large hill near the island's capital, Anuradhapura. There the king of Sri Lanka and his hunting party discover the monks and are soon converted to the Buddha's dharma. (Mahinda's Hill, Mihintale, remains an active centre for monks and lay pilgrims in Sri Lanka today.) The next day, Mahinda enters the capital and teaches dharma to the members of the king's court, who are converted. On the following day the largest space available—the royal elephant stable—is put into service as a hall of dharma instruction, whereupon everyone is converted.

These legends are presumably based on historical events, since one of Ashoka's inscriptions claims that he sent missionaries in groups of five to seek converts far and wide, even in the Hellenistic kingdoms to the west. The king of Sri Lanka could well have been receptive to the idea of an alliance with the great emperor on the mainland, in which case adopting the empire's religion and court rituals would have been an excellent way of signalling willingness to comply with the greater power. The king ordered the building of a proper temple, dharma hall, and **stupa**, and the temple grounds were made complete with the arrival of a Bodhi tree sapling brought from India by Mahinda's sister, herself a *bhikshuni*.

After receiving the proper equipment from India, the Sri Lankan king submitted himself to a new enthronement ritual carried out according to Ashoka's instructions. In this way the island of Sri Lanka became a cultural extension of Ashoka's empire while maintaining its sovereignty. This uniting of Buddhist leadership and Indian forms of kingship set the pattern for subsequent Buddhist rulers in mainland Southeast Asia, who became the lay leaders and the chief financial supporters of Buddhism in their respective domains.

Theravada Buddhism is still the main religion of Sri Lanka, although the sangha fell on such hard times in the eleventh century that there were not enough ordained *bhikshus* to continue. Buddhist rules require a minimum of five senior *bhikshus* to

Sites

Bangkok, Thailand

On the grounds of the Grand Palace in Bangkok is the temple housing a famous jade sculpture known as the Emerald Buddha. Murals depicting scenes from the life of the Buddha are painted on the walls surrounding one part of the palace grounds. The nearby Wat Pho temple complex is filled with interesting temples, including one with a 46-metre (150-foot) reclining Buddha image, and includes a training centre for Thai massage. Across the river is the picturesque Wat Arun, "Temple of the Dawn," where a tall **pagoda** sparkles at dawn and sunset.

officiate at an ordination. Thus *bhikshus* from Burma had to be imported to Sri Lanka to conduct a proper ordination. A similar appeal to *bhikshus* from Siam in the eighteenth century led to the revitalization of Theravada, with the establishment of a new ordination lineage. The majority of Sri Lankan monks today belong to the Siyam Nikaya ("lineage"), which has control of many of the main temples.

Sri Lanka was populated by various peoples from India, and many aspects of the island's culture reveal close ties to the predominantly Hindu mainland. Among the Hindu transplants to Sri Lanka is a version of the Indian caste system. Shakyamuni taught that people should be judged by their character rather than the social status of the hereditary occupational or clan group they were born into. In keeping with this principle, his sangha was open to all social groups. In Sri Lanka, however, the Siyam Nikaya—the most prestigious ordination lineage—today accepts only members from the Goyigama caste, the equivalent of India's vaishyas.

There are other *nikayas* in Sri Lanka that accept members regardless of caste. The most important of these is the Ramanna Nikaya, which was founded in the nineteenth century as a lineage dedicated to various reforms, including the elimination of caste restrictions.

Theravada in Southeast Asia

The spread of Buddhism into Southeast Asia took place in stages over many centuries. The names and boundaries of the region's kingdoms have changed frequently since that process began. "Southeast Asia," which is a modern term, originally referred to an area under Allied military command during the Second World War. In earlier European usage the region was called "the Indies" because of the assumption by explorers and traders from the sixteenth century onward that the cultures they encountered were all in some sense Indian. Today Buddhist culture remains dominant in much of mainland Southeast Asia, including Cambodia, Thailand, and Myanmar. It was also influential (as was Hinduism) in the Indonesian islands and the Malay peninsula, although Islamic religion and culture eventually became dominant there.

The traditional claim is that Buddhism was introduced to Southeast Asia in the third century BCE, when King Ashoka reportedly sent missionaries to the Mon people, who ruled a large region spanning present-day Cambodia and Thailand; yet there is little historical evidence of Buddhism in Southeast Asia until about the sixth century, long after Ashoka's time. The kingdoms of Southeast Asia during the early centuries of the Common Era are described as "Indianized." The religious affiliations of the Indianized kingdoms were sometimes Buddhist, sometimes Hindu. For example, the Cambodian temple known to us as Angkor Wat began as a Hindu Vishnu temple in the early twelfth century, but was rededicated for Buddhist use when the region's rulers converted. An account written by a seventh-century Chinese Buddhist pilgrim, together with some archaeological evidence, suggests that several of the early Buddhist sects were established in Southeast Asia. This diversity follows the pattern in India, where various schools of Buddhism coexisted for centuries before Theravada eventually prevailed. Some accounts of early Buddhism in Southeast Asia emphasize the working of miracles, a feature of Buddhist missionary efforts found later in Tibet and elsewhere. The use of chanting to invoke blessings and protective powers was also a feature of Buddhism in Southeast Asia, partly because some of the missionaries there came from the Vajrayana school (p. 232).

From the eleventh century through the fifteenth, Buddhism consolidated its position in the region, and by the end of this period Theravada was the majority religion of the Thai, Khmer (Cambodian), Burmese, and Lao (Laotian) peoples. It remains so today.

Myanmar (Burma)

The region most easily reached by Buddhist missionaries from India was Burma. By the eleventh century, the kingdom of Pagan (Bagan), in what is today Myanmar, had developed ties with the Theravada rulers of Sri Lanka. A temple enshrining a sacred relic—a tooth alleged to be from the Buddha, became the guardian and legitimizer of the kingdom.

With the dominance of Theravada in Burma, the Pali-language version of the *Tripitaka* became the official text in Burma, but in keeping with Buddhist practice elsewhere, it was written in the local script, in this instance Burmese. The Thai and Khmer sanghas likewise copied the Pali texts using their own scripts. At first glance, these alphabets bear little resemblance to one another, but they are all derived from Indian scripts and are distantly related to the alphabets of Semitic origin used in the Mediterranean world.

Cambodia

The area of Southeast Asia that corresponds to modern Cambodia was also influenced by various forms of Indian Buddhism as well as Hinduism before the fifteenth century. Since then, the Theravada school has been well established in Cambodia. During the period of the twentieth-century "killing fields," all sides of the political spectrum, including the communists, looked to Buddhism for legitimacy. "Paying respect" to the *bhikshus* is a time-honoured way for political leaders to show their continuity with Cambodia's past.

Thailand

The Thai people are thought to have migrated into Southeast Asia from southern China, where tribal groups speaking similar dialects still live. The history of the Thai spread into Thailand, formerly Siam, traces the gradual southward movement of the Thai people and their capital cities. During the

Sites

Angkor, Cambodia

Angkor (from a Sanskrit word meaning "city") is the name of the region in northern Cambodia that was the core of the Khmer Empire, which ruled much of Southeast Asia from the ninth century to the fifteenth. Of the hundreds of temples and shrines within the region, the most famous are the originally Hindu Angkor Wat and the Bayon temple, which was built roughly a century later and dedicated to the Buddha. The entire region is now an archaeological park and UNESCO World Heritage Site that attracts as many as 3 million tourists per year.

fifteenth century, Thai monks returning from Sri Lanka, where they were ordained in the Theravada tradition, gained favour with King Tiloraja, who ruled central Thailand from Chiangmai, a city well north of the modern capital, Bangkok.

Two of the most important kings of nineteenth-century Siam were Mongkut and his son Chulalongkorn. Both were active in reforming the sangha. King Mongkut (r. 1824–51) is revered by Thais under the name Rama IV and is known in the West as the king of *The King and I*—which has never been shown in Thailand because it portrays Mongkut in a disrespectful way.

Having been a monk for over 20 years, Mongkut set out to restore discipline and direction to the sangha after he became king. This endeavour led to the founding of a new ordination lineage called the Thammayut Nikaya. The name is a Thai version of a Pali word meaning "those who adhere to the dharma." This reform movement set the tone for modern Theravada not only in Thailand, but also elsewhere in Southeast Asia. For example, the king of Cambodia arranged for the establishment of the Thammayut Nikaya in his country in the nineteenth century.

Following in his father's footsteps, King Chulalongkorn, Rama V (r. 1868–1910), undertook to unite the various *nikayas* under a central administrative authority and standardize the training given to novices in meditation, dharma instruction, and the Pali language. The training standards and central administration are still important features in the Thai sangha.

Thai kings in the modern period, even today, have always spent time in a monastery. This monastic training is considered an important preparation for someone who, as king, will be lay head of the sangha and the guiding figure in Thai cultural life.

Buddhist discipline and orthodoxy are maintained through control of the right to ordain. Historically the kings of Burma, Cambodia, Siam, and Laos sought to regularize and consolidate religion in their kingdoms by establishing the Theravada ordination lineage as normative. Theravada may have appealed to the rulers because of its insistence on maintaining discipline and traditions and because, in adopting it, the rulers could bring their kingdoms into political alignment with other powerful kingdoms in Sri Lanka and mainland Southeast Asia.

Laos

Laos is a small country with close linguistic, ethnic, and cultural connections to Thailand. There is inscriptional evidence of Sri Lankan *bhikshus* bringing Theravada orthodoxy to Laos over 500 years ago. However, because of its proximity and common language, Thai Buddhism was more influential in Laos. In modern times, Laotians have travelled to Bangkok to attend one of the two large universities there that train *bhikshus*.

Summary

The history of Buddhism in mainland Southeast Asia may be summarized along the following lines. Before 1000, various early Buddhist sects as well as Mahayana and Vajrayana schools competed for support, but by the fifteenth century the rulers of the major kingdoms of the area had all embraced Theravada and imported senior *bhikshus* from Sri Lanka to re-ordain the indigenous monks in the Theravada lineage. Other forms of Buddhism gradually died out in most of Southeast Asia, and Theravada training centres and temples of national importance flourished under royal patronage.

Island Southeast Asia, by contrast, has become predominantly Muslim over the past five centuries, but both Buddhist monuments and Buddhist minorities survive. For example, although Buddhism is no longer practised in Indonesia, tourists still flock to the ruins of the majestic temple of Borobudur, which covers a hilltop with a geometrical arrangement of stupas representing the mountains that anchor the world, according to traditional Buddhist cosmology. Malaysia also has a sizable Buddhist minority, mainly among the Chinese population.

Theravada Practice: Rituals and Mindfulness

The most common Theravada ritual is the Buddha-puja, a service of respect for the Buddha. Typically, when visiting a temple, Buddhists quickly pay respect to the guardian spirit at the entrance and then place flowers on altars near the stupa and Bodhi tree before proceeding into the temple to place more flowers on the altar(s) there. They may also put coins into an offering box. Then they say prayers expressing their dedication to living according to the dharma. In front of the main altar, they perform the Buddha-puja, chanting praise to the Buddha and vowing to observe the Five Precepts. Unlike the "commandments" of the Judeo-Christian tradition, these precepts are moral rules that

Buddhists voluntarily undertake to follow. The Buddhist vows to refrain from

- taking life
- taking that which is not given
- sensual misconduct (sexual immorality)
- wrong speech (lying, slander, and the like) and
- intoxicants leading to the loss of mindfulness.

On holy days lay Buddhists may undertake to observe additional precepts.

Theravadins (those who follow Theravada) also perform a number of more elaborate "merit-making" rituals specifically designed to produce good karma. Of these rituals, two of the most important are the giving of alms to monks and the *dana* ceremony.

© Robert Harding Picture Library Ltd/Alamy

Lay Buddhists in Laos lower themselves in respect as they offer food to monks, who silently make their alms rounds early in the morning.

Almsgiving

Traditionally, members of the sangha would leave the monastery early each morning carrying bowls to collect their daily food. As they moved slowly through the streets without speaking, their eyes downcast to maintain a tranquil, composed state of mind, laypeople would come out of their houses, put cooked food into the alms bowls, and then bow low or prostrate themselves as a sign of respect.

The practice of going for alms is increasingly rare today. It is still common in Thailand, however, and efforts have been made to revive it in Sri Lanka. In other countries, such as Malaysia, the ritual is performed in the vicinity of the temple on important Buddhist occasions. People bring rice and food packets from home and put their offerings in the alms bowls as the *bhikshus* proceed along the road near the temple.

The Dana Ritual and Merit Transfer

The practice of giving food and other necessities to the sangha has developed into a ritual called *dana*, from the Sanskrit word for "giving." A *dana* might be held at a temple or a pilgrimage site, but is often held by a family in their home to celebrate some important occasion. The following description of a *dana* ceremony in a Sri Lankan home offers a glimpse of several other Buddhist rituals as well.

As the monks arrive at the door, their feet are washed by the men of the family. (If the guests were *bikshunis*, this hospitality ritual would be performed by the women of the family.) On entering the home, the *bhikshus* first bow before the Buddha altar. Then they seat themselves on the floor around the room and conduct a Buddha-puja, after which they chant from a collection of scriptures called *paritta*.

Preparations for the next ritual are made before the chanting begins and involve running a string from the Buddha image on the home altar to a pot containing water, then to the monks, and finally to all the laypeople. The monks and laypeople hold the string in their right hands during the chanting and dharma talk. The water and the string become sacred objects through the power of the chanting.

The chanting is followed by a merit-transfer ritual, in which the merit made by all present through their participation is transferred "to all living beings": "May the merit made by me now or at some other time be shared among all beings here infinite, immeasurable; those dear to me and virtuous as mothers or as fathers are, . . . to others neutral, hostile too. . . ."

In some respects merit transfer resembles the old Roman Catholic traditions of performing penance or purchasing "indulgences" for the benefit of deceased relatives: the Buddhist merit transfer is intended to help one's ancestors, and others, in the afterlife. Although the practice might seem to violate the early Buddhist principle that all of us must make our own karma, the scriptures say that Shakyamuni himself advocated it.

After the merit transfer ritual, the *bhikshus* cut the string into short pieces, which they tie around the right wrist of each male. A layperson ties a string around the wrists of the women, because monks and nuns are not supposed to come into contact with members of the opposite sex. The string is left on the wrist until it falls off.

Life-Cycle and Death Rituals

Early Indian Buddhists continued to follow the life-cycle rituals of what we now call Hinduism, and as Buddhism spread, converts in other regions similarly continued to celebrate their traditional life-cycle rituals. Thus there are no specifically Buddhist wedding or childhood rituals. It is in part for this reason that Buddhism has coexisted with the traditional belief systems of each country where it has established itself: Sri Lankan Buddhists continue to observe Indian rituals, Thai Buddhists still worship the traditional spirits, and Japanese Buddhists still visit Shinto shrines.

There is a Theravada funeral ritual, however, based on the ancient Indian cremation ceremony. The funeral includes a procession, ritual prayers, a water-pouring ritual, final prayers, and a communal meal. But the pattern varies from country to country, and cremation is not mandatory: where the cost of wood is prohibitive, it is replaced by burial.

A traditional Buddhist funeral in Sri Lanka illustrates the principal features of the cremation ceremony. The corpse is taken in a procession to the cemetery along a route prepared in advance by filling in potholes, cutting the grass and weeds beside the road, and placing flowers along the way. These preparations reflect traditions that have parallels in many parts of the ancient world (Christians may recall the preparations made for Jesus' procession into Jerusalem on Palm Sunday).

At the cemetery the body is placed in a temporary wooden structure above a funeral pyre. A brief service is then held that includes chants, prayers, and a ritual in which family members and friends take turns pouring holy water from one container into another while a long prayer is chanted. After the service the pyre is lit, ideally by the eldest son of the deceased. In the event that a crematorium is used instead of a funeral pyre, some aspects of the traditional ceremony, such as the water-pouring ritual, are postponed until the *dana* held on the seventh day after the death, but one or more *bhikshus* will still come to recite prayers over the body.

The loss of a loved one is always a difficult experience, but Buddhists prepare for it through years of prayer and meditation on the inevitability of death. One of Buddhism's strengths is the way it helps its followers to develop a realistic view of the end of life through rituals that remind the living of how all things pass away.

Buddhist death rituals do not end with the burial. On the sixth night after the death, a dharma-preaching service is held at the home, followed by a *dana* on the morning of the seventh day. Other memorial *dana* rituals are held at the home of the deceased after three months, on the eve of which *bhikshus* may be invited to chant all night long, and after one year. Family members and friends who live too far away to attend the funeral itself are able to participate in these memorials. After the passage of time has lessened the pain (*dukkha*) of losing a loved one, the memorial services provide an occasion for the family and friends to remember the happy times with the deceased and to enjoy a family reunion.

Vipassana: Mindfulness Meditation

Theravada Buddhists practise a simple form of meditation called **vipassana** ("insight" or "mindfulness"). While sitting in a meditational posture, practitioners concentrate on their breathing, focusing either on the sensation of air passing through the nostrils or on the rising and falling of the abdomen. Although the breaths are usually counted (in cycles of ten), the point is not to keep track of the number but to focus the mind. Unlike some forms of yoga, *vipassana* does not require practitioners to slow their breath rate. Practitioners may also cultivate mindfulness of other parts of the body, personal emotions, or relationships with others. The goal is to live in a totally mindful way.

Vesak, the Buddha Day Festival

Many Buddhist festivals developed out of earlier seasonal festivals, and there are regional variations. However, Buddhists in most places celebrate the day of the full moon in the "rains" month, known in Theravada countries as Vesak or Wesak (Sanskrit Vaishakha). In English-speaking countries this festival is often called "Buddha Day." According to Theravada Buddhist tradition, three major events in the life of Shakyamuni occurred on that day: his birth, his enlightenment, and his *parinirvana*.

One of the rock inscriptions recounting King Ashoka's accomplishments states that he organized a procession to be held annually on Vaishakha day. In contemporary Sri Lanka, the custom is for Buddhists to travel from place to place to see special paintings depicting scenes from the life of the Buddha. Talks are given on Shakyamuni's life, and special Buddha-pujas are performed.

❂ Mahayana, The Second Vehicle

The Mahayana ("Greater Vehicle") movement appears to have emerged around the first century CE. Although its origins are unclear, we know that its members were dismissing older forms of

Buddhism as Hinayana ("Lesser Vehicle") by the third or fourth century, and that around the same time it was becoming the dominant form of Buddhism across the region traversed by the Silk Road, from Central Asia to northern China. It remains the main form of Buddhism in China, Korea, and Japan.

Mahayana differed from Theravada in everything from the doctrines and scriptures it emphasized to its rituals and meditation practices. Whereas Theravada saw the discipline of the *bhikshu* as a precondition for enlightenment and liberation, Mahayana offered laypeople the opportunity to strive for those goals as well. Whereas Theravada focused on the historical Shakyamuni, Mahayana developed a framework in which he represented only one manifestation of buddhahood. Furthermore, whereas Theravada emphasized that the only way to enlightenment and liberation was through personal effort—that there was no supernatural force on which human beings could call—Mahayana populated the heavens with bodhisattvas dedicated to helping all those who prayed to them for assistance.

How did all these differences arise? A possible explanation is that Mahayana Buddhism developed from one or more of the eighteen early Indian sects. There is some evidence for a close connection between early Mahayana and two or three of the early Indian sects, especially the Mahasanghika (Great Sangha). However, it seems more likely that Mahayana Buddhism arose in southern India as part of a movement towards more liberal interpretation that spread across several of the early Indian sects.

Despite their differences, Mahayana and the earlier forms of Buddhism share a common core of values and moral teachings, practices (such as meditation, chanting, scripture study, and veneration of relics), and forms of monastic life and buildings. In short, Theravada and Mahayana are different vehicles (*yanas*) for travelling the same path to enlightenment.

Mahayana Doctrine

Mahayana Buddhism begins with the same basic teachings as Theravada, but gives more emphasis to some doctrines, such as Emptiness (discussed below in the context of the Madhyamaka School); interprets others, such as the role of the lay sangha and the doctrine of the Buddha Body, in new ways; and includes additional elements, such as the bodhisattva vow.

The Lay Sangha

The practice of venerating Shakyamuni at the stupas enshrining his relics began soon after his death. In time, many lay people began making pilgrimages to places with major relics, and new stupas were built in all Mahayana countries. (The veneration of sacred relics was an important part of several religions in this period, including Hinduism and Christianity.) Lay Buddhists came to believe that they could earn valuable karmic merit by making a pilgrimage.

This development marked a major shift away from early Buddhism, in which the religious role of laypeople had been restricted to providing material support for the sangha, and the prospects for lay progress along the spiritual path were limited. Anyone who wished to seek enlightenment more seriously was expected to "depart the world" and become a *bhikshu* or *bhikshuni*. Mahayana Buddhism, by contrast, offered laypeople the possibility of pursuing spiritual development and even attaining enlightenment while living in the world.

Doctrine of the Three Bodies (Trikaya)

To account for the various ways in which one could experience or refer to buddhahood, Mahayana developed a doctrine of "three bodies" (*trikaya*). The earthly manifestation body of a buddha is called the Appearance Body or Transformation Body (*nirmanakaya*). The heavenly body of a buddha that presides over a buddha-realm and is an object of devotion for Mahayana Buddhists is called the Body of Bliss (*sambhogakaya*). These are supported by the buddha as the absolute essence of the universe, called the Dharma Body (*dharmakaya*).

The Three Bodies doctrine calls attention not only to the oneness of all the buddhas that have appeared on earth, but also to the unity of the buddha-nature or buddha-potential in all its forms. That is, the *trikaya* doctrine envisions one cosmic reality (Dharma Body) that manifests itself in the form both of heavenly beings (Body of Bliss) and of humans such as Shakyamuni (Appearance Body). By connecting the earthly Buddha to the Dharma Body or Absolute, the doctrine of the three bodies also moved Mahayana Buddhism in the direction of theistic religion—in sharp contrast to the Theravada school, which continued to revere the Buddha not as a deity but as an exceptional human being.

Teaching by Expedient Means

The Sanskrit word *upaya* forms part of an expression frequently translated as "skill in means" or "skilful means." The word was used occasionally in Theravada's Pali texts with a more general sense, but the roots of the more technical sense that the word later acquired were already present. Shakyamuni's teachings were practical, even pragmatic, and he seems to have tailored his presentation of them to suit each audience's capacity. He urged his followers to use skill in guiding people to spiritual attainment, like the skillful boatman ferrying people to the other side of the river. The analogy of the raft or boat implies that when one has reached the other side, there is no further need of the raft for the onward journey.

The Lotus Sutra *and the Parable of the* Burning House

A Mahayana text that places a strong emphasis on *upaya* is the *Lotus Sutra*. It treats many Buddhist teachings as provisional: that is, as steps towards a more complete understanding. As an illustration of this perspective, the *Lotus Sutra* tells a story about a father whose children are inside a burning house. He persuades them to come out by promising them chariots that he does not actually have; this false promise may be a lie, but it serves an important purpose. Similarly, those just starting on the path are taught not the ultimate truth, but temporary formulations that will allow them to advance to a

point where they will be able to see the purpose of the earlier stages. From this perspective, even Shakyamuni's teaching is provisional, simply an expedient means of persuading human beings to start along the path. By treating earlier teachings as expedient means, Mahayana thinkers were able to shift the emphasis from Shakyamuni to celestial buddha figures and a notion of cosmic wisdom.

Bodhisattvas and Merit Transfer

Early Buddhism taught that every individual makes his or her own karma, and that there was no supernatural source of grace. The Mahayana school, however, proposed that grace was available in the form of merit transferred to humans from bodhisattvas. Mahayana cosmology envisions a multitude of spiritually advanced beings, all of them prepared to share their great merit with anyone who prays for help.

Bodhisattvas were not unknown in early Indian Buddhism: in a previous life Shakyamuni himself had become a bodhisattva when he vowed to attain buddhahood one day, and he remained a bodhisattva until the night of his enlightenment. Still, for most Theravada Buddhists, the highest goal was to reach the status of an Arhat. The Mahayana school sharply criticized this goal as self-centred because it was focused solely on achieving personal liberation. They maintained that those who take bodhisattva vows are dedicating themselves first and foremost to the salvation of all living beings. All Mahayana Buddhists were therefore encouraged to take the bodhisattva vow, pledging not only to attain buddhahood themselves but also to work towards the liberation of all beings.

The corollary of this innovation in Buddhist thought was Mahayana's introduction of the idea that humans could appeal to merit-filled beings in the heavens for assistance. Early Indian Buddhism had considered Shakyamuni, after his *parinirvana*, to be beyond the realm of direct involvement with human lives, and therefore it had no tradition of appealing to him for assistance. In some forms of Mahayana Buddhism, by contrast, worshippers not only venerate the bodhisattvas but petition them for blessings, much as Roman Catholic or Orthodox Christians venerate the saints and ask them for help.

Another important characteristic of Mahayana Buddhism is its extension of the concept of merit transfer. As we have seen, early Buddhism taught that merit—that is, karma—is made solely by the individual, not by any external agent such as a saint or a god. The only exception to this rule is the transfer of merit for the benefit of one's dead relatives and the welfare of all beings, as in the Theravada *dana* ritual described earlier. In Mahayana, by contrast, the buddhas and the bodhisattvas are believed to be capable of transferring merit from themselves to human beings. Thus devotees can appeal to their chosen bodhisattvas by name to ask for assistance in the same way that some Christians pray to their chosen saints to intercede for them.

Some important bodhisattvas have special functions. For example, Bodhisattva Manjusri is the guardian of Buddhist wisdom, and novices entering Buddhist training often call on him to guide and inspire them.

The bodhisattva known especially for compassion, Avalokiteshvara ("the Lord who looks down"), is popular in all Mahayana countries. Originally Avalokiteshvara was masculine, but in China he came to be venerated in female form under the name Guanyin. This change of gender is an example of the bodhisattva's power to take any shape necessary in order to benefit believers (the *Lotus Sutra* lists 33 examples of such "shape shifting"). Known as the "Bodhisattva of Compassion," Guanyin is the most venerated bodhisattva in Buddhist history, and has been called the "Virgin Mary of East Asia" by Westerners, since graceful statues of her are found everywhere. Many Mahayana women feel especially close to her because she is believed to bring children to those who lack them and to care for infants who die, as well as aborted fetuses.

Bodhisattva Maitreya (the "Friendly One") is expected to be the next buddha, the one who will turn the dharma wheel once again after the wheel set in motion by Shakyamuni has stopped turning. Some Mahayana Buddhists pray to Maitreya as the "future buddha," requesting that they be reborn when he comes, for it is thought to be easier to achieve enlightenment when there is a living buddha to follow.

The heavens in which the buddhas and bodhisattvas reside are known as "fields" or "realms." The belief in such "Buddha realms" is another characteristic of the Mahayana school. Those who venerate a certain buddha may be reborn into his heaven. As we shall see, this is a central belief of the **Pure Land** movement, which venerates a celestial buddha of "infinite life" and "infinite light" known in Sanskrit as Amitayus or Amitabha, in Chinese as Amituofo and in Japanese as Amida (the Japanese spelling is the one most commonly used in English).

The bodhisattvas have had enormous appeal as saviour figures in Mahayana Buddhism. In their compassionate self-sacrifice, they have been compared to the Christian Jesus.

Bodhisattva Vows

The practice of taking bodhisattva vows reflects the Mahayana emphasis on giving of oneself to help others. As we have seen, early Indian Buddhism taught that Shakyamuni's "bodhisattva vow" was a special case. Few Buddhists dared to think that they themselves were destined to become the buddha of some future era: they were content to hope that in some future life they could enter the sangha and achieve the status of Arhat ("worthy one" or saint).

It was the self-centred nature of this ambition, focused only on personal liberation, that Mahayana philosophers criticized. They argued that those who take bodhisattva vows are dedicating themselves to the salvation of all living beings. All Mahayana Buddhists—male or female, lay or monastic—were encouraged to take the bodhisattva vows declaring their intention to become buddhas someday, but also to remain active in helping to liberate all beings.

In practical terms, taking the bodhisattva vow meant vowing to be reborn in a heaven from which one could transfer merit to others. Although the possibility of helping others in this world by accepting rebirth as a human was not ruled out, the advanced bodhisattvas were thought to live in their own heavenly realms.

Mahayana Schools

The above overview of Mahayana doctrine suggests some substantial differences from Theravada Buddhism, especially regarding scriptures, the nature of the Buddha, and the efficacy of prayer. But there are also pronounced differences between the various ordination lineages, or "schools," that developed within the Mahayana tradition, first in India and eventually across East Asia. For example, the **Chan** (**Zen** in Japan) school downplays Buddha veneration and has much in common with Theravada, whereas the Pure Land school stresses the necessity of Amida Buddha's help. We will briefly discuss some of the more important schools of Mahayana thought, focusing on their beginnings (usually in India) and noting how their names changed as they spread across East Asia.

Madhyamaka

Early Buddhism taught that there were six perfections (*paramitas*), the sixth and most important of which was the perfection of a particular kind of wisdom known as *prajna*. This wisdom—not to be confused with worldly wisdom or scientific knowledge—is accessible only to those with a highly developed consciousness or awareness.

Mahayana thinkers put great emphasis on the development of *prajna* and wrote a number of texts on the subject, beginning as early as the first century BCE with the *Perfection of Wisdom in Eight Thousand Verses*. The two that were to become the most important were the *Heart Sutra* and the *Diamond Cutter Sutra*. In all these texts, the key to the highest

spiritual wisdom is awareness of the emptiness or nothingness (*shunyata*) of all things.

Sometime during the latter part of the second century, a brahmin from southern India converted to Buddhism and took the ordination name Nagarjuna. He wrote Buddhist devotional hymns and ethical guides, but his fame is based on philosophical works such as the *Mulamadhyamaka-karika* ("Fundamentals of the Middle Way").

Nagarjuna's philosophical position is called the "Middle Way" (Madhyamaka) because it refuses either to affirm or to deny any statement about reality on the grounds that all such statements necessarily fall short of expressing ultimate truth. All realities (dharmas) are equally "empty" of absolute truth or "self-essence." According to Nagarjuna's doctrine of Emptiness, everything in the phenomenal world is ultimately unreal. By a process of paradoxical logic he claims that Emptiness as ultimate reality is itself unreal, although it may be experienced directly in meditation. Nagarjuna summed up this paradox in a famous eightfold negation:

> Nothing comes into being,
> Nor does anything disappear.
> Nothing is eternal,
> Nor has anything an end.
> Nothing is identical,
> Or differentiated,
> Nothing moves hither,
> Nor moves anything thither (Chen 1964: 84).

For Madhyamaka and the later Mahayana schools that developed under its influence, including Zen, enlightenment demands recognition of the *shunyata* of all dharmas.

Of course Nagarjuna recognized that his own thinking was no less empty than any other. Thus he made it his philosophical "position" to refrain from taking any dogmatic position. A modern Japanese Buddhist professor reports that as a graduate student, he told his teacher he was uncertain of where he stood in relation to the various Buddhist philosophical schools. The teacher responded by implicitly likening him to Nagarjuna: "Your position is to have no position."

According to Nagarjuna's paradoxical logic, *nirvana* is dialectically identical to *samsara*, or the phenomenal world. In other words, each is present in the other. This is the most characteristic Madhyamaka teaching and also the most puzzling. Early Indian Buddhism had taken the two to be opposites, *samsara* being the temporal, worldly process of "coming to be and passing away," and *nirvana* being the eternal, unchanging goal of the spiritual quest; yet Madhyamaka holds that "*samsara* is *nirvana*, and *nirvana* is *samsara*." From the point of view of conventional wisdom, the two may be distinguished, but ultimately the distinction is not tenable. In fact, claims Madhyamaka, perfection of the higher wisdom brings the realization that no such distinction is tenable.

In the sixth century, a split developed around the teachings of two teachers, each of whom considered himself to be the true follower of Nagarjuna. Bhavaviveka (or Bhavya, c. 490–570) was willing to talk about levels of reality and degrees of insight, as long as it was understood that such distinctions applied only in the realm of conventional truth. That is, he accepted the mind's ability to make distinctions about reality within the realm of conventional truth, but recognized that no such distinctions could be made in the realm of absolute truth. The school he founded was known by the name Svatantrika because it accepted the validity of independent (*svatantra*) inference.

Bhavya's rival Buddhapalita (c. 470–550) rejected independent inference and argued that all statements of knowledge were ultimately self-contradictory.

Sanlun: Chinese Madhyamaka

The Sanlun ("Three Treatises") school is the Chinese extension of Nagarjuna's Madhyamaka ("Middle Way"). The monk Kumarajiva (334–414), famous as a translator of Buddhist texts into Chinese, introduced this teaching into China with his translation of two treatises by Nagarjuna and a third by Nagarjuna's disciple Aryadeva (or Deva, c.

300). These three works became the foundation of the Sanlun school.

The chief teaching of the Sanlun school is essentially a restatement of Nagarjuna's idea that everything is empty (*shunya*), because nothing has any independent reality or self-nature. An entity can be identified only through its relation to something else. In this unreal phenomenal world we function as in a dream, making distinctions between subject and object, *samsara* and *nirvana*, but with the higher wisdom comes understanding of the higher truth called *shunyata* or Emptiness.

Kumarajiva's disciple Seng Zhao (374–414) became an outstanding exponent of this system in China, producing three texts on Madhyamaka known as *Zhaolun, the Treatises of Zhao*. For him, the Middle Doctrine represented an effort to reconcile extremes and grasp the paradoxical reality that things both exist and do not exist—a reality that can be apprehended only through sagely wisdom, not through rational, worldly thought.

Yogacara or "Consciousness Only"

In the late fourth century, three Indian *bhikshus* named Maitreyanatha, Asanga, and Vasubandhu founded a new Mahayana school that rivalled Madhyamaka. Though usually called Yogacara ("Practice of Yoga") because it stresses meditation and uses a text by that name, it is also known as "Consciousness Only" (Vijnanavada), because it argues that we cannot truly know either the external world or ourselves. It holds that what most people assume to be realities are in fact nothing more than ideas and images taken from a "storehouse consciousness" (*alaya-vijnana*). As a consequence, we can never know if external objects exist. All we can ever know are the images in our consciousness—images that come from a repository shaped by past karmic actions and attachments.

For Yogacara, both the universe and the perceiver exist only in the process of perceiving. Even our "selves" and our karma are merely reifications of momentary awareness. Sensory impressions are "seeds" that lead to acts or thoughts:

A seed produces a manifestation,
A manifestation perfumes a seed.
The three elements (seed, manifestation, and
   perfume) turn on and on,
The cause and effect occur at the same time
(Chen 1964: 323).

According to this theory, the only way to avoid false substantialization is to so exhaust the consciousness, through yoga and spiritual cultivation, that it becomes identical to the ultimate reality called "thusness" (*tathata*), which corresponds to the "emptiness" of Madhyamaka. Critics from rival schools argued that the concept of the storehouse consciousness seemed to contradict the traditional Buddhist doctrine of no-self (*anatman*) and come close to affirming the Hindu notion of Atman that the Buddha had rejected. The Yogacara writers, however, were careful to point out that, unlike the Atman, it has no eternal, unchanging substance. Buddhist ideas of the link between one birth and the next as a "karma complex" or "migrating consciousness" were developed by Yogacara into the notion of a storehouse consciousness.

The Yogacara school's emphasis on "consciousness only" and the psychological origin of all perceptions may have arisen out of the experience of emptying the mind during Yogacara meditation—a practice quite different from the visualization practised in some other meditation traditions.

Faxiang: Chinese Yogacara

The Chinese version of the Yogacara or "Consciousness Only" school also has two names, Weishi ("Consciousness Only") and Faxiang ("Dharma Character"). First introduced into China in the sixth century, the school grew up around a text by Asanga entitled *Compendium of Mahayana*. It was his perplexity over the meaning of this work that spurred a monk named Xuanzang to set out for India in search of more scriptures; on his return, the Big Wild Goose Pagoda was built in Xi'an (the Chinese terminus of the silk route) to house the manuscripts he brought back. This temple, along with its smaller companion the Little Wild Goose Pagoda, remains an important centre of Buddhism in this historic city. (The story of Xuanzang's perilous journey to India is celebrated in Chinese Buddhist art and inspired the famous novel *Journey to the West*, best known in English under the title *Monkey: A Folk-Tale of China*.)

Although Faxiang did not survive as a vital sect, it had some influence on the development of other schools of thought, including Neo-Confucianism.

Pure Land Buddhism

The school dedicated to Amitabha (Amida) most likely began to take shape around the first century, some 500 years after Shakyamuni's *parinirvana*. According to an account in the *Larger Sutra on the Pure Land*, attributed to Shakyamuni himself, Amitabha was a buddha of a previous age who in an earlier life, as a young prince named Dharmakara, took 48 bodhisattva vows detailing his intention to strive for enlightenment and help others in specific ways. In a sense, some resemble a doctor's oath not to deny treatment to those who have no money to pay for it. In one of the most important vows (the eighteenth), Amitabha promises to establish a heavenly region—the "Pure Land" or "Western Paradise"—into which all beings who so desire can be reborn. No extraordinary effort will be required to earn rebirth in that land: admission will be free to all who have faith in Amitabha's compassionate power and make their desire for rebirth in his heaven known by thinking of him:

If, after my obtaining Buddhahood, all beings in the ten quarters should not desire in sincerity and trustfulness to be born in my country, and if they should not be born by only thinking of me for ten times, except those who have committed the five grave offences and those who are abusive of the true Dharma, may I not attain the Highest Enlightenment (Bloom 1965: 2–3).

In short, Dharmakara vows that he will strive to become a completely enlightened buddha on the condition that he can remain active in the work of helping all living beings towards liberation.

Suffering, old age, and death will be unknown in the Pure Land—the *sukhavati*, as opposed to the *dukkha-vati*, the land of suffering, that is the world. There will be food, drink, and music for all; the streets and buildings will be made of jewels; and the buddha's followers will be so uplifted by his merit that their progress towards nirvana will be easy. This notion of the "Pure Land" marked a remarkable transformation in the Buddhist idea of heaven. In early Buddhism, meritorious individuals could hope to be reborn in some kind of paradise. While there, they would be unable to "make" new merit or develop their higher wisdom. In other words, there was no path leading from heaven to nirvana: once the inhabitants' store of merit was exhausted, they would have to be reborn in human form. But for those in the Pure Land rebirth on earth will no longer be necessary.

The *Smaller Sutra on the Pure Land* spells out what is required to benefit from Amitabha's great store of merit. Those who had recollected and repeated his name before death would be reborn in his Pure Land. This rebirth would not be earned by the individual's meritorious works. Rather, rebirth in the Pure Land would be a gift made available through the infinite merits of the buddha Amitabha. Theologically, the Christian concept of salvation through faith in divine grace is a parallel.

A third text of early Pure Land Buddhism, the *Meditation on Amitayus Sutra*, offers detailed instruction in vision meditation. For those unable to undertake the rigorous training required to achieve a vision, however, it also offers an easier path. This is the formula that was to become central to Pure Land Buddhism: "Homage to Amitabha Buddha." Even the meritless or wicked could gain rebirth in the Pure Land through sincere repetition of the sacred formula.

The Pure Land school introduced into Buddhism a path to salvation based solely on faith. There is no equivalent to this path in the Theravada tradition. The *Smaller Sutra on the Pure Land* teaches that the only condition for rebirth in the Pure Land is faith in the infinite compassion of Amitabha, shown through prayerful and meditative repetition of his name. This reliance on an external power, called "other power," stands in sharp contrast to the self-reliance emphasized in early Buddhism. Such "other-reliance" was described as "cat grace," as opposed to the "monkey grace" of self-reliance—the idea being that a baby cat is picked up and carried by its mother, whereas a baby monkey has to reach for its mother and hold on.

Over the centuries that followed, Pure Land Buddhism spread from India to China, Korea, and Japan. Pure Land became the most popular of all Buddhist schools in East Asia.

Jingtu: Chinese Pure Land

In China, Pure Land is known as Jingtu and Amitabha Buddha as Amituofo. He is assisted by two bodhisattvas (*pusa* in Chinese), one of whom is Guanyin, the bodhisattva of compassion.

The recitation of praise to Amituofo is called *nianfo* in Chinese. During the recitation the devotee usually fingers a string of beads. Thus Pure Land Buddhism parallels some forms of Christianity in several ways, with a God-figure (Amida), a mediator (Guanyin), a doctrine of faith and grace, and a devotional practice not unlike the recitation of the rosary. (Some scholars think that the practice of using a string of beads to keep count while reciting a sequence of prayers originated in India.)

In China, Pure Land Buddhism has had a special appeal for the masses of people who seek not only ultimate salvation but also a power that will assist them in everyday life. Guanyin is particularly important in this respect, especially for women. She soon came to symbolize the "giver of children"—an adaptation that underlines the more worldly focus of Chinese Buddhism, compared with its Indian counterpart. Guanyin is associated with the medieval legend of the Chinese princess Miaoshan, killed by her parents to prevent her from becoming a nun. Sometimes seen holding a child, she recalls the Christian figure of the Madonna with child. It has been suggested that this pose reflects the influence of Christian art brought to

China by missionaries in the late seventeenth and early eighteenth centuries.

Jodo: Japanese Pure Land

In Japan, Pure Land Buddhism is called Jodo (from Chinese Jingtu), its Buddha is called Amida (from Amituofo), and the female bodhisattva is called Kannon (from Guanyin). Most Buddhists in Japan today belong to the Jodo school.

Pure Land Buddhism was introduced to Japan by a monk named Honen (1133–1212). A man of saintly reputation, Honen wanted to provide a simpler way to salvation for those unable to undertake the demanding program prescribed in the *Meditation on Amitayus Sutra*. The devotional practice that he taught relies entirely on faith in Amida's power of salvation, and consists in chanting the "Homage to Amida Buddha" mantra. Repetition of this phrase, called the *nembutsu* in Japanese, leads to a heightened state of consciousness, especially during services as the chanting quickens, building to a feverish pace. (For a detailed discussion of Pure Land in Japan, see Chapter 7.)

Honen's disciple Shinran (1173–1262) further developed Pure Land Buddhism in Japan, underlining the need for the "other-power" of Amida's grace in a "degenerate" age when Buddhist dharma was thought to be in a phase of decline. Condemning the magical and syncretic tendencies that he saw in other schools, Shinran taught the *nembutsu* as an act of faith and thanksgiving. In a moving passage about the salvation of the wicked, Shinran says:

> People generally think . . . that if even a wicked man can be reborn in the Pure Land, how much more so a good man! This latter view may at first sight seem reasonable, but it is not in accord with the purpose of the Original Vow, with faith in the Power of Another. The reason for this is that he who, relying on his own power, undertakes to perform meritorious deeds, has no intention of relying on the Power of Another and is not the object of the Original Vow of Amida. Should he, however, abandon his reliance on his own power and put his trust in the Power of Another, he can be born in the True Land of Recompense. . . . Amida made his Vow with the intention of bringing wicked men to Buddhahood. Therefore the wicked man who depends on the Power of Another is the prime object of salvation (Tannisho; Tsunoda 1958: 217).

Both Honen and Shinran met with opposition from rival schools and were exiled by the authorities, but they found wide support among the people. Shinran founded a new sect called "True Pure Land" (Jodo Shinsu) or Shin Buddhism. He also did

Document

Pure Land Buddhism: Honen's Testament

The method of final salvation that I have propounded is neither a sort of meditation, such as has been practised by many scholars in China or Japan, nor is it a repetition of the Buddha's name by those who have studied and understood the deep meaning of it. It is nothing but the mere repetition of the "Namu Amida Butsu," without a doubt of his mercy, whereby one may be born into the Land of Perfect Bliss. The mere repetition with firm faith includes all the practical details, such as the threefold preparation of mind and the four primordial truths. If I as an individual had any doctrine more profound than this, I should . . . be left out of the Vow of the Amida Buddha (Tsunoda 1958: 208).

something revolutionary: like Martin Luther, the sixteenth-century German priest whose demands for reform led to the Protestant Reformation in Europe, he chose to marry, maintaining that husband and wife are to each other as the bodhisattva Kannon is to the believer. In so doing he laicized Buddhism. Although this break with the tradition of monastic celibacy was widely opposed, today most Buddhist priests in Japan are married, and temples are usually passed down through their families; the oldest son is typically called the "temple son" and is expected to train for the priesthood so that he can continue the family tradition.

Chan (Zen) Buddhism

The founder of Chan Buddhism (better known in the West by its Japanese name, Zen) was Bodhidharma—the same sixth-century Indian monk who told King Wu that all his good works had earned him no merit at all. In sharp contrast to the Pure Land sect's emphasis on "other power," Chan emphasized "self-power" and the attainment of personal enlightenment through rigorous practice of meditation. Although there is no surviving evidence that a similar school existed in India,

Chan tradition traces Bodhidharma's lineage to the Buddha's disciple Kashyapa, whose intuitive insight is celebrated in the story of the "flower sermon" (see Focus box).

The Chinese pronunciation of the word *dhyana* or *jhana* was "*chan*": hence the name of the school that Bodhidharma founded, having gone to China to teach what he called a "mind to mind, direct transmission" of enlightenment, with "no dependence on words." Just as the Buddha relied on a single enigmatic gesture to deliver his "flower sermon," so Bodhidharma and later Chan (Zen) masters used surprising, shocking, paradoxical, or even violent actions to bring about the state of mind best known in the West by the Japanese term *satori*. One master twisted a disciple's nose so hard that the pain and indignity led to a breakthrough. Another shoved his disciple into a thorn bush, with the same result. Another would simply hold up a single finger. Other masters had their own signature methods. Many made impossible demands on their students, including the master who held up one hand and demanded to be told what sound it made: this was the origin of the familiar Zen **koan** "What is the sound of one hand clapping?" One master would instruct his disciples to imagine themselves

Focus

The Flower Sermon

This story begins with the disciples asking Shakyamuni Buddha for a dharma talk. He agrees, and the disciples prepare a place for the talk at an appropriate spot part way up Vulture Peak Mountain. The list of those wanting to attend includes the monks (from the earth level) as well as *nagas*, the mystical cobras of the underworld, and angels (*devatas*) from the heavenly realm. As the Buddha takes his seat on the teaching throne, all grow silent, eagerly waiting to hear his words. Instead of speaking, however, Shakyamuni simply holds up a white lotus flower.

All are dumbfounded except for Kashyapa, who in that moment experiences an intuitive flash of enlightenment. The Buddha acknowledges his understanding with a smile, and Kashyapa comes to be known as Kashyapa the Great (Mahakashyapa) and the first patriarch in a lineage that stresses the achievement of the state of mind called *dhyana* in Sanskrit and *jhana* in Pali—the state reached by the young Shakyamuni while meditating under the rose-apple tree.

Sites

Shaolin, China

The Shaolin monastery, in central China, is the home of Chan Buddhism as well as many of the East Asian martial arts traditions. A two-hour hike up a mountain path leads to Bodhidharma's cave, where he is said to have practised "wall-gazing" meditation for seven years. The story is that he began teaching self-defence exercises to his students as an antidote to their long hours of sitting meditation.

hanging by their teeth from a branch suspended over some danger then being asked a question that demands a response—a question such as "Do all persons have Buddha-nature?" If the disciple correctly answers "Yes," he will fall and die. But if he refuses to answer, he will seem to communicate an untruth. The master demands to know: "What would you do?" Since there is no logical way out of this dilemma, the correct answer must be found in some place other than the rational mind.

© VISUM Foto GmbH/Alamy

Dozens of elementary and high schools in the town of Shaolin combine academic studies in the mornings with martial arts training in the afternoons. Although most of the schools are Buddhist in orientation, two are Muslim; there are also some schools for girls, although the majority are male-only. The best students from each age group perform hourly for tourists, as in this photo.

In the early sixth century, Bodhidharma took this school of thought to China and settled into a cave in the mountains above the village of Shao-lin. He was known especially for meditating while facing the wall of his cave. Later legend has it that after nine years of "wall-gazing meditation," his legs atrophied. This is popularly recalled in the legless, egg-shaped Japanese dolls called Darumas (*daruma* is the Japanese word for "dharma"). Some Japanese buy Daruma dolls on New Year's Day, then take them home and make a wish for a good year while filling in the missing pupil of one of the doll's eyes. The following New Year, they will fill in the other pupil while thanking Daruma for the good year that has passed.

Bodhidharma's teaching is summed up in these four lines attributed to him:

A special transmission outside of doctrines. Not setting up the written word as an authority. Pointing directly at the human heart. Seeing one's nature and becoming a buddha (Robinson 1959: 332).

These lines put into words Kashyapa's "flower sermon" experience of the transmission of enlightened consciousness by direct contact between master and disciple, without the need for textual or doctrinal study.

Because of its distaste for book learning, Chan–Zen became known for its transmission of enlightenment "outside the scriptures," independent of "words or letters." The special Chan–Zen state of consciousness is transmitted only "from mind to mind"—from master to disciple—without the intervention of rational argumentation. It advocates the "absence of thoughts" to free the mind from external influences.

The Lineage of Chan Patriarchs

One winter day a Chinese man is said to have arrived at Bodhidharma's cave, hoping to be invited in to study under the master. But no such invitation was forthcoming. Hours passed and darkness fell but the man waited throughout the night, shivering in the ever deepening snow. In the morning Bodhidharma finally asked him what he wanted. He explained that he wanted a teacher who would open his mind to enlightenment. Bodhidharma refused, telling him it was hopeless for someone like him, with little wisdom and only feeble resolve, to expect any serious breakthrough. After several more hours, he came up with a plan. He cut off his left arm and presented it to Bodhidharma as proof of his resolve. Bodhidharma accepted him as a disciple.

The story continues with the new disciple, now named Huike, asking Bodhidharma for help in pacifying his anxious mind. The master replied by saying, "Bring me your mind so that I can pacify it." Huike explained that he had long sought his mind, but he could not find it. "So there," says Bodhidharma, "I have pacified your mind!" The one-armed Huike went on to become the first Han Chinese patriarch, after Bodhidharma's death. In Chan paintings he is often depicted in the act of handing his severed arm to Bodhidharma. There is a small temple dedicated to Huike at the monastery in Shaolin, with a statue of him standing in the snow just outside.

The lineage of patriarchs continued and the Chan school gradually spread to other areas. Most Chan monasteries in China, Korea, and Japan were located partway up a mountain, where the cool, dry atmosphere optimized the chances of a spiritual breakthrough. For this reason Chan Buddhism has been called the "mountain school."

HUINENG AND THE POETRY CONTEST

During the era of the fifth Chan patriarch, in the late seventh century, a young boy from southern China named Huineng arrived at the Shaolin monastery seeking admission as a novice. He was not accepted, perhaps because he spoke a southern dialect difficult for the northerners to understand. But Huineng stayed to work in the kitchen, pounding rice and helping to cook for the monks.

Huineng had made the long journey because he had learned that the monastery taught a radical new form of Buddhism that offered the possibility of a direct breakthrough to a higher level of consciousness, without undue dependence on knowledge of scriptures or the performance of rituals. He understood the essence of Buddhism to involve an intuitive, mystical experience, the "direct pointing of the mind" that Bodhidharma had taught.

When it came time for the aging fifth patriarch to choose his successor, candidates were asked to compose a poem (*gatha* in Sanskrit) expressing their state of enlightenment. The most senior disciple produced this verse:

> This body is the Bodhi-tree;
> The soul is like the mirror bright;
> Take heed to keep it always clean,
> And let no dust collect upon it (Suzuki 1991).

This poem captures the Chan point of view nicely. Instead of practising ritual veneration of the Buddha who was enlightened under a Bodhi tree long ago in a distant land, one is to think of one's own body, here and now, as the Bodhi tree,

the place of enlightenment. Mirrors in old China were made of shiny metal, and they needed to be polished daily to keep dust from marring the reflections. But Mahayana Buddhism also had a long tradition of comparing the purifying of the mind to the polishing of a mirror. A bright, shiny mirror perfectly reflects reality, and a pure mind should do the same. Thus the senior disciple's poem encourages regular meditation to keep the mind clear and pure. That night, however, Huineng produced a counter-poem:

> The Bodhi (True Wisdom) is not like the tree;
> The mirror bright is nowhere shining:
> As there is nothing from the first,
> Where does the dust itself collect? (Suzuki 1991)

This poem deepens the understanding of Chan enlightenment. It goes beyond merely bringing the enlightenment experience, symbolized by the Bodhi tree, to the "here and now." In denying the

Document

Chan Buddhism

The following extracts are from the Platform Sutra, *an important scripture attributed to the sixth Chan patriarch, Huineng, and compiled by one of his disciples in the early 700s.*

Meditation and Wisdom
Good friends, how then are meditation and wisdom alike? They are like the lamp and the light it gives forth. If there is a lamp there is light; if there is no lamp there is no light. The lamp is the substance of light; the light is the function of the lamp. Thus, although they have two names, in substance they are not two. Meditation and wisdom are like this (*The Platform Sutra of the Sixth Patriarch*, sec. 15; Yampolsky 1976: 137).

On Saving Oneself
Good friends, when I say "I vow to save all sentient beings everywhere," it is not that I will save you, but that sentient beings, each with their own natures, must save themselves. What is meant by "saving yourselves with your own natures"? Despite heterodox views, passions, ignorance, and delusions, in your own physical bodies you have in yourselves the attributes of inherent enlightenment, so that with correct views you can be saved. (*The Platform Sutra of the Sixth Patriarch*, sec. 21; Yampolsky 1976: 143).

imagery of the Bodhi tree and the mirror, it implies that the pure mind corresponds to the state of emptiness central to the Mahayana tradition.

The fifth patriarch called Huineng into his room, acknowledged his deep understanding, and awarded him the robe and staff of the office of patriarch—but with the advice that he should go back to the South. This he did, and even though he was still a layman, he began teaching the deep state of intuitive wisdom that became known in the West as *satori*, one of its names in Japanese. Eventually he was ordained and recognized as the true sixth patriarch. It was Huineng who spread Chan to the masses and into southern China, from which it was eventually taken to Korea, where it is known as Seon, and Japan, where it is called Zen.

Zen Sects: Linchi (Rinzai) and Caodong (Soto)

There are two main Zen sects, Linzai (Rinzai in Japan) and Caodong (Soto in Japan). The first is named after Linji, a famous ninth-century Chinese Chan monk who is said to have entered training as a shy young boy. After training diligently for more than a year, he was permitted to meet with the master, Huangbo. When the master asked why he had come, Linji humbly requested instruction in enlightenment, whereupon the master hit him hard with his stick.

When Linji told his teacher what had happened, he was advised to try again, which led to a second beating. After three such beatings Linji decided to leave training, thinking he was not worthy. The master allowed him to leave, but requested that he first visit an old hermit monk who lived farther up the mountain. The hermit, after hearing Linji describe what had happened, exclaimed, "Poor old Huangbo, he must have nearly exhausted himself hitting you!" This lack of sympathy so shocked and angered Linji that he experienced a breakthrough and burst out laughing. "Why the sudden change?" demanded the hermit. "There's not so much to old Huangbo's Zen after all" was the reply. Upon returning to Huangbo, Linji threatened to hit the master with his own stick. "Just get back to your training," said the master.

When Huangbo died, Linji succeeded him as master and gave his name to a new ordination lineage or sect. The Linji (Rinzai) sect stresses exactly the kind of "sudden enlightenment," or *satori*, that he experienced in response to Huangbo's apparently irrational behaviour. Subsequent masters in his sect continued to find that they could stimulate a breakthrough to Chan consciousness by delivering unexpected blows and shouts, or otherwise confounding their pupils.

At the centre of this approach is the **koan** (from Chinese **gongan**): a paradoxical anecdote that is specifically designed to defy rational understanding and force the student out of normal "heady" (reason- or word-centred) mode into a more intuitive, body-centred state of mind. The typical koan retells an incident in which, by doing something unexpected, a master sparked an enlightenment experience in his student. The point of the retelling is to evoke the same experience in successive generations of disciples. We will return to the subject of koan training in the Practice section below.

The second Zen sect, Caodong (Soto in Japan), seeks "gradual enlightenment" through long hours of *zazen* (sitting meditation). Both sects use koans and *zazen*, so the differences lie mainly in emphasis and tradition. Soto training relies more heavily on *zazen* and Rinzai on koans.

Mahayana Practice

Meditation

Meditation is central to all forms of Buddhism, including Mahayana. Monastic training involves careful attention to the posture of the body and the method of concentration. The goals include quieting the mind and heightening mental alertness, with the ultimate goal of breaking through into a state of pure mind known as the buddha-mind or emptiness (**shunyata**). In some Mahayana schools, terms such as "buddha-nature" and "buddha-mind" became virtual synonyms for "enlightenment."

The practice of meditation is particularly intense among monks of the Soto Zen school. One famous

Soto monk kept his seat cushion in the sleeve pocket of his robe so that he could practice seated meditation (**zazen**) whenever a moment of free time presented itself. When done in groups, the leader signals the beginning of the session by striking a bell. Typically, after roughly half an hour of *zazen* during which attention is focused on breathing, the bell is rung again, signalling that it is time to rise and practise walking meditation—focused on the slow lifting of the feet high off the ground—for a similar length of time. Then another bell signals a return to a period of seated meditation.

In the Pure Land tradition, as we have seen, rebirth is not earned by meritorious works and wisdom, as was the case with the path laid down by Shakyamuni, but is granted through the grace of Amida (Amitabha). The *Meditation on Amitayus Sutra* promises that whoever achieves a vision of Amida will be reborn in his Pure Land, and explains 16 forms of "vision meditation" designed to help the devotee achieve that goal and develop a special rapport with him. Such visualization would eventually become a central element in Vajrayana Buddhism.

Koan Training

The use of koans is a Zen practice identified with the Rinzai sect in particular. A standard collection of koans called the *Mumonkan* is used in training. The first koan presented to disciples is known as "Joshu's *Mu*." It tells of a time when the ancient master Joshu and a disciple were walking through the monastery grounds and saw one of the stray dogs that had made the monastery their home. The disciple asks Joshu, "Does a dog have buddha-nature?" Joshu replies "*mu*" ("no"; *wu* in the Chinese original). There are many layers to this reply. On the surface, we might say that the standard Buddhist answer to the question would obviously be "yes," since all living beings have buddha-nature. Yet Joshu answers with a word that seems to deny that fundamental doctrine. The key to this paradox lies in the fact that *mu*, "no," is the very word used in Buddhism to express emptiness, the "nothingness" state of mind that characterizes the buddha mind. Thus Joshu's negation is in reality an affirmation.

The correct response to the koan lies not in a rational answer to the master's question but in the experience of breaking through the confines of the rational mind. It is the master's task to reject all false responses to the koan until an intuitive breakthrough into a new level of consciousness is achieved. Disciples must report to the master regularly to respond to the assigned koan. Masters have been known to shout at or hit students who respond with inadequate "answers." Disciples' efforts to master their first koans might go on for days, months, or years, until one day the mental breakthrough occurs.

Mahayana Holidays

In Mahayana countries, the three anniversaries of the Buddha—his birth, his enlightenment, and his

---

Focus

Roshi Robert Aitken

Roshi Robert Aitken of the Zen Center in Hawaii tells a story from his time as one of a group of students who were assigned "Joshu's *Mu*" in Japan. One of the other students, frustrated at working on the koan in silence, began to shout: "mu! muU! muUU! muuuuuuuUU!." As the others worked on the koan in silence, he continued to shout, day after day. In the end, the master acknowledged his breakthrough, demonstrating that there is no single correct approach. Whatever the route taken, once a student has broken through to the first level of spiritual enlightenment, a second koan is assigned.

Mount Putuo, off the southern coast of China, is one of the four mountains that Chinese Buddhists hold to be most sacred, each of which is associated with a particular bodhisattva. Putuo is dedicated to Guanyin, and it includes a temple and a huge Guanyin statue.

parinirvana—are remembered on separate days, determined by the lunar calendar. Festivals honouring other buddhas and bodhisattvas are also observed, especially Guanyin's birthday. Different sects also celebrate the anniversaries of their patriarchs (for example, Nichiren in Japan).

Under the influence of the ancestor cults of China and Japan, the dead are honoured by an "all souls' day." In China this day is celebrated by burning paper boats to free the *preta* ("hungry ghosts") who have perished in violence. In Japan, at the feast called Obon, two altars are built, one for offerings to the dead ancestors and the other for the "ghosts." Traditionally, Chinese Buddhists avoided non-essential outside activity during the "ghosts" month, to lessen the risk of a ghostly encounter. Buddhism has also adopted local customs

surrounding occasions such as the beginning of the new year. In China pilgrimages are made to four sacred mountains, each dedicated to a different bodhisattva. In Japan the temple gong is struck 108 times on New Year's Eve, symbolizing forgiveness of the 108 kinds of bad deeds. Many Japanese gather at temples before midnight to hear the striking of the gong, but many more watch television coverage of the ceremony broadcast from a major monastery.

⊛ Vajrayana, The Third Vehicle

"Vajrayana"—from *vajra*, meaning both "diamond" and "thunderbolt"—is just one of several names for the third vehicle of Buddhism. The image of the

diamond suggests something so hard that it cannot be broken or split, while the thunderbolt suggests a very particular kind of power. Long before the emergence of Buddhism, the thunderbolt was the sceptre of the Hindu storm god Indra, the symbol of his power. It came to be represented by a wand shaped somewhat like an hourglass, or a three-dimensional version of the familiar symbol of infinity. Such wands are used regularly in Vajrayana rituals. Despite the thunderbolt connection, however, the symbolism of the wand is not physical or astronomical. Rather, the curved prongs represent various buddhas, and the power that the wand symbolizes is the power of the enlightened

Sites

Kathmandu, Nepal

There are two great Buddhist sites in Kathmandu, Nepal. Swayambhunath, nicknamed the "monkey temple" because it has even more monkeys than the usual temple, sits high on a hill, its Nepali-style "eyes" overlooking the countryside. The other, Bodhanath, is a Tibetan-style stupa surrounded by shops and cafés.

© Tuul/Hemis/Corbis

The eyes of the Swayambhunath Buddha survey the Kathmandu Valley in all four directions. The Nepali script for the number one, symbolizing unity, forms the "nose".

awareness—itself unbreakable, but capable of shattering spiritual obstacles such as ignorance, greed, or hatred. It remains a central symbol in the principal Vajrayana school today, Tibetan Buddhism.

Followers of Vajrayana refer to it as the "third turning of the wheel of dharma," the culmination of the two earlier vehicles, Theravada and Mahayana. This is exemplified in a system of Vajrayana training, which takes place in three stages named after the three vehicles. In the "Hinayana" phase of practice (corresponding to Theravada), beginners concentrate on basic moral discipline. In the "Mahayana" stage, they receive instruction in basic Mahayana doctrines. And in the third and highest stage, the Vajrayana, they learn the doctrines and practices that Vajrayana itself considers the most advanced.

The view of Vajrayana as the third turning of the wheel also makes sense in historical terms, for it is a more recent phenomenon than Theravada and Mahayana. Emerging in India during or after the third century, Vajrayana was subsequently taken to virtually all parts of the Buddhist world, although it disappeared from Southeast Asian (Theravada) countries centuries ago, and in East Asia had to settle for a minor role in relation to the more popular Mahayana schools. Where Vajrayana became the majority religion was in the region of Nepal and Bhutan, and across the Himalayas in Tibet and Mongolia. Hence some refer to Vajrayana as "northern" Buddhism—northern from the point of view of the Ganges region where Buddhism first developed (from that perspective, Theravada is "southern" and Mahayana "eastern").

Vajrayana Practice

Mantras

Vajrayana incorporates numerous elements that originated in India, in both Hindu and Buddhist practice, but in many cases gives them its own emphasis. An example is its use of mantras: sacred syllables or phrases thought to evoke great spiritual blessings when properly spoken or chanted.

Although mantras are also central to the Pure Land ("Homage to Amida Buddha") and Nichiren ("Homage to the Lotus Sutra") schools, the Vajrayana (also known as Mantrayana) tradition puts particular emphasis on sound, recalling the ancient brahminic tradition according to which the priests' chanting of the ritual formulas in itself had a special acoustic efficacy.

The best-known Vajrayana mantra is the phrase *Om mani padme hum*. The words are Sanskrit: *om* and *hum* are sacred syllables, not words per se; *mani* means "jewel"; and *padme* is "lotus." So in English we might say "O the jewel in the lotus," or simply "Om jewel lotus hum." But the phrase can be interpreted in several ways. Some Vajrayana practitioners see the jewel and lotus as symbolic of the male and female principles, and understand their union to represent the harmony of the male and female cosmic forces. Others understand the phrase to refer to the bodhisattva Avalokiteshvara in feminine form as the "jewelled-lotus lady." Some believe its six syllables refer to six realms of rebirth, or six spiritual perfections. Whatever the interpretation, the mantra evokes a cosmic harmony.

Mantras need not be spoken to be effective, however; they can also be written on banners or slips of paper and hung on trees or lines, or rotated in cylindrical containers called prayer wheels. The repetition achieved through rotation is thought to provide additional benefit.

Tantras

Another Indian tradition that Vajrayana incorporated is tantrism. "Tantric" Buddhism, like its Hindu counterpart, envisions cosmic reality as the interplay of male and female forces and teaches a set of practical techniques for tapping into the spiritual energy produced by that interplay. The image of a male figure in sexual embrace with his female consort is common in Vajrayana art. Known in Tibetan as the *yab–yum* (father–mother), this union of male and female symbolizes the coming together of the complementary elements essential to enlightenment, such as compassion and wisdom.

Thus a central component of tantric Buddhism is the concept of sexual union. Some tantric texts suggest that since the world is bound by lust, it must be released by lust as well. While the "right-hand" school understood this principle symbolically, the "left-hand" school interpreted it in a more literal fashion, practising ritual unions in which the man and woman visualized themselves as divine beings. Such practices, properly undertaken, would confront lust, defeat it, and transcend it. The texts that lay out such techniques are called tantras. The Tibetan canon includes a vast library of tantras under the heading *Kanjur* and various commentaries under the heading *Tanjur*.

The Vajrayana tantras classify the many buddhas and bodhisattvas in various families, which are often depicted in a sacred geometric design called a mandala. The "head" of the family occupies the place of honour in the centre of the design, surrounded by the other members, each of whom occupies a specific position.

Practitioners meditate on their chosen buddhas or bodhisattvas in order to achieve visions that will help them along the path to enlightenment. The Vajrayana guru initiates the disciple into the symbolic meanings of the various members of the family and their relationships, as well as the rituals required to develop inner wisdom.

Having built up a visualization, practitioners begin to identify with their chosen figures and tap into their energies. Visualizing themselves as identical with them, practitioners become aware of the centres of power ("chakras") in their own bodies and may perceive themselves to be at the centre of a sacred space defined by a mandala. At the culmination of this process of gradual enlightenment, initiates aspire to dissolve slowly into emptiness (*shunyata*), liberated from ego attachment.

A classic mandala pattern reflects tantric Buddhism's emphasis on the *Mahavairocana* ("Great Sun") *Sutra*. For example, a mandala might centre on Mahavairocana, surrounded by the buddhas of the four directions: Aksobhya in the east, Amida in the west, Amoghasiddhi in the north, and Ratnasam-bhava in the south, all of whom together represent the various emanations of buddhahood itself. It is also characteristic of tantric Buddhism to give female counterparts not only to the buddhas but to the bodhisattvas who accompany them; as a result, mandalas often include numerous figures.

These deities have dual aspects, pacific and angry, depending on their functions (e.g., to assist in beneficial activities or to repel evil forces). The union of wisdom and compassion, considered the key to enlightenment, is represented by the father–mother image evoked by the embrace of deities and their consorts.

Vajrayana in East Asia

Introduced to China in the eighth century under the name Zhenyan ("true word" or "mantra"), tantric Buddhism enjoyed only a brief period of popularity as a novelty there. In 806, however, a Japanese monk who had been studying in China introduced Zhenyan to his homeland. Shingon Buddhism, as it came to be known, flourished in Japan and is still practised there today.

Shingon tantrism is of the "right-hand" type. For the Shingon school, enlightenment consists in the realization that one's own Buddha-nature is identical with the Great Sun Buddha, Mahavairocana, and can be achieved in this life, in this world, through the esoteric teachings of Shingon.

Zhenyan was transmitted to Korea in the same period. Known there as Milgyo, it maintained a distinctive identity until the fourteenth century, when it was amalgamated with Mahayana schools.

Vajrayana in Tibet

Shakyamuni was born near the foothills of the Himalayas and converted his home region (now part of Nepal) a few years after his enlightenment. But the high Himalayan plateau was so difficult to reach that Buddhism made little headway there for the first 1,200 years of its history. It was not until the late eighth century that a few Buddhist missionaries found their way to Tibet at the invitation of Tibetan kings.

Vajrayana is said to have been established in Tibet by a *bhikshu* named Padmasambhava. Revered as Guru **Rinpoche** ("precious teacher"), he combined instruction in dharma with magical practices involving the world of the spirits. The figure of Padmasambhava is particularly identified with a school of Tibetan Buddhism known as the Nyingma ("ancient"), which traces its origins to his time.

The indigenous religion of the region when Buddhism arrived is known as Bon (a name meaning "truth" or "reality"). Little is known of Bon belief and practice in that era, but most scholars agree that its ritual objectives included the safe conduct of the soul to an existence in a land beyond death. To get the soul to that realm, the Bon priests would sacrifice an animal such as a yak, a horse, or a sheep during the funeral ritual. Kings were buried in large funeral mounds that resemble Chinese tomb mounds.

The Bon religion appears to have combined and interacted with Buddhism in Tibet, but elements of it have survived to the present day. One element that distinguishes Bon from Buddhism is the claim that it originated not in India but in a mythical region west of Tibet named Ta-zig (from the same root as "Tajikistan") or Shambhala. Today some Tibetans still identify themselves with Bon rather than Buddhism, while others practise both.

Tibetan Buddhism is divided among three main ordination lineages or orders. The best known, the Gelugpa, was founded by the reformer Tsongkhapa (1357–1419). On ceremonial occasions, members of this order wear large yellow hats, whereas members of the Kargyu and Karma-pa orders wear red and black hats, respectively. The ceremonial hats and robes of past masters are preserved in some Buddhist monasteries.

Buddhist nuns during morning chanting service in Lhasa, Tibet.

© Tom Salyer/Alamy

The Tibetan Book of the Dead

A unique feature of Tibetan Buddhism is the text called the Bardo Thodol ("Liberation by Hearing on the After-Death Plane"), better known as The Tibetan Book of the Dead. A set of written instructions concerning the afterlife, the Bardo Thodol was intended to be read aloud to the dying in order to help them achieve liberation during the three stages of the bardo state between death and subsequent rebirth.

During the first stage the dying person loses consciousness, experiences a transitional time of darkness, and then emerges into a world filled with strange objects unknown on the earthly plane. A brilliant light then appears. If the person recognizes the light as the Dharma Body of Buddha, he or she will attain liberation and experience nirvana rather than rebirth. More often, however, bad karma prevents people from recognizing the true nature of the light, and instead they turn away in fear. Thus most people then pass on to a second bardo stage, in which some consciousness of objects is regained. One may be aware of one's own funeral, for example. Peaceful deities appear for seven days, then wrathful deities appear for seven more days. These are all the Buddha in the Body of Bliss form, and those who meditate on them as such will experience liberation. Those who do not recognize them will gradually assume a new bodily form within a few weeks of death. Liberation is possible right up to the moment of rebirth, but karma keeps most people in the grip of samsara, the wheel of death and rebirth. In the third stage the individual's karma is judged and the appropriate rebirth is determined.

The Office of the Dalai Lama

To understand the office of Dalai Lama and the controversial Chinese claim that Tibet is a part of China, we need to understand the historic relationship between Tibet and the Mongols. As the rulers of China from 1222 to 1368, the Mongols did not invade Tibet. They did, however, appoint the head of the Shakya monastery to serve as their viceroy for the region. Some two centuries later, a Gelugpa missionary named Sonam Gyatso (1543–88) went to Mongolia and converted its ruler, Altan Khan, who created the title Dalai Lama ("Ocean of Wisdom") and bestowed it posthumously on Gyatso's two predecessors, designating Gyatso the third in the succession. With the sponsorship of the Mongol princes, the Gelugpas soon became the dominant sect in both Mongolia and Tibet.

The first Dalai Lama to become the temporal as well as the spiritual leader of Tibet was the fifth, Ngawang Lobsang Gyatso (1617–82). With Mongol aid he subdued the challenge of the rival Karma-pa lineage and constructed the famous Potala Palace in Lhasa. He recognized his teacher, Lobsang Chogye Gyaltsen (1569–1662), as an incarnation of the bodhisattva Amida and gave him the title Panchen Lama. The position of the Panchen Lamas still

Sites

Lhasa, Tibet, TAR, China

Lhasa is the site of the Potala Palace, the traditional home of the Dalai Lamas before the Chinese occupation of Tibet led the fourteenth Dalai Lama to relocate his headquarters in Dharamsala, India, in 1959. Other important Buddhist sites in Lhasa include the Jokhang temple and the Barkhor area that surrounds it, which is an important pilgrimage circuit.

exists, but has become controversial because the Dalai Lama and the Chinese government disagree on the identity of the legitimate Panchen Lama.

The fifth Dalai Lama also established diplomatic relations with the Manchu (Qing) dynasty, which came to power in China in 1644. As a result, Tibet became embroiled in the eighteenth-century rivalry between the Manchus in Beijing and the Oirots of Mongolia, and became a Manchu protectorate. These old Tibetan ties with Mongolia and China are the basis of modern China's claim to Tibet. The former Tibet is now divided into three Chinese provinces known collectively as the Tibetan Autonomous Region, or TAR.

Choosing a New Dalai Lama

Considered to be a manifestation of the bodhisattva Avalokiteshvara, each Dalai Lama is said to be the reincarnation of the previous one. When a Dalai Lama dies, a complicated search is undertaken to find a young boy who shows signs of being his reincarnation. The candidate must display intellectual qualities and personality characteristics similar to those of the deceased, and various objects are presented to the boy to see if he chooses ones that were the Lama's favourites. Finally, the State Oracle enters a trance state in order to contact the spirits to confirm the selection. The fourteenth and current Dalai Lama, Tenzin Gyatso, was chosen in this way

Focus

The Fourteenth Dalai Lama

Born: 6 July 1935, in a peasant farming village northeast of Lhasa. His name was Lhamo Thondup.

Signs: After the death of the thirteenth Dalai Lama, in 1933, the head of his corpse turned to the northeast, and a senior monk had a vision that included a monastery and a house with a distinctive guttering. When the party searching for his reincarnation finally found the house, in 1938, the three-year-old boy who lived there called one member of the party by name, and picked out the toys and other objects loved by the thirteenth Dalai Lama. He was then taken from his family to the monastery to begin training.

Instruction: After 18 months the boy was reunited with his family, who moved with him to Lhasa. In 1940 he was ordained as a novice and installed as the spiritual leader of Tibet. A long course of Buddhist studies followed.

High Office: An earthquake and threats of invasion from China prompted his installation as the political leader of Tibet in 1950, at age 15.

Exile: By 1959 the Chinese had taken over Tibet. To avoid arrest or worse, the Dalai Lama crossed the Himalayas to Dharamsala in northern India. From there he led the Tibetan government in exile until 2011, when he officially turned over the leadership to Lobsang Sangay, a Harvard-trained legal scholar. This brought to an end the tradition of joint religious and political leadership that began in the seventeenth century.

Writings: The Dalai Lama has travelled extensively and written numerous books on Tibetan Buddhism, meditation, and philosophy, as well as an autobiography, *Freedom in Exile*.

Politics: The Dalai Lama continues to use nonviolent means to advocate for the well-being of the Tibetan people. Negotiations with the Chinese government have so far not been fruitful. It remains to be seen whether his formal renunciation of political power will do anything to ease the tensions with China.

from a family of Tibetan descent living in China. A senior monk's vision played a key role in locating the boy.

⦾ Interaction and Adaptation in East Asia

China

Chinese converts interpreted a number of Buddhist ideas in ways that served to harmonize them with indigenous teachings, especially those associated with Daoism (see Chapter 6). The Buddhist concept of the afterlife, for example, was adapted to conform to Chinese tradition. Chinese Buddhists extended the vague notion of the underworld and a home with their ancestors into a system of many-layered heavens and hells, with a variety of saviour figures. Among them were Guanyin and the bodhisattva Dizang ("earth-store"; Jizo in Japanese), who relieves the suffering of those reborn in hell. Similarly, the scripture *Yulanpenjing* tells the story of a Buddhist monk named Mulian, who after his enlightenment sought to rescue his mother from hell. This Buddhist expression of filial piety was the basis for the "all souls' day" celebrated on the fifteenth day of the seventh month in China, Korea, and Japan, where it is known as Obon. Buddhism in turn had some influence on Chinese Daoism and folk religion, which incorporated the Buddhist idea of rebirth on a higher or lower level of life into the traditional system of retribution for good and evil.

However, the Buddhist tradition of monasticism was deeply alien to a social system based on kinship and veneration of ancestors. Not only were monks required to shave their hair, given by ancestors, but the practice of celibacy put the family lineage in jeopardy. Furthermore, endowments and donations enabled monasteries to acquire large areas of land and use serf labour to work the fields. Whereas Indian society respected the monks who begged for their living, Chinese society looked down on those who did no work. In time, therefore, Chinese monks incorporated labour into their discipline,

growing their own food. As a Chinese Zen master proclaimed, "A day without work is a day without eating."

At the same time, imperial officials saw Buddhism as a direct threat to the state's authority, as this seventh-century memorial to the first Tang emperor shows:

> Thus people were made disloyal and unfilial, shaving their heads and discarding their sovereign and parents, becoming men without occupation and without means of subsistence, by which means they avoided the payment of rents and taxes. . . . I maintain that poverty and wealth, high station and low, are the products of a man's own efforts, but these ignorant Buddhist monks deceive people, saying with one voice that these things come from the Buddha. Thus they defraud the sovereign of his authority and usurp his power of reforming the people (Hughes and Hughes 1950: 77).

Two centuries later, in 845, the Chinese state launched a campaign of persecution against Buddhism that led to the destruction of more than 40,000 temples and the laicization of 260,500 monks and nuns.

Folk Buddhism and the Milo Cult

The image of the "friendly" bodhisattva Maitreya underwent a transformation in China not unlike that of the Indian Avalokiteshvara into the Chinese Guanyin. Before the seventh century, Maitreya was a heroic figure, and he has more than once been the focus of political rebellions in China, including the one that led to the founding of the Ming dynasty (1368). Beginning in the fifteenth century, however, he began to appear as Milo, a laughing monk with a pot-belly, carrying a hemp bag and accompanied by small children. According to the legend, Milo used to travel from village to village, putting interesting objects into his sack along the way. Then, on arriving at the next village, he would give them out as presents for the children, like Santa Claus. With his happy-go-lucky nature (*maitri* means "friendly" in Sanskrit), his large belly, and his affinity for children, the "Happy Buddha" reflects the importance that Chinese culture attached both to children and to worldly prosperity. His image is still popular today on altars and as an artistic decoration, especially in restaurants.

Korea

Physical proximity created close links between China and Korea. The Han dynasty conquered the northern part of the peninsula in the late second century BCE and Buddhism was introduced roughly two centuries later, spreading from the northern kingdom of Koguryo first to Paekche in the southwest and then to Silla in the southeast. It became most influential after Silla conquered the other two kingdoms and united the country (668–935).

The new religion expanded on an unprecedented scale during the Silla period. Among the major schools of Buddhism introduced from China were the Theravada tradition of the *vinaya* (monastic discipline) and the Faxiang (Yogacara) school, which eventually developed into a syncretic tradition. The most influential school, however, was Chan ("Seon" in Korea), introduced in the early seventh century. Nine Seon monasteries, known as the Nine Mountains, were eventually established.

In a commentary on the *Flower Garland Sutra* the monk Wonhyo (617–86) sought to harmonize the various doctrinal trends of the period. He argued that the different teachings complement one another, and together make up one whole truth:

> The world itself is, essentially speaking, in everlasting Enlightenment. In other words, the essential base upon which the whole complex of relationships among the different living beings is standing, is the ultimate eternal reality which is . . . the source of life and light, . . . which make it possible for our life . . . to be truly human, to be enlightened (Rhi 1977: 202).

In the late twelfth century, a charismatic monk, Chinul (1158–1210), united the various schools to create the Jogye sect, which became the orthodox form of Buddhism in Korea. Nevertheless, Buddhist influence withered for several centuries after the Yi dynasty (1392–1910) adopted Confucianism as Korea's state ideology. Confucian scholars petitioned the court to restrict the number of Buddhist temples, supervise the selection of monks, and reorganize the ecclesiastical system while reducing the number of sects to facilitate state control. In the fifteenth century, temple properties were confiscated, serfs retained by monasteries were drafted into the army, and Buddhist monks were banned, especially in Seoul, the capital.

The institutional form that survived, the Jogye sect, remains the largest Buddhist denomination in South Korea today. Jogye monks living in the same monastery may recite *sutras*, worship the buddha Amitabha, or practise Seon meditation, each according to his own inclinations.

In Korea, as in other countries, new cults have emerged that owed their inspiration to Buddhist teachings. The best known is Won Buddhism, which was founded in the early twentieth century. This new religion seeks to modernize Buddhism by translating the sutras into modern Korean, emphasizing social service, especially in the cities, and permitting monks to marry. Its meditation object is an image of a black circle on a white background, representing the cosmic body of the Buddha, the *dharmakaya*.

Japan

Buddhism was first introduced to Japan from Korea in the mid-sixth century. It had taken almost 900 years to reach the extremities of East Asia, and it had been transformed along the way. Today Japanese Buddhism is mainly Mahayana, but with influences from other forms as well.

An important landmark for Buddhism in Japan was the warm reception it received from the regent, "Prince" Shotoku, who in 604 issued the "Seventeen-Article Constitution," a set of moral guidelines for the ruling class that extolled the value of harmony and urged reverence for the Three Gems. Welcoming Buddhism (as well as Confucianism) for its civilizing benefits, the prince became the centre of a Buddhist cult that still endures. The state offered protection for Buddhism, even building temples, and Japanese monks travelled to China to pursue further study.

How Buddhism developed in Japan—moving from the upper classes to the lower classes, interacting with the rituals and shrines associated with the traditional *kami* (spirits) of Japan, and developing new sects—will be explored in detail in Chapter 7.

◉ Cultural Expressions

Because Buddhism has been the principal religion of many Asian countries, cultural expressions of its influence are widespread.

Stupas and Pagodas

After the Buddha's *parinirvana*, several kings requested the honour of enshrining his cremated remains in their kingdoms. This created a dilemma that was brilliantly solved by the disciple in charge of funeral arrangements. He divided the remains into seven portions. The urn that had held the cremated remains and the cloth that had covered it were also given the status of primary relics, and so nine memorials were built over the nine original relics. But as Buddhism spread to other parts of India, additional memorials were needed to provide sites for Buddhist rituals. These memorials were built over other sacred objects, such as the cremated remains of Shakyamuni's major disciples, or even portions of the Buddhist scriptures.

The architecture of the memorials has a rich history. The Buddha had been asked before his death about the proper way to bury him, and his response was that a Tathagata's remains should be enshrined in a memorial stupa like that of a great ruler. There is evidence from as far away as Ireland that the preferred method of burial for Indo-Aryan rulers was to place their remains in an above-ground crypt, which was then covered with earth to form a large burial mound. Tables or platforms for offerings were then constructed in each of the four cardinal directions near the mound.

The funeral itself lasted seven days—the 28-day lunar month was divided into four such weeks—during which the mourners circumambulated the mound and placed food, water, and flower offerings on the altars. Circumambulation is always clockwise, the devotee keeping the shrine to his or her right—in Indian tradition, a much more auspicious side than the left. For the same reason, monks' robes keep the right shoulder bare while covering the left.

The cremated remains were placed in small caskets about the size of shoe boxes, richly decorated with jewels, each of which was interred in a crypt made of stone slabs. The crypt was then covered over with a large mound of earth and a layer or two of bricks, which were plastered and finally whitewashed. Then the builders erected a pole, which was fixed in a square frame on top of the mound and positioned over the crypt.

The pole represents Mount Meru, a cosmic mountain that in Indian mythology reaches from earth up towards the pole star, and around whose axis the world is thought to turn. The part of the pole that extends above its support base symbolizes the upper reaches of the heavens. The pole runs through a series of wooden disks that symbolize the levels of heaven. (The European parallel would be the notion of "heavenly spheres.") There are usually nine such layers, in keeping with Indian cosmology, which envisions nine levels of heaven and nine orbiting planetary bodies. The frame, the pole, and the nine layers later came to be built of stone because wooden parts were difficult to maintain.

There are several terms for these white memorial mounds. The Sanskrit *stupa* and its Pali equivalent, *thupa*, are cognate with the English word "tomb." Another term is *caitya*, which means "shrine," or in this case "burial shrine." The term used throughout East Asian Buddhism is "pagoda," which derives from another Sanskrit word for a monument, *dagoba*. It connotes "womb" in the sense that burial is the forerunner of a rebirth. Whether the

Sites

Kyoto, Japan

Kyoto, Japan's second capital, includes many famous sites among its 1,600 temples. Ryoanji is known for its Zen "rock garden" (the Japanese say "dry garden"). Byodoin Temple, located in a traditional tea-growing area, and Daigoji, with its scenic five-storeyed pagoda, are World Heritage Sites.

memorial structure is called stupa, *thupa*, *caitya*, or pagoda, nearly every Buddhist temple precinct in the world has one.

Many legends claimed that the relic of a particular stupa could be traced back to the Buddha himself. For example, important temples in Sri Lanka and Burma claimed to have an eye tooth of the Buddha enshrined in their stupas. Major Buddhist temples developed long chronicles detailing the legendary history of the relics enshrined in their stupas.

In addition to the large main stupa, a temple complex may often have smaller ones built as memorial crypts for important Buddhists of that particular temple. These small votive stupas add to the beauty and spiritual atmosphere of the temple grounds. Lay Buddhists sometimes strew flower petals at such locations and vow that they, too, will someday overcome death and achieve nirvana.

Building small stupas as an act of devotion was especially popular as a merit-making practice in Myanmar, where thousands of devotional stupas have been built through the centuries. Some are built to last, such as the ones located near the ancient Burmese city of Pagan, but most are temporary structures, such as the ones devout Buddhists make from sand at the shore. The merit comes from building the stupa in a devotional state of mind, and so it is not necessary that it endure for long.

The shape of the stupa or pagoda underwent changes through the centuries, especially when Buddhism spread to East Asia. There, pagodas eventually developed into elegant five- or seven-storeyed stone or wooden towers that devotees could either climb up or circumambulate. The storeys of the East Asian pagoda represent the various levels of the heavens symbolized by the wooden disks of the original Indian stupas. Pagoda architecture exaggerated the "heavenly section" of the original stupa, making it the dominant part of the structure.

Temples

Buddhist monasteries grew out of the simple refuges in which early monks lived during the rainy season—usually a collection of thatched huts located on the outskirts of a city. Wealthy devotees would earn merit by paying for the construction of permanent buildings, and over time a temple complex would take shape consisting of living quarters, a small shrine, and a meeting hall. Eventually, to accommodate large numbers of lay worshippers, the small shrine developed into a large temple housing images of the Buddha. Today, besides the stupa and temple, the grounds usually contain a Bodhi tree, dharma hall, monastery, library, and refectory, and are typically surrounded by an ornamental wall with elaborate entrances.

There are some similarities among temples in different parts of the ancient world. The typical ancient temple—whether in Israel, India, or elsewhere in southern and western Asia—is a rectangular building that is entered from one of the shorter sides. (In East Asian temples, access is from one of the longer sides.) Entering through a tall portico, the worshipper comes into an outer chamber that in some cases is open to the air and can hold large numbers of people. At the far end of the building is an image of the revered figure—or, in the Hebrew temple, some sort of throne but no image—flanked by attendant deities, angels, or supernatural

Sites

Ajanta Caves, India

Maharashtra state in west central India has two famous cave complexes. The Ajanta Caves, carved into a long, curving cliffside, are filled with Buddhist sculptures and paintings, and the stone temples were carved and painted to look like wooden temples. The Ellora site is similar, but includes Hindu and Jain as well as Buddhist caves.

animals. Often, but not always, there is an altar in front of the image where worshippers or priests representing them place flowers and other offerings. Songs of praise were usually sung, candles were lit, and incense was burned. Ritual attendants brought food and water to the deity's image, and waved fans to keep it cool in hot weather. In every way the image was housed and treated like royalty.

Although early Buddhism did not consider the Buddha to be a god, Buddhists followed the local temple practices. Thus they place flowers on altars or platforms at the base of the stupa and near the Bodhi tree, and then proceed into the temple to place flowers on the altar(s) there. They say prayers expressing their dedication to living according to the dharma.

Early cave temples carved in stone were clearly modelled after the simple huts that early sangha members dwelt in during the rainy season, when they settled down for a period of intense study and meditation. By the Gupta period in India (c. 320–540), Buddhist temples had taken on the rectangular shape and other architectural features of Hindu temples of the time.

In some regions of India, cliffside cave complexes were developed that included all the essentials of a temple complex, including separate caves for shrines, living areas, and even large dharma halls. The practice of creating cave complexes spread with Buddhism to China (for example, the Longmen caves) and elsewhere. Such caves took on a political role during the presidency of George W. Bush. In Afghanistan, the Taliban's destruction of some colossal cliffside bodhisattva images in 2001 helped to gain popular support for the US invasion.

In China, the rectangular wooden buddha hall reflected the influence of the tile-roofed imperial hall of state, with the buddha statue enshrined in the posture of an emperor. This style was the one that made its way to Japan, the best-known example being the Todaiji, the Great East Monastery in Nara, which houses a bronze image of Vairocana, the cosmic buddha, more than 16 metres (52 feet) high.

Images of the Buddha

It was almost 500 years after the *parinirvana* of the Buddha before the first image of him was created. Until then, it was apparently assumed, particularly in Theravada Buddhism, that no physical form could or should depict him. In the intervening years, the Buddha and his teaching were symbolized by the stupa and symbols such as his footprint, the Wheel of the Law, the Bodhi tree, or an empty seat. These symbols played an important role in the decoration of stupas, as well as their surrounding fences and gates.

The first images of the Buddha himself date from the first century CE, a time when the devotional aspects of Mahayana Buddhism were becoming increasingly popular. Statues and reliefs show the Buddha standing, seated in the lotus position of yogic meditation, seated with dangling legs, or reclining at the moment of the *parinirvana*. Specific hand gestures or **mudras**, similar to those found in Hindu portrayals of deities, convey specific meanings.

Buddhist iconography also includes the 32 major signs of Shakyamuni's status, the most obvious of which are the *usnisa* (the protuberance on the

a) "Teaching the Dharma": The *Dharmachakra* mudra symbolizes the Eightfold Path in particular, and Buddhist teaching in general.

b) "Fulfilling a Wish": The *Varada* mudra symbolizes compassion; performed with the right hand, it is often combined with the *Abhaya* mudra.

c) "Fear Not": The *Abhaya* mudra grants protection from fearsome things; performed with the left hand, it is often combined with the *Varada* mudra.

d) "Meditation": The *Dhyana* mudra symbolizes the meditator's calm, focused state of mind; a begging bowl is sometimes included just above the hands.

e) "Debate": The *Vitarka* mudra symbolizes rational discussion of truth and reality.

f) "Warding off Evil": The *Tarjani* mudra symbolizes the power of Dharma to protect from evil.

Figure 5.2 Hand Mudras

g) "Touching the Earth" or "Witness": The *Bhumisparsha* mudra recalls the way Shakyamuni called the earth as witness during his confrontation with Mara.

h) "Paying Respect": Disciples of the Buddha are typically shown performing the *Namaskara* mudra: the traditional Indian greeting of respect ("Namaste") to humans and deities alike.

Figure 5.2 Hand Mudras (*continued*)

top of his head that was supposed to be the locus of his supernatural wisdom) and elongated ear lobes. Some art historians think that these features were associated with royalty (elaborate hair styles, earlobes stretched by heavy earrings), but Buddhists see them as signs of Shakyamuni's supernatural nature. Other signs include wheel images on the soles of his feet, and fingers that are all the same length.

Buddhist iconography in China typically shows the Buddha encircled by his company like an emperor surrounded by his court. The Buddha is seated in a serene posture, flanked by his disciples Kashyapa and Ananda. Nearby stand the bodhisattvas and stern-looking Arhats (*lohans* in Chinese). The Four World Protectors or Heavenly Kings often stand guard at the entrance or along the sides of the entrance hall. Each of the four is associated with one of the cardinal directions, and each one holds a characteristic object.

Story Illustrations

Buddhist art, especially painting and relief carving, often illustrates scenes from the life of the Buddha or from the *Jataka* ("birth story") collections that recount the previous lives of Shakyamuni. The walls of temples are often lined with such art so that visitors can see the story of the Buddha's life unfold as they circumambulate the structure.

In ancient India, stupas located away from temple grounds were surrounded by an ornamental fence carved with scenes from the *Jatakas* and the Buddha's life. The great stupa in the complex at Sanchi, in central India, offers the most important example of such art. The fences that survive today are all made of stone, but the prototypes would have been carved in wood. The narrative illustration panels in temples continue the ancient pattern.

As Buddhism spread, other cultures developed their own distinctive iconography. In China, images of Shakyamuni gradually took on a more Chinese appearance, and the figure of Guanyin developed into the graceful, standing feminine form now found throughout East Asia. There is a distinctive Korean representation of Maitreya as a pensive prince with one leg crossed over the other knee. This pose spread to Japan at the time of "Prince" Shotoku. An example is the famous wooden statue of Maitreya in Kyoto's Koryuji temple, which was founded in 622 for the repose of Shotoku.

Zen Art and the Tea Ceremony

The highly ritualized tea ceremony was introduced by Zen monks and spread from monasteries to become one of the most familiar symbols of Japanese culture, expressed in everything from special tea bowls to distinctive tea houses. The Zen influence is also reflected in the minimalism of Japanese painting, in which empty space plays a central role, and the raked-sand gardens (the space accented only by the occasional boulder) typically found in the courtyards of Zen temples such as Ryoanji in Kyoto. Another cultural expression of Zen values is the Japanese art of flower arranging, which originated in the practice of creating floral offerings for altars and special ceremonies.

⦿ Buddhism in the Modern World

India

Buddhism's intellectual and institutional influence within India lasted for several centuries after the third-century BCE reign of Ashoka. It was only in the seventh century CE that it began to decline.

In the past, Buddhism had enjoyed the support of Indian royalty, but that support gradually disappeared as the northwest was overrun by Muslim armies and its royal patrons were replaced by Muslim rulers. A related factor may have been the loss of lay support for the monasteries as Hinduism absorbed a number of elements from Buddhism, including its ascetic dimension (celibacy, vegetarianism, non-violence, etc.). At the same time, many Hindus came to regard the Buddha as an avatar of Vishnu, a development that encouraged people to see Buddhism as part of Hinduism. Indian laypeople may have lost their motivation to support Buddhism rather than Hinduism. Buddhist monasteries throughout India were either abandoned or taken over and repurposed by other traditions. The fact that some of the most famous Buddhist scholar-monks left for Tibet, beginning in the eleventh century, suggests that the great Buddhist universities, such as the large one at Nalanda in the northeast, were in decline. As a result of this migration and the loss of lay adherents, Buddhism largely disappeared from India until the mid-twentieth century. It did survive in a few regions of eastern India, however, as well as in Tibet, Nepal, Bhutan, Sikkim, and Assam.

B.R. Ambedkar and the Mass Conversion of Dalits

One catalyst for the revival of Buddhism in India was Dr Bhimrao R. Ambedkar (1891–1956), the lead author of the Indian constitution. Although he was born into the "untouchable" Dalit class, his keen intelligence caught the attention of a brahmin teacher named Ambedkar, who formally adopted the boy so that he could have an upper-class name. This change of name allowed him to compete on a level playing field when he went for higher education. With the help of that teacher and the local Muslim ruler, the young Ambedkar earned an undergraduate degree in India and eventually a doctorate from the London School of Economics. On his return to India he became an active advocate for Dalit rights at a time when his older contemporary M.K. Gandhi was pursuing the same goal. The two disagreed, however, on the best way to that goal.

Ambedkar blamed Hinduism for the discrimination that Dalits faced. Hindu leaders such as Gandhi held out the hope that Hinduism could be reformed along lines that would eliminate, or at least greatly reduce, that discrimination, but Ambedkar foresaw that entrenched social and economic interests would make substantial reform impossible. Therefore he turned his back on Hinduism and set out to find a religion that would not discriminate against Dalits. He recognized in Buddhism a form of spirituality that was compatible with Indian cultural values, but that from its origins had spoken out in favour of the equality of all humans, regardless of birth status.

The history of Buddhism supports Ambedkar's view. The Buddha accepted both lay and ordained members into his movement without any regard for their caste status, and he taught his disciples to ask

A mass conversion ceremony held in Mumbai in 2007 recalled the original mass conversion of Dalits to Buddhism under Ambedkar's leadership in 1956. The people in red robes are Tibetan monks and nuns, many of whom now reside in India.

AP Photo/Rajesh Nirgude, File

not about caste but about character. The names of early Buddhist leaders suggest that all social classes were attracted to the movement. Social rank within the sangha was based solely on seniority as determined by date of ordination.

The Buddha also criticized the brahmin priests, and early Buddhist stories made fun of pompous brahmins who exploited the lower classes. One such story tells of a brahmin who gained great prestige with the king because he knew a magical charm that would cause fruit to ripen out of season. He had in fact learned the charm from a low-caste person, who revealed it only on the condition that he would answer truthfully if anyone inquired about the origin of the charm. When the king asked that question, however, the brahmin was too proud to admit that he had learned something from a Dalit. The lie broke the magic of the charm, and the brahmin fell into disgrace. Another story tells of the Buddha asking a low-caste Chandala woman for

water. She is pleasantly surprised that he is willing to accept a drink from her, because high-caste persons were thought to become impure themselves if they consumed anything touched by an "impure" low-caste person. (This story has a Christian parallel in the account of Jesus asking for water from a Samaritan woman at a well; John 4: 1–42.)

In 1956, at a large rally in the historic city of Nagpur, in the heart of Hindu India, Ambedkar and his wife publicly took the Three Refuges and the Five Precepts from a Buddhist monk, and thousands of Dalits followed their example. Since then, many more Dalits have converted to Buddhism; others have turned to Islam or Christianity. Shakyamuni's critique of social inequity has also contributed to a growing appreciation among Indian scholars of his place in Indian history. During the period of Buddhist–Hindu competition before Buddhism's decline, Hindus had claimed that Buddha was actually an *avatara* (incarnation) of Vishnu. Unlike Vishnu's other *avataras*—figures such as Rama and Krishna—the Buddha was said to have played a negative role, drawing undesirable people away from the "true" religion. That some modern Hindu scholars accept the Buddha as an important and admirable figure in the religious history of India marks a significant change.

Restoration of Monuments

Under the leadership of Buddhists from Sri Lanka, the Mahabodhi Society of India was formed in 1891 with the purpose of restoring the country's Buddhist pilgrimage sites and revitalizing Indian Buddhism. With the permission of the Indian government, the Society in 1953 took charge of Bodh Gaya, the once grand pilgrimage spot that commemorates Shakyamuni's enlightenment. It has restored several of the ancient stupas at Bodh Gaya with financial contributions from Buddhists around the world and has made the site an active pilgrimage and learning centre. The ancient pilgrimage site that commemorates Shakyamuni's birth at Lumbini has been identified in southern Nepal (on the border with India, northeast of Lucknow and southwest of Kathmandu) and has likewise been returned to active use. Sarnath (near Varanasi), the site of the first sermon, and Kushinagar (near modern Gorakhpur), the site of the *parinirvana*, have also been restored.

Theravada in Modern Sri Lanka

After the fifteenth century, Sri Lanka was colonized by the Portuguese, Dutch, and British in turn, all of whom promoted some form of Christianity. Buddhism declined in prestige but hung on, and in the late 1800s efforts to revitalize the tradition received an important boost from the founders of the Theosophical Society, Helena P. Blavatsky (1831–91) and Henry S. Olcott (1832–1907). Sinhalese Buddhists have been active ever since in publishing English-language materials on Buddhism, and they remain loyal to Theravada Buddhism despite the presence of largely Hindu India to the north and 500 years of Christian missionary efforts under the European colonial rulers. The Sinhalese take pride

in Sri Lanka's status as a stronghold of Theravada, which they regard as the purest form of Buddhism.

Since independence in 1948, Buddhism has had considerable influence on the policies of Sri Lanka's ruling parties, which draw support from the Sinhalese majority. This has led to feelings of oppression among members of the Hindu minority, most of whom are Tamils—descendants of people from Tamilnadu in South India who migrated to the island at various times over the past two millennia. (The Sinhalese are thought to have come from North India.) Conflict between the government and Tamil separatists seeking an independent homeland in the northern part of the island led to more than two decades of bloodshed, even though Hinduism and Buddhism alike teach non-violence. The civil war finally came to an end in 2009, but relations between the two religious communities remain severely strained.

Despite these political problems, Sri Lankan Buddhism continues its rich intellectual and ritual life. The symbolic centre of that life is the Temple of the Tooth in Kandy, where an eye tooth that is said to be a relic of Shakyamuni himself is enshrined. At the time of the Perahera festival, one of the miniature gold stupas that house the tooth is placed in a howdah on the back of an elephant and paraded through the streets of Kandy for several nights. Each night the parade becomes larger and grander, and on the final day the sacred relic is given a ritual bath in a nearby river.

Theravada in Modern Southeast Asia

Theravada also remains the most important vehicle across most of mainland Southeast Asia, though East Asian Mahayana traditions are dominant in Vietnam, Malaysia, and Singapore.

The end of Burmese kingship in the late nineteenth century, the years of British colonialism, and long periods of military rule since independence have severely weakened the Burmese sangha's traditional political influence. Its members have been cut off from significant contact with other Buddhist

Sites

Kandy, Sri Lanka

The Temple of the Tooth in Kandy, in the hills 100 kilometres (60 miles) northeast of Colombo, is the most important Buddhist site in Sri Lanka. The Perahera festival, held at the time of the full moon in August, is a spectacular 10-day event in which some Hindus also participate.

The Kandy Perahera, one of world's most elaborate religious rituals, features torchlit processions in which more than a hundred elaborately costumed elephants are paraded through the streets in groups of three. Groups of musicians and dancers come from surrounding villages, each with its own distinctive attire and dance style. Historically, providing dance troupes for the Perahera was an obligation that the villages owed to the king, but now it is done for the sake of pride and tradition.

countries, and its temples have fallen into disrepair. Yet the *bhikshus* are still important in the traditional village-centred society, and the recent easing of military control and movement towards democracy offer some hope for economic improvement, more freedom of expression, and a renewal of Buddhist values.

Similarly in modern Cambodia, the overthrow of Prince Norodom Sihanouk (r. 1941–55) meant the end of Buddhist kingship with its ideal of a government that provides for the basic human needs of all citizens. Since then, the Cambodian sangha's political influence has been limited. During the period of the communist Khmer Rouge under Pol Pot (r. 1975–9), many *bhikshus* were among the innocents slaughtered in the "killing fields." Yet by the late 1980s, the monthly newsletter of the coalition of movements opposed to the new pro-Vietnamese government, which included the remnants of the Khmer Rouge, proudly pictured Khmer Rouge soldiers and *bhikshus* working together on village projects. Today most laypeople of all political stripes remain Buddhists, and all factions appeal to Buddhist values to help legitimate their claims to power. At the village level, Buddhism continues to play its traditional role.

In Thailand Buddhism retains some political influence. The tradition of monastic training for the king continues, and members of the royal family take part in Buddhist ceremonial occasions. The most important are the rituals in which the king, at the beginning of each season, changes the clothing on the Buddha image in the famous Temple of the Emerald Buddha and gives the Buddha image a ceremonial bath. These rituals symbolize the close ties between Buddhism, the monarchy, and nationalism in Thailand.

In Laos—under communist rule since the 1960s—Buddhism has lost the governmental support that it had traditionally enjoyed throughout Southeast Asia. The traditional relationship of *bhikshus* and laity continues in the villages, however.

Finally, although Theravada has never gained a foothold in Vietnam, Theravada missionaries have recently had some success in Singapore and Malaysia, especially among English-speaking Chinese. Apparently some of the Chinese Mahayana Buddhists in Singapore have been attracted to Theravada as a purer form of Buddhism than the Chinese Mahayana schools that have incorporated numerous elements of Chinese folk religion into their practice. The Young Buddhist Association of Malaysia has been very active in encouraging dharma study among young Buddhists.

Several Buddhist reform movements are having an impact on Theravada Buddhism today. For example, retreat centres have been established in Thailand in an effort to reintroduce the practice of meditation among laypeople. The Thai reformer Buddhadasa Bhikkhu (1906–93) severely criticized what he saw as the complacency of Thai Buddhists, lay and ordained, and urged them to be more diligent in meditation and the study of dharma. Other Theravada Buddhists have concentrated on social reform. The Thai intellectual Sulak Sivaraksa (b. 1932) has argued effectively for a Buddhist vision of society in which the means of development are harnessed for the good of everyone rather than the profit of a few capitalists. He has founded several Buddhist organizations dedicated to that goal, including the Asian Cultural Forum on Development and the International Network of Engaged Buddhists.

Mahayana in Vietnam

It is difficult to say exactly when Buddhism was introduced to Vietnam. Theravada images and monastery foundations dating from before the ninth century have been found there, but Chinese Mahayana traditions—notably Thien (from Chan) and Tinh-do (from Chinese Jingtu, "Pure Land")—have been dominant ever since then. Thien is largely a monastic tradition, whereas Tinh-do is mainly a lay movement that spread during periods when there was a dearth of educated Thien monks. However, Vietnamese Buddhism is syncretic; the two sects have influenced each other, and all Thien monasteries also teach Pure Land practices.

In the early part of the twentieth century, Vietnamese Buddhism attempted to reform itself in response to modern challenges that included secularism and Christianity, but this effort was interrupted by the Second World War and the 1954 division of the country into a communist North and an anti-communist South, where the Roman Catholic president Ngo Dinh Diem (r. 1954–63) imposed a number of restrictions on Buddhists. It was in protest against these restrictions that, in May 1963, an elderly monk named Thich Quang Duc assumed the lotus position on a busy street in Saigon, had gasoline poured over him, then calmly struck a match and became a human torch. A number of monks and nuns followed his example over the next months, attracting worldwide attention and contributing to the fall of the Diem government.

At the same time, these self-immolations forced Buddhists to ask what the dharma is concerning suicide. The answer is ambiguous. It is clear that Shakyamuni forbade suicide: "[Monks], let no one destroy himself, and whosoever would destroy himself, let him be dealt with according to law" (Warren 1896: 437). In the Mahayana tradition, however, the *Lotus Sutra* appears to accept suicide when it is committed for a good cause. This is the case with the Medicine bodhisattva, a popular figure in China, who vows to offer his own body to heal human beings. According to the *Lotus Sutra*:

> he wrapped his body in a garment adorned with divine jewels, anointed himself with fragrant oils, with the force of supernatural penetration took a vow, and then burnt his body. The glow gave light all around to the world-spheres equal in number to the sands of eighty millions of Ganges rivers. Within them the Buddhas all at once praised him (Hurvitz 1976: 294–5).

Historically, Buddhist monks in China occasionally committed suicide as a demonstration of their piety or to protest persecutions. Sometimes they cut off parts of themselves, such as arms or fingers, and made offerings of them. It was this practice, together with the veneration of relics, that the Chinese Confucian scholar Han Yu (786–824) cited in his criticism of Buddhism in a text called the *Memorial on the Bone of Buddha*. Self-sacrifice is an important theme in the thought of Thich Nhat Hanh (b. 1926), a well-known Vietnamese monk who entered a monastery at the age of 16 and became not only a Thien (Chan–Zen) master but a poet and a peace activist. In response to the atrocities of the Vietnam war, he developed what he called an "engaged Buddhism" to bring the resources of Buddhist wisdom and meditation to bear on contemporary conflicts.

For Thich Nhat Hanh, the self-immolations of 1963 were acts not of self-destruction but of self-sacrifice, designed to call attention to the suffering of the people in Vietnam, and ought to be understood in the context of the Buddhist belief in the continuity of life beyond one human life span. Changing the world, for Thich Nhat Hanh, requires that we first change our awareness of ourselves and the world, especially through meditation and the "art of mindful living." Commenting on the *Heart Sutra*, he says:

> If you are a poet, you will see clearly that there is a cloud floating in this sheet of paper. Without a cloud, there will be no rain; without rain, the trees cannot grow; and without trees, we cannot make paper. If we look even more deeply, we can see the sunshine, the logger who cut the tree, the wheat that became his bread, and the logger's father and mother. Without all of these things, this sheet of paper cannot exist. . . . Everything co-exists with this sheet of paper. So we can say that the cloud and the paper "inter-are." We cannot just be by ourselves alone; we have to inter-be with every other thing (Nhat Hanh 1988: 3).

Buddhism in Modern China and Korea

China

In the 1920s, while Chinese intellectuals were advocating greater openness to Western ideas, a Chan monk named Taixu ("Great Emptiness") called for both political and monastic reform, as well as a restatement of dharma in such a way as to speak to modern Chinese society. Like other

Buddhist modernists, he believed that Buddhism should aspire to establish the heavenly Pure Land on earth.

Government policy regarding Buddhist communities varies depending on their ethnicity. Temples of the majority Han Chinese population are mostly self-governing, but minority Buddhist communities, especially Tibetans, are strictly regulated because they are perceived to constitute a potentially threatening separatist movement. For that reason, any display of support for the Dalai Lama is prohibited. Even so, many Tibetan Buddhists took part in anti-government protests during the run-up to the Beijing Olympics in 2008, and in recent years dozens (most of them monks and nuns) have sacrificed themselves in what may be the ultimate form of non-violent protest: self-immolation.

Korea

Because North Korea has been governed by a religion-suppressing communist regime since 1945, this section will focus exclusively on the South. Under Japanese occupation (1910–45), Korean Buddhism was freed from its subjugation to Confucianism. Monks—who had been banned from Seoul during the pro-Confucian Joseon dynasty (1392–1910)—were once again permitted to enter the city. However, religion was controlled and manipulated by the occupying power. Japanese influence led to the breakdown of monastic discipline: monks began to eat meat and marry. The renewal of Korean Buddhism had to await the country's liberation from Japan, and the process was further delayed by the devastating civil war of 1950–3. The more conservative Jogye Buddhists struggled against the married monks of the urban-based Taego order, and sought to restore the meditative, disciplinary, and scholastic orientations of traditional Korean Buddhism. The Jogye monks finally won official support for their efforts in 1954, when they regained control of virtually all the major monasteries. Today Korean Seon is said to have the strictest discipline of the Korean Buddhist sects. After the end of Japanese rule in 1945, partly in response to the growing influence of Christianity in Korea, Buddhists made an effort to influence students and intellectuals, especially through the spread of Seon meditation.

Tensions between Buddhists and Korea's large Christian population have been reflected in attacks on several Buddhist temples. Allegedly carried out by fundamentalist Christians who see Buddhism not as a religion to be respected but as an evil to be destroyed, these incidents have led many Buddhists to feel persecuted.

Buddhism and Modernity in Japan

In some ways, modern Japan resembles a museum of the history of religions, with exhibits that cover everything from the traditions of ancient Japan, through Indian and Chinese Buddhism, to Christianity and the secular ideologies of the West. Although Buddhism has left an indelible imprint on Japanese culture, it never became the state religion, or even the religion of the people as such. Today it is often described as the religion of the dead, whereas Shinto is called the religion of the living because of its association with the joys of life. So closely is Buddhism associated with the memorialization of the dead that the family shrine dedicated to the ancestors is called the *butsudan*—literally, the Buddhist altar. (For more on the complex interactions of Buddhism and other Japanese traditions, see Chapter 7.)

"Abortion Temples"

A few Buddhist temples have come to be known as "abortion temples" because they provide space on their grounds for shrines in memory of aborted fetuses. Grieving parents offer toys or treats appropriate to the ages their aborted offspring would have reached if they had lived. It may be that, in addition to honouring the unborn, parents hope to placate their spirits lest they become vengeful and seek to harm their living siblings.

The West and the Kyoto School

An interesting development in modern Japan is the Kyoto school of Buddhist philosophy. Its founder was Nishida Kitaro (1875–1945), who came of age in the early days of the Meiji Restoration, when Japan was looking to the West for ideas to help it modernize. In this context, Nishida sought to fuse Japanese Zen Buddhist ideas with continental European philosophy. In keeping with Zen's emphasis on direct experience, he wrote of what he called "pure experience"—"experience just as it is without the addition of the slightest thought or reflection." For example:

> the moment of seeing a colour or hearing a sound that takes place . . . before one has added the judgment that this seeing or hearing is related to something external. . . . When one has experienced one's conscious state directly, there is not as yet any subject or object; knowing and its object are completely at one. This is the purest form of experience (Nishida, *Zen no kenkyu*; Takeuchi 1987: 456).

This approach is consistent with Zen founder Bodhidharma's call for a "direct pointing of the mind."

Among Nishida's successors was Nishitani Keiji (1900–90). Nishitani's interest in bridging the gap between Zen thought and Christian theology played a role in the emergence of an international Buddhist–Christian dialogue movement in the 1970s.

Buddhism in the West

Alfred North Whitehead (1861–1947), the Anglo-American philosopher, once said that Christianity was "a religion seeking a metaphysic," whereas Buddhism was "a metaphysic generating a religion." For a long time, Western scholars were not certain whether Buddhism fitted their definition of "religion" at all, since—despite its rituals, scriptures, and monastic traditions—it did not centre on a personal deity.

Knowledge of Buddhism in Europe and North America was almost non-existent before the middle of the nineteenth century, but in 1879 a book entitled *The Light of Asia*—a moving poetic account of the life of Buddha, by Edwin Arnold—attracted wide public attention. Even so, it was not until the beginning of the twentieth century that a few Western seekers began to publish first-hand accounts of Buddhist meditational practice. By the 1930s, Buddhist societies had been established in Great Britain, France, and Germany.

The Spread of Zen

Buddhist influences in North America have tended to come more from the Mahayana and Vajrayana traditions than the Theravada. This has been the case ever since the World's Parliament of Religions conference in Chicago in 1893. Among the delegates was a Zen monk named Shaku Soyen (1856–1919), who later returned to America to spread Buddhism. His young translator, Daisetsu T. Suzuki (1870–1966), became the most influential Buddhist writer in North America.

Suzuki made two extended visits to the United States, and wrote many popular books sprinkled with stories of Zen masters and the koans with which they challenged their disciples. Especially as popularized by Alan Watts, these writings caught the attention of Westerners looking for alternatives to the personal theism or institutional structures of Christianity. Some Westerners have considered Zen a form of mysticism. Others have argued against this view on the grounds that there is no experience of union with a personal god in Zen.

On the other hand, if "mysticism" is understood to encompass a broader sense of the spiritual experience as a transformation of human consciousness, then Zen practitioners may well share some experience in common with Christian mystics such as Johannes "Meister" Eckhart (c. 1260–1327). Many

Westerners have been interested in Zen meditational practice as well. Catholic missionaries and theologians, coming from a long contemplative tradition, have sought to learn from Zen insights and techniques. At the same time, the Zen experience has attracted the attention of experts in depth psychology, as Daoist meditation has also done.

Zen was the first form of Buddhism to make significant numbers of converts in North America, but it was by no means the only one. Nichiren Shoshu, for example, was imported by immigrants from Japan. Immigrants also brought with them various Pure Land sects.

Vajrayana (Tibetan) Buddhism

Since the 1960s, two lineages of Vajrayana or Tibetan Buddhism have also gained converts in North America. The Kargyu lineage is represented both by the Naropa Institute in Boulder, Colorado, and by a community of Tibetans and converts based in Halifax, Nova Scotia, while the Dalai Lama's Gelugpa lineage has centres in New York and elsewhere.

Ethnic Congregations

Existing alongside and independent of the converts to Buddhism are East Asian Buddhists. Beginning in the late 1880s, Chinese and Japanese immigrants settled along the west coast of North America, especially in places like Hawaii, California, and British Columbia, and gradually found the financial resources to build temples similar to those in their homelands. The ethnic congregations were quite diverse. First-generation immigrants from different lands spoke different Asian languages, and their overseas-born descendants tended to speak English. In ritual and teaching, these congregations represented many branches of Buddhism.

The most popular form of Buddhism in East Asia is Pure Land, and that popularity is reflected among the ethnic Buddhist congregations of North America. There are networks of particular ethnic groups like the Buddhist Association of America and the Buddhist Association of Canada, which serve mainly immigrants of Chinese origin, and the Buddhist Churches of America (and of Canada), which serve True Pure Land followers, who are mainly ethnic Japanese. Similar, if smaller, groups with roots in Vietnam and Laos also have their own networks. Over time, some ethnic Buddhists have adopted Christian styles of worship, with pews, hymnals, and group leaders who take on all the responsibilities typically expected of North American clergy. Buddhist Sunday schools have been founded, Buddhist cemeteries consecrated, and Buddhist wedding rituals brought under the supervision of a *bhikshu*, now called a "priest."

In North America, ethnic Buddhists use their temples as community centres as well as places of worship. Visitors are welcome, but the emphasis on community affairs tends to limit congregation membership to people from the same ethnic community. Buddhist meditation centres, on the other hand, have attracted many Western converts. Umbrella organizations such as the Buddhist Council of Canada are helping to bring Western "meditation Buddhists" into closer contact with the ethnic Buddhist congregations.

The influence of Buddhist thought in the West has been greater than the relatively small number of Western Buddhists might suggest. Without necessarily becoming Buddhists, many people in the West have adopted modified versions of Buddhist meditational practices in order to calm their minds or to concentrate before athletic or artistic performances. In addition, Buddhist (and Hindu and Jaina) values such as non-violence and concepts such as rebirth and karma have spread well beyond the traditional religious context.

Recent Developments

Although Buddhism continues to spread far beyond the South Asian land of its origin, it has faced some setbacks in recent decades. In Sri Lanka and Southeast Asia it was weakened and challenged by the Christian missions and Western values introduced during the period of colonial domination. And the loss of kingship in most of the Buddhist countries of southern Asia has undermined the political support system that existed for many centuries. Like other religions, Buddhism has also been challenged and called into question by modern, secular ways of life. Buddhists generally do not consider the scientific world view to represent a serious challenge, since the Buddha himself emphasized rational thought and the causal principle of dependent origination. Still, the concepts of karma and rebirth do not fit comfortably into the standard scientific world view.

It is also true that *bhikshus* are no longer the main educators, social workers, dispute settlers, and advisers in Buddhist countries, especially in the major cities; their roles have been reduced to those of ritual leaders and directors of religious education. Yet Buddhists are not converting in any significant numbers to other religions, and most do make some effort to live according to Buddhist values.

The Female Sangha

Over time the *bhikshuni* sangha was allowed to die out in many Buddhist countries. The specific reasons may have varied, but in general the female order was vulnerable simply because it was relatively small and less well connected to political power than the male order was. In Sri Lanka, for instance,

when both sanghas were devastated by famine, the king imported a number of monks from Siam to revive the male order, but there is no evidence of any attempt to revive the female sangha. Recently, some effort has been made to revive the practice of *bhikshuni* ordination in Theravada countries.

Some Theravada women take the same 10 precept vows as male novices, consisting of the five that laypersons take, plus five more. In Sri Lanka a female order observing ten precepts was started in 1905 with the help of women from Burma, and in 1996 a new order of *bhikshunis*, adhering to all 235 precepts (the 227 that monks take plus eight that are specific to women) was established with the help of *bhikshus* from Sri Lanka and Korea. Some women's centres, or meditation centres open to both men and women, are named after Ayya Khema, a German Jewish woman who was ordained in 1988 and became a respected leader and author.

Even without ordination, however, many Theravada women pursue a very active religious life, both at home and in the temples. In Thailand Buddhist laywomen can take vows of poverty and service similar to those taken by Roman Catholic nuns. Some of these women say they would not seek ordination even if it were available because they feel they have more freedom to serve others if they are not bound by the *vinaya* rules. In modern times, Theravada has also moved towards greater

Document

Jewel Brocade

In The Sutra of Sagara, the Naga King, *which was translated into Chinese in the third century, a princess named Jewel Brocade cleverly uses the Mahayana doctrine of the emptiness of all things to refute a male disciple who represents the stereotypical patriarchal position. No distinction between male and female spiritual abilities is valid, she argues, because all distinctions are ultimately invalid:*

You have said: "One cannot attain Buddhahood within a woman's body." Then, one cannot attain it within a man's body either. What is the reason? Because only the virtuous have eyes of Emptiness. The one who perceives through Emptiness is neither male nor female. The ears, nose, mouth, body, and mind are also Empty (Paul 1979: 236).

acceptance of women's capacity for high religious achievement. A Thai laywoman named Upasika Kee Nanayon (1901–79), for instance, was revered by Buddhists of both sexes for her mastery of meditation and her instructional talks.

The status of women in the Mahayana tradition tended to be higher from the beginning. Certainly Mahayana took a more sympathetic view of laypeople in general than earlier forms of Buddhism did. The fact that Mahayana encouraged women as well as men to take the bodhisattva vow indicates that it considered women capable of enlightenment in a way that Theravada did not.

An order of Mahayana nuns following a discipline (*vinaya*) of the Dharmagupta sect has continued as an unbroken lineage in China and Taiwan, and some of their *bhikshunis* may now be found in many countries. The Rinzai Zen school has both nuns and female masters, although they are not as numerous as monks and male masters. And the founder of the Soto school, Dogen, taught females as well as males. By the late medieval period, however, the tradition of Soto convents had died out, and during the Tokugawa period Soto nuns were not allowed to teach, become masters, reside in the temple compounds, or conduct funeral rituals. Outside Japan, both Rinzai- and Soto-trained Zen masters give equal status to practitioners of both sexes.

Tibetan Buddhism has a long tradition of ordained women, several of whom have been in the forefront of Tibet's struggle against Chinese domination. Ani Pachen ("Great Courage") came to be known as Tibet's Joan of Arc after she led her clan in a rebellion against the Chinese takeover of Tibet in 1949. She was imprisoned and tortured, but refused to renounce either Buddhism or her loyalty to the Dalai Lama. On her release from prison in 1981, she again played a leading role in Tibetan demonstrations against Hanification before escaping to live among the Tibetans in exile in Dharamsala, India.

A Renewed Sense of Mission

According to the Buddhist understanding of long-term historical cycles, Shakyamuni began a new era by setting the wheel of dharma in motion again after a period of decline. Eventually the dharma will again go into decline, until the next buddha restarts the wheel. This somewhat pessimistic view of the future stands in sharp contrast to the views of many other religions, including Christianity. Yet the notion that organized Buddhism will eventually decline does not in any way diminish Buddhists' zeal or sense of mission.

In a sense, the many volunteer associations promoting Buddhist solutions to modern problems are performing the same functions as the Buddhist kings of the past who provided financial support as well as leadership in education, economic development, and social values. Thus meditation retreat centres offer help with modern problems such as stress and overdependence on material possessions. Such centres offer instruction in basic meditational posture and breathing techniques in order to help achieve calmness, mental focus, and insight into dharma truths. Most of them emphasize the importance of breaking through the normal bonds of ego, self-centredness, and the assumption of permanence. Buddhadasa Bhikkhu (1906–93), a Thai reformer, identified the fundamental problem as the attitude of "me and mine." This attitude may be characteristic of the human condition, but Buddhists believe that it is made worse by the materialistic and individualistic emphasis of contemporary values.

Buddhist Economics

Another problem currently being addressed by some Buddhist writers and organizations is the need for alternatives to modern schemes of economic development. The term "Buddhist economics" was first used by the economist E.F. Schumacher, who had exposure both to Gandhi's advocacy of small-scale, people-oriented development and to the efforts of U Nu, the devout Buddhist who in 1947 became the first prime minister of Burma, to implement "Buddhist Socialism" as a middle path between communism and capitalism. Not surprisingly, Buddhist economics proposes a middle path between the environmental and social disasters of overdevelopment on the one hand and the poverty of underdevelopment on the other. It advocates local-level, low-tech, people-oriented projects that will help everyone, and criticizes all projects that serve to make the rich richer and the poor poorer. Other advocates of Buddhist economics include the Thai monk Ven. Prayudh Payutto, who sees the Middle Path as the best way to sustainable development. Yet another Thai monk, Ven. Prabhavanaviriyakhun, has written a book entitled *Buddhist Economics* in which he argues that achieving sustainable development will require (as he puts it in the title of another book) "reforming human nature." This theme is also central to the social critic Sulak Sivaraksa, who laments the spread of consumer greed around the world. In a variation on Descartes's "I think, therefore I am," Sivaraksa says that the slogan of consumerism is "I shop therefore I am."

Cooperation among Buddhists

There is a growing spirit of cooperation among the branches of Buddhism in most parts of the world, and Buddhists in various countries are now forming networks across national borders. (One example is the International Network of Engaged Buddhists, based in Bangkok.) Many Buddhists now identify themselves first as Buddhists and only secondarily as Zen Buddhists or Theravada Buddhists. This trend is strengthened by the growing tendency of Buddhist periodicals and Internet sites to include articles by writers from a variety of Buddhist traditions.

The sense of common purpose has been strengthened by the international exposure of the Dalai Lama, who has travelled to most Buddhist countries and in every case has been very well received. Strictly speaking, the Dalai Lama is the spiritual head of just one order of Tibetan Buddhists, but by virtue of the stature of his office and his outstanding personal qualities, Buddhists everywhere recognize Tenzin Gyatso as their spokesperson in some sense. His forced exile is seen as a loss for Tibet, but in the long run it may provide the impetus that Buddhism needs to regain its traditional role as one of the world's most vigorous and successful religions.

✸ Summary

Buddhists understand Shakyamuni, the Sage of the Shakya clan, to be the latest in a long line of spiritual masters who have become fully enlightened, teaching Buddhas. In the 2,500 years since his birth, his followers have preserved the teachings of the Buddha and others as sacred texts, selections from which are chanted to bring understanding and blessing to all. Buddhist thought makes no sharp distinction between animals and humans, and holds that all living beings are reborn according to their karma and stage of spiritual progress along the path to enlightenment. Buddhism spread throughout Asia and beyond, and is organized by ordination lineages as subdivisions among three Vehicles: Theravada, Mahayana, and Vajrayana. No one individual holds authority over all Buddhists, but the current Dalai Lama is world-renowned as the face of Buddhism today. Although Buddhism is a missionary religion, its approach today is generally low-key, centred on activities such as meditation training and informal "dharma talks."

What gives Buddhism its energy? What makes it work for so many people in so many different times and cultures? The answer may lie in the continuing power of the Triple Gem to shape people's spiritual lives. Buddhists feel confident "taking refuge" in the Buddha not as a god but as a great human being; in the Dharma as a set of living teachings that go to the heart of reality; and in the Sangha as a community of people committed to following the Buddha's path as closely as possible. They also feel confident that, in the distant future, when the wheel of dharma set in motion by Shakyamuni ceases to turn, the future buddha Maitreya will appear on earth and turn the wheel yet again for the benefit of all beings.

Sacred Texts

Religion	Texts	Composition/ Compilation	Compilation/ Revision	Use
Buddhism: Theravada	*Tripitaka: Vinaya* (discipline), *Sutras* (sermons), and *Abhidharma* (further dharma)	Each of the various early sects had its own collection of texts, which were transmitted orally for several centuries before they were first written down in the 1st century BCE, in Sri Lanka.	Only the Theravada versions of the texts survive in full; commentaries include Buddhaghosa's *The Path of Purification* (5th century).	Study and discussion; selections called *Parittas* chanted as blessings in various rituals; and verses from the *Dhammapada* (part of the *Sutra* collection) often used for guidance in everyday life
Buddhism: Mahayana	*Lotus* and *Heart Sutras*, as well as hundreds of other sutras and commentaries	Some written in early 1st century CE; others said to have been recovered from hiding	Commentaries written on many major sutras	Chanted for study or blessing rituals; different Mahayana schools had their own favourite texts.
Buddhism: Mahayana, Pure Land	*Sukhavati* (Pure Land) *Sutras*, of various lengths	Composed during early centuries of CE	Commentaries written by major thinkers	Studied and chanted; the source of the Bodhisattva vows that Pure Land practitioners take
Buddhism: Mahayana, Chan	*Platform* and *Lankavatara Sutras*, among others; *Mumonkan* (koan collection)	Favourite Mahayana scriptures, plus stories of masters unique to Chan tradition	Numerous translations of teachings, updated frequently over time	Doctrinal, ritual, inspirational, educational; it can take years for students to work their way through the 48 koans of the *Mumonkan*.
Buddhism: Vajrayana	*Kanjur* (sutras and tantras)	Includes many Tibetan translations of Mahayana sutras	Commentaries called *Tanjur* expanded on the *Kanjur* texts.	Study, chanting, rituals

Discussion Questions

1. How does the life of the Buddha compare with that of Christ (or the leader of some other spiritual tradition)?

2. What were the main elements of the brahmin tradition that Buddhism rejected?

3. What role, if any, do deities play in Buddhism?

4. What does Buddhism mean by the goal of purifying the mind?

5. What is the status of Tibetan Buddhist culture in contemporary China?

6. Why does the Chinese government object when the leaders of other countries meet with the Dalai Lama?

7. Why has the *Bhikshuni sangha* been lost in several Buddhist countries? What efforts are being made to restore it?

8. What is "Engaged Buddhism"?

9. Why did Dr Ambedkar and many other Dalits convert from Hinduism to Buddhism?

10. Is it fair to call Buddhism a system of self-development rather than a religion?

Glossary

anatman "No-soul," the doctrine that the human person is impermanent, a changing combination of components.

Arhat/*lohan* A worthy one or saint, someone who has realized the ideal of spiritual perfection.

bhikshu, bhikshuni An ordained Buddhist monk and nun, respectively.

bodhisattva In Theravada, a being who is on the way to enlightenment or buddhahood but has not yet achieved it; in Mahayana, a celestial being who forgoes nirvana in order to save others.

Chan/Seon/Zen A tradition centred on the practice of meditation and the teaching that ultimate reality is not expressible in words or logic, but must be grasped through direct intuition; see also **koan** and *zazen*.

dana A "giving" ritual, in which Theravada families present gifts of food, at their homes or a temple, to *bhikshus* who conduct rituals including chanting and merit-transfer.

dharma In Buddhist usage, teaching or truth concerning the ultimate nature of things.

dukkha The suffering, psychological as well as physical, that characterizes human life.

Hinayana "Lesser Vehicle"; the pejorative name given by the Mahayana ("Greater Vehicle") school to earlier Indian Buddhist sects, of which Theravada became the most important.

karma The energy of the individual's past thoughts and actions, good or bad; it determines rebirth within the "wheel" of samsara or cycle of rebirth that ends only when *parinirvana* is achieved. Good karma is also called "merit."

koan/*gongan* A paradoxical thought exercise used in the Chan–Zen tradition to provoke a breakthrough in understanding by forcing students past the limitations of verbal formulations and logic.

lama "Wise teacher"; a title given to advanced teachers as well as the heads of various Tibetan ordination lineages.

Mahayana "Greater Vehicle"; the form of Buddhism that emerged around the first century in India and spread first to China and then to Korea and Japan.

mandala A chart-like representation of cosmic Buddha figures that often serves as a focus of meditation and devotion in the Mahayana and Vajrayana traditions.

mudra A pose or gesture in artistic representations of Buddha figures; by convention, each *mudra* has a specific symbolic meaning.

nirvana The state of bliss associated with final enlightenment; nirvana "with remainder" is the highest level possible in this life, and nirvana "without remainder" is the ultimate state. See also *parinirvana*.

pagoda A multi-storey tower, characteristic of Southeast and East Asian Buddhism, that developed out of the South Asian mound or stupa.

parinirvana The ultimate perfection of bliss, achievable only on departing this life, as distinct from the nirvana with the "remainder" achievable while one is still in the present existence.

prajna The spiritual wisdom or insight necessary for enlightenment.

Pure Land The comfortable realm in the western region of the heavens reserved for those who trust in the merit and grace of its lord, the celestial buddha Amitabha (Amida).

rinpoche A title of respect for Tibetan teachers or leading monks.

samadhi A higher state of consciousness, achieved through meditation.

sangha The "congregation" or community of Buddhist monks and nuns. Some forms of Buddhism also refer to the congregation of lay persons as a sangha.

Shakyamuni "Sage of the Shakya clan," a title used to refer to the historical figure of Siddhartha Gautama, the Buddha.

shunyata The Emptiness that is held to be ultimately characteristic of all things, stressed especially by Madhyamaka doctrine.

stupa Originally a hemispherical mound built to contain cremation ashes or a sacred relic; in East Asia the stupa developed into the tower-like pagoda.

sutra A discourse attributed either to Shakyamuni himself or to an important disciple.

Theravada "Teaching of the Elders," the dominant form of Buddhism in Sri Lanka and Southeast Asia.

Tripitaka "Three baskets"; the collection of early sacred writings whose three sections consist of discourses attributed to the Buddha, rules of monastic discipline, and treatises on doctrine.

Vaishakha/Vesak A Theravada festival held at the full moon around early May, marking Shakyamuni's birth, enlightenment, and *parinirvana*.

Vajrayana The tantric branch of Buddhism that became established in Tibet and the Himalayan region, and later spread to Mongolia and eventually back to India.

vinaya The rules of practice and conduct for monks; a section of the Pali canon.

vipassana "Insight" or "mindfulness" meditation practised by Theravada Buddhists.

zazen Sitting meditation in the Chan–Zen tradition.

Zen See **Chan**.

Further Reading

Amore, Roy C. 1978. *Two Masters, One Message.* Nashville: Abingdon. Compares and contrasts the figures of Buddha and Jesus.

Batchelor, Martine. 2006. *Women in Korean Zen: Lives and Practices.* Syracuse: Syracuse University Press. A good account based on ten years of Zen practice in Korea.

Dalai Lama. 1990. *Freedom in Exile: The Autobiography of the Dalai Lama.* New York: HarperCollins.

Dalai Lama, His Holiness The. 2002. *How to Practice: The Way to a Meaningful Life.* Trans. and ed. by Jeffrey Hopkins. New York: Pocket Books.

Fisher, Robert E. 1993. *Buddhist Art and Architecture.* London: Thames & Hudson. An overview of South and East Asian developments.

Gross, Rita M. 1993. *Buddhism after Patriarchy: A Feminist History, Analysis, and Reconstruction of Buddhism.* Albany: State University of New York Press. Material for provocative debate.

Lopez, Donald S., Jr. 2002. *The Story of Buddhism: A Concise Guide to Its History and Teachings.* New York: HarperCollins.

Queen, Christopher S., and Sallie B. King, eds. 1996. *Engaged Buddhism: Liberation Movements in Asia.* Albany: State University of New York Press. Twentieth-century activism from India and Thailand to Tibet and Japan.

Seager, Richard Hughes. 2000. *Buddhism in America.* New York: Columbia University Press.

Shaw, Ronald D.M., trans. 1961. *The Blue Cliff Records: The Hekigan Roku [Pi yen lu] Containing One Hundred Stories of Zen Masters of Ancient China.* London: M. Joseph. Koans especially prized by the Japanese.

Sivaraksa, Sulak. 2005. *Conflict, Culture, Change: Engaged Buddhism in a Globalizing World.* Somerville, MA: Wisdom Publications. A book by an important Thai Buddhist social critic.

Recommended Websites

http://lhamo.tripod.com/

A site focusing on women in Buddhism.

www.americanbuddhist.net

Offers a broad overview of Buddhism, including Buddhist activism.

www.buddhamind.info

A comprehensive site, including an ezine with cartoons, pictures, and much more.

www.dharmanet.org

A useful overview of the history and varieties of Buddhism in China, but does not address current issues.

www.dhamma.org

A good source on Theravada-style *vipassana* meditation.

www.freetibet.org

Site of the Free Tibet Campaign, a movement started by Tibetans in exile and their supporters.

www.sakyadhita.org

Site of The International Association of Buddhist Women, with links to various country sites including USA and Canada.

References

Bloom, Alfred. 1965. *Shinran's Gospel of Pure Grace*. Tucson: University of Arizona Press.

Chen, Kenneth. 1964. *Buddhism in China: A Historical Survey*. Princeton: Princeton University Press.

de Bary, William Theodore, ed. 1958. *Sources of Indian Tradition*. New York: Columbia University Press.

Dhammika, Sravasti, ed. 1989. *Buddha Vacana*. Singapore: Buddha Dhamma Mandala Society.

Horner, I.B. 1930. *Women under Primitive Buddhism: Laywomen and Almswomen*. New York: Dutton.

———, trans. 1967. *The Collection of the Middle Length Sayings (Majjhimanikaya)*. vol. 3. London: Luzac.

Hughes, Ernest R., and K. Hughes. 1950. *Religion in China*. London: Hutchinson.

Hurvitz, Leon. 1976. *Scripture of the Lotus Blossom of the Fine Dharma*. New York: Columbia University Press.

Nanamoli [formerly Osborne Moore], trans. 1972. *The Life of the Buddha as It Appears in the Pali Canon, the Oldest Authentic Record*. Kandy: Buddhist Publication Society Inc.

Nhat Hanh, Thich. 1988. *The Heart of Understanding: Commentaries on the Prajnaparamita Heart Sutra*. Berkeley: Parallax Press.

Nielsen, N.C., et al., eds. 1993. *Religions of the World*. 3rd ed. New York: St Martin's Press.

Paul, Diana Y., ed. 1979. *Women in Buddhism: Images of the Feminine in Mahayana Tradition*. Berkeley: Asian Humanities Press.

Rhi, Ki-Yong. 1977. "Wonhyo and His Thought." In Chai-Shin Yu, ed., *Korean and Asian Religious Tradition*, 197–207. Toronto: Korean and Related Studies Press.

Rhys Davids, Caroline A. 1964. *Psalms of the Early Buddhists*. vol. 1 (Psalms of Sisters). London: Luzac, for the Pali Text Society.

Rhys Davids, Thomas W., trans. 1881. Buddhist Sutras. In F. Max Müller, ed., *Sacred Books of the East*, 11. Oxford: Clarendon Press.

———, trans. 1890. The Questions of King Milinda, Part I. In F. Max Müller, ed., *Sacred Books of the East*, 35. Oxford: Clarendon Press.

Robinson, Richard H. 1959. "Buddhism: In China and Japan." In R.C. Zaehner, ed., *The Concise Encyclopedia of Living Faiths*, 321–47. London: Joseph.

Sivaraksa, Sulak, *Challenges to Governance in Southeast Asia*, www.sulak-sivaraksa.org/en/index.php?option=com_content&task=view&id=75&Itemid=103 accessed 1 February 2013.

Suzuki, D.T. 1991. *An Introduction to Zen Buddhism*. New York: Grove Press.

Takeuchi, Yoshinori. 1987. "Nishida Kitaro." In Mircea Eliade, ed., *The Encyclopedia of Religion* 10: 456–7. New York: Macmillan.

Tsunoda, Ryusaku. 1958. *Sources of Japanese Tradition*. New York: Columbia University Press.

Yampolsky, Philip, trans. 1976. *The Platform Sutra of the Sixth Patriarch*. New York: Columbia University Press.

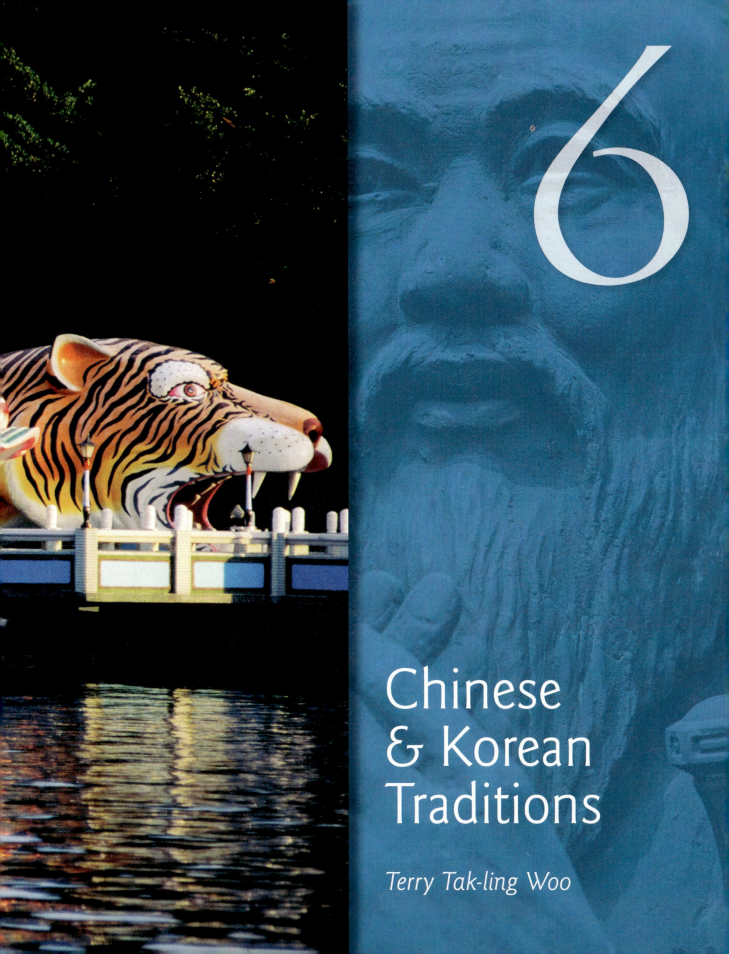

6

Chinese
& Korean
Traditions

Terry Tak-ling Woo

Traditions at a Glance

Numbers

Indigenous: East Asian traditions such as shamanism, Confucianism, and Daoism do not require exclusive membership: they also tend to be less institutionalized, with a much weaker sense of congregation, than monotheistic religions. Their membership is therefore very difficult to count.

Confucianism: The *World Christian Encyclopedia* estimates that there are 6.3 million Confucians in the world. Other sources also come within the range of 6 million, but because most of the East Asian world does not consider Confucianism to be a religion, the true number is impossible to gauge.

Daoism: As with Confucianism, the exact number of adherents is impossible to determine because of issues around definition; estimates range from 20 million to as many as 400 million.

Chinese folk or popular religion: Daoists will sometimes be counted as folk religionists. This category also includes numerous new religious movements and traditional sects whose devotees may consider their practices and beliefs to be more cultural than religious. Estimates range from 225 to 445 million.

Korean shamanism and popular religion: Reliable data are impossible to find, but estimates range from 1 to 7 million.

Distribution

Confucians and Daoists live mainly in East and Southeast Asia, Australia and New Zealand, Western Europe, and North America. Adherents of popular religions remain primarily in East Asia, with small pockets in diasporic communities in Australia, New Zealand, North America, and Europe.

Founders and Teachers

Mythical founders and heroes include Yao, Shun, and Yu in China, and Dangun in Korea. Famous first teachers—some mythical, some historic—include the Yellow Emperor, Confucius, and Laozi in China, and Choe Chung in Korea.

Deities

For Confucians, the place of a deity is filled either by Heaven or by Heaven and Earth together. For some Daoists, the Way functions as a deity, while others look to what is in effect a bureaucracy of deities. Popular religions, both Korean and Chinese, include literally hundreds of deities.

Authoritative Texts

Popular and shamanistic religions tend not to be textually oriented, although practitioners do read morality books (*shanshu*) about how to live a virtuous life. For Confucians, the classics from the Zhou and Han dynasties are the foundational texts.

For Daoists the situation is considerably more complex. While Laozi and, to a lesser degree, Zhuangzi (also known as the classic of Southern China) are basic to all Daoist groups, the various groups consider different scriptures and commentaries to be definitive. Included in the mix are revealed scriptures and writings on alchemy, utopian visions, and meditation, such as the *Unity of the Three*, and the Classics of *Great Peace*, *Salvation of Humanity*, and *Purity and Tranquility*.

For Buddhists, Mahayana texts such as the *Lotus*, *Vimalakirti*, *Heart*, *Diamond*, *Pure Land*, and *Flower Garland Sutras* are central, although different schools give priority to different texts. The only Chinese text that is considered "canonical" in the monotheistic sense is the *Platform Sutra* of the Chan school.

Noteworthy Teachings

Since none of the East Asian traditions are exclusive, believers are free to attend temples and

shrines of all kinds. Daoism, Confucianism, and Buddhism share cultural and social space even though they differ fundamentally in doctrine and vary greatly in practice. Popular religions continuously appropriate and syncretize teachings from all three traditions, as well as more recent religions like Islam and Christianity. All three elite religions share a utopian view of a peaceful and harmonious society whose members are devoted to self-cultivation and discipline, live frugally, serve the community, and try to be good. In addition, some schools of Buddhism look to an afterlife in the Pure Land of a celestial buddha such as Amituofo (Amitabha).

In this chapter you will learn about:

- the role that syncretism has played in the development of Chinese religiosity
- how the popular religions that continue to thrive today express the syncretic spirit
- how Confucianism, Daoism, and Buddhism argued against, influenced, and developed in relation to one another
- about the development and acceptance of a wide range of texts for a variety of needs
- the brutal challenges that Chinese religions have faced in modern times and how they have responded
- the importance of women and yin (the feminine principle) in Chinese religion.

"All religions teach people to be good" is a popular Chinese saying. This optimistic sentiment is not surprising when we consider that the classical texts that helped to define East Asian religions were composed during the chaotic and violent half-millennium (722–221 BCE) from the beginning of the Spring and Autumn period to the end of the Warring States. Because religion was inextricably linked to politics from the beginning, social harmony and stability in governance have been central concerns, along with physical sustenance and security.

✹ Overview

Chinese and Korean indigenous religious beliefs and practices are many-layered. The foundational layers of animism and shamanism remain visible today in traces of prehistoric tribal practices that, although they originated in different types of societies—some matriarchal, some patriarchal—in different parts of East Asia, reflected a common need to deal with the insecurities of life. Philosophers, shamans, and various other religious practitioners known as masters of the methods, including prognosticians, geomancers, and doctors of prescriptions, all sought to bring peace. Early Confucian and Daoist writings thus included a fair proportion of political teachings combined with metaphysical ruminations, advice on cultivating good health and moral character, instructions for achieving mystical union with the divine, and guidance on meditation. When Buddhism (*Fojiao*, "teaching of the Buddha") was later introduced from India and Central Asia, this was the religious landscape to which it had to adapt.

The central focus on peace and harmony had a profound effect on the nature of the religious questions that were posed and the solutions that were found. A shared aversion to violence led the various religions to be tolerant of differences and to embrace a generally inclusive and broadly syncretic ethos. This ancient syncretism is still visible today in the contemporary practice of folk religion.

Next time you go to a Chinese restaurant, take a look around and see if there is a shrine at the door, or perhaps the back of the sitting area. Chances are good that you will see a red shrine with three incense sticks in a censer, a small plate of fruit at the front, a candle on each side, and at least one figure standing in the centre. If the figure is holding a halberd or lance, it will represent Guan Gong, who symbolizes the Confucian virtues of integrity or loyalty (**zhong**) and the sense of what is right (**yi**).

Sites

Beijing, People's Republic of China

The Imperial Palace complex, also known as the Forbidden City, includes the Tiantan (Altar or Temple of Heaven), where the Ming and Qing emperors performed the grandest sacrifices. Beijing is also home to the Taimiao, the ancestral temple of both dynasties; a Confucian temple dedicated to scholar-officials; various Daoist and Buddhist temples; and the tombs of the later Ming emperors.

© Imagemore Co., Ltd./Corbis

The three tiers of the Temple of Heaven (Tiantan) symbolize the relationship between Heaven, Earth, and human beings; the circular shape expresses the belief that Heaven is round whereas the Earth is square. The emperor represented the people, and so he made offerings to Heaven and prayed for bountiful harvests. The temple complex was constructed in the fifteenth century.

Timeline

2357 BCE	Time of China's Sage kings Yao, Shun and Yu; some accounts place Dangun, the mythical founder of Old Joseon (Korea), in the same period
c. 2200–1750	Xia dynasty (China)
c. 1750–1046	Shang (Yin) dynasty (China)
c. 1046–256	Zhou dynasty (China)
722–479	Spring and Autumn period
551	Birth of Confucius (d. 479); some accounts place Laozi around the same time, some place him earlier, and others say that he never existed
479–221	Warring States period
c. 400–100	Huang–Lao school
c. 343	Birth of Mengzi (Mencius) (d. 289); Zhuangzi (369?–286?) was a slightly older contemporary
c. 310	Birth of Xunzi (d. 219), who witnessed the carnage of the late Zhou period
c. 300	Old Joseon (Korea)
221–206	Qin dynasty (China); destruction of Confucian texts by the First Qin Emperor
202 BCE–9 CE	Early (also Former or Western) Han dynasty; Confucian texts recovered and edited based partly on copies that had been preserved and partly on the recitations of scholars who had memorized them
25–220	Latter or Eastern Han
124	First state college for Confucian teachings established, along with state examination system
c. 50 BCE–668 CE	Three Kingdoms of Goguryeo, Baekje, and Silla (Korea)
c. 48 CE	Birth of Ban Zhao (d. 112), who advocated education for women
142	Zhang Daoling founds the Daoist Celestial Masters, also known as Orthodox Unity
220–589	Period of North–South disunion or Six Dynasties (China)
317	Northern China falls to invaders from North and Central Asia
c. 370–380	Buddhism introduced to Goguryeo and Baekje, and (later) Silla
527	Martyrdom of Yi Chadon overcomes opposition to Buddhism, which is made state religion of Silla
c. 530	Baekje monks travel to Japan to introduce Buddhism
618–907	Tang dynasty (China)
600s	Tang rulers send Daoist priests, texts, and images to Goguryeo
629–630	Chinese monk Xuanzang makes pilgrimage to India
647	Second Tang emperor orders the construction of Confucian temples with tablets commemorating 22 orthodox Confucians
661	Korean monks Wonhyo and Uisang start out for China

Continued

668–936	Kingdom of United Silla (Korea)
682	United Silla establishes the National Confucian College
824	Death of Han Yu, defender of Confucianism
890–936	Later Three Kingdoms (Korea)
918–1392	Goryeo period (Korea); Buddhism is the state religion
960–1279	Song dynasty (China)
1158–1250	Jinul synthesizes the practice-focused Seon (Chan) school and doctrinal schools like Hwaeom (Flower Garland)
1368–1644	Ming dynasty (China)
1392–1897	Joseon persecution of Buddhism
1400s	Both China's Empress Xu and Joseon's Queen Sohye write texts entitled *Instructions for the Inner Quarters*
1500s	Joseon Neo-Confucianism thrives in the commitment to communal responsibilities represented by Village Compacts and scholarly discussion like the Four-Seven Debates
1529	Death of Confucian Wang Yangming
1545–67	Korea's Queen Munjeong, ruling as regent for her young son, repeals many anti-Buddhist measures
1592–98	Imjin wars; Buddhist monks gain minimal acceptance by helping to drive Japanese invaders out of Korea
1644–1911	Qing (Manchu) dynasty (China)
1900s	East Asia is reconfigured in response to Western challenges; new religions are established and traditional ones renewed
1910–45	Japanese occupation of Korea
1911	Qing dynasty falls and China becomes a republic
1945	Korea divided between Democratic People's Republic (North) and Republic (South)
1949	People's Republic of China (PRC)
1950s	New Confucian movement finds a home in Hong Kong; Korean New Confucian Gim (Kim) Chungnyol travels to Taiwan to study with Fang Dongmei
1966–76	Communist government attempts to eradicate traditional Chinese values and practices in "Great Proletarian Cultural Revolution"
1980s	Revival of Daoism in China after more than a century of persecution
1989	Confucius' birthday officially celebrated in the PRC for the first time since 1949
2004	The first Confucius Institute opens in Seoul
2006	First World Buddhist Forum—the first government-sponsored religious conference held in China since 1949—opens in Hangzhou
2007	A week-long, privately funded International Forum on the *Daodejing* is approved by the government and held simultaneously in Xi'an and Hong Kong
2011	First International Daoism Forum held in the city of Hengyang, at the foot of Hengshan, one of the five sacred Daoist mountains

A traditional cap and a flowing beard signify the Daoist lineage ancestor Lu Dongbin, while a female figure will usually represent Guanyin, the Buddhist bodhisattva of compassion who sees and hears the suffering of all sentient beings. If there is no figure, the back panel of the shrine will often carry a verse of thanksgiving addressed to the local earth god.

When the Chinese speak of *sanjiao*, they are talking about the three (*san*) teachings, philosophies, or religions (*jiao*) of Confucianism, Daoism, and Buddhism. Collectively, these are sometimes described as the elite tradition. A much more diffuse fourth tradition, often described as folk or popular religion, honours an assortment of spirits that varies from place to place. While these four traditions have occasionally contested each other's teachings and legitimacy, for the most part they have coexisted in peace.

Ordinary people consult specialists from across the religious spectrum—Confucian teachers, Daoist priests, Buddhist monks, spirit mediums, astrologers, *fengshui* practitioners—although specialists in the elite traditions tend to be exclusive in their allegiances. Scholars have often noted that Chinese religions are more interested in right action than right belief. While this is true, right action is based on one common principle, for as varied as the three elite traditions are in their doctrines, rituals, and spiritual goals, they all agree on the central importance of avoiding socio-political conflict and chaos.

This common emphasis on harmony reflects a shared recognition that human temperaments and capacities vary. For example, the Confucian Xunzi talks about the different ways in which different people might understand particular religious rites. The Daoist *Daodejing* (*Classic of the Way and Power or Virtue*, also known as the *Laozi*) speaks of the universal, all-encompassing Way (**Dao**) as indefinable, beyond words, since any definition would necessarily be incomplete. And Buddhism uses the *Lotus Sutra*'s idea of "skillful means," along with the Chinese idea of doctrinal categorization, to reconcile different and even contradictory teachings.

The Classical Period to the Qin (c. 2300 BCE–206 BCE)

Confucian Beginnings

Origins

Not all of the philosophy that the West calls Confucianism originated with Kongzi or **Confucius** (c. 551–479 BCE).[1] Some of its seminal ideas can be found in the Five Classics: the *Classic* or *Book of Changes* (*Yijing*), the *Classic of Documents* or *Book of History* (*Shujing*), the *Classic of Odes* or *Book of Poetry* (*Shijing*), the *Records* or *Book of Rites* (*Liji*), and the *Spring and Autumn Annals* (*Chunqiu*). (A sixth work, the *Classic of Music* [*Yueji*], is now lost.) Some parts of these works may predate Confucius himself, who professed to be a transmitter of tradition rather than an innovator; and other parts appear to have been written after his time. Nevertheless, Confucius is revered as the first of three foremost classical philosophers in the Confucian tradition, the other two being **Mengzi** (Mencius c. 343–289 BCE) and **Xunzi** (c. 310–219 BCE).

Originating during the Zhou dynasty (c. 1046–256 BCE), the Classics were first standardized during the Han dynasty (202 BCE–220 CE) and they have formed a substantial part of the state examination curriculum since the establishment of the first state college in 124 BCE. The world they describe is the same one that shaped Daoism and Mohism as well as later folk beliefs and practices.

Historically, the Five Classics provided both the ideology that informed government policy and the framework in which that policy was implemented for some 2,000 years. They have also served as blueprints for good conduct within families, and as guidelines for individual moral and spiritual transformation.

The Classics record a society in transition. During the Shang era (c. 1750–1046 BCE) the world was understood to be under the control of anthropomorphic deities, ghosts, and spirits. In the Zhou era this "supernatural" worldview was gradually replaced by an increasingly humanistic ethos based on a new understanding that the world operated according to impersonal natural principles. The content of the Five Classics therefore ranges from descriptions of deities, ghosts, and spirits, and the rites (*li*) performed for them, to philosophical explanations of the natural principles underlying those rites. The primary source of those explanations, the *Book of Rites*, also explains how the rites serve the ultimate goal of Confucianism: the creation of a harmonious society through careful self-cultivation not for the sake of the self, but for the sake of the society. Over time, the Five Classics were reinterpreted with this goal in mind.

Confucian Concerns

The concerns addressed in the Five Classics can be categorized in four broad areas: individual, familial, political, and cosmic. The first duty of the exemplary Confucian (*junzi*) is to understand how to achieve and maintain peace, prosperity, and harmony.

The Classics make it clear that a peaceful, prosperous, and harmonious society cannot be achieved by men alone, for there can be no harmony in the state without harmony in the family—and the private realm of the family is the responsibility of the Confucian woman. They also explain how sacrifices and rituals give symbolic expression to the relationship between the outer world of politics and the inner world of the family. The essential function of rituals, ancestor rituals in particular, was to define, frame, and encourage right relationships, especially between men and women.

Each person has overlapping roles in society, and Confucians believe that the cultivation of correctness in human relationships is crucial to the establishment of a safe, secure, and stable society. There are five types of relationship: ruler and minister (state official), parent and child (traditionally, father and son), husband and wife, elder and younger siblings (often translated as "brothers"), and friends. They are hierarchical and guided by *ren* (goodness, humaneness, benevolence, and compassion). Except in the case of the "friends" relationship, the first person in each pair is deemed "senior" and expected to be especially considerate of how his or her actions will affect others; the second person is "junior" and is expected to maintain integrity and be upright and loyal.

Confucian Exemplars and Sages

The prototypes of the Confucian sage are three mythical "sage kings" named Yao, Shun, and Yu, whose stories are told in the first chapters of the *Classic of Documents*. The virtues they embody are civil, familial, and filial rather than military, and their stories are interpreted as implicitly criticizing rulers who govern by force.

Yao's reign was considered a success because he brought harmony to his domain and, most important, made sure that the common people he served were well fed and prosperous. In the simple agrarian society of his day, Yao's exemplary virtue was said to have radiated throughout the land.

The *Classic of Documents* recounts how, when it came time for him to retire, Yao recognized that his own son was not virtuous enough to be a good ruler. He asked his ministers to find a more appropriate successor, and they unanimously recommended a man of humble status named Shun. When Yao asked them why Shun would make a good king, they answered that he had managed to transcend his circumstances, living in harmony with his family and fulfilling his filial duties, even though his father was blind (literally and figuratively) and stupid, his stepmother deceitful, and his half-brother arrogant. In other words, Shun had not allowed his situation to overcome him, but had triumphed over adversity. Accordingly, Yao married his two daughters to Shun, observed his conduct for three years, and then offered him the throne.

The last sage king, Yu, is associated with the largely legendary Xia dynasty—the predecessors of the Shang. Yu's father was said to have thrown the natural cycle into chaos by building dams to contain floodwaters, but Yu dug deep canals to channel the water away. According to a chapter in the

Documents entitled "The Grand Model," this story was told to King Wu, the first king of Zhou, as a lesson in governance. Regarded as a blueprint for an equitable, prosperous, and harmonious society, the Grand Model was said to have been revealed to Yu as his reward for taking the "right action" to prevent disaster, working with nature (by channelling the water) rather than against it.

Divination and the Pantheon of Spirits

At least two related elements from the stories of the sage kings survived into the Shang dynasty: an intense interest in "right" governance and a belief in divine intervention through revelation to the king. We know, for instance, that the Shang kings took the role of shaman and practised divination, communicating directly with the spirits that were believed to hold the real power over the empire. Religious ritual was thus an indispensable part of governance in ancient China.

The Shang pantheon of spirits included human souls as well as natural elements and supernatural beings. At its apex, far above the natural realm, sat the Lord-on-High or Shangdi. Thought to be the ancestor-god of the Shang clan, he was the sky god, the only one who could command natural elements such as the rain, thunder, and wind. Below the Lord-on-High were the nature spirits believed to animate natural phenomena such as rivers and mountains; then the celestial spirits like the sun and moon; then "Former Lords" (*xiangong*) who were associated with the Shang but were not royal clan members; and, finally, direct ancestors, both male and female. Together, the cult of ancestors and the royal practice of divination cloaked the Shang kings in an aura of sacredness.

The Mandate of Heaven

After more than 700 years in power, the Shang dynasty fell to the Zhou. It was in the context of this power shift that the concept of the **Mandate of Heaven** (*tianming*) was developed.

When the first Zhou ruler, King Wu, died within a few years of taking the throne, his brother the Duke of Zhou served as regent for his young nephew. But the Duke returned the throne to the boy once he was old enough to rule. Such loyalty was revered in the early Confucian tradition, and the Duke's popularity rivalled that of Confucius himself. An exemplary Confucian sage, the personification of restraint, humility, and willingness to listen to advice, the Duke declared that Heaven had withdrawn the Mandate of Heaven from the Shang because their later kings had failed to provide for the people.

Document

On the Mandate of Heaven

The Mandate of Heaven appears in the Classic of Documents *in the form of a public announcement legitimating the Zhou overthrow of the Yin (an alternative name for the Shang):*

Heaven has rejected and ended the Mandate of this great state of Yin. Thus, although Yin has many former wise kings in Heaven, when their successor kings and successor people undertook their Mandate, in the end wise and good men lived in misery. Knowing that they must care for and sustain their wives and children, they then called out in anguish to Heaven and fled to places where they could not be caught. Ah! Heaven too grieved for the people of all the lands, wanting, with affection, in giving its Mandate to employ those who are deeply committed. The king should have reverent care for his virtue (D. Nivison in de Bary and Bloom 1999: 36).

In this way moral character became the primary determinant of the right to rule. The idea that good governance was a duty to Heaven reflected the Zhou belief in a moral force or supreme deity that ruled the world and took an interest in human affairs. How to encourage a king to rule ethically became a central concern for Confucians. In the *Classic of Odes*, King Wen (the father of Wu) is imagined addressing the last Shang king:

> King Wen said, Woe!
> Woe upon you, Yin and Shang!
> You have been the harsh oppressor,
> you have been grasping and crushing.
> You have been in the places of power,
> you have held the functions.
> Heaven sent recklessness down in you,
> and you rise by acts of force
> (Owen 1996: 20).

Thus the mandate to rule was taken away from the cruel and negligent Shang and passed to the virtuous Zhou. In this political transition, the term "god" (*di*) became associated with the earthly political ruler, while Heaven came to be portrayed as an impartial universal being or power, an intelligent cosmic moral force that cares for human welfare and so gives the people a wise and good king.

Humanization: The Transition from Shang to Zhou

With the establishment of the Zhou dynasty, the concept of Heaven gained ascendancy over the more personal Lord-on-High of the Shang. Although the interest in divination continued, the methods and materials used for the purpose changed over time, reflecting a change in the understanding of the universe. Eventually, the bones and tortoise shells used for divination were replaced by plant stalks—a change that reflected a conceptual shift away from an enchanted universe towards a more rational, impersonal one.

This shift did not mean that ancient beliefs and practices disappeared. The understanding that the world is controlled by ghosts, nature spirits, and celestial beings remains an integral part of Chinese religion, especially in folk traditions. Nevertheless, many Zhou thinkers diverged from their Shang predecessors in this regard. A number of schools developed and thrived. Legalists stressed the power of law in the advancement of human security and well-being; Naturalists concentrated on natural elements and processes (see Focus box); and Confucians promoted the importance of human relationships, beginning with familial affection. Philosophers came to see the world as regulated by impersonal

Focus

The Yin–Yang School

The Naturalists, also known as the yin-yang school, believed that those who followed the laws of nature would flourish while those who did not would perish. Yin–yang theory was later combined with the theory of the five "agents" or "elements" (*wuxing*)—metal, wood, earth, water, and fire—to form a theory of cycles that are generated and overcome.

For example, metal generates water, water generates wood, wood generates fire, fire generates earth, and earth in turn generates metal; then the cycle begins again. This cosmology suggests there is nothing in the world that cannot be defeated; and, at the same time, that there is no destruction from which growth cannot come.

processes, which they sought to understand in order to use them as models for human society.

The quest to understand natural processes was driven in part by the desire to find a natural—hence "correct"—foundation on which to structure a harmonious human society. The 64 hexagrams that are the basis of the *Classic of Changes*, a divination text originating in the early Zhou dynasty (c. 1000 BCE), were said to capture the metaphysical structure, transformations, and "Way" of the universe, providing both a general blueprint and a specific guide to correct behaviour for humans facing a cosmos in continual flux.

Rites: Performance and Principles

The section on "Principles of Sacrifice" in the *Records of Rites* explains that a ruler must have a wife as a helpmate in both state and familial duties. The principle of complementarity is reflected in the division of labour between king and queen, in the realms of activity prescribed for each, and in their gender-differentiated roles in ritual performance. The king and queen were together responsible for making offerings at the ancestral temple representing the imperial family; and at the altars of the land and grain representing the people and state; in this way they symbolically attended to their different duties in the outer-public and inner-private realms of male and female responsibilities.

This balance of yin and yang is reinforced by the first two trigrams in the *Classic of Changes*. *Qian* (Heaven and the creative) is represented by three solid lines ☰, while *kun* (Earth and the receptive) is represented by three broken lines ☷. The 64 trigrams that make up the *Changes* were

A *bagua* (eight trigrams) mirror is said to ward off evil spirits. This one contains the yin-yang symbol at its centre, surrounded by the eight trigrams and two circles.

iStockphoto/Thinkstock

understood to capture various transformations in the universe.

The rituals described in the *Rites* evolved over time, as did the understanding of their place in the lives of the individual, the state, and the society. Belief in their magico-religious efficacy was gradually replaced by a sense of their value in terms of discipline, education, and moral development. The deeply religious culture of the Shang was humanized by philosophers like Confucius during the later Zhou. In *Master Tso's Commentary* on the Spring and Autumn Annals, for example, a duke is reprimanded when he remarks that the spirits will protect him because his sacrificial offerings are "bountiful and pure":

> It is not simply that ghosts and spirits are attracted to human beings: it is virtue that attracts them. Hence . . . the *Book of History* says, "August heaven has no partial affections; it supports only the virtuous." It also says, "It is not the millet that is fragrant; it is bright virtue that is fragrant" (adapted from J. Legge in Sommer 1995: 25).

The shift from reliance on the supernatural efficacy of rituals to reliance on moral behaviour finds further support in the same text's story of a marquis who is rebuked for requesting an exorcism to ward off the evil threatened by the appearance of a comet in the sky: "If your virtue is not unclean, then why this exorcism? . . . Do not transgress against virtue, and people from all quarters will come to you" (ibid.: 26).

Confucius

Confucius spoke of himself as a transmitter of tradition rather than an innovator. On the connection between goodness and ritual, he famously said:

> Respect without ritual becomes tiresome, circumspection without ritual becomes timidity, bold fortitude without ritual becomes unruly, and directness without ritual becomes twisted (Sommer 1995: 46).

Confucius used the word *li* ("rites" or "ritual") to mean not only religious ritual but also the rules of social etiquette and everyday courtesy. He believed that *li* embodied the wisdom of the earliest Zhou tradition. He encouraged his students to practise *li* in all five fundamental relationships (emperor and minister, father and son, elder and younger brother, husband and wife, friends). At the same time he urged his students to seek the meaning, spirit, and principles behind the rites. Central to the Confucian understanding of history were the stories of the sage kings and the perfection they achieved by governing in accordance with the Way. According to "The Evolution of Rites" (*Liyun*), Confucius believed that the time of the sage kings was preceded by a utopian age:

> When the Great Way was practised, the world was shared by all alike. The worthy and the able were promoted to office and men practised good faith and lived in affection. Therefore they did not regard as parents only their own parents, or as sons only their own sons. The aged found a fitting close to their lives, the robust their proper employment; the young were provided with an upbringing, and the widow and widower, the orphaned and the sick, with proper care. Men had their tasks and women their hearths. They hated to see goods lying about in waste, yet they did not hoard them for themselves; they disliked the thought that their energies were not fully used, yet they used them not for private ends. Therefore all evil plotting was prevented and thieves and rebels did not arise, so that the people could leave their outer gates unbolted. This was the age of Grand Commonality [*Datong*] (B. Watson in de Bary and Bloom 1999: 342–3).

In time, greed and selfishness put an end to the Grand Commonality, ushering in the period of Lesser Prosperity. It was during this potentially chaotic era that the sage kings emerged as exemplars of correct, ethical governance. The primary source of Confucius' teachings on how to govern in such a period is the collection known as the *Analects* (*Lunyu*).

At the core of Confucius' ideal was the *junzi* (translated variously as "gentleman" or "noble"; the "authoritative," "exemplary," or "superior person"). The standard meaning of *junzi* was "son of a lord," indicating inherited social nobility, but in the *Analects* the word takes on a new meaning: this gentleman is a person of noble character, committed to the development of **de**—another word that underwent a shift in meaning with Confucius. Originally referring to a kind of magical charismatic power, in the *Analects* it signifies a moral power rooted in virtuous, ethical behaviour.

The fact that Confucius used these words in non-traditional ways did not mean that the meanings he gave them were new; the socio-political ideals he promoted were already present in the classic texts (*Odes*, *Documents*, *Spring and Autumn Annals*, and *Changes*). Confucius used the single word *ren* to capture virtues such as respect, liberality, trustworthiness, earnestness, and kindness. He believed that the most effective way to cultivate *ren* was through careful observance of *li*.

Above all, Confucius emphasized the importance of filial piety or devotion. The "Principles of Sacrifice," a chapter in the *Rites*, explains filial devotion as "caring for" one's parents according to the Way: that is, to the greatest extent possible without neglecting one's responsibilities in other relationships (8.2.1). But it could include everything from looking after one's own health to protecting family members even when they have committed a crime. Confucius understood ritual observance to be essential to the maintenance of harmony:

> Let there be no discord. . . . When one's parents are alive, one serves them in accordance with the rites; when they are dead, one buries them in accordance with the rites and sacrifices to them in accordance with the rites (2:5).

He also suggests that those who treat their parents and brothers with the proper respect will be equally loyal to a government ruling with the Mandate of Heaven. Thus Confucius explains that the "noble person concerns himself with the root; when the root is established, the way is born. Being filial and fraternal—is this not the root of humaneness?" (1:2).

Above all, humaneness is reflected in two characteristics: loyalty and empathetic understanding or reciprocity (4:15). Refining this idea, Confucius encapsulates his teachings in the "silver rule": "What you would not want for yourself, do not do to others" (15:23). The noble person is the one who puts the self aside and "relinquishes arrogance, boasting, resentment, and covetousness" (14:2).

Who can be a noble person? Anyone: all human beings are by nature similar. But there is a catch, for Confucius also teaches that individuals are set apart through their habits and actions (17:2). Thus even as he democratizes the idea of nobility, he creates a hierarchy of character based on moral cultivation. This hierarchy is all about the mastery of one's heart-mind (**xin**) and actions:

Sites

Qufu, Shandong province, People's Republic of China

The complex of monuments in the birthplace of Confucius, in Shandong, includes a temple, a cemetery, and a family mansion. The cemetery contains Confucius' tomb and the remains of more than 100,000 of his descendants.

Through mastering oneself and returning to ritual one becomes humane. If for a single day one can master oneself and return to ritual, the whole world will return to humaneness. . . . Look at nothing contrary to ritual; listen to nothing contrary to ritual; say nothing contrary to ritual; do nothing contrary to ritual (12:1).

Confucius believed that if the ruler wants goodness, the people will be good: "The virtue (*de*) of the exemplary person is like the wind, and the virtue of small people is like grass: When the wind blows over the grass, the grass must bend" (12:19). To re-create the Grand Commonalty, therefore, the good, the wise, and the humane must rule over small-minded and morally inferior people.

The Confucian mandate aims to limit the negative consequences of ignoble behaviour. When a recluse describes Confucius as "a scholar who withdraws from particular men" and suggests that instead he should withdraw from society, Confucius sighs and responds: "If the Way prevailed in the world, [I] would not be trying to change it" (18:6). Personal goodness alone is not enough: ethical nobility must be expressed, demonstrated, and reflected through action in the public realm.

Mengzi

The second most prominent classical thinker after Confucius is Meng Ke, whose name was latinized as Mencius. He lived more than a century after Confucius, in the fourth century BCE. By that time large conscript armies had replaced the elite chariot forces on which feudal rulers had relied in the past, resulting in a horrific increase in the human cost of war.

In an effort to stop the carnage, Mengzi travelled from state to state meeting with rulers, trying to persuade them to act in the interest of their people. He deplored the consequences of war:

In wars to gain land, the dead fill the plains;
in wars to gain cities, the dead fill the cities.

This is known as showing the land the way to devour human flesh. Death is too light a punishment for such men. Hence those skilled in war should suffer the most severe punishments . . . (4.A.14 Lau 1970: 124).

At the same time he tried to persuade rulers of the practical value of humaneness (*ren*), expanding on Confucius' understanding and placing the moral sense of what is right (*yi*) beside *ren*.

The book *Mencius* is a collection of conversations between Mencius and his disciples, his opponents, and the rulers of the various feudal states. Prominent among the issues discussed are human nature and government. Wishing to "follow in the footsteps of the three sages [King Yu of Xia, the Duke of Zhou, and Confucius] in rectifying the hearts of men, laying heresies to rest, opposing extreme action, and banishing excessive views" (ibid., 115), Mencius traced many of the problems of his day to the human "heart-mind" (*xin*), of which he identified four types. The heart-mind of compassion yields benevolence; that of shame leads to observance of rites; that of respect moves people to duty or right behaviour; and that of right and wrong brings wisdom (6.A.6 ibid., 163).

Mencius taught that sensitivity to others' suffering is innate, but that this predisposition must be consciously developed if a ruler is to govern compassionately, as the ancient kings did. In later times, a great man—teacher, scholar-official, or imperial minister—was needed to encourage the ruler to cultivate the heart-mind; and when the prince had become benevolent, dutiful, and correct, everyone else would seek to emulate him.

In contrast to Confucius, however, Mencius did not believe that the effect of the prince's character on the people was automatic or magical. He believed that even though human nature was essentially good, the common people needed supervision and discipline: otherwise, once their bellies were full and their bodies warmly clothed, they would degenerate to the level of animals driven only by material needs and desires, with no higher consciousness. The best way of nurturing the heart-mind of the people, Mencius taught, was neither to deprive them nor to give them more than they needed to survive, but to teach them to reduce their desires.

Mencius's belief in the ability of the mature heart-mind to arrive at sound conclusions allowed him to take some unconventional positions. He rejected the notion that filial piety demanded blind obedience. When someone suggested that Shun, the son-in-law of King Yao, had defied the rule of filial piety by failing to inform his parents of his marriage to Yao's two daughters, Mencius defended Shun on the grounds that his parents' heart-minds were not sufficiently developed for them to consent to his marriage. Shun's own heart-mind, by contrast, was so well developed that he was justified in acting independently, according to his own conscience.

Similarly, Mencius argued against blind adherence to the rule that unrelated men and women should not touch one another, pointing out that it would be inhuman for a man not to rescue his sister-in-law if she were drowning. On another occasion he remarked that if everything in the *Documents* were to be accepted without critical thought, it would be better if the text had never been written. Most famously, he drew on the Mandate of Heaven to argue that rebellion is justified when the ruler is causing his people to suffer. In short, for Mencius it is not enough simply to follow the classical teachings: we must use our heart-minds to determine the morally correct course of action.

But Mencius was not only a political thinker. He is sometimes described as a mystic because of his emphasis on **qi** (or *ch'i*): the "flood-like vital force, energy or ether" that appears simultaneously to give substance to virtue and to be nourished by it:

This is a *ch'i* which is, in the highest degree vast and unyielding. Nourish it with integrity and place no obstacle in its path and it will fill the space between Heaven and Earth. It is a *ch'i* which unites rightness and the Way. Deprive it of these and it will collapse. It is born of accumulated rightness and cannot be appropriated by anyone through a sporadic show of rightness. Whenever one acts in a way that falls below the standard set in one's heart, it will collapse (2.A.2; ibid., 77–8).

Mencius suggests that nourishing this vital force through constant practice in both public and private life is what permits human beings to achieve cosmic oneness and harmony. Virtue cannot be forced: it can be given substance only by following the heart-mind, behaving with integrity, and practising right action.

Xunzi

Xun Kuang or Xun Qing (c. 310–219 BCE), better known as Master Xun or Xunzi, was a generation younger than Mencius. Living at the end of the horrendously violent Warring States period, he likely witnessed the bloody conflict that ended in the conquest of the last feudal states by the first Qin emperor (Qin Shi Huang). So perhaps it is not surprising that Xunzi did not agree with Mencius on the innate goodness of human beings: he believed that human nature was evil, and that "goodness was the result of conscious activity" (Watson 1963: 157). Nevertheless, he did share the core Confucian beliefs in the possibility of sagehood and the value of culture and learning.

Xunzi believed that education and ritual were essential to the maintenance of the hierarchy required for a society to function in an orderly fashion. But he was not blind to the misuse and corruption of Confucian values. Like Mencius, who followed Confucius in criticizing the "village worthy" as someone who performed all the right actions but was insincere, Xunzi spoke out against "rotten Confucians" and people who "stole a reputation for virtue."

The collection known as the *Xunzi* was compiled and edited more than a century after Xunzi's time, during the Han dynasty. Its form marks a major departure from the recorded conversations of the *Analects* and *Mencius*: it consists mainly of essays in which Xunzi reflects on topics such as the original nature of human beings, learning, self-cultivation, government, and military affairs. The first chapter, "Encouraging Learning," underlines the necessity of effort to achieve moral progress:

> Learning should never cease. Blue comes from the indigo plant but is bluer than the plant itself. Ice is made of water but is colder than water ever is. A piece of wood as straight as a plumb line may be bent into a circle as true as any drawn with a compass and, even after the wood has dried, it will not straighten out again (Watson 1963: 15).

Why do human beings need to be "straightened out"? Because they are bent and warped with innate desires. Xunzi believed that these "evil" impulses would spark feelings of envy and hate if they were not curbed, as competition for scarce resources would lead to chaos. The guidance of sages and observance of ritual principles are necessary for transformation, for only then can people cultivate courtesy and humility. Xunzi's belief in the efficacy of rituals and education marked a further turn towards humanism.

In his chapter "A Discussion of Heaven," Xunzi continues Confucius' effort to humanize the Zhou tradition, rejecting the supernatural in favour of the rational and natural. He sees Heaven, Earth, and humanity as forming a trinity in which each component has its own role. As human beings, even sages do not seek to understand Heaven, let alone to take over its "godlike" role. Rather, humans should focus on the activities necessary for humans to live well and prosper. The noble person thus cherishes the power given to him by Heaven, but does not try to usurp its power.

Even though Xunzi understood the world to operate without supernatural intervention, he supported the performance of traditional rituals addressed to Heaven because he believed that they had been perfected by the ancient kings. Only a sage can fully understand the rites, he said; but the noble person finds comfort in performing them as a part of human culture, while the common person accepts them as a reflection of the reality of the spirit world. Xunzi took ritual and music out of the realm of magic by interpreting their functions in practical terms. Thus the purpose of teaching the rites (*li jiao*, another name for Confucianism) is to cultivate virtues such as courtesy and humility, which discourage aggression and promote harmony. Similarly, even if the performance of rituals cannot "satisfy fully the desires of the mouth and the stomach, the ears and the eyes," it can still produce satisfaction by "teach[ing] people to moderate their likes and dislikes and return to the proper human Way [*rendao*]" (de Bary and Bloom 1999: 344).

Daoism

Origins

Not everyone agreed with or believed in the Confucian way. Daoists developed a counterpoint and complement to the focus on social hierarchy, political involvement, emotional and moral discipline, and ritual regimentation. They did not seek to destroy, displace, or overturn Confucianism. Rather, Confucius was included in an anecdote in the book *Zhuangzi* (named after its putative author), and Daoism sought to include Confucian teachings while pointing out their limitations.

Historically, Daoism was understood to have two branches, philosophical and religious. Daoist philosophy traced its origins to the third and fourth centuries BCE, but Daoist religion was thought to have emerged only in the second century CE, with the formation of two millenarian groups (the Celestial Masters and Yellow Kerchiefs). Recent research however shows that philosophers at the Jixia Academy in the northeastern state of Qi, in present day Shandong, were already discussing ideas related to both philosophical and religious Daoism as early as the Warring States period, in the fourth century BCE.

© Michael Saso

Daoist nuns from the Quanzhen (Complete Truth) sect perform daily rituals on Wudang Mountain. The three head officiates wear the *lianhua guan* (lotus crown) and robes embroidered with trigrams. The yellow banners in the background mark the space as sacred and contain writing that resembles Chinese characters but is "heavenly," not of the human realm.

The literature of that time does not use the term "Daoist." However, it does refer to a Huang–Lao school, named for the mythical "Yellow Emperor" (Huangdi), and the legendary, historically dubious philosopher Laozi. Huang–Lao teachings correspond roughly to what we now consider philosophical Daoism; its teachings took shape around the early fourth century, when King Xuan of Qi offered sinecures—official appointments—at the Jixia Academy to scholars from various states, north and south, in the hope that they would discuss the problems of the day and find solutions to them.

Among those scholars were Mencius, Xunzi, the Naturalist Zou Yan of the **Yin-yang Five Phases** (*Wuxing* or five elements) school, and a student of the Huang–Lao teachings named Huan Yuan.

Philosophical Daoism

Philosophical Daoism is a term used to refer to an early prototypical Daoism concerned with ideas such as the nature of virtue, cultivation of the heart-mind, and attainment of good governance. Its early history has conventionally been associated with two main sources: the **Daodejing** (*Classic of the Way and Power*), a multi-layered, multi-authored verse text that is traditionally attributed to Laozi or the "old master"; and the **Zhuangzi**, which is named for the thinker whose ideas it purports to represent and is characterized by frequent use of humorous anecdotes. In fact, both works are collections of disparate texts written at different times by different authors.

This conventional view is changing. At least three new sources have proved helpful in reconstructing the early development of philosophical Daoism. Two of them are found in the *Guanzi*, a collection of writings traditionally attributed to a very early (seventh century BCE) figure named Guan Zhong; and the third is a bundle of silk manuscripts discovered in 1973.

Development Towards Religious Expression

Religious Daoism is widely associated with colourful rituals; belief in deities, ghosts, and spirits; meditation in search of mystical union with the Dao; and the ingestion of drugs in pursuit of immortality or transcendence. Thus it may appear to be diametrically opposed to philosophical Daoism. Yet the two streams do share a number of fundamental elements: the practice of self-discipline, the quest for transcendence of the ordinary self, the ideal of non-action (**wuwei**), and the assumption that religion and politics are embedded in one another.

What makes it difficult to recognize these common elements is the fact that religious Daoism also incorporates two traditions that are clearly not philosophical: a southern tradition of shamanism and a northern tradition known as the "way of recipes, methods, and immortality" (*fangxian dao*). Quite unlike the (northern) divinatory shamanism of the Shang and Zhou eras, this southern shamanism was distinctly non-philosophical and resolutely religious. Its character can be seen in a collection of texts called *Songs of the South* or *Songs of Qu* (*Quchi*), which features lavish descriptions of gods and goddesses, "serpentine cloud banners," "soaring phoenixes," and fabulous unions between humans and gods. The northern "way of recipes, methods, and immortality," for its part, centred on a quest for an elixir of everlasting life conducted by such "masters

Focus

The *Guanzi*

The *Guanzi* originated in the fourth century and took its current form in the first century BCE. It was categorized as Daoist during the Han, but later reclassified as Legalist and therefore neglected by students of Daoism. Recent research has found that two of its sections, both dealing with mental discipline, are directly relevant to the ideas in the two classical Daoist texts.

The first, *Techniques of the Mind I* (*Xinshu, Shang*), is written in verse but includes prose commentaries and addresses the broader concerns of government as well as methods of self-cultivation. The second, *Inward Training* (*Nei-yeh*), focuses exclusively on spiritual cultivation; it is written in verse and clearly bridges the streams of philosophical and religious Daoism.

The *Huang–Lao Silk Manuscripts* (*Huang–Lao boshu*) is the third new source for the study of classical Daoism. It is a bundle of silk manuscripts discovered around Changsha in Hunan province in 1973 and contains the teachings of the Huang–Lao group in both verse and prose. Included in the discovery were illustrations of "guiding and stretching" (**daoyin**), exercises similar to modern-day **taiji** (the sequence of slow-motion movements known in the West as Tai Chi).

of technical methods" as magicians, doctors, diviners, geomancers, astrologers, and exorcists. The integration of these very different traditions only adds to the difficulty of understanding the early history of what came to be called religious Daoism.

Different Streams of Daoism

The conjunction of the Daoist philosophical texts with the southern shamanistic tradition and the northern tradition of the masters of recipes and methods leading to immortality produced not just two but several distinctive streams in early Daoism. Three elements recur in the classical texts: the concept of the Dao as the One and the primary force in the universe; the need for inner discipline to empty the heart-mind of distractions in order to reach the

deep tranquillity necessary to experience unity with the One; and, finally, the use of the first two elements to achieve benevolent government.

In light of these elements, it has been suggested that the concerns of the classical texts can be classified in three groups: Individualist, Primitivist, and Syncretist. The Individualist stream is mystical, concerned mainly with inner cultivation and the experience of union with the cosmos, and is basic to all six of the classical texts. To this the second stream adds an appeal for a simple agrarian way of life; this Primitivist stream can be seen in the *Laozi* as well as in several chapters of the *Zhuangzi* (8–10 and the first part of 11). The third and last stream combines teachings of Laozi and Zhuangzi with those of other schools and is found in the later chapters of the *Zhuangzi*, *Techniques of the Mind I*,

© Imaginechina/Corbis

The Dragon Boat Festival (*Duanwujie*), held on the fifth day of the fifth month of the lunar calendar, commemorates the loyal Chu minister Qu Yuan (c. 340–278 BCE), who drowned himself after he was unjustly banished. The eating of sticky rice dumplings (*zongzi*) and boat racing recall the efforts that were made to keep fish from eating Qu's body.

and the *Huang–Lao* manuscripts. This Syncretist stream appears to have developed some time after the first two, likely during the early Han.

The exact chronology of the various writings is not known, but the *Daodejing* and *Inward Training* are generally considered to be the earliest. Anecdotes in the *Zhuangzi* that describe encounters between Confucius and Laozi would make the two men contemporaries, but the historical authenticity of the stories is questionable. The first seven chapters of the *Zhuangzi*, if they were in fact composed by Zhuang Zhou, also known as Master Zhuang (Zhuangzi, 369?–286? BCE) are also of some antiquity.

Finally, the *Songs of the South* are traditionally attributed in part to Qu Yuan, the famously righteous minister remembered in the Dragon Boat Festival on the fifth day of the fifth lunar month; but most of them were probably written about a century after his death in 278 BCE. Thus the poems are likely of a slightly later period than the other texts. Brief descriptions of the six sources follow.

Inward Training *in Daoist and Confucian Contexts*

Inward Training, a short text, is embedded in the recently discovered *Guanzi*. It is important for our study because it serves as a bridge between philosophical and religious Daoism and provides clear examples of the cultural beliefs and practices from the Zhou era that Confucians and Daoists shared.

Inward Training deals with the cultivation of the heart-mind. The early Daoists focused on a type of meditation known as "holding fast to the One." Thought to help the practitioner realize the Dao, this technique is mentioned in the *Daodejing*, *Zhuangzi*, *Techniques of the Mind I*, and *Huang–Lao* sources. Other themes from *Inward Training*, however—notably the concepts of the vital essence (*jing*), vital energy or breath (*qi*), and the numinous or the spirit (*shen*)—are uncommon in the philosophical texts. Yet they became core features of religious Daoism, in which the integration of these three elements through meditation and dietary practices was believed to confer longevity and even physical immortality or spiritual transcendence.

Inward Training recalls early Confucianism when it suggests that the virtue of an exemplary person has a kind of magical, mystical efficacy. The emperor in particular was believed to be capable of "righting" conditions in the empire without expending any vital energy, simply by virtue of his own attainment and embodiment of harmony. Section 9 uses the same terms that the Confucians do to describe the noble or exemplary person (*junzi*) who cultivates this power-virtue (*de*):

> Only exemplary persons who hold fast to the One are able to do this.
> Hold fast to the One; do not lose it,
> And you will be able to master the myriad things.
> Exemplary persons act upon things,
> And are not acted upon by them,
> Because they grasp the guiding principle of the One (Roth 1999, 62).

Like the ideal Confucian ruler, the Daoist one possesses a virtue-power that is capable of influencing lesser persons just as the wind causes the grass to bend.

Whereas Laozi and Zhuangzi suggest some antipathy towards Confucians, *Inward Training* does not. In fact, it hints at a shared desire for tranquillity and recovery of the individual's original or Heavenly nature. Later forms of Daoism, however, did include beliefs and practices that some later Confucians found abhorrent, including the use of esoteric sexual practices in religious ritual, the ingestion of cinnabar (a poisonous substance) to attain immortality, and its emphasis on escaping or transcending the world rather than serving it.

Laozi and the **Daodejing**

If the apparent incongruity of such practices seems puzzling, it may be helpful to remember the famous first line of the *Daodejing*: "The way that can be spoken of / Is not the constant way" (Lau 1963: 57). The dynamism and fluidity implied by this holy ineffability are characteristic of Daoism.

Unlike the authors (or editors) of *Inward Training*, Laozi takes a dim view of Confucian rites: "The rites are the wearing thin of loyalty and good faith / And the beginning of disorder" (Lau 1963: 99). Yet, like the Confucians, he wants to ensure that "the offering of sacrifice by descendants will never come to an end" (ibid., 115). The sage of the *Daodejing* shares with Confucius the ideal of discipline: the only difference is that he seeks to achieve it not through human-created rites but through the all-embracing cosmic Way.

The term *de* in the *Daodejing* refers to virtue-power, but this is no ordinary virtue. It embodies the mystic inner power attained through integrity and alignment with the unseen world, the power that allows a sage ruler to infuse his realm with the harmony he has achieved by "doing nothing," *wuwei*. (It's important not to take this phrase literally: in this context, "doing nothing" refers to a state of mind or being in which one can be so permeated by the Way that one acts in concert with it, free of self, intention, or ulterior motives.)

The Daoist sage models himself on the Dao, inviting it to dwell in him by making himself as empty as the hub of a wheel, the hollow of a cup, or the space in a room. Soft as the water that flows over and around rocks yet in time wears them down, and that occupies ravines and valleys, benefiting all things, he is spare in his desires. Overturning convention, he knows the honoured male but keeps to the traditionally subservient and humble female. He knows the symbolic goodness of white but keeps to the "hoodwinking," unenlightened black (ibid., 127). He embraces the One and remains an uncarved block, transcending dichotomies. He refuses to be sculpted with conventional virtues—though Laozi makes it clear that he also teaches conventional values:

What others teach I also teach.
"The violent will not come to a natural end."
I shall take this as my precept
(Lau 1963: 103).

Yet even as the *Daodejing* counsels against violence—just as the Confucian sages do—it criticizes as "false adornments" the Confucian concepts of the wise sage and righteous benevolence. It also finds fault with profit, ingenuity, and learning, declaring that they should be abolished. Simplicity, the Daoist sage suggests, should replace false values:

These three [the Confucian sage, benevolence, and ingenuity], being false adornments, are not enough
And the people must have something to which they can attach themselves:
Exhibit the unadorned and embrace the uncarved block,
Have little thought of self and as few desires as possible (Lau 1963: 75).

Unlike the Confucian who deals mainly with the good and the virtuous, the Daoist sage "abandons no one" (ibid., 84). He is said to have three treasures: compassion, frugality, and "not daring to take the lead in the empire" (ibid., 129). He is "drowsy," "muddled," "foolish," and "uncouth" (ibid., 77). He is inconspicuous and does not consider his own way to be the right one; he does not brag, boast, or contend with others (ibid., 79). He is self-effacing and "avoids excess, extravagance, and arrogance" (ibid., 87). Such a sage is capable of surviving even the tumult of the Warring States.

Zhuangzi

The current working copy of the *Zhuangzi* comes from an edition by Guo Xiang (d. c. 312 CE). Unlike the sage of the *Laozi*, the sage of the *Zhuangzi* shuns politics. Even more strikingly, in the *Zhuangzi* great sages, mythical rulers, and deities are not the only ones endowed with wisdom: a humble cook may also be wise. The fanciful and the historical exist alongside each other like black and white, or female and male. This aspiration to transcend dichotomies is at the core of Zhuangzi's teachings:

Everything has its "that," everything has its "this." From the point of view of "that" you cannot see it, but through understanding you can know it. . . . [The sage] illuminates all in the light of Heaven. He too recognizes a "this," but a "this" which is also "that," a "that" which is also "this." His "that" has both a right and a wrong in it; his "this" too has both a right and a wrong in it (Watson 1968: 39).

The sage allows his mind to wander in simplicity, blending with the vastness that is the Way. He follows things as they are and makes no room for personal views. In contrast to Laozi's "non-action," Zhuangzi describes a state of "self-so-ness" or spontaneity (**ziran**). Although the principle is not inconsistent with the Confucians' ideal of following the pattern in nature, it is expressed in remarkably different terms. The story of Cook Ding illustrates the Daoist position. When the prince asks the cook for advice on governing his empire, Ding counsels him to take the same approach to governance that he would take to carving an ox. Instead of hacking at the carcass, he would look for the hollows in the joints: in the same way, the ruler should not govern on the basis of preconceived rules and principles, but should examine the empire to determine where the hollows are.

The condition in which it is possible for a person to make a clear assessment, whether of an ox or an empire, is that of Oneness through emptiness (*xu*). In *Inward Training* this emptiness is achieved through physical discipline, while Zhuangzi adds an unexpected non-sectarian, perhaps cheeky, twist, setting Confucius up with his favourite disciple, Yan Hui. When the latter asks about the meaning of fasting, Confucius replies:

> Make your will one! Don't listen with your ears, listen with your mind. No, don't listen with your mind, but listen with your spirit. Listening stops with the ears, the mind stops with recognition, but spirit is empty and waits on all things. The Way gathers in emptiness alone. Emptiness is the fasting of the mind (ibid., 57–8).

In his attention to the spirit, the sage in the *Zhuangzi* takes an approach that is more reminiscent of *Inward Training* than of the practically focused Confucius and Laozi. This other-worldly orientation is confirmed in the image of the Holy Man who lives on Gushe Mountain, far away from human society. This is the sage as spiritual and cosmic healer. The themes of health, long life, and immortality are introduced in the *Zhuangzi* through reference to the mythical Yellow Emperor, who

Document

From the *Zhuangzi*

One chapter attributed to Zhuangzi is entitled "Fit for Emperors and Kings." It concludes with a little story about the damage that can be done by the imposition of sameness and conformity, even with the best intentions.

The emperor of the South Sea was called Shu [Brief], the emperor of the North Sea was called Hu [Sudden], and the emperor of the central region was called Hun-tun [Chaos]. Shu and Hu from time to time came together for a meeting in the territory of Hun-tun, and Hun-tun treated them very generously. Shu and Hu discussed how they could repay his kindness. "All men," they said, "have seven openings so they can see, hear, eat, and breathe. But Hun-tun alone doesn't have any. Let's try boring him some!"

Every day they bored another hole, and on the seventh day Hun-tun died (Watson 1968: 97).

does not appear in either *Inward Training* or the *Daodejing*. This sage-emperor is the putative author of the medical text *Inner Canon of the Yellow Emperor* (*Huangdi neijing*).

The Huang–Lao Silk Manuscripts, Techniques of the Mind I, *and* Songs of the South

The last three textual sources of early Daoism are the *Huang–Lao Silk Manuscripts, Techniques of the Mind I,* and *Songs of the South.* They were likely compiled through the late Zhou, Qin, and early Han periods. The first two are syncretic and similar to the *Daodejing* and *Zhuangzi,* but the *Songs* are distinctive in their literary quality and their descriptions of love between deities and humans.

The *Huang–Lao Silk Manuscripts* were sealed in a tomb in 168 BCE. The ideas they record are drawn from a variety of schools, but their underlying theme is said to be Laozi's ideal of the tranquil sage king who governs through non-action. The Huang–Lao scholars believed in the triad of Heaven, Earth, and humanity. These prototypical Daoists went further than the Confucians in discerning correspondences between Heaven, Earth, and human beings; they imagined the macrocosm of the universe reflected not only in the microcosm of human society but also in the individual human body. They were active at court during the early Han, but disappeared after Emperor Wu made Confucianism the state religion in the late second century BCE. Until these manuscripts were excavated in 1973, none of the writings they contain were known.

Like the Huang–Lao teachings, *Techniques of the Mind I* reflects the Daoist concerns outlined in *Inward Training,* the *Daodejing,* and the *Zhuangzi.* Echoing the *Daodejing,* it seeks to explain how self-cultivation—specifically, the practice of restraining desire and emptying the mind—can help an enlightened ruler attain the tranquillity necessary to respond harmoniously to any situation in its "self-so-ness." The text has two parts: one written in verse and tentatively dated to the mid-200s BCE and the other a line-by-line prose commentary dated to 180 BCE.

Women and the Feminine in the Classical Texts

Neither *Inward Training* nor the *Daodejing* discussed women. The latter talks abstractly about the "mother" and the "spirit of the valley," which it describes as both the "root of heaven and earth" and the "mysterious female" that never dies (Lau 1963: 62). Nor does Zhuangzi concern himself much with women: wives are mentioned only as companions in life who are grieved in death. There was an acceptance of the conventional gender roles. The Daoist Liezi is described as taking over the domestic realm of the feminine after he attains mature spiritual understanding:

> He went home and for three years did not go out. He replaced his wife at the stove, fed the pigs as though he were feeding people, and showed no preferences in the things he did. He got rid of the carving and polishing and returned to plainness, letting his body stand alone like a clod. In the midst of entanglement he remained sealed, and in this oneness he ended his life (Watson 1968: 97).

This association of sacred oneness with animals and the feminine is not surprising. Nor is Zhuangzi's implied criticism of Xunzi's Confucian-style "carving and polishing," given the Daoist preference for non-action and the natural. The theme of men seeking union with the feminine, and women with the masculine, becomes prominent in the poems of the south. Images of female power and divinity in themselves—without reference to men—appear only in the chapter entitled "The Great and Venerable Teacher," which mentions a teacher called the Woman Crookback and a Queen Mother of the West who heads the pantheon of goddesses. These are mythical characters, however: unlike the Confucian classics, the *Zhuangzi* does not celebrate any historical woman.

Mohism

Mohism was the third most influential religious system after Confucianism and Daoism in the pre-Han period before the introduction of Buddhism. Master Mo (Mozi, 470–391 BCE) coexisted with Confucians and Daoists, and his teachings shared similar aims and concerns with them, but Mohist ideas were also markedly different. Mozi taught an ungraded, undifferentiated love, a love of all without distinction (*jianai*). He believed that Heaven willed people to love one another, and that those who failed to do so would be punished. Mozi believed that the ultimate objective of government was to provide food, shelter, and security for all; and that members of a society should work to save each other from harm and deprivation. Why the school disappeared after the Han is not clear.

One Chinese scholar tells us that many Mohists were metallurgists by trade and had experience with chemical reactions in minerals. He suggested that Mohists brought their knowledge of the nature of various minerals, particularly gold and cinnabar, into the production of drugs that were consumed to achieve immortality. In this way, they and their knowledge were absorbed into groups that were interested in outer alchemy; these were in turn absorbed into the complex of Daoism and became a part of Daoist outer alchemy, which involved the ingestion of mineral "medicines" in order to achieve physical immortality.

⊛ Han Dynasty (202 BCE–220 CE)

State Confucianism, Huang–Lao and Religious Daoism, and the Introduction of Buddhism

Early Chinese religious beliefs and practices faded or were recontextualized in new ideas, rituals, and structures. Ancient shamanic traditions endured, and interest in the *Yijing* and divination persisted. While Confucianism eclipsed Huang–Lao Daoism

and the masters of the methods at court, Daoism re-emerged in the form of religious anti-Han rebel groups like the Yellow Kerchiefs and Celestial Masters. It was into this varied religious landscape that Buddhism was introduced.

Popular Beliefs and Practices Assimilated

The worship of deities continued into the Han. During a drought at the end of the Early or Western Han, it was the Queen Mother of the West (Xiwangmu) that ordinary folk appealed to. They travelled with branches or stalks of hemp, believing that these talismans of the Queen Mother would protect them. By the Latter Han, she had become the head deity of a paradise in the far west that was believed to connect Heaven and Earth, and where peaches of immortality grew; she also became the goddess who bestowed immortality and a protector-deity who granted wealth and children, a precursor to Guanyin (Avalokitesvara, or the One who Sees and Hears All), the Buddhist *pusa* (*bodhisattva* or enlightened being). Devotees would gather to worship and summon the Queen Mother with songs, dances, and the use of talismans (Lewis 2009: 198).

Political Daoism

The influence of the Huang–Lao thinkers during the early Han can be seen in the fact that the King of Huainan, Liu An, sponsored a collection of Huang–Lao writings called the *Masters of Huainan* (*Huainanzi*), a copy of which he presented to the Emperor Wu (his nephew) in 139 BCE. A comprehensive guide to just governance consisting of 21 essays on topics ranging from cosmology and astrology to inner cultivation and political thought, it emphasizes the ruler's need to still his passions and rid himself of prejudice so that he can respond appropriately to all situations.

The court historian Sima Tan (d. 110 BCE) was also a follower of the Huang–Lao school. The account of Daoism in his discourse "On the Six Lineages of Thought" corresponds closely to the contents of the *Huainanzi*, and in it he describes the Daoists approvingly as "permit[ting] the numinous essence within people to be concentrated and

© Pierre Colombel/Corbis

This sixth-century mural from the Mogao Caves (or Grottoes) at Dunhuang, in western China, shows four divinities, including, at left, the Queen Mother of the West—the pre-eminent female immortal in Daoism. In spite of her presence, Mogao is renowned as a Buddhist site, one of three extraordinary Buddhist cave-temple systems in north central and western China; the others are Yungang and Longmen. Beginning in 366 CE, more than 400 grottoes were carved out of the rock at Mogao alone and filled with Buddhist paintings, sculptures, and manuscripts. Among the subjects they depict are Amituofo in his western Pure Land, the bodhisattvas who help the suffering, and celestial beings who fly through the air.

unified," "mov[ing] in unison with the Formless and provid[ing] adequately for all living things" (H. Roth 1999 and S. Queen in de Bary and Bloom 1999: 279). By contrast, he describes the Confucians (who by that time were in the ascendant) as "erudite yet lack[ing] the essentials. They labour much yet achieve little. This is why their doctrines are difficult to follow completely" (ibid.). In short, Sima Tan distanced himself from the purposeful "right" action of the Confucians and made clear his preference for the Daoists:

> The essentials of the Great Way are simply a matter of discarding strength and avarice

and casting aside perception and intellect. One relinquishes these and relies on the techniques [of self-cultivation]. When the numen (*shen*, "spirit") is used excessively it becomes depleted; when the physical form labours excessively it becomes worn out. It is unheard of for one whose physical form and numen are agitated and disturbed to hope to attain the longevity of Heaven and Earth (H. Roth and S. Queen in de Bary and Bloom 1999: 279–80).

The concern for health and longevity in this account is typical of Daoism. And while Confucians would agree on the importance of renouncing avarice, they would argue in favour of strength (especially for men), perception, and intellect. Moreover, the Confucians focus on ritual performance in the social and political realms while the Daoists focus on the fasting of the mind, clearly reflecting their contrasting priorities.

Nevertheless, underlying both traditions is a fundamental emphasis on self-cultivation for the sake of harmony in the universe. Both Confucians and Daoists seek to control the heart-mind, especially the passions, in order to attain the tranquillity necessary to achieve union with the Way. Both believe that oneness with the Dao and, consequently, with Heaven and Earth allows us to transcend our ordinary selves in order that we may serve others.

The Introduction of Buddhism

Buddhism, like Daoism, emphasizes the importance of meditation, breath control, and abstinence from certain foods. Like both indigenous religions,

it values life, focuses on purity of the heart-mind and mastery of the passions. But its trajectory and methods tend to be more extreme. For example, the *Sutra in Forty-two Sections* stresses the undesirable effects of lust and the hindrance that it poses for a man's path toward enlightenment. The Buddha advises his monks this way: "You must be careful and not look at women. If you meet them, act as if you do not see them. Be careful not to talk to them. If they should speak to you, then be mindful and upright." During the Han dynasty, the features that Buddhism appeared to share with Confucianism and Daoism helped to mask its more fundamental differences. Sometimes Daoist terms and ideas were used to convey Buddhism to potential converts.

Confucianism

The Birth of Political State Confucianism

The victory of the Qin brought an end to the carnage and unified the Warring States. To minimize

Document

From the *Sutra in Forty-two Sections*

The Sutra in Forty-two Sections *is mentioned in the* Mouzi lihuo lun *(Master Mou's Disposing of Errors), a defence of Buddhism purportedly written by a Chinese convert at the end of the second century. But it was most likely composed in the fifth or sixth century, when Buddhism was at the height of its popularity and influence. Mouzi records the story of Emperor Ming, who dreams of a golden man, interpreted as the Buddha, and sends envoys to search for him. They arrive in Scythia, a Euroasian kingdom to the north of the Black and Caspian Seas, then copy and bring back to China the* Sutra in Forty-two Sections. *The following excerpts address the deleterious effects of passion, especially lust.*

Those who are addicted to the passions are like the torchbearers running against the wind; their hands are sure to be burned.

From the passions arises worry and from worry arises fear. Away with the passions, and no fear, no worry.

People cleave to their worldly possessions and selfish passions so blindly as to sacrifice their own lives for them. They are like a child who tries to eat a little honey smeared on the edge of a knife.

The Lord of Heaven offered a beautiful maiden to the Buddha, desiring to test the Buddha's intentions and teachings. The Buddha replied, "You are but a leather bag filled with filth, why do you come?" (quoted in Chen 1964: 34–5)

dissent, however, the first emperor ordered the destruction of almost all the scholarly books that might encourage deep reflection on social and political values, among them the Confucian classics. Although one copy of each work was preserved in the imperial library, those copies were destroyed in a fire when the capital was sacked. Thus when the Han dynasty (202 BCE–220 CE) replaced the short-lived Qin, a great many works had to be reconstructed. The *Changes* and books on practical subjects like agriculture, medicine, and forestry were spared, however.

The political and intellectual changes that took place during the Han would continue to shape imperial ideology as well as religious beliefs and practices for the next 2,000 years. To the four virtues identified by Mencius—humaneness, right action, ritual appropriateness, and wisdom—was added a fifth: trustworthiness. Also central to Han ideology were the notions that Heaven, Earth, and humankind form a trinity; and that the celestial and terrestrial powers respond to human entreaty. Confucian thinkers reflected the influence both of Xunzi and of a chapter in the *Rites* called "Centrality and Equilibrium" (*Zhongyong*; also translated as "Centrality and Harmony" or "The Doctrine of the Mean"): they believed that humans who were sincere in their efforts to bring about peace and harmony could share in the creative, transformative powers of Heaven and Earth.

Echoing Mencius and Xunzi, Han Confucians identified economic welfare as the basis of morality. The government, in particular the emperor, was obliged to provide both the physical sustenance and the moral education necessary for people to lead secure and happy lives. Following Xunzi, Han Confucians also promoted moral education through ritual, music, and literature.

Both a Confucian canon (in the form of the Five Classics) and political or state Confucianism were established during the Han. Philosophers seeking a holistic account of the universe and humankind's place in it tried to syncretize the Confucian tradition with other philosophies. The result was a Confucianism that blended ideas from traditional texts with those of thinkers such as the masters of technical methods, who sought to manipulate the cosmos; and the Naturalists, who developed the notions of *qi* and yin-yang–five phases. It was also during the Han that a number of influential non-canonical texts were written or compiled and edited, among them the *Biographies of Exemplary (or Virtuous) Women* (*Lienu zhuan*), *Admonitions (or Lessons) for Women* (*Nu jie*), and the *Classic of Filiality* (*Xiaojing*). *Exemplary Women* and *Admonitions* in particular defined what was expected of women and formed the foundation of a specifically female Confucian tradition.

The Compilation of the Five Classics

Han Confucians believed that Confucius himself had transmitted the Zhou tradition through the canonical texts, and that he had had a hand in the selection, compilation, and editing of all five Classics. However, later scholars have shown that a good portion of their content originated after Confucius' time.

The first classic, the *Changes*, which had been compiled and arranged in its current form over the course of the Zhou dynasty, assumed particular importance during the Han. It is divided into two parts: a series of short passages interpreting the 64 hexagrams, and ten appendices or "wings" that elaborate on those interpretations. The ten wings were traditionally attributed to Confucius.

Confucius is also said to have edited or written a short introduction to each section of the second classic, the *Documents*. Although some of the content is now thought to date from as late as the fourth century CE, this volume has historically been considered an accurate account of China's ancient rulers, from the sage kings to the early Zhou.

The third classic, the *Odes*, consists of roughly three hundred poems, mostly from the early Zhou, that Confucius is believed to have chosen and edited. They include songs from both ordinary people and the aristocracy and were often interpreted politically as expressions of popular sentiment—praising virtuous rulers and criticizing bad ones.

The fourth classic, the *Rites*, consists of three separate texts: *Rites of Etiquette and Ceremonials*

(*Yili*) for minor officials, *Rites* (or *Institutions*) *of Zhou* (*Zhou li* or *Zhou guan*), and the *Records* or *Book of Rites* (*Liji*), which explores the principles behind particular rites. The contents likely date from the mid- to late Zhou and the early Han and took their current form over time. Confucius is credited with the compilation and editing of some of these ritual texts, whose contents range from minutely detailed advice on how to live daily life to broad philosophical discussions of the meaning of state rituals and ceremonies.

The fifth and last classic, the *Spring and Autumn Annals*, is a terse chronicle of events in Confucius' native state of Lu from 722 to 481 BCE. Confucius is said to have compiled it from archival materials in order to express his judgments of past events. It was therefore used as a guide to moral laws and principles in the management of human affairs.

Map 6.1 Indigenous Chinese Religions

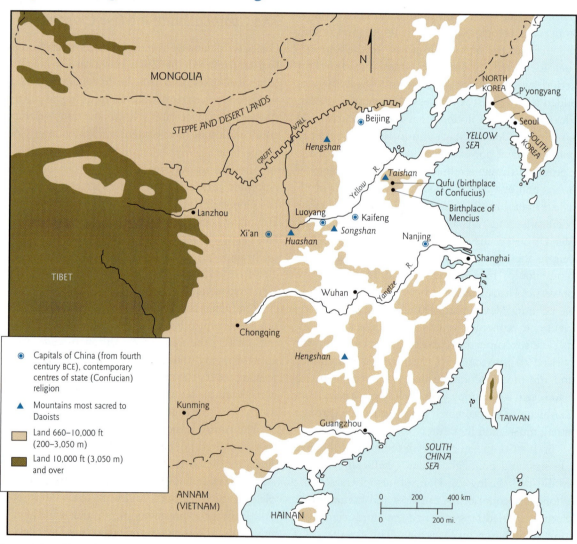

Source: Adapted from al Faruqi and Sopher 1974: 111.

Because the historical text is so brief, it is usually read with the help of commentaries.

The text-focused Confucians were the hardest hit by the Qin emperor's book burning. And it was the Confucians of the second and third centuries BCE who, more than any other group, took up the enormous task of retrieving and reassembling the lost texts. They compiled, edited, and annotated dictionaries and great works of history belonging to other schools in addition to their own.

Dong Zhongshu

The most influential Confucian at the early Han court was **Dong Zhongshu** (195?–105? BCE), who was largely responsible for persuading Emperor Wu to adopt Confucianism as state orthodoxy. Like many during the Han, Dong promoted a "natural model" of the way the world works, based on the idea of correlation between the macrocosm of Heaven and Earth and the microcosm of the human body.

Dong set out to integrate Confucian thought with the supernatural thinking of court diviners, the correlative thinking of the Huang–Lao movement (see the section on Daoism), and the yin-yang thinking of the Naturalist school. Tracing the Confucian interest in human nature and emotion through Mencius and Xunzi, Dong took ideas from both, then combined them with the Naturalist concept of vital force (*qi*) operating through the dynamics of yin and yang.

At the close of the Han, two rationalist scholars named Yang Xiong and Wang Chong deconstructed Dong's system of correlation, separating classical Confucian teachings from the yin-yang–five phases school, and cleared away some of his more extravagant accretions.

The Classic of Filiality

A version of the five relationships known as the three bonds was a central part of Han Confucianism; they concentrated on the distinction between the senior and junior roles encapsulated in emperor–minister, parent–child and husband–wife. The importance of the minister's role was especially clear in the *Classic of Filiality* (*Xiaojing*). According to tradition, this influential text comes from the school traced to Confucius' disciple Zengzi. By the Latter Han, *Filiality* and *Analects* were added to the list of Classics. Presented in the form of a conversation (probably apocryphal) between Zengzi and Confucius, the *Classic of Filiality* broadens the definition of filial devotion outlined in the *Rites*; it extends the notion of continuity between the human and spirit worlds through the veneration of ancestors and connects filial piety to the idea of the triad formed by Heaven, Earth, and human beings. Following the *Rites*, the work clearly establishes filiality as the foundation of all virtues and the basis of public morality:

> The Master [Confucius] said, "Loving one's parents, one dare not hate others. Revering one's parents, one dare not be contemptuous of others. When his love and reverence are perfected in service to parents, [the ruler's] moral influence is shed on all the people and his good example shines in all directions. . . ."
>
> The Master said, "Filiality is the ordering principle of Heaven, the rightness of the Earth, and the norm of human conduct. This ordering of Heaven and Earth is what people should follow; illumined by the brightness of Heaven and benefited by the resources of the Earth, all-under-Heaven (that is, the whole world) are thus harmonized. . . . (W.T. de Bary in de Bary and Bloom 1999: 326–7)

Women

According to the *History of the Former Han Dynasty* (*Han shu*), Liu Xiang (79–8 BCE) wrote the *Biographies of Exemplary Women* because he believed that women had a critical, albeit indirect and informal, role to play in government. To Liu's mind, the emperor would necessarily reflect the influence of his closest private counsellors, beginning with the empress. Drawing on the *Odes* and *Documents*, Liu identified seven types of women, six of which had contributed to the peace and prosperity of their countries and the good reputation of their families, and one of which had brought about the downfall of dynasties (Raphals 1998: 19):

1. Maternal rectitude
2. Sage intelligence
3. Benevolent wisdom
4. Chaste and obedient
5. Chaste and righteous
6. Skill in argument
7. Vicious and depraved.

Under "Maternal Rectitude" he tells the famous story of Mengmu, the widowed mother of Mencius. She is said to have moved three times, finally settling next to a school in order to facilitate her son's studies. The focus on education is strong. On one occasion, when Mengmu asked how his day at school had gone and Mencius answered nonchalantly "As usual," she took a knife and destroyed the cloth she had been weaving. The purpose of this dramatic gesture was to teach him that a man who does not take learning seriously is like a woman who neglects her responsibility to provide for her family. Mencius' mother is said to have been a motivating force in his life.

Ban Zhao

Like a man's moral development, a woman's cultivation began at home, in the family. Self-cultivation was especially important for women because the Han Chinese believed that a fetus would be influenced by the mother's mood, demeanour, and actions, and that the cultivation of proper behaviour in a child should begin in the womb.

As children mature, according to the *Rites*, boys and girls should be separated: they should no longer sit on the same mat or eat together after reaching the age of seven. At the age of ten, boys were sent out to study with teachers and girls were discouraged

from leaving the house. While boys learnt the six arts (rites, music, archery, chariot racing, calligraphy, and mathematics), girls were taught the domestic skills and encouraged to develop the mental discipline and fortitude that they would need as providers of material comfort, emotional succour, and moral guidance for their families.

In addition to learning how to weave, sew, and prepare food, girls were taught etiquette—the conventions of social behaviour required for harmonious relations—and how to perform the rituals, including the sacrifices required to express familial harmony: that is, to serve elders while they are alive through the principle of filial piety; and to keep peace with the ancestors with the rites of remembrance. At the age of 15 a girl's hair was pinned up as a ceremonial rite of passage signalling that she was ready for marriage.

Ban Zhao (c. 48–112 CE) said that she wrote *Admonitions for Women* out of concern for her daughters, who had not had the benefit of systematic training in their roles either as wives or as daughters- and sisters-in-law in their husbands' families. Ban did not want her daughters' lack of good manners to bring shame to their ancestors, family, and clan.

Born into a leading scholarly family, Ban was said to have taken over the compilation of the *History of the Former Han* after the deaths of her father and brother. Well-educated, socially prominent, and politically influential, Ban Zhao was typical of aristocratic women in Han society. According to one later history, she worked in the imperial libraries and supervised the writing of treatises on astronomy and the chronological tables of nobles. Recognizing Ban's erudition, the emperor appointed her as tutor to the women at court, and she later served as an advisor to Empress Deng, who became regent in 106 CE and remained in power for 15 years. *Admonitions* is divided into seven chapters:

1. Humility
2. Husband and wife
3. Respect and caution

4. Womanly qualifications
5. Whole-hearted devotion
6. Implicit obedience
7. Harmony with younger brothers- and sisters-in-law.

Deferring to tradition, Ban describes three ritual customs performed at the birth of a girl and then explains the principles behind them. First, whereas a baby boy was placed on the bed, a girl was placed below it, to signify that she was lowly and weak and must humble herself before others; second, she was given potsherds (broken pieces of pottery) to play with to signify she must work hard; and third, her birth was announced to the ancestors to mark the importance of her future role in the veneration of ancestors.

Ban drew on the classical tradition, Mencius, and Dong Zhongshu and belongs firmly in the Confucian lineage. She believed that relationships are founded on the cosmic principles of yin and yang, and Heaven and Earth. Because yang is distinctive in its rigidity, a man was honoured for his strength; and because yin is characteristically yielding, a woman was considered beautiful for her gentleness. Over time, the name Ban Zhao became synonymous with womanly erudition. Some 400 years after the Han, she was included in a list of exemplary women venerated in state sacrifices. And more than a millennium after her death, *Admonitions* was included in a collection called the Four Books for Women.

Daoism

Differentiation during the Han

The presentation of the Daoist *Masters of Huainan* to Emperor Wu by his uncle Liu An indicates that the Huang–Lao school remained active in the early years of the dynasty. It disappeared from the court after the emperor made Confucianism the state religion, in the late second century BCE (in fact, the gift may have been intended to stave off the Confucian influence). Nevertheless, Daoist practice continued to develop outside the palace, among the common people.

Inner and Outer Alchemy

In the mid-second century, during the Eastern Han, the first text on inner alchemy was published. Traditionally ascribed to Wei Boyang, an alchemist from the south, *The Seal of the Unity of the Three, in Accordance with the Book of Changes* or simply *The Seal of the Unity of the Three* (*Zhouyi cantong qi* or *Cantong qi, Kinship of the Three, Akinness of the Three, Triplex Unity*) was highly influential. "Three" refers to the three major subjects discussed: cosmology from the *Book of Changes*, *wuwei* from Daoism, and alchemy. Wei fused the three elements into a single doctrine. Like Dong Zhongshu before him, Wei too used correlative cosmology, drawing on yin-yang and five phases to describe the cosmos in relation to the Dao, the relative to the Absolute, multiplicity to Oneness, and time to timelessness.

The *Unity of the Three* offers a theoretical framework for meditation and clearly defines the Daoist practice of inner alchemy. The classical texts taught that the three vital elements of essence, energy, and numinous spirit ought to be returned to an early wholeness that had been broken and scattered; first by worldly activity, and then by the disruptive perception of things as divided and separate from each other. Practitioners sought to return to the Dao by reversing these processes through meditation—as though they were sculptures "unsculpting" themselves to recover their original unity with the 10,000 things and become once again uncarved blocks.

In practice, devotees sought to move from form to essence, from essence to vitality or vital energy, from vitality to spirit, and from spirit to emptiness or the Void. This ultimate Void is formless but can also be visualized as the highest deity: the Great One, Supreme Unity, or Supreme Oneness (Taiyi). Classical texts suggest various ways of achieving (or maintaining) this original unity: by "holding fast to the One (*shouyi*)," "sitting and forgetting," visualizing the cosmos within one's body, and following the internal circulation of vital energy.

Belief in physical immortality was strong during the Han. It was thought that an embryo containing or representing the True Self would be formed over a long period of inward concentration. This True Self—also known as the Spirit Embryo, Holy Embryo, Golden Embryo, Golden Elixir, the True Person Cinnabar of the North, the Golden Pill, the Pearl—was said to be born when the spirit had been purified and become indistinguishable from vital energy and essence. There were also some who believed that immortality could be achieved through the ingestion of cinnabar.

The Celestial Masters and Yellow Kerchiefs

Over time, the Confucian underpinnings of the Han regime were challenged by a combination of political corruption, natural disaster, and military turbulence. The resulting economic and social turmoil provoked uprisings, some of which reflected significant Daoist influences. At the same time, the *Classic of the Great Peace* (*Taipingjing*) was circulating, prophesying the coming of a celestial master who would bring peace to a time of surging chaos.

The Great Peace likely influenced both millenarian movements: the Celestial Masters and the Yellow Kerchiefs (*Taiping Dao* or "Way of Taiping"). Founded in 142 CE, the Celestial Masters (*Tianshi*; later renamed Orthodox Unity) traced its origins to a deified Laozi who revealed to **Zhang Daoling** the teachings of Orthodox Unity, and gave him a covenant establishing a new relationship between the gods and humans. A central feature of this covenant was the abolition of traditional blood sacrifices. No longer would the celestial or inner gods (who lived within the human body) be influenced by animal offerings. Instead, they would come to operate as a kind of celestial bureaucracy, modelled after the governmental bureaucracy of the Han, to whom believers could present their appeals just as they did to state officials in ordinary life. The priests were expected to provide their services without monetary reward and relied on an annual donation of five bushels of rice from devotees.

Initiates of the Celestial Masters gained access to esoteric sacred texts. The *Daodejing* was used in liturgy; practices included chanting and meditation; and purity chambers were provided for the cultivation of the Spirit Embryo. Talismans drawn on paper and offered to the deities served as contracts and guaranteed protection to the faithful. The sect established a theocracy in the state of Shu (Sichuan) and eventually became the state religion of the Wei kingdom. The Wei later dispersed the Celestial Masters across northern China, unintentionally aiding the spread of Daoism.

The Yellow Kerchiefs movement, based in Shandong, was established by three brothers named Zhang with the express purpose of challenging the Han regime in the name of the Yellow Emperor. They wore yellow kerchiefs because, according to calculations based on the Naturalist yin-yang–five phases system, a new dynasty associated with the colour yellow and the element earth would overthrow the Han (associated with blue, green, and wood). Like the Celestial Masters, the Yellow Kerchiefs practised confession, repentance of sins, meditation, and chanting; they also believed in inherited guilt, passed on from ancestors to descendants. They attracted a massive following, but their success was short-lived. When the Yellow Kerchiefs rose in rebellion in the year 184 (the beginning of a new 60-year cycle in the Chinese calendar), they were crushed and the movement disappeared.

Buddhism

It was during the Han that Eurasian merchants and monks from Parthia, Scythia, Sogdiana, and Bactria (in modern day Iran, Afghanistan, and the Central Asian Islamic states) and South Asian travellers, both monastic and secular, brought Buddhism to China. When Buddhism was first introduced, Confucianism was soon to become the official religion, and the various prototypical Daoist elements had yet to be synthesized. *Mouzi's Disposing of Errors* gives an account of Emperor Ming ("Bright," r.

57–75) dreaming of a golden man that a courtier interprets as the Buddha.

At first the Chinese had difficulty understanding the relationship between rebirth and the idea of no-self (**wuwo**, or *anatman*; see Chapter 5). If there was no enduring soul, what was reborn? Misunderstanding of this concept led Han Buddhists to erroneously teach the indestructibility of a soul that is bound to the cycle of rebirth through cause and effect (**yinguo** or karma). The idea of an enduring soul was familiar to the Chinese through the teachings about ancestors and immortality, but the idea of karma was something new. Contrary to the indigenous idea that descendants would inherit the sins of their ancestors, Buddhism suggested that the fruits or effects, both in reward and punishment, would be bound to the individual alone. As Xi Chao explains in *Essentials of the Dharma* (*Fengfayao*):

If the father performs some evil deed, the son does not suffer the consequences for him; if the son performs some evil deed, the father does not suffer the consequences for him. A good deed naturally brings about its own blessings, an evil deed its own calamity (Chen 1964: 70).

One unexpected development during the Han encounter between Buddhism and Daoism was the idea of *huahu* ("transforming the barbarians"). The theory went like this: When Laozi left China and, according to Daoist lore, travelled to the west, he became the Buddha and converted the western "barbarians" to Buddhism. Thus both traditions were considered members of one religious family. Altars were set up for Huang–Lao and the Buddha in the imperial palace, where worship was conducted without the animal sacrifices that were a standard part of both traditional Confucian state rituals and popular religion.

Sectarian rapprochement notwithstanding, the *Taipingjing* attacked Buddhism on four counts that reflected core Chinese concerns: it encouraged the abandonment of parents; to become a monk it was necessary to abandon wife and children; the requirement of celibacy defied the duty to procreate and thereby continue the family lineage; and the monks' dependence on alms promoted begging.

In time, Buddhism disentangled itself from Daoism and established its own communities of monks, nuns, and lay practitioners, which became more popular than their Daoist counterparts. Reciprocal relationships and mutual influence developed as the traditions matured: the native teachings influenced the evolution of Buddhism, and Buddhism in turn had a profound influence on the development of Confucianism and Daoism, the two indigenous Chinese traditions.

⊛ The Six Dynasties Period (220–589)

The Six Dynasties period, covering the Three Kingdoms (220–280), Jin Dynasty (265–420), and Southern and Northern Dynasties (420–589), was politically fractured, marked by struggle against "barbarian" invaders from North and Central Asia on the one hand and a foreign religion, Buddhism, on the other. The evolution of religious teachings in this period was shaped by the tension between China's hopes of preserving its traditional values and retaining its political independence, and its sometimes-grudging admiration and acceptance of an increasingly sinicized Buddhism. The absorption of Buddhist ideas, practices, liturgies, institutions, and organization would forever change the Chinese religious landscape.

Tensions and conflicts notwithstanding, Buddhist ideas attracted many. As those ideas began to permeate Chinese society, different spheres were allocated to each religion. Buddhism was seen as medicine for spiritual unease or disease and Confucianism continued to play an important role in family life despite its loss of official status and support. It survived over the next 400 years not only through individual study of the Five Classics, the *Analects*, and the *Classic of Filiality*, but also in family handbooks offering practical advice on everyday matters.

The development of large-scale religious organizations like the Celestial Masters was greatly strengthened by the new model of Buddhist monastic discipline. The nascent Daoist and Buddhist movements brought significant changes to Chinese society, for they went far beyond the traditional state- and family-centred cults such as those dedicated to Heaven, the gods of the soil and grain, or ancestors. Although Buddhism and Daoism respected the foundational values of filial piety and socio-political harmony, they did not show the traditional respect for socio-political hierarchies: thus monks and nuns refused to bow before kings. Under their influence, the imaginative boundaries of traditional Chinese religions expanded as well; for example, stories about popular deities came to involve previously unknown heavens and hells.

Confucianism

Interaction with Daoism and Buddhism

The fall of the Han dynasty, in 220, marked the beginning of what would be almost four centuries of instability. During this period, known as the Six Dynasties, China experienced repeated invasions from North and Central Asia. Confucianism lost the state support it had enjoyed under the Han and receded to the periphery, while those seeking personal well-being, political unity, and social harmony increasingly looked to Daoism and Buddhism.

Wang Bi

Among the Confucian literati was one who has also been described as a Neo-Daoist. In his short life (226–249), Wang Bi wrote extensive commentaries not only on the *Analects* and *Changes* (a text revered by Daoists as well as Confucians) but also on *Laozi*. Like the Seven Sages of the Bamboo Grove—famous Neo-Daoist eccentrics who were near-contemporaries of his (see p. 305)—Wang was interested in **xuanxue** (study of the "dark" or mysterious and profound), discoursing on the meaning of ideas such as being and nothingness, naturalness, the relationship of symbols and language to

reality, and the nature of the sage. Above all, Wang Bi emphasized the concept of principle (**li**, written differently in Chinese from the *li* meaning rites), which would become the linchpin for the Neo-Confucians of the Song period (960–1279), nearly a thousand years later.

Criticism of Buddhism

As Daoism and Confucianism drew closer together, both criticized Buddhism on the same grounds that the *Taipingjing* had. Leaving the family to become an itinerant monk meant abandoning the duties of filial piety and ancestor veneration, and monastic celibacy struck at the heart of Confucianism, for to produce no offspring, as Mencius observed, was the most unfilial act of all. There were also questions about Buddhist practices. To shave one's head, for instance, was construed as an act of gross disrespect, since it amounted to harming the body given by one's parents and ancestors. Industrious Confucians interpreted Buddhist monks' ascetic withdrawal from productive work as a shirking of responsibility, and the monastic tradition of begging for food as parasitism. In addition, Confucians and Daoists argued that Buddhism lacked authority because it did not originate in Chinese antiquity. If Buddhist teachings were important, why were they not mentioned in the Five Classics? Furthermore, the Buddhist renunciation of worldly pleasures went far beyond the Confucian ideal of moderation, effectively denying the value that Confucianism attributed to life in the world (de Bary and Hurvitz in de Bary 1972: 125–38).

The second-century Buddhist convert Mouzi defended Buddhism by arguing that there were many teachers the Five Classics did not mention, among them Laozi. Moreover, he noted that Taibo of the Zhou, whom Confucius praised for yielding his claim to the throne to his wiser younger brother, had cut his hair short and tattooed his body (like the Wu people of the region he had migrated to). Finally, Mouzi gave examples of men whom Confucius had praised even though they were childless, without property, and sometimes unconventional; he drew a parallel to a monk who "practises the way and substitutes that for the pleasures of disporting himself in the world. He accumulates goodness and wisdom in exchange for the joys of wife and children" (ibid., 134).

Finally, there was what seemed to be the extreme, even irrational nature of some Buddhist teachings. According to Mouzi, Confucians were baffled by the Buddhist practice of reflecting on the impurities of the body:

> The ascetic engages in contemplation of himself and observes that all the noxious seepage of his internal body is impure. Hair, skin, skull and flesh; tears from the blinking of the eyes and spittle; veins, arteries, sinew and marrow; liver, lungs, intestines and stomach; feces, urine, mucus and blood: such a mass of filth when combined produces a man. . . . awakened to the detestability of the body, concentrating his mind, he gains *dhyana* (ibid., 129).

This emphasis on the impurity of the human body was especially harsh for women, given the additional defilements of menstruation and childbirth. Although it contradicted the indigenous Chinese idea that the body is a gift from the ancestors, fundamentally good, the negativity of other Buddhist ideas about women was not inconsistent with Chinese ideas. Confucius himself once observed that women were difficult to deal with, becoming presumptuous when befriended and resentful when kept at a distance. And the depictions of "Vicious and Depraved" females in Liu Xiang's *Biographies of Exemplary Women* are quite in line with Buddhist notions of women's physical and spiritual impurity.

Buddhism

Amid the chaos of the Six Dynasties era, Chinese Buddhism developed in two distinctive streams. In the north, where many states were under the control of non-Han Turkic, Tibetan, and Mongolian rulers, Buddhism became involved in the political intrigues of dissenters attracted by monks' claims of mysterious powers such as clairvoyance

and the ability to make themselves invisible. In the south, where many Han scholars and officials had taken refuge, society was steeped in an apolitical Neo-Daoism that focused on Pure Conversation (*qingtan*); here Buddhism focused mainly on the study of texts and meditation and was only occasionally drawn into politics by its aristocratic supporters.

Hinayana (**Xiaocheng** or "Small Vehicle") as well as Mahayana (**Dacheng** or "Great Vehicle") traditions were practised in China. In this early period, meditation was more closely associated with the Hinayana than the Mahayana school, which was more interested in exploring what constitutes wisdom (**zhi** or *prajna*). Several texts on the Perfection of Transcendental Wisdom (*prajnaparamita*), such as the *Heart* (*Xinjing*) and *Diamond* (*Jingangjing*) *Sutras*, had been translated into Chinese by the end of the 300s. Many Mahayana texts were translated after the famous scholar-monk Kumarajiva arrived in 401, including the *Lotus Sutra* and *Vimalakirti* (*Weimojing*) *Sutra*.

Buddhism and Daoism

Nevertheless, the Chinese continued to think of Buddhism as a variant of Daoism. The confusion is understandable when we consider the similarities between them. The Perfection of Transcendental Wisdom writings teach a notion of emptiness or the void that recalls the Daoist belief in non-being. Drawing on the wisdom literature, the monk Zhi Dun taught that there is a transcendental absolute (*li*), an essence and ultimate truth that is expressed in the relative mundane world; this idea found echoes in Wang Bi's *li* or principle. Moreover, just as a buddha is free of all attachments, a sage is free from all desires; and in both, all dualities and distinctions disappear. As one Fan Ye (398–445) said:

> If we examine closely its teachings about purifying the mind and gaining release from the ties of life, and its emphasis upon casting aside both "emptiness" and "being," we see that it belongs to the same current as do the Taoist writings (Chen 1964: 64).

Sites

Xian, Shaanxi province, People's Republic of China

China's capital through many dynasties, Xian (formerly Chang'an) and its environs are home to the famous terracotta warrior guardians, numerous Daoist and Buddhist temples, and Huashan, one of the five sacred mountains of Daoism.

© Grant Rooney Premium/Alamy

The first five storeys of the Big Wild Goose Pagoda in Xian were built in 652 as a part of a temple complex designed to house Buddhist manuscripts and objects brought back by the famous monk Xuanzang from his pilgrimage to India. After it collapsed, some 50 years later, Empress Wu Zetian rebuilt and added five storeys to it in 704; the pagoda was reduced to its current height of seven storeys by an earthquake in 1556.

There were other similarities. Buddhism's dual focus on the cultivation of wisdom and of compassion echoed the traditional concern with security, stability, and harmony. And the Buddhist understanding that all things are ultimately incomplete and impermanent was in tune with Chinese cultural assumption of continual change. Moreover, the teachings on suffering and the path to liberation and enlightenment resonated with people living in a time of instability.

Reasons for the Popularity of Buddhism

People were attracted to Buddhism for many reasons, including its art (paintings and sculptures) and architecture (pagodas modelled after stupas); the promise of enlightenment, or at least a better chance at happiness or equanimity in this life; a well-tested, progressive program of precept-taking, chanting, meditation, and study to help the faithful achieve that goal; and the sophisticated philosophy, literary offerings, and erudition of its proponents. And even though some found the idea of leaving one's family unfilial, others were positively attracted to the idea of a religious community (*sangha* or *sengjia*) that was separate from the family and clan.

In the northern city of Chang'an (present-day Xian), Dao An (312–385), one of the first Chinese monks, focused on monastic discipline (*lu* or *vinaya*) and organized a cult dedicated to the future buddha Maitreya or Milo. On the other hand, the Central Asian monk Fo Tudeng (278?–349) attracted people by performing feats of magic such as creating a lotus out of a bowl of water; producing rain; using toothpicks to draw water out of dry wells; and predicting the future with great accuracy.

New ideas added to the fascination with Buddhism. Concepts such as **lunhui** (the cycle of rebirth, or *samsara*), **niepan** (extinction/release or *nirvana*), *yinguo* (cause and effect or karma), and narratives of heavens and hells offered the Chinese an entirely novel understanding of the cosmos. As Buddhism became ever more popular, it also offered new possibilities to women. Baochang's *Lives of Nuns* (*Biqiuni zhuan*) is a testament to the devotion and accomplishments of the first Chinese nuns, many

Document

From the *Lives of Nuns*

The Lives of Nuns, *by a sixth-century monk named Baochang, tells the stories of 65 Buddhist nuns who lived between 316 and 516. Two earlier efforts to capture the religious lives of women are the anonymous Buddhist* Song of the Sisters (Therigatha) *and Liu Xiang's Confucian* Biographies of Exemplary Women. *The following excerpt from Baochang's work tells of a young devotee who rejected a marriage arranged by her family.*

Sengduan had vowed that she would leave the household life rather than be married off. Nevertheless, her beauty of face and figure were well known in the region, and a wealthy family had already received her mother and elder brother's agreement to a betrothal. Three days before the marriage ceremony Sengduan fled in the middle of the night to a Buddhist convent whose abbess hid her in a separate building and supplied her with everything she needed. Sengduan also had a copy of the Bodhisattva Guanshiyin [Enlightened One Who Sees and Hears Everything in the World; another name for Guanyin] Scripture that she was able to chant from memory after only two days of study. She rained tears and made prostrations day and night without ceasing. Three days later, during her worship, she saw an image of the Buddha, who announced to her, "Your bridegroom's lifespan is coming to an end. You need only continue your ardent practice without harboring sorrowful thoughts." The next day her bridegroom was gored to death by an ox (Tsai: 49–50).

of whom were ordained in the fifth century by a quorum of nuns from Sri Lanka. Of course, their male counterparts were remembered as well, in parallel biographies like the *Lives of Famous Monks* (*Mingseng zhuan*), also by Baochang, and Huijiao's *Lives of Eminent Monks* (*Gaoseng zhuan*).

Power Struggle between Sengjia and State

It was not long before the growing wealth of the *sengjia* attracted charges of extravagance in the construction and decoration of its numerous monasteries. Monastics were accused of moral laxity, graft, and corruption. According to a memorial submitted to Emperor An of the Eastern Jin dynasty in 389,

> Monks [and] nuns . . . are vying with each other to enter into cliques and parties. . . . I have heard that the Buddha is a spirit of purity, far-reaching intelligence, and mysterious emptiness. He has based his doctrines upon the five lay commandments such as prohibiting intoxicating drinks and debauchery. But nowadays the devotees are vile, rude, servile, and addicted to wine and women (quoted in Chen 1964: 74–5).

Where the government was entrusted to monks and nuns, as in the case of the Eastern Jin (317–420), they were accused of meddling in politics and miscarriage of justice. With worldly and spiritual leaders in such close proximity, issues of precedence were sure to arise. In 403 Huan Xuan, who usurped power from the Eastern Jin, demanded that monks and nuns bow to him, as laypeople were obliged to.

The famous monk of Lu Shan (northern Jiangxi province), Hui Yuan (344–416), successfully argued against this command. The leader of a well-organized and strictly disciplined community that focused on the worship of the celestial Amituofo (Amitabha buddha) and entry into his Pure Land or Land of Bliss (*jingtu*) at death, he contended that Buddhism can be divided into two levels: the laity who, because they remain in the world, should obey all rules; and the monastics who, having left

home, have effectively abandoned the world, so no longer belong in the secular realm and therefore should not be required to adhere to its rules. Such were Hui Yuan's status and power of persuasion that Huan acquiesced.

The boundary between the monastic and secular worlds was porous. Confucian officials, untroubled by the conventional Confucian attitude that the afterlife cannot properly be known, would sometimes join a monastic community upon retirement. The retired scholar Bo Daoyou was one such example. He is quoted in the *Lives of Eminent Monks* as follows:

> Only now I have found the opportunity to roam freely through the mountain forests, and to let my mind indulge in the (study of) Confucian and Buddhist literature. Everything which touches my emotion becomes a poem! I go over the mountain peaks to gather medicinal (herbs), and I consume them in order to escape from disease—all this is abundant joy. The only thing which I regret is that I do not spend these days together with you [colleagues and friends] (Zurcher: 145)

Success and Subsequent Inter-religious Conflict

The popularity of Buddhism proved to be its undoing. While in the south hostility towards it was channelled into written form, in the north it resulted in full-blown persecution, once under Emperor Taiwu of Northern Wei in 446, and twice under Emperor Wu of Northern Zhou, in 574 and then again in 577.

Scholars suggest that Taiwu, whose tribe was likely of Turkish origin, was predisposed against Buddhism because he wanted to prove his acculturation to Chinese values. His antipathy was aggravated when he discovered that bows, arrows, spears, and shields had been found hidden in a Chang'an monastery; that men were becoming monks to avoid corvee labour and conscription; and worse yet, that monks were disregarding their vows of celibacy and secretly living with women in subterranean apartments. He was further out-raged when he learned that some monks had sold off grain intended for the poor in times of famine; and that the rich merchants who bought the grain had resold it at exorbitant prices.

To make things worse, the monastic system was a powerful organization operating alongside the state, and even its architecture rivalled that of the imperial buildings. Taiwu's Daoist–Confucian prime minister Cui Hao, whose brother and wife were both Buddhists, encouraged him to burn sutras, destroy temples, and reduce to slavery aris-tocratic members of the community, both monas-tics and lay believers. His measures were so extreme that even the Daoist Kou Qianzhi counselled against them. The other northern ruler to torment the Buddhists was Emperor Wu of the Northern Zhou. Unlike Taiwu, however, he included Daoists in his persecutions.

A different Emperor Wu, this one in the south, in the area of modern Nanjing, was a devout Bud-dhist himself. So great was his respect for the monastic community that Liang Wudi (502–549) ceded the responsibilities of governance to the monks and nuns—much to the dismay of officials who were more inclined towards Confucianism. The emperor was perceived to be too lenient in his punishment of convicted criminals and particularly idiosyncratic when, in an effort to raise funds for the monastic community, he presented himself to a temple as a simple monk and refused to leave until the palace had paid a very costly "ransom." Further straining his credibility and authority, he restored without sufficient investigation an official who had threatened to commit suicide. Liang Wudi was such an ardent Buddhist that he abolished all Daoist tem-ples in 517 and returned all Daoist priests, men and women, to lay life. Many Daoists fled north.

Ideas Central to Chinese Buddhism

Non-duality and Emptiness
As more Buddhist teachings made their way into China, it became clear that the Hinayana and Mahayana doctrines sometimes contradicted one another (see Chapter 5). The *Heart Sutra* (*Xinjing*), for example, presents the Madhyamaka (*zhonglun* or *san-lun*) teaching of non-duality, which negates Hinayana teachings such as the five components of personality (*skandhas* or *yun*). The second stanza of this short but essential sutra, often chanted in liturgy, begins with the bodhisattva of compassion, Avalokiteshvara or Guanyin, in a deep trance, recognizing that the five components are "in their own-being . . . empty (*kong*)," and that the same is true of "feelings, per-ceptions, impulses, and consciousness."

Doctrinal Categorization and Skillful Means
The *Lotus Sutra* offered a way of understanding these divergent teachings. Two ideas developed to account for the theoretical differences: doctrinal categorization or classification (*panjiao*) and skill-ful means (*upaya* or *fangbian*). The first term refers to the notion that the talks given by the historical Buddha can be classified into varying doctrines based on different periods and audiences. The sec-ond idea offers the reasons for this: the substance of the Buddha's lectures reflected both his own devel-opment and his skillful shaping of his ideas to suit the capacities of his audience (*sravaka* or *shengwen*). The famous story of the burning house (see Chapter 5) is reinforced by the following passage, also in the *Lotus Sutra*, according to which there is a single Buddha vehicle:

> [T]he Buddhas of the past used countless numbers of expedient means, various causes and conditions, and words of simile and par-able in order to expound the doctrines for the sake of living beings. These doctrines are all for the sake of the one Buddha vehicle (Watson 2002: 9).

Guanyin
Over time, the Chinese accepted the three baskets of the Hinayana, but privileged Mahayana teach-ings. In the *Lotus Sutra*, the Buddha himself says nothing about the classic Hinayana themes, but he does advise the faithful to call on Guanyin:

> If a woman wishes to give birth to a male child, she should offer obeisance and alms to

Bodhisattva Perceiver of the World's Sounds [Guanyin] and then she will bear a son blessed with merit, virtue, and wisdom. And if she wishes to bear a daughter, she will bear one with all the marks of comeliness, one who in the past planted the roots of virtue and is loved and respected by many persons (Watson 2001: 121).

The idea of a selfless being who defers enlightenment, is capable of taking on an infinite number of forms, and disregards socio-cultural and religious boundaries in order to aid all beings who suffer, had the effect of expanding and deepening Chinese religiosity. The *Lotus Sutra* continues:

If they [the people] need a monk, a nun, a layman believer, or a laywoman believer to be saved, immediately [Guanyin] becomes a monk, a nun, a layman believer, or a laywoman believer and preaches the Law for them. . . (ibid., 123).

The innumerable guises of Guanyin recall the first two lines of the *Daodejing*: "The way that can be spoken of / Is not the constant way; / The name that can be named / Is not the constant name" (Lau 1963: 57). And the *pusa's* compassion resonates with the ideal of the sage, central to both Confucian and Daoist teachings. But the Buddhist Guanyin introduced a stronger version of the indigenous ideas of transformation implicit in the *Book of Changes*: He/she is portrayed with a capacity to morph into any form in order to save those who need his/her help.

Lay Practice

Buddhism altered the Chinese religious landscape; it made accommodations to local ideals; and shifted its focus from monasticism to lay practice. One of the most popular sutras, the *Vimalakirti*, affirms non-duality through the parity of lay and monastic life and teaches that there is no need to abandon one's home and family in order to become enlightened. This lay orientation no doubt helped in the domestication and sinicization of Buddhism by

elevating the potential wisdom and status of the layperson.

In the sutra the Buddha's students—the recognized religious specialists of the tradition—all fear Vimalakirti, who is a wise, pure, celibate layman; one by one they tell the Buddha that Vimalakirti understands the teachings better than they do. The

This early image of Guanyin from the Northern Qi (550–560) clearly represents the bodhisattva as male—the robe and fineries lie on a flat chest. Later devotees, however, often understood "him" to be female. While Guanyin can take any form, s/he, like other bodhisattvas (but unlike buddhas), is usually sumptuously dressed and recognizable by Amituofo's face in her/his crown.

bodhisattva Shining Adornment tells how, when he met Vimalakirti coming from the "place of practice" and asked him where that place was, Vimalakirti replied:

> An upright mind is the place of practice, for it is without sham or falsehood. The resolve to act is the place of practice, for it can judge matters properly. A deeply searching mind is the place of practice, for it multiplies benefits. The mind that aspires to bodhi [enlightenment] is the place of practice, for it is without error or misconception (Watson 1997: 55-6).

The Mind in Both Aspects: Pure and Impure

The mind that is "upright" and "deeply searching," that "aspires to *bodhi*," illustrates two core Mahayana ideas: that Mind or Consciousness is crucial in the alleviation of suffering, and that it has two aspects—which means that those three positive characteristics can never be separated from their opposites: non-uprightness, not deeply searching, and not aspiring to *bodhi*. The first idea belongs to the Yogacara or Consciousness Only school (see Chapter 5), known as Faxiang in China. The second is an expression of the concept of the non-dual One Mind (*yixin*) found in the teachings on the Matrix of the Tathagata (*Tathagatagarbha* or *Rulaizang*) and discussed at length in the *Lankavatara Sutra* and a treatise entitled *The Awakening of Faith* (*Dacheng qixin lun*).

The two aspects of the One Mind may take several forms: the universal and the particular, the transcendental and the phenomenal, the pure and the impure. The Matrix (*garbha*) also has two aspects, symbolizing both the seed of the Tathagata (the Buddha) and the womb in which it may grow. It represents Buddha-nature and the capacity for enlightenment that are inherent in all human beings (a concept that parallels Confucian and Daoist ideas about sagehood). But it is important to understand that (in line with the concept of no-self) Buddha-nature has no substance: it is not a thing, even in the sense that a soul would be a thing. When the One Mind is unhindered by defilements, the luminosity of Buddha-nature will

be clear. Thus Buddha-nature is not something we possess, but something we are. The key to uncovering or cultivating the One Mind is meditation.

Mofa *or End Time*

From the beginning, Buddhism taught that the universe was in a phase of decline when Shakyamuni was born to set the wheel of dharma in motion again. The Three Stages School (*Sanjiejiao*), founded in the late sixth century, developed that idea, teaching that time was divided into three periods—those of the Correct Law, the Counterfeit Law, and the Decadent or Final Law—and that the Chinese were living during the last of the three, the end times (*mofa*). During the time of the Buddha, people were able to attain enlightenment through practice. During the time of false teachings, however, even though Buddhism is well established, it becomes increasingly formalized, so that fewer and fewer people are able to benefit from it. During the end time, humans are poisoned by greed, anger, or hatred, and ignorance or foolishness: thus they lose their aspiration for enlightenment and Buddhism is incapable of leading them to buddhahood.

Help from the Celestial Buddhas

So what if one is living in the end time, has family obligations that prevent one from becoming a monk or nun, and thus remains incapable of reaching enlightenment in lay life? What if one is too weak and undisciplined, overcome by greed, hatred, and ignorance? What if there were too many distractions, or conditions are too chaotic to permit a meditative life? One group of practitioners offered a solution: When you cannot do it on your own, ask to be reborn in the Pure Land (*sukhavati* or **jingtu**) of a celestial buddha.

The most prominent of these is the Pure Land or Western Paradise of Amituofo (Amitabha). According to the *Smaller Pure Land Sutra* (also known as the *Amitayus Sutra* or *Amituojing*), Amituofo's "light shines boundlessly and without hindrance over all the worlds in the ten directions" and "the people of his land last for innumerable, unlimited and incalculable kalpas [cycles of time]" (Inagaki 1994: 355). The *Smaller Sutra* is one of three **Pure Land** sutras; the other two are the *Larger Pure Land Sutra* (*Sutra* on the *Buddha of Infinite Life* or *Wuliangshoujing*) and the *Contemplation Sutra* (*Amitayurdhyana Sutra* or *Foshuoguanwuliangshoufojing*).

The *Larger Sutra* tells Pure Land devotees that Amituofo, in a previous incarnation as the bodhisattva Dharmakara, vowed to bring into his Western Paradise all who "sincerely and joyfully entrust themselves to me, and call my Name even ten times," "awaken aspiration for Enlightenment, (and) do various meritorious deeds," or "having heard my Name, concentrate their thoughts on my land . . . with a desire to be born there" (ibid., 244–5). The *Contemplation Sutra* describes 13 different visualizations, one of which is of Amituofo. It also says that if someone is so overwhelmed by evil that even on his deathbed he is unable to concentrate on Amituofo, then he should simply say 10 times "Homage to Amitayus Buddha" (*Namo Amituofo*), the mantra for rebirth into the Pure Land. The mantra can be used as a focus in silent meditation or chanted aloud.

Flower Garland

Another very important idea that shaped the development of Chinese Buddhism is found in the *Flower Garland Sutra* (*Avatamsaka* or *Huayan*): that is, the belief that all things are interpenetrated and interconnected.

Some Chinese schools, such as Tiantai and Huayan, were organized around a particular sutra (the *Lotus* and *Flower Garland* respectively), while others, such as **Chan** and Pure Land, were centred on a core practice. They formed two broad categories: those that drew on a particular teaching or doctrine, and those that focused on a particular practice, such as meditation or chanting. We will look at the most influential schools in the next section. In the meantime, let us return to Daoism and see how it was faring during this period.

Daoism

Buddhist Influences

Daoism benefited greatly from the introduction of Buddhism into China. It assimilated beliefs and practices from the imported tradition, blended them into the various streams that made up its own tradition—local folk practices, practices from the

Document

From the *Diamond Sutra*

Like the Heart Sutra, *the* Diamond Cutter (Vajracchedika *or* Jingang) *is one of the* Perfection of Transcendental Wisdom (prajnaparamita *or* boreboluomi) *sutras, which centre on the Madhyamaka teaching of emptiness (*kong*). Kumarajiva, a native of Kucha (in present day Xinjiang), was the first to translate the sutra into Chinese, around 400 CE. The* Diamond *is structured as a discourse on non-duality between the Buddha and his disciple Subhuti. The following verses come from Chapter 29, "Perfect Tranquillity" and 32 (the last chapter), "The Delusion of Appearances," respectively.*

Subhuti, if anyone should say that the Tathagata [*rulai*, "Thus-gone one," i.e., the Buddha] comes or goes or sits or reclines, he fails to understand my teaching. Why? Because Tathagata has neither whence nor whither, therefore is he called "Tathagata" (Price and Wong: 50).

Subhuti . . . in what manner may he explain them [the teachings] to others? By detachment from appearances—abiding in real truth. So I tell you:

Thus shall ye think of all this fleeting world:
A star at dawn, a bubble in a stream;
A flash of lightning in a summer cloud,
A flickering lamp, a phantom, and a dream
(ibid., 53).

masters of the methods, philosophical ideals, liturgy—and developed them in a variety of directions while remaining resolutely faithful to its own beliefs and practices.

Doctrines were reinterpreted in terms of *yinguo* (karma) and *lunhui* (rebirth), and rituals were adapted to reflect the new ideas about death that Buddhism had introduced. Both monastic and lay organizations and institutions were established, culminating in the construction of the first Daoist temple in the fifth century. Some Daoist leaders stayed active politically, but others turned inward and focused on individual cultivation.

Cultivation of stillness remained a focal point, as did the quest for transcendence. That quest took two distinctly different forms. For some practitioners it meant the pursuit of spiritual transcendence through meditation; for others it meant the pursuit of physical immortality through a number of methods including two extraordinary ones: a sexual ritual known as the joining of energy or the union of breaths and the ingestion of poisonous substances such as cinnabar (mercuric sulphide).

Mysterious Learning and Outer Alchemy

Contemporaries of the Confucian Wang Bi, the Seven Sages of the Bamboo Grove concentrated on private individual cultivation, and, like Wang, they were also interested in *xuanxue*. Discouraged from participating in public life after the fall of the Han, and inspired by Zhuangzi's notions of spontaneity, spiritual freedom, and non-attachment to convention, they gained a reputation for eccentric behaviour (one of them was said to have roamed around naked in his hermitage). Having fled the turmoil of northern China for the south, the Seven Sages engaged in "pure" or "light conversation" focused on metaphysical rather than political topics, and reflected Confucian and Buddhist as well as Daoist influences.

It was likely sometime in the 300s that the *Liezi*—the third most important Daoist "philosophical" text, after the *Daodejing* and *Zhuangzi*— was compiled, bringing together stories about one of the Daoist thinkers mentioned in the *Zhuangzi*.

A less important but still informative text, probably written in the 320s, was Ge Hong's *Baopuzi* ("The master who embraces spontaneous nature"). It is a collection of essays on classic Daoist themes, including methods of driving away harmful spirits, reaching the gods, and alchemical recipes for achieving longevity and immortality.

The Highest Clarity and Numinous Treasure Schools

Two new religious Daoist schools emerged in the latter part of the same century. Yang Xi, a medium and shaman, formed the Highest Clarity (Shangqing) school when he received scriptures from the immortal Lady Wei of the Heaven of Highest Clarity. Yang and his followers sought to become "true beings" or "perfected persons" (*zhenren*) through practices that included the use of outer alchemy to facilitate flights of ecstasy to the star deities who controlled human destiny. Highest Clarity devotees ate very little, believing that fasting would make their bodies light and radiant in their ascent to the heavens.

The second new school, Numinous Treasure (Lingbao), shows a great deal of Buddhist influence and was founded a few decades later by a grandnephew of Ge Hong. Ge Chaofu received from his Ge clan ancestors a series of revelations involving the Buddhist concepts of karma, rebirth, and cycles of time (*kalpas*). Whereas the Highest Clarity sect focused on the individual, followers of the Numinous Treasure looked outward to the local community and beyond to all of humanity, suggesting a synthesis of Daoist and Buddhist ideas. A text from this sect, the *Scripture for the Salvation of Humanity* (*Durenjing*), illustrates this synthesis well. It describes a great cosmic deity who is so concerned for the salvation of human beings that he sends an emissary to reveal the *Durenjing*. The deity and his emissary ferry the suffering masses from worldly misery to liberation and peace—the equivalent of the service performed by Amituofo and the historical Buddha Gautama himself.

Numinous Treasure focused especially on two kinds of ritual: purification (*zhai*) and communal renewal (*jiao*). These two categories continue to define the aims of Daoist practice today. The goals of the purification rituals were typical of this era: prevention of disease, warding off natural calamities, and salvation of ancestors. They were performed around a temporary altar and started with a cleansing of the body by bathing and fasting and purification of the heart-mind through the confession of sins. A communal feast was then held to celebrate the reinstatement of harmony between the gods and human beings. In community renewal rituals (still practised today), deities were invited down into the altar, incense was offered, and the faithful who sponsored the rituals were granted audiences with the gods, during which they would request favours for their communities.

☸ Sui and Tang (589–907)

China Reunited

In 589 China was reunited for the first time since the fall of the Han nearly 400 years earlier, and in 618 the Tang came to power. Daoism and Buddhism both reached new heights of popularity over the next three centuries of relative peace and prosperity; Confucianism too experienced a renewal that opened the way for the rise of Neo-Confucianism during the Song.

Confucianism

The second Tang emperor, Taizhong, established an academy for scholar-officials in the mid-600s where the curriculum was based on the classical texts of Confucianism, the students venerated Confucius alongside the Duke of Zhou, and—for the first time in Chinese history—it became possible for a commoner to work his way into officialdom. Taizhong also ordered all prefectures and districts to build Confucian temples for sacrifices to be performed by the literati. In 647 he installed in each temple 22 tablets commemorating orthodox Confucians of the Han era. A century later, in 739, the title "King of Manifest Culture" was bestowed on Confucius, who

now displaced the Duke of Zhou as the "uncrowned king" of Chinese civilization.

One of the responsibilities of the Confucian officials was to oversee rituals. Four new types of worship that drew on earlier ritual systems were established at the royal clan temples during the Tang dynasty: honouring Earth (through the gods of the land and harvest), Heaven, Confucius, and imperial ancestors. Within a century the Confucian temples began to display carved images of honoured figures, similar to the images in Buddhist temples representing buddhas, bodhisattvas, and arhats. Among the figures so honoured were Confucius himself, Yan Hui (his favourite disciple, who died young), his 72 disciples, and 10 historical figures admired by Confucians and known as the "Wise Ones." These images remained in the temples for seven or eight hundred years until—in an effort to differentiate Confucian temples from Buddhist ones—they were replaced by portraits.

In time, the Confucian curriculum for bureaucrats was expanded to include a total of 12 works, among them the *Analects* and the *Classic of Filiality*. The revival of interest in Confucian thought was reflected in three writers of particular interest to us here. Madame Zheng, author of the late seventh-century *Classic of Filiality for Women* (*Nu xiaojing*); **Han Yu** (768–824), a prominent scholar-official intent on reintroducing Confucianism to the people; and Han's contemporary Song Ruozhao, the daughter of an official, who wrote the *Analects for Women* (*Nu lunyu*) in the early ninth century.

Madame Zheng's Classic of Filiality for Women

The wife of a government official, Madame Zheng set out to create a female Confucian tradition starting from Ban Zhao. Her *Classic of Filiality for Women* emphasizes the importance of purity, filial piety, intelligence, and wisdom, so that women might guide their husbands by example. Zheng imagines Ban Zhao teaching a group of women that a wife should encourage her husband in good behaviour and guide him with "modesty and deference, [so that] he will refrain from being contentious" (T. Kelleher in de Bary and Bloom 1999: 826). Such a wife will use music and rites—in the broad sense that includes everything from formal courtesy to religious ritual—to moderate his emotions, so that he will be pleasant and easy to get along with. When the women ask if they must obey their husbands' every command, Madame Zheng has Ban respond indignantly—"What kind of talk is that!" Then, echoing the original *Filiality*, Ban cites historical examples of wives who corrected or criticized their husbands and explains:

> If a husband has a remonstrating wife, then he won't fall into evil ways. Therefore, if a husband transgresses against the Way, you must correct him. How could it be that to obey your husband in everything would make you a virtuous person? (ibid., 827)

Han Yu's Defence of Confucianism

Han Yu marks a point of renewal that is especially important in the history of Confucianism. He spoke for the tradition in a period when Daoism and Buddhism were flourishing, the former as the state religion and the latter as the religion of choice for both the elite and the masses. Although Confucian principles had been reintroduced into government, they had little popular currency. In an effort to bring Confucian teaching back to the centre of Chinese life after nearly six centuries on the periphery, Han Yu wrote *Essentials of the Moral Way* (*Yuandao lun*). In it he answers the question "What is the teaching of the former kings?" as follows:

> To love largely is called a sense of humaneness; to act according to what should be done is called rightness. To proceed from these principles is called the moral Way; to be sufficient unto oneself without relying on externals is called inner power. . . . Its methods are the rites, music, chastisement, and government. Its classes of people are scholars, peasants, craftsmen, and merchants. . . . (C. Hartman in de Bary and Bloom 1999: 569)

Song Ruozhao's Analects for Women

The *Analects for Women* (*Nu lunyu*) is usually attributed to Song Ruozhao, though some say that her sister Ruohua actually wrote the text. Like Ban Zhao, Song came from a scholarly family. She was appointed to the court as scholar, and was assigned to teach the imperial princesses. Focusing on emotional restraint and self-cultivation as the basis for good familial relationships and efficient household management, her treatise consists of eight sections:

1. Establishing oneself as a person
2. Learning how to work
3. Ritual decorum: learning proper etiquette
4. Rising early to begin household work
5. Serving one's parents-in-law
6. Serving a husband
7. Instructing sons and daughters
8. Managing the household.

The work of these writers and many others paved the way for the success of Neo-Confucianism during the Song and Ming dynasties. But Confucianism was not the only religious tradition that thrived during the Tang: so did Daoism and Buddhism.

Daoism

The founder of the Tang dynasty, Li Yuan, claimed descent from Laozi, and under his family's rule Daoism once again became the state religion. Some patriarchs from the Highest Clarity School held government posts, while others were invited to the capital, Chang'an (now known as Xi'an), to attend the emperors. One of the most famous Highest Clarity patriarchs of the period, Sima Chengzhen (647–735), emphasized the personal practice of inner alchemy, meditation, and longevity techniques in two essays: "On the Essential Meaning of the Absorption of Energy" (*Fuqi jingyi lun*) and "On Sitting in Oblivion" (*Zuowang lun*).

In the eighth century the "Brilliant Emperor" Xuanzhong wrote a commentary on the *Daodejing* and invited Sima Chengzen to court. Princesses were ordained as Daoist priestesses and performed state rituals for the protection of the empire. Colleges of Daoism were established, and the *Daodejing* was briefly included in state examinations. By 739 there were 1,137 abbeys for Daoshi and 550 for Nuguan (male and female Daoist priests respectively). Classical Daoism reached the height of its power and popularity during the Tang, but it did not undergo any substantial new development until Wang Chongyang's development of the Quanzhen (Complete Truth or Perfect Truth) during the Song dynasty.

Buddhism

The first two centuries of the Tang dynasty are often seen as the apex of Buddhism in China, a time when the "foreign" religion became thoroughly sinicized, immensely popular, and broadly influential. Monks visited the imperial court often, and several Chinese Buddhist schools developed around individual sutras. In addition, one sutra was used to legitimate the rise to a power of China's first and only female emperor. The *Great Cloud Sutra* (*Mahamegha Sutra* or *Dayunjing*) prophesied the imminent arrival of a female Maitreya (Milo), a salvational figure who would bring peace and prosperity to the land. After the death of her husband, the Emperor Gaozong, Wu Zetian claimed to be that salvational figure and ascended the throne as Empress Wu of the Zhou dynasty.

The two types of Buddhist schools, doctrinal and practical, were often described as two wings of a single bird. Among the schools of the former type that were influential during the Tang period were Tiantai, based on the *Lotus Sutra* and named after a mountain; Huayan, based on the sutra of the same name (the *Flower Garland*); and Faxiang (Yogacara, or Consciousness Only). Less prominent but nevertheless important to the monastic community was the school of Discipline (*Vinaya* or *Lu*), dedicated to the study and practice of the regulations that had governed monastic life since the time of the Buddha. Vajrayana Buddhism, known in China as Zhenyan (True Word or Mantra), was introduced in the 700s,

The only female emperor in Chinese history, Wu Zetian (625–705) flouted more than one Confucian norm. She committed "incest" when she married Gaozong even though she had been a concubine to his father, Tang Taizong. For a time after Gaozong's death, she ruled from behind the throne as the empress-dowager; then, encouraged by Buddhist monks and prophecies, she declared her own dynasty and took the throne herself.

but its practices were soon absorbed by other schools and it did not remain a separate entity for long.

Towards the end of the dynasty, the scholar-monk Zongmi (780–841) integrated Confucianism and Daoism into a Buddhist framework in his *Treatise on the Original Nature of Man*—a classic example of the Chinese tendency towards syncretism, reinforced by the idea of doctrinal categorization.

Late Tang Persecution of Buddhism

Zongmi's efforts notwithstanding, Daoist priests eventually persuaded Emperor Wuzong to put an

Document

From the *Platform Sutra*, fourth chapter, *"Samadhi and Prajna"*

The Tanjing (Platform Sutra) is the only "canonical" non-Indian Buddhist text. It is a record of the teachings of Huineng, the sixth patriarch of the Chan school. The sutra begins with his account of how he was enlightened on hearing a recitation of the Diamond Sutra. When he approached the fifth patriarch, Hongren, to teach him how to achieve buddhahood, the master rejected him saying that he was a "barbarian" from Guangdong. He replied that there might be northern men and southern men, but that they all had Buddha-nature in common. In the following passages, he explains that practising meditation and non-attachment does not mean having no thoughts, and that there is no "right" way to become enlightened.

Learned Audience, some teachers of meditation instruct their disciples to keep a watch on their mind for tranquillity, so that it will cease from activity. Henceforth the disciples give up all exertion of mind. Ignorant persons become insane from having too much confidence in such instruction. Such cases are not rare, and it is a great mistake to teach others to do this.

. . .

In orthodox Buddhism the distinction between the Sudden school and the Gradual school does not really exist; the only difference is that by nature some men are quick-witted, while others are dull in understanding. Those who are enlightened realize the truth in a sudden, while those who are under delusion have to train themselves gradually. But such a difference will disappear when we know own mind and realize our own nature. Therefore these terms *gradual* and *sudden* are more apparent than real (Price and Wong 1990: 95).

---

end to the spread of Buddhism in China. In 845 Wuzong issued an edict that summarized the charges laid against the foreign religion by defenders of China's native traditions: idleness and corruption of indigenous social values.

. . . through the Three Dynasties [Xia, Shang, and Zhou] the Buddha was never spoken of. It was only from the Han and Wei on that the religion of idols gradually came to prominence. So in this latter age it has transmitted its strange ways, instilling its infection with every opportunity, spreading like a luxuriant vine, until it has poisoned the customs of our nation . . .

Now if even one man fails to work the fields, someone must go hungry; if one woman does not tend her silkworms, someone will be cold. At present there are an inestimable number of monks and nuns in the empire, each of them waiting for the farmers to feed him and the silkworms to clothe him, while the public temples and private chapels have reached boundless number, all with soaring towers and elegant ornamentation sufficient to outshine the imperial palace itself . . . (B. Watson in de Bary and Bloom 1999: 585–6).

❀ The Song, Yuan, and Ming Dynasties (960–1644)

In the aftermath of the late Tang persecution, Buddhism was deeply wounded. The monastic community had been decimated, and the only schools that remained relatively healthy, with strong followings among ordinary people, were the two that focused on practice rather than study: Chan

(Meditation) and Jingtu (Pure Land). After the fall of the Tang, however, Daoism too was brought low, stripped of its status as the state religion. If the early Tang had favoured Buddhism and the late Tang had seen Daoism in the ascendant, the Song (960–1279) would prove to be a period of renewal for Confucianism, which synthesized ideas from both Daoism and Buddhism and reasserted itself at the state level as Neo-Confucianism.

Daoism

The Complete Truth School

The Daoist school of Complete Truth (*Quanzhen*; also translated as Perfect Realization, Perfect Truth, or Complete Perfection) was founded in the twelfth century and is still active today. Associated with the White Cloud Abbey in Beijing, it is distinctive in its monasticism—a feature that its founder, Wang Chongyang, modelled on Buddhism. Wang also argued against the superstitions and supernatural elements that had accrued to Daoism over time, and taught a more down-to-earth understanding of transcendence or immortality:

> Leaving the world does not mean that the body departs. . . . When you realize the Tao, your body will be in the sphere of the ordinary, but your mind will be in the realm of the sages. Nowadays, people want to avoid death forever and at the same time leave the ordinary world. They are very foolish, indeed, and have not even glimpsed the

true principle of the Tao (Kirkland 2004: 188).

In addition to discouraging supernatural expectations, Wang urged his disciples to read across all three of the major traditions, especially the Confucian *Classic of Filiality*, the Buddhist *Heart Sutra*, and the *Daodejing*. His "Fifteen Precepts for Establishing the Teaching" includes practical recommendations alongside more elevated principles. For example, he advises that to achieve the ideal of harmony in spirit and vital energy, the body must be well rested. He also recommends the use of herbs for healing, living a simple life, and maintaining good Daoist friends. The "basic motif of the art of self-cultivation," he wrote, is the "search for the hidden meaning of Nature and mind" (Sommer 1995: 202).

Sun Buer

Where Confucians have Ban Zhao, the Daoists have Sun Buer (1119–83). The wife of Wang Chongyang's disciple Ma Danyang, she became the only woman among Wang's "Seven Perfected" disciples. The following story is likely apocryphal, but it highlights the difficulties that women of her time faced in their search for enlightenment.

One day Sun heard Wang say that an immortal was expected to emerge in the city of Luoyang, far from her home in Shandong. She told Wang that she wished to go and cultivate transcendence there, but he withheld permission, telling her that her beauty would arouse men's desire, that she would be molested, and that the shame would kill her.

Sites

Wudangshan, Hubei province, People's Republic of China

Mount Wudang in Hubei is known for its many Daoist monasteries. It is also home to an organized complex of palaces and temples; most were built during the Ming dynasty (1368–1644), but some of its Daoist buildings date from as early as the seventh century. The complex contains some of the finest examples of Chinese art and architecture.

Undeterred, Sun went to her kitchen and asked the servants to leave her alone. Then she heated some oil, poured cold water into it, and stood over the wok as the boiling oil spattered over her face. When Wang saw her scars, he recognized her sincerity and agreed to teach her the methods of inner alchemy, but he advised her to hide her knowledge even from her husband. To ensure that she would be left alone, Sun pretended to be insane. When her husband told Wang, the latter replied that she could not otherwise become an immortal. Eventually, Sun slipped out of the house and travelled to Loyang, where she continued to behave like a madwoman.

Most of the townspeople left her alone, but—as Wang had anticipated—two men accosted her. When a rain of enormous hailstones helped her to evade them, the men realized her special nature and spread the story of her escape. Left in peace for 12 years, Sun attained her goal and became the only female master among the famed seven masters of the Complete Truth School.

Revival of Orthodox Unity

Daoism continued to thrive until the twelfth century, when Kublai Khan, the Mongolian ruler, extended his rule to the south. There he consolidated his control over religious life by giving exclusive authority to the Orthodox Unity sect, renamed for the revelations given to the Celestial Masters, which had survived through the dominance of Highest Clarity and Numinous Treasure. After the Mongols were overthrown, Orthodox Unity retained its position of authority, and its leader was entrusted with the compilation of the Daoist canon (*Daozang*), which was printed in 1445.

Confucianism

The Emergence of Neo-Confucianism

Meanwhile, the ongoing development of Confucianism culminated in the emergence of a new school that came to be known in the West as

Document

From Zhang Zai's *Western Inscription*

Zhang Zai (1020–77) took Zhou Dunyi's universal cosmology and expressed it in terms of a human family. The following excerpt from his Western Inscription *(Ximing) shows how he correlated the essential Confucian elements of self, family, humanity, and virtue to the broader elements of nature and the cosmos.*

Heaven is my father and Earth is my mother, and even such a small creature as I finds an intimate place in their midst.

Therefore that which fills the universe I regard as my body and that which directs the universe I consider as my nature.

All people are my brothers and sisters, and all things are my companions. The great ruler (the emperor) is the eldest son of my parents (Heaven and Earth), and the great ministers are his stewards. . . .

He who disobeys [the Principle of Nature] violates virtue. He who destroys humanity is a robber. He who promotes evil lacks [moral] capacity. But he who puts his moral nature into practice and brings his physical existence into complete fulfillment can match [Heaven and Earth].

One who knows the principles of transformation will skillfully carry forward the undertakings [of Heaven and Earth], and one who penetrates spirit to the highest degree will skillfully carry out their will. . .

In life I follow and serve [Heaven and Earth]. In death I will be at peace. (W.T. Chan in Sommer 1995: 188).

Neo-Confucianism. This development reached its apex with **Zhu Xi** (1130–1200), but much of Zhu's work drew on thinkers from the preceding century, among them Zhou Dunyi, Zhang Zai, and the brothers Cheng Yi and Hao, who studied with Zhou. Although the Neo-Confucians traced the roots of their philosophy to the ancient writings, much of their thinking reflected Buddhist and Daoist influences. Thus Zhou Dunyi (1017–73) advocated what he called "quiet-sitting"—a practice clearly modelled on Daoist and Buddhist meditation—and he based his most important work, "An Explanation of the Diagram of the Great Ultimate," on a Daoist representation of the creation of the material world.

For Zhou, the Great Ultimate and the Ultimate Non-being are identical. Through movement, yang is generated from the Ultimate Non-being/Great Ultimate. When its limit is reached, it becomes quiet and yin is generated. When yin reaches its limit, then activity, or yang, begins again. Thus the alternation between stillness and movement produces yin and yang, which in turn give rise to the five vital elements—fire, water, earth, metal, and wood—each of which has its own specific nature. When Ultimate Non-being interacts with the essences of yin-yang and the five elements, a mysterious union occurs, from which Heaven and Earth come into being.

Zhu Xi and the School of Principle

Working from Zhou's cosmology, the School of Principle (*Lixue*) explicitly linked *li*, the principles or patterns of nature, to human relationships and theories about education and government. Zhu Xi, considered the founder of this new school, synthesized the ideas of the earlier Song thinkers and gave Confucianism a metaphysical bent while drawing authority from classical Confucian writings.

Zhu focused on the nature, place, and function of self in the Great Ultimate. His thinking on this subject was not new. Like Han Confucians and other Chinese philosophers, he understood human beings to be part of the fabric of the universe. Although he was interested in Buddhist-style "quiet

sitting," Zhu was quintessentially Confucian in his focus on self-cultivation. He distinguished Confucian concerns and teachings clearly from Buddhist ones by drawing on the authority of the ancient *Book of Rites*.

Zhu commented on "Centrality and Equilibrium" and "The Great Learning" (*Daxue*), another chapter from the *Rites*, in which self-discipline or self-cultivation is the first link in a chain that extends from the individual through the family to the state and recalls the ideal of the Grand Commonality. A famous passage from "The Great Learning" argues that proper self-cultivation begins with the acquisition of knowledge:

> In antiquity, those who wanted to clarify their bright virtue throughout the entire realm first had to govern their states well. Those who wanted to govern their states well first had to manage their own families, and those who wanted to manage their families first had to develop their own selves. Those who wanted to develop themselves first rectified their own minds, and those who wanted to rectify their minds first made their thoughts sincere. Those who wanted to make their thoughts sincere first extended their knowledge. Those who wanted to extend their knowledge first had to investigate things (Sommer 1995: 39).

Women in Neo-Confucianism

Neo-Confucianism continued to thrive from the Song through to the Ming dynasty (1368–1644). After the Ming regained control from the Mongols, the education of women—esteemed as the first teachers, the transmitters of culture to the young—received renewed attention. Empress Xu, the wife of the third Ming emperor, wrote *Instructions for the Inner Quarters* (*Neixun*) under the inspirational influence of Empress Ma, her mother-in-law. The latter had often challenged her cruel, hot-tempered husband, believing it was her duty to serve as inner counsellor and Mother of the people. Empress Xu's *Instructions* reflects the same sense of a woman's

Focus

Zhu Xi on Human Nature

Following Zhou Dunyi and Zhang Zai, Zhu Xi believed human beings—like everything else in the universe—to be the product of the interaction between heavenly "principle" and the material forces of yin-yang and the five elements. Thus human beings possessed both principle and material force. Like Mencius, Zhu Xi believed human nature to be intrinsically good, an expression of Heaven-given principle. Yet human action was not necessarily good. Zhu Xi attributed this apparent contradiction to the effects (or lack thereof) of material force on the three aspects of human personality: heavenly nature (i.e., principle), human feelings, and mind. Reflecting Zhou's cosmology, Zhu wrote that "Nature is the state before activity begins and feelings are the state when activity has started, and the mind includes both of these states" (W.T. Chan in Sommer 1995: 192). Nature, being Heaven-given, is always good; but feelings can be good or bad, while the mind is the master and "unites and apprehends both nature and the feelings, but it is not united with them" (ibid.). The mind brings nature and feelings together but remains a separate entity.

broader responsibility. When a set of "Four Books for Women" (*Nu sishu*) was compiled during the Ming, Empress Xu's work was one of them, along with Ban Zhao's *Admonitions*, Song Ruozhao's *Analects*, and Madame Zheng's *Filiality*.

Wang Yangming

Approximately three centuries after Zhu Xi's death, **Wang Yangming** (1472–1529) challenged his view that the process of self-cultivation must begin with studying the classical texts and learning about the outside world. He argued that our moral sense or intuition of the good is innate, within our heart-minds, and takes precedence over any external learning; this teaching became known as *Xinxue*, the School of the Heart-Mind.

Buddhism

Developments in Chan

Critics of Wang Yangming charged that his focus on the heart-mind reflected the influence of Buddhism. It is true that his emphasis on intuitive, innate knowing resonated with both the Chan view of enlightenment and the general Mahayana belief in the universality of Buddha-nature. These elements are expressed in the lines attributed to the founder of the Chan school, Bodhidharma (see Chapter 5): "Directly pointing to the human mind / Achieving Buddhahood by seeing one's nature."

The Chan of the early Tang period had developed broadly into two schools with different notions on how to achieve enlightenment: a Northern "gradual" school and a Southern "sudden" school associated with the sixth patriarch, Huineng (see Chapter 5).

By the end of the Tang dynasty, the two schools of Chan thought were represented by two distinct lineages—Linji and Caodong—both of which survive today. New literary genres also developed: discourse records (*yulu*) of individual masters, and "lamp" or "flame" records of lineages were later edited into collections of *gongan* (public documents or case records). A record of a Chan master's spontaneous encounter with a student became a *gongan* when a living master wrote a commentary on the exchange and formally "proved" himself to be a part of the lineage of enlightened masters. Eventually,

Sites

Guangzhou, Guangdong province, People's Republic of China

It was in Guangzhou that Huineng (638–713), the sixth Chan patriarch and reputed author of the *Platform Sutra*, was enlightened. His remains are enshrined in the Nanhua Temple, north of Guangzhou city.

the cases became pedagogical tools used to bypass the student's intellect and spark sudden enlightenment. A critical phrase or head-word from a selected case would be assigned to a student and put to use in meditation.

Gongan thus served as a metaphor for principles of reality beyond individual opinions. Famous collections of these stories and their commentaries include the *Book of Serenity* (*Congronglu*), *Blue Cliff Record* (*Biyanlu*), and the *Gateless Gate* (*Wumenguan*), variously collected and edited in the twelfth and thirteenth centuries. (See the document box for a comparison of Chan and Daoist dialogue on the Buddha and the Dao respectively.)

Document

Excerpts from the *Gateless Gate* and *Zhuangzi*

Scholars have noted a general eccentricity in Chan dialogues that is shared by Zhuangzi. The two excerpts that follow, the first from the Chan Gateless Gate and the second from the Zhuangzi, point to an earthy irreverence in both Buddhism and Daoism.

A Chan gongan:
A monk asked [Yunmen Wenyan, c. 863–949]: "What is Buddha?" [Yunmen] answered him: "Dried dung."

[Wumen's] comment: It seems to me [Yunmen] is so poor he cannot distinguish the taste of one food from another, or else he is too busy to write readable letters. Well, he tried to hold his school with dried dung. And his teaching was just as useless.
　　Lightning flashes,
　　Sparks shower.
　　In one blink of your eyes
You have missed seeing (Reps 1989 [1960]: 106–7).

A dialogue from *Zhuangzi*:
Master Tung-kuo asked Chuang Tzu, "This thing called the Way—where does it exist?"
　　Chuang Tzu said, "There's no place it doesn't exist."
　　"Come," said Master Tung-kuo, "you must be more specific."
　　"It is in the ant."
　　"As low a thing as that?"
　　"It is in the panic grass."
　　"But that's lower still!"
　　"It is in the tiles and shards."
　　"How can it be so low?"
　　"It is in the piss and shit!"
　　Master Tung-kuo made no reply (Watson 1968: 240–1).

Popular Buddhism

The second school of Buddhism to survive the Tang persecution relatively well, Jingtu, continued to offer comfort to the faithful with the promise of an afterlife in the "pure land" of a celestial Buddha who would free them of the prospect of rebirth into the realm of suffering (see Chapter 5). In time, other forms of popular Buddhism did develop, but they tended to be more prosaic in their promises. The monk Zhuhong (1535–1615), for example, classified actions in terms of merit and demerit. Actions of merit were grouped in four categories—"loyal and pious," "altruistic and compassionate," "beneficial to the Three Jewels," and "miscellaneous good deeds"—and had merit points assigned to them: to "offer medicine to a sick person" was worth one merit point; to "help a person recover from a slight illness," five; points to "help a sick man on the road back to return home," 20 points; and to "rescue one person from the death penalty," 100 points. Conversely, anyone who failed to "help a person in serious illness" would receive two demerit points; and the penalty for murder was 100 points. According to this scheme, those who earned 10,000 points would see their wishes granted; but if at death their demerit points exceeded their merits, their descendants would suffer for it (Chen 1964: 437–8).

The schedule of merits and demerits was adapted from a monk who had learnt it when he was a Daoist, which may explain the non-Buddhist idea of transference of ancestral demerit points to suffering descendants. Another indication of the fluidity and plurality of religious practice in that period can be seen in the fact that many of Zhu's followers were Confucians.

Popular Religion

Popular religion continued to thrive. The White Lotus Society is thought to have originated in the eleventh and twelfth centuries as a lay movement dedicated to Amituofo. Over time, however, it incorporated other elements, including Daoist longevity practices and millenarian expectations surrounding a messianic Milo. Its clergy married, it provided social services, and its scriptures featured common folk motifs such as apocalyptic change and the attainment of paradise. White Lotus members played a substantial role in establishing the native Ming by overthrowing the Mongols, who had established Tibetan Buddhism as the state religion. But the first Ming emperor so feared the Society's power that he sought to suppress it. In time, "White Lotus" became a pejorative term, used by officials to refer to any religious group they considered suspect.

✸ The Qing Dynasty and Republican Period (1644–present)
The Challenges of Modernity

The Qing Manchus retained Tibetan Buddhism as the state religion, but they accepted the functional structure of Chinese religions and continued to use Confucianism for government. However, radical changes brought by the Europeans beginning in the mid-nineteenth century led to a historic break from dynastic rule in 1911, and a shift to republicanism.

The end of the Qing, in the early twentieth century, was marked by a great deal of hostility against traditional beliefs and practices. By mid-century "China" had splintered into the People's Republic of China (PRC) on the mainland, the Republic of China on the island of Taiwan, and the British Crown Colony of Hong Kong, existing alongside sizable Chinese communities in the city-state of Singapore and elsewhere in Southeast Asia, as well as a global diaspora.

Yet despite the persecution that traditional institutions and folk spiritualities have suffered over the last 120 years, popular annual celebrations, folk religious practices, Confucianism, Daoism, and Buddhism continue to thrive in areas outside the mainland. Moreover, many religious beliefs and practices have experienced a renaissance in the PRC itself since the 1980s.

Confucianism

Encounter with the West and Modernization

In 1838 the Qing emperor appointed Lin Zexu to put an end to the opium trade initiated by the British in hopes of balancing their trade deficit with China. In addition to confiscating and destroying vast quantities of the drug, Lin composed an open letter of protest to Queen Victoria:

> The wealth of China is used to profit the barbarians [the British]. . . . By what right do they then in return use the poisonous drug [opium] to injure the Chinese people? Let us ask, where is your conscience? I have heard that the smoking of opium is very strictly forbidden by your country; that is because the harm caused by opium is clearly understood. Since it is not permitted to do harm to your own country, then even less should you let it be passed on to the harm of other countries—how much less to China! (S.Y. Teng and J. Fairbank in deBary and Lufrano 2000: 203).

As a Confucian minister, Lin framed his argument in moral terms: the fact that opium was outlawed in Britain, he reasoned, made it all the more reprehensible for the British to sell it to the Chinese.

The British responded to this high-minded appeal with the first Opium War (1839–42; a second war would follow in 1856–60). The defeat of the hopelessly outgunned Chinese is a watershed in East Asian history, presaging the end of the dynastic system and ultimately leading to a profound reassessment of the traditional Confucian way of thinking. The final military nail in the coffin was Japan's victory in the Sino-Japanese War of 1894–5. That Japan—a former vassal state—had succeeded

not only in modernizing itself along Western lines but in defeating China meant that radical reform was necessary. Some reformers urged the abandonment of all traditions; others argued that certain aspects of China's cultural heritage should be preserved. Among the latter was Kang Youwei (1858–1927), who believed that Japan's adoption of Shinto as the state religion had saved Japan from the stultifying influence of Buddhism, given it a strong national identity, and helped it to focus on modernization. He argued that Confucianism could play a similar role for China, but his attempts at establishing Confucianism as a state religion failed and the ancient teaching continued to lose ground.

"New Confucians" in Post-dynastic China

Soon after Kang, Sun Yatsen, the founding father of modern republican China, found precedents for democracy in Confucian philosophers, specifically Mencius and the Neo-Confucian Cheng Yi. He identified three principles as fundamental to democracy—nationalism, citizen rights, and the welfare of human beings—and argued that they represented "a completion of the development of . . . three thousand years of Chinese ideas about how to govern and maintain a peaceful world" (Bell and Hahm 2003: 9).

Sun Yatsen's insights notwithstanding, state Confucianism was disestablished following the fall of the Qing and the formation of the Chinese Republic in 1911, and the great writer Lu Xun described it as a teaching that "cannibalized" people. But scholar-teachers such as Fang Dongmei—a professor of Chinese philosophy who settled in Taiwan after the communist takeover of the mainland—encouraged the ongoing development of Confucianism in the diaspora.

Diaspora Attempts to Reconstruct Chinese Culture

In 1958 a group of "New Confucians" based in Hong Kong responded to Western critics of China with an English-language "Manifesto for a

Reappraisal of Sinology and the Reconstruction of Chinese Culture."

Following a discussion of "what the West can learn from Eastern thought," the authors concluded with a few remarks on the direction of the future "intellectual development of China and of the world." First, since "The expansion of Western civilization has brought the peoples of the world into close contact and unfortunately has also produced much friction," they called for the cultivation of "an attitude of respect and sympathy toward other cultures," "genuine compassion and commiseration." Second, since "scientific learning is inadequate" to that end, they called for "a different kind of learning, one that treats [Man] as a conscious, existential being [and] applies understanding to conduct, by which one may transcend existence to attain spiritual enlightenment." Finally, in their third and last point, they suggested that the end product of that new learning would be "a moral being that . . . can truly embrace God" (quoted by J. Berthrong in de Bary and Lufrano 2000: 559).

Even though they clearly identified themselves with the Confucian tradition, the authors included Daoism and Buddhism in their discussion; and their use of the Christian term "God" shows their willingness to adopt foreign concepts. Their efforts are still visible and embodied in contemporary academics and politics respectively by scholars such as Du Weiming (Tu Weiming) of Harvard and John Berthrong of Boston University; the controversial Daniel A. Bell, a Canadian who describes himself as a Confucian philosopher and scholar, who is teaching at the Center for International and Comparative Political Philosophy at the prestigious Tsinghua University in Beijing; and Lee Kuan Yew, the first President of Singapore, who tried (unsuccessfully) to introduce both Confucian and religious studies into the new republic's high schools.

Winds of Change in the People's Republic of China

Since the 1980s, the PRC has reintroduced state Confucian ritual in the form of the annual celebration of the sage's birthday (the Republic of China, Taiwan, has always celebrated it). It is celebrated twice: once on 28 September and a second time on the 27th day of the lunar month. A renewed interest in Confucian values can also be seen in the fact that some elementary schools have integrated classical literature into their curricula, along with a focus on rites and ethics, and introduced traditional garb such as the scholar's robe into their classrooms.

Scholars also note that the Chinese government's emphasis on a "harmonious society," non-interference in foreign policy, soft diplomacy, the establishment of Confucius Institutes outside China, and the development of online sites for Chinese language and culture all reflect the Confucian concern to promote social security and stability through the disciplined self-cultivation of individual persons.

Daoism and Popular Religion

Even as Neo-Confucianism became entrenched as state ideology during the Qing dynasty (1644–1911), Daoism continued to inspire popular morality books and a variety of practices from meditation to *taiji* and **qigong** (breath exercises that help the movement of vital energy through the body). However, it suffered enormous setbacks after the Opium Wars, when Western-inspired reformers began to attack traditional beliefs and practices.

Daoism, with its Eight Immortals (legendary figures who play a role not unlike that of human saints) and its elaborate liturgies inviting the deities into this realm, can be difficult to distinguish from folk religion. Modernizers and advocates of change perceived both Daoism and folk religion as superstitious and hostile to progress, especially after the failure of the state-sponsored anti-Western uprising (1899–1901) mounted by the Yihequan ("Righteous and Harmonious Fists") movement—known in the West as the "Boxer Rebellion." The Boxers had believed they could drive out the foreigners on the strength of their martial arts skills alone, which they expected to render them impervious to Western guns and cannon.

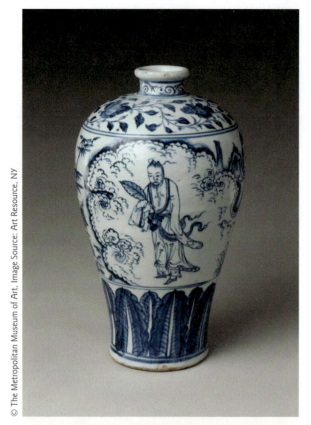

This Ming dynasty bottle shows Zhongli Quan, one of the eight Daoist "Immortals" who serve as patrons of various groups and trades. Recognizable by his two topknots, exposed belly, and fan, Zhongli is believed to have been a successful Han general who discovered the Dao only after he had experienced defeat for the first time; he is also said to have had an impressive knowledge of alchemy.

© The Metropolitan Museum of Art. Image Source: Art Resource, NY

Buddhism

Reform and Modernization

Of the three elite religions, Buddhism has been the most successful in modernizing itself. A leader in that effort was a layman named Yang Wenhui (1837–1911). He published Buddhist texts, started a school for monastics in Nanjing, and inspired Tan Sitong (1865–98) to propose a process through which millennia-old institutional and cultural barriers in Chinese society might be cleared away. In his book *Renxue* ("On Benevolence") Tan argued that the Confucian notion of *ren* was the same as Mohism's *jianai* (love without distinction), Buddhism's *cibei* (compassion), and Christianity's love. Appealing to Huayan ideas of interpenetration and interconnectedness, he described a state of oneness or non-differentiation in which communication between people is always possible. Tragically, he was beheaded for plotting against the Qing government, but his wife, Li Run, remained true to his ideal of non-differentiation and established a school for girls in his hometown in rural Hunan—a feat unheard of in the early twentieth century.

Elsewhere, several monks also worked to revive and reform Buddhism. Yinguang (1861–1940) was a conservative monk credited with reviving the Pure Land school, while Taixu (1890–1947) argued that of all religions, Buddhism was the one most compatible with modern science; he also advocated a modern education for monastics. He made his reputation as an activist in 1912 when he and another monk, Renshan, announced that they had petitioned the government for permission to open a new school for monastics and planned to use the monastery's resources to run it.

The monk-officers of the temple successfully prevented the construction of the school. But the seeds of Humanistic Buddhism—a Buddhism for the human realm (*renjian fojiao*)—had been sown. Instead of retreating into meditation or study of the scriptures, monastics and laypeople alike were encouraged to become "engaged" in the world: in education, social work, medicine, politics. In 1929 the Chinese Buddhist Association was established in Shanghai and charged with reforming and reviving Buddhism in China.

Government Treatment of Religion

In 1949 the PRC guaranteed freedom of religion. The official policy, in line with Marxist historical materialism, stated that to coerce religious people without material improvement and transformation of society was "useless and positively harmful." Nevertheless, in 1950 the Chinese Buddhist Association decamped to Taiwan with the Nationalist government and was replaced by a state-administered Buddhist Association. And in 1966 the government launched the Cultural Revolution. Fuelled by the Marxist notion of religion as an opiate that blunts the masses' instinct for justice and hinders advancement towards a utopian society, the "revolutionaries" systematically targeted temples and shrines of all traditions—folk, Daoist, Confucian, Buddhist—and persecuted people of faith. By the mid-1970s the social and economic foundations of traditional Chinese society had been destroyed, and the government acknowledged that a new approach was necessary. Today, working within an ethos of liberal development, the Chinese government recognizes five religions as "legitimate": Buddhism, Daoism, Roman Catholicism, Protestantism, and Islam. (It considers Confucianism to be a philosophy rather than a religion.) At the same time, although it is not officially recognized, popular religion is experiencing a revival in the PRC.

Popular Religion

A loose collection of beliefs and practices centred on the power of deities, ghosts, and spirits, popular religion is non-institutional and may draw elements from any of the more established traditions, including Christianity and Islam. Spirits of all kinds are seen as compassionate helpers, regardless of tradition.

The goals that practitioners of popular religion seek to secure have remained remarkably stable through the ages: children (especially sons), happiness, academic success, prosperity, safety at work (especially in occupations such as fishing and policing), even political change. They can be divided into two streams: personal religiosity and political activism.

One important element in personal religiosity is the belief that the spirits or souls of the deceased continue to intervene in the human world; and that their potentially malevolent power can be harnessed for the benefit of the living. This belief finds expression not only in ancestral tablets in temples, or family shrines and altars dedicated to ancestors, but also in the kinds of shrines in commercial establishments described at the beginning of this chapter. In addition, devotees believe that numerous local folk heroes and heroines continue to protect the living after they have become spirits. Likewise, buddhas, bodhisattvas, and Daoist perfected beings are believed to help people through the many challenges in life.

But popular religion can also be externalized in a less individual, more dogmatic and partisan way. When an idea such as the Mandate of Heaven or a messianic figure such as Milo (Maitreya) is incorporated into popular religion, it can give rise to a politically charged movement like the White Lotus Society, the Boxers, or the Heavenly Kingdom of Great Peace.

The most recent example in the PRC is the Buddho-Daoist Energy of the Wheel of Law, better known as Falun Dafa or Falun Gong. Its founder, Li Hongzhi, teaches the virtues of truthfulness, compassion, and forbearance, along with a form of meditation that he claims minimizes the need for doctors. The PRC government objects to this practice (likely because it recalls the superstitions of the Boxer Rebellion) as well as the group's frequent anti-government demonstrations both in China and in the diaspora.

At the beginning of the twenty-first century, Daoism and folk religion are re-establishing themselves in the PRC while becoming rooted in many different parts of the world. Daoism is especially popular in Europe and the Americas, where its dual focus on living a simple and balanced life and promoting health, longevity, and transcendence through specific bodily practices are increasingly valued.

Recent Developments

Study after study tells us that the Chinese, with their Korean, Japanese, and Vietnamese neighbours, are the least religious of all ethnic groups.

This calls into question the term "religion" and how it is understood. If we consider the humanistic bent of Confucianism and the syncretic, diffuse, unstructured, and provisional nature of Chinese folk religion then Chinese traditions fit badly into the monotheistic frame of reference. Even so, in this section we will look at some developments in contemporary Chinese "religious" beliefs and practices.

Revival of Confucianism

The first two generations of the twentieth-century New Confucians wrote from the cultural margins—Hong Kong, Taiwan, Singapore, Boston—during the period when China was lagging substantially behind the West developmentally. Yet by the late 1970s, less than three decades after the formation of the People's Republic, it was clear that communism had failed to improve the conditions of life for the people. Thus in 1978 a process of economic and political reform began and a new constitution was adopted. Rapid industrial and economic growth followed: half a billion people were lifted out of poverty between 1981 and 2004, and by 2012 China had achieved exceptional economic stability, despite a global financial disaster that continued to threaten the European and North American economies. Despite (or because of) this remarkable success on the level of basic material security, some long-standing problems remained and some new ones surfaced: social alienation, ecological degradation, lack of spiritual direction, and continuing infractions of human rights.

Aspirations to prosperity were accompanied by wariness of full-scale Westernization—an irony, given that the guiding ideology of the Chinese state is Marxist historical materialism. Confucian values such as integrity, right action, and trustworthiness; loving respect for family and community; and belief in the unity of human beings with the cosmos were recommended by political and academic leaders as antidotes to dual ills: first, a spiritual malaise that communism failed to ease; and second, the perceived poisons of market capitalism and the hyper-individualism of neo-liberalism. Traditional values, including Confucian ideals, became integral to China's efforts to combat corruption, promote ethical conduct, build strong familial and communal relationships, discourage rabid consumerism, and mitigate the effects of radical individualism.

The New Confucianism that had developed in the diaspora was harnessed in an effort to neutralize international fears that rapid economic growth would turn China into an imperialistic superpower. In 1984, just six years after the process of economic and political reform began, the state-supported China Confucius Foundation was created with the explicit mandate to expand the influence of Confucianism both internally and internationally, through academic and cultural exchanges. Ten years later, the International Confucian Association was inaugurated with a mandate to advance Confucianism so as to promote freedom, equality, peaceful development, and prosperity around the world.

Designed to promote Chinese language and culture globally, the first Confucius Institute was symbolically established in Seoul, South Korea, in 2004. By 2007 there were close to 200 Institutes around the globe, all supported by the Chinese government. The Confucius Institute/Classroom website offers a cyber-classroom with information on teaching materials, tests, teachers, and scholarships.

None of this activity is explicitly "religious" in the Western sense. Yet the Chinese government's strategy of persuasion through education, both in and outside China, clearly recalls the traditional Confucian concern for moral development as a fundamental element in the development of a peaceful society. The contemporary need for stability and security, the failure of communism, the distrust of capitalism, and the ultimate goal of prosperity have combined to give rise to a secular Confucianism with spiritual overtones.

Daoism Under Reconstruction

Daoism has been popular in the West in a way that Confucianism has not. The *Daodejing* is one of the most translated books in the world, and Zhuangzi is treasured for his humour as well as his teachings on spontaneity or "going with the flow." Daoist teachings were integral to the counterculture movement of the 1960s, and some Westerners continue to cherish the Daoist ideal of *wuwei* and *ziran*.

Daoism has also been used to encourage "green" ecological thinking in Taiwan. In China, however, it has only recently begun to receive state support. It was only in 2007 that a government approved a week-long, privately funded International Forum on the *Daodejing* that was held simultaneously in Xi'an and Hong Kong. In the summer of 2011, a privately sponsored international academic conference was held at the foot of Hengshan (Nanyue), one of the five sacred Daoist mountains; and in October of the same year, the First International Daoism Forum was held there.

As mainland Chinese become prosperous enough to turn their attention to the critical state of the natural environment, the importance of the Daoist emphasis on achieving harmony with the cosmos is increasingly recognized.

Folk Religiosity

Many popular religious groups focus on cultivating inner calm and peace. Like Confucianism and Daoism, they too have gone global. Some are organized around a particular teacher, as in the case of Falun Dafa. Others are organized around the anticipated arrival of a Milo-like figure, as in the case of the Taiwan-based Yiguandao (Unity, Pervasive Truth or Consistent Way) movement, which teaches that during these end times, people must repent their sins, take up vegetarianism, and reunite with the Eternal Mother. Still other movements are syncretic, combining elements from Confucianism, Daoism, Buddhism, Christianity, and Islam; one of these movements, Tien De or Tiande (Heavenly Virtue), professes to use cosmic energy and spiritual healing to cure disease.

Humanistic Buddhism: A Religion for This World

Buddhism is the most successful and popular "Chinese" religion in the West. Engaged or Humanistic Buddhism flourished in Taiwan after defecting from the PRC. Three groups influenced by the reformist Taixu have been particularly active in growing global Buddhism: Foguangshan (Buddha's Light Mountain), Fagushan (Dharma Drum Mountain) and Cizi (Tzu Chi or Compassionate Relief). All three have attracted strong participation from laypeople.

Foguangshan claims to be ecumenical, accepting all the teachings of eight traditional schools: Tiantai, Huayan, Sanlun, Faxiang, Lu, Zhenyan, Chan, and Jingtu. Education is their primary focus: the group has three universities, one of which is the University of the West in Rosemead, California. Its stated principles are to "propagate Buddhist teachings through cultural activities" such as concerts and art exhibitions; "nurture talents through education" from kindergarten to university; "benefit societies through charitable programs," like medical care and childcare; and "purify human hearts and minds through Buddhist practice." The founder of Fagushan, Sheng Yen (1930–2009), was a modern scholar-monk who wanted to raise the status of Buddhism and the quality of monasticism in Taiwan. To nurture first-class researchers, he founded the Chung-Hwa Institute of Buddhist Studies and Dharma Drum University. Then, "to uplift the character of humanity and to build a pure land on earth," he instituted an ongoing campaign for "Six Ethics of the Mind": Family Ethics, Living Ethics, School Ethics, Environmental Ethics, Workplace Ethics, and Ethics between Ethnic Groups.

The third group, Cizi or Tzu Chi (Compassionate Relief), has the distinction of having been founded by a nun. Cheng Yen (1937–) shaved her own head after her prayers for her mother's recovery from illness had been answered; but by conventional Buddhist standards she was not properly tonsured and was therefore not recognized as a nun until she took refuge with the pre-eminent Chan scholar-monk Yinxun (Yin Shun). The Cizi foundation began when three Catholic nuns observed that while Buddhism was well respected in Hualien, where Cheng Yen was living, it was not well organized to help people. On the basis of that insight and with the help of housewife-disciples, she established Cizi as a charitable foundation to assist the sick and the poor. Cizi is active in disaster relief in Taiwan and around the world.

☸ Korean Religions

This section will concentrate on the historical development of religions on the Korean peninsula. Theoretically, traditional Korean religiosity can be classified as non-theistic at the elite level and polytheistic at the popular level. In practice, though, like its Chinese counterpart, it tends to be syncretic. Thus neither of these categories necessarily excludes the other. It is even possible to identify a quasi-monotheistic belief in a purposeful and creative Way (or Heaven, or Heaven-and-Earth)

This early twentieth-century painting of the Mountain God shows him with several symbols of longevity: a crane to the left, a deer to the right, and pine trees in the foreground. The Mountain God is a good illustration of syncretism in Korea; he is variously portrayed as the legendary founder Dangun, a Confucian sage, a Daoist immortal, and a Buddhist bodhisattva.

coexisting with both the polytheistic belief in ancestral spirits and nature deities and the non-theistic belief in an impersonal natural Way.

Korea and China: A Shared History

Ancient Korean culture shows influences from both continental East Asia and Central Asia. Migration from China may have been underway as early as 1000 BCE, and there are traces of Chinese influence in settlements from c. 300 BCE. Political relations between the two populations have always reflected a mixture of kinship and antipathy, relatedness and differentiation.

The earliest written records of Korea are Chinese. Sima Qian's *Records of the Grand Historian* describes Wiman, one of the later kings of the proto-state of Old Joseon (Choson), as a refugee from northern China who ruled over Chinese refugees and indigenous inhabitants at Wanggeom (Wanggom; present-day Pyongyang) in the sixth and fifth centuries BCE. Another Chinese source, the sixth-century *History of the Wei Dynasty*, tells how the mythical king Dangun (Tangun) founded Old Joseon during the time of China's legendary sage King Yao. Further evidence of the connection between these ancient peoples can be seen in the Wu family shrine in the Chinese coastal province of Shandong: built in 147 CE, it is engraved with the myth of Dangun.

Old Joseon

An early Korean source, now lost, started with Dangun's divine ancestors, his grandfather Hwanin and father Hwanung. Hwanin knew that his son wanted to descend from heaven and live in the world of human beings, so he settled Hwanung in a cave in one of the highest mountains, Mount Taebaek.

But Hwanung was not alone in the cave: a bear and a tiger were also living there, and they asked him to transform them into human beings. So Hwanung gave them a bundle of sacred mugworts and 20 cloves of garlic, with instructions to eat these foods and avoid the sunlight. After 21 days the bear became a woman, but the tiger had failed to avoid the light and therefore was not transformed. The woman remained alone, unable to find a husband, so she prayed for a child. In response to her prayers, Hwanung transformed himself, lay with her, and gave her a son, Dangun Wanggeom.

This foundation myth became a marker of national identity in the thirteenth century, when Korea faced a series of Mongol invasions (1231–70). According to the *Memorabilia of the Three Kingdoms* (*Samguk yusa*), compiled during that period by the monk Iryeon (Iryon), the god Hwanung descended into the human world and married a she-bear who gave birth to Dangun (a bear cult is still current among the Ainu people of Japan as well as some Siberian tribes in Russia). Yi Suenghyu (Yi Sunghyu) in his *Songs or Rhymed Record of Emperors and Kings* (*Chewang ungi*; 1287) gives a variant account in which the great king Hwanung gave medicine to his granddaughter to change her into a human being; she then married a tree god and bore Dangun (a tree cult was prevalent in the southern portion of the Korean peninsula). Interestingly, there is no reference to Dangun in the official *History of the Three Kingdoms* (*Samguk sagi*), compiled a century earlier, under Confucian inspiration, by Gim Busik (Kim Pusik).

The Three Kingdoms (c. 50 BCE–668 CE)

The proto-state of Old Joseon was followed by the Three Kingdoms of Goguryeo (Koguryo), Baekje (Paekche), and Silla. Goguryeo's foundation myth (found in a collection from the thirteenth century) tells how its founder Jumong (Chumong), who eventually took the title King Dongmyeong (Tongmyong), was born from an egg after the sun—Haemosu, the Son of Heaven—shone on the breast of his mother, the eldest daughter of the River Earl. In both style and content, this poem recalls the *Songs of the South*. After ruling for 19 years, Dongmyeong forsook his throne and rose to heaven. Goguryeo

Document

The Lay of King Dongmyeong (Tongmyong)

From the Collected Works of Minister I (Yi) of Korea

In early summer, when the Great Bear stood in the Snake,
Haemosu came to Korea,
A true Son of Heaven.
He came down through the air
In a five-dragon chariot,
With a retinue of hundreds,
Robes streaming, riding on swans,
The atmosphere echoed with chiming music.
Banners floated on the tinted clouds.
. . .

North of the capital was the Green River,
Where the River Earl's three beautiful daughters
Rose from the drake-neck's green waves
To play in the Bear's Heart Pool.
Their jade ornaments tinkled.
Their flowerlike beauty was modest—
They might have been fairies of the Han River banks,
Or goddesses of the Lo River islets.
The king, out hunting, espied them,
Was fascinated and lost his heart.
Not from lust for girls,
But from eager desire for an heir.
(Lee et al. 1993: 24).

was linked very closely to Baekje, whose founder, King Onjo, is said to have been Dongmyeong's son.

Silla's foundation myth, like Old Joseon's, was recorded in Iryeon's *Memorabilia*. Like King Dongmyeong, King Hyeokgeose (Hyokkose) ("Bright"), the founder, was born from an egg, a red one in this case. His birth was announced by an eerie lightning-like emanation from a well. When the people cracked open the egg, they found inside it a beautiful boy. When they bathed him he emitted light; the "birds and beasts danced for joy, heaven and earth shook, and the sun and the moon became bright" (Lee et al. 1993: 33). Soon after, a dragon appeared near a well and brought an infant girl from under her left rib. The child's features were lovely except for a beak-like lip, which fell off after she was bathed in the river. When the two reached the age of 13, they married and became king and queen.

Daoism

Korea's foundation myths contain several elements reminiscent of the shamanist stream in Daoism,

including nature deities (the River Earl), marriage between gods and human beings (Hwanung and the bear-woman), and ascension into heaven (King Dongmyeong). In Silla, the people believed in the Holy Mother, a mountain goddess who was the guardian of the country. She was said to live on a mountain to the west of the capital, recalling the Queen Mother of the West in the *Zhuangzi*.

These apparently Daoist elements have led some scholars to suggest that the cult of the Holy Mother was a composite of an indigenous mountain deity and a Daoist immortality cult. In the *Memorabilia* there is an account of the Holy Mother appearing to a Buddhist nun who was seeking to repair a Buddha Hall. This "immortal fairy," who knows "the art of the immortals," is said to be the daughter of a Chinese emperor who had learned the way of immortality. After settling in Korea, she gave birth to a holy man who became the first ruler of Silla; the story suggests that "perhaps" this was Hyeokgeose.

This mythological syncretism is reinforced in Silla's history. In the 700s Gim Jiseong (Kim

Document

The Holy Mother of Mount Fairy Peach

The phrases "art of the immortals" and "art of longevity" refer to Daoism: by emphasizing that the Holy Mother embraced both Daoism and Buddhism, the passage underlines the syncretic nature of Korean religion.

During the reign of King Chinpyong [579–632], a nun . . . wished to repair a hall for the Buddha . . . but could not carry out her desire. A beautiful immortal fairy, her hair adorned with ornaments, appeared in the nun's dreams and consoled her: "I'm the holy goddess mother of Mount Fairy Peach [Mount West], and I am pleased that you would repair the Buddha Hall. I offer you ten *kun* of gold . . . ." The holy mother, originally the daughter of a Chinese emperor, was named Saso. Early in her life she learned the art of the immortals. . . . When Saso first came to Chinhan, she gave birth to a holy man who became the first ruler of Silla—perhaps he was Hyokkose. . . . Saso donated gold to make a Buddha image, lighted incense for the living beings, and initiated a religion. How could she be merely one who learned the art of longevity and became a prisoner in the boundless mist? (Lee et al. 1993: 94).

Chisong), a vice-minister of state, kept one image each of Amitabha, the buddha of the West, and Maitreya, the buddha of the Future. He read Mahayana literature but also enjoyed Laozi and the first chapter of the *Zhuangzi*, "Free and Easy Wandering." Echoes of Daoist scripture continued into the 1400s, during the staunchly Neo-Confucian Joseon or I (Yi) dynasty, when one minister, disappointed in his ruler, left the court to spend the rest of his life wandering as a monk, writing poetry and telling stories, and other literary men (much like the Seven Sages of the Bamboo Grove) retired from official life to engage in metaphysical conversation.

Murals in Goguryeo tombs suggest that the Daoist cult of immortality merged with local Korean beliefs in prognostication. At the start of the dynasty, the Tang court sent a memorial asking about Daoism in Korea, along with an adept and seven other envoys, plus a copy of the *Daodejing*. In the same period, a Buddhist monastery in the region of what is now the border between North Korea and China was converted into a Daoist temple; and in 643, at the request of the Goguryeo king, eight Daoist priests were sent there from China. By 650, the Daoist influence at the Goguryeo court was so strong that a monk who opposed the state's adoption of Daoism fled and sought refuge in Baekje.

Shamanism

With its focus on deities, ghosts, and spirits, Daoism found deep resonance in Korean shamanism (*mugyo*). Each village had its own deity: a local mountain god or goddess in inland regions and a dragon king by the sea. Two spirit-generals, female and male, were responsible for all activities below and above the earth respectively.

Traditional household deities included the gods of the hearth, the roof beam (in the main room where guests were received and family corpses laid out), and the outhouse. Shamans (*mudang*) were summoned in cases of demonic disturbance and they regularly performed rituals at community celebrations and ceremonies of thanksgiving.

Buddhism

A Buddhism that was focused on karma and the search for happiness was introduced to Goguryeo by a Chinese monk in 372 and to Baekje by the Indian monk Marananta in 384; both received imperial support. In Silla the people initially supported Buddhism, as did King Pophung and his minister Yi Chadon, but the majority of aristocrats resisted it until 527: then Yi arranged his own martyrdom, predicting that it would be accompanied by a miracle capable of winning over the aristocracy. The prediction came true, and the king was able to make Buddhism the state religion. In 540 King Chinhung established the Hwarang (Flower Youth) for aristocratic young men and introduced the five precepts (p. 215) as part of the ethical foundation for the group. And in 661 two monks named Wonhyo (617–686) and Uisang (625–702) set out on a trip to China in search of new teachers.

In the end they did not travel far. One night, while waiting out a rainstorm, they unknowingly slept in an ancient tomb and drank water that had collected in a human skull. The next morning Wonhyo was horrified to see what he had used as a drinking vessel; then he realized that his response had been determined solely by his mind. Having achieved enlightenment, Wonhyo returned home, left the monastery, and developed what came to be known as "interpenetrated Buddhism" (*tongbulgyo*), harmonizing the teachings of the Samron (Sanlun or Madhyamaka) and Yusik or Yugagyo (Weishi or Yogacara) schools and integrating into his practice the Jeongto (Pure Land) practice of reciting or remembering the Buddha's name as well. Wonhyo's *tongbulgyo* reflected the teachings of his friend Uisang, who had completed the trip to China and returned to found the Hwaeom school—the Korean version of the Huayan (Flower Garland) tradition.

The influence of Korean Buddhism spread beyond Korea's borders. The work of Wonhyo and Uisang influenced the Huayan patriarch, Fazang, in Tang China and the first mission to Japan was made during this period too. In 577 a second mission of scholars was sent abroad on the invitation of the Japanese rulers.

United Silla, Later Three Kingdoms, and Goryeo (668–1392)

Confucianism

Today Korea has the largest network of Confucian shrines in the world. The process of Confucianization started during the late Three Kingdoms period but it was not until the **Goryeo** (Koryo) period (918–1392), when Buddhism was at its height, that Confucianism became firmly rooted. King Taejo ("Ultimate Ancestor"), who united the Three Kingdoms that splintered from Silla and founded Goryeo in 918, was an ardent Buddhist but he also encouraged Confucian learning.

Taejo rejected Silla's tradition of governance by a hereditary aristocracy and adopted instead the examination-based bureaucratic system of Tang China. He is also said to have left for his successors a list of "Ten Injunctions" that reflected his syncretic approach, bringing together Buddhist, Confucian, and indigenous perspectives. The first injunction, for example, clearly honours the Buddhist tradition:

> The success of the great enterprise of founding our dynasty is entirely owing to the protective powers of the many Buddhas. We therefore must build temples for both Son [Meditation] and Kyo (Textual) Schools and appoint abbots, that they may perform the proper ceremonies and themselves cultivate the way (Lee 1985: 132).

But the third injunction pays tribute to the Confucian tradition:

> . . . if the eldest son is not worthy of the crown, let the second eldest succeed to the throne. If the second eldest, too, is unworthy, choose the brother the people consider the best qualified for the throne.

And the fourth injunction emphasizes the primacy of indigenous traditions:

In the past we have always had a deep attachment for the ways of China and all of our institutions have been modelled upon those of Tang. But our country occupies a different geographical location and our people's character is different from that of the Chinese. Hence, there is no reason to strain ourselves

Sites

Mount Gaya and Cheongju City, South Korea

The Goryeo period is famous for its printing projects involving Buddhism. Two projects stand out: the massive Tripitaka Koreana, carved on roughly 80,000 woodblocks, and the first book in the world (1377) to be printed using movable metal type.

Entitled *The Monk Baegun's Anthology of the Great Buddhist Patriarchs' Seon Teachings* but better known as *Jikji* (*Straight Pointing*), it was printed at the recently excavated Heungdeok Temple in Cheongju and is now housed in the National Library of France.

© John Van Hasselt/Sygma/Corbis

The *Tripitaka Koreana*, now kept at Haeinsa (Temple of the Ocean Mudra) on Mount Gaya, is the most complete collection of Buddhist texts in the world. Engraved in Chinese characters on 80,000 woodblocks, it was completed between 1237 and 1248. This immense government-sponsored project was undertaken in an effort to win the Buddha's protection against invasion by the Mongols.

unreasonably to copy the Chinese way . . . (H. Kang in Lee 1993: 263).

Soon after this, the influence of Confucianism was further reinforced when Choe Chung (948–1068) established a private Confucian Academy.

Buddhism

A new era began around 800 CE with the establishment of the Seon (Chan or Meditation) school (initially nine schools, the "nine mountains"). Although the established Gyo (doctrinal) schools resisted its innovations, two monks, Uicheon (1055–1101) and Jinul (1158–1210), effectively synthesized the Seon and Gyo.

Jinul brought together the two views on enlightenment, sudden and gradual, with the dictum "sudden enlightenment followed by gradual practice." He integrated *gwanhwa* (meditating on the word) or *gongan* practice into Seon, turned his back on the excesses of other Buddhist schools, and established a new community of pure-minded and disciplined Seon practitioners on Mount Jogye (Jogye Order).

Joseon (1392–1910)

Confucian Antipathy to Buddhism

In Korea as in China, Buddhism's success eventually led to corruption and backlash. The founder of the Joseon dynasty, another Taejo, banned the building of new Buddhist temples and stopped the growth of the monastic population. And his son

Taejong continued the effort: temples were disestablished, and their estates and workers, including slaves, confiscated; a great deal of damage done to Buddhist sculptures; and Buddhist activities were confined to specific areas—in particular, outside the cities and on the mountains.

Around the same time, Buddhist funerals and memorial rituals were discontinued and families began installing shrines for ancestral tablets in their homes, in accordance with Confucian custom. Eventually, the responsibility for performing the rites of ancestor veneration was entrusted to the first son, who became the only one with the right of inheritance. This system of primogeniture put an end to the Goryeo system under which female as well as male offspring were entitled to inherit and couples could hold property jointly.

There were moments of reprieve. Queen Munjeong, a devout Buddhist who governed for her young son, Myeongjong (r. 1545–67), repealed many of the anti-Buddhism laws. The Buddhists themselves, successfully fighting alongside others against the Japanese during the Imjin Wars (1592–98), won back respect and regained some lost ground.

Neo-Confucianism

Nevertheless, the process of Confucianization advanced. During the early 1500s, the philosopher Jo Gwangjo (Cho Kwang-jo) continued to root out superstitions deemed incompatible with Confucianism. He encouraged government by moral suasion and instituted a system of local self-government based on the idea of a village code or "Family

Sites

Seoul, South Korea

The Changdeokgung Palace (Palace of Prospering Virtue) complex was established by Taejong, the first king of the Joseon dynasty. It includes Jongmyo, the oldest and most authentic of the surviving Confucian royal shrines, which are dedicated to the ancestors of Joseon. It houses tablets bearing teachings of the royal family.

Compact," outlined by the Chinese Neo-Confucian Zhu Xi in a work entitled *Lu Family Compact with Additions and Deletions*. At the heart of this system was a notion of reciprocity expressed in mutual encouragement of morality, mutual supervision of conduct, mutual decorum in social relations, and mutual aid in times of hardship or disaster.

Zhu Xi's influence extended beyond the world of practical politics into the metaphysical realm. He believed that human beings have in them both a Principle or pattern of nature that is wholly good, and a vital or material force that can be good or bad. The latter is good when desires and emotions are expressed in appropriate balance and bad when a lack or an excess is expressed. This inspired a famous exchange of letters between the Korean philosophers I Hwang (Yi Hwang or Toegye) and I I (Yi I or Yulgok) in the mid-1500s.

At the centre of this exchange, known as the "Four–Seven Debate," was the relationship between the four heart-minds—which, according to Mencius, reflect the fundamental goodness of human nature—and the seven emotions (happiness, anger, sorrow, fear, love, hate, and desire)—which, according to "Centrality and Equilibrium," cause some human actions to be less than good when they are extreme and not expressed in correct proportion.

Both taking Zhu Xi as their starting point, I Hwang and I I arrived at different conclusions. I Hwang argued that principle or pattern in nature (*i*) rises and material force (*ki*) follows, implying that human nature is mixed from the beginning. I I, on the other hand, argued that if principle pervades everything, is uniform and undifferentiated, then it must be material force that initiates action, implying that human nature is originally wholly good. Behind the philosophers' quest for a deeper understanding of human nature was the commitment to psychological–moral transformation of the self—the Neo-Confucian equivalent of the self-cultivation emphasized in classic Confucianism.

The search for efficacious methods of self-improvement was not limited to men. In early Joseon Korea, as in Ming China, women's education became a focal point. Three prominent publications written by or for women were Queen Sohye's *Instructions for the Inner Quarters* (*Naehun*; 1475); a letter written by the seventeenth-century Confucian Song Siyol on the occasion of his daughter's marriage, emphasizing the importance of a mother's influence on her children; and a letter from Lady Hyegyeong (Hyegyong, 1735–1815) to her nephew in which she sought to impress on him the importance of Confucian virtues: being honest and conscientious, respectful of elders, affectionate and filial at home, and compassionate to paternal aunts.

As Neo-Confucianism became increasingly entrenched at the state level and Daoism was gradually assimilated into Joseon culture, Buddhist monastics argued for reconciliation of the various religions—in effect, syncretism. As the sixteenth-century monk Hyujeong (Hyujong) wrote in his *Mirror of Three Religions* (*Samga kwigam*): "An ancient man said: 'Confucianists plant the root, Taoists grow the root, and Buddhists harvest the root'" (Lee et al. 1993: 662). Nevertheless, Confucianism retained its dominant position.

◉ Recent Developments: 1897 to the Present

The late-nineteenth to mid-twentieth centuries marked a seismic change for Korea, forcing it to contend with Japanese imperialism and the increasing presence of the West.

Korean responses to the increasingly politically dominant and culturally influential West varied. One of the few English-speaking politicians of the time, Yun Chiho (1864–1945), favoured wholesale Westernization and an end to the relationship with a radically weakened and defeated China, which was then known as the "sick man of East Asia." Yet Korea was still implicitly expected to play the subordinate role. Yun, like his contemporaries in China, argued that if Koreans were poor and oppressed, her women degraded, families weak, and officials cruel, it was Confucianism that was to blame.

Yun's antipathy towards Confucianism was not unreasonable, for in addition to being seen as regressive and oppressive, it was associated with

Japanese imperialism. During Japan's occupation of Korea (1910–45), Confucianism was used as an imperial tool: the old Royal Confucian Academy was renovated and institutions like the Society for the Promotion of the Confucian Way were established to aid the imposition of Japanese culture on the Koreans.

Contemporary Confucianism

Other Korean scholars agreed that Korea's adherence to the conservative teachings of Zhu Xi, which focused on maintaining the status quo through mastery of classical literature, had held it back. However, like the Chinese New Confucians, they also believed that a renewed transnational Confucianism based on the traditional values of filial piety, chastity, and frugality could help to bring peace, security, and stability to the whole world. Among those scholars was Bak Eunsik (Pak Unsik, 1859–1925), who preferred the Confucianism of Wang Yangming even though Wang had been overshadowed by Zhu Xi in Korea.

Bak Eunsik saw hope in Wang Yangming's emphasis on the "manifesting" of the naturally "clear character" through a Mencian cultivation of the heart-mind and the uncovering of the innate goodness in human beings. Everyone, according to Wang, has the "innate knowledge of the good," but it is the noble person who nourishes and expresses it best. The exemplary person commiserates with other people in their suffering, with birds and animals about to be slaughtered, with broken plants, and even shattered tiles and stones. Bak was not alone in his choice of Wang's Confucianism as a response to modernity.

Gim Chungnyol (Kim Chungnyol), a professor of East Asian philosophy who studied with the New Confucian Fang Dongmei in the 1950s and 1960s, was an activist in the Korean democracy movement in the 1970s and 1980s. He believed that Confucianism could serve as an antidote to the excesses of capitalist industrialization. But the movement for the revival of Confucianism in Korea is not monolithic.

So Chonggi, for one, was critical of authoritarian rule even if it were Confucian. Nevertheless, like Bak, he believed that Confucianism could be good for Korea. Differentiating between "royal," "official," and "scholar" Confucianisms, he criticized all three for their narrow focus on "ethical politics," "ritual politics," and "eremitic politics," respectively. In their place he proposed a Confucianism of the people, based on their moral purity and creative capacities.

The recent establishment of an Institute of Confucian Cultural Studies as part of a nationwide network—headquartered at Sungkyunkwan University's Academy of East Asian Studies—suggests a revival of scholarly interest in the Confucian tradition. Yet despite the elitist interest in Confucianism, recent census data show that popular support for Confucianism as a religion is not strong.

Buddhism

The 35 years of Japanese occupation were particularly difficult for the Buddhists. A 1911 Temple Ordinance virtually dismantled the traditional system, replacing it with the Japanese system. The Japanese Governor-General gave temple abbots the right to private ownership and inheritance, replacing the traditional collective governance by the community. Monks from pro-Japan factions also began to adopt Japanese customs that violated standard monastic rules, such as marrying and having children. Then the 1920 Temple Ordinance gave the Japanese government direct oversight of the 31 main temples in the country; and following the invasion of China in 1937 Korean temples increasingly came under Japanese control. After the defeat of the Japanese in 1945, deep rifts developed between the "Japanized" monks and those who had remained celibate. In time the Jogye Order became the dominant school and took over the management of the temples from the married priests.

Since the 1960s, Buddhism has grown by adopting a Protestant model of active missionizing, encouraging lay associations and focusing on youth. The South Korean government has devoted a great deal of resources to restoring and reconstructing historic temples.

Won Buddhism

Won or Circle Buddhism (Wonbulgyo) is a twentieth-century school that can be placed in the Seon tradition because of its practice of meditation and its emphasis on learning to harness the mind. The circle that is its symbol stands for ultimate reality and the belief that, in the words of its founder, Sotaesan (1891–1943), "All beings are of one Reality and all things and principles originate from one source, where the truth of no birth and no death and the principle of cause and effect operate on an interrelated basis as a single, perfect organ."

Today Won Buddhism has a global presence.

North Korea

In 1953 the Korean peninsula was divided into two parts. North Korea, like the PRC, is communist, and although its laws support religious freedom, in practice religion is barely tolerated. There are reports that Buddhism fares a little better than Christianity, but it still has a very limited presence in the country.

South Korea

In the early 2000s, census data showed that nearly half of South Korea's population professed to have no religion—a similar pattern to the Chinese. Those who did claim an institutional affiliation were almost equally divided between Buddhism and Christianity (mainly Protestant, especially Pentecostal).

Unspecified affiliations accounted for less than 1 per cent of the population, while Confucianism came last at a negligible 0.3 per cent and the indigenous shamanic tradition was statistically invisible. The apparent lack of institutional affiliation and personal dedication to either shamanism or Confucianism is striking. Yet both these traditions still seem pervasive in Korean life.

There are more than 200 new religions in South Korea. Their beliefs and practices are syncretic, often considered "cultural" rather than "religious," and may not be captured in census statistics. But they demonstrate well the pervasiveness of Korean religiosity and its multiple sources of influence: from ancient indigenous shamanism through the older foreign religions of Confucianism, Daoism, and Buddhism to more recent arrivals such as Christianity.

Some modern progressives urge the revival of folk traditions rather than Confucianism as a way of reclaiming Korean culture, especially because the credibility of Confucianism in Korea was so profoundly compromised by its function in Japanese imperialism, as well as its inability to arrest the military, political, and cultural advance of the West. Others, however, see shamanism as mere superstition and call for it to be rooted out. A sampling of new religious movements shows that Korean religious responses to modernity are diverse.

The oldest of the new movements, the Religion of the Heavenly Way or Cheondogyo (Chondogyo), was founded by Choe Je-u in 1860, in response to Catholicism. It syncretizes Korean, Chinese, and Christian values; and combines monotheism and belief in the equality of all human beings with the broad East Asian vision of religious practice as enabling humans to live in harmony with the universe.

Another response to the dominance of Western culture and growing globalization is the Religion of the Great Ancestors (Daejonggyo), which sees itself as a revival of ancient Korean shamanism. Founded in 1910 by Na Chol, it depicts God as Korean and presents the heavenly triad of indigenous ancestors—Hwanin, Hwanung, and Dangun—as an alternative to the Christian Trinity.

Other new religions have been influenced by the Daoist internal alchemy aimed at longevity and spiritual transcendence. Thus Dahn Yoga focuses on health and well-being. Its founder, Ilchi (One Finger or Pointing the Way) Lee (1951–) is also the president of the Korea Institute of Brain Sciences, the University of Brain Education, and the Global Cyber University in South Korea. He is also the

© Seoul Shinmun/epa/Corbis

Students wearing traditional costumes perform during one of the regular celebrations of Confucius held at Sungkyunkwan University in Seoul.

founder of the Tao Fellowship and the International Brain Education Association, a non-profit that promotes brain education.

⊛ Summary

The ancient popular beliefs and practices at the root of the elite religions of China and Korea do not claim exclusive truth. They come from many different places and cultures. Yet most of them share a single aspiration to harmony—individual and communal, earthly and cosmic. Furthermore, many see the achievement of harmony as dependent on the disciplined transcendence of self. Although individual groups vary in their specific goals and methods, they have all tended to believe that basic human desires—for material well-being, health, familial joy, personal security, social stability, spiritual maturity, and, ultimately, release from the cycle of rebirth—should be harnessed and directed towards the care of others: family and friends, the community, the state, and the natural world.

Like Korea's, China's religious culture has undergone significant transformations over the last 1500 years, incorporating new influences—from Confucianism, Daoism, and Buddhism to Christianity—without abandoning its indigenous shamanistic traditions. Today both societies remain pluralistic and syncretic. None of the traditional religions have disappeared. Buddhism has thrived in Taiwan while Christianity has flourished in Hong Kong and South Korea. New religious movements have developed in Taiwan and Hong Kong; and there are now more than 200 active new ones in South Korea. But religious freedom remains elusive in the People's Republic and North Korea. How the various religions will develop and interact with one another remains to be seen.

Sacred/Foundational Texts

Religion	Classical and Sacred Texts	Composition/ Compilation Process	Compilation/ Revision Process	Use (Oral, Legal, Ritual)
Confucianism (Texts are understood to come from sages and are not considered "sacred")	*Book of Music, Poetry, History, Changes, Rites* and the *Spring* and *Autumn Annals*	5th–3rd centuries BCE	175 CE stone engraving of the Classics after the burning of the books in 213 BCE; the Book of Music is lost	Used for home education; curriculum assigned for state examination and official learning
Confucianism	*Classic of Filial Piety, The Analects, Er Ya* (the earliest Chinese dictionary), three commentaries on the *Spring and Autumn Annals* and *Rites* in three sections (*The Rites of Zhou, The Book of Rites,* and *Ceremonial Rites*)	7th–10th centuries	The Five Classics increased to Nine and then Twelve Books and inscribed on stone	As above
Confucianism	Zhu Xi formulates standard texts into the *Four Books* (*Great Learning, Centrality and Equilibrium* both from the *Book of Rites, Mencius, The Analects*) and *Five Classics* from ancient times	10th–13th centuries	With *Mencius*, the Twelve Classics become Thirteen	As above
Confucianism	Four Books for women include *Admonitions for Women, Filial Piety for Women, Analects for Women,* and *Instructions for the Inner Quarters*	1st–2nd centuries	7th–9th centuries see two new additions; *Instructions* is added in the 15th century; *Filial Piety* replaced by a *Handy Record of Rules for Women*	Education for women
Daoism (early texts seen primarily as words of wisdom from sages)	*Daodejing*	Contested but early 3rd century BCE generally accepted	3rd century CE Wang Bi commentary	Liturgical use and acts as basis for movements seeking legitimacy from Laozi
Daoism	*Zhuangzi*	First seven chapters attributed to namesake; 4th to 3rd centuries BCE	Guo Xiang believed to be the compiler of the current text	Known as the *Classic of South China* (*Nanhuajing*) and used in education
Daoism	*Techniques of the Mind* and *Inward Training*	4th century BCE	Both were lost to the main tradition and "found" recently in the Legalist *Guanzi*	Likely used as meditation manual
Daoism	*Classic of the Great Peace*	1st century CE	Reassembled in 6th century after its destruction in 3rd century	Ritual use and instructional manual

Continued

Sacred/Foundational Texts (Continued)

Religion	Classical and Sacred Texts	Composition/ Compilation Process	Compilation/ Revision Process	Use (Oral, Legal, Ritual)
Daoism	*Master Who Embraces Spontaneous Nature or Simplicity*	320s	14th century saw the combination of the "inner" and "outer" sections of the current text	Used as manual for external alchemy
Daoism	High Clarity scriptures	Revealed 364 to 379	Edited into *Pronouncements of the Perfected* by Tao Hongjing	Doctrinal and ritual use
Daoism	*Scripture for the Salvation of Humanity* of the Lingbao school	Revealed 4th century	12th century; 61-chapter version presented to Song emperor	Used in recitation
Daoism	*Fifteen Precepts for the Establishing of the Teaching*	12th century	Collected as part of Wang Chongyang's writings	Doctrinal for Complete Truth school
Buddhism	Three Baskets of the Theravada/Hinayana	Originals from India; see chapter on Buddhism	Most translated during the third to sixth centuries	Used in study and as reference for monastic law
Buddhism	Many; core to Chinese and Korean practice are treatises like *The Awakening of Faith*; sutras like *The Pure Land* (in three volumes), *The Lotus, Flower Garland, Platform of Hui-neng, Vimalakirti,* and others (see the chapter on Buddhism); and Recorded Sayings by Chan masters like Baegan's *jikji.* Wumen's *Gateless Gate,* and the *Blue Cliff Records*	Most from South Asia except for *The Platform Sutra* and records of sayings from masters of the Chan school; and *The Awakening of Faith* which has no Sanskrit original	Most translated during the fourth to sixth centuries	See Chapter 5
Popular tradition	Innumerable tracts of religious rituals and devotion	Throughout history	New writings appear based on new movements	Instructional and ritual

Discussion Questions

1. How does the popular shrine described at the beginning of this chapter illustrate the syncretic quality of Chinese religion?

2. What assumptions and values do Confucianism and Daoism share? What sets them apart?

3. Would you consider Confucianism to be patriarchal, misogynist, and oppressive for women? Explain your position, using evidence from China and Korea.

4. What are some of the core spiritual concerns in the early prototypical Daoist texts? How did they influence the goals, methods of cultivation, and institutional development of religious Daoism?

5. Compare and contrast classical and Neo-Confucianism. What accounts for their differences?

6. What qualities would make an ideal Buddhist woman?

7. How would you characterize the relationship between Daoism and Buddhism through the dynasties?

8. Explore points of tension and convergence between Confucianism, Daoism, and Buddhism.

9. What allows for such disparate groups as the Seven Sages of the Bamboo Grove and Complete Truth to coexist under the umbrella of Daoism? What makes them both Daoist?

10. Who are the "New Confucians"? What issues are they tackling? What are their goals?

11. How do you understand Engaged or Humanistic Buddhism? How does it differ from traditional Buddhism?

12. How have Chinese religious traditions tried to "modernize" themselves?

13. Recall the Korean foundation myths outlined in this chapter. What do they suggest about the nature of Korean culture and religiosity?

14. Explore the development of modern Korean Buddhism and outline some of its challenges.

15. In this book, the religious traditions of East Asia have been organized geographically in two groups: "China and Korea" and "Japan." Would a different organization, based on the traditions—indigenous shamanism (as in Shinto and *mugyo*), Daoism, Confucianism, and East Asian Buddhism—be more appropriate or less so? Why?

Glossary

Ban Zhao (c. 48–112 CE) The influential female Confucian scholar who wrote *Admonitions* (or *Lessons*) *for Women*.

Chan From Sanskrit *dhyana* (meditation); the Buddhist school known as Seon in Korea and Zen in Japan.

Confucius (551–479 BCE) The first teacher of Confucianism, known in Chinese as Kongzi or Kongfuzi.

Dao/dao Either the "Way" in the sense of the Ultimate or the "way" in the sense of the path taken by followers of a particular tradition.

Daodejing The *Classic of the Way and Power or Virtue* is the multi-authored foundational Daoist text purportedly written by Laozi.

de Power or virtue.

Dong Zhongshu (195?–105? BCE) The most prominent Confucian of the Early Han, who helped establish Confucianism as the state religion.

five phases The generative and destructive cycles between metal, wood, water, fire, and water represent a dynamic view of the cosmos. The concept is also translated as five agents or elements depending on the meaning. See *wuxing*.

Han Yu (768–824) Played a pivotal role in the revival of Confucianism in a period when it was overshadowed by Daoism and Buddhism.

Huayan Flower Garland Buddhism; Hwaeom in Korea.

Jingtu Pure Land Buddhism.

junzi A person of exemplary or authoritative behaviour, especially in Confucianism; traditionally translated in English as "gentleman," implying the virtues of the upper class; a superior person, or one of virtue and exceptional character.

Laozi The "Old Master"; the putative patriarch of Daoism and author of the *Daodejing*; may or may not have been an actual historical figure.

li The single English transliteration used for two different Chinese words. *Li* in the first sense refers to ritual practice and decorum and is usually translated as "rites." *Li* in the second sense refers to the pattern in a natural material such as wood or stone; it was used by the Neo-Confucians to designate the force that pervades the cosmos and is translated as "principle."

lohan Arhat; an enlightened disciple of the Buddha.

lunhui Rebirth or *samsara*.

Mencius (c. 343–289 BCE) The second most prominent Confucian thinker, known in Chinese as Meng Ke, Master Meng, or Mengzi; he believed that human nature is inherently good.

pusa Bodhisattva; an enlightened being who foregoes release/liberation to stay in the world and help others.

qi material force or vital energy.

qigong A "breath" discipline or set of exercises used to enhance health and spiritual well-being; also the vital or material energy or force that animates everything in the universe.

ren The central Confucian virtue, usually translated as "humaneness," "benevolence," "goodness," or "compassion."

taiji The "Great Ultimate," understood to coexist with the Ultimate of Non-being; also the term for the slow-motion exercise sequence widely known in English as Tai Chi.

Wang Yangming (1472–1529) The Ming Confucian who challenged Zhu Xi's understanding of self-cultivation and established the Neo-Confucian School of Mind.

wuwei "Not-doing" as a way of being in the world: a state not of "doing nothing" but of acting without intention or self-interest; an ideal for both Daoists and Confucians, though most prominently associated with the former.

wuxing Five agents, elements, or phases. See also **five phases** and **yin-yang**.

xin The single English transliteration used for two different Chinese characters: the first is translated throughout this chapter as "heart-mind" when discussing Daoism and Confucianism and is associated with both the thinking and feeling capacities; the same character also refers to Mind or Consciousness in Buddhism. The second character means

trustworthiness, a quality valued by Daoists and Confucians alike.

Xunzi (c. 310–219 BCE) The third most important classical Confucian thinker; he believed that human nature is evil and that conscious effort is required to develop goodness.

yi A moral sense of what is right, what is required and appropriate for a situation; most often used in conjunction with *ren*.

yinguo Cause and effect or karma.

yin-yang wuxing "Yin" and "yang" originally referred to the shady and sunny sides of a mountain, but in time they came to be associated with female and male qualities and, more broadly, complementary forces in the universe. *Wu* means "five" and *xing* can be translated as "element," "agent," "force," or "phase." Together, these terms specify the dynamic nature of the universe—a concept integral to the Naturalist school of thought, which was popular during the Han dynasty.

Zhang Daoling According to tradition, he established the oldest surviving Daoist school, the Way of the Celestial Masters, after Laozi appeared to him in a vision in 142 CE.

Zhuangzi (369?–286?) The second most important early Daoist thinker, after Laozi; also the title of the book attributed to him.

Zhu Xi (1130–1200) The most important member of the Neo-Confucian School of Principle. He synthesized early Song Confucian writings, focused on book learning, and sought to find the principle/pattern common to Nature.

ziran Spontaneity or "self-so-ness."

Further Reading

Bell, Daniel A., and Chaibong Hahm, eds. 2003. *Confucianism for the Modern World*. Cambridge: Cambridge University Press. Draws from Chinese, Korean, and Japanese texts and histories to argue that Confucianism is relevant to our world.

Buswell, Robert E., ed. 2007. *Religions of Korea in Practice*. Princeton: Princeton University Press. Presents primary-source selections regarding ordinary devotional beliefs and practices as well as critical analysis; also includes a helpful introductory essay by Don Baker.

Elman, Benjamin A., ed. 2002. *Rethinking Confucianism: Past and Present in China, Japan, Korea, and Vietnam*. Los Angeles: UCLA Asian Pacific Monograph Series. Explores issues of gender and national variations, and asks who represents Confucianism.

Kirkland, Russell. 2004. *Taoism: The Enduring Tradition*. London: Routledge. An introductory text by an author who believes Daoism has been misrepresented and seeks to offer a new perspective.

Kohn, Livia, ed. 1993. *The Taoist Experience: An Anthology*. Albany: SUNY Press. Primary sources (with brief notes) for a range of philosophical, liturgical, and alchemical texts, mostly from medieval Daoism.

Lopez, Donald S., ed. 1996. *Religions of China in Practice*. Princeton: Princeton University Press. Includes essays on the religious practices of ethnic minorities such as the Manchus and Yi; Stephen Teiser's introductory essay provides a helpful overview.

Miller, James. 2003. *Daoism: A Short Introduction*. Oxford: Oneworld. Covers the historical development, political involvement, and physical practices of Daoism as well as its understanding of nature.

Rainey, Lee Dian. 2010. *Confucius and Confucianism: The Essentials*. London: Wiley-Blackwell. A delightfully accessible introduction to the origins and development of Confucianism, with an account of its contemporary relevance.

Robinet, Isabelle. 1993. *Taoist Meditation: The Mao-Shan Tradition of Great Purity*. Julian F. Pas and Norman J. Giradot, trans. Albany: SUNY Press. A detailed study of the Shangqing (Highest Clarity) tradition.

Wu, Ch'eng-en. 1970 [1943]. *Monkey*. Arthur Waley, trans. New York: Grove Press. A fictional look at popular religious beliefs and practices in medieval China.

Yao, Xinzhong. 2000. *An Introduction to Confucianism*. Cambridge: Cambridge University Press. Focuses on China; Korea and Japan are dealt with very briefly.

Yu, Anthony. 2005. *State and Religion in China*. Chicago and La Salle, IL: Open Court. Argues persuasively that religions in China have always been closely involved with worldly politics.

Recommended Websites

www.orientalarchitecture.com

Asian Historical Architecture offers photographs of numerous religious sites in China, Korea, and other countries in Asia, with brief historical notes and descriptions of how the buildings are used.

www.clickkorea.org/

A general-interest site, sponsored by the Korea Foundation; to access essays on Korean religions, select the main category "Thought & Religion" and then choose from six subcategories.

www.stanford.edu/~pregadio/index.html

"The Golden Elixir: Taoism and Chinese Alchemy" is hosted by Fabrizio Pregadio of Stanford University, who gives a concise introduction to Daoism and includes an impressive list of sources on alchemical beliefs and practices in Daoism.

eng.taoism.org.hk

The Taoist Culture and Information Centre offers an insider's view of Daoism's history and place in the world today. The site is sponsored by a Daoist temple in Hong Kong and maintained with the help of scholars from North America, Europe, and China.

www.chinakongzi.org

The Chinese-language site of the China Confucius Foundation (CCF). Established in 1984, the CCF dedicated to promoting the teachings of Confucius.

www.ica.org.cn

The mandate of the International Confucian Association is to advance the study of Confucianism in order to promote peace and prosperity around the world. Its site is also available in Chinese.

english.hanban.org/node_10971.htm

The English-language site of the Confucius Institute/Classroom offers information on teaching materials, tests, teachers, and scholarships.

college.chinese.cn/en

The Confucius Institute Online; the contents of this site are available in many languages, including Chinese, French, German, Russian, Korean, Spanish, Japanese and Arabic.

www.fgs.org.tw/english/index.html

Foguangshan (Buddha's Light Mountain) is an ecumenical group that favours Pure Land teachings; it is based in Gaoxiong in southern Taiwan.

www.dharmadrum.org/

Fagushan (Dharma Drum Mountain) is a Chan group headquartered in New Taipei city in Taiwan.

tw.tzuchi.org/en/

Tzu Chi (Compassionate Relief), also transliterated as Cizi, is a Taiwanese group, led by the nun Zhengyan, involved primarily in healthcare.

References

al Faruqi, I., and D.E. Sopher, eds. 1974. *Historical Atlas of the Religions of the World*. New York: Macmillan.

Bell, Daniel A., and Chaibong Hahm, eds. 2003. *Confucianism for the Modern World*. Cambridge: Cambridge University Press.

Chen, Kenneth. 1964. *Buddhism in China. A Historical Survey*. Princeton, New Jersey: Princeton University Press.

Ch'oe, Yongcho, Peter Lee, and W. Theodore de Bary, eds. 2000. *Sources of Korean Tradition*. Vol. II. New York: Columbia University Press.

Cissell, Tsai Kathryn Ann, tr. 1994. *Lives of the Nuns: Biographies of Chinese Buddhist Nuns from the Fourth to Sixth Centuries*. Honolulu: University of Hawai'i Press.

Cleary, Thomas. 1989. *Immortal Sisters: Secret Teachings of Taoist Women*. Berkeley: North Atlantic Books.

de Bary, Theodore, ed. 1972. *The Buddhist Tradition in India, China and Japan*. New York: Vintage Books.

———, and Irene Bloom, comp. 1999. *Sources of Chinese Tradition*, 2nd edn. Vol. 1. New York: Columbia University Press.

———, and Richard Lufrano, comp. 1999. *Sources of Chinese Tradition*, 2nd edn. Vol. 2. New York: Columbia University Press.

Fung, Yu-lan. 1934/1953. *A History of Chinese Philosophy*. Vol. 2. Derk Bodde, trans. Princeton: Princeton University Press.

Inagaki, Hisao, trans. 1994. *The Three Pure Land Sutras*. Kyoto: Nagata Bunshodo.

Jochim, Christian. 1986. *Chinese Religions: A Cultural Perspective*. Englewood Cliffs, NJ: Prentice-Hall.

Kirkland, Russell. 2004. *Taoism: The Enduring Tradition*. New York and London: Routledge.

Lau, D.C., trans. 1970. *Mencius*. Middlesex and New York: Penguin.

———, trans. 1963. *Lao Tzu: Tao Te Ching*. Middlesex and New York: Penguin.

Lee, Ki-Baik. 1985. *A New History of Korea*. Edward Wagner, trans. Cambridge, MA: Harvard University Press.

Lee, Peter H., et al., eds. 1993. *Sourcebook of Korean Civilization*. Vol. I. New York: Columbia University Press.

Lewis, Mark Edward. 2009. *China Between Empires: The Northern and Southern Dynasties*. Cambridge, MA, and London: The Belknap Press of Harvard University Press.

Little, Reg. 1995. "Confucius in Beijing: The Conference of the International Confucian Foundation." *Culture Mandala: The Bulletin of the Centre for East-West Cultural and Economic Studies*. Vol. 1, issue 2, article 4. Available at http://epublications.bond.edu.au/cm/vol1/iss2/4.

Owen, Stephen, ed. and trans. 1996. *An Anthology of Chinese Literature*. New York, London: W.W. Norton.

Pregadio, Fabrizio. 2006. *Great Clarity: Daoism and Alchemy in Medieval China*. Stanford: Stanford University Press.

Price, A.F. and Wong Mou-lam. 1990 (1969). *The Diamond Sutra & The Sutra of Hui-neng*. Boston: Shambhala.

Raphals, Lisa. 1998. *Sharing the Light: Representations of Women and Virtue in Early China*. Albany: SUNY Press.

Reps, Paul, comp. 1989 (1960). *Zen Flesh, Zen Bones: A Collection of Zen and Pre-Zen Writings*. New York, London, Toronto, Sydney, Auckland: Anchor Books, Doubleday.

Roetz, Heiner. 2008. "Confucianism between Tradition and Modernity, Religion, and Secularization: Questions to Tu Weiming." *Dao* 7: 367-380.

Roth, Harold D. 1999. *Original Tao: Inward Training and the Foundations of Taoist Mysticism*. New York: Columbia University Press.

Sommer, Deborah, ed. 1995. *Chinese Religion: An Anthology of Sources*. New York, Oxford: Oxford University Press.

Watson, Burton, trans. 2001. *The Essential Lotus: Selections from the Lotus Sutra*. New York: Columbia University Press.

———. 1997. *The Vimalakirti Sutra*. New York: Columbia University Press.

———. 1968. *The Complete Works of Chuang Tzu*. New York: Columbia University Press.

———. 1963. *Xunzi: Basic Writings*. New York: Columbia University Press.

Note

1. Some scholars prefer 552, based on scientific dating of an eclipse mentioned in the records of the time.

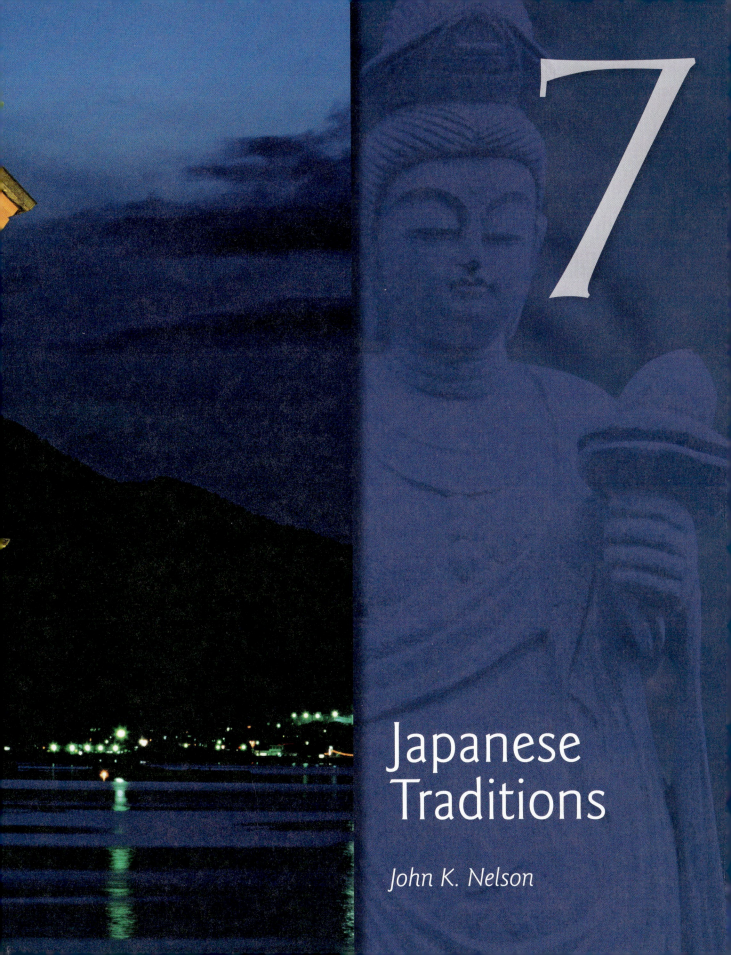

7

Japanese Traditions

John K. Nelson

Traditions at a Glance

Numbers

All numbers are based on self-assessment by the groups concerned. Because most Japanese religions are complementary rather than exclusive, the numbers of adherents reported by various sects may reflect periodic participation rather than ongoing membership.

Shinto: Estimates range from 3.5 million self-described adherents to more than 100 million if annual New Year's visits to shrines are counted as indicating "Shinto" affiliation.

Buddhism: Estimates range from 85.1 million, based on a 1999 government assessment of membership in the major denominations, to more than 100 million.

"New" religions: Estimates range from 10 to 30 million worldwide.

Christianity: Generally estimated at a little under 1 million nationwide.

Distribution

Buddhism, Shinto, and "new" religions are practised in every part of Japan, as well as in overseas communities. Japan itself counts approximately 75,000 Buddhist temples and more than 80,000 Shinto shrines, although many of the latter do not have resident priests.

Founders

Shinto is an ethnic religion with no founder. Important founders of new Buddhist schools include Saicho (Tendai), Kukai (Shingon), Eisai (Rinzai Zen), Dogen (Soto Zen), Honen (Pure Land), Shinran (True Pure Land), and Nichiren (Nichiren).

Deities

Shinto has a vast number of deities, many of which are specific to local communities. The Sun Goddess, Amaterasu, has been promoted as the supreme deity since the late 1800s because of her affiliation with the imperial household. However, one of the most widely distributed deities is Hachiman, associated with military valour.

The primary deities in Buddhism include the Medicine Buddha, the Cosmic Buddha, and Amida, the Buddha of the Pure Land, along with various bodhisattvas associated with compassion, healing, and deliverance from hell.

Authoritative Texts

Since the nineteenth century the primary texts for Shinto have been the *Kojiki: Record of Ancient Matters* and the *Nihon Shoki*. Individual Buddhist denominations and "new" religions all have their own primary texts.

Noteworthy Teachings

Shinto emphasizes harmony with nature, sincerity, and ritual purity. Each Buddhist denomination (Tendai, Shingon, Rinzai Zen, Soto Zen, Pure Land, True Pure Land, and Nichiren) and "new" religion (Tenrikyo, Kurozumikyo, Rissho Koseikai, etc.) likewise emphasizes key teachings that differentiate it from competing sects: secrets about the nature of reality, how universal salvation can be achieved through faith in the Buddha of the Pure Land, the perfection of the *Lotus Sutra*, the necessity of performing memorial rites for ancestral spirits, and so on.

The great "floating" torii gate at the Itsukushima Shinto shrine. Each of the main posts is a giant camphor tree said to be some 500 years old (Source: GARDEL Bertrand/hemis.fr/Getty Images).

In this chapter you will learn about

- the interactivity of diverse religious traditions and practices in Japan
- the features and interventions of spiritual and religious agents
- the myths, history, and development of Japan's major religious traditions
- the strong influence that politics has had on religion in Japan
- the transitions and transformations of religious practice in the modern and contemporary periods.

Japanese religions have served the aspirations, anxieties, and concerns of the people living on the Japanese islands for several millennia. Long before the establishment of shrines to local deities and Buddhist temples in the third and sixth centuries respectively, local clans had developed close relationships with both deities of the natural world and the spirits of their ancestors. Reciprocity was a key dynamic of these relationships, in which humans sent their petitions to the deities, accompanied by ritual offerings, and the deities were expected to respond by bestowing blessings in the form of bountiful harvests, plentiful children, stable political and social conditions, and so on. There was brand-name loyalty to the ancestral spirits of one's own household and clan; yet there was also acknowledgement of the powers of the many other deities (**kami**) associated with natural phenomena such as fire, water, climate, mountains, and the spirits of animals and plants. When (as often happened) things went wrong—when the harmonious balance of the relationship between humans and spirits was disturbed by plague, famine, earthquake, typhoons, war, death—efforts to restore it via rituals were renewed. This pattern is common to all Japanese religions and will serve as a point of departure and return throughout the following discussion.

To discuss Japan's religious traditions with any degree of accuracy, it is necessary to juggle and juxtapose perspectives from cultural studies, history, politics, and anthropology, as well as religious studies. Even then, to encompass all the diverse and complex traditions that inform Japanese society in the present day is a challenge. Shinto, or the "way of the *kami*," is often said by its priests to be more than 2,000 years old. And yet history shows us that it has gone through several transformations, some as recently as 150 years ago. Buddhism likewise defies easy assumptions; for example, only a small segment of priests and practitioners have anything to do with meditation. Layered on an even older tradition of venerating ancestral spirits, the major contemporary Buddhist denominations (of which there are seven, with very different perspectives and practices) have their roots in the medieval period and yet must continually reinvent themselves to retain the financial support of the Japanese people. Nearly every temple has a homepage, and many priests use Facebook and Twitter to stay in touch with their parishioners and supporters, but there is no guarantee that a younger generation highly skeptical of religion in general will develop affiliations with local temples. It is no exaggeration to say that Japanese religious traditions force us to rethink the social, cultural, and individual dimensions of religion in a rapidly changing world.

✺ Overview

The Rousing Drum

In a small city deep in the mountains of central Japan, tens of thousands of people—some laughing, chatting, and yelling; others quietly expectant—fill the evening streets for the festival of the "rousing drum." At 9:30 an enormous drum, a metre and a half (five feet) in height, will emerge from the city's main Shinto shrine, having been blessed by priests in solemn rituals. It will then be hoisted and affixed to a platform that will be carried through the streets by as many as 170 men. Adding to the weight of the platform will be two male strikers, one on each side of the drum, and eight "guardians" representing local officials. But the weight is only part of the challenge that the bearers will

City of Hida

The *okoshidaiko* or "rousing drum" festival takes place every spring in the city of Furukawa, Nagano prefecture. Smaller drums from neighbourhood associations try to topple a large drum representing the city government and main Shinto shrine as it is carried through the streets.

face, for as the drum makes its way through the streets it will be "attacked" by neighbourhood teams with their own (smaller) drums mounted on platforms, who will attempt to fight through the mass of guardians at ground level and occupy a position of honour immediately behind the main drum.

Fuelled by generous amounts of sake, the ensuing clashes seem anything but conducive to community solidarity. The festival is like a steam vent designed to release the pressure created by class and economic differences. In fact, injuries are common; parked vehicles are frequently damaged, and houses belonging to greedy landlords or stingy merchants may be vandalized. Old-timers still remember with pride the year when festival-goers trashed the local police station. Yet the event is promoted by both municipal and tourist associations as representing "the spirit of Furukawa."

Mr Sato's Funeral

After nearly a week of preparation, the funeral for Mr Sato Hideo (in Japan, the surname precedes the given name) is unfolding with the precision of a military operation. In a building constructed specifically for funerals, on the grounds of a large temple, the casket sits at the front of a hall decorated by hundreds of white chrysanthemums. A portrait of Mr Sato, smiling and grandfatherly, has been placed in the centre of the display, surrounded by candles and food offerings that recall a Buddhist altar.

Professional funeral directors, men and women wearing black suits, black armbands, and white

Timeline

c. 8000 BCE	Hunter-gatherers produce sophisticated cord-pattern pottery, arrowheads, and human figures with possible religious significance
c. 450–250 CE	Immigration from north Asia introduces new technology, cultural forms, language, religious rituals, etc.
c. 250–600	Kofun period; rulers interred in massive burial mounds (*kofun*), with grave goods and clay models (*haniwa*) of attendants that indicate complex local hierarchies in this life and the next
538	Introduction of Buddhism; Yamato clan establishes its dominance
594	"Prince" Shotoku (*Shotoku taishi*) promotes Confucian principles alongside Buddhism; later acknowledged as patron saint of Buddhism in Japan
600s	Early temple building; ruler referred to as "heavenly sovereign" (*tenno*)
710–794	Nara period; capital city, Heijokyo, located on site of present-day Nara
712, 720	Compilation of two key texts (*Kojiki*, *Nihon Shoki*) used to legitimate imperial rule and aristocratic privileges; more than a thousand years later, these texts would be used in the campaign to revitalize "Shinto"
752	Dedication of Todaiji temple and completion of its Great Buddha image
785	Saicho, founder of Tendai sect, establishes a temple on Mount Hiei near Kyoto
794–1184	Heian period; capital city, Heiankyo, moved to what is now Kyoto
834	Kukai, founder of Shingon sect, establishes a monastery on Mount Koya
1039	Tendai monks attack monasteries of rival Buddhist sects
1052	Beginning of the "Final Decline of the Buddhist Dharma" (age of *mappo*) marked by fires, famines, earthquakes, wars, pestilence, etc.
1175	Honen begins propagating "Pure Land" Buddhism
1185–1333	Kamakura period, characterized by dominance of the samurai class; capital moved to Kamakura
1200	Eisai establishes Rinzai Zen school with support of the samurai
1233	Dogen establishes Soto Zen school
1253	Nichiren forms a sect centred on recitation of the *Lotus Sutra*
1254	Honen's disciple Shinran introduces "True Pure Land" Buddhism
1274, 1281	Attempted invasions by Mongol armies are thwarted when violent storms, called "divine winds" (*kamikaze*), sink many of their ships
1430–1500	Major fires, famine, epidemics, social disorder; Onin War (1467) devastates Kyoto and marks start of regional power struggles
1474–1550	True Pure Land peasant protest movement spreads throughout the country
1542	Systematization of Shinto shrines, priestly certification via Yoshida clan
1549	Christianity enters Japan with the Jesuit Francis Xavier

Continued

1573–1602	Gradual centralization of political power; Oda Nobunaga, Toyotomi Hideyoshi, and Tokugawa Ieyasu establish military regimes that subdue regional lords
1603–1867	Edo Period; Tokugawa clan dominates all political, military, and bureaucratic activity; country closed to outside trade in 1633
1638	Shimabara rebellion; Christianity banned
1644–1860	Rise of Neo-Confucian teachings as challenge to Buddhist dominance
1705	First major pilgrimage of commoners to Ise Grand Shrines
1812	Beginning of movement to revitalize Shinto
1853–1867	Commodore Matthew Perry arrives in Japan and demands open ports; Christian missionaries return; regional wars between feudal and imperial forces end with defeat of Tokugawa shogunate
1868	New Meiji government orders separation of *kami* and buddhas, resulting in destruction of temples and religious art throughout the country
1879	Establishment of Yasukuni Shrine, where the spirits of military dead are venerated
1890–1944	State campaign to establish ideology centred on notions of imperial divinity, sacred nature of Japan, and military conquest
1936–1945	War in the Pacific, ending in the systematic destruction of most major and many minor Japanese cities
1945–1953	Allies occupy Japan; emperor renounces divinity; Shinto's status as state religion revoked
1995	Aum Shinrikyo attack on Tokyo subway; government passes new laws regulating religion organizations and activity
2011	Great Eastern Japan Earthquake of 11 March kills more than 19,000 people and causes a meltdown of three nuclear reactors, as well as tremendous property damage. In the aftermath, Japan's religious organizations provide substantial material and spiritual relief.

gloves, direct the proceedings in soft yet commanding voices. Hired by the family and subcontracted by the temple, they have orchestrated every part of the ceremony: the syrupy background music, the guest books, the arrangements for voluntary donations, the refreshments for guests, transportation to the crematorium for relatives.

As the mourners file in, three at a time, each one takes a pinch of sand-like incense and sprinkles it on glowing charcoal before bowing to the portrait. Although ceiling exhaust fans are set on high, smoke soon fills the room—but no one leaves for fresh air. In three hours, after the funeral has concluded and the body has been cremated at a high-tech facility nearby, family members and close relatives will use special chopsticks to select astonishingly white bone fragments for the urn.

All the identities Mr Sato assumed in the course of his 83 years—son, brother, soldier, father, businessman, civil servant, poetry aficionado, grandfather, gardener, world traveller—are now consigned to the past as he takes on his final role, that of "ancestor." This will remain Mr Sato's identity for the next 33 years—the time it will take before his spirit fully leaves this world and enters into the undifferentiated collectivity of the family's "distant" ancestors. Until then, his spirit must be venerated regularly with rituals, offerings, and grave visitations, lest it take offence and seek retribution.

Performing Belief

A young woman in her early twenties, dressed completely in black except for red shoes and screaming red hair, walks towards a large public park with a Fender electric guitar slung over her shoulder. It's early Sunday afternoon and her band, the Killers, is about to put on a concert of very loud atonal music known as "Visual Kei"—similar to punk, but less structured and rhythmic. She hopes that a talent agent she's invited to several previous performances will finally show up and offer them a contract. How could he resist, after he's seen the drummer (a cute girl with a green mohawk, yellow bikini top, and numerous body piercings) launch an exploding canister above the crowd, releasing a giant paper spider web, while the "music" becomes a car-crash of metal, sirens, and sparks flying from a spinning metal wheel?

As is her custom before one of these park performances, she veers off the main path and enters the compound of a small temple. Using a ladle from a stone basin filled with clean water, she purifies her hands and mouth. Then, in the main hall, she joins her hands together and bows to the **bodhisattva** of compassion, Kannon, who bestows her mercy on all who ask. Before leaving, she makes sure to stop in front of a small shrine to Benten, deity of

music and performance, where she bows, claps her hands twice, throws a coin into the coffer, and asks that today's concert be the best ever, that the talent agent actually show up, and that he give them the break they need. Were a foreign researcher to stop her and ask if she is "religious," she would likely say "no way!" before telling him, in no uncertain terms, to get lost.

Persistent Themes

The preceding vignettes present a challenge to Western cultural assumptions about the nature of "religious" belief and practice in general.

It's important to emphasize from the start that, in Japan, religious belief generally takes a back seat to religious activity. Taking action—if only to purchase an amulet from a Shinto shrine or a Buddhist temple—may significantly reduce anxiety about an upcoming examination, a relationship problem, or a health condition. The choice of shrine or temple to visit in order to obtain the most beneficial blessing for a particular situation is often determined by local custom or the recommendations of neighbours, relatives, or co-workers, based on their own experience.

A traditional approach to Japanese religions would emphasize the most important doctrines, institutions, incidents, and leaders associated with the three major traditions: Buddhism, Confucianism, and Shinto. This chapter will certainly touch on all of these. However, recent scholarship has

Sites

Neighbourhood Temples and Shrines

One of the easiest ways to become acquainted with Japanese religious traditions is to visit local (Buddhist) temples and (Shinto) shrines. They are usually open to the public and at festival time may offer opportunities for direct participation. Most

Japanese take pride in their cultural history, and so religious institutions—with their traditional architecture, worldviews, and robed priests—provide a ready example of continuities that can extend over a thousand years.

questioned the validity of this approach. Scholars now generally agree that for much of Japanese history, these grand traditions—one of which did not exist as such until the late nineteenth century—were neither discrete nor autonomous. The Japanese language had no equivalent to the word "religion" until the 1880s, when, as part of a government modernization campaign, the characters meaning "teachings" (*kyo*) and "sect" (*shu*) were combined to form *shukyo*. Lack of specific "religion," however, does not necessarily mean any lack of religious belief, feeling, or orientation (Pye 2004). Japan has no fewer than seven major and sixteen minor schools of Buddhism; countless "new religions," most of them founded in the wake of that modernization campaign; and more than 80,000 different *kami*—the individual spirits associated with specific natural phenomena, powers, and places. So it's not surprising that people might feel confused when asked whether they adhere to the teachings of one particular sect. Most Japanese people have no trouble tolerating doctrinal diversity at the popular level. Nor do most of their religious traditions require adherence to a particular set of beliefs. In fact, these traditions, with their specific doctrines and ritual practices, have been subordinate to the themes outlined below for more than a thousand years.

Seeking Benefits

Central to most religious traditions in Japan is the pragmatic desire to secure various benefits, either in this world or in the next. It matters little to the

John K. Nelson

Tendai and Shingon Buddhists in Japan perform a purification and blessing ritual that has its roots in ancient India. Participants in the "consecrated fire" ritual (*homa* in Sanskrit, *gomadaki* in Japanese) inscribe wooden slats with their names and a prayer or petition; their requests are then transported into the spirit realm via the fire and chanting of the priests.

average person whether a given place of worship is devoted to the Buddha or to a particular local *kami*: the important thing is that the prayers offered there help him or her deal with a specific situation, whether healing an illness, resolving a conflict, starting a new business, taking an examination, finding a marriage partner, or conceiving a child. A person may visit both temples and shrines, engage priests to perform rituals, and make regular offerings until the desired outcome is obtained—or until it seems clear that all those efforts have failed. Then he or she may well have little to do with any organized religion until the next problem arises. "Turning to the gods in a time of trouble" is a well-known expression that summarizes the pragmatic attitude of the average person in Japan towards religious institutions and beliefs.

To those who identify themselves as Christians, Jews, or Muslims, this kind of behaviour may smack more of self-interest than of religion. Where are the moral codes, the commandments, the sacred texts that guide all aspects of life? Where is the congregation of fellow believers with whom the faithful can share their sorrows and joys? How is it possible to draw from multiple religious traditions without violating at least some basic principles?

One way to understand the diversity of religion in Japan is to imagine religious life as a marketplace in which consumers decide which shops to patronize on the basis of cost, product availability, and benefits received. Variables of time, place, and occasion also enter into consumers' calculations: thus a religious "product" appropriate for the end of summer—for example, the ritual prescribed to protect the ripening rice crop from insects, typhoons, or fire—is not the same ritual required to protect one's business from financial trouble or one's soul from the flames of hell. Just as consumers go to different stores, depending on the kinds of goods they need to buy, so Japan's religious consumers know which traditions offer the appropriate assistance for the situation at hand.

A person may shop around for the right religious "product" or service, but once a decision is made, a reciprocal relationship is created that entails certain obligations and expectations. In exchange for tangible assistance from a spiritual agent—whether *kami*, bodhisattva, or buddha—one must show one's gratitude not only by performing various formal rituals but by treating that agent with special respect. Japanese literature is full of exemplary stories in which an ungrateful or arrogant person who has offended one or more of the deities ends up chastened and contrite.

Religious and Spiritual Agents

Let's look more closely at the spiritual agents that require such attention and care. One of the most fundamental themes of Japanese culture and civilization has been the idea that there is a kind of life-energy that circulates throughout the phenomenal world, and that humans can align themselves with it through worship of the *kami*. Highly mobile and fluid, capable of entering any object useful for exercising their power, *kami* can be found in flowing water, rain, mountains, clouds, fire, earth, and wind, as well as in certain animals that serve as their agents, messengers, and avatars. Their peaceful side (*nigimitama*) is beneficial and helps humans prosper, while their destructive side (*aramitama*) can only be endured and appeased through rituals.

Mythology

We can see examples of these dynamics in the myths explaining the origins of what would become "Japan." The basic contours of Japan's creation myth first took shape in the **Kojiki**, a collection of regional stories compiled in 712 CE with the purpose of legitimating the dominance of the Yamato clan by associating it with the divine origins of Japan. However, these stories were not widely known until the nineteenth or even the twentieth century, when they were circulated as part of a campaign by the state to create a cultural heritage that citizens of the new nation could share.

The positive and peaceful side of the primordial *kami* couple, Izanagi and his "wife" Izanami, can be seen in their creation of the islands that make up Japan and the primary elements of the phenomenal world. After a false start produces a "leech baby," which must be cast aside, the two successfully

Map 7.1 Japan: Major Cities and Religious Sites

Source: Adapted from Young 1995: 211

create all the dimensions of the natural world: seas, straits, winds, trees, mountains, plains. Then suddenly, with neither warning nor rationale, Izanami gives birth to the deity of fire and in the process suffers burns that lead to her death. As her grieving partner consigns her to the land of the dead, he laments: "Alas, I have given my beloved spouse in exchange for a mere child!" (Philipi 1985: 57).

The destructive side of the *kami* is then revealed in several examples. First, the enraged Izanagi kills the fire deity and journeys to the gates of Yomi (the netherworld) to beseech his wife to return so that they can continue creating the world. Although she has eaten from the hearth of Yomi, she agrees to negotiate with the gods of the underworld on the condition that Izanagi does not look at her. Of course he cannot resist taking a peek and is shocked to see her corpse full of "squirming and roaring maggots" (ibid., 62). As he attempts to flee the underworld, she cries out, "He has shamed me!" and, furious at this betrayal of trust, sends her "hags" to stop him. After several narrow escapes, Izanagi leaves the land of the dead and uses a huge boulder to block the opening. As a final example of a *kami*'s vengeful side, Izanami vows that she will cause 1,000 of Izanagi's subjects to die each day, but he counters that he will cause 1,500 to be born.

Izanagi then bathes in a river to purify himself after this ghastly encounter with death and its defilements. As he does so, the female *kami* of the sun, **Amaterasu**, is born from his left eye; she will become the primary deity associated with the imperial family. She is followed by the male moon *kami*, which springs from Izanagi's right eye; then the last imperial *kami*, associated with the land, issues from his nose. Izanagi rejoices: "I have borne child after child, and finally . . . have obtained three noble children" (ibid., p. 71).

What we learn from this myth is that the *kami* are constantly at work in the natural world, and that they are responsible for both its blessings and its destructive powers. *Kami* may also enter into human beings, enabling them to perform heroic tasks, such as unifying warring clans or chiselling a tunnel through solid rock so that a riverside community can gain access to a road. Whenever the well-being of individuals, families, and communities is threatened, you can be sure that the *kami* will be petitioned for help.

✸ Foundations

Japanese history has no written records from the first four centuries of the Common Era. However, Chinese accounts from the fourth century describe "the land of Wa" (Japan) as ruled by a female queen who used "black magic and witchcraft" to control the *kami* and thus maintain power. The belief that early kings and "emperors" (second to fifth century CE) embodied the *kami* served to legitimize their rule as a function of divine will.

When these rulers died, earthen mounds of all sizes and shapes (more than 10,000 in all, called **kofun**) were built to house their tombs, into which were deposited various items that they would need in the netherworld. Unlike their counterparts in Egypt and China, however, the Japanese did not sacrifice human beings to accompany their masters into the next life. Instead, they relied on clay models called **haniwa** to provide the servants, musicians, shamans, and soldiers that the ruler would require for life in the next world. These early rulers became guardian spirits of the clans, communities, and regions they once ruled, assuming positions alongside the local *kami*. We can still visit some of their ancient burial sites: at Mount Miwa near Nara

Sites

Izumo Shrine

Izumo Shrine is located in Shimane prefecture on the Japan Sea coast, and is a registered "National Treasure" for the architecture of its main sanctuary. It is one of Japan's oldest shrines, mentioned in several myths and ancient accounts of the founding of the nation. A visit to the shrine is considered advantageous to those seeking a marriage partner.

(in central Japan) and Yoshigaoka (in northwestern Kyushu), at Asuka and Sakai (both located in central Japan; these rivalled the Great Pyramid of Cheops in the number of slave labourers their construction required), and near Miyazaki (in eastern Kyushu).

These traditions changed dramatically after 538 CE, when the ruler of what is today western Korea wrote to the Japanese king praising Buddhism as a religion "superior to all others" (see the Document box below). Buddhism offered a whole new set of deities that could be petitioned to protect the ruler and maintain the status quo. The clans that were especially devoted to *kami* worship did not simply roll over and submit to this alien religion; there was prolonged contention and conflict over how to accommodate new foreign influences within the existing local orders.

For its first 150 years in Japan, Buddhism was sustained mainly by clans with ties to Korean immigrants from earlier centuries. But in time its new rituals, its promises of "liberation" and "salvation," and its unique teachings attracted increasing state patronage. Meanwhile, a steady stream of immigrants fleeing ongoing wars in southern China and the Korean peninsula brought to Japan valuable cultural knowledge—in everything from

architecture and philosophy to astrology and divination to courtly protocol—that contributed significantly to the development of the fledgling state. Among the influences brought from the mainland were a number of concepts and practices that we now associate with religious Daoism. Attention was clearly paid to the movement of the stars, for example: the constellations painted on the ceilings of imperial tombs help to link the Japanese court to its counterparts in Korea and China, where the same constellations can be found. Stories about magical peaches ("Momotaro") and time-travel ("Urashima Taro") also contain themes that can be traced to Daoist ideas about immortality and alchemy. Even elements of the material culture that came to symbolize the imperial household—the mirror, sword, and jewel, as well as the colour purple—have roots in continental Daoist practices, which themselves were influenced by the older traditions of shamanism (Senda 1988: 133–8).

Japan's first Buddhist temple was constructed in 596 CE with the assistance of Korean builders, and the first Buddhist rituals were conducted there by specialists (both men and women) from the Korean kingdom of Baekje. Incredibly, temples established in those early years are still in existence at places like Shitennoji (in Osaka), Horyuji (in Nara; the

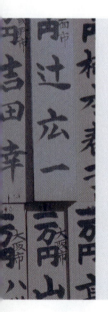

Document

From the Nihon Shoki

Japan's second oldest book after the Kojiki *(712), the* Nihon Shoki *("Chronicles of Japan," 720) combines origin myths with more factual accounts of the reigns of early emperors. The following extract purports to be from the Korean document recommending Buddhism to the Japanese king.*

This Dharma is superior to all others. It is difficult to grasp and difficult to attain. Neither the Duke of Zhou nor Confucius was able to comprehend it.

It can give rise to immeasurable, limitless merit and fruits of action, leading to the attainment of supreme enlightenment. The treasure of this marvelous Dharma is such that it is as if one owned a wish-fulfilling gem that granted every desire. Every prayer is granted and nothing is wanting. Moreover, from distant India to the three kingdoms of Korea, all receive these teachings and there is none who does not revere and honour them (*Nihon Shoki* account in Bowring 2006: 15).

Sites

Nara

Nara was Japan's capital from 710 to 784, and today it is the location of many World Heritage sites. Todaiji Temple, said to be the world's largest wooden building, houses a colossal Buddha image. Both Kofukuji and Horyuji Temples feature ancient five-storeyed pagodas, and the latter is home to the world's oldest wooden building. Kasuga (Shinto) Shrine hosts a famous lantern festival in late summer. There is even a festival dedicated to the deer that roam freely through Nara Park.

temple complex includes the world's oldest wooden building, from the early seventh century), and Todaiji (also in Nara).

Todaiji

It's worth pausing for a moment to look more closely at the founding of the Todaiji temple, because it brings together many of the themes we've been discussing. Ostensibly a "Buddhist" institution, designed to house a monumental bronze statue of the Cosmic Buddha (Vairocana), the temple was conceived by the emperor Shomu in the early 740s in response to a series of earthquakes and poor harvests. Before starting construction, he sent a high-ranking priest to the distant island of Kyushu to ask a powerful *kami* named Hachiman whether the project should proceed. Not only did the *kami* approve, he demanded to be transported to the construction site so as to oversee the local deities and keep them from interfering. His shrine still stands on a hillside overlooking the reconstructed temple (which, at two-thirds the size of the original structure, remains the world's largest wooden building, and has been designated a World Heritage Site by the United Nations).

What we see at Todaiji is the use of Buddhism both as a source of additional protection in the form of rituals and prayers, and as a worldview that, without discrediting older ideas about the *kami*, adapted them to fit into a Buddhist cosmos. Japan's rulers took advantage of both religious systems to help control the many variables threatening the stability of their regimes: from poor harvests and natural disasters to epidemic disease, court intrigues, and continuing immigration—as well as threats of invasion—from the continent.

Despite the many centuries that have passed since the completion of the Todaiji temple in 752, aspects of this story are still relevant today. Temples and shrines still conduct rituals for the health of the emperor and the stability of the nation. Rituals continue to be seen as generating a variety of benefits that address this-worldly concerns. And though Westerners tend to see the two dominant religious traditions in Japan as discrete entities, most Japanese do not distinguish between them. As a result there is considerable interaction between Buddhist and Shinto concepts and activities.

Other Spiritual Agents

The role of the bodhisattva in Mahayana Buddhist traditions was discussed at some length in Chapter 5. In Mahayana thought, a bodhisattva is an enlightened being who chooses to delay entry into nirvana in order to help all the living beings who have not yet been released from worldly suffering.

The bodhisattva with the greatest reputation for intervening in human affairs is undoubtedly Kannon, who arrived in Japan from China under the name Guanyin but originated in India as a bodhisattva called Avalokiteshvara. Although, as divine beings, bodhisattvas have no sex, they have generally been imagined as male. In a culture with a strong tendency to associate qualities such as generosity, caring, and sympathy with women rather than men, depictions of Kannon's features in sculpture and painting over time became increasingly feminine. Today Kannon is usually depicted as female.

In Japan, Kannon is committed to alleviating the suffering she perceives (*kan*) and hears (*on*). Countless "miracle" tales testify to her powers of intercession, especially in desperate situations, when people are facing calamity and death. She was very popular with the warrior class since she confers the "gift of fearlessness" in the midst of terror and trouble. The economic golden years of the 1980s saw a revival of interest in Kannon: her cult was promoted at pilgrimage sites and in temples, and

giant statues of her were erected in various places, some reaching 108 metres (354 feet) in height; 108 is the number of the human frailties that Kannon is said to help overcome (Reader 1991: 191, 157, 36).[1] While all the traditional attributes of Kannon are still present, her benign, all-embracing, and motherly qualities have received special attention, attracting a new generation of devotees.

Another bodhisattva who has provided comfort to millions of Japanese is known as Jizo (Ksitigarbha in Sanskrit), or, more respectfully and affectionately, Ojizo-sama. Known for his ability to descend into hell and free tormented souls, he also protects children and travellers. With his shaved head, staff, and wish-fulfilling jewel (which lights the darkness), Jizo is an easily recognizable figure, and statues of him can often be seen standing at

John K. Nelson

Jizo is a popular bodhisattva believed to help travellers and the souls of children arrive safely at their destinations. The statues at this temple in central Osaka were purchased by women who had aborted their fetuses and entrusted the care of their spirits to the temple. The faded red cloths symbolize a child's bib.

crossroads or near main thoroughfares. In addition, since the 1970s he has taken on the job of conducting the souls of deceased children and aborted fetuses to salvation. Anyone visiting a temple in Japan today is likely to see neat rows of Jizo statues, many with bibs, little berets on their shaved heads (he is a monk, after all), and offerings of coins or pebbles at their feet. A woman who has aborted a pregnancy or suffered a miscarriage may arrange for a temple to care for the soul of the fetus; for a fee of perhaps 30 dollars a month, the temple will perform periodic rituals and offerings to appease the unhappy and potentially dangerous spirits of the unborn.

Unsettled Spirits

How can the spirit of an unborn child be dangerous? This tradition has complex roots, combining native Japanese, Korean, and Chinese folk beliefs and practices with Daoist dynamics and Buddhist demonology. In ancient times, the spirits of people who had lost their lives to powers beyond their control were expected to become angry and very possibly vengeful. In order to calm these spirits, periodic rituals of acknowledgment and pacification were required. This belief appears to have been in place since prehistoric times, and it permeates Japanese attitudes towards death even today. One of Japan's most respected scholars of death and dying, Gorai Shigeru, believes that all Japanese funeral and memorial rites reference this tradition, in which the spirits of the dead must be placated before they can become benevolent ancestral influences (Shigeru 1994: 105).

At the level of the state, to neglect or ignore the vengeance-seeking spirits of assassinated rivals or powerful enemies killed in battle was to invite retribution in any number of forms: storms, earthquakes, droughts, infertility, sickness. Spirit appeasement was therefore high on the list of state-sponsored ritual activities. When Buddhism came to Japan in the early sixth century, it took up its share of that activity, which until then had been the exclusive domain of shamans. In fact, controlling unsettled spirits has been one of the most enduring responsibilities for all Japan's religious traditions.

❀ Pivotal Developments in Japanese Religious History

During the formative Nara period (710–794), the government set up a ministry to manage the shrines of the *kami*. At the same time, a council of senior Buddhist priests formed the Sangha Office to oversee the behaviour, training, and duties of Buddhist monks. The growing Buddhist organization was represented through various bureaus (library, textiles, art and architecture) within the Ministry of Central Management.

This administrative control and bureaucracy helped to set the stage for the Nara and Heian periods. The same basic administrative structure would remain in place for nearly 350 years, reasserting itself whenever a strong centralized government took charge. Knowing all too well from Chinese history how religious organizations and ideas could undermine the state, the early Japanese rulers carefully monitored all religious appointments and construction projects, none of which was permitted to proceed without their supervision.

Tendai and Shingon

For three centuries Buddhism remained the preserve of the Nara elite, who commissioned temples dedicated to their ancestors, consigned their second or third sons to Buddhist monasteries, and sponsored Buddhist art as a way to cultivate religious merit. In 804, however, two monks named Saicho (767–822) and Kukai (774–835) travelled to China for further study, and there they encountered some important new perspectives, one of which emphasized the written word. The *Lotus Sutra*, which had originated in north India and been translated into Chinese (in 209 CE and again in 406), was thought to be a vehicle for enlightenment and salvation *simultaneously*. It taught that there is only one vehicle to salvation—the body we live in, here and now—and that we all have the potential to become buddhas ourselves. The priests who had mastered the teachings advocated in the *Lotus Sutra* saw themselves as instrumental to the welfare of the state.

When Saicho and Kukai returned to Japan, they took with them volumes of teachings and commentaries, paintings, mandalas, and ritual implements, as well as letters from Chinese masters testifying to their grasp of these powerful new teachings. It might sound like little more than a wholesale borrowing of religious "software" from another culture, but the traditions founded by these two monks—Tendai by Saicho and Shingon by Kukai—helped to domesticate Buddhist teachings and rituals in very pragmatic ways.

For one thing, both Tendai and Shingon taught a kind of short-cut approach that put the possibility of enlightenment and salvation within the reach of the common person: anyone (not just monks and nuns) could actually *become* a buddha in this lifetime. Through a combination of incantation, ritual gestures, meditation, visualization, and austerities, individuals could connect with and obtain benefits from deities in other spheres of existence. Whereas previous schools of Buddhism viewed the human body as problematic because of its fragility, desires, and impermanence, the new doctrines, which we now identify as "tantric" or "esoteric," attributed a spiritual value to the physical body: much as geothermal steam and seismic activity can be transformed into electricity, bodily desires could be harnessed through ritual and directed towards the quest for salvation and enlightenment.

The fact that both sects chose to establish their headquarters on sacred mountains—Tendai on Mount Hiei, northeast of what is today Kyoto, and Shingon on Mount Koya, some 70 kilometres (43 miles) from Kyoto—suggests that they continued to respect the local *kami*. Indeed, we can see the consolidation of the relationship between Buddhism and *kami* worship as continuing throughout Japanese social and religious history.

The Japanese phrase **honji suijaku** (which comes from the *Lotus Sutra* and means "manifestation from the original state") helps to explain the implications of this relationship. *Honji*, meaning the "original ground," refers to the fundamental reality and power of various buddhas and bodhisattvas, while *suijaku* refers to the "trace" or particular form in which the deity chooses to manifest him- or herself in Japan. Thus the *kami* of a particular mountain or powerful clan came to be seen as the "provisional manifestation" (*gongen*) of a particular buddha or bodhisattva. Today Buddhist and Shinto deities are

John K. Nelson

A young *bugaku* dancer performs on the grounds of Osaka's Shitennoji temple. Established in 593 CE, the temple has been in continuous operation ever since.

clearly differentiated in theory, but for many centuries the *honji suijaku* principle made them interdependent, although the Buddhist deities were usually superior.

As Buddhism expanded from the ninth century onward, it increasingly overshadowed the traditional ritual practices centred on *kami*. The *honji suijaku* principle was applied to local shrines as a way both to incorporate their deities and to allow them to achieve salvation along more obviously Buddhist lines. The four main *kami* of Kasuga Shrine in Nara—two associated with agriculture and two with war—were linked to Buddhist counterparts: Shakyamuni Buddha, the bodhisattva Kannon, the Medicine Buddha, and the Buddha of the future.

A number of rituals honouring *kami* and buddhas could be performed by priests of either tradition. We are fortunate to have the early eleventh-century diary of a high-ranking noblewoman who served as the chief spiritual medium (*saiin*) at the Kamo Shrine in Kyoto, a shrine ranked second in importance only to the Grand Shrine of Amaterasu at Ise (pronounced *ee-say*). A devout Buddhist concerned with reaching salvation in the Pure Land (about which we will hear more in a moment), she nonetheless served in a ritual capacity for the Kamo deities for nearly four decades.

❋ New Emphases in Japanese Religious Practice

New Sects in the Kamakura and Muromachi Periods

Around the world, people deeply affected by changing political, economic, and cultural conditions have often been open to innovations in religious belief or practice that promise to help them cope with challenging new circumstances. In Japan, not just one but three new types of Buddhist practice emerged during the Kamakura period (1185–1333): Pure Land, Nichiren, and Zen. Significantly, these are the three principal forms of Buddhism still practised in Japan today. At the same time, innovations in *kami* worship laid the foundations for what would eventually come to be known as "Shinto."

The relative stability of the Heian period ended in a war that overthrew the courtly families in power since the early days of Japanese civilization and resulted in the destruction of numerous temples, including the magnificent Todaiji. Once the imperial capital of Kyoto was under the control of the new regime, which drew its power from the warrior elite that we call **samurai**, the centre of

Focus

Taboo Terms at Shinto Shrines

In an effort to resist total assimilation into the influential new tradition, the priests and priestesses of major shrines developed a kind of code for referring to Buddhism without adopting its vocabulary. Thus Shakyamuni Buddha became the "Central One," a temple a "tiled roof," and sutras "dyed paper." Buddhist monks, with their shaved heads, were called "long hairs," death became "getting well," and illness was "slumber" (Felicia Bock, cited in Bowring 2005: 191).[2] Using these terms, the participants in a *kami* ritual could acknowledge the importance of Buddhist concepts while keeping a certain distance from them.

Sites

Kamakura

Kyoto had been the centre of political and religious power in Japan for only 200 years when a samurai-led army from the north seized power and moved the capital to Kamakura. Between 1185 and 1333, the once-small fishing village became home to grand temples, shrines, and palaces. One of the most famous large Buddha statues in the world can be found in Kamakura, some 50 kilometres (30 miles) southwest of Tokyo.

political power shifted north to Kamakura, a region near what is today Tokyo.

For the aristocrats, priests, doctors, and merchants living in the Kyoto region, moving the capital was an unmitigated disaster. Yet they were predisposed to expect conflict, corruption, and vice because a popular Buddhist teaching had predicted that the year 1052 would mark the beginning of the degenerate age known as **mappo**, during which the Buddhist dharma would decline. Social chaos and bloody political disorder were accompanied by a series of natural disasters, including earthquakes, typhoons, pestilence, and famine. Living at a time before the science behind such disasters was understood, people sincerely believed they were trapped in a kind of hell on earth.

Pure Land Salvation

It is no wonder, then, that a new interpretation of Buddhism promising salvation gained widespread acceptance among elites and commoners alike. Prior to this development, Buddhism had been almost exclusively the faith of the former. While there had been individual monks who worked with the common people—men like Gyoki (668–749), renowned as a bodhisattva for his charity and public works, and Kuya (903–972), who used song and dance to convey the dharma to the lower classes—it was not until Genshin (942–1017) organized Pure Land beliefs into a coherent system that Buddhism began to attract wide public attention. To make the

doctrine of salvation more compelling, his *Essentials of Salvation* (*Ojo yoshu*, completed in 985) described in graphic, often terrifying detail the six realms of existence (hell, hungry ghosts, demonic beings, animals, human beings, and heavenly beings) through which every living creature must pass, in multiple incarnations, before reaching the perfection of the Pure Land.

For the first time in Japan, groups of Buddhist monks began to concern themselves with the salvation of the ordinary person, although it would take another 200 years before a new institutional form emerged to give practical expression to their concern. It was a Tendai monk, frustrated by his sect's preoccupation with politics and managing the profits from its vast landholdings, who developed Pure Land Buddhism as we know it today. Honen (1133–1212) believed it was impossible for people in an age of *mappo* to attain salvation by traditional means (following the precepts, chanting sutras, meditating, worshipping the Buddhist deities). He argued that the saving grace of Amida did not discriminate according to social rank, past karma, or present activity: sincere faith and repeated recitation of the **nembutsu**, "*Namu Amida Butsu*," alone were enough. In this way Honen opened the door to what was then the radical notion of universal salvation.

This concept might sound pleasingly democratic to modern ears, but at the time it was thought to be subversive of the entire monastic enterprise. Taken to its logical conclusion, the principle of universal salvation meant there was no difference between a lay person and a learned monk. Honen was banished from the Kyoto region in 1207, along with one of his prominent disciples, Shinran (1173–1262). Earlier that year, Shinran had scandalized both temple and courtly communities by marrying—a "degenerate" practice that was fairly common among monks (as was keeping a concubine) but was never made public. Shinran reasoned that if the power of Amida Buddha was great enough to save even those of the lowest social status, then marriage would not be an obstacle to achieving salvation.

Honen's exile lasted only four years, but Shinran was banished for seven. According to popular biographies, he used this time to preach and organize among farmers and fishermen, refining his "True Pure Land" doctrine to the point of maintaining that a *single* sincere repetition of the *nembutsu* would secure salvation. Shinran believed human beings to be incapable of mustering the disciplined "self-power" (*jiriki*) necessary for attaining salvation: therefore we must rely on "other-power" (*tariki*) for deliverance from suffering.

In the tumultuous disorder of the Kamakura period (and beyond), True Pure Land teachings gained wide popular support, but detractors were still powerful. In 1227, monks from the Tendai temples on Mount Hiei desecrated Honen's grave and burned copies of his major works. True Pure Land practice was spread around the country via small groups called *ko*, where emphasis was on *nembutsu* practice. Around 1450, the eighth hereditary leader of the True Pure Land movement, Rennyo (1415–99), began to systematize the teachings and organize the scattered True Pure Land communities into a well-disciplined religious group. Taking advantage of a time of widespread civil unrest, he drew on the existing networks of True Pure Land followers to create a kind of militant security force dedicated to protecting the sect's Honganji temple (in what is today the city of Osaka).

The result was a new development in Japanese Buddhism: bands of armed peasants and low-ranking samurai loyal to the True Pure Land tradition rose up against those they considered to be oppressors. These were not the first Buddhists to take aggressive action: as early as 1039, "monk warriors" from the Tendai monastery on Mount Hiei had attacked rival sects and temples, and even challenged the legitimacy of the imperial court itself. Four centuries later, however, the True Pure Land insurrection was led not by monks but by masterless samurai and common people. With nothing to lose and salvation guaranteed through their faith in Amida Buddha, fearless True Pure Land militias were able to hold their own against experienced armies and sometimes even overwhelm them. By 1500 they controlled several provinces as well as what is today the city of Osaka, where their fortress temple was never breached, although they were finally defeated and brought at least partially under control by the warlord Oda Nobunaga (1534–82) in the 1580s.

Rinzai Zen and Kamakura Culture

Zen Buddhism became established in much the same way as Pure Land, but with an important difference: Zen was imported directly from China, and its development benefited from the leadership of Chinese masters who immigrated to Japan in the thirteenth century. Although the seeds of Zen meditation can be found in Tendai doctrines as early as the ninth century (when a practice referred to as "constantly sitting" was introduced), it was not until the latter part of the twelfth century that the tradition took root in Japan, imported by a Japanese monk who had encountered it during a visit to China in 1168.

The word "Zen" is the Japanese version of the Chinese *chan*, itself a translation of the Sanskrit term for meditation, *dhyana*. Whereas the Pure Land traditions emphasized recitation of the name of Amida Buddha as the path to salvation, the Chan/Zen tradition emphasized the practice of seated meditation as the path to enlightenment and, eventually, salvation.

A Tendai monk named Eisai (1141–1215) travelled to China in 1168 expecting to find the traditions from which Tendai and Shingon had originated in the ninth century, only to discover that those traditions had been superseded by Chan Buddhism. Chan temples had survived a nation-wide campaign of persecution, launched in 845, that had targeted the esoteric traditions because of their lavish wealth, landholdings, political meddling, and "parasitic" monks and nuns who did nothing for society. By contrast, Chan monks worked with their hands and displayed little of the elaborate trappings that characterized other traditions.

Although Eisai stayed in China for only six months, he studied Chan doctrines for the next 20 years while continuing to fulfil his duties as a Tendai priest. A second trip to China in 1187 gave him the opportunity to study with an eminent Chan master in the Linji (Rinzai in Japanese) trad-ition, who certified Eisai's enlightenment before he returned to Japan in 1191. In addition to his knowledge of Chan, Eisai imported other Buddhist and Confucian teachings—as well as a plant from which a hot drink could be made to keep sleepy monks awake during meditation. His work "Drink Tea and Prolong Life" is credited with promoting tea in Japan; and the tea ceremony (developed a century later) was deeply influenced by Zen aes-thetics and symbolism.

In an effort to legitimate his new school of Bud-dhism and attract the patronage of the military rulers in Kamakura, Eisai wrote a treatise entitled "The Propagation of Zen for the Protection of the Country." Emphasizing outer discipline and inner wisdom, this work caused his temporary exile from all Tendai temples in the Kyoto region. After a short time in Kamakura, where he secured patrons for his teachings and established a small temple, he returned to Kyoto and in 1202 built the city's first Zen temple, Kenninji, in what is today the Gion entertainment district. Its many rebuildings have preserved a number of cultural treasures as well as beautiful examples of classic Zen landscape gar-dens and architecture.

It's worth asking why a samurai warrior would be attracted to a somewhat austere Chinese tradi-tion focused on the achievement of "sudden enlight-enment" through the practice of seated meditation (*zazen*) and the mental exercise of the koan. One reason was that the kind of mind cultivated through those practices was conducive to a particularly rich type of artistic expression. Zen-inspired poetry, sto-ries, paintings, and sculpture were valued for their subtle and elegant evocation of concepts such as emptiness, the cycle of rebirth (*samsara*), imperma-nence, and enlightenment (*satori* in Japanese), and those who associated themselves with such art easily acquired a highly valued aura of refinement. At the same time, in a society that accorded the highest status to the warrior, Zen-style discipline was valued as a way of training the mind and body to endure hardship, pain, and even the finality of death.

The Rinzai tradition was assisted in its institu-tional development by its ongoing relationship with

Sites

Kyoto

Japan's capital for more than a thousand years (794–1869), Kyoto abounds in temples and shrines. Toji is a Buddhist temple with Japan's tallest pagoda. Ryoanji is a Zen temple with a world-renowned rock and sand garden. The picturesque (but tour-ist-thronged) Kinkakuji, or Golden Pavilion, was built as a **shogun's** palace and is now part of a Zen temple. Japan's first Zen temple (Kenninji), its sec-ond most important Shinto shrine (Kamigamo), and the famous Kiyomizu Temple, built on the side of a mountain overlooking the city, are also worth see-ing, along with the Imperial Palace and Nijo Castle.

Tendai roots, he is regarded as the founder of the Rinzai lineage.

Soto Zen: The Gradual Path

The other major Zen school, also based on a Chinese tradition, promotes "gradual enlightenment" through the practice of "just sitting" without any conceptual or metaphoric stimulation. The story of Soto Zen and its founder Dogen (1200–53) is problematic in that the only source of information is the tradition itself.

According to the standard accounts, Dogen studied on Mount Hiei in the Tendai tradition, but was troubled by a persistent question: if humans are born with an innate Buddha-nature, as Tendai doctrines maintained, why should they need to make any effort to achieve enlightenment? After studying at Kenninji with Eisai's successor, the young monk somehow gained a place with an official mission to China in 1223, in the course of which he encountered the Caodong tradition.

Whether Dogen actually made the trip or this part of the tale was invented by later Soto leaders to legitimize their tradition is unclear; in any event, the Caodong emphasis on integrating body and mind via *any* activity became central to the kind of liberation promoted by Dogen. Supposedly, a conversation with a monastery cook helped him understand the importance of "enlightened activity" and led to his own spiritual awakening.

On his return to Kyoto in 1227, it became apparent to Dogen that his Soto Zen could not hope to compete with either the still dominant Tendai or the increasingly influential Rinzai Zen school. Leaving the capital, he sought out local aristocrats and wealthy rural landowners who were more receptive than urban samurai to his new way to liberation. The Eiheiji monastery he founded in 1244 (near present-day Fukui city) is still the headquarters of the Soto denomination, and it continues to function as a monastery, training young monks in "just sitting" *zazen* coupled with rigorous study and physical labour.

In the countryside the popularity of Soto Zen grew rapidly after priests in the early fifteenth

John K. Nelson

The Kenninji temple in Kyoto marked its 800th anniversary by commissioning this powerful painting by Koizumi Junkasu for its ceiling.

the ruling samurai class in Kamakura. Adopted from China, Rinzai's temple building and political alliances prospered because of the "Five Mountain" monastery system, which made five top temples into administrative outposts of the government. The Five Mountain temples, through their many subtemples and affiliations, helped to monitor local conditions and implement new laws for the military rulers. The same system was soon applied to several major Zen temples in Kyoto as well, including Nanzenji, Tenryuji, and Kenninji.

Just as two schools of Pure Land Buddhism developed in close proximity to each other, so it was with Zen. Although Eisai never renounced his

Focus

Dogen and the Cook

As a young monk travelling in China, the founder of the Soto Zen school, Dogen, encountered an old priest who was serving in the office of *tenzo* (head cook). Dogen felt the *tenzo* was working too hard for a person of his age, so he asked him, "Reverend sir, why don't you do *zazen* or read the ancient texts? What is the use of working so hard as a cook, drying these mushrooms in the blazing sun?" The *tenzo* laughed for a long time and then he said, "My foreign friend, it seems you don't really understand Zen practice or the words of the ancients."

Hearing the elder monk's words, Dogen felt ashamed and surprised. He asked, "What is practice? What are words?" The *tenzo* said, "One, two, three, four, five." Dogen asked again, "What is practice?" and the *tenzo* replied, "Everywhere, nothing is hidden" (adapted from Dogen 1996).

century introduced a new practice that would help to transform the religious landscape of Japan. Dogen's teachings were important within a monastic setting, but local warlords, wealthy farmers, and other patrons were—like most upper-class Japanese—more concerned with salvation than with enlightenment. In part because Zen offered direct, intuitive transmission of enlightenment, its priests were said to embody the very mind of Shakyamuni Buddha. Who better, then, to lead the spirit of a deceased loved one towards the ultimate liberation? In this era, only the clergy were entitled to funeral services; therefore the corpse of a commoner was symbolically ordained as a monk or nun (Bodiford 1992). This brilliant innovation not only gave regular people access to funeral and memorial services but helped to gain a wide following for Soto Zen.

Nichiren

The last new Buddhist sect of the Kamakura period was founded by a charismatic priest who drew on the Tendai tradition of reciting mantras but embraced the teachings of the *Lotus Sutra* as the only possible path to salvation, not only for the individual but for the nation. Believing that it provided an all-encompassing guide to both secular and spiritual affairs, Nichiren (1222–82) instructed his followers to study its teachings and chant the mantra "*namu myoho renge kyo*" ("Hail the marvellous teaching of the *Lotus Sutra*!"). To Nichiren, other types of Buddhism were merely provisional, introductory teachings, no longer relevant in the age of *mappo*.

After being expelled from his monastery in Kyoto, he travelled to Kamakura where he preached on street corners the radical message that "the *nembutsu* is hell, Zen is a devil, and Shingon is the nation's ruin." He was exiled twice for subversive teaching and avoided execution only because of a divine intervention that, according to his own account, shattered the executioner's sword as it was about to fall on his neck. Nichiren's 1260 work "On Establishing the True Dharma to Bring Peace to the Nation" (*Ankoku-ron*) established him as a pioneer in the politicization of religion. If the nation suffered invasions, plagues, and social disorder, he argued, it was the fault of the ruler who had not adopted the *Lotus Sutra* as his guide to sound governance.

When the Mongol dynasty actually invaded Japan in 1274, Nichiren's warnings were seen as a kind of prophecy, and he was pardoned. Weary of continual confrontation, he accepted an offer of land at Mount Minobu (not far from Mount Fuji). The temple he established there became both a memorial to Nichiren's teachings and a training facility for the next generation of disciples. Men like Niko, Nissho, and Nichiko proselytized widely, and though they were persecuted by the authorities and ostracized by other Buddhist sects, they succeeded in establishing a network of temples throughout central Japan. However, each had different ideas about what should be emphasized, leading to centuries of factionalism. It's important to note that some of Japan's most prominent "new religions"—Soka Gakkai (which has branches all over the world and counts a number of Hollywood celebrities among its adherents), Rissho Koseikai, Nichiren Shoshu—trace their roots to one or another of these denominations.

Confucianism and the Beginnings of Shinto

We've focused thus far on the development and differentiation of Buddhist sects in the Kamakura and Muromachi periods. But there were two other developments—the introduction of Confucianism and the beginnings of Shinto—that also deserve attention for their influence on the development of the modern Japanese state.

You will recall that a number of Chinese Chan masters went to Japan in the thirteenth century to head Rinzai Zen temples, and that Japanese Tendai monks in the same period once again travelled to China to obtain new teachings and texts. Among the fruits of this cultural exchange were the teachings of Confucius. Although Confucian ideas (dating from the fifth century BCE) had been present at the very beginning of Japanese civilization in the sixth century CE, they had not developed into a distinct body of knowledge or ritual practices. During the political and social disruptions of the Kamakura and Muromachi periods, however, Japan's ruling classes began to take a new interest in religions and philosophies that promoted order in society.

Confucian values, as interpreted by the scholar Zhu Xi (1130–1200), laid out the "Way" that every member of society—ruler, minister, parent, friend, child—should follow, as determined by his or her position in that society. Awareness of the responsibilities in each relationship would promote reciprocity between superiors and subordinates, which in turn would foster a stable and harmonious society. Zen monks found these teachings to resonate with their own monastic and religious traditions, and so they were taught within the Five Mountain system and recommended to rulers by their Buddhist advisers for nearly 400 years. We will see in the next historical period how these Confucian seeds grew into a vast tree that branched out to cover all of Japanese society.

The Emergence of "Shinto"

And what of the older religion based on the ritual veneration of natural and human spirits called *kami*? Recent scholarship has demonstrated that it was only in the medieval period that "Shinto" began to take form as a distinct and self-conscious organization. After the fall of the imperial forces in 1185, the Ise Grand Shrines, dedicated to the Sun Goddess Amaterasu, lost their main source of financial support, and by the early fifteenth century were in obvious decline. Fearful of further decay, their priests devised new strategies to attract support from a wider range of sources.

In the early eleventh century, the imperial household had ceased making regular pilgrimages to Ise in favour of the Kumano shrines, some 80 kilometres (50 miles) to the west. Therefore the priests opened up Ise to visits from samurai and lower-ranking officials and developed new rituals for them. Purification was of primary importance, but now, in recognition of the institutional power of Tendai and Shingon and the doctrine of *honji suijaku*, Ise ritual practices were coupled with Buddhist notions of enlightenment so that, instead of competing, the two traditions complemented one another. At one time there were more than 300 Buddhist temples on the Ise shrine grounds.

With its emphasis on rituals rather than texts, the "way of the *kami*" had always lacked the kind of conceptual structure that was so highly developed within Buddhism. By creating their own theological rationale, Ise priests reversed the *honji suijaku* principle that the *kami* were lesser manifestations of the original buddhas and bodhisattvas. They argued that *kami* were indigenous to the land of Japan, and that although they could have Buddhist counterparts, they were not subordinate to Buddhist deities. With new doctrines in place, pilgrimage at an all-time high, and increasing interest in the power of Ise's main deities to provide benefits even for common people, a foundation was in place for the *kami* tradition to assume a new importance in the life of the nation. An organized system began to emerge in 1542, when the central government granted the powerful Yoshida clan the authority to appoint and demote shrine priests outside Ise. Today, in part because of Ise's appeal as a source of Japanese cultural identity and its association with imperial mythology, the Ise Grand Shrines receive over 5 million visitors annually.

⊛ Continuities of Religious Practice

The opening pages of this chapter described several contemporary religious practices involving access to benefits, control of spirits, and petitions to deities concerning problems. Many of these customs can be traced back to the end of the Muromachi period (1333–1573), with further elaboration in the Tokugawa (1600–1867) and modern (1868–1945) eras. As a way of reviewing and expanding on those themes, let's revisit two of the most important for individuals and institutions alike: access to benefits and veneration of spirits.

The variety of benefits (*riyaku*) that worshippers may seek is almost endless: from good health and financial prosperity to individual salvation in the afterlife, fertility and beneficial weather to enlightened governance. Equally diverse are the religious

John K. Nelson

The Itsukushima shrine complex on the island of Miyajima is about 90 minutes by train and ferry from Hiroshima. The iconic torii gate is at the far left.

practices believed to help bring about these conditions. Here are just a few examples:

- Individuals, families, businesses, entire communities, or even political leaders can contract religious specialists to conduct rituals at a temple or shrine. In most cases, petitioners address their requests to a particular spiritual agent (buddha, bodhisattva, or *kami*) that is believed capable of exerting a beneficial influence on the situation in question. However, household altars that commemorate Buddhist or Shinto deities are also widespread. Until very recently, many homes had both a Buddhist altar (where ancestral spirits are venerated alongside Buddhist deities) and a Shinto altar (honouring the local and regional *kami* that protect the family). In most cases, the care and religious observances thought necessary for each type of household altar have been the responsibility of the family's female members.

- By purchasing amulets or talismans, individuals can establish an informal relationship with the deity of a particular temple or shrine. Like a kind of battery, however, the spiritual energy invested in these objects becomes depleted over the course of a year, so that purchasers must return regularly for replacements.

- Undertaking a pilgrimage to a sacred place is another way of accessing benefits in this world and beyond. We saw how imperial pilgrimages to the Kumano and Ise shrines became popularized in the medieval and modern periods. Even today, the 88 sacred temples of the island of Shikoku are regularly visited by more than 100,000 pilgrims a year. Some walk the entire route of 1,400 kilometres (870 miles) at once, but most take buses or private transportation and complete the route in segments, as time permits. Smaller, less demanding pilgrimage routes exist all over Japan, each of which is believed to provide pilgrims with some kind of spiritual benefit.

- Monetary donations and the performance of good deeds for a temple/shrine or its priests are thought to generate merit beneficial to one's spiritual condition.

- Grand festivals (*matsuri*) involving the entire community generate benefits not only for those who participate but even for those who do not. Although many Buddhist temples also have adopted this practice, it is especially common for Shinto shrines to periodically remove their central object of worship and place it in a portable shrine that can be paraded through the community. In large communities, the *matsuri*

Sites

Ise Shrines

The Ise Shrines in south-central Japan are associated with the imperial *kami* Amaterasu and are said to receive over 5 million visitors a year. The forests that surround the inner (*Naiku*) and outer (*Geku*) shrines contain some of the few old-growth trees remaining in all the world and have been designated a World Heritage site. The main sanctuaries are rebuilt every 20 years, ensuring that the shrines remain pristine and free from decay. This practice also means that ancient wood-joinery techniques are passed on to the next generation of builders.

can be a major annual event commanding a staggering degree of financial, personal, and administrative commitment. The "rousing drum" festival mentioned at the beginning of this chapter involves an entire city of 74,000, while the Tenjin Matsuri held in central Osaka attracts crowds of nearly 2 million.

The second widespread religious practice is the veneration and memorialization of spirits. Unlike Western religious traditions, in which the spirits of the deceased have no lingering engagement with this world, the religious traditions of East Asia and Japan in particular maintain that the spirits of the dead continue to play an active part in the lives of the living. Whoever the deceased may have been in life—a religious leader, a soldier killed in war, the sweetest grandmother in the world—his or her spirit may become angry or vengeful in death; therefore periodic rituals are required long after the funeral to ensure that this does not happen. If the spirits are satisfied with the respect they receive, they can become benign and beneficial allies to those who perform the rituals.

One of Japan's great holidays is the Obon festival, held in mid-August in most parts of the country, when the spirits of the dead are said to return to this world to enjoy some entertainment—perhaps a community dance on the grounds of a temple or in a public park—and receive ritual offerings of food and drink from their loved ones. In addition, individuals and families regularly memorialize departed family members at household altars (*butsudan*). In the past, the size and shape of these home altars followed guidelines, but today more people are choosing to express their spirituality through altars specially designed to complement the interiors of their homes.

The household altar is just one example of the material impact that religious traditions and practices have had on Japanese culture. From paintings and sculpture, architecture and landscape design, to ritual attire and habits of personal hygiene derived from purification rituals, the list of cultural influences is almost endless. Let's consider just a few of the things that a visitor to Japan would likely encounter in the course of a week.

Even before leaving the international airport, a visitor might see an example of *ikebana*, the Japanese art of flower arranging. Having developed in Buddhist temples, where the spare, deceptively simple arrangements were used in memorial services, the practice of *ikebana* eventually filtered through all social classes. Today there are many different styles of *ikebana*, but most still share a few basic features, including organic materials (not necessarily flowers—stems and leaves are at least as important), sensitivity to the season, balanced composition, and poetic or religious symbolism (a classic three-part arrangement, for instance, is likely to symbolize heaven, earth, and humanity).

A similar combination of natural materials, restrained composition, and religious symbolism is found in the Japanese garden. The art of garden design also developed first at temples, where a few artfully placed rocks in a bed of gravel might symbolize islands in the sea of eternity. Gardens were later constructed in imperial palaces and, as the centuries passed, on the estates of wealthy aristocrats, samurai, and merchants. Today even the most humble residence will often have a carefully tended garden that evokes ancient cultural values. The temple has also been a major influence on architecture. The sweeping roof lines, overhanging eaves, and verandas of the classic temple have constituted the dominant paradigm for builders for over a thousand years. Inside the house, one room would typically be modelled on the abbot's quarters in a temple, with a hanging scroll painting in an alcove, an *ikebana* arrangement, and open space conveying a calming sense of space in harmony with form. Even ultramodern high-rise condominiums still try to incorporate the alcove into their designs.

The influence of Japan's religious traditions can also be seen in both literature and popular culture. The minimalism of image and language in the *haiku*, for example, is said to derive from Zen's emphasis on penetrating to the essence of reality. In its 17 syllables, the *haiku* typically gives us both sharply defined detail and a connection to a wider universe, as in this example from the late 1600s, composed by one of Japan's most celebrated poets, Matsuo Basho, in the late 1600s:

> The sea darkens;
> the plaintive calls of the wild ducks
> are faintly white.

Another art form that uses minimalism to evoke deep emotions and reflection on the nature of reality is Noh theatre, in which Buddhist themes are prevalent. The slow, mesmerizing cadences of the masked actors—who speak in a manner reminiscent of the ritual chanting heard at temples and shrines—usually convey a lesson of some kind, whether about karma, the consequences of desire, or the spiritual power of priests.

Our final examples from popular culture are the postwar phenomena of *anime* and *manga*. Both genres abound in references to religious practices, individuals with spiritual powers gained through ascetic training (*shugyo*), and divinities who use their powers for both good and evil ends. The early comics of Osamu Tezuka (1928–89) and the feature films of the animator Miyazaki Hayao (b. 1941; *Totoro*, *Princess Mononoke*, *Spirited Away*) are full of allusions to Japan's religious and spiritual history.

⊛ Global and Domestic Trends
Christianity, New Religions, and Native Learning

It's now time to bring our discussion of Japanese religious traditions more fully into the modern

© Alex Hunter/Alamy

The *kami* at Kanda Shinto Shrine are known for helping in business ventures and the search for a spouse. Aspiring artists create self-portraits on wooden plaques as a way to personalize their petitions to the deities—and to advertise their talents.

period. We often talk about "globalization" as a phenomenon of the late twentieth century, but in fact the worldwide exchange of people, ideas, and goods began several centuries earlier. In the fifteenth century, while Japan was in the midst of a series of wars over local territory, European powers such as Spain, Portugal, Holland, and England were navigating the globe, claiming new territory for their kings and the Christian church. The first Europeans to reach Japan were some shipwrecked Portuguese sailors who arrived there in 1543, but they were soon followed by Jesuit missionaries led by Francis Xavier (1549). The Jesuits' strategy for missionary work combined religious proselytizing with the lucrative incentive of trade via Portuguese ships travelling between Macao (near what is today Hong Kong), India, Mozambique, and Europe.

Christianity's Rise and Fall

Had Japan not been in a state of ongoing internal conflict, it is doubtful that the Jesuits would have been permitted to enter at all. Yet because of a unique convergence of social and political factors, they were able to broker agreements with a number of local warlords. It was also a stroke of luck that the first Europeans arrived during the rise to power of Japan's first military unifier, Oda Nobunaga. Highly distrustful of the Tendai warrior-monks as well as the True Pure Land militias, Nobunaga hoped Christianity would drive a wedge into the strength of Buddhism in Japan. He and his vassals also profited handsomely from the trading opportunities that came with the missionaries.

By 1571 Nobunaga's military and economic power had grown to the point that he was able to attack Mount Hiei, destroying every building on the mountain (along with priceless manuscripts, pictures, and sculptures) and killing more than 3,000 priests and attendants. The example was not lost on the True Pure Land sect, which had also become politicized and taken up arms: only one more major battle was required to bring them under control. It also served as a warning to the early Christian missionaries.

Although Nobunaga died in 1582 (assassinated by one of his own vassals), his chief aide quickly established himself as a visionary leader and patron of religion. Toyotomi Hideyoshi (1537–98) not only continued the unification effort that Nobunaga had begun, but embarked on a building and consolidation campaign among Buddhist and Shinto sects that led to the construction of many of the temples and shrines we see today. So great were his economic resources that he even tried twice to take the Korean peninsula in preparation for an invasion of China (neither attempt succeeded).

Hideyoshi's tolerance extended beyond Buddhism to Christianity, which by 1590 may have acquired as many as 100,000 converts, though not all the conversions were voluntary: some were forced by local warlords seeking to facilitate trade first with the Portuguese and later with the Spanish and Dutch. However, after a Spanish ship ran aground in Shikoku in 1596 and its captain threatened military reprisals to be delivered by an armada stationed in the Philippines, new legal restrictions were imposed on Christian missionaries. A number of European missionaries and Japanese converts were expelled and some were put to death.

The third of Japan's unifiers and supreme military leaders (shoguns), Tokugawa Ieyasu (1548–1616), at first tolerated the Catholic presence, largely because of the lucrative trade that missionaries helped facilitate. Over time, however, he came to see its priests as meddlesome in local affairs and thus disruptive of the social order he was trying to build after years of conflict. Ieyasu's successors cracked down hard on Christian activities, beginning in the 1620s, requiring all adults to register at the local Buddhist temple; those who resisted or refused to step on an image of Jesus or Mary were arrested and threatened with torture if they did not recant their Christian faith.

In 1637 an estimated 25,000 oppressed peasants and rogue samurai warriors took over an abandoned castle in Shimabara, on the southwestern island of Kyushu, and mounted an armed insurrection. Using Christian symbols on their flags, this rag-tag army held off the government's forces for nearly seven months. Dutch ships were called in to bombard the rebel fortifications, but with little effect. It was only when the rebels ran out of food and gunpowder that an army of more than 125,000 was able to storm the fortifications and kill all those within, effectively ending the last resistance to the Tokugawa regime.

With the defeat of the Shimabara rebels, Japan closed the door not only on Christianity but on Europe. From 1641 to 1853, the only port open to the outside world was Dejima, a small artificial island near Nagasaki, and it was rigidly controlled. Christianity did not entirely disappear, however. Rather, it went into hiding in remote valleys and on far-flung islands. Believers adopted Buddhist practices but continued reciting mass and worshipping images of the Virgin Mary disguised as the bodhisattva Kannon.

Unification and Stability

As part of its effort to establish stability after half a century of political turmoil, the Tokugawa regime imposed laws that would restructure Japanese society into four distinct classes: samurai, farmers, artisans, and merchants. This structure (like the temple registration law) was inspired by the Confucian doctrines introduced to Japan by Chinese Zen monks some 400 years earlier. In addition, a number of newer Confucian texts discovered in Korea during Hideyoshi's attempted invasions were now reinterpreted in ways that would promote, above all other values, the overall stratification and regulation of society. Each social class was given specific guidelines regarding occupation, travel, and civic duties, with infractions punishable by the confiscation of property, imprisonment, or execution. Likewise, the central government imposed regulations on both Buddhist and Shinto institutions, requiring them to adopt a hierarchical organizational model that held sect leaders and branch priests alike accountable for adhering to the rules. The Tokugawa shoguns had Zen priests as some of their closest advisers in the early years. Buddhist priests continued to provide counsel, but as the regime tightened its control over the nation, it also sought advice from Neo-Confucian scholars.

The overall mood of society was changing as well. During the medieval period, Buddhism had flourished because its doctrines of salvation in the next life offered hope to people whose prospects in this life were bleak. Now, with growing economic prosperity in the cities and order imposed by a police state (although taxation and famine still sparked occasional rebellions in the countryside), Neo-Confucianism became more relevant to Japan. Scholars and intellectuals developed ideologies that were critical of Buddhism and emphasized what they considered to be truly "Japanese."

We have already seen how Buddhism benefited from state patronage but also suffered because of its involvement in political affairs. Temple building increased dramatically with the imposition of the temple-registration requirement; the numbers

Sites

Nikko

Nikko's religious architecture and dramatic mountain setting have become major tourist attractions. Rinnoji is a Buddhist temple founded in the eighth century by the famous monk Shonin, who also established the nearby Futarasan Shrine, dedicated to the *kami* of the surrounding mountains. The Toshogu, the tomb of the first Tokugawa shogun, is open to visitors. Look for the beautiful ceremonial bridge and the famous carving of the three monkeys who "see no evil, hear no evil, and speak no evil."

of Soto Zen temples alone multiplied from several thousand to 17,500 in this period. At the same time, however, the growing emphasis on political rather than spiritual matters was reflected in a breakdown of morality among many priests (Williams 2005). As one seventeenth-century Confucian scholar noted, "the freedom with which they [Buddhist priests] eat meat and engage in romantic affairs surpasses that of even secular men" (Jansen 2000: 217). Although Buddhism remained central to ritual life, it was losing its vitality as a force in society. It is not surprising, therefore, that alternative religious perspectives and practices began to emerge towards the end of the Tokugawa period.

Religion Meets Modernity

The first of the "new religions" originated in an 1838 revelation to the wife of a wealthy farmer. Nakayama Miki said that "God the Parent" (*oyasama*) had chosen her to transmit divine truths about how to live happily and honourably. She was imprisoned a number of times for her beliefs, but, as the Tokugawa regime was ending she succeeded in establishing the new religion known as Tenrikyo. Another new religion called Kurozumikyo traced its origins to a revelation "received" by a Shinto priest (he claimed to have experienced "divine union" with Amaterasu). And Konko-kyo (1859) was based on a privileged communication between a farmer and a *kami* who supposedly turned out to be the saviour of mankind.

Scholars in particular were eager for new philosophies that would explain the meaning of life and the individual's purpose in society. Government officials produced almanacs and calendars promoting Neo-Confucian principles regarding social regulation, and counselled village head men accordingly. Hayashi Razan and Yamazaki Ansai were key figures in this movement, as was Yamaga Soko (1622–85), the scholar who codified samurai ethics to create the "way of the warrior" known as **bushido**. "Native Learning" or **Kokugaku** (literally, "study of one's country") argued the superiority of all things Japanese over their foreign counterparts, including the superiority of native spiritual traditions over Buddhism and Confucianism.

Some scholars argued that for convincing evidence of Japan's superiority, one needed only to consider the story of Noah and the flood, which Japan had survived untouched. Likewise, the reason Japan had not produced medical breakthroughs was that it was essentially pure and less polluted than other countries (ibid., 209). Scholars like Motoori Norinaga (1730–1801) tried to use ancient texts such as the *Kojiki* (which contains the rather bizarre foundation myth of Izanagi and Izanami) to discover fundamental truths about the will of the *kami* regarding the roles of a ruler and his subjects. The logical implication was that the solution to the country's growing political problems and the threats it faced from abroad lay in direct imperial rule—although to voice this opinion publicly would surely have led to charges of treason.

In 1825, during the last decades of the 250-year-old shogunate, the scholar and samurai Aizawa Seishisai (1781–1863) advocated the unification of religion and the state, on the model of the European colonial powers that were slowly encircling and threatening Japan's sovereignty. He urged the adoption of Shinto as the national faith and the sun deity Amaterasu as the primary *kami* as a way to enhance national polity (*kokutai*). Although these ideas created controversy at the time, they later became central to the leaders of samurai clans in the far west and south.

In 1868, following a brief civil war, those clans overthrew the Tokugawa regime. Well aware of how far behind Japan had fallen during its period of isolation, and fearing colonization by Europeans and Americans, the new government embarked on an unprecedented program of industrialization, militarization, and nation-building. This agenda, legitimized by a new emphasis on the emperor's status as a direct descendant of the *kami* (exactly as Aizawa had recommended four decades earlier), would dramatically alter Japan and the Asian region in both positive and negative ways.

◉ Recent Developments

Nationalism and Shinto

How does a government create a nation of citizens where only feudal loyalties had existed before? This was the daunting challenge that faced the social planners of the Meiji government (1868–1911). The term *meiji* means "enlightened rule," and its adoption signified a paradigm shift away from clan rule to a parliamentary system. In its effort to follow the examples of other modern nation states, where religion served to legitimate both domestic and foreign policies, the Meiji government promoted a kind of national cult based on the emperor and his associations with various *kami*.

The Meiji state subjected Buddhism to a brief but dramatic period of persecution, in part because it had served the Tokugawa feudal regime so well. Institutions that had been fully syncretic, combining worship of buddhas and *kami*, were now split apart. Their ritual specialists were either forced into lay life or re-educated as government-certified Shinto priests. Even more extreme was the brief period (1868–72) when Buddhist temples, icons, and artifacts were destroyed by over-zealous officials. At temple cemeteries all over Japan one can still see the remains of Buddhist statues decapitated during this period.

The Meiji government embarked on ambitious programs of education, industrialization, and militarization modelled on Western precedents. Shinto was designated the official religion of the state, although adherence to it was described as a matter of "civic duty" rather than religious conviction. Not everyone supported these policies, of course, but it became increasingly difficult and dangerous to resist the state's agendas. A series of wars with China (1894–95), Russia (1904–5), and Korea (1910)—which cost the lives of approximately 80,000 young men while gaining Japan overseas resources that it would use to expand its manufacturing and military base—inspired a general patriotic fervour that drowned out all but the most courageous voices of opposition.

It was during this period that the government sponsored the establishment of a shrine dedicated to the veneration of the spirits of soldiers who had died in the service of the nation. Although Shinto shrines had traditionally avoided association with the impurity of death, at Yasukuni Shrine in Tokyo Shinto-style rituals were combined with Buddhist ancestor worship and shamanic traditions of spirit appeasement and control. After all, as young men cut down in the prime of life, Japan's military dead were at high risk of becoming unsettled and vengeful spirits. The emperor and his household, high-ranking government officials, and leading businessmen,

Document

The Great Way

The "father" of modern Shinto studies as an academic discipline was Tanaka Yoshito (1872–1946). The following excerpt comes from his 1936 book Shinto Gairon.

The Japanese people, being endowed with a true Japanese spirit, sincerely hold an absolute faith in shrines. . . . Buddhism and Christianity are merely religions and nothing more; but Shinto and shrines are politics, as well as morality, as well as a great religion. A combination of these three aspects, that is the Way of the Gods. It is the Great Way of the subjects of Japan (Tanaka Yoshito [1936] in Breen and Teeuwen 2000: 328).

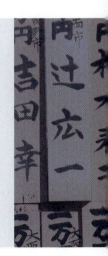

intellectuals, and even Buddhist priests all visited the shrine regularly, alongside bereaved family members, to pay their respects to the military dead. According to government policies and educational curriculum, there was no greater glory than to die for the nation and be enshrined at Yasukuni. An imperial edict on education instructed the youth of Japan that, "should emergency arise," they were expected to "offer [themselves] courageously to the State; and thus guard and maintain the prosperity of Our Imperial Throne coeval with heaven and earth" (Hardacre 1989: 122). The well-known "divine wind" (*kamikaze*) missions undertaken in desperation at the end of the Second World War to attack American naval vessels in the Pacific were extreme expressions of this ideology.

Several of Japan's prime ministers have insisted on visiting Yasukuni Shrine despite constitutional guidelines that prohibit the state from favouring a particular religion. Each visit set off protests and sometimes violent anti-Japanese demonstrations in China and Korea—both of which had been occupied by the Japanese military during the war. They objected not so much to the practice of honouring the military dead as to the inclusion of 14 men that Allied courts after the war had identified as "class-A" war criminals. These officers were the ones who were said to have orchestrated and carried out Japan's punitive and bloody military campaigns against its neighbours.[3] The debate over how to honour Japan's war dead in a more inclusive and secular manner remains a volatile and controversial issue that regularly attracts global media attention.

Postwar Restructuring and Religious Adaptation

After Japan's devastating defeat in 1945, a period of occupation by the Allied forces laid the groundwork for its transformation into a stable democracy. The emperor was obliged to renounce his divinity and Shinto was stripped of its status as the *de facto* state religion. In the spiritual void that followed a war in which so much had been lost, constitutional guarantees of religious freedom encouraged a proliferation of new religious movements. Among them were Soka Gakkai and Rissho Koseikai (both based on the *Lotus Sutra*), Shinnyo-en (derived from Shingon), and others such as Mahikari (True Light) and Perfect Liberty Kyodan (Obaku Zen), each of which claims to have more a million followers today.

Much of the success of these movements can be attributed to the sense of community they provided to people uprooted by urbanization and industrialization, and to the teachings they offered to deal with life's problems. Some smaller religious groups have, for one reason or another, seen it as their role to serve as agents of radical personal and social transformation. The most extreme example was the Aum Shinrikyo cult ("the Supreme Truth of Aum"), established in 1987. Aum was responsible for a number of crimes and murders, including a sensational sarin gas attack on the Tokyo subway system in 1995 that killed 12 people and injured 5,000. According to the group's leader, Asahara Shoko, Japanese society was so thoroughly corrupt that it needed to be "cleansed" by an apocalypse. As a result of these attacks, the Japanese government began instituting more rigorous laws to monitor all religious organizations.

Japan's 75,000 Buddhist temples benefited greatly from the economic bubble and into the present. A number of Zen temples in both rural and urban settings began offering retreats for company employees and school groups as a way to foster spiritual discipline that could benefit individuals competing for success at work or in higher education. With so many families buoyed by the rising tide of the Japanese economy, a desire to venerate one's ancestors in style fostered an expansion for the mortuary industry (morticians, priests, crematoriums, memorial stone manufacturers, cemeteries, and so on) and enriched these players significantly. In urban areas particularly, a kind of "memorial boom" created a thriving marketplace for a wide range of services. From the staging of elaborate funerals and the giving of posthumous Buddhist names, to the performance of rituals

John K. Nelson

A Japanese Buddhist temple can be compared to a franchise business in that it is affiliated with a particular brand yet operates independently. Each temple is required by law to have a board of trustees who work with the temple's priest to ensure stability and continuity. Here, temple trustees relax after a ritual commemorating ancestral spirits, one of the key functions of Buddhism in Japan.

memorializing an aborted fetus or deceased household pet and the scattering of cremated remains in a designated forest, there has been great innovation in meeting (and nurturing) a need for memorial services (called *kuyo*).

Because of the close association of Buddhist priests and temples with the business of funerals, "funeral Buddhism" has become a common derogatory term, applied to temples that depend on the income generated by funerals and memorials. Temples have also benefited financially from the sale of grave plots on their property, so that the presence of several gleaming new gravestones beside a temple is often a telling sign of its prosperity. Many people have been turned off by this trend, seeing it as hypocritical for Buddhism—a religious tradition

dedicated to the alleviation of human suffering— to profit from situations of grief and loss. Younger generations in particular object to supporting their family or neighbourhood temple (membership fees can vary widely, from $300 at a smaller temple to more than $1,000 at prestigious one) just so that they will be in good standing when someone finally dies and they require a funeral and memorial services. An increasing number of rural Buddhist temples no longer have resident priests and some have been forced to sell lands and buildings prior to closing or merging with other temples in the area. In urban areas especially, increasing numbers of people are holding non-religious funerals and thus avoiding the expense of purchasing a grave on temple property.

⊛ Summary

Today the religious traditions of Japan appear to be entering a new and what might be called experimental phase. Ancient shrines and temples still attract many visitors, but most people are more interested in history, aesthetic surroundings, and sacred art than having an experience that could be characterized as "religious." In response to some of the current perceptions of Buddhism in contemporary society, a number of progressive priests have been directing their temples to engage more directly with the problems of society, offering community services, providing sanctuary for victims of domestic violence, and working to protect the environment against unnecessary development. The earthquake and tsunami of 11 March 2011 (in which over 19,000 people lost their lives), and subsequent nuclear meltdown at Fukushima—the so-called "triple disaster"—gave religious specialists of all faiths a highly visible role in providing material and spiritual care for the survivors. Many temples became shelters for people who had lost their homes, and priests in the affected regions as well as volunteers nation-wide helped survivors cope with the emotional and psychological after-effects. The nuclear disaster in particular has caused much soul-searching among Japan's religious leaders, and many have lobbied their denominations to produce statements that acknowledge their failure to address the dangers of nuclear power.

The current period is one of great challenges for the ancient and yet rather new Shinto tradition as well. Scholars continue their efforts to craft a system of ethical and religious principles that can

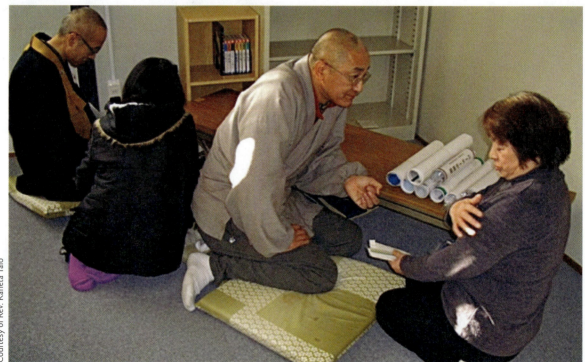

Courtesy of Rev. Kaneta Taiō

Buddhist priests played active roles in providing material, psychological, and spiritual relief after the earthquake and tsunami of 11 March 2011. "Café de Monk" priests and volunteers travelled between temporary housing settlements to offer victims a chance to speak with a priest.

Document

The Japan Buddhist Federation's Appeal for a Lifestyle without Dependence on Nuclear Power

The following statement is excerpted from a longer document drafted by leaders of Japan's largest national organization of Buddhist denominations. Even though the word "Buddhist" appears in the singular form, the differences in thought and practice between Buddhist schools are significant. The statement represents a rare moment of intra-faith cooperation and agreement for the Buddhist Federation.

We, the Japan Buddhist Federation, will strive to reduce our dependence on such nuclear power that threatens life, and to realize a society based on sustainable energy. We must choose a path in which personal happiness is harmonized with human welfare, instead of wishing for prosperity at the expense of others. We would like to make an appeal for building societies that protect each and every life . . . , letting go of excessive materialistic greed, finding contentment in the feeling of moderation, and living in humility with nature (translated by Sakai and Watts, 2012).

hold their own in a crowded spiritual commons. In urban areas, local festivals hosted by Shinto shrines continue to attract broad-based participation, especially among women, who for generations were barred simply because of their gender. In many rural areas, however, it is becoming difficult to find enough people even to carry the portable shrine around the streets of the village. New religions continue to develop and dissipate on the strengths and weaknesses of savvy public relations, charismatic leaders, and the social support offered by a community of like-minded believers.

Even so, there is an increasing tendency to move away from traditional religious affiliations, especially when they impose financial demands. It is predicted that, as Japan's baby-boomers age and pass away, their funeral rituals will become less identifiably Buddhist and more like the eclectic services typical of North America and Europe. Although young people appear distrustful of organized religion in general, partly because of a series of financial scandals and partly because of the Aum terror attack, many still seem interested in more individual spiritual pursuits. Books related to the occult, fortune-telling, and the spirit world always seem to sell well. This suggests that one of the most ancient of all Japan's religious traditions—"turning to the gods in times of trouble"—will likely remain a guiding paradigm resulting in new and innovative forms of religious practice.

Sacred Texts

Religion	Text	Composition/ Compilation	Compilation/ Revision	Use
Shinto	*Kojiki*	8th century; compiled by O no Yasumaro at emperor's request	13th, 15th, 19th, 20th century versions	Legitimates imperial rule; provides myth for founding of Japan; select parts used in ritual purification; ideological use
Shinto	*Nihon Shoki*	8th century; Prince Toneri; O no Yasumaro	13th, 15th, 19th, 20th century versions	More historical than the *Kojiki*, it has been more useful to scholars researching the origins of Japanese civilization
Tendai Buddhism	*Lotus Sutra*; writings of founder, Saicho; other esoteric Buddhist texts	3rd century China, brought to Japan in early 9th century	Translations are updated; commentaries added periodically	Ritual, doctrinal, and ideological
Shingon Buddhism	Mahavairocana and Vajrasekhara *sutras*	7th century (India)	Periodic updates, new translations, and commentaries	Doctrinal, ritual, inspirational, educational
Rinzai Zen Buddhism	Various *sutras*, including the *Lankavatara*; apocryphal stories of enlightened masters; koans	12th century (and earlier)	Numerous translations of teachings, updated frequently over time	Doctrinal, ritual, inspirational, educational
Soto Zen Buddhism	*Heart, Diamond,* and *Lankavatara Sutras*; writings of Dogen	13th, 16th, 18th century texts and commentaries	Periodic updates, new translations, and commentaries	Doctrinal, ritual, inspirational, educational
Pure Land Buddhism	*"Infinite Life"* Sutra	3rd century	Periodic updates, new translations, and commentaries	Doctrinal, ritual, inspirational, educational
True Pure Land Buddhism	*Tannisho*, sayings of Shinran the founder	13th century version	Periodic updates and commentaries	Doctrinal, ritual, inspirational, educational
Nichiren Buddhism	*Lotus Sutra*; writings of founder, Nichiren	13th century version	Translations are updated; commentaries added periodically	Doctrinal, ritual, inspirational, educational

Discussion Questions

1. Why is it common for a contemporary Japanese to visit a Buddhist temple and on the same trip stop at a Shinto shrine to purchase an amulet, yet say he or she is "not religious"?

2. What are several of the principal spiritual agents in Japan that interact with human beings and the natural world?

3. Discuss two of Japan's most popular bodhisattvas and some of their powers to help human beings in moments of crisis.

4. How did the monks Saicho and Kukai help to establish what can be called "Japanese Buddhism" in the eighth century?

5. Identify and differentiate the three types of Buddhism that emerged in the medieval period. Sometimes referred to collectively as "Kamakura Buddhism," these denominations are still among the most popular forms of Buddhist practice in contemporary Japan.

6. What are some of the contributions of Zen Buddhism to Japanese culture? Be sure to reference both aesthetic and political aspects.

7. Explain why accessing spiritual benefits, or *riyaku*, has more meaning for Japanese people than the teachings of particular religious denominations.

8. What role did religion play in the creation of a "modern Japan" between the latter part of the nineteenth century and the Second World War?

Glossary

Amaterasu Female deity of the sun, born from the eye of the primordial deity Izanagi following his purification; enshrined at Ise as the patron deity of the imperial family.

aramitama The rough or violent side of the *kami*, responsible for natural disasters, illness, political disorder, etc.

bodhisattva A Buddhist "saint" who has achieved spiritual liberation but chooses to remain in this world to help alleviate the suffering of individuals.

bushido Literally, the "way of the warrior"; an ethical code that combined a Confucian-style emphasis on loyalty with the discipline of Zen.

haniwa A clay effigy representing a servant, soldier, etc., interred with a ruler to serve him in the afterlife.

honji suijaku Literally, "manifestation from the original state"; the concept that *kami* are manifestations of buddhas or bodhisattvas.

jiriki Literally, "self-power"; the principle that individuals can attain liberation through their own abilities and devotional activities.

kami The spirits that animate all living things, natural phenomena, and natural forces. Shrines were built to accommodate their presence during rituals.

kofun Burial mounds, dating from the second to the sixth centuries CE.

Kojiki A collection of stories commissioned to legitimate the imperial regime by linking it with Japan's mythical origins. It was published in 712 CE but was soon replaced by the *Nihongi* and

remained largely forgotten until the eighteenth century.

Kokugaku Literally, "learning about one's country"; the intellectual movement of the eighteenth and nineteenth centuries that privileged Japanese culture and ideas over those from abroad.

mappo The period of "decline of the (Buddhist) dharma," thought to have begun in 1052; a time of social disorder, during which individuals could not achieve liberation without the aid of buddhas and bodhisattvas.

nembutsu The key prayer of the Pure Land traditions: *Namu Amida Butsu* ("praise to the Amida Buddha").

nigimitama The benevolent side of the *kami*, associated with peace, prosperity, good health, and ample harvests.

samurai A popular term for the *bushi* ("warrior"), who served regional warlords in various capacities; samurai made up the top 5 per cent of society during the Edo period (1603–1867).

shogun The supreme military commander of Japan, appointed by the emperor and effectively ruling in his name.

tariki The "outside power," offered by buddhas and bodhisattvas, without which individuals living in the age of the Buddhist dharma's decline (*mappo*) would be unable to achieve liberation.

Further Reading

Ambros, Barbara. 2012. *Bones of Contention: Animals and Religion in Contemporary Japan*. Honolulu: University of Hawaii Press. A thorough exploration of the newly popular practice of memorializing pets and what it implies for both Japanese society and its Buddhist traditions.

Bowring, Richard. 2006. *The Religious Traditions of Japan, 500–1600*. Cambridge: Cambridge University Press. A comprehensive and highly readable account of Japanese religious history covering more than 1,000 years.

Covell, Stephen. 2005. *Japanese Temple Buddhism: Worldliness in a Religion of Renunciation*. Honolulu: University of Hawaii Press. A pioneering examination of contemporary temple Buddhism, with an emphasis on the Tendai denomination.

Jaffe, Richard. 2002. *Neither Monk nor Layman: Clerical Marriage in Modern Japanese Buddhism*. Princeton: Princeton University Press. An engaging analysis of the tension between the historical image of Buddhist priests as monks and the modern expectations that priests will have families and run their temples like businesses.

Nelson, John. 1996. *A Year in the Life of a Shinto Shrine*. Honolulu: University of Hawaii Press. A study of what goes on behind the scenes at a major Shinto shrine in the city of Nagasaki.

———. 2005. *Spirits of the State: Japan's Yasukuni Shrine*. 28 min. Documentary film, distributed by Films for the Humanities (www.films.com). A documentary, made for university audiences, about the controversy surrounding Yasukuni Shrine, where the spirits of the military dead are enshrined and venerated by the state.

———. 2013. *Experimental Buddhism: Innovation and Activism in Contemporary Japan*. Honolulu: University of Hawaii Press. A study of priests from all of Japan's Buddhist denominations, evaluating the crisis facing temples in Japan today, and documenting some of their creative responses to their loss of patronage and declining social significance.

Prohl, Inken, and John Nelson, eds. 2012. *Handbook of Contemporary Japanese Religions*. Leiden: Brill. More than 20 scholars contributed chapters survey postwar and contemporary developments in Japanese religions and religious practices.

Reader, Ian. 2005. *Making Pilgrimages: Meaning and Practice in Shikoku*. Honolulu: University of Hawaii Press. A detailed study of the Shikoku pilgrimage, including the religious significance of the 88 sacred temples that make up the route.

Rowe, Mark. 2011. *Bonds of the Dead: Temples, Burial, and the Transformation of Contemporary Japanese Buddhism*. Chicago: University of Chicago Press. A groundbreaking book that explores Japanese Buddhism's reliance on mortuary rituals in the postwar period.

Schnell, Scott. 1999. *The Rousing Drum: Ritual Practice in a Japanese Community*. Honolulu: University of Hawaii Press. An ethnographic look at a major festival in a small mountain city and what it means to the cultural identity of the local people.

Swanson, Paul, and Clark Chilson, eds. 2006. *The Nanzan Guide to Japanese Religions*. Honolulu: University of Hawaii Press. A very useful compilation of scholarly articles on many topics related to Japanese religions.

Thal, Sarah. 2006. *Rearranging the Landscape of the Gods: The Politics of a Pilgrimage Site in Japan, 1573–1912*. Chicago: University of Chicago Press. A comprehensive history of the wrenching changes forced on a former Buddhist temple, now converted to a major Shinto shrine.

Watsky, Andrew. 2004. *Chikubushima: Deploying the Sacred Arts in Momoyama Japan*. Honolulu: University of Hawaii Press. One of the best studies of the artistic, architectural, and aesthetic contributions of the sixteenth-century Toyotomi regime to the religious landscape of Japan.

Williams, Duncan. 2005. *The Other Side of Zen: A Social History of Soto Zen in Tokugawa Japan*. Princeton: Princeton University Press. Surprising and often shocking in its account of corruption and exploitation among priests from the sixteenth to the nineteenth centuries, this study reveals the "dark" side of institutional Zen, which dominated Japanese society for more than 250 years.

Recommended Websites

www.nanzan-u.ac.jp/SHUBUNKEN/publications/jjrs/jjrsMain.htm

http://nirc.nanzan-u.ac.jp/youkoso.htm

A semi-annual journal dedicated to the academic study of Japanese religions.

www2.kokugakuin.ac.jp/ijcc

The English-language website for the Institute of Japanese Culture and Classics at Kokugakuin University, specializing in Shinto studies. Many online publications.

global.sotozen-net.or.jp/eng/index.html

The English-language website of the Soto Zen school introduces key teachings and practices. (Each Buddhist denomination has a similar site; many temples also have their own sites.)

www.jodo.org

An English-language website offering a variety of resources on Pure Land Buddhism.

www.onmarkproductions.com/html/buddhism.shtml

A photo library devoted to artwork, especially sculpture, depicting Buddhist and Shinto deities in Japan.

References

Bodiford, William M. 1992. "Zen in the Art of Funerals: Ritual Salvation in Japanese Buddhism." *History of Religions* 32.

Bowring, Richard. 2005. *The Religious Traditions of Japan: 500–1600.* Cambridge: Cambridge University Press.

Breen, John, and Mark Teeuwen. 2000. *Shinto in History: Ways of the Kami.* Honolulu: University of Hawaii.

Dogen, Eihei. 1996. "Tenzo kyokun: Instructions for the Tenzo." Yasuda Hoshu and Anzan Hoshin, trans. White Wind Zen Community. Retrieved online at www.wwzc.org/translations/tenzokyokun.htm.

Hardacre, Helen. 1989. *Shinto and the State: 1868–1945.* Princeton: Princeton University Press.

Jansen, Marius. 2000. *The Making of Modern Japan.* Boston: Harvard University Press.

Kamens, Edward. 1990. *The Buddhist Poetry of the Great Kamo Priestess: Daisaiin Senshi and Hosshin Wakash.* Michigan monograph series in Japanese studies no. 5. Ann Arbor.

MacWilliams, Mark. 2012. "Religion and Manga." In *Handbook of Contemporary Japanese Religions,* ed. Inken Prohl and John Nelson. Leiden: Brill.

Philipi, Donald L. 1985. *The Kojiki.* Tokyo: Tokyo University Press.

Pye, Michael. 2004. "The Structure of Religious Systems in Contemporary Japan: Shinto Variations on Buddhist Pilgrimage." Occasional Paper No. 30, Centre for Japanese Studies. University of Marburg.

Reader, Ian. 1991. *Religion in Contemporary Japan.* Honolulu: University of Hawaii Press.

Sakai, Jin and Jonathan Watts. 2012. *This Precious Life: Buddhist Tsunami Relief and Anti-Nuclear Activism in Post 3/11 Japan.* Yokohama: International Buddhist Exchange Center.

Senda, Minoru. 1988. "Taoist Roots in Japanese Culture." *Japan Quarterly* 35, 2.

Shigeru, Gorai. 1994. *Nihonjin No Shiseikan ("Japanese views of death").* Tokyo: Kadokawa Shoten.

Williams, Duncan. 2005. *The Other Side of Zen: A Social History of Soto Zen in Tokugawa Japan.* Princeton: Princeton University Press.

Young, W.A. 1995. *The World's Religions.* Englewood Cliffs: Prentice-Hall.

Notes

1. One of these colossal statues of Kannon appears at the end of the 2006 film *Kamikaze Girls* as the backdrop for a battle between an all-girl motorcycle gang and one of the protagonists.
2. For more on the *saiin* tradition, see Edward Kamens, *The Buddhist Poetry of the Great Kamo Priestess: Daisaiin Senshi and Hosshin wakashu,* Michigan monograph series in Japanese studies no. 5 (Ann Arbor: Center for Japanese Studies, University of Michigan, 1990).
3. For a treatment of this topic suitable for classroom use, see my documentary film *Spirits of the State: Japan's Yasukuni Shrine* (2005, Films for the Humanities).

8

Current Issues

Amir Hussain and Roy C. Amore

In this chapter you will learn about:

- some of the ways in which religion and politics have interacted in recent decades
- fundamentalism
- how religious traditions around the world are responding to issues such as bioethics, environmental responsibility, gender, and sexuality
- religious diversity.

Most of the chapters in this book have concentrated on individual religious traditions. In this concluding chapter we broaden our focus and look at some general issues relevant to religions around the world.

⊛ Religion and Politics

Once upon a time, many in the West regarded religion as a kind of cultural fossil. Aesthetically rich or anthropologically intriguing? Yes. But relevant to today's hard-nosed world of economics and politics? Hardly at all. Those of us who studied religion were often asked how we could waste our lives on something that had so little to do with the modern world. In the secular intellectual climate of the 1960s, some philosophers and even theologians announced that God was dead. That announcement proved to be premature.

Religion has been a major factor in many of the events that have shaken the world since 1970. One such event occurred in 1979, when the Shah of Iran was deposed in an "Islamic Revolution." That a nation of 40 million people would be ready to sacrifice lives and livelihoods to defend religious values was a concept utterly alien to development economists and politico-military strategists in the West. Meanwhile, not only in Iran but elsewhere, Muslims were turning their backs on modernity and secularism in general and the modern West in particular. In increasing numbers, Muslim men from Algeria to Zanzibar started to grow beards and wear turbans, and more Muslim women than ever before adopted the *hijab* (head scarf).

A second event of 1979 that was to have profound repercussions was the Soviet Union's invasion of Afghanistan. From across the Muslim world, volunteers were taken to Afghanistan and trained by the United States to fight for the country's liberation. They were called *mujahidin*, and at the time—before the end of the cold war—they were widely seen as what US President Ronald Reagan called "freedom fighters."

Among the supporters of Afghanistan's "holy war" was Osama bin Laden (1957–2011), a wealthy Saudi who helped fund and train *mujahidin*. The Soviet troops were withdrawn in 1988, but bin Laden emerged as the leader of al Qaeda ("the base"), an extremist organization. In 1996 bin Laden issued a *fatwa* (religious legal opinion) calling for the overthrow of the Saudi government and the removal of US forces in Arabia; in 1998 he declared war against Americans generally; and in 2001 he was accused of masterminding the 9/11 attacks. In response to those attacks, the United States went to war first in Afghanistan and then in Iraq. To understand the modern world, we now realize, we need to take into account the meanings that traditional religions have for their adherents.

Another eventful year was 1989, when the communist order of eastern Europe and the Soviet Union began to crumble. Hopes for democracy, peace, and progress were high. But when the restraints of the socialist order were loosened, old identities resurfaced, and with them passions that most outsiders had assumed to be long dead. Feuds and ethno-religious divisions in the Balkans, the Caucasus, and Central Asia erupted into bitter conflict. Samuel Huntington, in his book *The Clash of Civilizations and the Remaking of World Order*, argued that the old world order based on the conflict between communism and capitalism has been replaced by a new one based on the differences among civilizations defined primarily along religious lines.

In India, Hindu nationalists have for decades demanded the construction of a Hindu temple in Ayodhya on the hill that is sacred to Hindus generally because of its association with the princely hero Rama. Since 1527, however, that hill had been

The Dalai Lama meeting with US President Barack Obama in February 2010 (Official White House Photo by Pete Souza).

Sites

Ayodhya, India

A city in the Indian state of Uttar Pradesh that is sacred to Hindus as the birthplace of Rama—the hero of the epic *Ramayana* who is said to be an incarnation of the god Vishnu and is worshipped by some devotees as the supreme deity himself. For nearly 500 years, Ayodhya was also the site of the Babri Mosque, named for the first Mughal emperor, Babur, and hence an important site for Indian Muslims. The city also has many other temples associated with characters from the *Ramayana*, as well as other mosques and former Buddhist sites.

occupied by the Babri mosque. Then in 1992 a Hindu rally at the site turned violent: the mosque itself was destroyed, and more than 2,000 people, mostly Muslims, were killed in the nation-wide rioting that followed. Among the forces suspected of provoking the violence was the Hindu nationalist Bharatiya Janata Party (BJP). It has become the main opposition to the Congress Party, and although it has never won a majority of seats at the national level, it did lead a coalition government from 1998 to 2004.

In Sri Lanka the struggle of Hindu Tamil **separatists**, led by the Liberation Tigers of Tamil Eelam, to establish an independent homeland led to a bitter and protracted civil war (1983–2009) that ended in the defeat of the separatists. Although the war was originally a struggle for regional autonomy, it took on a religious dimension because the Tamil Tigers and their supporters were mostly Hindu, whereas the central government was dominated by ethnic Sinhalese, who were mostly Buddhist. This sparked a resurgence of Buddhist fervour among the Sinhalese majority. For the first time in history, monks ran for public office, leading to the formation of a pro-Buddhist party that elected several monks to parliament. Now that the civil strife has ended, the challenge is to rebuild a state in which Sri Lankans of all religions can feel welcome and represented in parliament.

A similar separatist movement has led to separatist strife against the majority Buddhist government by Islamic groups in the southern part of Thailand that borders Malaysia and has a majority ethnic Malay, Muslim population.

In China religious minorities such as the Muslim Uighurs and the Buddhist Tibetans have renewed their struggles against the repressive tendencies of the national government.

☸ Fundamentalism

In most cases the leading figures in the resurgence of religious fervour have come from the ultraconservative or "**fundamentalist**" end of the religious spectrum. A brief review of the rise of fundamentalism may help to explain why.

Now widely used to refer to ultraconservative religious movements, the term "fundamentalism" originated in the United States, where a series of booklets entitled *The Fundamentals* was published from 1910 to 1915. Affirming the "inerrancy" (infallibility) of the Bible and traditional Christian doctrines, the booklets were distributed free to Protestant clergy, missionaries, and students through the anonymous sponsorship of "two Christian laymen" (William Lyman Stewart and his brother Milton, both of whom were major figures in the Union Oil Company of California). By 1920, defenders of biblical inerrancy were being described as "fundamentalists."

Fundamentalism is a modern phenomenon, a reaction against the values associated with secularism and modernity. Above all, perhaps, what

In June 2012, opponents of US President Obama's health-care plan in Charleston, SC, argued that requiring employers to provide insurance coverage for contraception would infringe on their religious freedom.

fundamentalists reject is the modern tendency to locate ultimate authority in human institutions such as courts and legislatures rather than divine scriptures and religious leaders. If they interpret their scripture as condemning homosexuality, for example, they resist all efforts to legalize same-sex marriage as a human right. Fundamentalists do not necessarily denounce science, but on specific issues where science differs from their interpretation of scripture, they side with scripture as the ultimate authority. For Christian fundamentalists, the main conflict with science has centred on the perceived conflict between the biblical stories of creation and the consensus of modern science. They understand the Bible to affirm that the world was created by

God in six days, only a few thousand years ago, and that everything in existence originated at that time. By contrast, science maintains that the universe has existed for many billions of years, that our planet formed some time later, and that all life on earth is the product of evolution through countless generations.

The test case for fundamentalism came in 1925, when a Tennessee high-school teacher named John T. Scopes was brought to trial for violating a newly enacted state law that banned the teaching of evolution on the grounds that it contradicted the Bible. The court found for the prosecution, conducted by the famed orator William Jennings Bryan (1860–1925) against the defence of Clarence Darrow

(1857–1938), and fined Scopes $100. So extensive was the news coverage of the case, however, that fundamentalism itself was effectively put on trial in the court of public opinion, where Darwin, Scopes, and Darrow emerged the clear victors. What earned the Scopes case the nickname the "monkey trial" and made it a *cause célèbre* was the idea that humans were not the special creations of God but a species of primate descended from the same common ancestor as gorillas and chimpanzees. Although Scopes's conviction was overturned in 1927 on the technical grounds that the fine was too high, it would be another 40 years before the Tennessee law banning the teaching of evolution was repealed.

The word "fundamentalism" can have various meanings, but almost all of them are pejorative: even conservative Protestants tend to describe their own views as "evangelical" and use "fundamentalist" only to refer to more extreme views. In addition to denoting an orthodoxy based on the inerrancy of scripture, "fundamentalism" generally suggests orthopraxy—conformity to a straitlaced code of social and personal conduct—and a militant defence of their tradition as they understand it. Fundamentalists have been known to attack as diabolical those they believe to be subverting that tradition by expressing doubt or taking more liberal positions on some issues.

Fundamentalists perceive a struggle between good and evil forces in the world, and they have a greater-than-average readiness to believe that evil is tangibly manifested in social groups and forces with which they take issue, such as advocates of homosexual rights or free choice in abortion. They

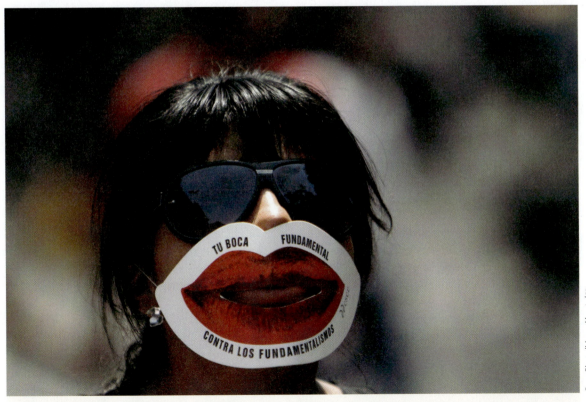

© AP Photo/Marco Ugarte/CP

At a demonstration in Mexico City in 2011 in favour of legalizing abortion, an activist wears a mask that reads "Your mouth is fundamental against fundamentalism".

also tend to believe that the apocalypse—a final battle between the forces of good and evil in this world—is imminent.

Since the 1970s the term "fundamentalist" has been widely used to describe ultraconservative movements in religious traditions other than Christianity—especially those movements that have taken their beliefs into the political realm. Some scholars object to the use of a term with specifically Christian roots to refer to different traditions. Nevertheless, from the popular perspective there are enough similarities among the various ultraconservative movements around the world to justify the term's extension to other cultures.

The term "fundamentalist" has also been applied in India to the conservative Hinduism embraced by the Sangh Parivar ("family of associations"), a collective term for Hindu nationalist organizations, including the BJP. The most important "parent" in this was the RSS, "National Volunteer Association," founded in 1925 by K.B. Hedgewar (1889–1940) to promote the idea of India as a Hindu nation. To counter the growing strength of the All-India Muslim League (a political party that was calling for the creation of a separate Muslim state), Hedgewar started a boy's club that met early in the morning for military style drills, physical exercises and instruction in traditional Hindu values. His emphasis on the Hindu nation inspired the formation of many other Hindu nationalist organizations.

Central to Hindu nationalist thought is the concept of **Hindutva**, a term coined in the 1920s by the writer and independence activist V.D. Sarvakar. It literally means "Hindu-ness" and refers to an attitude that can manifest itself in a wide range of ways, from taking pride in Hindu traditions to claiming that Hinduism is the only true Indian religion, demanding that Indians of other faiths accept Hindu dominance, and promoting sectarian violence.

❂ Bioethics

An important challenge facing religious communities in the twenty-first century is the unprecedented power over human life and death made available by developments in biological research and medical technology. This power is especially troubling for the Western religions, which have traditionally considered humans to be sacred, set apart from all other beings. In Islam, for example, the human being is created expressly to serve as God's representative on earth:

> Behold, your Lord said to the angels: "I will create a vicegerent on earth." They said: "Will You place therein one who will make mischief there and shed blood while we celebrate Your praises and glorify Your holy name?" God said: "I know what you do not" (Q. 2: 30).

Central to the notion of the human being as sacred is the notion of the soul. The Christian understanding of the soul was economically expressed by the Anglican writer C.S. Lewis: "You don't have a soul, you are a soul. You have a body." Hinduism likewise teaches that the soul (*atman*) is the eternal and therefore the more important part of the human being; in fact, one of the Hindu terms for soul is *dehin*, meaning "that which possesses a body." In Islam, the soul is believed to enter the body at a certain stage of its development in the womb:

> And truly We created the human being out of wet clay, then we made it a drop in a firm resting place, then We made the seed a clot, then We made the clot a lump of flesh, then We made (in) the lump of flesh bones, then We clothed the bones with flesh, then We caused it to grow into another creation, so blessed be God, the best of the creators" (Q. 23: 12–14).

Modern Muslims take great pride in the history of science and medicine associated with Islam. Following an injunction of the Prophet Muhammad "to seek knowledge even unto China" (that is, to the end of the then-known world),[1] Muslims never really experienced the kind of tension between religion and science that Western Christianity did. To

Demonstrating against the gang rape and death of Jyoti Singh Pandey in December 2012, a protestor in Gauhati, India suggested a link between violence against women and the selective abortion of female fetuses.

discover scientific truths about the world was to learn more about God who created the world. Thus universities were established in the Islamic world as early as the ninth century; one of the earliest accounts of the duties of the doctor was written by a ninth-century physician named Ishaq ibn Ali Rahawi; and in the tenth century another Muslim physician named al-Razi (known in the West as Rhazes) wrote numerous treatises on medicine, pharmacy, and medical ethics.

The situation with Eastern religious traditions is somewhat different. One reason is that modern medical technologies have only recently arrived in Asia, and still are not readily available to many people. Abortion, however, has long been an issue for Buddhists and Hindus. Even though all Eastern traditions condemn it, abortion is relatively common in most Asian countries, especially Japan, India, China, and South Korea. According to the World Health Organization and The Guttmacher Institute, the abortion rate in Asia in the period from 1995 to 2008 was approximately the same as for the whole world: approximately 28 induced abortions for each 1,000 women of child-bearing age (Sedgh, 2012).

The Buddhist scriptures have little to say about abortion itself, but the Buddhist ethic of non-violence has been understood to apply to abortion no less than to any other form of harm. In the Theravada countries of Southeast Asia abortion is typically illegal, but covert abortions are common. Japanese Buddhists have developed a special memorial service, called *mizuko kuyo*, for aborted fetuses, and some temples set aside special areas where family members may go to honour their memory.

As well as all the usual motivations for abortion, Hindus in India face two additional pressures. One is the persistence of an unusually onerous **dowry** system under which the family of a bride is expected to provide the groom's family with generous compensation. Because the family can rarely afford to pay the entire debt before the wedding, the payments are often spread over several years, like a mortgage. The dowry system is not sanctioned in traditional Hindu law, but neither governmental legislation nor the condemnation of some Hindu leaders has been able to put an end to it. Thus the birth of a daughter means that the family faces the prospect of a terrible burden when she comes of marital age: not only will it have to pay for both the wedding and the dowry, but after marriage the girl will go to live with—and work for—the family of her husband. Conversely, a baby boy brings the prospect not only of receiving a significant financial reward when he marries, but of gaining an additional labourer or income earner in the form of his wife.

Under these circumstances, many families use modern medical technology to find out the sex of a prospective child before birth, and some give in to the economic pressures and abort female fetuses. The other factor contributing to the rise of abortion in India is the government's ongoing effort to control the growth of the country's population. Unlike China, India has not resorted to forced birth control, but it has put in place incentives to limit reproduction. For example, a village that manages to keep its birth rate low is eligible to receive special grants for community development projects, such as roads, wells, or community centres. Thus community leaders sometimes put heavy pressure on women who already have children to undergo sterilization in order to prevent additional pregnancies. This approach may have the unintended effect of encouraging abortion.

❂ The Environment

After creating the first humans, according to the Bible (Genesis 1: 28), God gave them "dominion . . . over all the earth": the fish of the sea, the birds of the air, and every living thing. This verse was traditionally interpreted as a grant of power and a licence for unlimited exploitation of the earth's resources, but today it is generally understood differently, as a command to take responsibility for the environment.

An influential early advocate of this "greener" interpretation was Lynn White, who in 1967 published an article entitled "The Historical Roots of Our Ecologic Crisis." In it he argued that the traditional reading of Genesis had played a significant part in the degradation of the earth. This article prompted a shift in attitude among many Jews and Christians, towards an understanding of "dominion over the earth" that emphasized stewardship of God's creation rather than exploitation of it. This awareness can be seen in churches such as the Canadian Memorial Church in Vancouver, which has embraced an environmental mission: "To cultivate a spiritual understanding of Creation, and to adopt and promote awareness of a spiritually-principled approach to planetary sustainability."

According to the Qur'an, God offered the responsibility for this universe as "a Trust to the heavens and the earth and the mountains; but they refused to undertake it, being afraid thereof" (Q. 33: 72). Thus the "Trust" passed from the physical world to the one part of creation that was willing to take it: the human being. The verse concludes with the following words: "The human being was indeed unjust and foolish." In suggesting that we would behave foolishly and without justice to the earth, this passage underlines the necessity of wisdom and justice in the exercise of the profound responsibility that humans have been given.

Faced with the evidence of humans' failure to serve as responsible stewards, Muslims, Jews, and Christians are reflecting on their fundamental religious teachings and discovering in them the bases for a new environmental ethic.

In sharp contrast to their Western counterparts, most Eastern religious traditions have never made any radical distinction between humans and nature or between humans and other animals. Hinduism understands all animals to have a soul (*atman*), and holds that reincarnation may take place in either a human or an animal body. Jainism goes even

© Roy C. Amore

Monks at Drepung Monastery near Lhasa, Tibetan Autonomous Region, China, use solar heaters to boil water in kettles, which they will pour into the waiting containers for their morning tea break.

further, teaching that plants as well are animated by a kind of soul. Jainism and Buddhism alike emphasize the ethic of non-violence and denounce any human activity that causes unnecessary harm to living things.

Ajai Mansingh (1995) defends Hinduism's "natural theology," based on reasoning and observation of nature rather than revelation, as better equipped to understand the dynamic relationship between the divine and the world than the more static Creator/creation approach of most Western religions. Certainly attitudes towards the environment may be shaped by practical as well as theoretical concerns. As Bina Agarwal (1992) points out, rural women in India have more at stake in the environmental arena than do most people in the West,

male or female, since so many of them still have the daily chore of fetching water for their households. The distances they must travel, especially in the dry months, are often increased by the pressures of human population growth and environmental degradation. The same is true for women who have to make regular trips to gather fodder for their animals. Their understanding of environmental issues is informed by direct experience.

A number of Buddhists, including the Dalai Lama and Sulak Sivaraksa, have applied the Buddhist ethic of moderation to environmental issues. Sulak argues that human greed is responsible for the redirection of vast quantities of natural resources to support cash crops, causing suffering on the part of local people as well as harm to the

Document

The Dalai Lama on the Common Ground between Buddhism and Science

On the philosophical level, Buddhism and modern science share a deep suspicion of any notion of absolutes, whether conceptualized as a transcendent being; as an eternal, unchanging principle such as soul; or as a fundamental substratum of reality. Both Buddhism and science prefer to account for the evolution and emergence of the cosmos and life in terms of the complex interrelations of the natural laws of cause and effect.

From the methodological perspective, both traditions emphasize the role of empiricism. . . . This means that in the Buddhist investigation of reality, at least in principle, empirical evidence should triumph over scriptural authority, no matter how deeply venerated a scripture may be. . . . I have often remarked to my Buddhist colleagues that the empirically verified insights of modern cosmology and astronomy must compel us now to modify, or in some cases reject, many aspects of traditional cosmology as found in ancient Buddhist texts. . . .

So, a genuine exchange between the cumulative knowledge and experience of Buddhism, and modern science on wide-ranging issues pertaining to the human mind, from cognition and emotion to understanding the capacity for transformation inherent in the human brain, can be deeply interesting and potentially beneficial as well. . . . The compelling evidence from neuroscience and medical science of the crucial role of simple physical touch for even the physical enlargement of an infant's brain, during the first few weeks powerfully brings home the intimate connection between compassion and human happiness (His Holiness The Dalai Lama 2008: 190–2).

environment. One of the first to bring these ecological concerns to wide public attention was the economist E.F. Schumacher, in his book *Small Is Beautiful* (1973). Schumacher called for a "Buddhist economics" designed to meet the needs of all the planet, as opposed to a traditional business economics designed to maximize profits. But of course this approach is not confined to Buddhism: M.K. Gandhi's preference for small-scale, locally based technology, together with his call for all to work for the benefit of all, has inspired organizations around the world dedicated to environmental responsibility and human-centred development.

⚛ Gender and Sexuality

In 2000, two advertising campaigns in Los Angeles featured images of veiled women. One campaign was for the opening of the renovated Aladdin Hotel and Casino in Las Vegas, a day's drive across the desert. Billboards featured the head and shoulders of an attractive Middle Eastern woman with an enticing smile, wearing a delicate veil that covered her hair and lower face. The image was a classic example of the "erotic Orient" myth—the harem girl whose sensuality so shocked (and sometimes titillated) the Victorians.

The other campaign was for the *Los Angeles Times*. Entitled "Connecting Us to the Times," it included television commercials as well as print ads and billboards. In each case, an image of bikini-clad women on a beach was juxtaposed with an image of women covered from head to toe in full black robes. In many ways, this campaign was more troubling than the first example. It's no surprise that a Las Vegas casino would use sex to sell itself, but why would a respected newspaper choose that approach? In this case, the veiled women suggested a suppressed sexuality that underlined the overt sexuality of the women in bikinis. The ads were criticized not only by Muslim groups, but also by 200 *Times* employees who objected to the use of women's bodies—covered or uncovered—to sell their product. As a result, the *Times* cancelled the campaign.

These examples are recent and specifically North American, but the distorted images they present point to a tendency to distort the image of Muslim women that is rooted in prejudice and misunderstanding.

When discussing the roles and lives of women today, it is essential to keep in mind that individual circumstances vary just as widely for them as for any other group. To be a woman in North America is a very different experience for a university professor than it is for an unemployed mother of four who never finished high school. Or look at the roles of women in political life. In both Canada and the United States, women are theoretically equal to men, yet neither country has elected a female leader. (Kim Campbell's short stint as prime minister in 1993 was the result of the midterm resignation of Brian Mulroney, not a national election.) By contrast, Indonesia, Pakistan, Bangladesh, and Turkey (all predominantly Muslim), India (predominantly Hindu) and Sri Lanka (predominantly Buddhist) have elected women as leaders. It would be no less simplistic to assume that North America is necessarily progressive in its treatment of women than it would be to assume that the other regions of the world are necessarily oppressive.

Many religious traditions are also beginning to rethink their positions on sexuality. Islam is among the majority of Western religious traditions that recognize only heterosexual relationships as valid, and Muslims often speak out against homosexuality. However, there are Muslims who identify themselves as lesbian–gay–bisexual–transgendered–intersex–questioning (LGBTIQ), and they are forming support groups. One such group, with branches in several Canadian cities including Toronto and Vancouver, is Min al-Alaq, which takes its name from a Qur'anic phrase (96: 2) that translates literally as "from the clot." The implication is that members consider all believers, whatever their sexual orientation, to come "from the same clot of blood."

Homosexuality has played a major role in Christian church politics as well. The international family of churches led by the Archbishop of Canterbury, the head of the Church of England, has been particularly hard hit by controversy over homosexuality. Until recently these churches constituted one big family known as the Anglican Communion, but in recent years a major split has taken place, largely over the question of whether or not the Church should bless same-sex marriages and ordain persons openly living in same-sex relationships. James Packer, a well-known conservative Anglican theologian, officially resigned his membership in a Vancouver-area diocese in 2008 because its head favoured allowing the ritual blessing of same-sex unions. Earlier that year several conservative congregations broke away from the Anglican Church of Canada to form the Anglican Network of Canada. They recognize a South African bishop as their spiritual head and pride themselves on adhering to biblical tradition, which in their view considers homosexuality a sin. (In fact, although some local divisions of the Anglican Church of Canada have endorsed same-sex blessings, so far the Church as a whole has not done so.)

Among Jews, the Union for Reform Judaism has been at the front of the struggle for LGBTIQ rights. In 2011 they participated in the "It Gets Better" campaign for teens.

Most Eastern traditions are just beginning to discuss such issues. In fact, it is only recently that India has officially recognized the existence of homosexuality within its borders. Buddhist ordination rules prohibit the admission to the sangha of a category of persons that has been understood to include homosexuals and transsexuals. But most sanghas insist that monks and nuns remain celibate in any case, so questions about sexual orientation rarely arise. (The one exception is Japan, where married Buddhist priests are common.) In general, Buddhist societies in Asia are socially conservative and frown on homosexual relationships, although the Buddhist culture of Thailand has a

Document

Reform Judaism and LGBTIQ Teens

Statement by Rabbi David Saperstein, Director of the Religious Action Center of Reform Judaism:

Unfortunately, even as we celebrate the growing acceptance of marriage equality and the end of "Don't Ask, Don't Tell," we know that members of the LGBT community still face stigma and discrimination. This is especially true for teens who, all too often, are bullied because of their real or perceived sexual orientation or gender identity.

When we hear the word "bullying" we often think merely of name calling, but LGBT youth sadly endure far much worse than that. According to the Suicide Prevention Resource Center, more than sixty percent of LGBT youth reported that they felt unsafe at school as a result of bullying related to their sexual orientation; more than forty percent were physically harassed (i.e. shoved or pushed) and nearly twenty percent were assaulted (i.e. punched, kicked, attacked with a weapon). The effects of enduring this are severe: the Center estimates that 30% of all lesbian, gay, bisexual, and transgender youth have attempted suicide at some

point—a rate that is three times that of their heterosexual counterparts.

That is why messages of hope, not hate, are so vital.

As Jews we believe in the inherent dignity of all people, for we read in the Torah, "So God created the human beings in [the divine] image, creating [them] in the image of God, creating them male and female" (Gen. 1:27). As human beings, we have a responsibility to ensure that the spark of the Divine presence in each individual is respected. To that end, we hope that our participation in the It Gets Better campaign will remind LGBT youth who are struggling that they are valued and loved.

In addition, we will continue our efforts to make it better for LGBT youth, as we advocate for passage of legislation to enhance anti-bullying efforts in schools, including the Safe Schools Improvement Act and the Student Non-Discrimination Act. [This statement] is a continuation of the Reform Movement's decades of work on behalf of LGBT equality and rights as well as our longstanding commitment to fighting bigotry, wherever it may arise.

long tradition of accepting males who cross-dress as females.

A major factor in India's movement towards greater openness has been the **Bollywood** film industry. Just a few years ago, the leading lady in an Indian film could not even be kissed on camera, but now physical expressions of affection—even suggestions of gay or lesbian sexuality—are increasingly common. Still, many traditionally minded Hindus and Muslims are shocked by the new openness.

Chinese society is also becoming more open and permissive about homosexuality. China no longer lists homosexuality as a mental illness, and gay–lesbian pride parades are now held annually in Shanghai. In the past, in China as elsewhere, many gay males married and raised families, but now gay men's wives—called *tongqi*—are forming support groups and calling attention to their plight ("Gay marriage gone wrong," 2012).

Japanese society has traditionally avoided any public discussion of homosexuality, but that is starting to change. One indicator of the change is that Tokyo Disneyland now allows same-sex marriages to be performed at its theme park (Westlake, 2012).

⚛ Religious Diversity

"Aren't all religions pretty much the same?" Most students of religion will be asked this question, or some version of it, more than once in their careers. As scholars we might want to unpack the proposition. What aspect of religion are we talking about—teachings? practices? implications for society? Still, it would probably be safe to assume that the questioner considers all religions to be of equal value and deserving of equal respect. And in the multicultural society of twenty-first-century North America, most of us would probably agree. This was not the case 100 years ago, when North American society was overwhelmingly Christian and most of the Christian churches were actively engaged in missionary work. Missionary activity presumes a difference among religions—a difference so consequential that believers cannot keep silent about it, but must spread the word.

For its first three centuries, Christianity was an affinity-based movement whose members were not born into it but actively chose to join. In the early fourth century, however, with the imperial favour of the emperor Constantine (r. 306–37), the missionary religion became a state religion as well. Christianity converted several entire populations by first converting their rulers. In its earlier centuries, Islam likewise succeeded in persuading a significant number of nations to convert, perhaps partly because it offered improved juridical status, including especially tax exemption, to those who became Muslims. Christianity's spread after the 1490s was closely associated with European military and cultural expansion. Priests accompanied soldiers in Mexico and Peru, and the sponsoring Spanish and Portuguese regimes took it as their responsibility to save the souls of the Indigenous peoples whose bodies they enslaved. The cultural–religious imperialism of Catholic countries in the sixteenth century was matched in the nineteenth by that of Protestant England, notably in Africa.

Muslim rule in northern India began with the establishment of the Delhi sultanate in the thirteenth century. This was the first region where Islam did not succeed in converting the entire population. Only in the Indus Valley, Bengal, and the mid-southern interior did Muslims become the majority; the rest of the subcontinent remained predominantly Hindu.

In the later centuries of its expansion, Islam grew not through military conquest, but through trade and the missionary activity of the Sufis in particular. The devotional life of the Sufis resonated with the Hindu and Buddhist meditational piety already present in Southeast Asia and provided Islam with an entrée to that region, in which it became dominant. Similarly in Africa south of the Sahara, traders and Sufis were the principal vehicles of Islam.

Dialogue in a Pluralistic Age

Today we often use the term "**pluralism**" to denote a combination of two things: the fact of diversity, and the evaluation of that diversity as desirable. This use of the word, which has become standard since the mid-twentieth century, reflects a convergence of developments and trends.

But let us be clear about what we mean by it. First, pluralism is not the same thing as diversity. People from many different religions and ethnic backgrounds may be present in one place, but unless they are constructively engaged with one another, there is no pluralism.

Second, pluralism means more than simple tolerance of the other. It's quite possible to tolerate a neighbour about whom we know nothing. Pluralism, by contrast, demands an active effort to learn.

Third, pluralism is not the same thing as relativism, which can lead us to ignore profound differences. Pluralism is committed to engaging those differences, to gain a deeper understanding both of others' commitments and of our own. It is also important to recognize that pluralism and

Focus

Missionary Religions

The fact that a mere three traditions—Buddhism, Christianity, and Islam—claim the allegiance of over half the world's population reflects the success of their missionary activities. All three are "universal" rather than "ethnic" religions: that is, they direct their messages to all human beings, regardless of heredity or descent. And all three were strongly motivated from the start to spread their messages far and wide.

By the time Buddhism emerged in what is now northern India, Indian society was already stratified into four broad social classes. Whether those distinctions had ethnic connotations in the time of the Buddha may be debated. What is clear is that Buddhism set caste and class status aside as irrelevant to the achievement of spiritual purity and liberation.

Christianity began as a sect of Judaism, a religion focused almost exclusively on the relationship of one particular nation to God. But the early Christians decided that it was not necessary to be a Jew in order to become a Christian. Early Christian teaching understood the new covenant to apply to all humans who accepted Jesus as their Lord, regardless of ethnicity.

Islam believes the Prophet Muhammad to have been the last in a long line of prophets sent by God to different peoples. And although the Qur'an explicitly addresses the people of Arabia, it was understood from the start to incorporate the messages delivered to other groups by earlier prophets and to represent God's final revelation to humanity at large.

In general, Buddhist, Muslim, and Christian missionaries have been more successful in recruiting converts from the traditional religions of small-scale tribal societies than from the other major religions. The reasons may have something to do with the material culture and technologies—including writing systems—of the major civilizations, which have conferred powerful advantages on those who possess them. Scriptural literatures have given the major traditions a special authority among cultures that were primarily oral, allowing them to use the content of their scriptures to shape social values. The early missionary spread of Theravada Buddhism is credited to King Ashoka. We do not know enough about the Indigenous traditions in many of the regions where Theravada spread to determine why its teachings were accepted. In the case of China, however, it seems that the Daoist interest in magic and healing techniques may have helped Mahayana Buddhism gain an initial foothold.

In the twentieth century, some Christian denominations began to curtail their missionary activity, partly because the returns on the resources invested were too small. Generations of European missionary effort in the eastern Mediterranean had made almost no inroads into Islam. And in the years around 1960, when many African countries were struggling for independence from European rule, Christian missionaries in West Africa particularly suffered from identification with colonial interests as well as the former slave trade. Thus Christian missionaries in Africa were largely replaced by an emerging generation of Indigenous church leaders. Another factor in the Christian churches' retreat from missionary work, however, was an increasing respect for other communities and traditions.

A coalition of diverse American faith leaders came to Washington, DC, for a day of interfaith action to urge the US Congress and President Obama to protect the poor and the vulnerable in the "fiscal cliff" negotiations of December 2012.

dialogue are happening around the world, not just in North America.

The current situation has been shaped by increasingly intimate intercultural contact. Within the lifetimes of people still alive today, transportation and communication have been transformed almost beyond recognition. As late as 1950, travel between North America and East Asia was rare, but now tens of thousands of people fly across the Pacific every day. And new technologies allow us to be in touch with almost any part of the world in an instant. Migration has also increased significantly. Since the end of the Second World War, the demographic profile of European and North American cities has been transformed by the arrival of populations from other parts of the world who have brought their Muslim, Hindu, Buddhist, and other traditions with them. Though apprehensive at first, Western societies have made some progress towards understanding those traditions.

Change in the evaluation of diversity is reflected in many aspects of contemporary life, large and small. In some cases old institutions have been retained, but with new rationales. For instance, Sunday—the Christian day of religious observance—remains the day of reduced business activity in many jurisdictions. The arguments for legislation preserving Sunday store closing, however, now revolve around issues such as fairness, family time, and opportunities for recreation.

We should distinguish pluralism from secularism. Secularism means the exclusion (in principle) of all religious groups, institutions, and identities from public support and public decision-making. Pluralism, on the other hand, means equal support, acceptance, and participation in decision-making for multiple religious groups. Whereas recreational arguments for Sunday closing are secularist, arguments for school holidays on the Jewish New Year or the Muslim festival ending the Ramadan fast are pluralist. Up to a point, secularism and pluralism go hand in hand in the West because both seek to limit the role that Christianity can play in setting the society's standards. Where they differ is in what they propose as alternatives. Pluralism places a parallel and a positive value on the faith and practice of different communities. It often does so on the assumption that any religion is beneficial to society so long as it does no harm to other religions. It can also presume that the effort to understand a neighbour's religion—whatever it may be—is beneficial to society. Essentially, pluralism downplays the differences between religions and focuses instead on the values they share. In its scale of priorities, harmony in the society as a whole is more important than the commitments of any particular religion.

Interfaith Dialogue

The word "dialogue" comes from a Greek root meaning to argue, reason, or contend. Some Christian writers have pointed to the apostle Paul as an early proponent of interfaith dialogue because he is described as "arguing and pleading about the kingdom of God" with the Jews (*Acts* 19: 8–9). Paul was a missionary, however, and missionaries—by definition—believe they are possessed of a truth that it is their mission to spread. Missionary argumentation therefore bears little resemblance to dialogue in the modern sense, which demands openness to other points of view.

Dialogue is also a literary form, almost always designed to advance the author's point of view. The Greek philosopher Plato was a master of the dialogue form, using questioners and objectors as foils (or comedic "straight men") to demonstrate the

invincible logic of his own ideas and those of his mentor Socrates.

The Hindu *Upanishads* also take the form of dialogues: yet they too were composed to advance specific arguments. Similarly, in the Buddhist story of the sage Nagasena answering the questions of King Milinda, the questioner is like a puppet whose only function is to bring out the views that the author is already committed to.

True openness to alternative points of view is rare in any of the premodern traditions, but we do find instances of it. One highly significant example was Akbar, the Mughal emperor of India from 1556 to 1605. As a Muslim ruler of a mainly Hindu population, Akbar could have taken a tolerant stance towards Hindu spirituality on purely practical grounds, but he was a genuine seeker of religious insight. Therefore he summoned to his court representatives of all the religious communities within his domain and pursued conversations with them late into the night. From those conversations Akbar drew the components of an eclectic new religion that he called Din-i Ilahi ("divine faith"). Although Akbar's synthesis did not endure for long after his death, it reflected a remarkable phenomenon in his society: a widespread perception that despite their communal boundaries, Hindus and Muslims shared a devotional spirituality.

Conservative Muslims disapproved of Akbar's openness to heretical views. This is nothing new. Traditional religions may encourage disputation when the outcome is not in question. But Akbar's explorations were open-ended. A dialogue in which both sides are equal is something that orthodoxy cannot control. To those committed to a fixed position, such dialogue implies a threat.

The World's Parliament of Religions, convened in Chicago in 1893, was an adventure in dialogue that brought together representatives of many—though not all—of the world's faiths to present their religious goals and understandings. The conference reflected the existing religious scene and at the same time affected its future development by creating opportunities for Vedanta to present itself as the definitive form of Hinduism, Zen to claim to represent Buddhism, and the Baha'i faith to appear as an overarching synthesis of religion.

Understanding of interfaith dialogue has grown considerably since 1948, when the World Council of Churches was formed. Experienced dialogue participants emphasize that such exercises require both parties to set aside their claims to exclusivity: each must work to understand the other on his or her own terms. Both participants must also be open to the possibility of revising their views in the light of what they learn in the encounter—though this is easier said than done. Even the best-intentioned participants may be tempted to read their own views into others'. The influential Roman Catholic theologian Karl Rahner (1904–84), for instance, referred to people of other faiths as "anonymous Christians"—Christians who simply did not recognize the fact. By the same token, could not Rahner himself have been an anonymous Buddhist?

The goal of dialogue in the modern sense is "understanding." But "understanding" can be a slippery term in the context of religion. Academic students of religion understand particular traditions by explaining them: by describing as accurately as possible what they require of their adherents and how they have developed to become what they are. For those people, understanding may be informed by sympathy, but it is not the same as participation or identification. Similarly, the participants in dialogue understand each other by identifying one another's commitments, but that is not to say that they identify with those commitments. Particularly in the area of Jewish–Christian–Muslim dialogue, there have been calls for complete solidarity on complex and hotly debated issues, characterized by one critic as "ecumenical blackmail." Does true understanding of Judaism require uncritical endorsement of Israel's policies towards the Palestinians? If one truly "understands" Islam, must one agree with Iran's theocratic government and its suppression of democracy? Does understanding Hinduism mean accepting polytheism or animal sacrifice? No. Real understanding is not a matter of agreement or acquiescence, but a quest for a patient and appreciative relationship that can persist despite disagreement.

The Question of Value

For more than three decades, the 1978 Jonestown tragedy—in which 914 members of a religious community called the Peoples Temple died in a mass suicide—has stood as a challenge to the idea that all religions are equally valuable and deserving of respect. The community's founder, the Reverend Jim Jones (1931–78), who took his own life alongside his followers, had aspirations to overhaul the world order that were compatible with a reformist and utopian strand in Protestant (and Marxist) thought; one of his objectives in founding the movement had been to improve the living standards of the poor. But he also sought from his followers an uncritical dedication to his personal leadership that many found disturbing. Having moved the community from the US to rural Guyana in 1972, Jones ordered the mass suicide when he became convinced that evil forces were closing in and the only honourable escape was death.

History repeats itself. The Jonestown story recalls the Jewish Zealots at the fortress of Masada who are said to have committed mass suicide when they were surrounded by Roman troops in 73 CE. Suicide and the psychology of martyrdom have been linked at various times by Christian groups, and in other traditions as well. A similar interpretation has been applied to the conduct of the followers of David Koresh (Vernon Wayne Howell, 1959–93), 85 of whom perished with him when their heavily armed religious commune outside Waco, Texas, was stormed by US law enforcement forces for firearms violations in 1993. To approve of Masada's defenders while condemning the "Branch Davidians" at Waco would amount to deciding what constitutes a provocation worth resisting to the death.

Jim Jones and David Koresh were both leaders of movements that sought to recruit and retain converts. That is not unusual in missionary religions: Buddhism, Christianity, and Islam have all done the same, as have numerous "new religious movements" since the late 1960s. If modern pluralistic society proclaims the freedom to preach or follow religion without state intervention, fairness demands that the same freedom be extended to all.

Nevertheless, my freedom to practise or promote a religion is limited by the freedom of others to know what I am offering and to refuse it if they so choose. In a pluralistic society, religious groups forfeit their right to acceptance if they engage in coercion (psychological or physical) or illegal activities (such as narcotics abuse, firearms abuse, or tax fraud). Critics of movements such as the Unification Church (the "Moonies"), or ISKCON (the Hare Krishna movement), or the Church of Scientology are particularly alarmed when recruits are instructed to sever all ties with their families—even though there have been parallels to such demands in the early Christian movement and in some religious orders—and the families of such recruits have often resorted to equally coercive methods to retrieve and "deprogram" them.

By the early twenty-first century, some of the new religions had achieved a degree of institutional maturity and public acceptance. Most of these organizations are compatible with mainstream religions in that they help their members cope with their lives and encourage good citizenship. Like mainstream religions, in one way or another they address the human condition.

The last point is important. Religions are not all the same, but many may be humanly acceptable if they in fact benefit human beings; an appropriate test is suggested by Jesus' words in the Sermon on the Mount: "you shall know them by their fruits" (Matthew 7: 16). On some occasions, when they have lived up to their ideals, all the major traditions have passed that test; on other occasions, when they have fallen short of their ideals, the same traditions have failed. Typically, though, the various traditions see their distinguishing features as eminently valuable in themselves. If all religions were of equal worth, if there were no fundamentally important differences, why would anyone choose one of them over another? Pluralism may be socially desirable, but it poses a serious theological challenge. Does it really require us to modify our own doctrinal claims?

We personally are convinced that it does. Affirmations of religious "truth" that used to be understood as statements of fact are now increasingly regarded as perspectival—true "for me"—rather than universal claims. Today, thinkers from various backgrounds are presenting their traditions as symbolic accounts of the world and metaphorical narratives of the past. What is more, they argue that this is the way the various traditions should have been seen all along, and that literal interpretation has always been a mistake.

Pluralism demands that religious traditions adapt to a world that is becoming ever more interconnected. Here we think of the work of Wilfred Cantwell Smith, perhaps the greatest Canadian scholar of religion in the twentieth century. Professor Smith founded the Institute of Islamic Studies at McGill University in Montreal. He then moved to Harvard University, where he directed the Center for the Study of World Religions. One of his most important books was *Towards a World Theology: Faith and the Comparative History of Religion* (1981). In it he argued that our various religious traditions were best understood in comparative context, "as strands in a . . . complex whole":

> What those traditions have in common is that the history of each has been what it has been in significant part because the histories of the others have been what *they* have been. This truth is newly discovered; yet truth it has always been. Things proceeded in this interrelated way for many centuries without humanity's being aware of it; certainly not fully aware of it. A new, and itself interconnected, development is that currently humankind *is* becoming aware of it, in various communities (Smith 1989: 6).

Although current events make us painfully aware of the differences that separate the world's religions, it is more crucial today than ever to appreciate the complex connections they share. That is exactly what we are trying to do in this book: to deepen understanding of our interconnected religious worlds.

Discussion Questions

1. What are some of the points of intersection of religion and politics?

2. What did the word "fundamentalism" originally mean, and how is it used today in connection with the world's religions?

3. How are Western religious traditions dealing with issues of sexuality, especially challenges to traditional heterosexual norms?

4. Have religious traditions helped or hurt the environment?

5. Is religious pluralism the same thing as relativism?

6. How does the Eastern view of animals compare with the traditional Western one?

Glossary

Bollywood India's thriving film industry, from "Bombay" and "Hollywood."

dowry The price paid by the bride's family to conclude a marriage contract; traditionally paid before the marriage, but now often spread over many years.

fundamentalism A very conservative form of religion that typically affirms the literal truth of its scriptures and doctrines and attributes ultimate authority to them.

Hindutva "Hindu-ness" or "India-ness," an affirmation of pride in traditional Indian culture and Hinduism.

pluralism A cultural attitude that welcomes a variety of political, religious and other stances.

separatists Persons who advocate to separating a region to form a new nation.

References

Agarwal, Bina. 1992. "The Gender and Environment Debate: Lessons from India." *Feminist Studies* 18, 1 (Spring 1992), 119–58.

Brockopp, Jonathan. 2003. *Islamic Ethics of Life: Abortion, War and Euthanasia*. Columbia: University of South Carolina Press.

Dalai Lama, His Holiness The. 2008. *In My Own Words: An Introduction to My Teachings and Philosophy*. Trans. Rajiv Mehrotra. London: Hay House.

"Gay marriage gone wrong." 2012. Retrieved 6 Feb. 2013 from www.economist.com/blogs/analects/2012/07/attitudes-towards-homosexuality.

Mansingh, Ajai. 1995. "Stewards of Creation Covenant: Hinduism and the Environment." *Caribbean Quarterly* 41, 1 (March 1995), 59–75.

Sajoo, Amyn. 2004. *Muslim Ethics: Emerging Vistas*. London: I.B. Tauris in association with The Institute for Ismaili Studies.

Saperstein, David. 2011. "Reform Movement Reminds LGBT Teens that 'It Gets Better.'" Retrieved 6 Feb. 2013 from Religious Action Center of Reform Judaism, http://rac.org/Articles/index.cfm?id=22448&pge_prg_id=11071&pge_id=2541.

Schumacher, E.F. 1973. *Small Is Beautiful: Economics as if People Mattered*. New York: Harper and Row.

Sedgh, Gilda et al. 2012. "Induced Abortion: Incidence and Trends Worldwide from 1995 to 2008." Retrieved 6 February 2013 from www.thelancet.com/journals/lancet/article/PIIS0140-6736%2811%2961786-8/fulltext.

Smith, Wilfred Cantwell. 1981. *Towards a World Theology: Faith and the Comparative History of Religion*. London: Macmillan, and Philadelphia: Westminster.

Westlake, Adam. 2012. "Gay Marriage Debate: Japan Next, Hope Equal Rights Activists." Retrieved 6 Feb. 2013 from http://japandailypress.com/gay-marriage-debate-japan-next-hope-equal-rights-activists-307751.

Note

1. Some Islamic scholars have questioned the authenticity of this *hadith*.

Credits

The authors gratefully acknowledge the use of the following material:

Document box, page 36: Wendy Doniger O'Flaherty, ed. and trans. *The Rig Veda: An Anthology, One Hundred and Eight Hymns* (Harmondsworth: Penguin, 1981).

Document box, page 40: From *The Principal Upanisads*, ed. S. Radhakrishnan (Amherst, NY: Humanity Books, 1992), pp. 230–4. Copyright © 1992 Humanity Books. All rights reserved. Used with permission of the publisher; www.prometheusbooks.com

Document box, page 43: from the *Bhagavad-Gita*, translated by Barbara Stoler Miller, translation copyright 1986 by Barbara Stoler Miller. Used by permission of Bantam Books, a division of Random House, Inc. Any third party use of this material, outside of this publication, is prohibited. Interested parties must apply directly to Random House, Inc. for permission.

Document boxes, pages 64 and 65: from *Songs of the Saints of India* translated by Hawley & Jurgensmeyer (1988) 21 lines from "Kabir" & "Catuverdi" © Oxford University Press, Inc. By permission of Oxford University Press, USA.

Document box, page 271: Theodore de Bary and Irene Bloom, comp. 1999. *Sources of Chinese Tradition*, 2nd edn. Vol. 1. New York: Columbia University Press, trans D. Nivison, page 36. Reprinted with permission of the publisher.

Excerpt, page 272: from *An Anthology of Chinese Literature: Beginnings to 1911*, edited by Stephen Owen, translated by Stephen Owen. Copyright © 1996 by Stephen Owen and The Council for Cultural Planning and Development of the Executive Yuan of the Republic of China. Used by permission of W.W. Norton & Company, Inc.

Excerpts, pages 274, 287, 291, 297, 307, 309: Theodore de Bary and Irene Bloom, comp. 1999. *Sources of Chinese Tradition*, 2nd edn. Vol. 1. New York: Columbia University Press, trans. B. Watson, page 342–3. Reprinted with permission of the publisher.

Excerpts, pages 283, 284, 285: Watson, Burton.1968. *The Complete Works of Chuang Tzu*. New York: Columbia University Press, page 37, 97, and 240–1. Reprinted with permission of the publisher.

Document box, page 288 and excerpts pages 295, 297, 300: Ch'en, Kenneth; *Buddhism in China*. © 1964 Princeton University Press, 1992 renewed PUP. Reprinted by permission of Princeton University Press.

Document box, page 299: Cissell, Tsai Kathryn Ann, tr. 1994. *Lives of the Nuns: Biographies of Chinese Buddhist Nuns from the Fourth to Sixth Centuries*. Honolulu: University of Hawai'I Press, pages 49-50.

Document box, page 309 and excerpt in Sites box, page 313: Chan, Wing-Tsit; *A Source Book in Chinese Philosophy* © 1963 Princeton University Press, 1991 renewed PUP. Reprinted by permission of Princeton University Press.

Document box, page 324: Lee, Peter H., et al., eds. 1993. *Sourcebook of Korean Civilization*. Vol. I. New York: Columbia University Press page 24. Originally published in The Korea Journal, Vol. 13, 7.

Document box, page 325: Lee, Peter H., et al., eds. 1993. *Sourcebook of Korean Civilization*. Vol. I. New York: Columbia University Press, page 94. Reprinted with permission of the publisher.

Excerpts, pages 326–7 and 327–8: H. Kang in Lee, Peter H., et al., eds. 1993. *Sourcebook of Korean Civilization*. Vol. I. New York: Columbia University Press, page 263. Reprinted with permission of the publisher.

Box Design Photos:

Chapter openers, Timelines, and running heads: Chapter 2: Hemera Technologies/AbleStock.com/Thinkstock; Chapter 3: Alan Lagadu/Thinkstock; Chapter 4: hanoded/iStockphoto.com; Chapter 5: Borirak/Thinkstock; Chapter 6: Sebastiaan de Steigter/Thinkstock; Chapter 7: Photos.com/Thinkstock

Focus box: moggara12/Thinkstock

Sites boxes: Chapter 1: Margaret and Alan Smeaton/Thinkstock; Chapter 2: javarman2/Thinkstock; Chapter 3: Nilesh Bhange/Thinkstock; Chapter 4: Caroline Vancoillie/Thinkstock; Chapter 5: eAlisa/Thinkstock; Chapter 6: javarman2/Thinkstock; Chapter 7: Urbanangel/Dreamstime.com/GetStock.com; Chapter 8: Nenand Cerovic/Dreamstime.com

Document boxes: Chapter 1: David Crowther/Thinkstock; Chapter 2: Amanda Lewis/Thinkstock; Chapter 4: The Schøyen Collection, MS 4464, http://www.schoyencollection.com/religions_files/ms4464.jpg; Chapter 5: Alexander Studentschnig/Thinkstock; Chapter 6: emily2k/Thinkstock; Chapter 7: Ciprian Catusanu/Thinkstock; Chapter 8: David Crowther/Thinkstock

Index